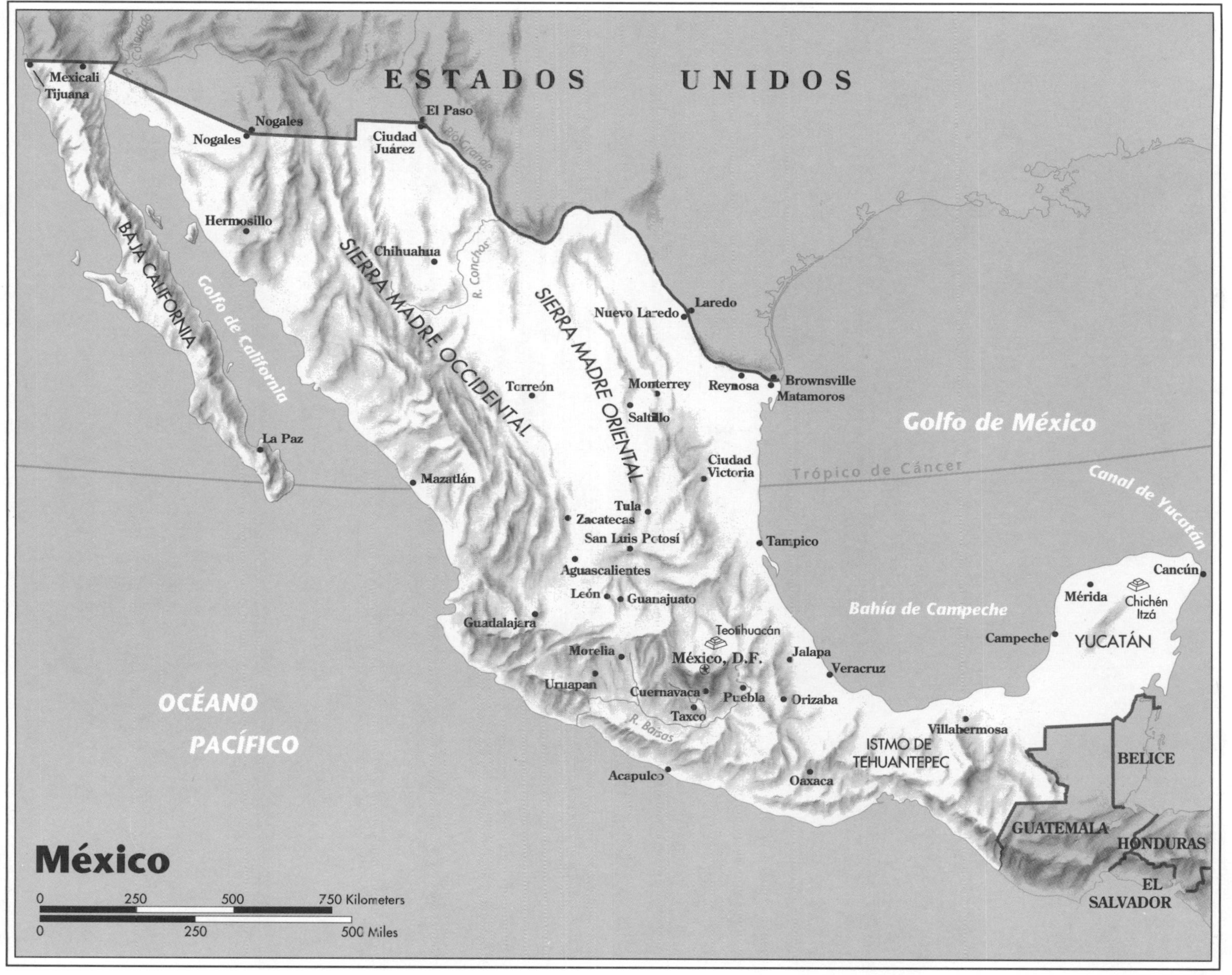

ESTADOS UNIDOS
Mexicali
Tijuana
Nogales
Nogales
El Paso
Ciudad Juárez
Río Grande
Hermosillo
Chihuahua
R. Conchos
BAJA CALIFORNIA
Golfo de California
La Paz
SIERRA MADRE OCCIDENTAL
SIERRA MADRE ORIENTAL
Nuevo Laredo
Laredo
Torreón
Monterrey
Saltillo
Reynosa
Brownsville
Matamoros
Golfo de México
Trópico de Cáncer
Ciudad Victoria
Mazatlán
Tula
Zacatecas
San Luis Potosí
Tampico
Canal de Yucatán
Aguascalientes
León
Guanajuato
Guadalajara
Bahía de Campeche
Cancún
Mérida
Chichén Itzá
Campeche
YUCATÁN
Teotihuacán
México, D.F.
Morelia
Jalapa
Veracruz
Uruapan
Cuernavaca
Puebla
Orizaba
Taxco
R. Balsas
OCÉANO PACÍFICO
Villahermosa
ISTMO DE TEHUANTEPEC
BELICE
Acapulco
Oaxaca
GUATEMALA
HONDURAS
EL SALVADOR
México
0 250 500 750 Kilometers
0 250 500 Miles

# ¿Cómo se dice...?

SEVENTH EDITION

Ana C. Jarvis

Chandler Gilbert Community College

Raquel Lebredo

California Baptist University

Francisco Mena-Ayllón

University of Redlands



Houghton Mifflin Company   Boston   New York

*Director, World Languages: New Media and Modern Language Publishing:* Beth Kramer
*Sponsoring Editor:* Amy Baron
*Development Editor:* Rafael Burgos-Mirabal
*Senior Project Editor:* Carol Newman
*Senior Production/Design Coordinator:* Jodi O'Rourke
*Senior Manufacturing Coordinator:* Priscilla Bailey
*Marketing Manager:* Tina Crowley Desprez

*Cover Image: Forms, Symbols, and Images,* 1967, José Gurvich.



Printed in the U.S.A.

Library of Congress Catalog Card Number: 2001131512

Student Text ISBN: 0-618-10366-X

456789-VH-05 04 03

# CONTENTS

Lección
15

Lección
16

Lección
17

# An Overview of Your Textbook's Main Features

**Provides focus for learning.** The **Lesson Opener** presents the thematic topic and an outline of the lesson's communicative goals and grammatical structures.

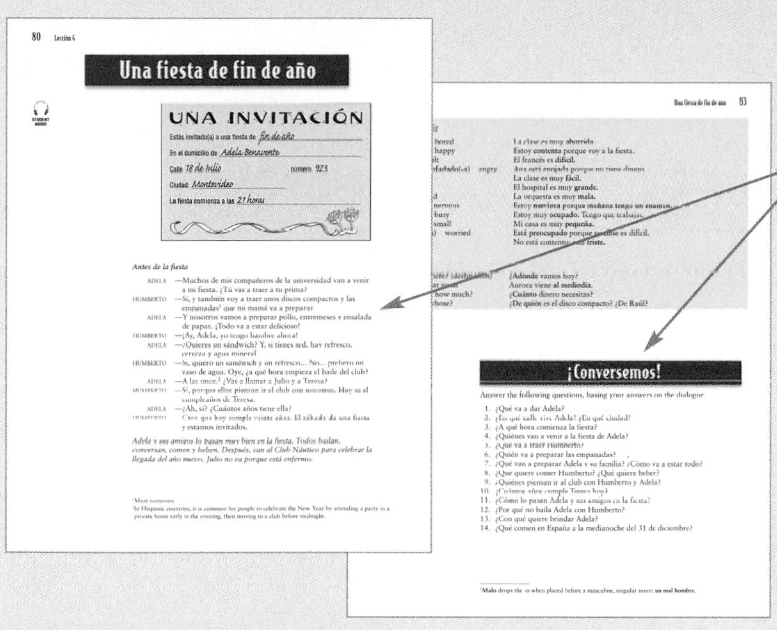


**Offers a natural setting for introducing language.** The **Opening Passage** serves as a lively, realistic context in which to learn the lesson's vocabulary and structures. The ***¡Conversemos!*** comprehension questions provide immediate reinforcement. Translations appear in Appendix D.

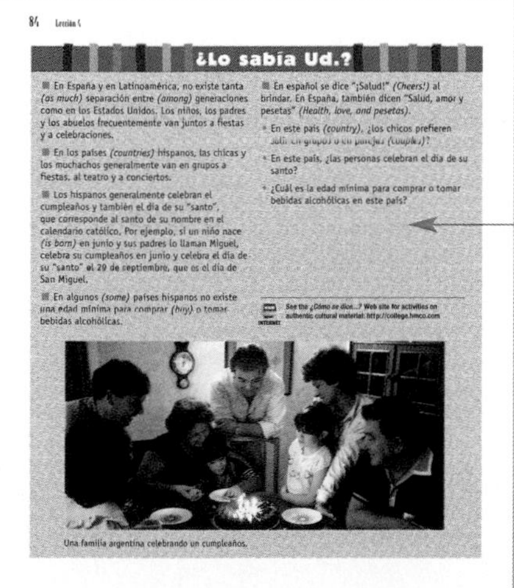


**Leads to an understanding of the cultures of the Spanish-speaking world.** Written in simple Spanish, the *¿Lo sabía Ud.?* culture notes convey information on cultural themes or points mentioned in the lesson's opening passage.

# Provides a solid foundation for building communication skills.

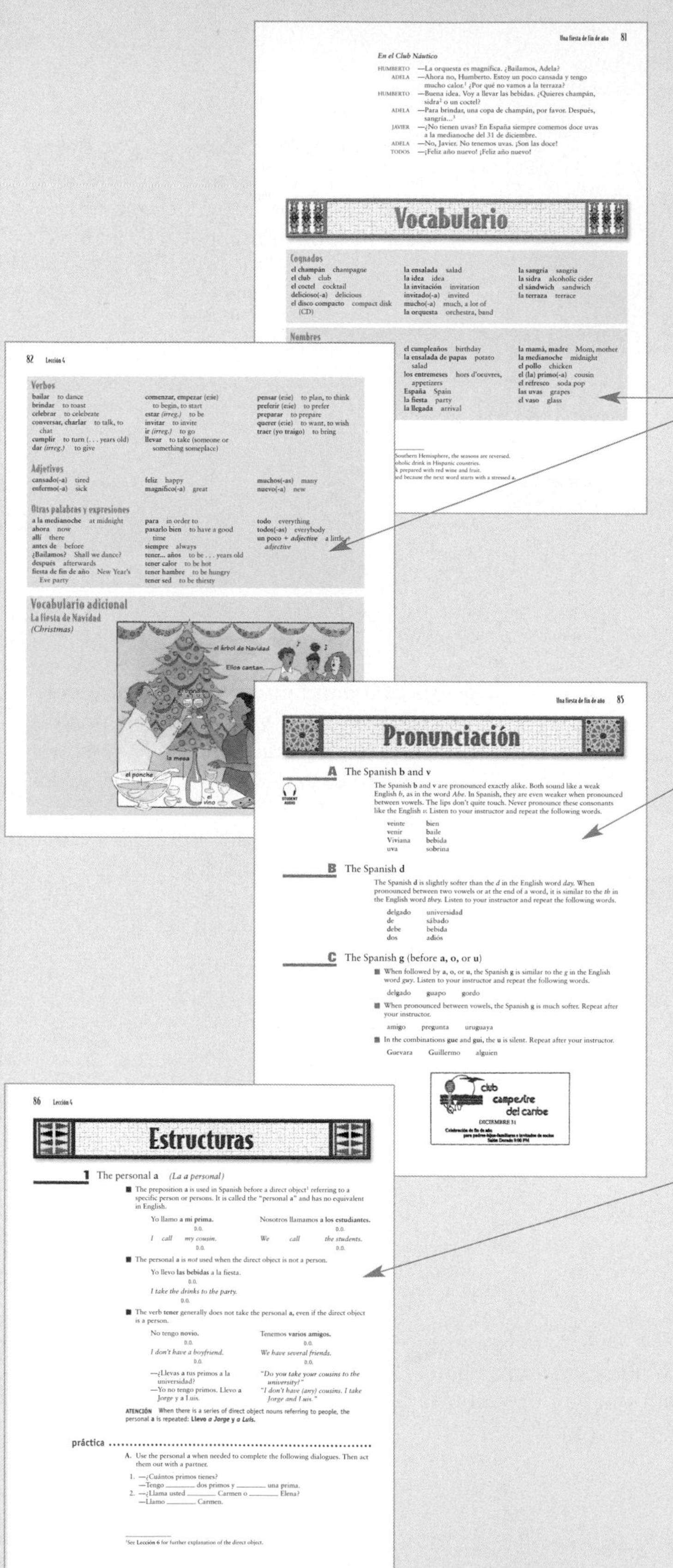



*En el Club Náutico*

HUMBERTO —La orquesta es magnífica. ¿Bailamos, Adela?
ADELA —Ahora no, Humberto. Estoy un poco cansada y tengo mucho calor.[1] ¿Por qué no vamos a la terraza?
HUMBERTO —Buena idea. Voy a llevar las bebidas. ¿Quieres champán, sidra[2] o un coctel?
ADELA —Para brindar, una copa de champán, por favor. Después, sangría...[3]
JAVIER —¿No tienen uvas? En España siempre comemos doce uvas a la medianoche del 31 de diciembre.
ADELA —No, Javier. No tenemos uvas. ¡Son las doce!
TODOS —¡Feliz año nuevo! ¡Feliz año nuevo!

## Vocabulario

**Cognados**

**el champán** champagne, **el club** club, **el coctel** cocktail, **delicioso(-a)** delicious, **el disco compacto** compact disk (CD), **la ensalada** salad, **la idea** idea, **la invitación** invitation, **invitado(-a)** invited, **mucho(-a)** much, a lot of, **la orquesta** orchestra, band, **la sangría** sangria, **la sidra** alcoholic cider, **el sándwich** sandwich, **la terraza** terrace

**Nombres**

**el cumpleaños** birthday, **la ensalada de papas** potato salad, **los entremeses** hors d'oeuvres, appetizers, **España** Spain, **la fiesta** party, **la llegada** arrival, **la mamá, madre** Mom, mother, **la medianoche** midnight, **el pollo** chicken, **el (la) primo(-a)** cousin, **el refresco** soda pop, **las uvas** grapes, **el vaso** glass



**Verbos**

**bailar** to dance, **brindar** to toast, **celebrar** to celebrate, **conversar, charlar** to talk, to chat, **cumplir** to turn (. . . years old), **dar** *(irreg.)* to give, **comenzar, empezar (e:ie)** to begin, to start, **estar** *(irreg.)* to be, **invitar** to invite, **ir** *(irreg.)* to go, **llevar** to take (someone or something someplace), **pensar (e:ie)** to plan, to think, **preferir (e:ie)** to prefer, **preparar** to prepare, **querer (e:ie)** to want, to wish, **traer (yo traigo)** to bring

**Adjetivos**

**cansado(-a)** tired, **enfermo(-a)** sick, **feliz** happy, **magnífico(-a)** great, **muchos(-as)** many, **nuevo(-a)** new

**Otras palabras y expresiones**

**a la medianoche** at midnight, **ahora** now, **allí** there, **antes de** before, **¿Bailamos?** Shall we dance?, **después** afterwards, **fiesta de fin de año** New Year's Eve party, **para** in order to, **pasarlo bien** to have a good time, **siempre** always, **tener... años** to be . . . years old, **tener calor** to be hot, **tener hambre** to be hungry, **tener sed** to be thirsty, **todo** everything, **todos(-as)** everybody, **un poco +** ***adjective*** a little + *adjective*

**Vocabulario adicional**
**La fiesta de Navidad**
*(Christmas)*





## Pronunciación

**A** The Spanish **b** and **v**

The Spanish **b** and **v** are pronounced exactly alike. Both sound like a weak English *b*, as in the word *Abe*. In Spanish, they are even weaker when pronounced between vowels. The lips don't quite touch. Never pronounce these consonants like the English *v*. Listen to your instructor and repeat the following words.

veinte, venir, Viviana, uva, bien, baile, bebida, sobrina

**B** The Spanish **d**

The Spanish **d** is slightly softer than the *d* in the English word *day*. When pronounced between two vowels or at the end of a word, it is similar to the *th* in the English word *they*. Listen to your instructor and repeat the following words.

delgado, de, debe, dos, universidad, sábado, bebida, adiós

**C** The Spanish **g** (before **a**, **o**, or **u**)

- When followed by **a**, **o**, or **u**, the Spanish **g** is similar to the *g* in the English word *guy*. Listen to your instructor and repeat the following words.
  delgado guapo gordo
- When pronounced between vowels, the Spanish **g** is much softer. Repeat after your instructor.
  amigo pregunta uruguaya
- In the combinations **gue** and **gui**, the **u** is silent. Repeat after your instructor.
  Guevara Guillermo alguien

club campestre del caribe
DICIEMBRE 31



## Estructuras

**1** The personal a *(La a personal)*

- The preposition **a** is used in Spanish before a direct object[1] referring to a specific person or persons. It is called the "personal **a**" and has no equivalent in English.
  Yo llamo **a mi prima.** — *I call my cousin.*
  Nosotros llamamos **a los estudiantes.** — *We call the students.*
- The personal **a** is *not* used when the direct object is not a person.
  Yo llevo **las bebidas** a la fiesta. — *I take the drinks to the party.*
- The verb **tener** generally does not take the personal **a**, even if the direct object is a person.
  No tengo **novio.** — *I don't have a boyfriend.*
  Tenemos **varios amigos.** — *We have several friends.*
  —¿Llevas **a** tus primos a la universidad? — *"Do you take your cousins to the university?"*
  —Yo no tengo primos. Llevo **a** Jorge y a Luis. — *"I don't have (any) cousins. I take Jorge and Luis."*

**ATENCIÓN** When there is a series of direct object nouns referring to people, the personal **a** is repeated: **Llevo *a* Jorge y *a* Luis.**

**práctica**

A. Use the personal **a** when needed to complete the following dialogues. Then act them out with a partner.

1. —¿Cuántos primos tienes?
   —Tengo ______ dos primos y ______ una prima.
2. —¿Llama usted ______ Carmen o ______ Elena?
   —Llamo ______ Carmen.

[1]See **Lección 6** for further explanation of the direct object.

- The *Vocabulario* section lists all active vocabulary, new words, and expressions introduced in the opening passage, as well as *Vocabulario adicional,* or words and phrases related to the lesson theme.

- Now appearing in Lecciones 1–18, the ***Pronunciación*** section contains pronunciation and linking exercises designed to acquaint you with the basic Spanish sounds; with sounds, words, and expressions that are challenging for English speakers; and with natural speech.

- The *Estructuras* section presents an average of four or five clear and succinct grammar points in English with more examples of practical use that can be consulted for independent study and reference. Each structure is immediately followed by ***Práctica*** exercises that range from controlled drills to open-ended activities, including illustration-based activities.

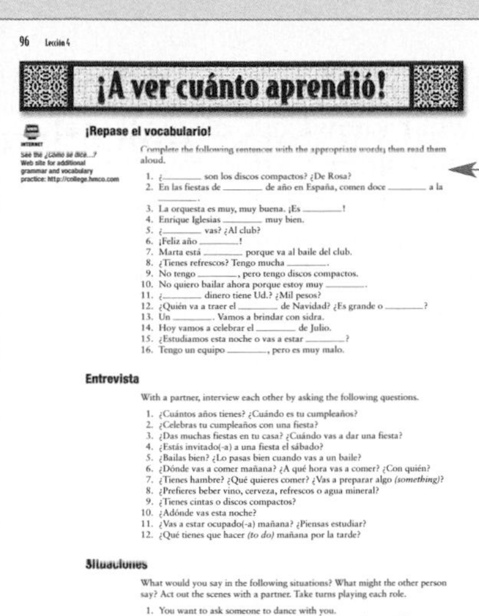

96 Lección 4

# ¡A ver cuánto aprendió!

## ¡Repase el vocabulario!

INTERNET
See the *¿Cómo se dice...?* Web site for additional grammar and vocabulary practice: http://college.hmco.com

Complete the following sentences with the appropriate words, then read them aloud.

1. ¿_____ son los discos compactos? ¿De Rosa?
2. En las fiestas de _____ de año en España, comen doce _____ a la _____.
3. La orquesta es muy, muy buena. ¡Es _____!
4. Enrique Iglesias _____ muy bien.
5. ¿_____ vas? ¿Al club?
6. ¡Feliz año _____!
7. Marta está _____ porque va al baile del club.
8. ¿Tienes refrescos? Tengo mucha _____.
9. No tengo _____, pero tengo discos compactos.
10. No quiero bailar ahora porque estoy muy _____.
11. ¿_____ dinero tiene Ud.? ¿Mil pesos?
12. ¿Quién va a traer el _____ de Navidad? ¿Es grande o _____?
13. Un _____. Vamos a brindar con sidra.
14. Hoy vamos a celebrar el _____ de Julio.
15. ¿Estudiamos esta noche o vas a estar _____?
16. Tengo un equipo _____, pero es muy malo.

## Entrevista

With a partner, interview each other by asking the following questions.

1. ¿Cuántos años tienes? ¿Cuándo es tu cumpleaños?
2. ¿Celebras tu cumpleaños con una fiesta?
3. ¿Das muchas fiestas en tu casa? ¿Cuándo vas a dar una fiesta?
4. ¿Estás invitado(-a) a una fiesta el sábado?
5. ¿Bailas bien? ¿Lo pasas bien cuando vas a un baile?
6. ¿Dónde vas a comer mañana? ¿A qué hora vas a comer? ¿Con quién?
7. ¿Tienes hambre? ¿Qué quieres comer? ¿Vas a preparar algo *(something)*?
8. ¿Prefieres beber vino, cerveza, refrescos o agua mineral?
9. ¿Tienes cintas o discos compactos?
10. ¿Adónde vas esta noche?
11. ¿Vas a estar ocupado(-a) mañana? ¿Piensas estudiar?
12. ¿Qué tienes que hacer *(to do)* mañana por la tarde?

## Situaciones

What would you say in the following situations? What might the other person say? Act out the scenes with a partner. Take turns playing each role.

1. You want to ask someone to dance with you.
2. You are having a party. Offer one of your guests a selection of beverages.

**Presents opportunities to actively use the language in the classroom.** The *¡A ver cuánto aprendió!* review section consists of a series of progressively more open-ended activities, including personalized pair activities, activities for vocabulary review, and pair and small group activities. The section ends with a writing activity on a topic related to the thematic goals of the lesson.

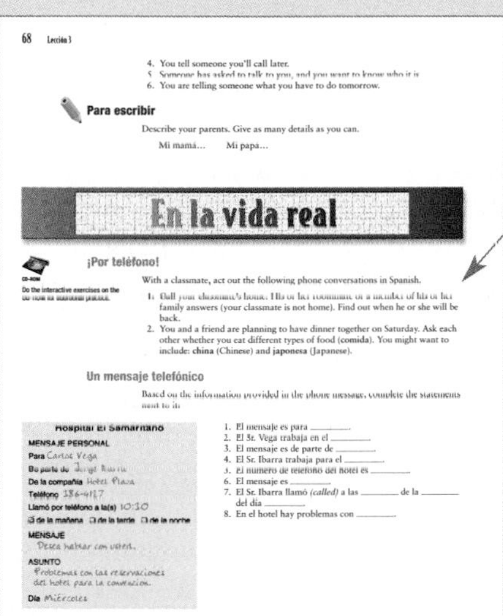

68 Lección 3

4. You tell someone you'll call later.
5. Someone has asked to talk to you, and you want to know who it is.
6. You are telling someone what you have to do tomorrow.

## Para escribir

Describe your parents. Give as many details as you can.

Mi mamá... Mi papá...

# En la vida real

## ¡Por teléfono!

CD-ROM
Do the interactive exercises on the CD-ROM for additional practice.

With a classmate, act out the following phone conversations in Spanish.

1. Call your classmate's home. His or her roommate or a member of his or her family answers (your classmate is not home). Find out when he or she will be back.
2. You and a friend are planning to have dinner together on Saturday. Ask each other whether you eat different types of food (**comida**). You might want to include: **china** (Chinese) and **japonesa** (Japanese).

## Un mensaje telefónico

Based on the information provided in the phone message, complete the statements next to it.

Hospital El Samaritano
MENSAJE PERSONAL
Para Carlos Vega
De parte de Jorge Ibarra
De la compañía Hotel Plaza
Teléfono 386-4127
Llamó por teléfono a la(s) 10:10
☑ de la mañana ☐ de la tarde ☐ de la noche
MENSAJE
Desea hablar con usted.
ASUNTO
Problemas con las reservaciones del hotel para la convención.
Día Miércoles

1. El mensaje es para _____.
2. El Sr. Vega trabaja en el _____.
3. El mensaje es de parte de _____.
4. El Sr. Ibarra trabaja para el _____.
5. El número de teléfono del hotel es _____.
6. El mensaje es _____.
7. El Sr. Ibarra llamó *(called)* a las _____ de la _____ del día _____.
8. En el hotel hay problemas con _____.

**Reinforces learning while strengthening communication skills.** Often based on authentic material, the activities in ***En la vida real*** ask you to synthesize what you've learned in order to communicate in real-life situations.

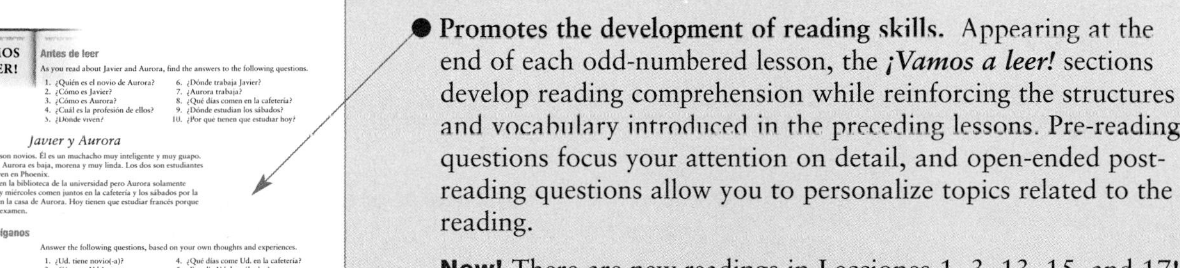

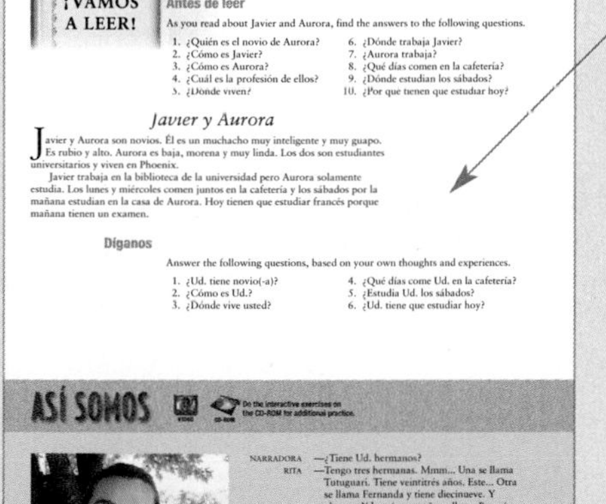

70 Lección 3

## ¡VAMOS A LEER!

### Antes de leer

As you read about Javier and Aurora, find the answers to the following questions.

1. ¿Quién es el novio de Aurora?
2. ¿Cómo es Javier?
3. ¿Cómo es Aurora?
4. ¿Cuál es la profesión de ellos?
5. ¿Dónde viven?
6. ¿Dónde trabaja Javier?
7. ¿Aurora trabaja?
8. ¿Qué días comen en la cafetería?
9. ¿Dónde estudian los sábados?
10. ¿Por qué tienen que estudiar hoy?

### *Javier y Aurora*

Javier y Aurora son novios. Él es un muchacho muy inteligente y muy guapo. Es rubio y alto. Aurora es baja, morena y muy linda. Los dos son estudiantes universitarios y viven en Phoenix.

Javier trabaja en la biblioteca de la universidad pero Aurora solamente estudia. Los lunes y miércoles comen juntos en la cafetería y los sábados por la mañana estudian en la casa de Aurora. Hoy tienen que estudiar francés porque mañana tienen un examen.

### Díganos

Answer the following questions, based on your own thoughts and experiences.

1. ¿Ud. tiene novio(-a)?
2. ¿Cómo es Ud.?
3. ¿Dónde vive usted?
4. ¿Qué días come Ud. en la cafetería?
5. ¿Estudia Ud. los sábados?
6. ¿Ud. tiene que estudiar hoy?

## ASÍ SOMOS

Do the interactive exercises on the CD-ROM for additional practice.

NARRADORA —¿Tiene Ud. hermanos?
RITA —Tengo tres hermanas. Mmm... Una se llama Tutuguari. Tiene veintitrés años. Este... Otra se llama Fernanda y tiene diecinueve. Y ahora... Y la más pequeña se llama Bensaír y también tiene diecinueve años.

NARRADORA —¿Cómo es su mejor amiga?
RITA —Es una persona muy dinámica. Baila ballet. Toma clases de equitación. Habla inglés, francés y es muy alegre.

**Promotes the development of reading skills.** Appearing at the end of each odd-numbered lesson, the ***¡Vamos a leer!*** sections develop reading comprehension while reinforcing the structures and vocabulary introduced in the preceding lessons. Pre-reading questions focus your attention on detail, and open-ended post-reading questions allow you to personalize topics related to the reading.

**New!** There are new readings in Lecciones 1, 3, 13, 15, and 17!

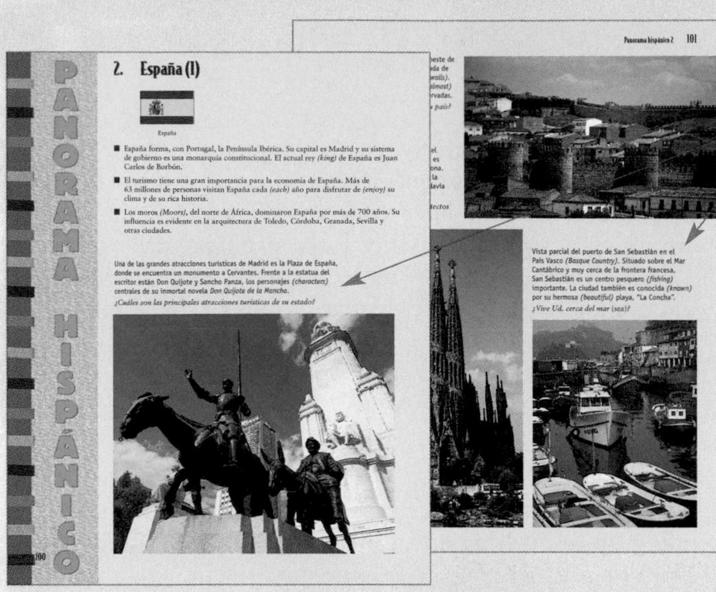

Panorama hispánico 2 101

PANORAMA HISPÁNICO

2. España (I)

España

- España forma, con Portugal, la Península Ibérica. Su capital es Madrid y su sistema de gobierno es una monarquía constitucional. El actual rey (*king*) de España es Juan Carlos de Borbón.
- El turismo tiene una gran importancia para la economía de España. Más de 63 millones de personas visitan España cada (*each*) año para disfrutar de (*enjoy*) su clima y de su rica historia.
- Los moros (*Moors*), del norte de África, dominaron España por más de 700 años. Su influencia es evidente en la arquitectura de Toledo, Córdoba, Granada, Sevilla y otras ciudades.

Una de las grandes atracciones turísticas de Madrid es la Plaza de España, donde se encuentra un monumento a Cervantes. Frente a la estatua del escritor están Don Quijote y Sancho Panza, los personajes (*characters*) centrales de su inmortal novela *Don Quijote de la Mancha*.
*¿Cuáles son las principales atracciones turísticas de su estado?*

Vista parcial del puerto de San Sebastián en el País Vasco (*Basque Country*). Situado sobre el Mar Cantábrico y muy cerca de la frontera francesa, San Sebastián es un centro pesquero (*fishing*) importante. La ciudad también es conocida (*known*) por su hermosa (*beautiful*) playa, "La Concha".
*¿Vive Ud. cerca del mar (sea)?*

100

**Expands your knowledge of geography, history, and culture.** After every two lessons, the ***Panorama hispánico*** photo essays explore the culture, geography, economy, and history of the Hispanic world. Regions featured include South America, the Caribbean, the United States, Canada, Central America, Mexico, and Spain.

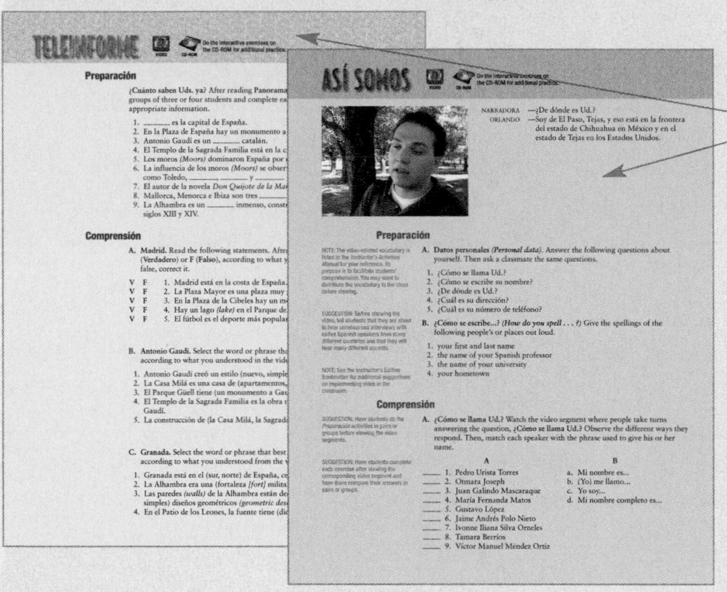

TELEINFORME

Preparación

¿Cuánto saben Uds. ya? After reading Panorama ... groups of three or four students and complete ... appropriate information.

1. ______ es la capital de España.
2. En la Plaza de España hay un monumento a ...
3. Antonio Gaudí es un ______ catalán.
4. El Templo de la Sagrada Familia está en la c...
5. Los moros (*Moors*) dominaron España por ...
6. La influencia de los moros (*Moors*) se obser... como Toledo, ______ y ______
7. El autor de la novela *Don Quijote de la Ma...*
8. Mallorca, Menorca e Ibiza son tres ______
9. La Alhambra es un ______ inmenso, constr... siglos XIII y XIV.

Comprensión

A. Madrid. Read the following statements. After... (Verdadero) or F (Falso), according to what y... false, correct it.

V F 1. Madrid está en la costa de España.
V F 2. La Plaza Mayor es una plaza muy ...
V F 3. En la Plaza de la Cibeles hay un m...
V F 4. Hay un lago (*lake*) en el Parque de...
V F 5. El fútbol es el deporte más popular...

B. Antonio Gaudí. Select the word or phrase th... according to what you understood in the vid...

1. Antonio Gaudí creó un estilo (nuevo, simple...
2. La Casa Milá es una casa de (apartamentos, ...
3. El Parque Güell tiene (un monumento a Gau...
4. El Templo de la Sagrada Familia es la obra ... Gaudí.
5. La construcción de (la Casa Milá, la Sagrad...

C. Granada. Select the word or phrase that best ... according to what you understood from the v...

1. Granada está en el (sur, norte) de España, ce...
2. La Alhambra era una (fortaleza [*fort*] milita...
3. Las paredes (*walls*) de la Alhambra están de... simples) diseños geométricos (*geometric desi...*
4. En el Patio de los Leones, la fuente tiene (di...

ASÍ SOMOS

NARRADORA —¿De dónde es Ud.?
ORLANDO —Soy de El Paso, Tejas, y eso está en la frontera del estado de Chihuahua en México y en el estado de Tejas en los Estados Unidos.

Preparación

A. Datos personales (*Personal data*). Answer the following questions about yourself. Then ask a classmate the same questions.

1. ¿Cómo se llama Ud.?
2. ¿Cómo se escribe su nombre?
3. ¿De dónde es Ud.?
4. ¿Cuál es su dirección?
5. ¿Cuál es su número de teléfono?

B. ¿Cómo se escribe...? (*How do you spell . . . ?*) Give the spellings of the following people's or places out loud.

1. your first and last name
2. the name of your Spanish professor
3. the name of your university
4. your hometown

Comprensión

A. ¿Cómo se llama Ud.? Watch the video segment where people take turns answering the question, ¿Cómo se llama Ud.? Observe the different ways they respond. Then, match each speaker with the phrase used to give his or her name.

| A | B |
|---|---|
| ____ 1. Pedro Urista Torres | a. Mi nombre es... |
| ____ 2. Otmara Joseph | b. (Yo) me llamo... |
| ____ 3. Juan Galindo Mascaraque | c. Yo soy... |
| ____ 4. María Fernanda Matos | d. Mi nombre completo es... |
| ____ 5. Gustavo López | |
| ____ 6. Jaime Andrés Polo Nieto | |
| ____ 7. Ivonne Iliana Silva Orneles | |
| ____ 8. Tamara Berrios | |
| ____ 9. Víctor Manuel Méndez Ortiz | |

**Broadens exposure to native speech and the cultures of the Spanish-speaking world.** Through a series of previewing, viewing comprehension, and expansion activities, the ***Teleinforme*** sections (after even-numbered lessons) and the ***Así somos*** sections (after odd-numbered lessons) support viewing of authentic as well as adapted footage. Each ***Teleinforme*** features footage from the region covered in the preceding ***Panorama hispánico*** photo essay. The ***Así somos*** footage consists of unrehearsed interviews with native Spanish speakers on topics related to the lesson theme.

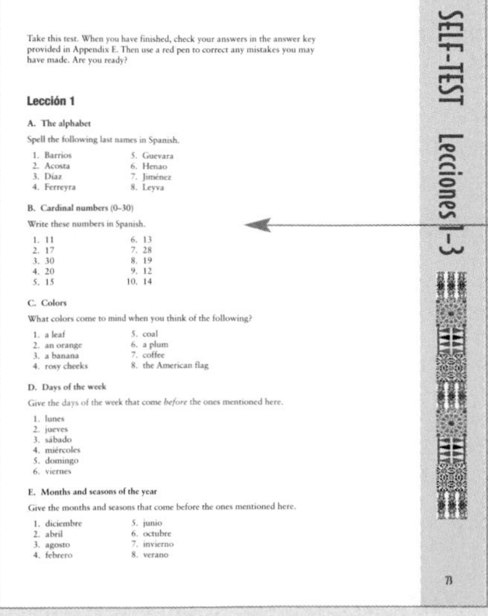

SELF-TEST Lecciones 1–3

Take this test. When you have finished, check your answers in the answer key provided in Appendix E. Then use a red pen to correct any mistakes you may have made. Are you ready?

Lección 1

A. The alphabet

Spell the following last names in Spanish.

| | |
|---|---|
| 1. Barrios | 5. Guevara |
| 2. Acosta | 6. Henao |
| 3. Díaz | 7. Jiménez |
| 4. Ferreyra | 8. Leyva |

B. Cardinal numbers (0–30)

Write these numbers in Spanish.

| | |
|---|---|
| 1. 11 | 6. 13 |
| 2. 17 | 7. 28 |
| 3. 30 | 8. 19 |
| 4. 20 | 9. 12 |
| 5. 15 | 10. 14 |

C. Colors

What colors come to mind when you think of the following?

| | |
|---|---|
| 1. a leaf | 5. coal |
| 2. an orange | 6. a plum |
| 3. a banana | 7. coffee |
| 4. rosy cheeks | 8. the American flag |

D. Days of the week

Give the days of the week that come *before* the ones mentioned here.

1. lunes
2. jueves
3. sábado
4. miércoles
5. domingo
6. viernes

E. Months and seasons of the year

Give the months and seasons that come before the ones mentioned here.

| | |
|---|---|
| 1. diciembre | 5. junio |
| 2. abril | 6. octubre |
| 3. agosto | 7. invierno |
| 4. febrero | 8. verano |

73

**Encourages self-assessment of learning objectives.** Following Lecciones 3, 6, 9, 12, 15, and 18, the **Self-Tests** contain exercises designed to review the vocabulary and structures of the three preceding lessons.

# Preface

*¿Cómo se dice...?*, Seventh Edition, is a complete, flexible program designed to present the fundamentals of Spanish to two- and four-year college and university students. This edition continues to feature the balanced, eclectic approach to language instruction that has made *¿Cómo se dice...?* one of the most widely used programs of its kind. To achieve its goal of helping attain linguistic proficiency, *¿Cómo se dice...?*, Seventh Edition, systematically involves you in activities requiring the communicative use of all four language skills: listening, speaking, reading, and writing. Because cultural awareness is as important to successful communication as linguistic competence, special care has been devoted in the Seventh Edition to providing up-to-date, practical insights into the cultural diversity of the Spanish-speaking world. Since it is essential to understand the underlying philosophy and organization of the program to use it to greatest advantage, the student's text and other components are described in detail below.

## The Student's Text

The organization of this central component of the *¿Cómo se dice...?*, Seventh Edition, program reflects its emphasis on the active use of Spanish for practical communication in context. The student's text is organized in eighteen lessons. Each lesson focuses on a high-frequency communicative situation and contains the features listed below.

**Objectives:** Each lesson begins with a list of grammatical and communicative objectives.

**Opening passages and *¡Conversemos!*:** New vocabulary and structures are first presented in the context of a conversation in idiomatic Spanish dealing with the high-frequency situation that is the lesson's central theme. An English translation of the opening passages is provided in Appendix D for you to verify meaning deduced from context. A headset icon indicates that the opening passages are recorded on the Student Audio. Comprehension questions on the opening passages *(¡Conversemos!)* follow the vocabulary section to provide immediate reinforcement of the vocabulary and communicative functions presented in the opening passage.

***Vocabulario:*** All new words and expressions introduced in the opening passages are listed by parts of speech or under the headings *Cognados* and *Otras palabras y expresiones*. The *Vocabulario adicional* section offers thematic groupings of other words and phrases related to the lesson theme; many are presented through illustrations to help you assimilate them more readily. Entries in these lists are to be learned for active use.

***¿Lo sabía Ud.?:*** These notes expand on cultural information and themes introduced in the opening passages in simple, easy-to-read Spanish. Follow-up questions invite cross-cultural comparisons.

**Pronunciación:** Lessons 1–9 *(Pronunciación)* present and practice the sounds of the Spanish language with special attention to features that pose difficulty for English speakers. Lessons 10–18 *(Pronunciación en contexto)* focus on several sounds or words from the lesson opening passage that may pose pronunciation challenges. The target words and phrases are presented as part of sentences from the opening passage in which they originally appear to address these pronunciation issues in context. A headset icon indicates that the pronunciation sections are recorded on the Student Audio.

**Estructuras and Práctica:** Each new grammatical structure featured in the opening passage is explained clearly and concisely in English so that the explanations may be used independently as an out-of-class reference. All explanations are followed by numerous examples of their practical use in natural Spanish. The *¡Atención!* head signals exceptions to the grammar rules presented or instances where knowledge of an English structure may interfere with learning the equivalent Spanish structure. After each explanation, the *Práctica* activities offer immediate reinforcement of new concepts through a variety of structured and communicative activities.

**¡A ver cuánto aprendió!:** This series of progressively less structured activities allows you to synthesize the lesson's new vocabulary and structures. *¡Repase el vocabulario!* uses a variety of proven activity formats to review new vocabulary presented in the lesson. *Entrevista* has you interview a classmate on topics related to the main lesson theme. *Situaciones* involves pairs or small groups of learners in using new structures and vocabulary in brief conversational exchanges. *Para escribir* guides you to express yourself in writing in a variety of formats, such as notes, postcards, letters, dialogues, and compositions.

**En la vida real:** This section develops oral proficiency by using authentic documents and role-plays to involve you in more complex and extended communicative tasks, such as planning an event, asking for information, or solving a problem. Each lesson includes an activity that involves reading and using information gained from an authentic text, for example, a newspaper ad or a travel brochure. Most of the activities are designed for work in pairs or small groups, and all of them require spontaneous use of Spanish in practical, meaningful, communicative tasks intended to motivate and to underscore the usefulness of language study.

In addition, the following features appear at regular intervals throughout the student's text:

**Así somos:** All odd-numbered lessons end with a series of activities designed for use with the candid interview segments of the *Así somos* modules of the *¿Cómo se dice...?* video, which reinforce the lesson themes. The previewing, post-viewing, and expansion activities use a variety of formats, including true/false, sentence completion, questions, matching, and multiple choice.

**¡Vamos a leer!:** Right before the *Así somos* video activities section, every odd-numbered lesson features a reading section that reinforces the structures and vocabulary presented in the text. Five readings are new to the Seventh Edition. The first four readings are related to the lesson themes; the final five readings consist of authentic literary selections that provide an appealing introduction to reading literature in Spanish. To develop reading skills, *Antes de leer,* a series of pre-reading questions, precedes each selection. Personalized, open-ended questions *(Díganos)* follow each reading and provide opportunities to discuss your own opinions and experiences in relation to the reading topic or theme.

**Self-Tests:** The Self-Tests, which appear after Lessons 3, 6, 9, 12, 15, and 18, enable you to review the structures, vocabulary, and cultural information of the three preceding lessons. Organized by lesson and by grammatical structure, the Self-Tests help you to determine quickly what material you have mastered and which concepts to target for further review. An answer key is provided in Appendix F for immediate verification.

***Panorama hispánico* and *Teleinforme:*** These sections, which appear after each even-numbered lesson, focus on the life-style, culture, geography, economy, and history of specific regions of the Spanish-speaking world. The full-color *Panorama hispánico* photo essays feature captions in simple Spanish; each caption ends with a question that invites cross-cultural comparison. The *Teleinforme* sections, which reinforce the content of the photo essays, include previewing, post-viewing, and expansion activities designed to enhance comprehension of the authentic footage featured in the *Teleinforme* modules of the ***¿Cómo se dice…?*** video.

**Reference Materials:** The following sections provide useful reference tools throughout the course:

- *Maps:* Colorful, up-to-date maps of the Hispanic world appear on the inside front and back covers of the textbook for quick reference.
- *Appendixes:* Appendix A summarizes the sounds and key pronunciation features of the Spanish language, with abundant examples; this section is also recorded on the Student Audio so you can hear and practice proper pronunciation of the Spanish sounds outside of the classroom. Conjugations of high-frequency regular, stem-changing, and irregular Spanish verbs constitute Appendix B. Appendix C is a glossary of all grammatical terms used in the text, with examples. Appendix D provides English translations of the opening passages. Appendix E is the answer key to the Self-Tests. Appendix F provides a list of the Spanish names of more than 100 professions and occupations to facilitate personalized classroom discussion.
- *Vocabularies:* Spanish-English and English-Spanish glossaries list all active, core vocabulary introduced in the *Vocabulario* lists that follow the opening passages and in the *Estructuras* sections. Active vocabulary is identified by the number of the lesson in which the word or phrase first appears. The Spanish-English vocabulary also lists passive vocabulary, which consists of those words glossed by an English equivalent in the text.

## Supplementary Materials

**Student Audio:** A free ninety-minute audio (in cassette or CD) containing recordings of the opening passages, the pronunciation sections, and the introduction to Spanish sounds from Appendix A is packaged with each copy of the student's text. This cassette is designed to maximize exposure to the sounds of natural spoken Spanish and improve your pronunciation.

**Workbook/Laboratory Manual:** Each lesson of the Workbook/Laboratory Manual is correlated to the corresponding lesson in the student's text and is divided into two sections. The *Workbook Activities* section offers an array of writing activities—sentence completion, sentence transformation, fill-in charts, dehydrated sentences, answering questions, crossword puzzles, and illustration-based exercises—that reinforce the structures and vocabulary presented in the textbook. Reading comprehension passages appear after each odd-numbered lesson to further skill development in that area. *Check Your Progress* sections provide a comprehensive review of key vocabulary and structures after every two lessons. The *Laboratory Activities* section includes pronunciation, structure, listening comprehension, and dictation exercises to be used in conjunction with the Audio Program. An answer key for all written exercises with discrete answers in both the Workbook and the Laboratory sections is provided for self-correction.

**Audio Program:** The complete Audio Program to accompany the *¿Cómo se dice...?* Workbook/Laboratory Manual, Seventh Edition, is available for purchase. The textbook opening passages are included as listening and pronunciation exercises in each lesson; they are dramatized once at natural speed, then reread with pauses for repetition. They are followed by comprehension questions, an open-ended activity that elicits responses appropriate to given situations, structured grammar exercises, a listening comprehension activity, and a dictation. A comprehensive review section of questions follows Lessons 9 and 18. Answers to all exercises, except for those that require a written response, are provided on the audio.

***¿Cómo se dice...?* Multimedia CD-ROM 3.0:** This new CD-ROM is an interactive multimedia program featuring short clips from the *¿Cómo se dice...?* Video with accompanying transcripts and access to a bilingual glossary. The clips are supported by a variety of comprehension and interpretation activities to help hone your listening skills. Language practice exercises corresponding to the language points presented in *¿Cómo se dice...?* are also included on this CD-ROM. The exercises contain links to a grammar reference that provides additional review of grammatical concepts.

***¿Cómo se dice...?* Video:** This revised video program provides a unique opportunity to develop listening skills and cultural awareness through multiple levels of viewing materials: unrehearsed interviews with native speakers from sixteen Spanish-speaking countries on a wide variety of topics, authentic as well as adapted footage, and images of everyday life. The video consists of eighteen modules that correlate to the *Así somos* and *Teleinforme* sections in the student's text. Filmed during the Semana Panamericana at the Universidad Autónoma de Guadalajara in Mexico, the nine *Así somos* modules reinforce the lesson themes, vocabulary, and language functions. They enable you to see, hear, and interact with Hispanics in authentic settings. In each module, students listen to a series of basic questions posed by María Isabel, the host, and the interviewees' responses. The segment concludes with María Isabel asking the viewers a question to which they provide a personalized response. The special *Entrevista* section, which appears at the end of Lessons 3, 7, 13, 15, and 17, features interviews with selected professionals. The nine *Teleinforme* modules present a broad cultural overview of the Hispanic world through authentic as well as adapted television footage from a number of Hispanic countries. Each *Teleinforme* includes two to four clips with a wide range of content: interviews, travelogues, festivals, and commercials. The content reinforces in a visually appealing and lively manner the material presented in the *Panoramas hispánicos*.

**The *¿Cómo se dice...?* Web Site and Spanish Web Resources:** The upgraded student's web site features web search activities related to the content of the lessons in the textbook. A self test for each lesson serves as an additional check of your progress in Spanish. This version of the *¿Cómo se dice...?* Web Site also includes a new flashcard feature designed to help review terms, images, and definitions. Audio- and video-based activities are now part of the web site. In addition, the Spanish Web Resources page provides links to authentic Spanish sites, maps of the Spanish-speaking world, and downloadable generic transparencies. The web site is accessible at *http://spanish.college.hmco.com/students*.

***¿Cómo se dice...?* Blackboard/WebCT ePack:** This new component provides materials in online formats to those institutions moving to online instruction.

## Acknowledgments

We wish to express appreciation to the following colleagues for the many valuable suggestions they offered in their reviews of the Seventh Edition.

Richard Auletta, LIU, Brookville, NY
Ann Baker, University of Evansville
Joanne de la Parra, Queen's University
Roxana Levin, St. Petersburg Junior College
Li McCleod, University of Saskatchewan
Kathy McConnell, Point Loma Nazarene University
Matthew Tornatore, Truman State University

We also extend our sincere appreciation to the Modern Languages Staff of Houghton Mifflin Company, College Division: Beth Kramer, Director; Amy Baron, Sponsoring Editor; Rafael Burgos-Mirabal, Development Editor; Carol Newman, Senior Project Editor; Jodi O'Rourke, Production/Design Coordinator; Priscilla Bailey, Senior Manufacturing Coordinator; and Henry Rachlin, Senior Designer.

*Ana C. Jarvis*
*Raquel Lebredo*
*Francisco Mena-Ayllón*

We would like to hear your comments on and reactions to *¿Cómo se dice...?*, Seventh Edition. Reports on your experiences using this program would be of great interest and value to us. Please write us care of Houghton Mifflin Company, College Division, 222 Berkeley Street, Boston, MA 02116–3764 or e-mail us at college_mod_lang@hmco.com.

# About the Authors

**Ana C. Jarvis,** a native of Paraguay, was born in Asunción and attended school in Buenos Aires, Argentina. She received her Ph.D. in Spanish from the University of California, Riverside, in 1973. Presently an instructor of Spanish at Chandler-Gilbert Community College in Chandler, Arizona, Dr. Jarvis previously taught at Mesa Community College, the University of California, Riverside, San Bernardino Valley College, Brigham Young University, and Riverside City College. In addition to authoring numerous Spanish textbooks, she has published several short stories in Spanish and is presently at work on a novel. In 1988 she was chosen "Faculty Member of the Year" at Chandler-Gilbert Community College.

**Raquel Lebredo** was born in Camagüey, Cuba. She attended school in Havana and later enrolled at the University of Havana, where she received a Ph.D. in Education in 1950. She was subsequently employed as an elementary school principal, and taught literature and language at a preparatory school in Havana. After living in Spain for a period of time, she moved in 1968 to the United States. Dr. Lebredo was awarded a Ph.D. in Spanish from the University of California, Riverside, in 1973. Since then she has taught Spanish at Claremont Graduate School, Crafton Hills College, the University of Redlands, and California Baptist University, and has authored several Spanish textbooks. In 1985 she was chosen "Faculty Member of the Year" by the student body at California Baptist University, and in 1991 she received a YWCA "Women of Achievement" award.

**Francisco Mena-Ayllón,** a native of Madrid, Spain, received his Ph.D. in Spanish from the University of California, Riverside, in 1973. He has taught Spanish language and literature courses at the University of California, Riverside, Oberlin College, California State University, Chico, the University of Redlands, and Crafton Hills College. In addition to authoring numerous Spanish textbooks in the United States, he has published a book about Federico García Lorca and several volumes of his own poetry. His poetry has been published in Spain, Latin America, and the United States. His work has also been included in several anthologies of contemporary Spanish poets, and he is listed in *Quién es quién en las letras españolas, 1978* (Who's Who in Spanish Letters), as an important contributor to contemporary Spanish literature.

# ¿Cómo se dice...?

# ¡Mucho gusto!

Lección 1

## OBJECTIVES

### Pronunciation

The Spanish **a** and **e**

### Structure

The alphabet • Cardinal numbers 0–30 • Colors • Days of the week • Months and seasons of the year • Subject pronouns • Present indicative of **ser**

### Communication

You will learn some greetings and farewells, how to introduce yourself and say where you are from and what your profession is, how to get people's phone numbers, and how to talk about days of the week and dates.

# ¡Mucho gusto!

¡Buenos días! Me llamo Juan Carlos Mirabal y soy de California. Soy estudiante de la Universidad de California. ¿Y tú? ¿De dónde eres?

¡Buenas tardes! Me llamo Laura Estévez y soy de Arizona. ¿Cómo te llamas tú? ¿Eres estudiante? Yo soy maestra.

¡Hola! Me llamo María Luisa Vargas Peña y soy de Nuevo México. Soy secretaria. Y yo me llamo Marcos Fuentes y soy de Tejas. Soy analista de sistemas. ¿Ustedes son estudiantes?

¿Qué tal? Me llamo Marisa Barrios y soy mexicana. Soy dentista. ¿Ustedes son norteamericanos?

¡Buenas noches! Me llamo Rafael Hernández y soy de Tejas. Soy piloto. ¿Cómo están ustedes? ¿Bien?

Me llamo Beatriz López y soy de Puerto Rico. Soy profesora de español. ¿Cómo estás? ¿Qué hay de nuevo?

—¡Hasta luego!
—¡Hasta mañana!
—¡Nos vemos el lunes!
—¡Adiós!
—¡Chau!

# Vocabulario

## Cognados *(Cognates)*[1]

**el (la) dentista**[2] dentist
**el (la) estudiante** student
**mexicano(-a)**[3] Mexican
**el (la) piloto** pilot
**el (la) profesor(-a)** professor
**el (la) secretario(-a)** secretary
**la universidad** university

## Nombres *(Nouns)*

**el (la) analista de sistemas**[4] systems analyst
**el español**[5] Spanish (language)
**el lunes** Monday
**el (la) maestro(-a)** teacher (at elementary school level)
**el (la) profesor(-a) de español**[4] Spanish teacher

## Verbo *(Verb)*

**ser** to be

## Adjetivo *(Adjective)*

**norteamericano(-a)**[3] North American

## Saludos y despedidas *(Greetings and farewells)*

**adiós** good-bye
**buenas noches** good evening, good night
**buenas tardes** good afternoon
**buenos días** good morning
**chau**[6] bye
**hasta luego** see you later
**hasta mañana** see you tomorrow
**hola** hello
**Nos vemos.** See you.

## Otras palabras y expresiones *(Other words and expressions)*

**¿cómo?** how
**de** from
**dónde** where
**Mucho gusto.** How do you do? Nice to meet you.
**tú** you *(familiar)*
**usted (Ud.)** you *(formal)*
**y** and

*Note:* Vocabulario = Vocabulary
[1]words that are very similar in both languages
[2]Nouns ending in **-ista** are used for both feminine and masculine.
[3]When modifying a feminine pronoun or noun, the adjective will end in **-a**. Notice also that adjectives of nationality are not capitalized.
[4]English uses a noun with the function of an adjective. Spanish uses the **de** phrase: **analista de sistemas; profesora de español.**
[5]Names of languages are not capitalized in Spanish.
[6]from the Italian "ciao"

## Preguntas y respuestas útiles *(Useful questions and answers)*

**¿Cómo te llamas tú?**[1] What is your name?
**Me llamo...** My name is . . .
**¿Cómo está usted?** How are you? *(formal)*
**¿Cómo estás?** How are you? *(familiar)*
**¿Cómo están ustedes?** How are you? (when speaking to more than one person)
**¿Qué tal?** How is it going? *(familiar)*
**¿Qué hay de nuevo?**[2] What's new?
**bien** fine, well
**muy bien** very well
**no** no, not
**no muy bien** not very well

## Vocabulario adicional *(Additional vocabulary)*

### Otras profesiones *(Other professions)*

**el (la) auxiliar de vuelo**
flight attendant

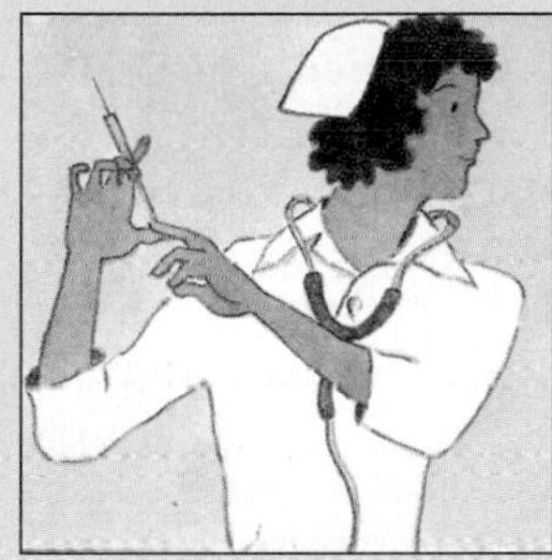

**el (la) enfermero(-a)**
nurse

**el (la) médico(-a)**
doctor (medical)

**el (la) programador(-a)**
programmer

**el (la) recepcionista**
receptionist

[1]**¿Cómo se llama usted?** is used in a formal situation.
[2]Possible answers: **No mucho.** *(Not much.)* or **Nada.** *(Nothing.)*

### Títulos *(Titles)*

**doctor** (**Dr.**) doctor[1] *(masculine)*
**doctora** (**Dra.**) doctor *(feminine)*
**profesor** professor, teacher, instructor *(masculine)*
**profesora** professor, teacher, instructor *(feminine)*
**señor** (**Sr.**) Mr., sir, gentleman
**señora** (**Sra.**) Mrs., madam, lady
**señorita** (**Srta.**) Miss, young lady

## ¡Conversemos!

Team up with a classmate and respond appropriately to the following questions.

1. ¿Juan Carlos Mirabal es de California o de Arizona? ¿Es estudiante o profesor?
2. ¿De dónde es Laura Estévez? ¿Es estudiante o maestra?
3. ¿María Luisa es recepcionista o secretaria? ¿Cuál es la profesión de Marcos?
4. ¿Marisa Barrios es norteamericana o mexicana? ¿Es enfermera o dentista?
5. ¿De dónde es Rafael Hernández? ¿Es auxiliar de vuelo o piloto?
6. ¿Beatriz López es puertorriqueña o mexicana? ¿Es médica o profesora?

*Note:* **¡Conversemos! = Let's talk!**

[1]In most Spanish-speaking countries, lawyers and members of many other professions who hold the equivalent of a Ph.D. are addressed as **doctor** or **doctora.**

## ¿Lo sabía Ud.?

- María es un nombre *(name)* muy popular en España *(Spain)* y en Latinoamérica. Frecuentemente se usa con otros *(with other)* nombres: **Ana María, María Isabel, María Teresa, María Luisa,** etc. Se usa también como segundo nombre *(middle name)* para hombres *(men)*: **José María, Luis María,** etc.
- En los países *(countries)* hispánicos las personas generalmente usan dos apellidos *(last names)*: el apellido del padre *(father's)* y el apellido de la madre *(mother's)*. Por ejemplo *(For example)*, los hijos de María **Rivas** y Juan **Pérez** usan los apellidos **Pérez Rivas.**
- En una guía telefónica *(phone book)* en español, alfabetizan *(they alphabetize)* los nombres según *(according to)* los dos apellidos; por ejemplo:

  Peña Aguilar, Rosa
  Peña Aguilar, Sara Luisa
  Peña Gómez, Raúl
  Quesada Álvarez, Javier
  Quesada Álvarez, Octavio
  Quesada Benítez, Ana María

UNIVERSIDAD NACIONAL

Nombre
Ana Luisa Méndez Díaz

Número de identidad
80259956

Fecha de expedición
20 julio 01

Válido hasta
31 diciembre 2006

Firma
Ana Luisa Méndez Díaz

- ¿Cuál *(What)* es un nombre muy popular en inglés *(English)*?
- ¿Cuáles son sus *(your)* dos apellidos?

See the *¿Cómo se dice...?* Web site for activities on authentic cultural material: http://spanish.college.hmco.com/students

*Note:* ¿Lo sabía Ud.? = Did you know?

## Pronunciación

### A The Spanish a

The Spanish **a** is pronounced like the *a* in the English word *father.* Listen to your teacher and repeat the following words.

| | |
|---|---|
| Ana | Ágata |
| Marta | sábado |
| llamas | mayo |
| analista | hasta mañana |

## B The Spanish e

The Spanish **e** is pronounced like the *e* in the English word *eight*. Listen to your teacher and repeat the following words.

| | |
|---|---|
| qué | usted |
| enero | Pepe |
| Ester | teléfono |
| secretaria | Teresa |

## 1 The alphabet *(El alfabeto)*

| Letter | Name | Letter | Name | Letter | Name |
|---|---|---|---|---|---|
| a | a | k | ka | s | ese |
| b | be | l | ele | t | te |
| c | ce | m | eme | u | u |
| d | de | n | ene | v | ve |
| e | e | ñ | eñe | w | doble ve |
| f | efe | o | o | x | equis |
| g | ge | p | pe | y | i griega |
| h | hache | q | cu | z | zeta |
| i | i | r | ere | | |
| j | jota | rr | erre | | |

### práctica

**A.** Spell these well-known acronyms in Spanish.

| | |
|---|---|
| 1. FBI | 5. NBA |
| 2. IBM | 6. NHF |
| 3. NAACP | 7. CIO |
| 4. PTA | 8. AFL |

**B.** A Spanish-speaking person may not know how to spell your name. If that person wants to write it, he or she might ask, **¿Cómo se escribe?** *(How do you spell it?)*. Learn how to spell your name in Spanish and ask other members of the class how to spell theirs.

## 2 Cardinal numbers 0–30 *(Números cardinales 0–30)*

| | | | |
|---|---|---|---|
| 0 cero | 7 siete | 14 catorce | 21 veintiuno |
| 1 uno | 8 ocho | 15 quince | 30 treinta |
| 2 dos | 9 nueve | 16 dieciséis[1] | |
| 3 tres | 10 diez | 17 diecisiete | |
| 4 cuatro | 11 once | 18 dieciocho | |
| 5 cinco | 12 doce | 19 diecinueve | |
| 6 seis | 13 trece | 20 veinte | |

**ATENCIÓN** **Uno** changes to **un** before a masculine singular noun: **un profesor** *(one professor)*. **Uno** changes to **una** before a feminine singular noun: **una profesora** *(one professor)*.

### práctica

A. To ask someone for his or her phone number, say, "**¿Cuál es tu**[2] **número de teléfono?**" *(What is your phone number?)*. Ask several members of the class for their phone numbers.

B. Complete the following series of numbers.

1. dos, cuatro,... treinta
2. uno, tres, cinco,... veintinueve
3. cero, tres,... dieciocho
4. cero, cuatro,... veintiocho

## 3 Colors *(Colores)*

■ You will see different colors in the classroom. Learn how to say them in Spanish.

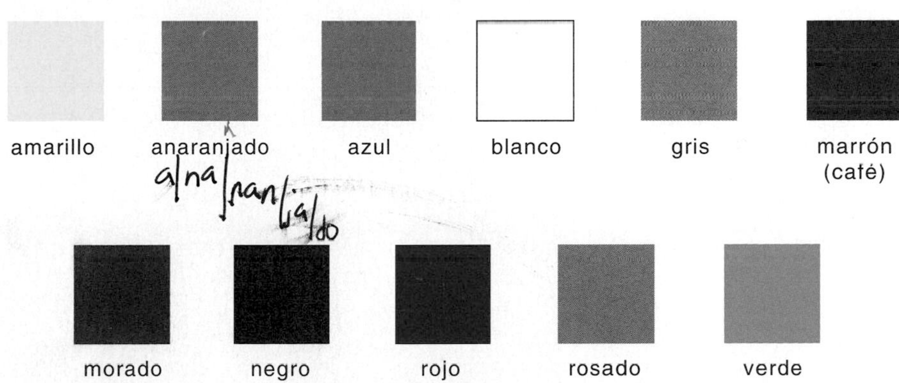


[1]The numbers 16 to 29 may also be spelled as separate words: **diez y seis..., veinte y uno...,** and so on.
[2]**tu** = *your* (when addressing a friend or a very young person). Say, "**¿Cuál es su número de teléfono?**" when addressing someone as **usted.**

## práctica

A. To ask someone whether he or she likes something, you say, "**¿Te gusta...?**"[1] To say that you like something, say, "**Me gusta...**" Conduct a survey of your classmates to find out which color is the most popular in class, following the model.

MODELO: —¿Qué color te gusta?
—*Me gusta el color rojo.*

B. *A splash of color!* This is an open-air market in Guatemala. With a partner, takes turns naming the colors that you see here in Spanish. You will need to include:

**claro** *light*
**oscuro** *dark*
(i.e., **azul oscuro** = *dark blue*)

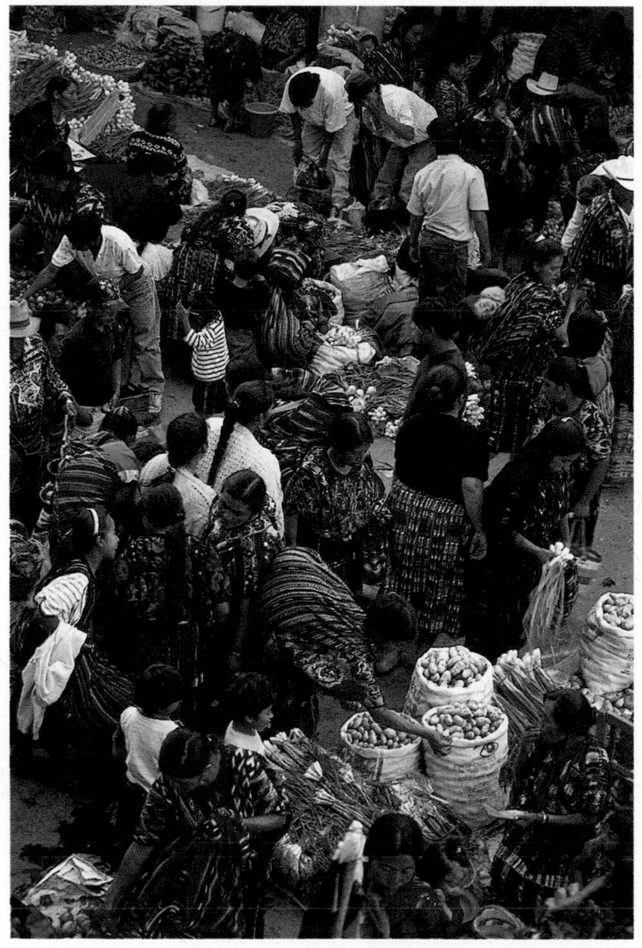

[1]When addressing someone as **usted**, use **¿Le gusta...?**

## 4 Days of the week *(Los días de la semana)*

**SEPTIEMBRE**

| LUNES | MARTES | MIÉRCOLES | JUEVES | VIERNES | SÁBADO | DOMINGO |
|---|---|---|---|---|---|---|
| | | 1 | 2 | 3 | 4 | 5 |
| 6 | 7 | 8 | 9 | 10 | 11 | 12 |
| 13 | 14 | 15 | 16 | 17 | 18 | 19 |
| 20 | 21 | 22 | 23 | 24 | 25 | 26 |
| 27 | 28 | 29 | 30 | | | |

—¿Qué día es hoy? **¿Jueves?** *"What day is today? Thursday?"*
—No, hoy es **viernes.** *"No, today is Friday."*

- In Spanish-speaking countries, the week starts on Monday.
- Note that the days of the week are not capitalized in Spanish.
- The days of the week are masculine in Spanish. The masculine definite articles **el** and **los** are often used with them to express *on.*

### práctica

A. The person asking these questions is always a day ahead. Respond, following the model.

MODELO: —¿Hoy es lunes?
*—No, hoy es domingo.*

1. ¿Hoy es miércoles?
2. ¿Hoy es domingo?
3. ¿Hoy es viernes?
4. ¿Hoy es martes?
5. ¿Hoy es sábado?
6. ¿Hoy es jueves?

B. Using the calendar sheet on this page, students take turns asking a classmate what day a certain date falls on.

MODELO: —¿Qué día es el 18 de septiembre?
*—Es sábado.*

## 5 Months and seasons of the year *(Los meses y las estaciones del año)*

El invierno

La primavera

El verano

El otoño

- To ask for the date, say:

  —¿Qué fecha es hoy? — *"What's the date today?"*

- When giving the date, always begin with the phrase **"hoy es el..."**

  —Hoy es el veinte de mayo. — *"Today is May twentieth."*

- Begin with the number, followed by the preposition **de** *(of)*, and then the month.

  **el quince de agosto** — *August fifteenth*
  **el diez de septiembre** — *September tenth*

  —¿Qué fecha es hoy? **¿El primero de mayo?** — *"What's the date today? May first?"*
  —No, hoy es **el treinta de abril.** — *"No, today is April thirtieth."*

**ATENCIÓN** **Primero** *(First)* is the only ordinal number used with dates. Also, the months are not capitalized in Spanish.

## práctica

A. Give the Spanish equivalent of the following dates.

1. July fourth
2. October thirty-first
3. January first
4. May fifth
5. February twelfth
6. December twenty-fifth
7. March twenty-first
8. April second
9. June twentieth
10. September ninth
11. August thirteenth
12. November eleventh

B. Indicate in which season the following months fall in the Northern Hemisphere.

1. febrero
2. agosto
3. mayo
4. enero
5. octubre
6. julio
7. abril
8. noviembre

C. Conduct a survey of your classmates to find out which season is the most popular, following the model. Which one is the least popular?

MODELO: —¿Qué estación te gusta?
*—Me gusta el (la) ________.*

## 6 Subject pronouns *(Pronombres personales usados como sujetos)*

| Singular | Plural |
|---|---|
| **yo** *I* | **nosotros** *we* (masc.) |
| | **nosotras** *we* (fem.) |
| **tú** *you* (familiar) | **vosotros** *you* (masc., familiar) |
| | **vosotras** *you* (fem., familiar) |
| **usted** *you* (formal) | **ustedes** *you* (formal) |
| **él** *he* | **ellos** *they* (masc.) |
| **ella** *she* | **ellas** *they* (fem.) |

- The **tú** form is used as the equivalent of *you* to address a friend, a coworker, a relative, or a child. The **usted** form is used in general to express deference or respect. In most Spanish-speaking countries today, young people tend to call each other **tú** even if they have just met. If in doubt, use **usted.**
- The plural form of **tú** is **vosotros(-as)**, which is used only in Spain. In Latin America, the plural form **ustedes** (abbreviated **Uds.**) is used as the plural form of both **usted** (abbreviated **Ud.**) and **tú.**
- The masculine plural forms can refer to the masculine gender alone or to both genders together.

**Ellos** (**Luis y Carlos**) son de Panamá. — *They (Luis and Carlos) are from Panama.*
**Ellos** (**María, Marta y Raúl**) son de España. — *They (María, Marta, and Raúl) are from Spain.*
**Nosotros** (**Ana María, Carlos y yo**) somos estudiantes. — *We (Ana María, Carlos, and I) are students.*

## práctica

**A.** Identify the personal pronoun that corresponds to each picture below.

**B.** Say whether you would use **tú, usted,** or **ustedes** to address the following people.

1. the president of the university
2. two strangers
3. a new classmate
4. your instructor
5. your best friend
6. your neighbor's children

C. What pronouns would be used to refer to the following persons?

1. Teresa y José
2. María y Verónica
3. Victoria y yo *(fem.)*
4. Enrique y yo
5. Carlos y Roberto
6. usted y Patricia

## 7 Present indicative of ser *(Presente de indicativo del verbo ser)*

| **ser** *to be* | | |
|---|---|---|
| **Singular** | | |
| yo | soy | *I am* |
| tú | eres | *you are* (fam.) |
| Ud. / él / ella | es | *you are* (form.) / *he is* / *she is* |
| **Plural** | | |
| nosotros(-as) | somos | *we are* |
| vosotros(-as) | sois | *you are* (fam.) |
| Uds. / ellos / ellas | son | *you are* (form.) / *they are* (masc.) / *they are* (fem.) |

- The verb **ser,** *to be,* is irregular. Its forms, like the forms of other irregular verbs, must be memorized.
- The verb **ser** is commonly used to express identity, place of origin, occupation, and nationality.

| | |
|---|---|
| —¿Ud. **es** profesor?[1] | *"Are you a teacher?"* |
| —No, **soy** estudiante. | *"No, I'm a student."* |
| —¿Carlos Paz **es** mexicano?[1] | *"Is Carlos Paz Mexican?"* |
| —Sí, **es** de Guadalajara. | *"Yes, he's from Guadalajara."* |
| —¿Quién **es** él? | *"Who is he?"* |
| —**Es** Héctor Díaz. | *"He is Héctor Díaz."* |
| —¿De dónde **es**? | *"Where is he from?"* |
| —**Es** de Ecuador. | *"He is from Ecuador."* |

[1]The indefinite article is not used after the verb **ser** when describing profession, nationality, religion, or party affiliation unless an adjective follows the noun: **Ella es católica. Ana es una profesora excelente.**

## práctica

**A.** Say where these people are from, using the information found in the illustrations. Also, say the capital of each country.

MODELO: yo
*Yo soy de Venezuela. La capital de Venezuela es Caracas.*

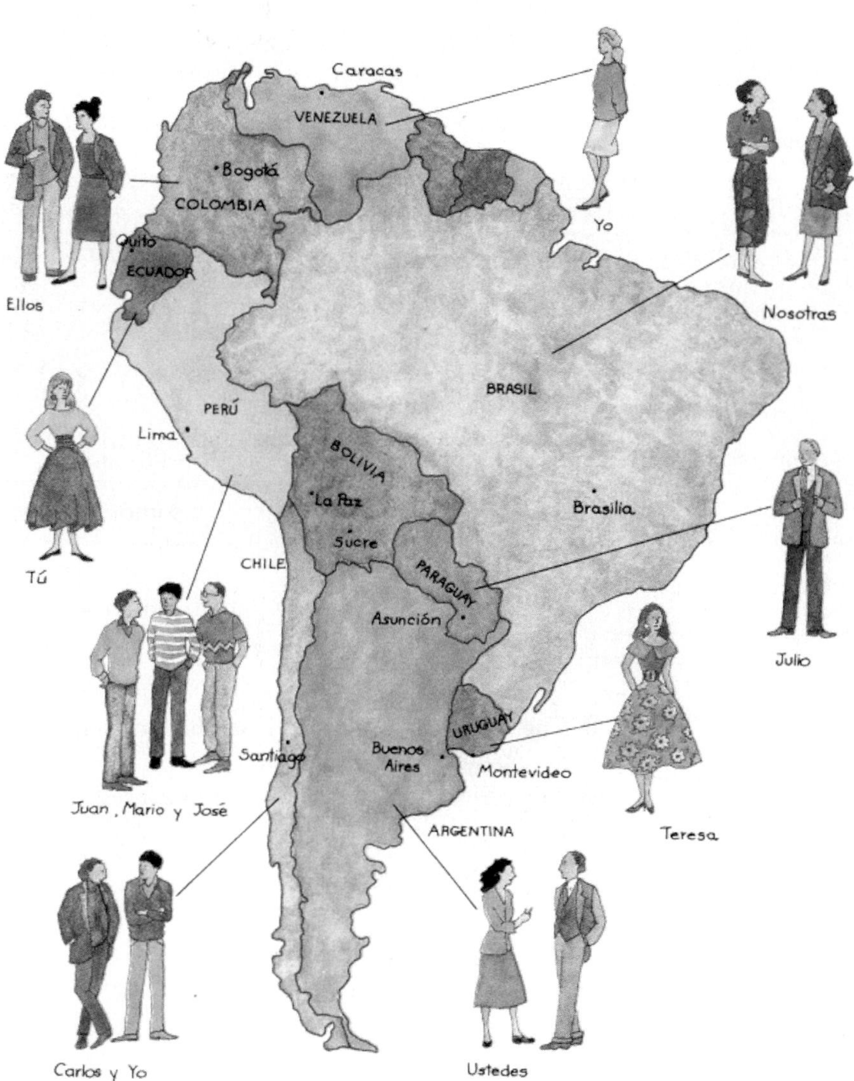


1. Teresa
2. Carlos y yo
3. Juan, Mario y José
4. tú
5. ellos
6. nosotras
7. Uds.
8. Julio

**B.** Say what nationality everyone is, using the list below. Follow the order used in Exercise A.

MODELO: yo
*Yo soy venezolana.*

| | | |
|---|---|---|
| argentino(-a) | chileno(-a) | uruguayo(-a) |
| boliviano(-a) | ecuatoriano(-a) | venezolano(-a) |
| brasileño(-a) | paraguayo(-a) | |
| colombiano(-a) | peruano(-a) | |

# ¡A ver cuánto aprendió!

INTERNET

See the *¿Cómo se dice...?* Web site for additional grammar and vocabulary practice: http://spanish.college.hmco.com/students

## ¡Repase el vocabulario!

Complete the following sentences using vocabulary learned in **Lección 1.**

1. Buenos ________. ¿Cómo ________ ustedes?
2. Me ________ Carlos Sandoval. ¿Cómo te ________ tú?
3. Yo ________ de Guadalajara.
4. Ella es ________ de español.
5. Julio es analista de ________.
6. David es ________; es de California.
7. Hola, ¿qué hay de ________?
8. Lupe es ________; es de Acapulco.
9. ¿Cómo estás? ¿________?
10. ________ luego, Antonio.
11. Nos ________ el lunes.
12. Eduardo es auxiliar de ________.

## Entrevista

With a partner, interview each other by asking the following questions.

1. ¿Cómo te llamas?
2. ¿Cómo estás?
3. ¿Tú eres norteamericano(-a)?
4. ¿De dónde eres?
5. ¿Tú eres profesor(-a) o estudiante?
6. ¿Cuál es tu número de teléfono?
7. ¿Qué día es hoy?
8. ¿Qué color te gusta?

---

*Note:* ¡A ver cuánto aprendió! = Let's see how much you learned!

## Situaciones

What would you say in the following situations? What might the other person say? Act out the scenes with a partner. Take turns playing each role.

1. You encounter your instructor in the morning and ask how he or she is.
2. At the mall, you run into a friend you haven't seen for a while.
3. You meet a friend's twelve-year-old daughter and ask how she is.
4. You leave your instructor's office. You have an appointment with him or her tomorrow.
5. You say good-bye to a friend and add that you will see him or her on Monday.
6. You meet an older person and want to know what his or her name is.
7. You want to know what day today is.
8. You ask someone what today's date is.

## Sumas y restas *(Additions and subtractions)*

Solve these arithmetic problems, using the following mathematical terms.

+ **más** − **menos** = **son**

| | | |
|---|---|---|
| 1. 8 + 15 = | 3. 30 − 13 = | 5. 27 − 12 = |
| 2. 18 − 14 = | 4. 7 + 11 = | 6. 16 + 9 = |

## Por teléfono *(By phone)*

Imagine that you and a classmate are in Madrid, Spain. Take turns reading the telephone numbers you must call according to the following needs.

1. You are having car trouble.
2. You need to cash a check.
3. You need some medicine.
4. You want to send roses to a friend.
5. You want to see a play.
6. You have to travel by plane.
7. You need to have your picture taken.
8. You want to report an accident.

Estación de Policía 911

Banco Nacional 701-8965

Farmacia "La Gran Vía" 475-0432

Aerolíneas Mexicanas 943-7510

Aeropuerto de Barajas 431-7068

Fotografía "Marín" 562-0437

Museo de Arte 792-3587

Hospital Municipal 482-3157

Apartamentos de lujo 987-3065

Dr. Manuel Vega Dentista 470-9265

Florería "Carrón" 952-0038

Estación de Ómnibus 493-7196

Taller de Mecánica "San Carlos" 356-7932

Servicio de Ambulancia 498-6530

9. A friend needs to go to the emergency room.
10. You need a place to live.
11. You want to buy a plane ticket to Mexico.
12. You want to see Picasso's paintings.
13. One of your friends has been hospitalized.
14. You want to travel to a nearby city.
15. You have a toothache.

### Para escribir *(To write)*

Following the style of the introductions on pages 2 and 3, write your own.

## En la vida real

CD-ROM

Do the interactive exercises on the CD-ROM for additional practice.

### Encuentros *(Encounters)*

Imagine that you and a classmate meet outside of class. How would you greet each other in Spanish? How would you find out each other's complete name and phone number? How would you say good-bye? Act out this situation with a partner. You may want to include these additional phrases:

| | |
|---|---|
| **¿Cómo te va?** | *How is it going (for you)?* |
| **Hasta la vista.** | *Until I see you again.* |

### Presentaciones

The class will be divided into groups of four. Each student will say who he or she is and where he or she is from. One member of the group will introduce his or her partners to the rest of the class.

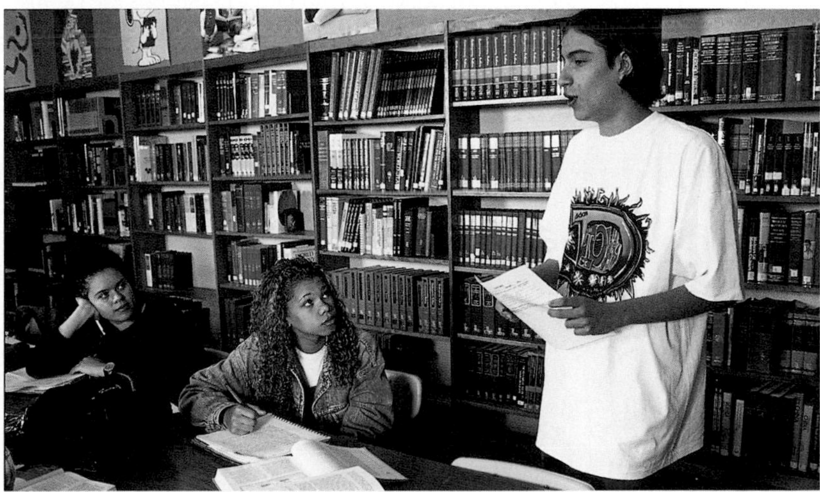

---

*Note:* En la vida real = In real life.

## Antes de leer *(Before reading)*

As you read the information below, find the answers to the following questions:

1. ¿Cuál es la profesión de José María Estévez y de Esmeralda Olmos?
2. ¿Son mexicanos?
3. ¿David Smith es norteamericano o mexicano?
4. ¿Es profesor?
5. ¿Rosalba Rojas es mexicana o cubana?
6. ¿Es enfermera?
7. ¿De dónde es Rafael Burgos?
8. ¿Cuál es la profesión de Rafael Burgos?

## *Mis compañeros°*

° My classmates

José María Estévez y Esmeralda Olmos son dos actores de televisión. Son de Guadalajara.
David Smith es de Tejas. Es estudiante.
Rosalba Rojas es de La Habana. Es médica.
Rafael Burgos es de San Juan. Es piloto.

## Díganos... *(Tell us . . .)*

1. ¿Cómo se llama usted?
2. ¿Es usted norteamericano(-a)?
3. ¿De dónde es?
4. ¿Es usted estudiante o profesor(-a)?

*Note:* ¡Vamos a leer! = Let's read!

CD-ROM Do the interactive exercises on the CD-ROM for additional practice.

NARRADORA —¿De dónde es Ud.?

ORLANDO —Soy de El Paso, Tejas, y eso está en la frontera del estado de Chihuahua en México y en el estado de Tejas en los Estados Unidos.

## Preparación

A. **Datos personales** *(Personal data)*. Answer the following questions about yourself. Then ask a classmate the same questions.

1. ¿Cómo se llama Ud.?
2. ¿Cómo se escribe su nombre?
3. ¿De dónde es Ud.?
4. ¿Cuál es su dirección?
5. ¿Cuál es su número de teléfono?

B. **¿Cómo se escribe...?** *(How do you spell . . . ?)* Give the spellings of the following people's or places out loud.

1. your first and last name
2. the name of your Spanish professor
3. the name of your university
4. your hometown

## Comprensión

A. **¿Cómo se llama Ud.?** Watch the video segment where people take turns answering the question, **¿Cómo se llama Ud.?** Observe the different ways they respond. Then, match each speaker with the phrase used to give his or her name.

| A | B |
|---|---|
| _____ 1. Pedro Urista Torres | a. Mi nombre es... |
| _____ 2. Otmara Joseph | b. (Yo) me llamo... |
| _____ 3. Juan Galindo Mascaraque | c. Yo soy... |
| _____ 4. María Fernanda Matos | d. Mi nombre completo es... |
| _____ 5. Gustavo López | |
| _____ 6. Jaime Andrés Polo Nieto | |
| _____ 7. Ivonne Iliana Silva Orneles | |
| _____ 8. Tamara Berríos | |
| _____ 9. Víctor Manuel Méndez Ortiz | |

**B. Soy de...** Match each person's name with his or her country of origin.

| | A | B |
|---|---|---|
| _____ | 1. Jaime | a. Puerto Rico |
| _____ | 2. Pedro | b. Colombia |
| _____ | 3. Víctor Manuel | c. España |
| _____ | 4. Leonardo | d. El Salvador |
| _____ | 5. Juan | e. Paraguay |
| _____ | 6. Héctor | f. Bolivia |
| _____ | 7. Gustavo | g. Ecuador |
| _____ | 8. Milka | h. Estados Unidos |
| _____ | 9. Otmara | i. México |
| _____ | 10. Orlando | j. Panamá |

**C. ¿Verdadero *(True)* o falso?** Read the following statements. Circle **V** (**Verdadero**) or **F** (**Falso**) according to what you understood from the video. If a statement is false, correct it.

V F 1. La dirección de Carolina es avenida El Cortijo 230 en Monte Rico, Lima.
V F 2. La dirección de Sofía es Andama 130, Interior 1.
V F 3. La dirección de Milka es calle Santa Cruz, 31.
V F 4. La dirección de Leonardo es Las Delicias, calle 14 en Ponce, Puerto Rico.

**D. Números de teléfono.** Match each statement with the name of the person who said it.

| | A | B |
|---|---|---|
| _____ | 1. 4-35-17-09 | a. Carolina |
| _____ | 2. 33-22-51 | b. Zaida |
| _____ | 3. Mi teléfono es el 6-32-96-22. | c. Juan |
| _____ | 4. Es el 6-38-68-36. | d. Milka |
| _____ | 5. Mi teléfono en Caracas es 241-32-01. | e. Gustavo |

## Ampliación

**A. Las nacionalidades.** Complete the following sentences with the nationality that matches the native country of each person.

1. Otmara es de Panamá; es _________.
2. Juan es de España; es _________.
3. Tamara es de Puerto Rico; es _________.
4. Víctor es de México; es _________.
5. Carolina es de Perú; es _________.
6. Jaime y Ángela son de Colombia; son _________.

**B. ¿Cuál es la dirección de...?** Take turns interviewing a classmate to find out the addresses of the following locations.

1. su restaurante favorito
2. su casa
3. la casa de sus padres
4. la casa de su mejor amigo(-a)

# El primer día de clases

Lección 2

## OBJECTIVES

### Pronunciation

The Spanish **i**, **o**, and **u**

### Structure

Gender and number • Definite and indefinite articles • Cardinal numbers 31–100 • Telling time • Present indicative of regular **-ar** verbs • Negative and interrogative sentences • Possession with **de**

### Communication

You will learn vocabulary related to the classroom, useful questions and answers, and some polite expressions.

# El primer día de clases

SRTA. ALBA —*(En la puerta)* Con permiso. Buenos días, profesor.
PROFESOR —Buenos días. Pase y tome asiento, por favor.
SRTA. ALBA —Muchas gracias.
PROFESOR —Señorita Alba, el[1] doctor Díaz.
SRTA. ALBA —Mucho gusto, doctor Díaz.
DR. DÍAZ —El gusto es mío, señorita Alba.
SRTA. ALBA —¡Perdón!, profesor, ¿qué hora es?
PROFESOR — Son las once y media.
SRTA. ALBA —¿A qué hora es la clase hoy?
PROFESOR —Es a las tres de la tarde.

LUISA —¿Cuál es tu dirección, Mario?
MARIO —Calle Magnolia, número 98.
LUISA —Ah, también necesito la dirección de Pedro. Él es amigo de Rocío, ¿no?
MARIO —Sí. La dirección es avenida Olmos, número 175.
RAÚL —Mario, ¿cuántos estudiantes hay en la clase?
MARIO —Hay cuarenta estudiantes.

ESTUDIANTE —Profesor, ¿cómo se dice "de nada" en inglés?
PROFESOR —Se dice *"you're welcome."*
ESTUDIANTE —¿Qué quiere decir *"to return"*?
PROFESOR —Quiere decir "regresar."

[1]When you are speaking about a third person (indirect address) and use a title with the name, the definite article is required.

LAURA —¿Tú trabajas, Daniel?
DANIEL —Sí, yo trabajo en un hospital. ¿Y tú?
LAURA —Yo no trabajo; solamente estudio.
DANIEL —¿Cuántas clases tomas?
LAURA —Tomo cinco clases. Oye, ¿tú tomas francés este semestre?
DANIEL —No, porque yo ya hablo francés. Tomo una clase de alemán con el Dr. Smith.
LAURA —Yo no hablo francés, pero hablo un poco de italiano y de portugués.

# Vocabulario

## Cognados

**la clase** class
**el italiano** Italian *(language)*
**el hospital** hospital
**el portugués** Portuguese *(language)*

## Nombres

**el alemán** German *(language)*
**el (la) amigo(-a)** friend
**la avenida** avenue
**la calle** street
**la clase de alemán** German class
**el día** day
**la dirección, el domicilio** address
**el francés** French *(language)*
**el inglés** English *(language)*
**el número** number
**la puerta** door
**la tarde** afternoon

## Verbos

**estudiar** to study
**hablar** to talk
**necesitar** to need
**regresar** to return
**tomar** to take
**trabajar** to work

## Otras palabras y expresiones

**ah** oh
**con** with
**¿cuál?** what?, which?
**¿Cuántos(-as)?** How many?
**de la tarde** P.M.
**el primer día de clases** the first day of classes
**en** in, at
**en inglés** in English
**este semestre** this semester
**hay** there is, there are
**hoy** today
**oye** listen
**porque** because
**sí** yes
**solamente** only
**también** too, also
**un poco de** a little
**ya** already

## Preguntas y respuestas útiles

**¿A qué hora...?** At what time . . . ?
**A la (las)...** At . . . *(when referring to time of day)*
**¿Cómo se dice...?** How do you say . . . ?
**Se dice...** You say . . . , One says . . .
**¿Cuál es tu dirección?**[1] What's your address?
**Mi dirección es...** My address is . . .
**¿Qué hora es?** What time is it?
**Son las...** It's . . . *(when referring to time of day)*
**¿Qué quiere decir...?** What does . . . mean?
**Quiere decir...** It means . . .

## Expresiones de cortesía

**Mucho gusto.** Pleased to meet you.
**El gusto es mío.** The pleasure is mine.
**Con permiso.** Excuse me.
**Perdón.** Pardon me.
**Pase.** Come in.
**Tome asiento.** Have a seat.
**Por favor.** Please.
**Muchas gracias.** Thank you very much.
**De nada.** You're welcome.

# Vocabulario adicional

## En la clase *(In the class)*

---

[1]When addressing someone as **Ud.**, say, **¿Cuál es su dirección?**
[2]Also "watch"
[3]Ballpoint pen

## ¡Conversemos!

Team up with a classmate and respond appropriately to the following questions or statements.

1. Mucho gusto, señor (señora, señorita).
2. Muchas gracias.
3. ¿Cuántos estudiantes hay en la clase?
4. ¿Cómo se dice *"please"* en español *(Spanish)*?
5. ¿Qué quiere decir "con permiso"?
6. ¿Cuál es la dirección de Mario?
7. ¿Dónde trabaja Daniel?
8. ¿Cuántas clases toma Laura este semestre?
9. ¿Daniel habla francés o portugués?
10. ¿Laura habla italiano?

## ¿Lo sabía Ud.?

- Para los horarios *(schedules)* de aviones *(planes)*, trenes, ómnibus, teatros, televisión y algunas *(some)* invitaciones, se usa el sistema de veinticuatro horas. Por ejemplo, las cuatro de la tarde son las dieciséis horas.
- En España y en Latinoamérica, muchas personas estudian inglés en la escuela secundaria *(high school)* y en la universidad.

- ¿Se usa el sistema de 24 horas en los Estados Unidos *(United States)*?
- ¿Qué idioma *(language)* toma la mayoría de los estudiantes norteamericanos en la escuela secundaria?

INTERNET

See the *¿Cómo se dice...?* Web site for activities on authentic cultural material: http://spanish.college.hmco.com/students

## Pronunciación

### A The Spanish i

STUDENT AUDIO

The Spanish **i** is pronounced like the double *e* in the English word *see*. Listen to your teacher and repeat the following words.

| | |
|---|---|
| sí | dirección |
| dice | domicilio |
| inglés | necesitar |
| días | hospital |
| cinco | |

## B The Spanish o

The Spanish **o** is a short, pure vowel. It corresponds to the *o* in the English word *no*, but without the glide. Listen to your teacher and repeat the following words.

| | |
|---|---|
| luego | número |
| no | noche |
| como | ocho |
| doctor | teléfono |

## C The Spanish u

The Spanish **u** is shorter in length than the English *u*. It corresponds to the *ue* sound in the English word *Sue*. Listen to your teacher and repeat the following words.

| | |
|---|---|
| estudiar | Susana |
| usted | puerta |
| mucho | universidad |
| luz | gusto |

## 1 Gender and number *(Género y número)*

### A. Gender, Part I

- In Spanish, all nouns—including those denoting non-living things—are either masculine or feminine.

| Masculine | | Feminine | |
|---|---|---|---|
| el hombre | el lápiz | la mujer | la ventana |
| el profesor | el estudiante | la profesora | la estudiante |
| el cuaderno | el secretario | la tiza | la secretaria |

- Most nouns that end in **-o** or denote males are masculine: **cuaderno** *(notebook);* **hombre** *(man).*
- Most nouns that end in **-a** or denote females are feminine: **mesa** *(table);* **profesora** *(female professor);* **mujer** *(woman).*

**ATENCIÓN** Some common exceptions include the words **el día** *(day)* and **el mapa** *(map),* which end in **-a** but are masculine, and the word **la mano** *(hand),* which ends in **-o** but is feminine.

- Here are some helpful rules to remember about gender:
- Some masculine nouns ending in **-o** have a corresponding feminine form ending in **-a: el secretario/la secretaria.**
- When a masculine noun ends in a consonant, the corresponding feminine noun is often formed by adding **-a: el profesor/la profesora.**
- Many nouns that refer to people use the same form for both genders: **el estudiante/la estudiante.** In such cases, gender is indicated by the article **el** (masculine) or **la** (feminine).

## práctica

Place **el**[1] or **la**[1] before each noun.

1. mapa
2. tiza
3. escritorio
4. señor
5. doctora
6. profesora
7. pizarra
8. libro
9. mujer
10. puerta
11. ventana
12. pluma
13. hombre
14. día
15. secretario
16. mano
17. cuaderno
18. doctor
19. silla
20. señora

### B. Plural forms

- The plural of nouns is formed by adding **-s** to words ending in a vowel and **-es** to words ending in a consonant.

señora → señoras
silla → sillas
libro → libros
reloj → relojes
borrador → borradores
lección → lecciones

**ATENCIÓN** Note that the plural form of **lección** does not have a written accent. See Appendix A.

- When a noun ends in **-z**, change the **-z** to **c** and add **-es.**

lápiz → lápices
luz *(light)* → luces

- When the plural is used to refer to two or more nouns of different genders, the masculine form is used.

dos secretarias y un secretario → tres secretarios

## práctica

Give the plural of the following nouns.

1. mapa
2. reloj
3. tiza
4. lápiz
5. ventana
6. puerta
7. lección
8. escritorio
9. borrador
10. día
11. luz
12. profesor

---

[1]**el** = *the* (m.); **la** = *the* (f.)

## 2 Definite and indefinite articles *(Artículos determinados e indeterminados)*

### A. The definite article

- Spanish has four forms that are equivalent to the English definite article *the*.

| | Masculine | Feminine | English |
|---|---|---|---|
| Singular | el | la | *the* |
| Plural | los | las | |

**el** profesor — **los** profesores
**la** profesora — **las** profesoras
**el** lápiz — **los** lápices

**ATENCIÓN** It is a good idea to learn new nouns with their corresponding definite articles—this will help you to remember their gender.

### B. The indefinite article

- The Spanish equivalents of *a (an)* and *some* are as follows.

| | Masculine | Feminine | English |
|---|---|---|---|
| Singular | un | una | *a (an)* |
| Plural | unos | unas | *some* |

**un** libro — **unos** libros
**una** silla — **unas** sillas
**un** profesor — **unos** profesores

## práctica

A. Identify the following objects or people using the appropriate definite article.

1. 

2. 

3. 

4. 

5. 

6.  

**B.** Identify the following objects or people using the appropriate indefinite article.

**C.** With a partner, take turns saying what you need. Use the appropriate indefinite article.

MODELO: Yo necesito un lápiz.

## 3 Cardinal numbers 31–100 *(Números cardinales 31–100)*

| | |
|---|---|
| 31 | **treinta y uno** |
| 32 | **treinta y dos** (and so on) |
| 40 | **cuarenta** |
| 41 | **cuarenta y uno** (and so on) |
| 50 | **cincuenta** |
| 53 | **cincuenta y tres** |
| 60 | **sesenta** |
| 68 | **sesenta y ocho** |
| 70 | **setenta** |
| 77 | **setenta y siete** |
| 80 | **ochenta** |
| 84 | **ochenta y cuatro** |
| 90 | **noventa** |
| 95 | **noventa y cinco** |
| 100 | **cien (ciento)** |

■ Note that **y** appears only in numbers between 16 and 99.

## práctica

When saying phone numbers, people in many Spanish-speaking countries tend to say the first number alone and the rest of the numbers in pairs. Using this system, give the names and phone numbers of the specialists the following people would call for each situation.

1. Your nephew has a bad case of acne.
2. Your best friend thinks she is pregnant.
3. Your grandmother has blurred vision.
4. Your friend's child is sick.
5. Your neighbor has frequent chest pains.

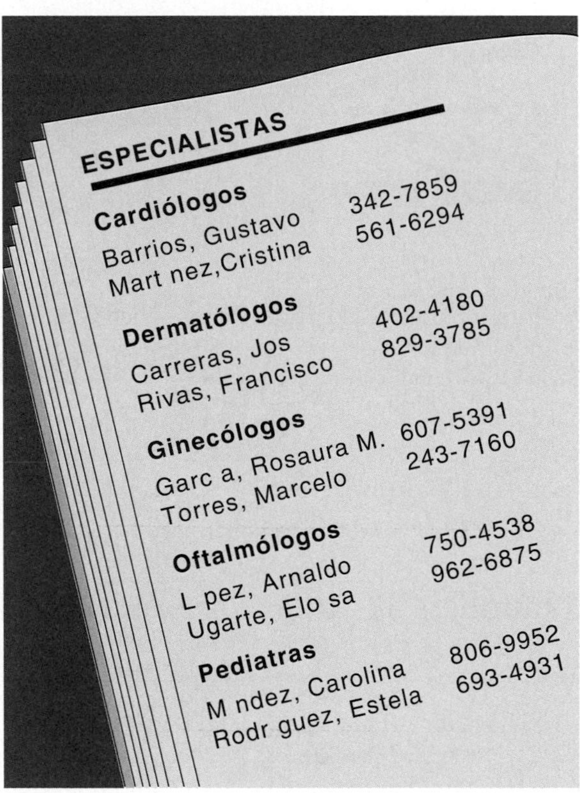

ESPECIALISTAS
Cardiólogos
Barrios, Gustavo 342-7859
Mart nez,Cristina 561-6294
Dermatólogos
Carreras, Jos 402-4180
Rivas, Francisco 829-3785
Ginecólogos
Garc a, Rosaura M. 607-5391
Torres, Marcelo 243-7160
Oftalmólogos
L pez, Arnaldo 750-4538
Ugarte, Elo sa 962-6875
Pediatras
M ndez, Carolina 806-9952
Rodr guez, Estela 693-4931


## 4 Telling time *(La hora)*

■ To ask what time it is, say, "**¿Qué hora es?**" To tell the time in Spanish, the following word order is used:

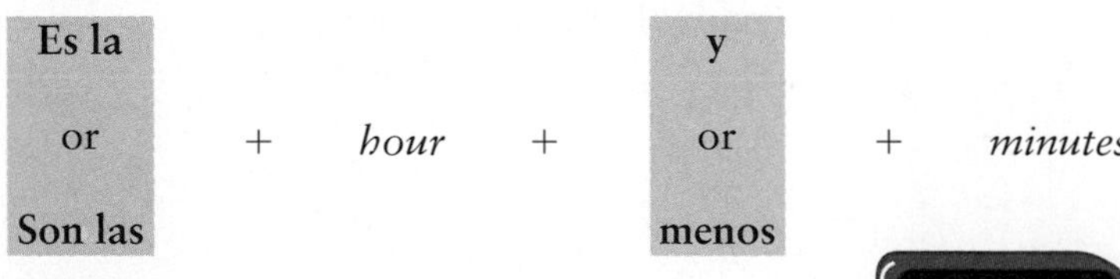


■ **Es** is used with **una.**

**Es** la una.

- **Son** is used with all the other hours.

  **Son** las cuatro.

- The feminine definite article is always used before the hour, since it refers to ***la* hora.**

  Es **la** una y media.

  Son **las** diez y cuarto.

- The hour is given first, then the minutes.

  Son las **once** menos **veinte.**

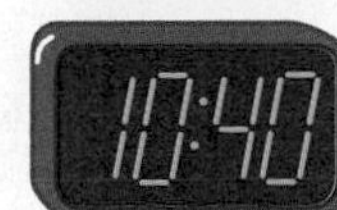

- The equivalent of *past* or *after* is **y.**

  Es la una **y** veinticinco.

- The equivalent of *to* or *till* is **menos.** It is used with fractions of time up to a half hour.

  Son las ocho **menos** cinco.

**ATENCIÓN** The equivalent of *at* + *time* is **a** + **la(s)** + *time.*

| | |
|---|---|
| —¿Qué hora es? | *"What time is it?"* |
| —Son las cinco menos diez.[1] | *"It's ten to five."* |
| —¿A qué hora es la clase? | *"At what time is the class?"* |
| —La clase es a las cinco. | *"The class is at five o'clock."* |

- To specify whether the time is A.M. or P.M., use **de la mañana** or **de la tarde,** respectively.

| | |
|---|---|
| —¿La clase es a las 7 de la mañana? | *"Is the class at 7* A.M.*?"* |
| —No, ¡es a las 7 de la tarde! | *"No, it's at 7* P.M.*!"* |

- To indicate that an activity takes place at an undefined time in the morning or in the afternoon, use **por la mañana** or **por la tarde,** respectively.

| | |
|---|---|
| —¿Estudiamos por la mañana? | *"Shall we study in the morning?"* |
| —No, por la tarde. | *"No, in the afternoon."* |

[1]It is becoming increasingly popular to substitute **y quince** for **y cuarto, y treinta** for **y media,** and **y treinta y cinco, y cuarenta,** etc., for **menos veinticinco, menos veinte,** and so on.

## práctica

**A.** With a partner, take turns giving the time indicated on the clocks in the illustration. Start with clock number one.

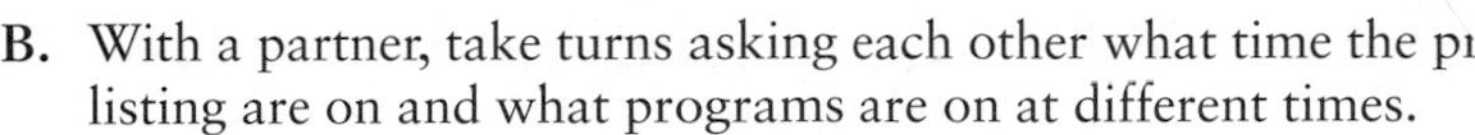

**B.** With a partner, take turns asking each other what time the pı listing are on and what programs are on at different times.

MODELOS: —¿A qué hora es "Telediario"?
*—Es a las seis.*

—¿Qué hay a las seis?
*—"Telediario."*

| Programación del Canal 36 | | | |
|---|---|---|---|
| **Viernes** | | | |
| ***6:00*** | Telediario | ***9:00*** | Noticiero Televisa |
| ***6:50*** | Noticias Internacionales | ***9:30*** | Música |
| ***7:00*** | Religión | ***10:00*** | Fútbol |
| ***7:30*** | Música Latina | ***11:00*** | Noticias de última hora |
| ***8:00*** | "María" (Telenovela) | | |

## 5 Present indicative of regular -ar verbs *(Presente de indicativo de los verbos regulares terminados en -ar)*

■ Spanish verbs are classified in three main patterns of conjugation, according to the infinitive ending. The three infinitive endings are **-ar, -er,** and **-ir.**

| **hablar** *to speak* | | | |
|---|---|---|---|
| **Singular** | | | |
| **yo** | hablo | Yo **hablo** español. | *I speak Spanish.* |
| **tú** | hablas | Tú **hablas** francés. | *You* (inf.) *speak French.* |
| **Ud.** | habla | Ud. **habla** alemán. | *You* (form.) *speak German.* |
| **él** | habla | Él **habla** italiano. | *He speaks Italian.* |
| **ella** | habla | Ella **habla** portugués. | *She speaks Portuguese.* |
| **Plural** | | | |
| **nosotros(-as)** | hablamos | Nosotros **hablamos** español. | *We speak Spanish.* |
| **vosotros(-as)** | habláis | Vosotros **habláis** francés. | *You* (inf.) *speak French.* |
| **Uds.** | hablan | Uds. **hablan** alemán. | *You* (form.) *speak German.* |
| **ellos** | hablan | Ellos **hablan** italiano. | *They* (masc.) *speak Italian.* |
| **ellas** | hablan | Ellas **hablan** portugués. | *They* (fem.) *speak Portuguese.* |

—¿Qué idioma **hablas?** — *"What language do you speak?"*
—Yo **hablo** español. — *"I speak Spanish."*
—¿Y Pierre? — *"And Pierre?"*
—Él **habla** francés. — *"He speaks French."*

■ Regular verbs ending in **-ar** are all conjugated as **hablar** in the chart on page 35. Some other common **-ar** verbs are:

| | | | |
|---|---|---|---|
| **desear** | *to want, wish* | **necesitar** | *to need* |
| **estudiar** | *to study* | **regresar** | *to return* |
| **llamar** | *to call* | **trabajar** | *to work* |

—¿Uds. **estudian** por la noche? — *"Do you study in the evening?"*
—No, nosotros **estudiamos** por la tarde. — *"No, we study in the afternoon."*

—¿Qué **necesitas** tú? — *"What do you need?"*
—Yo **necesito** un libro. — *"I need a book."*

**ATENCIÓN** Notice that the verb forms for **Ud., él,** and **ella** are the same. In addition, **Uds., ellos,** and **ellas** share common verb forms. This is true for all verbs in all tenses.

■ The infinitive of Spanish verbs consists of a stem (such as **habl-**) and an ending (such as **-ar**).

■ The stem **habl-** does not change. The endings change with the subject.

■ The Spanish present tense is equivalent to three English forms:

Yo **hablo** inglés. { *I speak English.* / *I do speak English.* / *I am speaking English.* }

■ Because the verb endings indicate who is performing the action, the subject pronouns are frequently omitted.

**Necesito** un lápiz. — *I need a pencil.*
**Estudiamos** inglés. — *We study English.*
Hoy **trabajo.** — *I work today.*

■ Subject pronouns can, however, be used for emphasis or clarification.

—¿**Ellos** hablan inglés? — *"Do they speak English?"*
—**Ella** habla inglés y **él** habla alemán. — *"She speaks English, and he speaks German."*

■ In Spanish, as in English, when two verbs are used together, the second verb remains in the infinitive.

—¿Con quién **necesita hablar** Ud.? — *"With whom do you need to speak?"*
—**Necesito hablar** con Roberto. — *"I need to speak with Roberto."*

## práctica

**A.** Complete the following dialogues, using the present indicative of the verbs given. Then act them out with a partner.

1. estudiar
   —¿Qué ________ Uds.?
   —________ alemán.
2. trabajar
   —¿Tú ________ en el hospital por la noche?
   —No, ________ por la tarde.
3. regresar
   —¿Cuándo *(When)* ________ Uds.?
   —Yo ________ el lunes y Jorge ________ el miércoles.

4. hablar —¿Qué idioma *(language)* ________ ellos?
—Carlos ________ español y Michele ________ francés.
—¿Cuántos idiomas ________ tú?
—________ tres: español, italiano y portugués.

5. necesitar —¿Qué ________ Uds.?
—________ unas tizas.

6. tomar —¿Cuántas clases ________ Ud.?
—Yo ________ cinco clases.

B. What language do these people speak?

1. Pierre
2. Hans
3. Carlos
4. Vittorio y Pietro
5. John
6. un señor de Portugal

C. Interview a classmate, using the following questions. When you have finished, switch roles.

1. ¿Dónde trabajas? *(name of city)*
2. ¿Qué idiomas hablas?
3. ¿Qué idioma estudias?
4. ¿Estudias por la mañana, por la tarde o por la noche?
5. ¿Qué necesitas?
6. ¿A qué hora regresas a casa *(home)*?

D. Talk about what is going on in these drawings, using the subject pronouns given and the verbs **trabajar, hablar, necesitar, regresar, llamar, estudiar,** and **desear.**

## 6 Negative and interrogative sentences *(Oraciones negativas e interrogativas)*

### A. Negative sentences

- To make a sentence negative, simply place the word **no** in front of the verb.

| | |
|---|---|
| Yo trabajo en el hospital. | *I work at the hospital.* |
| Yo **no** trabajo en el hospital. | *I don't work at the hospital.* |
| Ella habla inglés. | *She speaks English.* |
| Ella **no** habla inglés. | *She doesn't speak English.* |

- If the answer to a question is negative, the word **no** will appear twice: at the beginning of the sentence, as in English, and in front of the verb.

| | |
|---|---|
| —¿Habla Ud. español? | *"Do you speak Spanish?"* |
| —**No,** yo **no** hablo español. | *"No, I don't speak Spanish."* |

The subject pronoun may be omitted.

| | |
|---|---|
| —No, no hablo español. | *"No, I don't speak Spanish."* |

### B. Interrogative sentences

- In Spanish, there are several ways of asking a question to elicit a *yes* or *no* answer.

¿**Ud.** habla español?<br>
¿Habla **Ud.** español?<br>
¿Habla español **Ud.**?<br>
} **Sí,** yo hablo español.

- These three questions ask for the same information and have the same meaning. The subject may be placed at the beginning of the sentence, after the verb, or at the end of the sentence.

- Note that written questions in Spanish begin with an inverted question mark.

- Another common way to ask a question in Spanish is to add tag questions such as **¿no?** and **¿verdad?** at the end of a statement.

| | |
|---|---|
| Ud. habla español, **¿verdad?** | *You speak Spanish, don't you?* |

- Questions that ask for information begin with an interrogative word, and the verb, not the subject, is placed after the interrogative word.

| | |
|---|---|
| ¿Dónde **trabajas** tú? | *Where do you work?* |
| ¿Cuándo **regresan** ellos? | *When do they return?* |
| ¿Qué **necesita** Ud.? | *What do you need?* |
| ¿Quién **es** el profesor? | *Who is the professor?* |

**ATENCIÓN** Spanish does not use an auxiliary verb, such as *do* or *does,* in negative or interrogative sentences.

## práctica

**A.** With a partner, take turns answering the following questions in the negative.

1. ¿Tú hablas francés?
2. ¿Tú trabajas en un hospital?
3. ¿Tú necesitas el libro de español?
4. ¿Tú regresas a la clase a las cinco?
5. ¿Tú estudias por la noche?
6. ¿Tú eres de Madrid?

**B.** Write the questions that will elicit each of the following answers.

1. — ______________________
   —Sí, nosotros estudiamos inglés.
2. — ______________________
   —No, yo no trabajo en el hospital hoy.
3. — ______________________
   —Somos de Colombia.
4. — ______________________
   —No, nosotros no hablamos alemán.
5. — ______________________
   —Ellos necesitan los bolígrafos.
6. — ______________________
   —Ella trabaja en la universidad.
7. — ______________________
   —Carlos regresa a las ocho de la noche.
8. — ______________________
   —No, no soy enfermera.

## 7 Possession with de *(El caso posesivo)*

■ The **de** + *noun* construction is used to express possession or relationship. Spanish does *not* use the apostrophe.

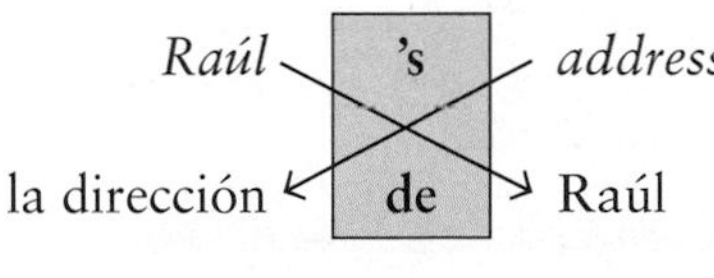


*(the address of Raúl)*

| | |
|---|---|
| la clase **de la Dra. Peña** | *Dr. Peña's class* |
| el libro **de Dora** | *Dora's book* |

**ATENCIÓN** Note the use of the definite article before the words **dirección, clase,** and **libro.**

| | |
|---|---|
| —¿Quién es Francisco Acosta? | *"Who is Francisco Acosta?"* |
| —Es **el profesor de Carmen.** | *"He is Carmen's professor."* |
| —¿Cuál es **la dirección de Irene?** | *"What is Irene's address?"* |
| —Calle Magdalena, número seis. | *"Six Magdalena Street."* |

## práctica

**A.** Express possession or relationship as it is shown in each drawing (e.g., the Spanish equivalent of María's professor.)

1.

la señorita
Martínez
los libros

2.

3.

la señora López
los estudiantes

4.

5.

6.

**B.** Give the following phrases in Spanish.

1. Miss Vera's students
2. Carmen's maps
3. Jorge's clock
4. Marta's notebooks
5. Amanda's friends
6. Javier's chair
7. Mrs. Valle's class
8. the young lady's phone number

C. The students will take turns asking other members of the class if they need certain items.

MODELO: —David, ¿tú necesitas el libro de John?
—*Sí, yo necesito el libro de John.*
*(No, yo no necesito el libro de John.)*

# ¡A ver cuánto aprendió!

## ¡Repase el vocabulario!

INTERNET

See the *¿Cómo se dice...?* Web site for additional grammar and vocabulary practice: http://spanish.college.hmco.com/students

A. Review the words referring to people and objects you see in the classroom, then name the numbered items below, using the definite article.

B. Supply the missing words and read aloud.

1. ¿Qué ________ es? ¿Las nueve?
2. ¿Cómo se ________ "puerta" en ________?
3. Tome ________, por favor.
4. ¿Qué clases ________ Sergio este ________?
5. ¿Cuántos estudiantes ________ en la clase?

6. ¿Qué ________ decir *"the pleasure is mine"?*
7. ¿Dirección? ________ Martí, ________ treinta.
8. ¿A qué ________ es la clase?
9. Hoy es el primer ________ de clases.
10. Rosa no trabaja; ________ estudia.
11. Yo hablo un ________ de portugués.
12. ¿Es una calle o una ________?

## Entrevista

With a partner, interview each other by asking the following questions.

1. ¿Tú trabajas los sábados?
2. ¿Tú trabajas o solamente estudias?
3. ¿Tú estudias por la mañana, por la tarde o por la noche?
4. ¿Tú tomas una clase de historia este semestre?
5. ¿Cuántas clases tomas este semestre?
6. ¿Tú hablas italiano? (¿portugués?)
7. ¿Cómo se dice *"door"* en español?
8. ¿Qué quiere decir "domicilio"?
9. ¿Necesitas un lápiz? (¿una pluma?)
10. ¿Qué hora es?
11. ¿A qué hora regresas a casa *(home)?*
12. ¿Cuál es tu dirección?

## Situaciones

What would you say in the following situations? What might the other person say? Act out the scenes with a partner. Take turns playing each role.

1. In class, you're not sure how to say "you're welcome" in Spanish.
2. You need to know a classmate's address.
3. You can't remember what time your Spanish class meets. Your roommate is also in the class.
4. You are with Dr. Cortés and your teacher, who have never met before.
5. Your elderly neighbor stops by to say hello. You invite him to sit down.
6. You don't know what time it is. The person next to you on the bus is wearing a watch.

## Para escribir *(To write)*

Complete the following dialogues.

1. *Julia talks with a classmate.*

JULIA —____________________
ELENA —Me llamo Elena Martínez.
JULIA —____________________
ELENA —Soy de Madrid.
JULIA —____________________
ELENA —486-3497.
JULIA —____________________
ELENA —Calle Roma, número veintiocho.

2. *Professor Mena and Mr. Roberto Soto are in the classroom. Today is Friday.*

PROF. MENA —¿Cómo se llama usted, señor?
ROBERTO —____________________
PROF. MENA —Mucho gusto, señor Soto.
ROBERTO —____________________
PROF. MENA —¿Qué día es hoy?
ROBERTO —____________________
PROF. MENA —¿Cómo se dice "*thirty-five*" en español?
ROBERTO —____________________
PROF. MENA —¿Qué quiere decir "*Until I see you again*"?
ROBERTO —____________________
PROF. MENA —Muy bien. Hasta luego, señor Soto.
ROBERTO —____________________

3. *A student thanks her teacher.*

MARISA —____________________
PROFESORA —De nada, señorita García. Hasta luego.
MARISA —____________________

# En la vida real

## Presentaciones *(Introductions)*

**CD-ROM**

**Do the interactive exercises on the CD-ROM for additional practice.**

Form groups of three. After one person introduces the other two, make small talk: find out everybody's address, how many classes everybody is taking, and talk about what day it is and what time it is. You might want to include the following words or phrases:

| | |
|---|---|
| **A sus órdenes.** | *At your service.* |
| **Encantado.** (If you are male)<br>**Encantada.** (If you are female) | *Charmed (It's a pleasure).* |

## Horario de clases

This is María Elena's schedule. With a classmate, try to figure out when her classes are.

MODELO: —¿Cuándo es la clase de tenis?
—*La clase de tenis es los sábados.*
—¿A qué hora?
—*A las nueve.*

| HORA | LUNES | MARTES | MIÉRCOLES | JUEVES | VIERNES | SÁBADO |
|---|---|---|---|---|---|---|
| 8:00-9:00 | Psicología | | Psicología | | Psicología | |
| 9:00-10:00 | Biología | | Biología | | Biología | Tenis |
| 10:00-11:30 | | Historia | | Historia | | |
| 12:15-1:00 | | | ALMUERZO[1] | | | |
| 1:00-2:00 | Literatura | | Literatura | | Literatura | Laboratorio de Biología |
| | | | | | | |
| 5:00-6:30 | | Educación Física | | Educación Física | | |
| | | | | | | |
| 7:00-8:30 | Arte | | Arte | | | |

## Mi horario

With the help of a dictionary and/or your instructor, work with a classmate to make up each other's schedules.

## Un inventario de la clase

With a classmate, conduct an inventory of everything in your classroom, using **hay.**

MODELO: Hay una pizarra en el salón de clases.

[1]lunch

# 1. El español en los Estados Unidos y en Canadá

Estados Unidos

Canadá

- Más de *(More than)* 30 millones de hispanos viven *(live)* en los Estados Unidos. Los hispanos son el grupo minoritario de mayor crecimiento *(growth)* en la nación. Los estados con la mayor concentración de hispanos son Nuevo México, Tejas, California, Nueva York, New Jersey y la Florida.
- Los nombres de muchas ciudades, estados y zonas geográficas de los Estados Unidos vienen del español: Arizona, California, Los Ángeles, El Paso, Sierra Nevada y Río Grande, por ejemplo. En Canadá, la gran península al este del país tiene un nombre de origen hispano: Labrador *(Farmer)*.
- El español es el idioma extranjero *(foreign)* más popular en las escuelas y universidades de los Estados Unidos. Más de 650.000 estudiantes universitarios estudian español cada año *(each year)*.
- En Canadá hay más de 200.000 habitantes de habla hispana; la mayoría de ellos son de España, Chile, El Salvador y México. La mayor parte vive en Toronto, Montreal y Vancouver.

Durante la época colonial, las órdenes religiosas españolas establecieron misiones en el suroeste de los Estados Unidos, y muchas aún *(still)* existen. La Misión de San Francisco de Asís es la más famosa de Nuevo México.

*¿Cuáles son otras atracciones turísticas en el suroeste?*

En muchas partes de los Estados Unidos hay servicios bilingües de tipo social, educativo y legal para los residentes hispanos.

*¿Hay muchas personas de habla hispana en su ciudad?*

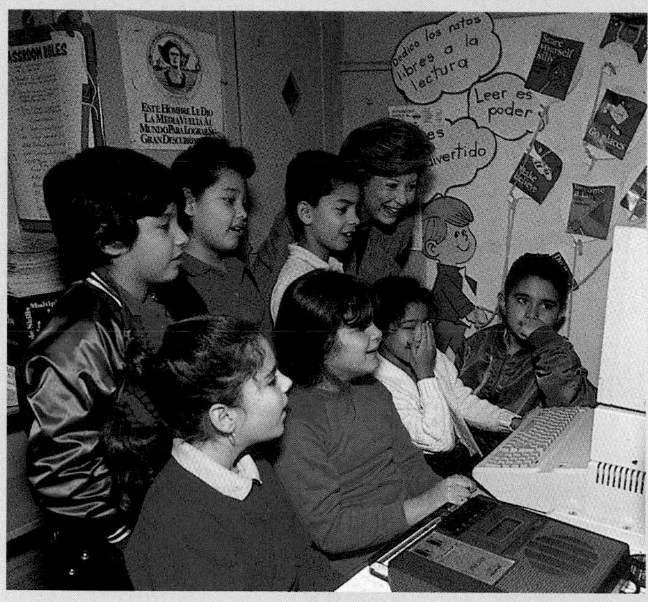


Los programas de educación bilingüe ayudan *(help)* a muchos niños hispanos en sus estudios primarios.

*¿La educación bilingüe es una buena idea?*

En muchas ciudades norteamericanas hay periódicos *(newspapers)* y revistas *(magazines)* en español. Muchos hispanos los leen *(read them)* porque tienen más información sobre *(about)* la comunidad latina. (Los Ángeles, California)

*¿Qué periódicos lee Ud.?*

Las emisoras de televisión hispanas son una fuente *(source)* de información importante en ciudades como Nueva York, donde vive *(live)* más de un millón de puertorriqueños, más que en San Juan, la capital de Puerto Rico. En la foto, un grupo musical anima la carroza *(float)* de una estación de televisión hispana de Nueva York.

*¿Qué canales de televisión mira Ud.?*

En "La Pequeña Habana", un barrio *(neighborhood)* hispano de la ciudad de Miami, las tiendas, los cafés, los restaurantes y los mercados tienen nombres en español, y el español es el idioma más hablado *(spoken)*.

*¿Cómo se llama el barrio de Ud.?*

La comida *(food)* mexicana es tan *(so)* popular en los Estados Unidos que para muchos norteamericanos la primera clase de español es en un restaurante.

*¿Le gusta la comida mexicana? ¿Cuál es su plato favorito?*

En muchas de las grandes ciudades de Canadá hay fiestas y actos interculturales en los que se nota *(one notes)* la influencia hispana. La música hispana, especialmente la mexicana, la salsa, el merengue y el tango, son muy populares. En varias ciudades también se celebra el "Cinco de Mayo".

*¿Celebran fiestas hispanas en su ciudad? ¿Cuáles?*

TELEINFORME

VIDEO

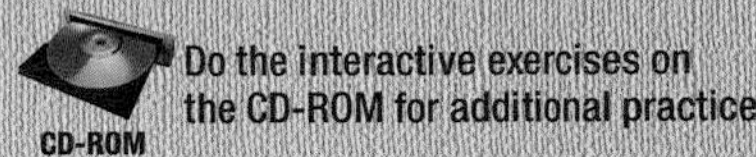
CD-ROM
Do the interactive exercises on the CD-ROM for additional practice.

## Preparación

**¿Cuánto saben Uds. ya?** After reading **Panorama hispánico 1,** get together in groups of three or four students and complete each statement with the appropriate information.

1. Hay más de ______ millones de hispanos en los Estados Unidos.
2. Muchos hispanos viven en los estados de ______, ______, ______, ______, ______ y ______.
3. En muchas ciudades de los Estados Unidos existen programas de ______ bilingüe para los niños hispanos.
4. Hay ______ y ______ en español en muchas grandes ciudades norteamericanas.
5. La Pequeña Habana está en la ciudad de ______, en el estado de ______.

## Comprensión

A. **Anuncios.** Read the following slogans in Spanish. Match the slogan with the name of the company in the second column according to what you understood in the video.

| A | B |
|---|---|
| 1. Su dinero vale mucho *(is worth a lot)* y muchas cosas más. | a. AT&T |
| 2. La mejor decisión *(the best decision)*. | b. Kodak |
| 3. De familia en familia. | c. Maybelline |
| 4. Colores vivos *(bright)* y reales. | d. Ford |
| 5. ¡Qué momento! ¡Qué sabor...! | e. McDonald's |
| 6. Los cosméticos que le ayudan a embellecerse *(help to make you beautiful)*. | f. Sears |

B. **El Festival de la calle Ocho.** Select the word or phrase that best completes each statement according to what you understood in the video.

1. El Festival de la calle Ocho de la Pequeña Habana se celebra (todos los años, cada semana).
2. La Pequeña Habana está en (Miami, Los Ángeles).
3. (Muchas, Pocas) personas disfrutan del festival.
4. De noche coronan (a la reina, al rey) en un concurso de belleza *(beauty pageant)*.
5. Hay una carrera *(road race)* a lo largo *(along)* de (Miami, la calle Ocho).

## Ampliación

A. **Publicidad.** In groups of three or four, try to guess the meaning of the following words. Then brainstorm a list of companies that might advertise their products in Spanish to the Spanish-speaking communities in the U.S. Choose one company and write an original Spanish slogan for a particular product.

1. cosméticos
2. perfumes
3. champú
4. aspirinas
5. automóviles
6. televisores
7. computadoras
8. servicios telefónicos

B. **Un festival típico.** In pairs or small groups, describe a typical festival or celebration in your town, state, or country. Use the following questions as a guide. Then compare your celebrations to the one you see in the video.

1. ¿Cómo se celebra el festival?
2. ¿Dónde se celebra?
3. ¿Cuándo se celebra?
4. ¿Cuáles son las actividades más importantes?
5. ¿Qué hacen *(do)* de día?
6. ¿Qué hacen de noche?

# Por teléfono

Lección 3

## OBJECTIVES

### Pronunciation

Linking

### Structure

Gender, Part II • Possessive adjectives • Cardinal numbers 101–1,000 • Descriptive adjectives: Forms, position, and agreement with articles and nouns • Present indicative of regular **-er** and **-ir** verbs • Present indicative of the irregular verbs **tener** and **venir**

### Communication

You will learn vocabulary used to make and to receive phone calls.

# Por teléfono

*Raquel, Pedro, Marisa, y Carmen son estudiantes universitarios que viven en Los Ángeles, y son muy buenos amigos. Raquel desea ser médica, Pedro desea ser abogado, y Marisa y Carmen desean ser maestras. Pedro es moreno, alto y muy simpático. Las chicas son inteligentes y bonitas.*

*Raquel desea hablar con Pedro.*

MARISA —¿Sí?
RAQUEL —Hola. ¿Está Pedro?
MARISA —No, no está. Lo siento.
RAQUEL —¿A qué hora regresa?
MARISA —A las nueve de la noche.
RAQUEL —Entonces llamo[1] más tarde.
MARISA —Muy bien. Adiós.

*Carmen habla con su amiga Marisa.*

MARISA —Bueno.
CARMEN —Hola. ¿Está Marisa?
MARISA —Sí, con ella habla... ¿Carmen?
CARMEN —Sí. ¿Qué tal, Marisa?
MARISA —Muy bien, gracias. ¿Qué hay de nuevo?
CARMEN —Nada. ¡Oye! ¿Dónde comemos[1] mañana? ¿En la cafetería?
MARISA —No, mañana tengo que escribir un informe y debo leer varios artículos en la biblioteca.
CARMEN —Yo también tengo que estudiar para un examen.
MARISA —Entonces nos vemos[1] el martes.

*Pedro habla con Raquel.*

ROSA —Dígame.
PEDRO —Hola. ¿Está Raquel?
ROSA —Sí. ¿Quién habla?
PEDRO —Pedro Morales.
ROSA —Un momento por favor.
RAQUEL —*(A Rosa)* ¿Quién es?
ROSA —Es tu amigo Pedro.
RAQUEL —Hola, Pedro. ¿Qué tal?
PEDRO —Bien, ¿y tú?
RAQUEL —Más o menos.
PEDRO —¿Por qué? ¿Problemas sentimentales?
RAQUEL —No, problemas económicos. ¡Necesito dinero!

[1]The present indicative is often used in Spanish to express a near future.

PEDRO —¡Yo también! Oye, ¿tú tienes que trabajar en el hospital esta noche?

RAQUEL —No, hoy no trabajo por la noche. Los lunes mi novio y yo estudiamos en la biblioteca.

PEDRO —¿Tú vienes a mi casa mañana?

RAQUEL —No, porque mañana tengo que ir a otro hospital a solicitar trabajo.

PEDRO —Entonces, adiós.

ROSA —*(A Raquel)* Oye, ¿cómo es tu amigo Pedro? ¿Es guapo?

RAQUEL —Es guapo y muy inteligente, pero… tiene novia.

# Vocabulario

## Cognados

**el artículo** article
**la cafetería** cafeteria
**el examen** exam
**inteligente** intelligent

## Nombres

**el (la) abogado(-a)** lawyer
**la biblioteca** library
**la casa** house, home
**la chica, muchacha** girl, young woman
**el chico, muchacho** boy, young man
**el dinero** money
**el informe** report
**la noche** evening, night
**la novia** girlfriend, fiancée, bride
**el novio** boyfriend, fiancé, groom
**el trabajo, el empleo** job, work

## Verbos

**comer** to eat
**deber** must, have to, should
**escribir** to write
**leer** to read
**solicitar** to apply
**tener** to have
**venir** to come
**vivir** to live

## Adjetivos

**alto(-a)** tall
**bonito(-a), lindo(-a)** pretty
**bueno(-a)**[1] good
**moreno(-a)**[2] dark, brunet
**otro(-a)** another, other
**simpático(-a)** charming, nice
**universitario(-a)** related to university
**varios(-as)** several

[1]**Bueno** becomes **buen** when used before a masculine singular noun.
[2]**Castaño** is used as the equivalent of *brown* when describing hair or eye color.

## Otras palabras y expresiones

**a** at, to, in order to
**bueno, dígame** hello *(answering the phone)*
**¿Cómo es...?** What is . . . like?
**con ella habla** this is she *(speaking)*
**de** of
**en** on, in, at
**entonces** then, in that case
**¿Está... + *(name)*?** Is . . . *(name)* there?
**esta noche** tonight
**lo siento** I'm sorry
**mañana** tomorrow
**más o menos** so-so, more or less
**más tarde** later
**nada** nothing
**no está** he or she is not here
**o** or
**para** for
**pero** but
**¿por qué?** why?
**por teléfono** on the phone
**problemas económicos** financial problems
**problemas sentimentales** love problems
**que** who, that
**¿quién?** who?
**¿quién es?** who is it?
**¿Quién habla? ¿De parte de quién?** Who is speaking?
**su** his, her, its, your *(formal)*, their
**tener que + *infinitive*** to have to + infinitive *(do something)*
**tengo que ir** I have to go
**un momento** one moment

# Vocabulario adicional

## Características

| | |
|---|---|
| **antipático(-a)** unpleasant | Antonio no es **antipático;** es muy simpático. |
| **bajo(-a)** short | Marco es **bajo;** no es alto. |
| **delgado(-a)** thin, slender | Roberto es alto y **delgado.** |
| **feo(-a)** ugly | Paco no es **feo;** es guapo. |
| **gordo(-a)** fat | ¿María es delgada o **gorda?** |
| **guapo(-a)** handsome | Mario es muy **guapo.** |
| **optimista**[1] optimist | Yo soy muy **optimista.** |
| **pelirrojo(-a)** red-headed | Teresa es **pelirroja.** |
| **pesimista**[1] pessimist | Pedro es muy **pesimista.** |
| **realista**[1] realist | Debemos ser **realistas.** |
| **rubio(-a)** blond | Sergio es **rubio.** |

[1]The ending of this kind of adjective (**-ista**) does not change, regardless of gender: **el profesor optimista, la profesora optimista.**

## Datos personales (*Personal data*)

**lugar donde trabaja** place of employment
**nombre del esposo (de la esposa)** husband's (wife's) name
**nombre y edad de los hijos** children's names and ages
**número de la licencia de conducir** driver's license number
**número de seguro social** social security number
**ocupación** occupation
**profesión** profession

**SOLICITUD DE TRABAJO** *(Job Application)*

Apellidos y nombre García López, Susana
*(Surnames and first name)*

Fecha de nacimiento *(Date of birth)*
Día 7 *(Day)* Mes 12 *(Month)* Año 80 *(Year)*

Número de identidad 86407423
*(Identification number)*

Edad 22 años
*(Age)*

Dirección Calle 6, 258 Ciudad Caracas *(City)* Zona postal 70-824 *(Zip Code)*

Teléfono 862-4221

Nacionalidad Venezolana Lugar de nacimiento Caracas *(Place of birth)*

Estado civil: *(Marital status)* ☑ Soltero(-a) *(Single)* ❑ Casado(-a) *(Married)* ❑ Divorciado(-a) *(Divorced)* ❑ Viudo(-a) *(Widowed)*

Sexo *(Sex)* ❑ Masculino ☑ Femenino

**Educación**

| Institución | Años |
|---|---|
| Universidad de Caracas | 1997-2001 |
| Instituto San Pedro | 1993-1997 |

**Experiencia**

| Compañía | Años |
|---|---|
| Farmacia Bernardino | 2001 (6 meses) |

# ¡Conversemos!

Answer the following questions, basing your answers on the dialogue.

1. ¿Pedro desea ser abogado o maestro?
2. ¿Raquel desea hablar con Marisa o con Pedro?
3. ¿Pedro regresa a las nueve de la mañana o de la noche?
4. ¿Carmen habla con Marisa o con Raquel?
5. ¿Carmen y Marisa comen o no comen en la cafetería?

6. ¿Marisa tiene que leer o escribir varios artículos?
7. ¿Carmen tiene que estudiar para una clase o para un examen?
8. ¿Pedro es el novio o un amigo de Raquel?
9. ¿Raquel necesita libros o dinero?
10. ¿Pedro necesita un reloj o necesita dinero también?
11. ¿Raquel trabaja o estudia en la biblioteca esta noche?
12. ¿Raquel tiene que solicitar trabajo en un hospital o en una universidad?

## ¿Lo sabía Ud.?

- Contestando el teléfono *(Answering the phone)*:
En España *(Spain)*: "Diga", "Dígame", "¿Sí?"
En Cuba y en otras regiones del Caribe: "Oigo"
En México: "Bueno"
En Argentina: "¿Sí?", "Hable", "Hola", "¿Aló?"
- En Latinoamérica y en España los estudiantes frecuentemente estudian juntos *(together)*.
- "Español" y "castellano" son *(are)* equivalentes.
- "El español es el idioma nativo de unos *(about)* 400.000.000[1] de personas.

- ¿Cómo contestan el teléfono en los Estados Unidos?
- ¿En los Estados Unidos los estudiantes estudian juntos?
- ¿Hay muchas *(many)* personas en los Estados Unidos que hablan español?

Estudiantes de la Universidad Iberoamericana, Ciudad de México, haciendo investigación en la biblioteca.

[1]Note that in Spanish numbers, a period is used instead of a comma to indicate thousands.

See the *¿Cómo se dice...?* Web site for activities on authentic cultural material: http://spanish.college.hmco.com/students

# Pronunciación

## Linking

STUDENT AUDIO

- In Spanish, a final consonant is always linked with the next initial vowel sound.

  el‿amigo    los‿hospitales[1]    problemas‿económicos

- When two identical consonants are together, they are pronounced as one.

  es‿simpática    Voy con‿Norma.

- When two identical vowels are together, they are pronounced as one long vowel.

  Rodolfo‿Ochoa    Habla‿Ana.

- The final vowel of one word is linked with the initial vowel of the following word to form one syllable.

  la‿amiga de‿Olga    trabaja‿esta noche    hablo‿español

# Estructuras

## 1 Gender, Part II *(Género, Parte II)*

In **Lección 2** you learned that words that end in **-o** in Spanish are generally masculine, and those that end in **-a** are generally feminine. Here are other useful rules to help you determine the gender of nouns that do not end in **-o** or **-a**.

- Nouns ending in **-sión, -ción, -tad, -dad,** and **-umbre** are feminine.

| | | | |
|---|---|---|---|
| la televi**sión** | *television* | la ciu**dad** | *city* |
| la conversa**ción** | *conversation* | la universi**dad** | *university* |
| la liber**tad** | *liberty, freedom* | la certid**umbre** | *certainty* |

- Many words that end in **-ma** are masculine.[2]

| | | | |
|---|---|---|---|
| el poe**ma** | *poem* | el cli**ma** | *climate* |
| el telegra**ma** | *telegram* | el idio**ma** | *language* |
| el progra**ma** | *program* | el proble**ma** | *problem* |
| el siste**ma** | *system* | el te**ma** | *subject, theme* |

[1]In Spanish the letter **h** is silent.

[2]Some feminine words end in **-ma,** such as **la cama** *(bed)* and **la rama** *(branch).*

- You must learn the gender of nouns that have other endings and that do not refer to male or female beings. Remember that it is helpful to memorize each noun with its corresponding article.

| | |
|---|---|
| **la** pared | **el** reloj |
| **el** lápiz | **la** luz |
| **el** borrador | |

## práctica

**A.** Read the following words, adding the corresponding definite article (**el, la, los,** or **las**).

1. pared
2. mesa
3. turismo
4. hospital
5. problemas
6. ciudad
7. sociedad
8. borrador
9. mano
10. lumbre *(fire)*
11. libertad
12. idiomas
13. organización
14. día
15. solución
16. conversación
17. universidad
18. muchedumbre *(crowd)*

**B.** With a partner, take turns asking each other whether or not you need certain items in your classroom.

MODELO: —¿Necesitas un borrador?
—*Sí, necesito un borrador.*
—*No, necesito una tiza.*

## 2 Possessive adjectives *(Los adjetivos posesivos)*

**Forms of the Possessive Adjectives**

| Singular | Plural | |
|---|---|---|
| **mi** | **mis** | *my* |
| **tu** | **tus** | *your* (fam.) |
| **su** | **sus** | *your* (form.), *his*, *her*, *its*, *their* |
| **nuestro(-a)** | **nuestros(-as)** | *our* |
| **vuestro(-a)** | **vuestros(-as)** | *your* (fam.) |

| | |
|---|---|
| —¿**Tu** novio es de Buenos Aires? | *"Is your boyfriend from Buenos Aires?"* |
| —No, **mi** novio es de Asunción. | *"No, my boyfriend is from Asunción."* |

- Possessive adjectives always precede the nouns they introduce. They agree in number with the nouns they modify.

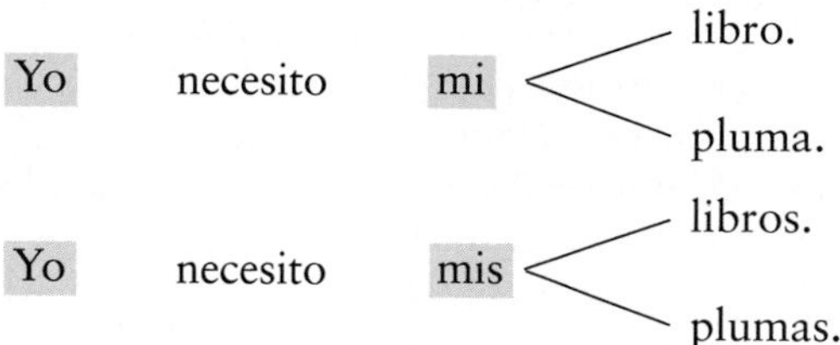


Yo necesito mi libro.

Yo necesito mis libros.

- **Nuestro** and **vuestro** are the only possessive adjectives that have the feminine endings **-a** and **-as.** The others take the same endings for both genders.

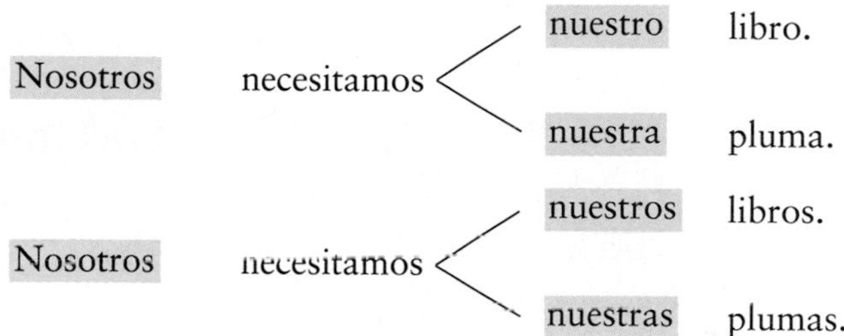

Nosotros necesitamos nuestro libro.
nuestra pluma.
Nosotros necesitamos nuestros libros.
nuestras plumas.


- Possessive adjectives agree in gender with the thing possessed and *not* with the possessor. For example, two male students referring to their female professor will say ***nuestra* profesor*a*.**

- Because **su** and **sus** each have several possible meanings, the form **de él** (or **de ella, de ellos, de ellas, de Ud.,** or **de Uds.**) can be substituted to avoid confusion. The "formula" is: *article* + *noun* + **de** + *pronoun.*

| | |
|---|---|
| sus plumas | las plumas **de él** (**ella, Ud.,** etc.) |
| su libro | el libro **de él** (**ella, Ud.,** etc.) |

## práctica

**A.** Complete the following dialogues, using the Spanish equivalent of the words in parentheses. Then act them out with a partner.

1. —¿A qué hora es la clase ________? *(your)*
   —________ clase es a las ocho. *(Our)*
2. —¿Cuál es ________ dirección, Anita? *(your)*
   —________ dirección es calle Lima, 230. *(My)*
3. —¿Necesita Ud. ________ libros, señora? *(your)*
   —No, necesito ________ cuadernos. *(my)*
4. —¿Es la casa ________? *(his)*
   —No, es la casa ________. *(her)*
5. —¿De dónde es el profesor ________? *(your)*
   —________ profesor es de Montreal. *(Our)*
6. —¿Con quiénes hablan Teresa y Victoria?
   —Hablan con ________ amigas. *(their)*

**B.** Answer the following questions in the negative, using possessive adjectives.

1. ¿Estela es la novia de Alberto?
2. ¿Necesitas tu libro de español?
3. ¿La profesora de Uds. es de México?
4. ¿Carlos y Daniel son tus amigos?
5. ¿El doctor Paz y la doctora Ruiz son los profesores de Uds.?
6. ¿Tú necesitas mis cuadernos?
7. ¿Tú necesitas la dirección de los chicos?
8. ¿Marisa y Olga son las amigas de Claudia?

## 3 Cardinal numbers 101–1,000 *(Números cardinales 101–1.000)*

| | | | |
|---|---|---|---|
| 101 | **ciento uno** (and so on) | 600 | **seiscientos** |
| 200 | **doscientos** | 700 | **setecientos** |
| 300 | **trescientos** | 800 | **ochocientos** |
| 400 | **cuatrocientos** | 900 | **novecientos** |
| 500 | **quinientos** | 1.000 | **mil** |

- To ask how much a single item costs, say, "**¿Cuánto cuesta?**" For multiple items, use "**¿Cuánto cuestan?**"

| | |
|---|---|
| —¿Cuánto cuesta el escritorio? | *"How much does the desk cost?"* |
| —Cuesta ciento cincuenta dólares. | *"It costs a hundred and fifty dollars."* |
| —¿Cuánto cuestan las ventanas? | *"How much do the windows cost?"* |
| —Cuestan mil cien dólares. | *"They cost eleven hundred dollars."* |

- When counting beyond 100 (101 to 199), **ciento** is used.
- **Y** appears only in numbers between 16 and 99. It is not used to separate thousands, hundreds, and tens from each other: **mil quinientos ochenta y seis.**
- In Spanish, one does not count in hundreds beyond 1,000; thus, 1,100 is expressed as **mil cien.** After 1,000, thousands are counted **dos mil, tres mil,** and so on. Note that Spanish uses a period rather than a comma to indicate thousands.
- When modifying a feminine noun, the feminine form is used: **doscientas sillas.**

### práctica

**A.** Complete the following series of numbers.

1. cien, doscientos, trescientos,… mil
2. diez mil, veinte mil, treinta mil,… cien mil
3. ciento diez, doscientos veinte, trescientos treinta,… mil cien

**B.** With a partner, look at the illustration at the top of the next page and ask each other how much everything costs.

MODELO: —¿Cuánto cuesta la silla?
—*La silla cuesta ciento ochenta dólares.*

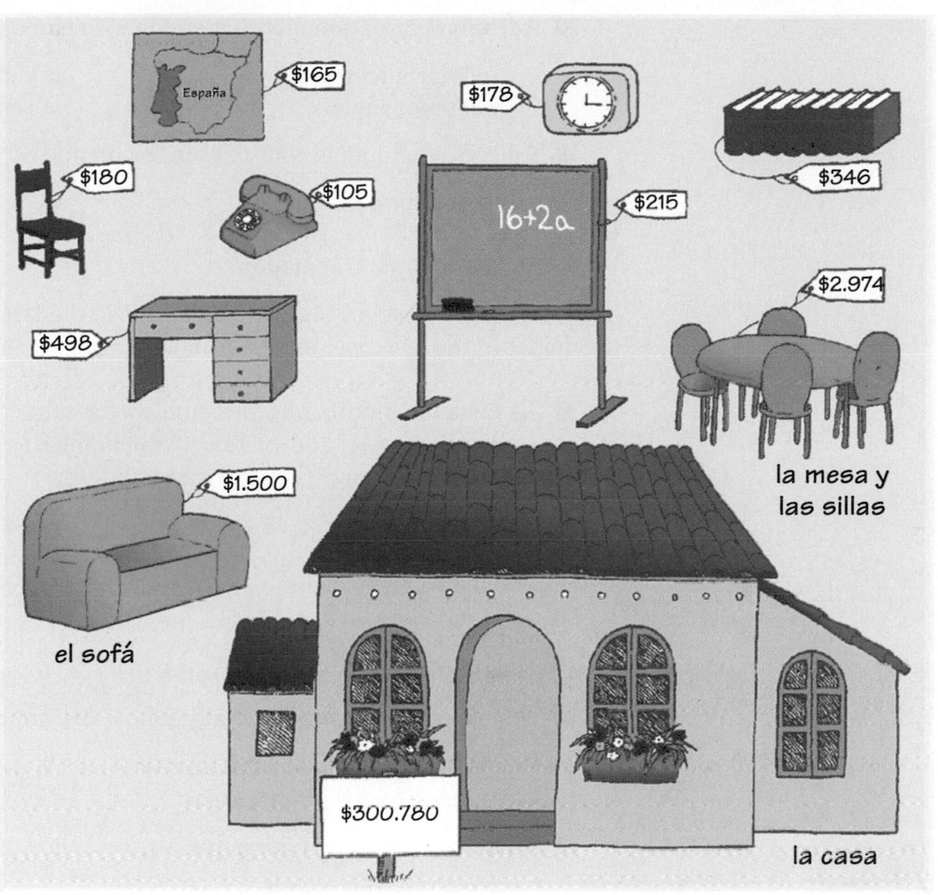


## 4 Descriptive adjectives: Forms, position, and agreement with articles and nouns *(Adjetivos calificativos: Formas, posición y concordancia con artículos y nombres)*

### A. Forms of adjectives

- Descriptive adjectives identify characteristics or qualities such as color, size, and personality. In Spanish, these adjectives agree in gender and number with the nouns they modify. Adjectives ending in **-o** are made feminine by changing the **-o** to **-a.**

| | |
|---|---|
| el muchach**o** mexican**o** | la muchach**a** mexican**a** |
| el chic**o** rubi**o** | la chic**a** rubi**a** |
| el lápiz roj**o** | la plum**a** roj**a** |

- Adjectives ending in **-e** or in a consonant have the same form for the masculine and the feminine.

| | |
|---|---|
| el chico inteligente | la chica inteligente |
| el esposo feliz *(happy)* | la esposa feliz |
| el libro fácil *(easy)* | la clase fácil |

- Adjectives of nationality that end in a consonant add an **-a** in the feminine.

| | |
|---|---|
| el muchacho español | la muchacha españo**la** |
| el señor inglés | la señora ingles**a** |

- Adjectives ending in **-or, -án, -ón,** or **-ín** add an **-a** in the feminine.

el alumno trabajad**or**
la alumna trabajad**ora** } *the hard-working student*

**ATENCIÓN** Adjectives that have an accent in the last syllable of the masculine form drop it in the feminine: **inglés** → **inglesa.**[1]

- To form the plural, adjectives follow the same rules as nouns. Adjectives ending in a vowel add **-s;** adjectives ending in a consonant add **-es;** adjectives ending in **-z** change the **-z** to **c** and add **-es.**

| | |
|---|---|
| norteamerican**a** | norteamerican**as** |
| españo**l** | españo**les** |
| feli**z** | feli**ces** |

## B. Position of adjectives

- Descriptive adjectives generally follow the noun.

| | |
|---|---|
| Miguel es un chico **inteligente.** | *Miguel is an intelligent boy.* |
| Necesito dos plumas **rojas.** | *I need two red pens.* |

- Adjectives denoting nationality always follow the noun.

El profesor **mexicano** trabaja en la universidad.

## C. Agreement of articles, nouns, and adjectives

- In Spanish, the article, noun, and adjective agree in gender and number.

| | |
|---|---|
| **un** muchach**o** alt**o** | **una** muchach**a** alt**a** |
| **los** muchach**os** alt**os** | **las** muchach**as** alt**as** |

- When an adjective modifies two or more nouns, the plural form is used.

la sill**a** y la mes**a** **rojas**

- If two nouns described together are of different genders, the masculine plural form of the adjective is used.

la chic**a** mexican**a**
el chic**o** mexican**o** } la chic**a** y el chic**o** mexican**os**

[1]For rules on accent marks, see Appendix A.

## práctica

**A.** With a partner, take turns asking the following questions. In your answers, contradict what is stated.

MODELO: —¿Rosaura es alta?
—*No, es baja.*

1. ¿El novio de Adriana es rubio?
2. ¿Las mujeres son gordas?
3. ¿Los muchachos son bajos?
4. ¿Tu profesora es antipática?
5. ¿La novia de Daniel es fea?
6. ¿Tú eres optimista?
7. ¿El hermano de Olga es delgado?
8. ¿Ellas son morenas?

**B.** Describe the following people, places, or things, using as many descriptive adjectives as possible.

1. Julia Roberts
2. Ricky Martin
3. Roseanne
4. Nueva York
5. su mejor *(best)* amigo
6. las chicas de la clase
7. los chicos de la clase
8. el presidente de los Estados Unidos

## 5 Present indicative of regular -er and -ir verbs *(Presente de indicativo de los verbos regulares que terminan en* **-er** *y en* **-ir***)*

| **comer** *to eat* | | **vivir** *to live* | |
|---|---|---|---|
| yo | com**o** | yo | viv**o** |
| tú | com**es** | tú | viv**es** |
| Ud. / él / ella | com**e** | Ud. / él / ella | viv**e** |
| nosotros(-as) | com**emos** | nosotros(-as) | viv**imos** |
| vosotros(-as) | com**éis** | vosotros(-as) | viv**ís** |
| Uds. / ellos / ellas | com**en** | Uds. / ellos / ellas | viv**en** |

■ Other verbs conjugated like **comer:**

**aprender** *to learn*
**creer** *to believe, to think*
**leer** *to read*
**beber** *to drink*
**vender** *to sell*
**deber** *must, should, ought to*

—¿Dónde **comen** Uds.? — *"Where do you eat?"*
—Nosotros **comemos** en la cafetería y Elsa **come** en su casa. — *"We eat in the cafeteria and Elsa eats at her house."*

—¿Qué **lees** tú? — *"What are you reading?"*
—**Leo** mi libro de español. — *"I'm reading my Spa*

■ Other verbs conjugated like **vivir:**

| | |
|---|---|
| **abrir** *to open* | **escribir** *to write* |
| **recibir** *to receive* | **decidir** *to decide* |

—¿Dónde **viven** Uds.? *"Where do you live?"*
—**Vivimos** en la calle Magnolia. *"We live on Magnolia Street."*

—¿Tú **escribes** con lápiz o con pluma? *"Do you write with a pencil or with a pen?"*
—**Escribo** con bolígrafo. *"I write with a (ballpoint) pen."*

## práctica

**A.** Complete the following dialogues, using the present indicative of the verbs given. Then act them out with a partner.

1. comer —¿Dónde ________ Uds.?
   —________ en la cafetería.
2. vivir —¿Dónde ________ tú?
   —________ en la calle Montalvo.
3. recibir —¿Cuánto dinero ________ Uds.?
   —Yo ________ quinientos dólares y él ________ cuatrocientos.
4. leer —¿Qué periódico *(newspaper)* ________ ellos?
   —________ el *Times*.
5. vender, creer, abrir —¿Dónde ________ (ellos) sándwiches?
   —En la cafetería, pero yo ________ que (ellos) no ________ la cafetería hasta *(until)* las siete.
6. beber —¿Qué ________ Uds.?
   —Nosotros ________ Coca-Cola y Ana ________ 7-Up.
7. deber —¿Qué ________ estudiar (yo)?
   —Ud. ________ estudiar alemán.
8. escribir —¿Uds. ________ en inglés?
   —No, ________ en español.

**B.** Describe what these people do, must do, or decide to do, using **-er** or **-ir** verbs.

1. Yo / café
2. Nosotros / español
3. Uds. / el *Times*
4. Carlos y Rosa / con una pluma roja
5. Tú / la puerta
6. Las chicas / en un apartamento
7. Ud. / tacos
8. Nosotros / estudiar hoy
9. Susana / tomar portugués

**C.** Interview a classmate, using the following questions and two questions of your own. When you have finished, switch roles.

1. ¿Dónde vives?
2. ¿Dónde comes?
3. ¿Comen sándwiches tú y tus amigos?

4. ¿Bebes Sprite o Coca-Cola?
5. ¿Aprendes mucho en la clase de español?
6. En la clase, ¿leen Uds. en español?
7. ¿Lees bien el español?[1]
8. ¿Escribes en español o en inglés?
9. ¿Vendes tus libros?
10. ¿Qué periódico lees tú?
11. ¿Debes trabajar mañana?
12. ¿Reciben mucho dinero tus amigos?

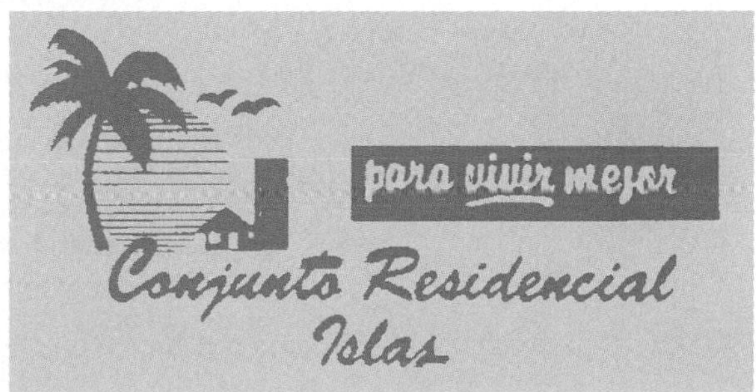


**D.** Take turns asking the instructor the questions in the preceding activity. Make sure to use the **Ud.** form.

## 6 Present indicative of the irregular verbs **tener** and **venir**
*(Presente de indicativo de los verbos irregulares **tener** y **venir**)*

| **tener** *to have* | | **venir** *to come* | |
|---|---|---|---|
| yo | **tengo** | yo | **vengo** |
| tú | **tienes** | tú | **vienes** |
| Ud. / él / ella | **tiene** | Ud. / él / ella | **viene** |
| nosotros(-as) | **tenemos** | nosotros(-as) | **venimos** |
| vosotros(-as) | **tenéis** | vosotros(-as) | **venís** |
| Uds. / ellos / ellas | **tienen** | Uds. / ellos / ellas | **vienen** |

—¿Cuántas clases **tienen** Uds.? — *"How many classes do you have?"*
—**Tenemos** dos. ¿Cuántas **tienes** tú? — *"We have two. How many do you have?"*
—Yo **tengo** cuatro. — *"I have four."*

**ATENCIÓN** **Tener que** means *to have to,* and it is followed by an infinitive. Olga **tiene que trabajar** hoy. *Olga has to work today.*

[1]The definite article is used with names of languages except after the prepositions **en** and **de,** or after the verbs **hablar** and usually **estudiar.**

| | |
|---|---|
| —¿A qué hora **vienen** Uds.? | *"What time are you coming?"* |
| —Sergio y yo **venimos** a las dos, y Olga **viene** a la una. | *"Sergio and I are coming at two and Olga is coming at one."* |
| —¿Tú **tienes que** venir a la universidad mañana? | *"Do you have to come to the university tomorrow?"* |
| —No. | *"No."* |

## práctica

**A.** Give each of the following sentences a logical ending.

1. Yo tengo un examen de español y ella...
2. Uds. vienen los sábados y nosotros...
3. Ella tiene veinte dólares y nosotros...
4. Ana viene con Roberto y tú...
5. Ellos vienen a las seis y yo...
6. Nosotros tenemos dos mapas y ellos...

**B.** Interview a classmate, using the following questions.

1. ¿Tienes mi número de teléfono?
2. ¿Tienes mi dirección?
3. ¿Tiene la profesora tu número de teléfono?
4. ¿Vienen Uds. a la universidad por la noche o por la mañana?
5. ¿Tienes que solicitar otro trabajo?
6. ¿A qué hora vienen Uds. a la clase de español?
7. ¿Vienes a la clase con tus amigos?
8. ¿Vienes a clase los sábados?
9. ¿Vienen los estudiantes a clase los domingos?

**C.** Say what the following people have to do, using **tener que** + *infinitive*.

1. Silvia tiene un examen mañana.
2. John tiene una amiga de Madrid que no habla inglés.
3. Nosotros necesitamos dinero.
4. Necesito escribir y no tengo pluma.
5. Necesito hablar por teléfono con Marta, y ella no está.

**D.** Make a list of tasks or errands for the week; then, with one or two classmates, take turns asking each other what you have to do (**¿Qué tienes que hacer?**) each day.

MODELO: el lunes: leer un libro
—¿Qué tienes que hacer el lunes?
—*Tengo que leer un libro.*

# ¡A ver cuánto aprendió!

**INTERNET**

See the *¿Cómo se dice...?* Web site for additional grammar and vocabulary practice: http://spanish.college.hmco.com/students

## ¡Repase el vocabulario!

Complete the following sentences using vocabulary learned in **Lección 3;** then read them aloud.

1. Tengo que escribir un ________ para mi clase de francés.
2. ¿Las chicas estudian en la ________ o en su casa?
3. Nosotros ________ sándwiches en la cafetería.
4. Teresa ________ estudiar porque mañana ________ un examen.
5. ¿Tienes problemas ________ o económicos? ¿Necesitas ________?
6. ¿No está? ________ más tarde.
7. ¿Ella es rubia, ________ o ________?
8. —¿Está Rosaura? —Con ________ habla.
9. ¿Eres optimista o pesimista? ¿O eres ________?
10. Nosotros somos estudiantes ________.
11. Tengo que leer ________ artículos.
12. ¿En qué calle ________ tú?

## Entrevista

With a partner, interview each other by asking the following questions.

1. ¿Tú trabajas esta noche?
2. ¿Tienes que trabajar mañana?
3. ¿Qué tienes que estudiar hoy?
4. ¿Tú debes estudiar más *(more)*?
5. ¿Tú aprendes mucho en la clase de español?
6. ¿Cuántos idiomas hablas tú?
7. ¿Tú vienes a la universidad los sábados?
8. ¿Hablas por teléfono con tus amigos?
9. ¿Cómo es tu mejor amigo?
10. ¿Qué periódico *(newspaper)* lees?
11. Yo necesito 500 dólares. ¿Cuánto dinero necesitas tú?
12. ¿Tú comes comida *(food)* italiana? ¿Mexicana?

## Situaciones

You are talking on the telephone. What would you say in the following situations? What might the other person say? Act out the scenes with a partner. Take turns playing each role.

1. You want to know whether your friend Carlos is at home.
2. Someone calls and asks for your sister, who is at home.
3. Someone asks to speak to you.

4. You tell someone you'll call later.
5. Someone has asked to talk to you, and you want to know who it is.
6. You are telling someone what you have to do tomorrow.

### Para escribir

Describe your parents. Give as many details as you can.

Mi mamá... Mi papá...

## En la vida real

CD-ROM

Do the interactive exercises on the CD-ROM for additional practice.

### ¡Por teléfono!

With a classmate, act out the following phone conversations in Spanish.

1. Call your classmate's home. His or her roommate or a member of his or her family answers (your classmate is not home). Find out when he or she will be back.
2. You and a friend are planning to have dinner together on Saturday. Ask each other whether you eat different types of food (**comida**). You might want to include: **china** (Chinese) and **japonesa** (Japanese).

### Un mensaje telefónico

Based on the information provided in the phone message, complete the statements next to it.

**Hospital El Samaritano**

MENSAJE PERSONAL

Para Carlos Vega

De parte de Jorge Ibarra

De la compañía Hotel Plaza

Teléfono 386-4127

Llamó por teléfono a la(s) 10:30

☑ de la mañana ☐ de la tarde ☐ de la noche

MENSAJE

Desea hablar con usted.

ASUNTO

Problemas con las reservaciones del hotel para la convención.

Día Miércoles

1. El mensaje es para ________.
2. El Sr. Vega trabaja en el ________.
3. El mensaje es de parte de ________.
4. El Sr. Ibarra trabaja para el ________.
5. El número de teléfono del hotel es ________.
6. El mensaje es ________.
7. El Sr. Ibarra llamó *(called)* a las ________ de la ________ del día ________.
8. En el hotel hay problemas con ________.

## La solicitud

Imagine that you are applying for a job. Fill out the application with your own personal data.

**SOLICITUD DE TRABAJO**

Apellidos y nombre ______________________

Fecha de nacimiento
Día Mes Año

Número de identidad ______________________

Edad ________

Dirección ________ ________

Ciudad ________

Zona postal ________

Teléfono ________

Nacionalidad ________

Lugar de nacimiento ________

Estado civil: ❑ Soltero(-a) ❑ Casado(-a) ❑ Divorciado(-a) ❑ Viudo(-a)

Sexo ❑ Masculino ❑ Femenino

**Educación**

| Institución | Años |
| --- | --- |
| | |
| | |

**Experiencia**

| Compañía | Años |
| --- | --- |
| | |
| | |

## Antes de leer

As you read about Javier and Aurora, find the answers to the following questions.

1. ¿Quién es el novio de Aurora?
2. ¿Cómo es Javier?
3. ¿Cómo es Aurora?
4. ¿Cuál es la profesión de ellos?
5. ¿Dónde viven?
6. ¿Dónde trabaja Javier?
7. ¿Aurora trabaja?
8. ¿Qué días comen en la cafetería?
9. ¿Dónde estudian los sábados?
10. ¿Por qué tienen que estudiar hoy?

## *Javier y Aurora*

Javier y Aurora son novios. Él es un muchacho muy inteligente y muy guapo. Es rubio y alto. Aurora es baja, morena y muy linda. Los dos son estudiantes universitarios y viven en Phoenix.

Javier trabaja en la biblioteca de la universidad pero Aurora solamente estudia. Los lunes y miércoles comen juntos en la cafetería y los sábados por la mañana estudian en la casa de Aurora. Hoy tienen que estudiar francés porque mañana tienen un examen.

## Díganos

Answer the following questions, based on your own thoughts and experiences.

1. ¿Ud. tiene novio(-a)?
2. ¿Cómo es Ud.?
3. ¿Dónde vive usted?
4. ¿Qué días come Ud. en la cafetería?
5. ¿Estudia Ud. los sábados?
6. ¿Ud. tiene que estudiar hoy?

## ASÍ SOMOS

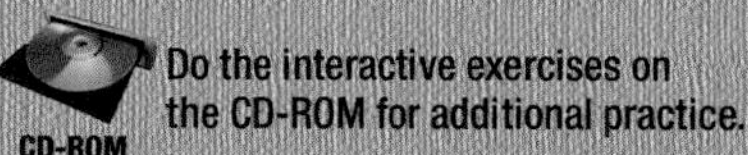


Do the interactive exercises on the CD-ROM for additional practice.

NARRADORA —¿Tiene Ud. hermanos?

RITA —Tengo tres hermanas. Mmm... Una se llama Tutuguari. Tiene veintitrés años. Este... Otra se llama Fernanda y tiene diecinueve. Y ahora... Y la más pequeña se llama Bensaír y también tiene diecinueve años.

NARRADORA —¿Cómo es su mejor amiga?

RITA —Es una persona muy dinámica. Baila ballet. Toma clases de equitación. Habla inglés, francés y es muy alegre.

## Preparación

**A. Descripciones.** With a partner, answer the following questions based on your own information. You will hear answers to these same questions when you watch the video. After viewing the video, compare your answers with those you hear.

1. ¿Cuál es su profesión u ocupación?
2. ¿Es Ud. casado(-a)?
3. ¿Cómo es su novio(-a)?
4. ¿Tiene Ud. hermanos?
5. ¿Cómo es su mejor amigo(-a)?

**B. En una entrevista.** Make a list of the questions you might expect to hear during a job interview. Share your questions with the class.

## Comprensión

**A. Profesiones.** Match each person's name with his or her profession or occupation.

| A | B |
|---|---|
| _____ 1. Manuel | a. Es gerente *(manager)* de la Librería de Cuba. |
| _____ 2. Ricardo | b. Es piloto. |
| _____ 3. José | c. Es estudiante. |
| _____ 4. Rosalía | d. Es médico cirujano *(surgeon)*. |
| _____ 5. Héctor | e. Es ingeniero *(engineer)*. |

**B. ¿Verdadero o falso?** Read the following statements. Circle **V** (**Verdadero**) or **F** (**Falso**) according to what you understood from the video. If a statement is false, correct it.

V F 1. Yolanda no es casada.
V F 2. Carolina no tiene novio.
V F 3. Orlando es casado.

**C. ¿Cómo es?** Complete the following statements with the appropriate adjective from the list below.

alegre *(happy)*
sincero(-a)
serio(-a)
trabajador(-a) *(hard-working)*
alto(-a)
guapo(-a)

1. El novio de Paola es _________ y _________.
2. El novio de Milka es _________ y _________.
3. La novia de Juan es _________ y _________.

D. **¿Verdadero o falso?** Read the following statements. Circle **V** (**Verdadero**) or **F** (**Falso**) according to what you understood from the video. If a statement is false, correct it.

V F 1. Ivonne tiene dos hermanos y dos hermanas.
V F 2. Carolina tiene tres hermanos.
V F 3. La mejor amiga de Carolina es delgada y estudia periodismo.
V F 4. La mejor amiga de Milka tiene ojos azules y pelo rubio.

E. **Entrevista** *(Interview)*. Watch the video segment called *Entrevista* at the end of Lesson 3. Select the word or phrase that best completes each statement, according to what you understood from the interview.

1. El nombre completo de Yurida, la persona entrevistada *(the interviewee)*, es (Guzmán Robles, Yurida Guzmán Robles, Vanesa Rinconada).
2. Yurida busca *(is looking for)* un nuevo (trabajo, teléfono, apartamento).
3. Rinconada Buganvillas, 3597 es donde (vive, trabaja, estudia) Yurida.
4. El teléfono de Yurida es (813-08-37, 803-04-36, 813-04-37).
5. Estudió *(She studied)* en la (Universidad Autónoma de México, Universidad Autónoma de Guadalajara).

## Ampliación

A. **Mi novio(-a) ideal.** Interview a classmate about his or her ideal boyfriend or girlfriend. First, make a list of the questions you would ask him or her. Then make a list of the adjectives to describe this ideal person. Compare the answers with the rest of the class.

B. **Un(-a) nuevo(-a) compañero(-a) de cuarto.** You are doing a telephone interview of a potential roommate in your university apartment. What questions would you ask to elicit the following responses?

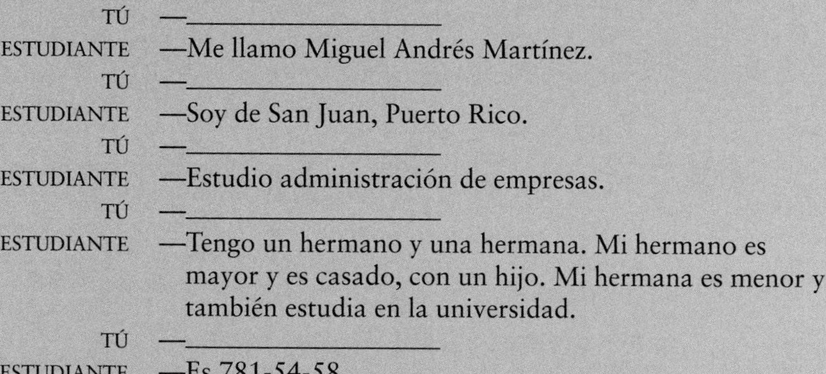

TÚ —____________________
ESTUDIANTE —Me llamo Miguel Andrés Martínez.
TÚ —____________________
ESTUDIANTE —Soy de San Juan, Puerto Rico.
TÚ —____________________
ESTUDIANTE —Estudio administración de empresas.
TÚ —____________________
ESTUDIANTE —Tengo un hermano y una hermana. Mi hermano es mayor y es casado, con un hijo. Mi hermana es menor y también estudia en la universidad.
TÚ —____________________
ESTUDIANTE —Es 781-54-58.

Take this test. When you have finished, check your answers in the answer key provided in Appendix E. Then use a red pen to correct any mistakes you may have made. Are you ready?

## Lección 1

### A. The alphabet

Spell the following last names in Spanish.

1. Barrios
2. Acosta
3. Díaz
4. Ferreyra
5. Guevara
6. Henao
7. Jiménez
8. Leyva

### B. Cardinal numbers (0–30)

Write these numbers in Spanish.

1. 11
2. 17
3. 30
4. 20
5. 15
6. 13
7. 28
8. 19
9. 12
10. 14

### C. Colors

What colors come to mind when you think of the following?

1. a leaf
2. an orange
3. a banana
4. rosy cheeks
5. coal
6. a plum
7. coffee
8. the American flag

### D. Days of the week

Give the days of the week that come *before* the ones mentioned here.

1. lunes
2. jueves
3. sábado
4. miércoles
5. domingo
6. viernes

### E. Months and seasons of the year

Give the months and seasons that come before the ones mentioned here.

1. diciembre
2. abril
3. agosto
4. febrero
5. junio
6. octubre
7. invierno
8. verano

### F. Subject pronouns and the present indicative of the verb *ser*

Complete the following dialogue, using the present indicative of the verb **ser.**

—¿De dónde ________ ustedes?
—Nosotros ________ de California. ¿De dónde ________ tú?
—Yo ________ de Tejas.
—Y Carlos y María?
—Carlos ________ de Arizona y María ________ de Nuevo México.
—¿De dónde ________ los profesores?
—De Nueva Jersey.

### G. Just words . . .

Match each question in column A with the best response in column B.

| | A | | B |
|---|---|---|---|
| 1. | ¿Cómo están ustedes? | a. | No, médica. |
| 2. | ¿Cómo te llamas? | b. | No, martes. |
| 3. | ¿Qué hay de nuevo? | c. | Soy analista de sistemas. |
| 4. | ¿Ud. es enfermera? | d. | Cuatro-dos-seis-veintidós-treinta. |
| 5. | ¿Cuál es su profesión? | e. | De Buenos Aires. |
| 6. | ¿Ella es la secretaria? | f. | No, él es auxiliar de vuelo. |
| 7. | ¿De dónde eres tú? | g. | Bien, gracias. |
| 8. | ¿Qué día es hoy? | h. | No, estudiantes. |
| 9. | ¿Hoy es lunes? | i. | No, la recepcionista. |
| 10. | ¿Cuál es tu número de teléfono? | j. | Ana María Belgrano. |
| 11. | ¿Uds. son profesores? | k. | Miércoles. |
| 12. | ¿Carlos es piloto? | l. | Nada. |

### H. Culture

Answer the following questions based on the **¿Lo sabía Ud.?** section.

1. ¿Cuál es un nombre muy popular en España y en Latinoamérica?
2. ¿Se usa también para hombres? Dé *(Give)* un ejemplo.

## Lección 2

### A. Gender and number and definite articles

Place **el, la, los,** or **las** before each noun.

1. _____ pizarra
2. _____ luz
3. _____ lápices
4. _____ día
5. _____ libros
6. _____ relojes
7. _____ mapa
8. _____ plumas
9. _____ pared
10. _____ pupitre

### B. Gender and number and indefinite articles

Place **un, una, unos,** or **unas** before each noun.

1. _____ tizas
2. _____ borradores
3. _____ mano
4. _____ hombres
5. _____ mujer
6. _____ secretario
7. _____ profesores
8. _____ papel

### C. Cardinal numbers (31–100)

Write the following numbers in Spanish.

1. 38
2. 100
3. 91
4. 85
5. 72
6. 57
7. 46
8. 63

### D. Telling time

Use the clues given to say at what time the following classes are.

1. la clase de español / 10:30 A.M.
2. la clase de inglés / 1:15 P.M.
3. la clase de literatura / 8:40 P.M.

### E. Present indicative of *-ar* verbs and negative and interrogative sentences

Complete the following dialogues, using the Spanish equivalent of the words in parentheses.

1. —¿Dónde _______ tú?
   —Yo _______ en la universidad.
   —¿A qué hora _______ a tu casa?
   —A las cuatro.
   *(work / work / return)*
2. —¿Uds. _______ por la mañana?
   —No, nosotros _______ por la mañana.
   —¿Cuántas clases _______ ustedes?
   —Cinco.
   *(study / don't study / take)*
3. —¿Qué _______ Carlos y Aurora?
   —Carlos _______ lápices y Aurora _______ bolígrafos.
   *(need / needs / needs)*
4. —¿ _______ llamar más tarde, Anita?
   —Sí, yo _______ más tarde.
   *(Do you wish / will call)*
5. —¿ _______ inglés en la clase?
   —No, nosotros _______ inglés en la clase.
   *(Do you speak / don't speak)*

### F. Possession with *de*

Give the Spanish equivalent of each phrase.

1. Miss Vega's students
2. Amanda's professor *(masc.)*
3. Paco's friends

### G. Just words . . .

Complete the following sentences using vocabulary from **Lección 2.**

1. No es una calle; es una ________.
2. Mi ________ es: calle Olmos, número 124.
3. ¿Cómo se ________ *"door"* en español?
4. ¿Qué ________ decir "borrador"?
5. Tome ________, por favor.
6. En Berlín hablan ________ y en París hablan ________.
7. ¿________ estudiantes hay en la clase? ¿Treinta?
8. Con ________. Buenos días, profesora.
9. Elsa no trabaja; ________ estudia.
10. Pedro habla un ________ de portugués.

### H. Culture

Answer the following questions based on the **¿Lo sabía Ud.?** section.

1. Si usamos el sistema de 24 horas, ¿qué hora es cuando decimos *(when we say)* "las 18 horas"?
2. En España y en Latinoamérica, ¿qué idioma extranjero *(foreign language)* estudian muchos estudiantes en la escuela secundaria?

## Lección 3

### A. Gender, Part II

Place **el, la, los,** or **las** before each noun.

1. _____ desilusión
2. _____ libertad
3. _____ programas
4. _____ universidad
5. _____ muchedumbre *(crowd)*
6. _____ ciudades
7. _____ sistema
8. _____ lecciones
9. _____ problemas
10. _____ conversación

### B. Possessive adjectives

Give the Spanish equivalent of the words in parentheses.

1. Necesito ________ y ________. *(my ballpoint pen / my books)*
2. ________ es muy grande, pero ________ es pequeña. *(His house / her house)*
3. ________ es de Colombia. Es una mujer muy inteligente. *(Our professor)*
4. ________ son de Buenos Aires. *(Our friends)*
5. ¿Tú necesitas ________, Anita? *(your pencils)*
6. ________ habla español. ¿Qué idioma habla ________? *(Their professor / your (pl.) professor)*

### C. Cardinal numbers (101–1,000)

Write the following numbers in Spanish.

1. 195
2. 286
3. 371
4. 460
5. 553
6. 644
7. 732
8. 827
9. 918
10. 1.513

### D. Descriptive adjectives

Change the articles and the adjectives according to the nouns in parentheses.

1. El chico es alto. (chica)
2. La pizarra es pequeña. (escritorio)
3. Los chicos son norteamericanos. (chicas)
4. Es un hombre muy simpático. (mujer)
5. Necesito los lápices rojos. (plumas)

### E. Present indicative of regular *-er* and *-ir* verbs

Complete the following sentences using the Spanish equivalent of the verbs in parentheses.

1. Nosotros ________ mucho en la clase de español. *(learn)*
2. ¿Tú ________ en la cafetería? *(eat)*
3. Yo ________ que Elena habla alemán. *(think)*
4. ¿Ustedes ________ muchos libros? *(read)*
5. Carlos ________ champán. *(drinks)*
6. Usted ________ estudiar. *(must)*
7. Ellos ________ sus libros. *(sell)*
8. Yo ________ las ventanas. *(open)*
9. Ellos ________ muchas cartas *(letters)*. *(receive)*
10. Nosotros ________ en inglés. *(write)*

**F. Just words . . .**

Match each question in column A with the best response in column B.

| A | B |
|---|---|
| 1. ¿Ana es tu novia? | a. No, soy realista. |
| 2. ¿Dónde estudian? | b. Sí, ¡y muy simpática! |
| 3. ¿Estudian esta noche? | c. Menéndez. |
| 4. ¿Cómo estás? | d. No, es muy guapo. |
| 5. ¿Es bonita? | e. Enfermera. |
| 6. ¿Está Jorge? | f. En la biblioteca. |
| 7. ¿Eres pesimista? | g. No, es rubia. |
| 8. ¿Es feo? | h. No, es muy antipática. |
| 9. ¿Es simpática? | i. No, mañana. |
| 10. ¿Cuál es su apellido? | j. De Mauricio Díaz. |
| 11. ¿Estado civil? | k. Más o menos. |
| 12. ¿Ocupación? | l. No, es bajo. |
| 13. ¿Es morena? | m. No, es una amiga. |
| 14. ¿Es alto? | n. Soltero. |
| 15. ¿De parte de quién? | o. Con él habla. |

**G. Culture**

Answer the following questions based on the **¿Lo sabía Ud.?** section.

1. ¿Cómo contestan el teléfono en México?
2. "Español" y "castellano", ¿son equivalentes?

# Una fiesta de fin de año

Lección 4

## OBJECTIVES

### Pronunciation

The Spanish **b**, **v**, **d**, and **g** (before **a**, **o**, or **u**)

### Structure

The personal **a** • Contractions • Expressions with **tener** • Present indicative of the irregular verbs **ir**, **dar**, and **estar** • **Ir a** + *infinitive* • Present indicative of **e:ie** stem-changing verbs

### Communication

You will learn vocabulary related to party activities, foods, and beverages.

# Una fiesta de fin de año

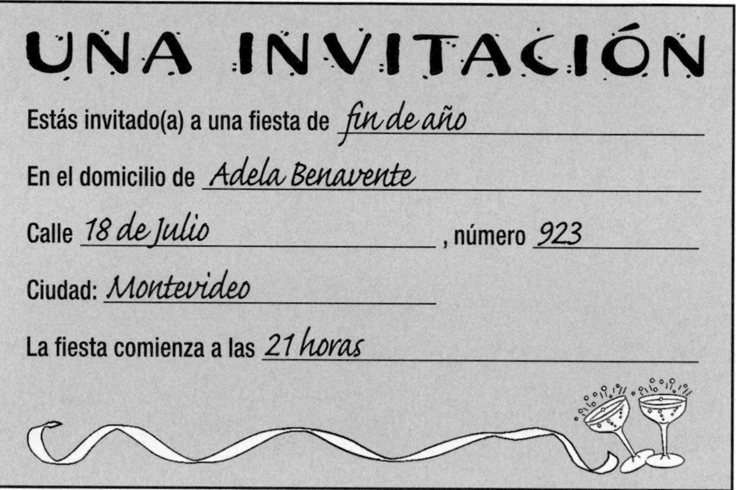
UNA INVITACIÓN

Estás invitado(a) a una fiesta de fin de año

En el domicilio de Adela Benavente

Calle 18 de Julio, número 923

Ciudad: Montevideo

La fiesta comienza a las 21 horas

*Antes de la fiesta*

ADELA —Muchos de mis compañeros de la universidad van a venir a mi fiesta. ¿Tú vas a traer a tu prima?

HUMBERTO —Sí, y también voy a traer unos discos compactos y las empanadas[1] que mi mamá va a preparar.

ADELA —Y nosotros vamos a preparar pollo, entremeses y ensalada de papas. ¡Todo va a estar delicioso!

HUMBERTO —¡Ay, Adela, yo tengo hambre ahora!

ADELA —¿Quieres un sándwich? Y, si tienes sed, hay refresco, cerveza y agua mineral.

HUMBERTO —Sí, quiero un sándwich y un refresco... No... prefiero un vaso de agua. Oye, ¿a qué hora empieza el baile del club?

ADELA —A las once.[2] ¿Vas a llamar a Julio y a Teresa?

HUMBERTO —Sí, porque ellos piensan ir al club con nosotros. Hoy es el cumpleaños de Teresa.

ADELA —¿Ah, sí? ¿Cuántos años tiene ella?

HUMBERTO —Creo que hoy cumple veinte años. El sábado da una fiesta y estamos invitados.

*Adela y sus amigos lo pasan muy bien en la fiesta. Todos bailan, conversan, comen y beben. Después, van al Club Náutico para celebrar la llegada del año nuevo. Julio no va porque está enfermo.*

---

[1]Meat turnovers

[2]In Hispanic countries, it is common for people to celebrate the New Year by attending a party in a private home early in the evening, then moving to a club before midnight.

*En el Club Náutico*

HUMBERTO —La orquesta es magnífica. ¿Bailamos, Adela?

ADELA —Ahora no, Humberto. Estoy un poco cansada y tengo mucho calor.[1] ¿Por qué no vamos a la terraza?

HUMBERTO —Buena idea. Voy a llevar las bebidas. ¿Quieres champán, sidra[2] o un coctel?

ADELA —Para brindar, una copa de champán, por favor. Después, sangría...[3]

JAVIER —¿No tienen uvas? En España siempre comemos doce uvas a la medianoche del 31 de diciembre.

ADELA —No, Javier. No tenemos uvas. ¡Son las doce!

TODOS —¡Feliz año nuevo! ¡Feliz año nuevo!

# Vocabulario

## Cognados

**el champán** champagne
**el club** club
**el coctel** cocktail
**delicioso(-a)** delicious
**el disco compacto** compact disk (CD)
**la ensalada** salad
**la idea** idea
**la invitación** invitation
**invitado(-a)** invited
**mucho(-a)** much, a lot of
**la orquesta** orchestra, band
**la sangría** sangria
**la sidra** alcoholic cider
**el sándwich** sandwich
**la terraza** terrace

## Nombres

**el agua**[4] water *(fem.)*
**el agua mineral** mineral water
**el baile** dance
**la bebida** drink, beverage
**la cerveza** beer
**el (la) compañero(-a) de clase** classmate
**la copa** glass, goblet
**el cumpleaños** birthday
**la ensalada de papas** potato salad
**los entremeses** hors d'oeuvres, appetizers
**España** Spain
**la fiesta** party
**la llegada** arrival
**la mamá, madre** Mom, mother
**la medianoche** midnight
**el pollo** chicken
**el (la) primo(-a)** cousin
**el refresco** soda pop
**las uvas** grapes
**el vaso** glass

[1]In the Southern Hemisphere, the seasons are reversed.
[2]An alcoholic drink in Hispanic countries.
[3]A drink prepared with red wine and fruit.
[4]**El** is used because the next word starts with a stressed **a.**

## Verbos

**bailar** to dance
**brindar** to toast
**celebrar** to celebrate
**conversar, charlar** to talk, to chat
**cumplir** to turn (. . . years old)
**dar** *(irreg.)* to give
**comenzar, empezar** (e:ie) to begin, to start
**estar** *(irreg.)* to be
**invitar** to invite
**ir** *(irreg.)* to go
**llevar** to take (someone or something someplace)
**pensar** (e:ie) to plan, to think
**preferir** (e:ie) to prefer
**preparar** to prepare
**querer** (e:ie) to want, to wish
**traer** (yo traigo) to bring

## Adjetivos

**cansado**(-a) tired
**enfermo**(-a) sick
**feliz** happy
**magnífico**(-a) great
**muchos**(-as) many
**nuevo**(-a) new

## Otras palabras y expresiones

**a la medianoche** at midnight
**ahora** now
**allí** there
**antes de** before
**¿Bailamos?** Shall we dance?
**después** afterwards
**fiesta de fin de año** New Year's Eve party
**para** in order to
**pasarlo bien** to have a good time
**siempre** always
**tener... años** to be . . . years old
**tener calor** to be hot
**tener hambre** to be hungry
**tener sed** to be thirsty
**todo** everything
**todos**(-as) everybody
**un poco** + *adjective* a little + *adjective*

# Vocabulario adicional

## La fiesta de Navidad

*(Christmas)*

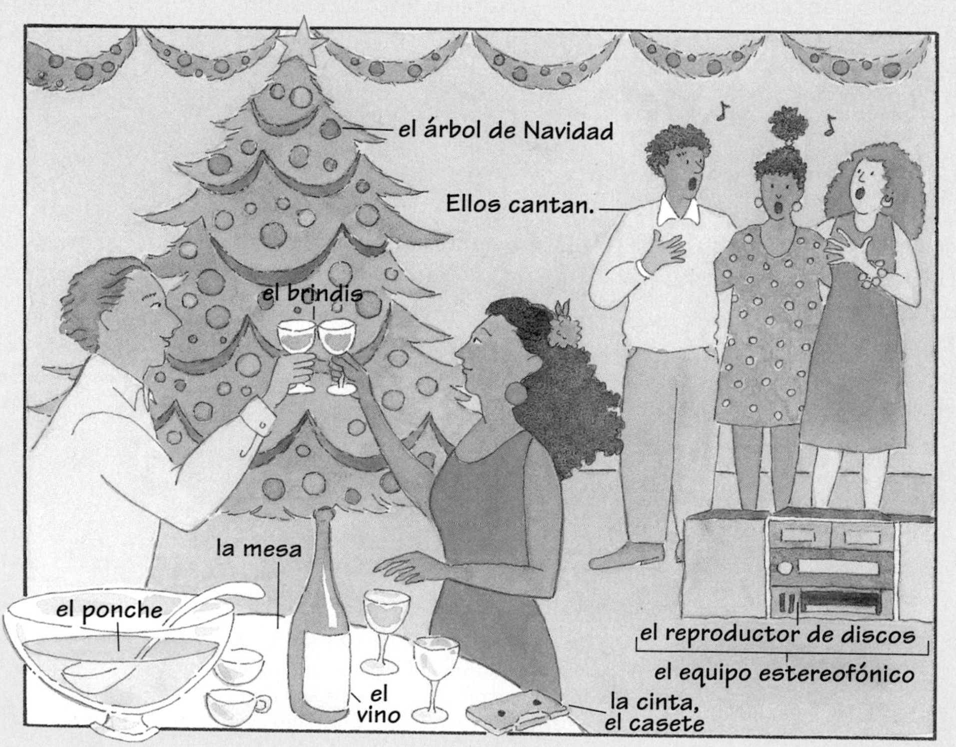

## Para describir

**aburrido(-a)** bored — La clase es muy **aburrida.**
**contento(-a)** happy — Estoy **contenta** porque voy a la fiesta.
**difícil** difficult — El francés es **difícil.**
**enojado(-a), enfadado(-a)** angry — Ana está **enojada** porque no tiene dinero.
**fácil** easy — La clase es muy **fácil.**
**grande** big — El hospital es muy **grande.**
**malo(-a)**[1] bad — La orquesta es muy **mala.**
**nervioso(-a)** nervous — Estoy **nerviosa** porque mañana tengo un examen.
**ocupado(-a)** busy — Estoy muy **ocupado.** Tengo que trabajar.
**pequeño(-a)** small — Mi casa es muy **pequeña.**
**preocupado(-a)** worried — Está **preocupado** porque su clase es difícil.
**triste** sad — No está contento; está **triste.**

## Para aclarar

**¿adónde?** where? *(destination)* — ¿**Adónde** vamos hoy?
**al mediodía** at noon — Aurora viene **al mediodía.**
**¿cuánto(-a)?** how much? — ¿**Cuánto** dinero necesitas?
**¿de quién?** whose? — ¿**De quién** es el disco compacto? ¿De Raúl?

# ¡Conversemos!

Answer the following questions, basing your answers on the dialogue.

1. ¿Qué va a dar Adela?
2. ¿En qué calle vive Adela? ¿En qué ciudad?
3. ¿A qué hora comienza la fiesta?
4. ¿Quiénes van a venir a la fiesta de Adela?
5. ¿Qué va a traer Humberto?
6. ¿Quién va a preparar las empanadas?
7. ¿Qué van a preparar Adela y su familia? ¿Cómo va a estar todo?
8. ¿Qué quiere comer Humberto? ¿Qué quiere beber?
9. ¿Quiénes piensan ir al club con Humberto y Adela?
10. ¿Cuántos años cumple Teresa hoy?
11. ¿Cómo lo pasan Adela y sus amigos en la fiesta?
12. ¿Por qué no baila Adela con Humberto?
13. ¿Con qué quiere brindar Adela?
14. ¿Qué comen en España a la medianoche del 31 de diciembre?

[1]**Malo** drops the **-o** when placed before a masculine, singular noun: **un mal hombre.**

## ¿Lo sabía Ud.?

- En España y en Latinoamérica, no existe tanta *(as much)* separación entre *(among)* generaciones como en los Estados Unidos. Los niños, los padres y los abuelos frecuentemente van juntos a fiestas y a celebraciones.
- En los países *(countries)* hispanos, las chicas y los muchachos generalmente van en grupos a fiestas, al teatro y a conciertos.
- Los hispanos generalmente celebran el cumpleaños y también el día de su "santo", que corresponde al santo de su nombre en el calendario católico. Por ejemplo, si un niño nace *(is born)* en junio y sus padres lo llaman Miguel, celebra su cumpleaños en junio y celebra el día de su "santo" el 29 de septiembre, que es el día de San Miguel.
- En algunos *(some)* países hispanos no existe una edad mínima para comprar *(buy)* o tomar bebidas alcohólicas.
- En español se dice "¡Salud!" *(Cheers!)* al brindar. En España, también dicen "Salud, amor y pesetas" *(Health, love, and pesetas)*.
  - En este país *(country)*, ¿los chicos prefieren salir en grupos o en parejas *(couples)*?
  - En este país, ¿las personas celebran el día de su santo?
  - ¿Cuál es la edad mínima para comprar o tomar bebidas alcohólicas en este país?

See the *¿Cómo se dice...?* Web site for activities on authentic cultural material: http://spanish.college.hmco.com/students

Una familia argentina celebrando un cumpleaños.

# Pronunciación

## A The Spanish b and v

The Spanish **b** and **v** are pronounced exactly alike. Both sound like a weak English *b,* as in the word *Abe.* In Spanish, they are even weaker when pronounced between vowels. The lips don't quite touch. Never pronounce these consonants like the English *v.* Listen to your instructor and repeat the following words.

| | |
|---|---|
| **v**einte | **b**ien |
| **v**enir | **b**aile |
| **V**i**v**iana | **b**e**b**ida |
| u**v**a | so**b**rina |

## B The Spanish d

The Spanish **d** is slightly softer than the *d* in the English word *day.* When pronounced between two vowels or at the end of a word, it is similar to the *th* in the English word *they.* Listen to your instructor and repeat the following words.

| | |
|---|---|
| **d**elga**d**o | universi**d**a**d** |
| **d**e | sába**d**o |
| **d**e**b**e | bebi**d**a |
| **d**os | a**d**iós |

## C The Spanish g (before a, o, or u)

- When followed by **a, o,** or **u,** the Spanish **g** is similar to the *g* in the English word *guy.* Listen to your instructor and repeat the following words.

  del**g**ado **g**uapo **g**ordo

- When pronounced between vowels, the Spanish **g** is much softer. Repeat after your instructor.

  ami**g**o pre**g**unta uru**g**uaya

- In the combinations **gue** and **gui,** the **u** is silent. Repeat after your instructor.

  **Gue**vara **Gui**llermo al**gui**en

club
campestre
del caribe
DICIEMBRE 31
Celebración de fin de año
para padres-hijos-familiares e invitados de socios
Salón Dorado 9:00 PM

## 1 The personal a (*La a personal*)

- The preposition **a** is used in Spanish before a direct object[1] referring to a specific person or persons. It is called the "personal **a**" and has no equivalent in English.

| | |
|---|---|
| Yo llamo **a mi prima.** (D.O.) | Nosotros llamamos **a los estudiantes.** (D.O.) |
| *I call my cousin.* (D.O.) | *We call the students.* (D.O.) |

- The personal **a** is *not* used when the direct object is not a person.

Yo llevo **las bebidas** a la fiesta. (D.O.)

*I take the drinks to the party.* (D.O.)

- The verb **tener** generally does not take the personal **a**, even if the direct object is a person.

| | |
|---|---|
| No tengo **novio.** (D.O.) | Tenemos **varios amigos.** (D.O.) |
| *I don't have a boyfriend.* (D.O.) | *We have several friends.* (D.O.) |
| —¿Llevas **a** tus primos a la universidad? | *"Do you take your cousins to the university?"* |
| —Yo no tengo primos. Llevo **a** Jorge y **a** Luis. | *"I don't have (any) cousins. I take Jorge and Luis."* |

**ATENCIÓN** When there is a series of direct object nouns referring to people, the personal **a** is repeated: **Llevo *a Jorge* y *a Luis*.**

### práctica

A. Use the personal **a** when needed to complete the following dialogues. Then act them out with a partner.

1. —¿Cuántos primos tienes?
   —Tengo ________ dos primos y ________ una prima.
2. —¿Llama usted ________ Carmen o ________ Elena?
   —Llamo ________ Carmen.

[1]See **Lección 6** for further explanation of the direct object.

3. —¿Tu amigo lleva ________ Rosa a la biblioteca?
   —No, lleva ________ su novia.
4. —¿Adónde lleva usted ________ los libros?
   —A la clase.
5. —¿Tienes ________ muchos amigos?
   —Sí, tengo ________ muchos amigos.
6. —¿Qué lees?
   —Leo ________ el libro de español.

**B.** With a partner, decide which members of the class you'll call, take, or invite to a party. Give reasons for your choices.

## 2 Contractions *(Contracciones)*

- There are only two contractions in Spanish: **al** and **del.** Both the preposition **a** *(to, toward)* and the personal **a** followed by the article **el** contract to **al.**

| | | | | |
|---|---|---|---|---|
| Llevo | **a** | + | **el** | profesor. |
| Llevo | **al** | profesor. | | |

- The preposition **de** *(of, from)* followed by the article **el** contracts to **del.**

| | | | | |
|---|---|---|---|---|
| Tiene los libros | **de** | + | **el** | profesor. |
| Tiene los libros | **del** | profesor. | | |

| | |
|---|---|
| —¿Llevas **al** amigo de Ana?<br>—No, llevo a las primas de Eva. | *"Are you taking Ana's friend?"*<br>*"No, I'm taking Eva's cousins."* |
| —¿La casa es **de la** Sra. Vega?<br>—No, es **del** Sr. Parra. | *"Is it Mrs. Vega's house?"*<br>*"No, it's Mr. Parra's."* |

**ATENCIÓN** **A** + **el** and **de** + **el** must always be contracted to **al** and **del.** None of the other combinations (**de la, de las, de los, a la, a las, a los**) is contracted: **Llaman *a los* hijos *de los* profesores.**

## práctica

**A.** Complete the following dialogues, using **de la, de las, del, de los, a la, a las, al,** or **a los.** Then act them out with a partner.

1. —¿De dónde vienes?
   —Vengo ________ club. ¿Y tú?
   —Yo vengo ________ hospital.
2. —¿A qué hora llamas ________ chicas?
   —________ dos.
3. —¿Los mapas son ________ Sr. Vega?
   —No, son ________ Srta. Ruiz.
4. —¿Tienes que ir ________ club?
   —No, tengo que ir ________ biblioteca.
5. —¿Adónde llevas ________ chicos?
   —________ clase ________ Sr. Peña.

**B.** With a partner, take turns asking and answering the following questions, using the cues provided.

1. ¿De quién son los libros? (profesor)
2. ¿De quién es el escritorio? (Srta. Paz)
3. ¿A quiénes llevas a la universidad? (chicos)
4. ¿A quién invitan ustedes? (Sr. Vega)
5. ¿A quiénes llaman los chicos? (muchachas)
6. ¿Adónde llevan a las muchachas? (club)
7. ¿De dónde vienen ustedes? (club)
8. ¿Los libros son de los muchachos? (no, muchachas)

## 3 Expressions with **tener** *(Expresiones con **tener**)*

■ Many useful idiomatic expressions that use *to be + adjective* in English are formed with **tener** + *noun* in Spanish.

| | |
|---|---|
| tener (mucho) frío | *to be (very) cold* |
| tener (mucha) sed | *to be (very) thirsty* |
| tener (mucha) hambre | *to be (very) hungry* |
| tener (mucho) calor | *to be (very) hot* |
| tener (mucho) sueño | *to be (very) sleepy* |
| tener (mucha) prisa | *to be in a (great) hurry* |
| tener (mucho) miedo | *to be (quite) afraid, scared* |
| tener cuidado | *to be careful* |
| tener razón | *to be right* |
| no tener razón[1] | *to be wrong* |
| tener... años de edad | *to be . . . years old* |

—¿**Tienes calor?** *"Are you hot?"*
—Sí, y también **tengo** mucha **sed.** *"Yes, and I'm also very thirsty."*

—¿Deseas comer pollo? *"Do you want to eat chicken?"*
—No, gracias, no **tengo hambre.** *"No, thank you, I'm not hungry."*

—¿Cuántos **años tienes?** *"How old are you?"*
—**Tengo** diecinueve **años.** *"I'm nineteen years old."*

**ATENCIÓN** Note that Spanish uses **mucho(-a)** *(adjective) + noun* (as in **mucha hambre**) the way English uses *very + adjective* (as in *very hungry*).

[1]Incorrectness is also conveyed by the expression **estar equivocado(-a).**

## práctica

**A.** ¿Qué tienen?

1. Jorge

2. Yo

3. Tú

4. La profesora

5. Ud.

6. Felipe

7. Marisa y Elena

8. Ella

B. Interview a classmate, using the following questions. When you have finished, switch roles.

1. ¿Qué bebes cuando tienes sed? ¿Y cuando tienes frío?
2. ¿Qué comes cuando tienes hambre?
3. ¿Cuántos años tienes?
4. ¿Cuántos años tiene tu mamá? ¿Y tu papá *(Dad)*?
5. En tu familia, ¿quién tiene razón siempre? ¿Y en la clase?
6. ¿Tienes miedo a veces *(sometimes)*?

C. Which expression with **tener** would you use in each of the following situations?

1. You are in the Sahara desert in the middle of summer.
2. A big dog is chasing you.
3. You have only a minute to get to your next class.
4. You are in Alaska in the middle of winter.
5. You haven't eaten for an entire day.
6. You got up at four A.M. and it is now midnight.
7. You just ran for two hours in the sun.
8. You are blowing out thirty candles on your birthday cake.

## 4 Present indicative of the irregular verbs **ir, dar,** and **estar** *(Presente de indicativo de los verbos irregulares **ir, dar** y **estar**)*

| | **ir** *to go* | **dar** *to give* | **estar** *to be* |
|---|---|---|---|
| yo | voy | doy | estoy |
| tú | vas | das | estás |
| Ud. / él / ella | va | da | está |
| nosotros(-as) | vamos | damos | estamos |
| vosotros(-as) | vais | dais | estáis |
| Uds. / ellos / ellas | van | dan | están |

—Susana **da** una fiesta hoy. ¿Tú **vas?**
—No, no **voy** porque **estoy** muy cansada.
—Entonces invito a tu hermana. ¿Dónde **está?**
—**Está** en la universidad. Viene a las tres.

*"Susana is giving a party today. Are you going?"*
*"No, I'm not going because I am very tired."*
*"Then I'm inviting your sister. Where is she?"*
*"She is at the university. She is coming at three o'clock."*

■ The verb **estar,** *to be,* is used here to indicate current condition (**Estoy muy cansada.**) and location (**Está en la universidad.**). **Ser,** another equivalent of the

English verb *to be,* has been used up to now to refer to origin (**Él es de Chile.**), nationality (**Ellas son mexicanas.**), characteristics (**Jorge es rubio.**), profession (**Elsa es profesora.**), and time (**Son las doce.**).

- Other frequent uses of **dar** are **dar un examen, dar una conferencia** *(lecture),* and **dar una orden** *(order).*

## práctica

**A.** Complete the following conversation, using the appropriate forms of the verbs **ir, dar,** and **estar.** Then act out the dialogue with a partner.

JOSÉ —Rosa, ¿tú ________ a la fiesta que ________ Estrella el sábado?
ROSA —Sí, ________ con Inés. ¿Tú ________ también?
JOSÉ —Sí. Oye, ¿estudiamos esta noche? El Dr. Vargas y la Dra. Soto ________ exámenes mañana.
ROSA —Ay, José, ________ muy cansada.
JOSÉ —Pero, Rosa, ¡tú siempre ________ cansada!
ROSA —No siempre. ¿Por qué no estudias con Jorge y Raúl? Ellos no ________ al club esta noche.
JOSÉ —Buena idea. ¿Dónde ________ ellos ahora?
ROSA —________ en la universidad.

**B.** Interview a classmate, using the following questions. When you have finished, switch roles.

1. ¿Cómo estás?
2. ¿Estás contento(-a) o triste hoy?
3. ¿Quién no está en clase hoy?
4. ¿Está muy ocupado(-a) el profesor (la profesora)?
5. ¿El profesor (la profesora) da exámenes fáciles o difíciles?
6. ¿Adónde vas los sábados por la noche con tus amigos?
7. ¿Van Uds. a un club? (¿A cuál?)
8. ¿Con quién vas a las fiestas?
9. ¿Das muchas fiestas en tu casa?
10. ¿Das una fiesta de fin de año? ¿De Navidad?
11. ¿Adónde van Uds. mañana? ¿Por qué?
12. ¿Dónde están tus amigos ahora?

**C.** Complete the following sentences in a logical manner.

1. Roberto está allí y nosotros...
2. Yo doy una fiesta esta noche y tú...
3. Tú vas a la universidad y yo...
4. Yo estoy muy enojado(-a) y ellos...
5. Nosotros damos una fiesta de Navidad y él...
6. Ellos van hoy y nosotros...
7. Ella está nerviosa y su novio...

D. Here is a list of places that people go to:

| | |
|---|---|
| la playa *(beach)* | el concierto *(concert)* |
| la piscina *(swimming pool)* del club | el museo *(museum)* |
| el teatro *(theatre)* | el parque *(park)* |
| el cine *(movies)* | la tienda *(store)* |

Imagining that you or you and one classmate are walking around town, walk around the class. You will bump into several of your classmates. Ask them where they are going now.

MODELO: —¡Hola! ¿Adónde vas?
—*Voy al cine. ¿Y tú?*
—*Yo voy a la tienda.*

After everyone sits down, the instructor will ask where everyone is going.

## 5 Ir a + *infinitive* *(Ir a + infinitivo)*

■ **Ir a** + *infinitive* is used to express future action. It is equivalent to the English expression *to be going (to) + infinitive*. The "formula" is as follows:

| **ir** *(conjugated)* | + **a** + | *infinitive* |
|---|---|---|
| Voy | a | **trabajar.** |
| *I am going* | | *to work.* |

| | |
|---|---|
| —¿En qué universidad **van a estudiar** Uds.? | *"At what university are you going to study?"* |
| —**Vamos a estudiar** en la Universidad de Costa Rica. | *"We're going to study at the University of Costa Rica."* |
| —¿Ud. **va a dar** una conferencia? | *"Are you going to give a lecture?"* |
| —Sí, **voy a dar** una conferencia el viernes. | *"Yes, I'm going to give a lecture on Friday."* |
| —¿Tú **vas a cantar?** | *"Are you going to sing?"* |
| —No, **voy a bailar.** | *"No, I'm going to dance."* |

### práctica

A. What do you think these people are going to do? Consider where they are and what time of day it is.

MODELO: —José / en el hospital / por la tarde
—*José va a trabajar en el hospital por la tarde.*

1. Yo / en mi casa / por la noche
2. Los estudiantes / en la clase / por la mañana
3. Nosotros / en el club / por la noche

4. Tú / en la cafetería / a las doce
5. El profesor / en la universidad / por la tarde
6. Julio y Teresa / en la terraza / a las diez de la noche
7. Susana / en su casa / por la mañana
8. Uds. / en la fiesta / por la noche

B. What are these people going to do? With a partner, take turns asking and answering questions, using the information in the illustrations.

MODELO: —¿Con quién va a bailar Marisol?
—*Va a bailar con Tito.*

Marisol

1. Roberto

2. Elisa

3. Julio y Estrella

4. Daniel

5. Eduardo

6. Graciela

C. Interview a classmate, using the following questions. When you have finished, switch roles.

1. ¿Dónde vas a comer hoy?
2. ¿Con quién vas a comer?
3. ¿A qué hora van a comer Uds.?
4. ¿Qué van a comer?
5. ¿Qué van a tomar Uds.?
6. ¿Qué vas a hacer *(to do)* mañana por la tarde?
7. ¿Qué van a estudiar tú y tus amigos?
8. ¿Qué van a hacer Uds. por la noche?
9. ¿Dónde vas a trabajar mañana?
10. ¿Tu amigo(-a) va a trabajar también?

## 6 Present indicative of **e:ie** stem-changing verbs *(Presente de indicativo de los verbos que cambian en la raíz* ***e:ie****)*

- Some Spanish verbs undergo a stem change in the present indicative. For these verbs, when **e** is the last stem vowel and it is stressed, it changes to **ie** as follows.

| **preferir** *to prefer* | | | |
|---|---|---|---|
| yo | prefiero | nosotros(-as) | preferimos |
| tú | prefieres | vosotros(-as) | preferís |
| Ud. / él / ella | prefiere | Uds. / ellos / ellas | prefieren |

—¿A qué hora **piensas** ir a la fiesta? — *"What time are you planning to go to the party?"*
—**Prefiero** ir a las diez. ¿Y tú? — *"I prefer to go at ten. And you?"*
—Yo **no quiero** ir. Estoy cansado. — *"I don't want to go. I'm tired."*

—¿A qué hora **empiezan** a[1] estudiar Uds.? — *"What time do you start to study?"*
—**Empezamos** a las tres. — *"We start at three."*

- Note that the stem vowel is not stressed in the verb forms used with **nosotros(-as)** and **vosotros(-as)**; therefore, the **e** does not change to **ie.**
- Stem-changing verbs have the same endings as regular **-ar, -er,** and **-ir** verbs.

[1]The preposition **a** is used after **empezar** and **comenzar** when they are followed by an infinitive.

■ Some verbs that undergo this change:

**cerrar** *to close*
**comenzar** *to begin, to start*
**empezar** *to begin, to start*
**entender** *to understand*
**pensar** *to think*
**pensar** *(+ **infinitive**)* *to plan (to do something)*
**perder** *to lose*
**querer** *to want, to wish, to love*

## práctica

**A.** Complete the following dialogues, using the verbs given. Then act them out with a partner, expanding each dialogue by adding one or two sentences.

1. preferir —¿Dónde ________ comer Uds.? ¿En la cafetería o en su casa?
—________ comer en nuestra casa.
2. querer —¿Qué ________ comer Uds.?
—Rosa ________ comer pollo y Oscar y yo ________ comer entremeses.
3. pensar —¿Adónde ________ ir Uds. el domingo?
—________ ir al club.
4. cerrar —¿No ________ (ellos) la cafetería los sábados?
—No, creo que no ________ la cafetería los sábados.
5. perder —Cuando Uds. van a Las Vegas, ¿________ mucho dinero?
—Sí, ________ mucho.
6. empezar —¿A qué hora ________ Uds. a trabajar?
—Nosotros ________ a las ocho y Luis ________ a las nueve.

**B.** You have just enrolled at a new university, and some current students are helping to orient you. Compare their routines and preferences with your own.

1. Comenzamos las clases a las nueve.
2. No entendemos inglés.
3. Pensamos trabajar mañana.
4. Queremos ir al club.
5. Preferimos beber refrescos.
6. No cerramos las ventanas por la noche.

**C.** Interview a classmate, using the following questions. When you have finished, switch roles.

1. ¿Entienden tú y tus amigos inglés?
2. ¿Entiendes una conversación en español?
3. ¿Entiendes la lección?
4. ¿Quieres tomar un refresco?
5. ¿Prefieres Coca-Cola o Sprite?
6. ¿Quieren Uds. comer en su casa o en la cafetería?
7. ¿Piensas ir a un baile el sábado?
8. Para bailar, ¿prefieres una orquesta o discos compactos?

**D.** With a classmate, prepare four questions to ask your instructor, using stem-changing verbs.

# ¡A ver cuánto aprendió!

**INTERNET**

See the *¿Cómo se dice...?* Web site for additional grammar and vocabulary practice: http://spanish.college.hmco.com/students

## ¡Repase el vocabulario!

Complete the following sentences with the appropriate words; then read them aloud.

1. ¿________ son los discos compactos? ¿De Rosa?
2. En las fiestas de ________ de año en España, comen doce ________ a la ________.
3. La orquesta es muy, muy buena. ¡Es ________!
4. Enrique Iglesias ________ muy bien.
5. ¿________ vas? ¿Al club?
6. ¡Feliz año ________!
7. Marta está ________ porque va al baile del club.
8. ¿Tienes refrescos? Tengo mucha ________.
9. No tengo ________, pero tengo discos compactos.
10. No quiero bailar ahora porque estoy muy ________.
11. ¿________ dinero tiene Ud.? ¿Mil pesos?
12. ¿Quién va a traer el ________ de Navidad? ¿Es grande o ________?
13. Un ________. Vamos a brindar con sidra.
14. Hoy vamos a celebrar el ________ de Julio.
15. ¿Estudiamos esta noche o vas a estar ________?
16. Tengo un equipo ________, pero es muy malo.

## Entrevista

With a partner, interview each other by asking the following questions.

1. ¿Cuántos años tienes? ¿Cuándo es tu cumpleaños?
2. ¿Celebras tu cumpleaños con una fiesta?
3. ¿Das muchas fiestas en tu casa? ¿Cuándo vas a dar una fiesta?
4. ¿Estás invitado(-a) a una fiesta el sábado?
5. ¿Bailas bien? ¿Lo pasas bien cuando vas a un baile?
6. ¿Dónde vas a comer mañana? ¿A qué hora vas a comer? ¿Con quién?
7. ¿Tienes hambre? ¿Qué quieres comer? ¿Vas a preparar algo *(something)*?
8. ¿Prefieres beber vino, cerveza, refrescos o agua mineral?
9. ¿Tienes cintas o discos compactos?
10. ¿Adónde vas esta noche?
11. ¿Vas a estar ocupado(-a) mañana? ¿Piensas estudiar?
12. ¿Qué tienes que hacer *(to do)* mañana por la tarde?

## Situaciones

What would you say in the following situations? What might the other person say? Act out the scenes with a partner. Take turns playing each role.

1. You want to ask someone to dance with you.
2. You are having a party. Offer one of your guests a selection of beverages.

3. Your friend is hungry. You have plenty of food in the house.
4. You call a friend to say that you are going to bring the drinks for a party.
5. It's 12:00 A.M. on January 1.
6. It's your best friend's birthday.
7. You tell a friend how old you're going to be (turn) in . . . (the month of your birthday).

## Para escribir

Look at the photo and make up a story about the people you see. Give their names, describe them, and say how they are related. Say who is giving the party, the occasion for the party, what they are doing, and so on.

# En la vida real

CD-ROM

Do the interactive exercises on the CD-ROM for additional practice.

## Una visita

With a classmate, plan activities you would have in your hometown to entertain a visitor from a Spanish-speaking country. Give your visitor a name and decide which country he or she is from. In your plans include a party, visits to places of interest, and outdoor activities. Decide who is going to do what, and include food and drinks you are going to offer your visitor.

Some additional words or phrases you may want to include are:

**la hamburguesa** *hamburger*
**el perro caliente** *hot dog*
**el pollo frito** *fried chicken*
**el cine** *movie theater*
**la discoteca** *disco*
**el museo** *museum*
**el teatro** *theater*
**la montaña** *mountain*
**el picnic** *picnic*
**la playa** *beach*
**el partido** *(game)* **de** { **béisbol** / **básquetbol** / **fútbol** *(soccer)* / **fútbol americano** }

## Un espectáculo

In Spain, you and a classmate come across this ad about a show and decide to go see it. What information can you get from the ad? After reading the ad, take turns answering the questions that follow.

MADRID ABIERTO

**«Holiday on Ice», en el Palacio de Deportes**

❊❊❊❊❊❊

***Música y acrobacias en una fiesta sobre hielo***

Setenta artistas del patinaje, de diversas nacionalidades, participan en el espectáculo musical «Holiday on Ice», que se presenta en Madrid solamente hasta el 2 de agosto, antes de continuar hacia Valladolid y Bilbao.

El «show» ofrece dos horas de números musicales, bailes y acrobacias dedicadas a México y a Rusia. La «danza de los platillos» y las acrobacias de los hermanos Ribelli son lo mejor.

El espectáculo se presenta a las 21,30 horas. Hay entradas desde 500 a 1.400 pesetas, con precios especiales para los niños menores de doce años. Venta anticipada por las tardes, de 18 a 21 horas, en el **Palacio de Deportes de la Comunidad** (avenida Felipe II, 19).

**Zdenek Pazdirek, doble campeón checoslovaco.**

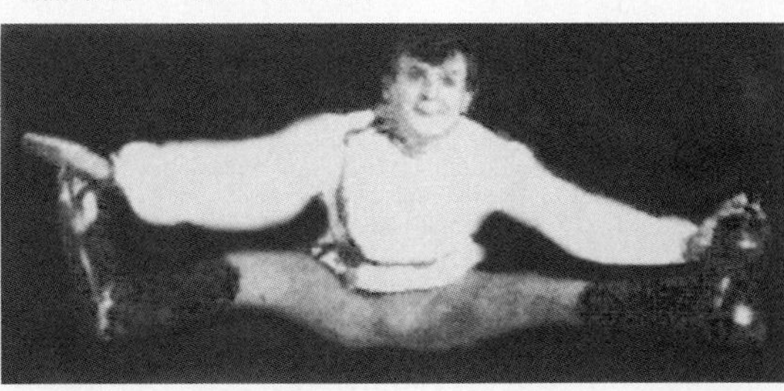

1. ¿Cómo se llama el espectáculo?
2. ¿Dónde presentan el espectáculo?
3. ¿Hasta *(Until)* cuándo va a estar en Madrid el grupo?
4. De Madrid, ¿adónde va el grupo?

5. ¿Cuántos artistas hay en el grupo?
6. ¿Son todos mexicanos?
7. ¿A qué países dedican los artistas el espectáculo?
8. ¿El espectáculo es a las nueve y media de la mañana o de la noche?
9. En España no usan dólares; usan pesetas. ¿Cuánto dinero necesitan Uds. para comprar las entradas *(buy the tickets)?*
10. ¿En qué calle está el Palacio de Deportes de la Comunidad?

## ¡Damos una fiesta!

Get together with two or three students and plan a party. Discuss the following:

1. how much money you have
2. when you are going to have the party
3. where you are going to have the party
4. whom you are going to invite
5. what you are going to eat and who is going to bring the food
6. what you are going to drink and who is going to bring the drinks
7. what you are going to do
8. who is going to bring the CDs and tapes
9. what kinds of music you want

PANORAMA HISPÁNICO

# 2. España (I)

España

- España forma, con Portugal, la Península Ibérica. Su capital es Madrid y su sistema de gobierno es una monarquía constitucional. El actual rey *(king)* de España es Juan Carlos de Borbón.
- El turismo tiene una gran importancia para la economía de España. Más de 63 millones de personas visitan España cada *(each)* año para disfrutar de *(enjoy)* su clima y de su rica historia.
- Los moros *(Moors)*, del norte de África, dominaron España por más de 700 años. Su influencia es evidente en la arquitectura de Toledo, Córdoba, Granada, Sevilla y otras ciudades.

Una de las grandes atracciones turísticas de Madrid es la Plaza de España, donde se encuentra un monumento a Cervantes. Frente a la estatua del escritor están Don Quijote y Sancho Panza, los personajes *(characters)* centrales de su inmortal novela *Don Quijote de la Mancha*.

*¿Cuáles son las principales atracciones turísticas de su estado?*

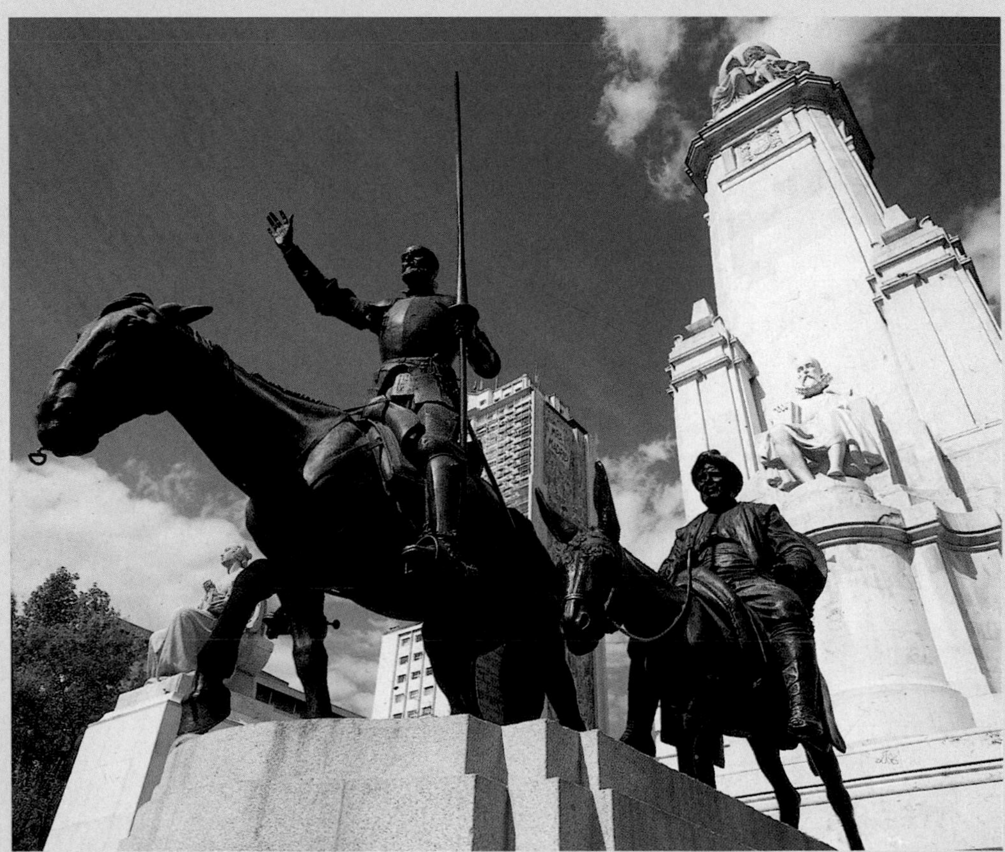

La ciudad de Ávila, situada al noroeste de Madrid, está completamente rodeada de murallas románicas *(Romanesque walls)*. Aunque las murallas tienen casi *(almost)* 1.000 años, están muy bien conservadas.

*¿Hay ciudades como Ávila en su país?*

El Templo de la Sagrada Familia, del arquitecto catalán Antonio Gaudí, es un símbolo de la ciudad de Barcelona. Gaudí murió en 1926 sin terminar la construcción de la iglesia, que todavía no está acabada *(finished)*.

*¿Cómo se llaman algunos arquitectos norteamericanos famosos?*

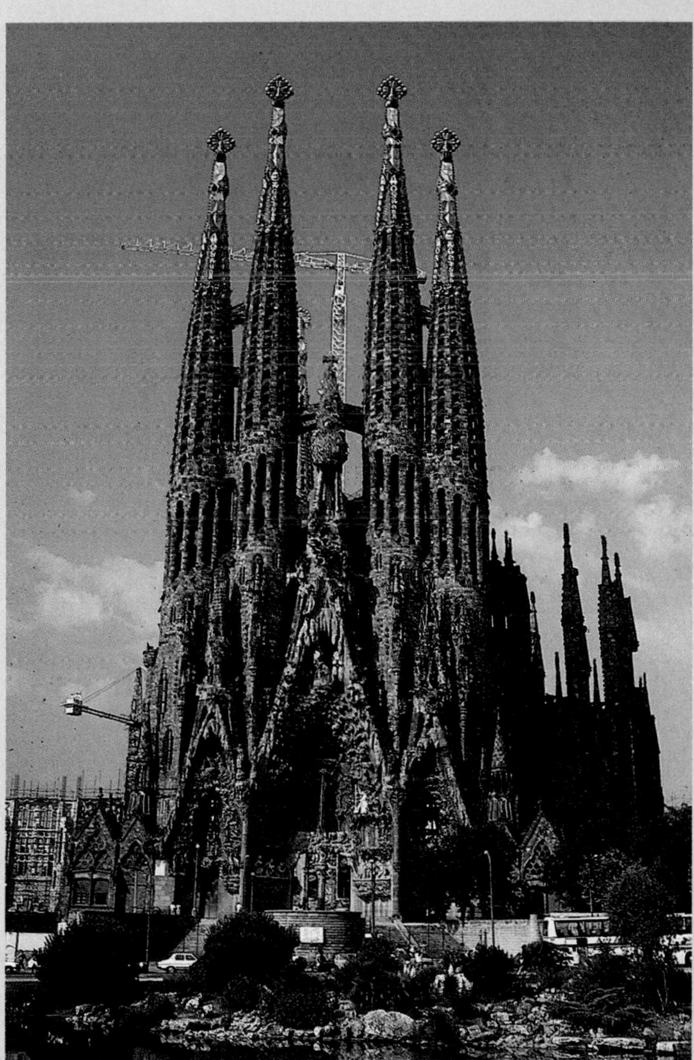

Vista parcial del puerto de San Sebastián en el País Vasco *(Basque Country)*. Situado sobre el Mar Cantábrico y muy cerca de la frontera francesa, San Sebastián es un centro pesquero *(fishing)* importante. La ciudad también es conocida *(known)* por su hermosa *(beautiful)* playa, "La Concha".

*¿Vive Ud. cerca del mar* (sea)*?*

El pueblo de Alcázar de San Juan, en la región de La Mancha. Esta región, una extensa llanura *(plain)*, y sus molinos de viento *(windmills)* son famosos en todo el mundo gracias a la novela *Don Quijote de la Mancha*, de Miguel de Cervantes.

*¿Qué sabe Ud. de Don Quijote?*

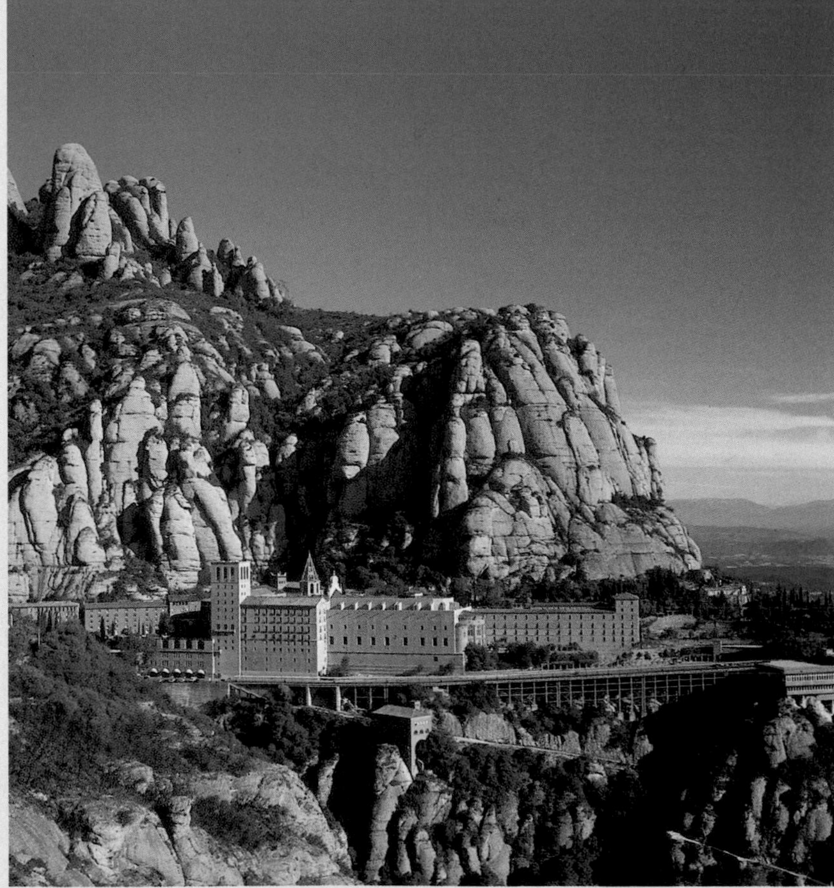

El Monasterio de Montserrat, situado en la montaña del mismo *(same)* nombre, cerca de Barcelona, es famoso por la estatua de la Virgen María y el Niño. La Virgen de Montserrat, a la que los catalanes llaman "la Moreneta", por su color negro, es la patrona de Cataluña. En el monasterio hay varios museos y una de las bibliotecas más importantes de España.

*¿Hay algún museo importante en su ciudad? ¿Cuál?*

Las ferias *(fairs)* son muy populares en toda España. La feria de abril de Sevilla, que se celebra después de la Semana Santa *(Holy Week)*, es una de las más famosas del país.

*¿Dónde hay ferias en su país?*

El Patio de los Leones de la Alhambra de Granada. La Alhambra es un palacio inmenso, construido por los árabes en los siglos XIII y XIV. Los salones y jardines del palacio forman una especie *(sort)* de laberinto.

*¿Dónde está su edificio favorito?*

Mallorca, Menorca e Ibiza, las Islas Baleares, están situadas en el Mar Mediterráneo y pertenecen a España. Más de cinco millones de turistas visitan estas islas todos los años. Sin embargo, las islas aún conservan muchas de sus típicas aldeas *(small towns)* de pescadores, como la que vemos en la foto.

*¿Qué islas pertenecen a los Estados Unidos?*

Do the interactive exercises on
the CD-ROM for additional practice.

## Preparación

**¿Cuánto saben Uds. ya?** After reading **Panorama hispánico 2,** get together in groups of three or four students and complete each statement with the appropriate information.

1. _______ es la capital de España.
2. En la Plaza de España hay un monumento a _______.
3. Antonio Gaudí es un _______ catalán.
4. El Templo de la Sagrada Familia está en la ciudad de _______.
5. Los moros *(Moors)* dominaron España por más de _______ años.
6. La influencia de los moros *(Moors)* se observa en la arquitectura de ciudades como Toledo, _______, _______ y _______.
7. El autor de la novela *Don Quijote de la Mancha* es _______.
8. Mallorca, Menorca e Ibiza son tres _______ en el mar Mediterráneo.
9. La Alhambra es un _______ inmenso, construido por los _______ en los siglos XIII y XIV.

## Comprensión

**A. Madrid.** Read the following statements. After watching the video, circle **V** (**Verdadero**) or **F** (**Falso**), according to what you understood. If the statement is false, correct it.

V F 1. Madrid está en la costa de España.
V F 2. La Plaza Mayor es una plaza muy grande.
V F 3. En la Plaza de la Cibeles hay un monumento a Cervantes.
V F 4. Hay un lago *(lake)* en el Parque del Buen Retiro.
V F 5. El fútbol es el deporte más popular entre los madrileños.

**B. Antonio Gaudí.** Select the word or phrase that best completes each statement according to what you understood in the video.

1. Antonio Gaudí creó un estilo (nuevo, simple) de arquitectura.
2. La Casa Milá es una casa de (apartamentos, edificios).
3. El Parque Güell tiene (un monumento a Gaudí, mosaicos de vivos colores).
4. El Templo de la Sagrada Familia es la obra más (ambiciosa, insignificante) de Gaudí.
5. La construcción de (la Casa Milá, la Sagrada Familia) continúa hasta hoy día.

**C. Granada.** Select the word or phrase that best completes each statement according to what you understood from the video.

1. Granada está en el (sur, norte) de España, cerca de la sierra Nevada.
2. La Alhambra era una (fortaleza *[fort]* militar, fuente *[fountain]*).
3. Las paredes *(walls)* de la Alhambra están decoradas con (complicados, simples) diseños geométricos *(geometric designs)*.
4. En el Patio de los Leones, la fuente tiene (diez, doce) leones.

## Ampliación

A. **Dos culturas.** With a partner, make a list of counterparts you can find in your local area, city, state, or country for each of the following items.

1. Madrid
2. el monumento de la Cibeles, Madrid
3. la Plaza Mayor, Madrid
4. el Parque del Buen Retiro, Madrid
5. el Templo de la Sagrada Familia, Barcelona
6. la Casa Milá, Barcelona
7. el Generalife, Granada

B. **Quiero visitar...** Interview a partner to determine which of the Spanish cities in the video segment he/she would like to visit. Use the following questions as a guide. Share your observations with the rest of the class.

1. ¿Te gusta Madrid? ¿Barcelona? ¿Granada?
2. ¿Qué lugares *(places)* quieres visitar? ¿Por qué?
3. ¿Cuáles son algunos de los monumentos que quieres ir a ver?

# Planes para un fin de semana

Lección 5

## OBJECTIVES

### Pronunciation

The Spanish **p**, **t**, **c**, and **q**

### Structure

Comparative forms • Irregular comparative forms • Present indicative of **o:ue** stem-changing verbs • Present progressive • Uses of **ser** and **estar** • Pronouns as objects of prepositions

### Communication

You will learn vocabulary related to family relationships and personal characteristics.

# Planes para un fin de semana

STUDENT AUDIO

*Carol, una estudiante de los Estados Unidos, está en España. Asiste a la Universidad de Salamanca y vive en una pensión cerca de la Plaza Mayor. Quiere aprender a*[1] *hablar español perfectamente y por eso nunca pierde la oportunidad de practicar el idioma. Ahora está hablando con dos amigos españoles en un café al aire libre. Están comiendo sándwiches y bebiendo café.*

LUIS —Oye, Carol, ¿puedes ir con nosotros a Madrid este fin de semana?

CAROL —No, no puedo... Tengo que escribir muchas cartas: a mi abuela, a mi tío, a mi hermano...

LUIS —Tú echas de menos a tu familia, ¿no?

CAROL —Sí, ...especialmente a mi hermano mayor.

CARMEN —¿Cómo es tu hermano? ¿Rubio? ¿Moreno?

CAROL —Es rubio, delgado y de estatura mediana. Estudia medicina.

CARMEN —¡Muy interesante! ¿Cuándo viene a España? ¿En el verano?

CAROL —No, va a viajar a México con su esposa y sus dos hijas.

CARMEN —¡Bah! Es casado... ¡Qué lástima! ¿No tienes otro hermano?

CAROL —No, lo siento. Aquí tengo una fotografía de mis sobrinas.

CARMEN —*(Mira la foto)* ¿Éstas son tus sobrinas? ¡Son muy bonitas!

CAROL —Empiezan a[1] asistir a la escuela el quince de septiembre.

LUIS —¡Oye! ¿Por qué no vas a Madrid con nosotros? Es más interesante que escribir cartas...

CAROL —¿Van en coche?

LUIS —No, preferimos ir en autobús. Es tan cómodo como el coche, no cuesta mucho y no tenemos que conducir.

CAROL —¡Buena idea! Yo nunca manejo en Madrid. ¿Y adónde piensan ir?

CARMEN —Al Museo del Prado. Allí están algunos de los cuadros más famosos del mundo.

LUIS —¡Es muy interesante! ¡Y Madrid tiene unos restaurantes muy buenos! Nosotros siempre almorzamos en Casa Botín que, para mí, es el mejor de todos.

CAROL —Vale. ¡Vamos a Madrid!... ¡Si no llueve! Porque si llueve no voy.

CARMEN —No, hija[2], no va a llover.

CAROL —¿Cuándo volvemos?

LUIS —El sábado por la noche o el domingo.

CARMEN —Ah, Luis, la fiesta de Marisol es mañana. ¿Dónde es?

LUIS —Es en su casa. ¿Quieren ir conmigo?

CARMEN —Sí, vamos contigo.

LUIS —¡Magnífico! Estén listas a las nueve.

---

[1]The preposition **a** is used after **aprender** and **empezar** when they are followed by a verb in the infinitive.

[2]In this context, "hija" is the equivalent of "child" or "dear."

# Vocabulario

## Cognados

**¡Bah!** Bah!
**especialmente** especially
**la familia** family
**famoso(-a)** famous
**la fotografía, la foto** photograph, photo
**interesante** interesting
**la medicina** medicine
**el museo** museum
**la oportunidad** opportunity
**perfectamente** perfectly
**el plan** plan
**el restaurante** restaurant

## Nombres

**la abuela** grandmother
**el autobús, el ómnibus** bus
**el café** coffee
**el café al aire libre** sidewalk cafe
**la carta** letter
**el coche, el carro, el automóvil, el auto** car, automobile
**el cuadro, la pintura** painting, picture
**la escuela** school
**la esposa** wife
**los Estados Unidos** United States
**el fin de semana** weekend
**el hermano** brother
**la hija** daughter
**el mundo** world
**la pensión** boarding house
**la plaza** town square
**la sobrina** niece
**el tío** uncle

## Verbos

**almorzar (o:ue)** to have lunch
**asistir(a)** to attend
**conducir (yo conduzco), manejar** to drive
**costar (o:ue)** to cost
**echar de menos, extrañar** to miss (feel homesick for)
**llover (o:ue)** to rain
**mirar** to look at
**poder (o:ue)** to be able to, can
**practicar** to practice
**viajar** to travel
**volver (o:ue)** to return

## Adjetivos

**casado(-a)** married
**cómodo(-a)**[1] comfortable
**este** this *(m.)*
**mayor** older, bigger
**mejor** better, best

## Otras palabras y expresiones

**algunos(-as)** some
**aquí** here
**cerca (de)** close (to), near
**cuando** when
**de estatura mediana** of medium height
**éstas** these
**estén listas** be ready
**más** more
**nunca** never
**por eso** that is why
**¡qué lástima!** what a pity!
**si** if
**tan... como** as . . . as
**vale** okay *(Spain)*
**vamos** let's go

[1]**incómodo(-a)** uncomfortable

## Vocabulario adicional

### La familia

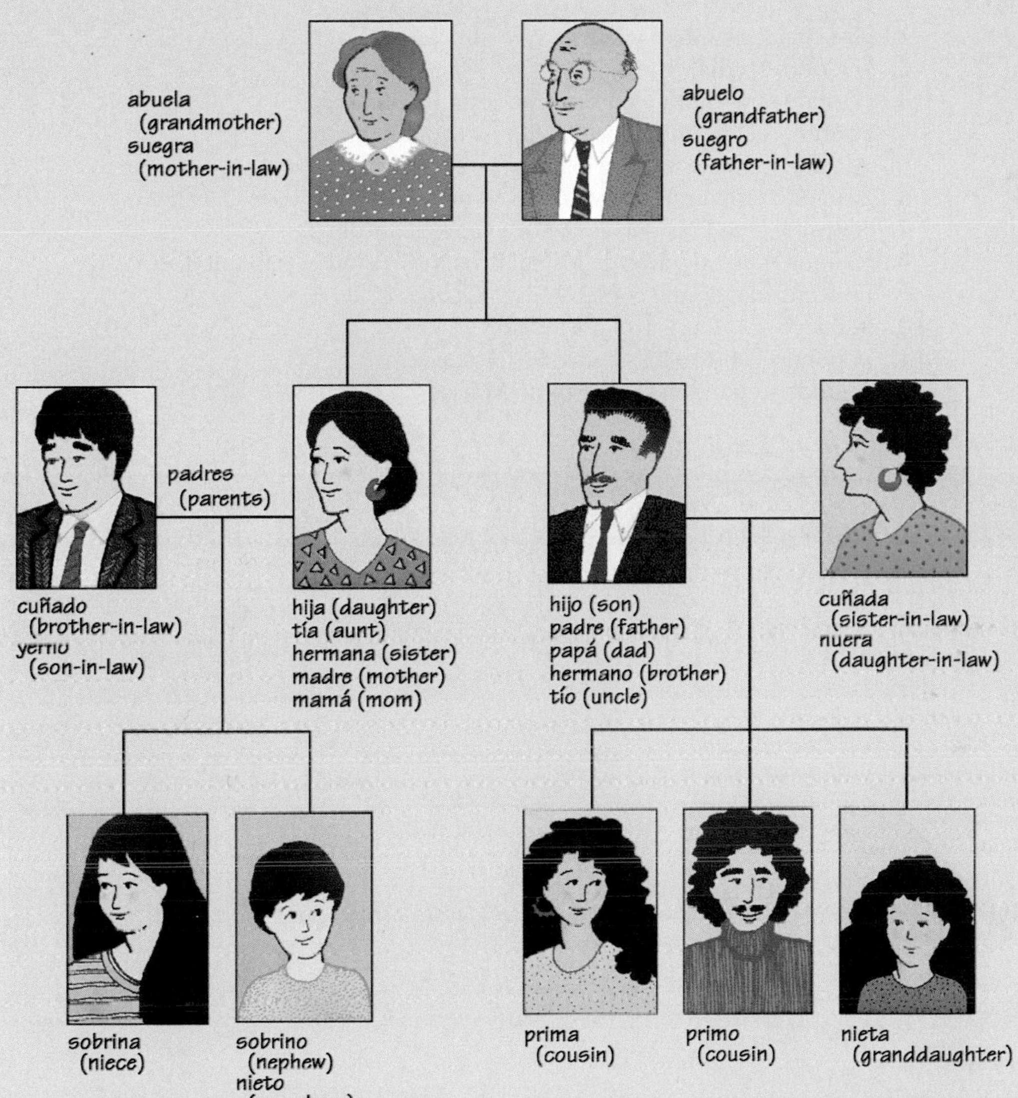


### Otros miembros de la familia

| | | |
|---|---|---|
| **la hermanastra** | stepsister | Elsa no es mi hermana; es mi **hermanastra.** |
| **el hermanastro** | stepbrother | Oscar es mi **hermanastro.** |
| **la hijastra** | stepdaughter | Elena es mi **hijastra.** |
| **el hijastro** | stepson | Julio es el **hijastro** de María. |
| **la madrastra** | stepmother | Mi **madrastra** se llama Dolores. |
| **la media hermana** | half sister | Yo tengo dos **medias hermanas.** |
| **el medio hermano** | half brother | Pedro es mi **medio hermano.** |
| **el padrastro** | stepfather | No es mi padre; es mi **padrastro.** |

## ¡Conversemos!

Answer the following questions, basing your answers on the dialogue.

1. ¿De dónde es Carol y dónde vive ahora?
2. ¿Dónde estudia?
3. ¿Dónde está ahora y con quiénes está hablando?
4. ¿Cómo es el hermano de Carol?
5. ¿Con quién va a viajar a México?
6. ¿Cuándo empiezan a asistir a la escuela las sobrinas de Carol?
7. ¿Por qué cree Luis que es mejor viajar en autobús?
8. ¿Dónde están algunos de los cuadros más famosos del mundo?
9. En Madrid, ¿dónde comen Luis y Carmen?
10. Si llueve, ¿va a ir Carol a Madrid?
11. ¿Cuándo vuelven los chicos a Salamanca?
12. ¿Dónde y cuándo es la fiesta de Marisol?

## ¿Lo sabía Ud.?

- La Universidad de Salamanca es una de las universidades más antiguas y famosas del mundo. Además de los cursos regulares para españoles, ofrece muchas clases para estudiantes extranjeros *(foreign)*.
- El Museo del Prado es uno de los museos más importantes del mundo. Tiene una colección de más de 2.000 cuadros y más de 300 esculturas. Allí están representados los grandes pintores españoles—Goya, Murillo, Velázquez, El Greco y otros. También hay cuadros de otros pintores europeos famosos.
- En la mayoría de los países hispánicos, las universidades no tienen residencias universitarias *(dorms)*. Los estudiantes viven con su familia o en pensiones, donde el precio incluye el cuarto y la comida *(room and board)*.
- El café al aire libre es una parte importante de la cultura hispánica, donde la gente *(people)* conversa mientras come y toma algo *(something)*.
- En los países de habla hispana, la fecha *(date)* se escribe con el día antes del mes: 2-5-01 equivale al dos de mayo del 2001.

• ¿Puede Ud. nombrar *(name)* dos universidades norteamericanas muy famosas?

La Universidad de Salamanca, la más antigua de España.

• ¿En qué ciudad está el famoso Museo Metropolitano de Arte?

• ¿En qué ciudades de este país hay cafés al aire libre?

See the *¿Cómo se dice...?* Web site for activities on authentic cultural material: http://spanish.college.hmco.com/students

# Pronunciación

## A The Spanish p

The Spanish **p** is pronounced like the English *p* as in the word *sparks*, but with no expulsion of air. Listen to your instructor and repeat the following words.

| | | |
|---|---|---|
| perfectamente | tiempo | oportunidad |
| pintura | papá | septiembre |
| pensión | primo | poder |

## B The Spanish t

The Spanish **t** is pronounced by placing the tongue against the upper teeth, as in the English word *stop*. Listen to your instructor and repeat the following words.

| | | |
|---|---|---|
| nieta | restaurante | practicar |
| tío | carta | auto |
| otro | este | foto |

## C The Spanish c

The Spanish sound for the letter **c** in the combinations **ca, co,** and **cu** is /*k*/, pronounced as in the English word *scar*, but with no expulsion of air. Listen to your instructor and repeat the following words.

| | | |
|---|---|---|
| café | coche | cuñado |
| nunca | cómodo | cuánto |
| calle | simpático | cuándo |

## D The Spanish q

The Spanish **q** is always followed by a **u**; it is pronounced like the *c* in the English word *come*, but without any expulsion of air. Listen to your instructor and repeat the following words.

| | | |
|---|---|---|
| Quintana | Roque | quien |
| que | quiere | orquesta |
| aquí | queso | Quevedo |

## 1 Comparative forms *(Formas comparativas)*

### A. Comparisons of inequality

- In Spanish, the comparative of inequality of most adjectives, adverbs, and nouns is formed by placing **más** *(more)* or **menos** *(less)* before the adjective, the adverb, or the noun and **que** *(than)* after it.

| | | | | |
|---|---|---|---|---|
| **más** *(more)* / **menos** *(less)* | + | *adjective* or *adverb* or *noun* | + | **que** *(than)* |

—¿Tú eres **más alta que** Ana? — *"Are you taller than Ana?"*
—Sí, ella es mucho **más baja que** yo. — *"Yes, she is much shorter than I."*

**ATENCIÓN** **De** is used instead of **que** before a numerical expression of quantity or amount.

Luis tiene **más de** treinta años. — *Luis is over thirty years old.*
Hay **menos de** veinte estudiantes aquí. — *There are fewer than twenty students here.*

### B. Comparisons of equality

- To form comparisons of equality with adjectives, adverbs, and nouns in Spanish, use the adjectives **tanto, -a, -os, -as,** or the adverb **tan... como.**

| *When comparing adjectives or adverbs:* | *When comparing nouns:* |
|---|---|
| **tan** *(as)* bonita / tarde + **como** | **tanto** *(as much)* dinero / **tanta** plata *(money)* / **tantos** *(as many)* libros / **tantas** plumas + **como** |

—¿Vas en autobús? — *"Are you going by bus?"*
—Sí, es **tan** cómodo **como** el coche. — *"Yes, it's as comfortable as the car."*

—Tengo mucho trabajo. — *"I have a lot of work."*

—Yo tengo **tanto** trabajo **como** tú. — *"I have as much work as you (do)."*

## C. The superlative

■ The superlative construction is similar to the comparative. It is formed by placing the definite article before the person or thing being compared.

| *definite article* | + | *(noun)* | + | **más** or **menos** | + | *adjective* | + | **de** |
|---|---|---|---|---|---|---|---|---|

—¿Quieres ir al Museo del Prado? — *"Do you want to go to the Prado Museum?"*

—Sí, allí están **los cuadros más famosos de** España. — *"Yes, the most famous paintings in Spain are there."*

—Juan no es muy inteligente. — *"Juan is not very intelligent."*

—No, **es el**[1] **menos inteligente de** la familia. — *"No, he is the least intelligent (one) in the family."*

**ATENCIÓN** Note that the Spanish **de** translates to the English *in* after a superlative.

Son los cuadros más famosos **de** España. — *They are the most famous paintings in Spain.*

Es la chica más bonita **de** la clase. — *She is the prettiest girl in the class.*

## práctica

A. Complete the following sentences, using the Spanish equivalent of the words in parentheses.

1. Tu primo es ________ tú. *(fatter than)*
2. Tú eres ________ que él. *(much thinner)*
3. Mi cuñado es ________ que ella, pero estudia mucho. *(less intelligent)*
3. Mi suegra tiene ________ años, pero mi suegro tiene ________. *(less than fifty / more than seventy)*
4. Mi abuela tiene ________ mis padres. *(as much money as)*
5. Carlos tiene ________ yo. *(as many CDs as)*
6. Mi sobrina es ________ su mamá. *(as tall as)*
7. Tu tía habla español ________ mi padre. *(as well as)*
8. Aquí hay ________ allí. *(as many girls as)*

---

[1] As in English, the noun may be omitted.

**B.** Compare the people in the picture below with each other.

1. María es ________ Rosa.
2. Rosa es ________ María.
3. Carlos es ________ Rosa y que María.
4. Carlos es ________ Juan.
5. Juan es ________ Carlos.
6. Juan es ________ María.
7. Juan es el ________ de todos.
8. Carlos es el ________ de todos.

**C.** Establish comparisons between the following people and things, using the adjectives provided and adding any necessary words.

1. Michael Jordan / Danny De Vito (alto)
2. Cuba / Canadá (pequeño)
3. la clase de español / la clase de alemán (difícil)
4. coche / ómnibus (cómodo)
5. Puerto Rico / Argentina (grande)
6. Jim Carrey / Antonio Banderas (guapo)

Now find a partner. Take turns comparing more people and things.

## 2 Irregular comparative forms *(Formas comparativas irregulares)*

■ The following adjectives and adverbs have irregular comparative and superlative forms in Spanish.

| *Adjective* | *Adverb* | *Comparative* | Superlative |
|---|---|---|---|
| bueno | bien | mejor | el (la) mejor |
| malo | mal | peor | el (la) peor |
| grande | | mayor | el (la) mayor |
| pequeño | | menor | el (la) menor |

—El restaurante El Dorado es muy **malo.** — *"The El Dorado Restaurant is very bad."*
—Sí, pero la cafetería de la universidad es **peor.** — *"Yes, but the university's cafeteria is worse."*

—Eva es una **buena** estudiante. — *"Eva is a good student."*
—Sí, es **la mejor** de la clase. — *"Yes, she's the best in the class."*

- When the adjectives **grande** and **pequeño** refer to size, the regular forms are generally used.

Tu casa es **más grande** que la de Carolina. — *Your house is bigger than Carolina's.*

- When these adjectives refer to age, the irregular forms are used.

Ella es **mucho mayor** que yo. — *She is much older than I.*
Teresa es **menor** que Carlos. — *Teresa is younger than Carlos.*
Ella es **la menor** de todos. — *She is the youngest of all.*

## práctica

**A.** Answer the following questions with complete sentences.

1. Mi sobrina tiene siete años y mi sobrino tiene cinco. ¿Quién es mayor? ¿Quién es menor?
2. Mi tío tiene cuarenta años y mi tía tiene treinta y ocho. ¿Quién es menor? ¿Quién es mayor?
3. ¿Quién habla mejor el español, tú o el profesor (la profesora)?
4. Pedro tiene una "B" en inglés; Antonio tiene una "C"; y José tiene una "F". ¿Quién es el peor estudiante? ¿Quién es el mejor estudiante?

Now write three original comparative situations, using the ones you have just completed as models. When you have finished, take turns giving and responding to situations with a partner.

**B.** Interview a classmate, using the following questions. When you have finished, switch roles.

1. ¿Tú eres mayor o menor que tu mejor amigo(-a)?
2. ¿Tu mamá es menor que tu papá?
3. ¿Quién cocina *(cooks)* mejor, tú o tu mamá?
4. ¿Quién crees tú que es el (la) mejor estudiante de la clase?
5. ¿Cuál crees que es la mejor universidad de los Estados Unidos?
6. ¿Cuál crees tú que es la mejor película *(film)* del año? ¿Y la peor?
7. De los restaurantes que tú conoces, ¿cuál es el mejor? ¿Y el peor?
8. ¿Quiénes crees tú que conducen mejor: los hombres o las mujeres?

**C.** With a partner, take turns comparing yourselves to members of your families, friends, and other members of the class.

## 3 Present indicative of **o:ue** stem-changing verbs
### *(Presente de indicativo de los verbos que cambian en la raíz* ***o:ue****)*

| **poder** *to be able* | |
|---|---|
| pu**e**do | podemos |
| pu**e**des | podéis |
| pu**e**de | pu**e**den |

- Some verbs undergo a stem change in the present indicative. For these verbs, when **o** is the last stem vowel and it is stressed, it changes to **ue.**

| | |
|---|---|
| —¿A qué hora **vuelven** Uds.? | *"At what time are you returning?"* |
| —**Volvemos** a las doce. | *"We'll return at twelve o'clock."* |
| —Entonces comemos a las doce y media. | *"Then we'll have lunch (eat) at twelve-thirty."* |

- Note that the stem vowel is not stressed in the verb forms used with **nosotros(-as)** and **vosotros(-as)**; therefore, the **o** does not change to **ue.**
- Other verbs that undergo this change:[1]

| | |
|---|---|
| **almorzar** *to have lunch* | **llover** (impersonal) *to rain* |
| **contar** *to tell, to count* | **morir** *to die* |
| **costar** *to cost* | **recordar** *to remember* |
| **dormir** *to sleep* | **volar** *to fly* |
| **encontrar** *to find* | **volver** *to return* |

## práctica

**A.** Interview a classmate, using the following questions. When you have finished, switch roles.

1. ¿Almuerzas en la cafetería o en tu casa?
2. ¿Cuánto cuestan los sándwiches en la cafetería?
3. ¿Cuántas horas duermes?
4. ¿Cuentas ovejas *(sheep)* para dormir?
5. ¿Hasta *(Up to)* qué número puedes contar en español?
6. ¿Encuentras difícil o fácil la clase de español?
7. ¿Cuándo vuelves a tu casa?
8. ¿Llueve mucho en tu ciudad?

**B.** Marité is talking to her roommate, who is sound asleep. Complete the story, supplying the missing (**o:ue**) verbs. Then read it aloud.

MARITÉ —¡Teresa, me voy! No _______ mis libros. ¿Dónde están? No _______ ir a mi clase sin *(without)* mis libros. ¡Oye! Hoy

[1]For a complete list of stem-changing verbs, see Appendix B.

______ con Pedro en la cafetería; no tengo dinero y los sándwiches en la cafetería ______ tres dólares. ¡Ay, Teresa!, hoy tengo que llamar a Marta y no ______ su número de teléfono. ¡Teresa!, ¿tú ______ el número de Marta? ¡Oye! ¿Roberto ______ a San Francisco hoy? ¿Vas al aeropuerto con él? *(Mira por la ventana.)* ¡Ay, cómo ______! Necesito tu impermeable *(raincoat)*. ¡Ah!, hoy ______ a casa a las cinco. *(Abre la puerta de Teresa.)* ¡Teresa! ¡Teresa! ¿Por qué no contestas *(answer)*?

TERESA —*(Mmm...)* Nunca ______ dormir cuando tú estás en casa.

MARITÉ —Tú ______ mucho. No necesitas dormir más. Me voy. Nos vemos.

C. Arnaldo is very nosy and is always asking questions. Here are the answers. What are his questions?

1. ¿______? Mi equipo estereofónico cuesta $1.000.
2. ¿______? Nosotros almorzamos en el restaurante.
3. ¿______? Volvemos a casa a las cinco.
4. ¿______? No, yo no duermo mucho.
5. ¿______? No, no recuerdo el número de teléfono de Ana.
6. ¿______? Vuelo a Los Ángeles los domingos.
7. ¿______? No, no puedo ir a tu casa esta noche.

D. With a classmate, prepare four or five questions to ask your instructor, using stem-changing (**o:ue**) verbs.

## 4 Present progressive *(Estar + gerundio)*

■ The present progressive describes an action that is in progress. It is formed with the present tense of **estar** and the **gerundio,** which is equivalent to the English present participle (the *-ing* form of the verb).

**Gerundio**

| **hablar** | **comer** | **escribir** |
|---|---|---|
| habl **-ando** | com **-iendo** | escrib **-iendo** |
| *speaking* | *eating* | *writing* |

Yo estoy comiendo.
*I am eating.*

—¿**Estás estudiando**? *"Are you studying?"*
—No, **estoy escribiendo** una carta. *"No, I am writing a letter."*

—¿Qué **estás tomando**? *"What are you drinking?"*
—**Estoy tomando** café. *"I'm drinking coffee."*

- The following forms are irregular:

  pedir: **pidiendo** | dormir: **durmiendo**
  decir: **diciendo** | traer: **trayendo**
  servir: **sirviendo** | leer: **leyendo**

  —¿Daniel **está leyendo**? — *"Is Daniel reading?"*
  —No, **está durmiendo**. — *"No, he's sleeping."*

- Note that as shown with **traer** and **leer**, the **i** of **-iendo** becomes **y** between vowels.

**ATENCIÓN** In Spanish, the present progressive is *never* used to indicate a future action. The present tense is used in future expressions that would require the present progressive in English.

**Trabajo** mañana. — I'm working tomorrow.

- Some verbs, such as **ser, estar, ir,** and **venir,** are rarely used in the progressive construction.

## práctica

**A.** With a partner, take turns asking each other what the following people are doing (**haciendo**).

1. Tú...

2. Yo...

3. Raúl y Sara

4. Eva...

5. La profesora...

6. Nosotros... y el chico...

**B.** Complete the following dialogues, using the present progressive of the verbs given. Then act them out with a partner, adding a sentence or two to each dialogue.

1. comer —¿Qué ________ tú?
   —Yo ________ ensalada.
2. leer —¿Qué libro ________ Uds.?
   —________ *Don Quijote.*
3. servir —¿Qué ________ Uds.?
   —Yo ________ refrescos y Luisa ________ vino.
4. decir —¿Qué ________ Juan Carlos?
   —No ________ nada.
5. estudiar —¿José ________?
   dormir —No, ________.

**C.** With a partner, discuss what you think these people are doing. Give two or three possibilities for each situation.

1. la secretaria / en la oficina
2. los estudiantes / en la clase
3. los chicos / en la cafetería
4. el profesor / en la universidad
5. los muchachos y las muchachas / en la fiesta
6. el Sr. Vega / en su cuarto
7. el camarero *(waiter)* / en el restaurante
8. la Srta. Barrios / en un café al aire libre

## 5 Uses of ser and estar *(Usos de ser y estar)*

The English verb *to be* has two Spanish equivalents, **ser** and **estar.** As a general rule, **ser** expresses *who* or *what* the subject is *essentially,* and **estar** indicates *state* or *condition.* **Ser** and **estar** are *not* interchangeable.

### A. Uses of *ser*

**Ser** expresses a fundamental quality and identifies the essence of a person or thing.

- It describes the basic nature or character of a person or thing. It is also used with expressions of age that do not refer to a specific number of years.

  La orquesta **es** buena.
  Yo **soy** joven *(young).*

- It describes the material that things are made of.

  Las mesas **son** de metal.

- It is used to denote nationality, origin, and profession or trade.

  Sandra **es** norteamericana.
  Yo **soy** de Caracas.
  Mi mamá **es** profesora.

- It is used with expressions of time and with dates.

  Hoy **es** miércoles, cuatro de abril.
  **Son** las cuatro y cuarto de la tarde.

- It is used with events as the equivalent of *taking place*.

  La fiesta **es** en el club Los Violines.

- It is used to indicate possession or relationship.

  Los discos compactos **son** de Julia.
  Antonio **es** el hermano de Raúl.

## práctica

Interview a classmate, using the following questions and two of your own. When you have finished, switch roles.

1. ¿Eres norteamericano(-a)? ¿De dónde eres?
2. ¿De qué ciudad eres?
3. ¿Cómo es tu mamá?
4. ¿Quién es tu mejor amigo(-a)?
5. ¿Es alto(-a) o bajo(-a)?
6. ¿Eres feliz?
7. ¿Dónde son tus clases?
8. ¿Qué día es hoy?
9. ¿Qué fecha es hoy?
10. ¿Qué hora es?

### B. Uses of estar

**Estar** is used to express more transitory qualities and often implies the possibility of change.

- It indicates place or location.

  Mi prima no **está** aquí. ¿Dónde **está**?

- It is used to indicate condition.

  Mis amigos **están** muy cansados.
  Sara **está** enferma.

- With personal reactions, it describes what is perceived through the senses—that is, how a person or thing seems, looks, tastes, or feels.

  El ponche **está** delicioso.

- It is used in the present progressive tense.

  Yo **estoy** estudiando y Ana **está** leyendo.

## práctica

**A.** Imagine that you and a friend are at a party at the Club Náutico, and answer the following questions.

1. ¿En qué calle está el club?
2. ¿Los amigos de Uds. están en el club?
3. ¿Sus amigos están contentos o tristes?

4. ¿Cómo están los entremeses? ¿Deliciosos?
5. ¿Quiénes están en la terraza?
6. ¿Tu mamá está en la fiesta?

**B.** Complete the following dialogues, using the appropriate forms of **ser** or **estar.** Then act them out with a partner.

1. —¿De dónde ________ tu mamá? ¿________ mexicana?
   —Sí, pero ahora ________ en California.
   —¿Tu mamá ________ profesora?
   —No, ________ médica.
2. —¿Olga ________ tu prima?
   —No, ________ mi hermana.
   —¿Cómo ________ ella?
   —________ alta, morena y delgada. ________ muy bonita.
   —¿Dónde ________ ella ahora?
   —________ en su casa.
3. —¿Qué hora ________?
   —________ las siete.
   —¿Dónde ________ la fiesta de Navidad?
   —________ en el Club Náutico. ¿Tú vas a ir?
   —No, ________ muy cansada.
4. —¿Qué ________ comiendo tú?
   —________ comiendo arroz con pollo.
   —¿________ rico *(tasty)*?
   —Sí, ________ delicioso.
5. —¿Ése *(That)* ________ tu escritorio?
   —Sí, ________ mi escritorio.
   —¿________ de metal?
   —No, ________ de madera *(wood)*.
6. —¡Oye! ¿Qué día ________ hoy?
   —Hoy ________ jueves.

C. With two or three other students, prepare a description of a famous person. Include as much information as possible (nationality, profession, physical characteristics, etc.). Read your description to the rest of the class and see who can identify your subject.

## 6 Pronouns as objects of prepositions *(Pronombres usados como objetos de preposición)*

- The object of a preposition is the noun or pronoun that immediately follows it: **La fiesta es *para María (ella)*. Ellos van *con nosotros*.**

| *Singular* | | *Plural* | |
|---|---|---|---|
| **mí** | *me* | **nosotros(-as)** | *us* |
| **ti** | *you* (fam.) | **vosotros(-as)** | *you* (fam.) |
| **Ud.** | *you* (form.) | **Uds.** | *you* (form.) |
| **él** | *him* | **ellos** | *them* (masc.) |
| **ella** | *her* | **ellas** | *them* (fem.) |

—¿Hablan de **mí**? — *"Are you talking about me?"*
—No, no hablamos de **ti**; hablamos de **ella.** — *"No, we are not talking about you; we're talking about her."*

—¿Vas **conmigo** o con Carlos? — *"Are you going with me or with Carlos?"*

—No voy **contigo;** voy **con él.** — *"I'm not going with you; I'm going with him."*

- Only the first- and second-person singular, **mí** and **ti,** are different from regular subject pronouns.
- **Mí** and **ti** combine with **con** to become **conmigo** *(with me)* and **contigo** *(with you),* respectively.

## práctica

A. Complete the following dialogues, using the Spanish equivalent of the words in parentheses. Then act them out with a partner, adding a sentence or two to each dialogue.

1. —¿Carlos va ________? *(with me)*
   —No, no va ________; va ________. *(with you / with her)*
2. —¿Para quién son los discos compactos, Paquito? ¿________ o ________? *(For him / for her)*
   —Son ________. *(for me)*
   —¿________? *(For you)*
   —Sí, señor.
   —¿Los cuadros son ________? *(for you, pl.)*
   —No, son ________. *(for them, fem.)*

B. Interview a classmate, using the following questions and two questions of your own. When you have finished, switch roles. Use the appropriate prepositions and pronouns in your responses.

1. ¿Hablas con tus amigos en la clase?
2. ¿Puedes estudiar español conmigo?
3. ¿Trabajas para tus padres?
4. ¿Vives cerca de tus abuelos?
5. ¿Hablas mucho con tus amigos por teléfono?
6. ¿Puedo ir contigo a la biblioteca?

# ¡A ver cuánto aprendió!

## ¡Repase el vocabulario!

INTERNET

See the *¿Cómo se dice...?* Web site for additional grammar and vocabulary practice: http://spanish.college.hmco.com/students

Match each question in column A with the best response in column B; then read them aloud.

| A | B |
|---|---|
| 1. ¿Dónde está tu familia? | a. No, es de estatura mediana. |
| 2. ¿Qué estudias? | b. Sí, es mi cuñada. |
| 3. ¿Estás incómoda? | c. El 3 de septiembre. |
| 4. ¿Vamos al museo mañana? | d. Medicina. |
| 5. ¿Practicas el español? | e. Pienso ir a Salamanca. |
| 6. ¿Pedro es menor que Juan? | f. No, es mi sobrina. |
| 7. ¿No tienen dinero para ir a un hotel? | g. Sí, ¡qué lástima! |
| 8. ¿Es la hermana de tu esposo? | h. ¡Vale! |
| 9. ¿Es tu prima? | i. Sí, es el hijo de mi hija. |
| 10. ¿Van en ómnibus? | j. En Canadá. |
| 11. ¿Cuándo es tu cumpleaños? | k. No, por eso van a una pensión. |
| 12. ¿Qué planes tienes para el fin de semana? | l. No, vamos en coche. |
| 13. ¿Es tu nieto? | m. Sí, mi silla es muy pequeña. |
| 14. ¿Van a perder la oportunidad de ir a México? | n. Sí, nunca pierdo la oportunidad. |
| 15. ¿Es alta? | o. No, es mayor. |

## Entrevista

With a partner, interview each other by asking the following questions.

1. ¿Tú eres más alto(-a) o más bajo(-a) que tu papá?
2. ¿Tu mamá es alta, baja o de estatura mediana?
3. ¿Tu mamá es mayor o menor que tu papá?

4. ¿Cuál es tu clase más interesante?
5. ¿Tú quieres aprender a hablar español perfectamente?
6. ¿Dónde almuerzas generalmente?
7. ¿Cuál es el mejor restaurante de la ciudad donde tú vives?
8. Generalmente, ¿a qué hora vuelves a tu casa?
9. ¿Adónde piensas ir este fin de semana y qué piensas hacer?
10. Este verano, ¿vas a viajar o vas a asistir a la universidad?
11. ¿Cuál crees tú que es la ciudad más bonita del mundo?
12. ¿Tú tienes tanto dinero como tus padres?

## Situaciones

What would you say in the following situations? What might the other person say? Act out the scenes with a partner. Take turns playing each role.

1. A Spanish exchange student is visiting your home, and you don't want to miss the opportunity to speak Spanish.
2. Someone asks about your weekend plans.
3. You are with a friend who has never seen pictures of your family, and you just happen to have some in your wallet.
4. You are trying to get a reluctant friend to go with you somewhere.

## Para escribir

Write a composition describing two members of your family. Include the following information for each person:

color of hair and eyes (**pelo y ojos**)
age
current residence
place of employment or study
marital status and number of children
other personal characteristics (Establish comparisons between the other members of your family and yourself.)

# En la vida real

CD-ROM

Do the interactive exercises on the CD-ROM for additional practice.

## Objetivos

You and a classmate have a goal: to someday speak Spanish like native speakers and to learn as much as possible about the culture of Spanish-speaking countries. Come up with a list of things you are going to do to reach that goal.

Here are some additional words and phrases you may want to include:

**escuchar** *(to listen to)* { **canciones** *(songs)* / **las cintas del laboratorio de lenguas** / **programas de radio** }
**gente** *people*
**películas españolas y latinoamericanas** *Spanish and Latin American movies*
**revistas** *magazines*
**tener correspondencia** *to correspond*
**visitar países de habla hispana** *to visit Spanish-speaking countries*

## Árbol genealógico *(Family tree)*

Prepare your family tree, following the model on page 109. Call it "**Mi árbol genealógico.**" Be sure to include each family member's relationship to you.

Abuelos maternos | Abuelos paternos

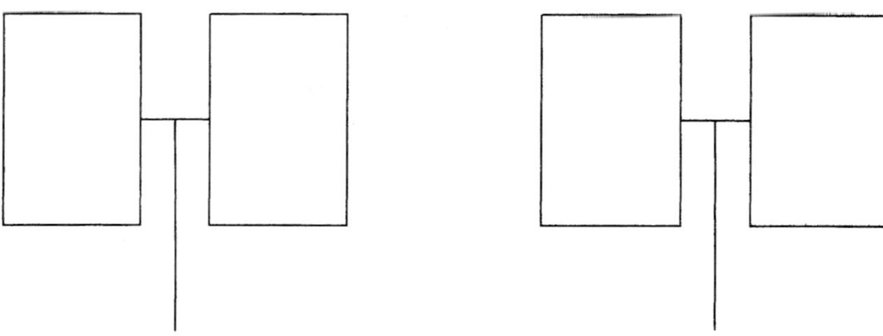

## ¿Quieres ver mis fotos?

Bring pictures of your relatives to class and tell a classmate who they are, giving information about each one. Ask each other any pertinent questions.

## ¿A qué museo vamos?

You and a friend want to go to a museum. Read the following ads and answer the questions.

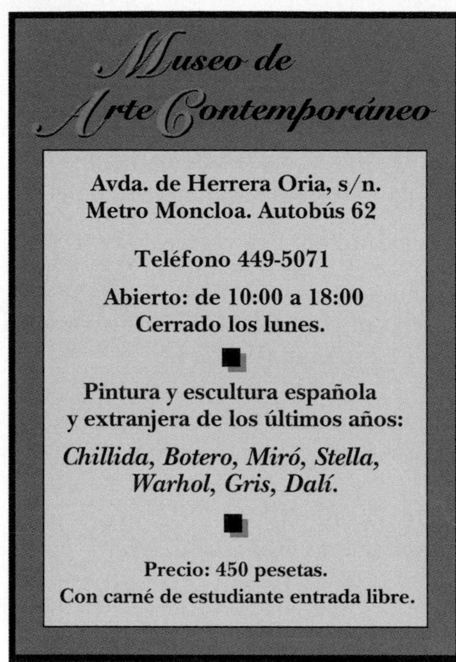


**MUSEO DEL PRADO**

**Paseo del Prado, s/n.**
**Metro Atocha. Autobús 27**
**Abierto: de 10:00 a 17:00**

**Instalado en un edificio del siglo XVIII.**

- **Muestra de los grandes pintores españoles de los siglos XII al XVIII: Goya, Zurbarán, Velázquez, El Greco, Murillo**
- **Pinturas de las escuelas italianas, flamencas, holandesa, etc.: Rafael, Rembrandt, Rubens, etc.**

**Precio: 600 pesetas.**
**Con carné de estudiante entrada gratuita.**
**Sábados entrada libre.**

1. ¿En qué calle está el Museo de Arte Contemporáneo?
2. ¿Pueden Uds. ir al Museo de Arte Contemporáneo el lunes? ¿Por qué?
3. ¿Cuánto cuesta la entrada *(ticket)* al Museo de Arte Contemporáneo?
4. ¿Cuánto pagan *(pay)* los estudiantes para visitar el Museo de Arte Contemporáneo?
5. ¿Qué metro *(subway)* deben Uds. tomar para ir al Museo del Prado?
6. ¿Pueden ir en autobús también? ¿En cuál?
7. El Museo del Prado, ¿es antiguo *(old)* o moderno?
8. ¿En cuál de los dos museos es más barata *(cheap)* la entrada?
9. En el Museo del Prado, ¿encuentran Uds. solamente cuadros de pintores españoles?
10. ¿En qué museo no es necesario pagar los sábados?

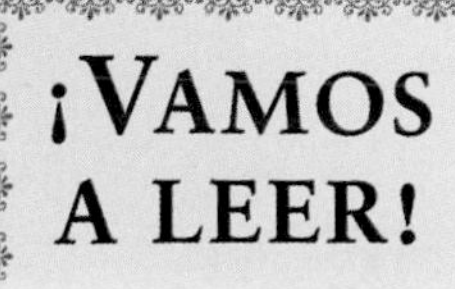


### Antes de leer

As you read the following dialogue, find the answers to these questions.

1. ¿Cuál es el apellido de Ana María?
2. ¿De dónde es?
3. ¿Dónde está su familia?

4. ¿Qué está estudiando Ana María en la universidad?
5. ¿Por qué no son fáciles las clases para ella?
6. ¿La muchacha trabaja? ¿Dónde?
7. ¿Ud. cree que Ana María va mucho a la playa?
8. ¿Con quiénes piensa ir a Disney World?
9. ¿Cuánto tiempo va a estar ella en Miami?
10. ¿Cuándo piensa regresar a Chile? ¿Por qué?

## *Una entrevista*°

interview

Ana María Estévez estudia en la Universidad Internacional de la Florida. Ella es de Chile, pero ahora su familia y ella viven en Miami. Hoy la entrevistamos° para el periódico de la universidad.

**la...** we are interviewing her

PERIODISTA —¿Qué clases estás tomando en la universidad, Ana María?
ANA MARÍA —Matemáticas, historia del arte, inglés y sociología. Las clases son muy difíciles para mí porque no hablo muy bien el inglés.
PERIODISTA —¿Trabajas también?
ANA MARÍA —Sí, trabajo en el laboratorio de lenguas.°

languages

PERIODISTA —¿Te gusta Miami?
ANA MARÍA —Sí, especialmente la playa.°

beach

PERIODISTA —¿Piensas ir a Disney World?
ANA MARÍA —Sí, pienso ir con unos amigos cubanos. Son unos chicos muy simpáticos y divertidos.°

entertaining

PERIODISTA —¿Cuánto tiempo° vas a estar en Miami?

**¿Cuánto...?** How long

ANA MARÍA —Unos cuatro años.
PERIODISTA —¿Piensas regresar a Chile?
ANA MARÍA —Algún° día, porque la verdad° es que echo mucho de menos a mi familia.

Some / truth

## Díganos

Answer the following questions, based on your own thoughts and experiences.

1. ¿Cuál es su apellido?
2. ¿Dónde vive y estudia Ud.?
3. ¿Dónde vive su familia?
4. ¿Cuántas clases toma Ud.? ¿Son fáciles o difíciles?
5. ¿Va Ud. a la playa? ¿Con quién?
6. ¿Son divertidos sus amigos?
7. ¿A quiénes echa Ud. de menos?

# ASÍ SOMOS

VIDEO

CD-ROM
Do the interactive exercises on the CD-ROM for additional practice.

NARRADORA —¿Cómo es su familia?

TAMARA —Mi papá se llama Carlos y trabaja en administración. Mi mamá se llama Neri; trabaja eh... como psicóloga. Tengo dos hermanas que son menores que yo. Yo soy la hija mayor y que está actualmente estudiando. Estamos todos estudiando.

## Preparación

A. **¿Cómo es su familia?** Answer the following questions about your family.

1. ¿Cuántos hermanos(-as) tiene?
2. ¿Cómo se llaman sus hermanos?
3. ¿Cuántos años tienen?
4. ¿Cómo se llama su tío(-a) favorito(-a)?
5. ¿En qué ciudad vive su tío(-a) favorito(-a)?
6. ¿Cuál es su profesión?

B. **¿Cómo te diviertes?** Interview a classmate about his or her favorite leisure activities using the following questions.

1. ¿Qué haces los fines de semana?
2. ¿Prefieres ir al cine o al teatro?
3. ¿Vas a los museos?
4. ¿Vas a las discotecas a bailar?
5. Este fin de semana, ¿piensas ir al parque?
6. ¿Practicas algún deporte?

## Comprensión

A. **¿Verdadero o falso?** Read the following statements. Circle **V** (**Verdadero**) or **F** (**Falso**) according to what you understood from the video. If a statement is false, correct it.

V F 1. Carolina tiene un hermano que tiene 24 años y una hermana que tiene 17 años.
V F 2. La abuela de Juan vive con su familia.
V F 3. El padre y la madre de Jaime trabajan.
V F 4. Tamara es la menor de su familia.
V F 5. Tamara tiene cuatro hermanas.

**B. Planes de familia.** Select the word or phrase that best completes each statement, according to what you understood from the video.

1. Por lo general, Yolanda sale (a pasear, a comer) con su esposo los domingos.
2. En la familia de Rita, (siempre, de vez en cuando *[sometimes]*) comen todos juntos los domingos.
3. Héctor está con (su familia, sus amigos) durante el fin de semana.
4. Los domingos Olga está con (sus niños, sus amigas).

**C. ¿Qué piensan hacer este fin de semana?** Read the statements below and match each weekend activity with the name of the person who said it in the video. More than one activity may correspond with one person.

| A | B |
|---|---|
| _____ 1. Rita | a. salir a comer |
| _____ 2. Ivonne | b. ir a bailar a discotecas |
| _____ 3. Pedro | c. ir a la playa |
| _____ 4. Carolina | d. salir a algún lugar o estar en mi casa |
| _____ 5. Tamara | e. salir con mis amigos |
| _____ 6. Héctor | f. estudiar |
| _____ 7. Milka | g. ir a la fiesta de los latinoamericanos |

## Ampliación

**A. Un árbol genealógico.** Make a list of the questions you may need to ask someone about their family. Then, interview a classmate about his or her family and create their family tree based on what you learn. Be sure to include information on names, ages, and relationships *(el parentesco)* of the various family members.

**B. Durante el fin de semana.** Work with two or three other students to make a list in Spanish of all the activities that you might do on a typical weekend. Then, divide the activities into two categories: *Actividades con mis amigos* and *Actividades con mi familia.* Share your observations with the class.

# Un viaje a Perú

Lección 6

## OBJECTIVES

### Pronunciation

The Spanish **j**, **g** (before **e** or **i**), and **h**

### Structure

Present indicative of **e:i** stem-changing verbs • Affirmative and negative expressions • Verbs with irregular first-person forms • **Saber** vs. **conocer** • Direct object pronouns • Weather expressions

### Communication

You will learn vocabulary related to travel: obtaining information about accommodations, asking about transportation, and checking in at a hotel.

# Un viaje a Perú

*Teresa, una profesora mexicana, va a pasar sus vacaciones en Perú. Ella acaba de llegar a Lima, donde piensa pasar unos días antes de ir a Machu Picchu para conocer las famosas ruinas de los incas. Teresa muestra su pasaporte y luego pasa por la aduana. En el aeropuerto Teresa ve objetos de oro y de plata, y compra algunos para su familia.*

*Teresa va a la oficina de turismo para conseguir información.*

TERESA —Buenos días, señor. ¿Tiene Ud. una lista de hoteles y pensiones? Yo no conozco Lima.

EMPLEADO —Sí, señorita. Aquí la tiene.

*Teresa lee un anuncio sobre el hotel Bolívar.*

## HOTEL BOLÍVAR

El mejor hotel de Lima, situado en el centro de la ciudad y cerca de muchos lugares de interés, es el favorito de miles de turistas que visitan nuestra hermosa capital. Tenemos amplios cuartos con vista a la calle o interiores. Todas las habitaciones tienen baño privado, aire acondicionado y televisor.

El hotel tiene dos restaurantes que ofrecen comida internacional y servicio de habitación. Aceptamos tarjetas de crédito y cheques de viajero. Para hacer reservaciones, llame al teléfono 285-3946

TERESA —Quiero ir al hotel Bolívar. ¿Dónde puedo tomar un taxi?

EMPLEADO —Vaya a la segunda puerta a la derecha. También hay un ómnibus que la lleva al centro.

*En el hotel Bolívar, Teresa pide una habitación.*

TERESA —Necesito una habitación sencilla con baño privado, por favor.

EMPLEADO —Tenemos una con vista a la calle que cuesta 208 soles[1] por día. También hay otra interior en el segundo piso por 130 soles.

TERESA —Son un poco caras. ¿No tiene alguna más barata?

EMPLEADO —No, no hay ninguna. Ahora hay pocos cuartos libres.

TERESA —Prefiero el cuarto interior. ¿A cómo está el cambio de moneda?

EMPLEADO —No sé... Voy a averiguarlo. Por favor firme aquí.

---

[1]Peruvian currency

*Teresa firma el registro.*

TERESA —Quiero cenar en mi habitación. ¿Hasta qué hora sirven la cena?
EMPLEADO —La sirven hasta las once.
TERESA —¿Puede alguien llevar mis maletas al cuarto, por favor?
EMPLEADO —Sí, en seguida viene el botones a llevarlas. Aquí tiene la llave.

*Como hace calor, Teresa decide ir a la piscina.*

# Vocabulario

## Cognados

**el aeropuerto** airport
**amplio(-a)** ample
**la capital** capital
**favorito(-a)** favorite
**el hotel** hotel
**la información** information
**el interés** interest
**internacional** international
**interior** interior
**la lista** list
**el objeto** object
**la oficina** office
**el pasaporte** passport
**privado(-a)** private
**el registro** register
**la reservación, la reserva** reservation
**las ruinas** ruins
**el taxi** taxi
**el turismo** tourism
**el, la turista** tourist
**las vacaciones**[1] vacation

## Nombres

**la aduana** customs
**el aire acondicionado** air conditioning
**el anuncio** ad
**el baño, el cuarto de baño** bathroom
**el botones** bellhop
**la cena** dinner, supper
**el centro** downtown (area)
**el cheque de viajero** traveler's check
**la comida** food
**el cuarto, la habitación** room
**el (la) empleado(-a)** clerk
**la llave** key
**el lugar** place
**la maleta, la valija** suitcase
**el oro** gold
**la piscina** swimming pool
**el piso** floor
**la plata** silver
**el servicio de habitación (cuarto)** room service
**la tarjeta de crédito** credit card
**el televisor** T.V. set
**el viaje** trip, journey

[1]**vacaciones** is always used in the plural in Spanish.

## Verbos

**aceptar** to accept
**averiguar** to find out
**cenar** to have dinner, supper
**comprar** to buy
**conocer (yo conozco)** to know, to be acquainted
**conseguir (e:i)** to get, to obtain
**firmar** to sign
**hacer (yo hago)** to make, to do
**llegar** to arrive
**mostrar (o:ue), enseñar** to show
**ofrecer (yo ofrezco)** to offer
**pasar** to spend (time), to pass
**pasar (por)** to go through, by
**pedir (e:i)** to ask for, to request
**saber (yo sé)** to know
**servir (e:i)** to serve
**ver (yo veo)** to see
**visitar** to visit

## Adjetivos

**alguno(-a)** some, any
**barato(-a)** inexpensive, cheap
**caro(-a)** expensive
**hermoso(-a)** beautiful
**libre** vacant
**pocos(-as)** few
**segundo(-a)** second
**sencillo(-a)** single, simple
**situado(-a)** located
**unos(-as)** a few

## Otras palabras y expresiones

**¿A cómo está el cambio de moneda?** What is the exchange rate?
**a la derecha**[1] to the right
**acabar de +** ***infinitive*** to have just + *past participle*
**alguien** someone, somebody
**Aquí las tiene.** Here they are. (Here you have them.)
**con vista a** overlooking
**en seguida** right away
**Firme aquí.** Sign here.
**hace calor** it's hot
**hasta** until
**llame** call
**luego** then, afterwards
**ninguno(-a)** none, not any
**por** per, for
**que** which
**sobre** about
**vaya a** go to

[1]**a la izquierda:** to the left

## Vocabulario adicional

### En el hotel

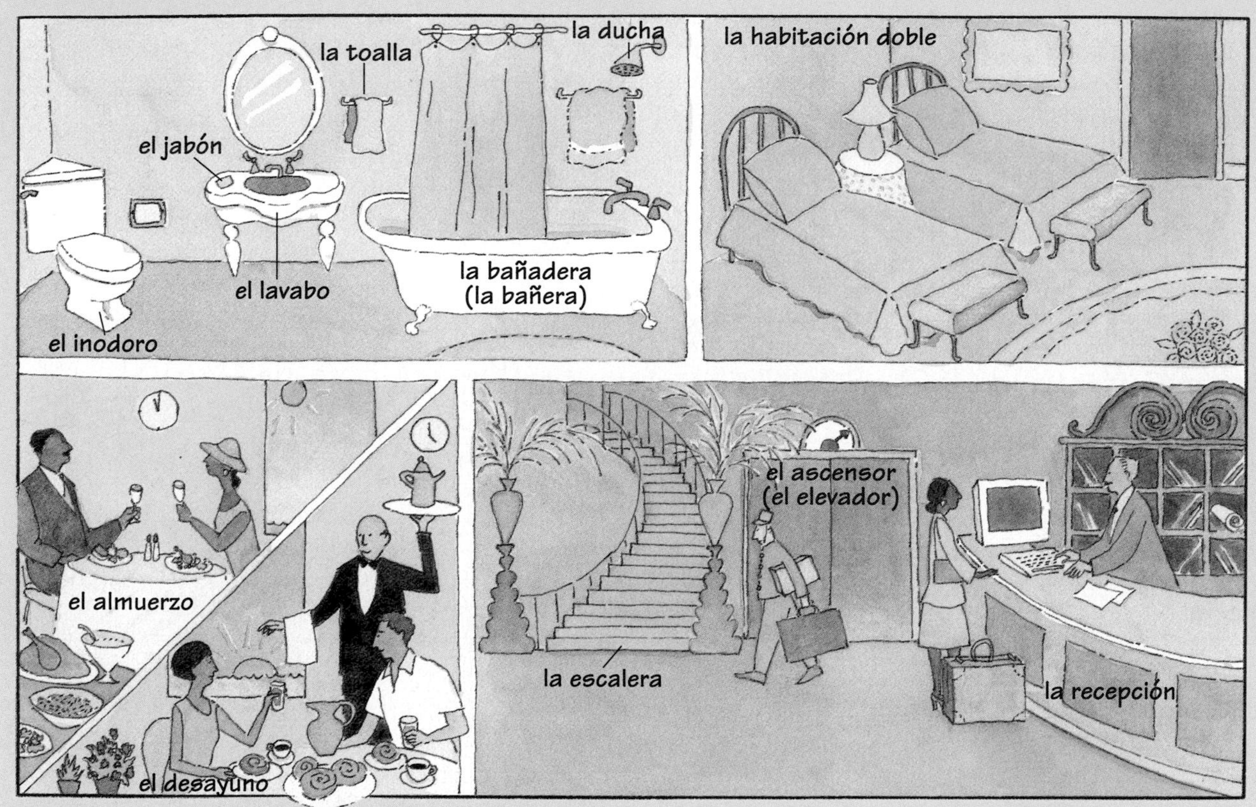


### Para el turismo

| | |
|---|---|
| **la cámara de video** video camera | ¿Tiene Ud. una **cámara de video**? |
| **la cámara fotográfica** camera | Voy a llevar mi **cámara fotográfica.** |
| **cancelar** to cancel | Voy a **cancelar** la reservación. |
| **confirmar** to confirm | Deseo **confirmar** la reservación. |
| **la embajada** embassy | ¿Dónde queda la **embajada** norteamericana? |
| **la lista de espera** waiting list | Estoy en la **lista de espera.** |
| **la tarjeta de turista** tourist card | Los norteamericanos necesitan una **tarjeta de turista** para visitar México. |

## ¡Conversemos!

Answer the following questions, basing your answers on the dialogue.

1. ¿Qué ruinas famosas hay en Perú?
2. ¿Qué muestra Teresa y por dónde pasa?

3. ¿Qué compra Teresa en el aeropuerto?
4. ¿Para qué va Teresa a la oficina de turismo?
5. ¿Qué lee Teresa?
6. ¿Dónde está situado el hotel Bolívar?
7. ¿Qué tienen todos los cuartos del hotel?
8. ¿Qué aceptan en el hotel Bolívar?
9. ¿Teresa pide una habitación sencilla o una doble?
10. ¿Qué cuarto prefiere Teresa? ¿Por qué?
11. ¿Hasta qué hora sirven la cena?
12. ¿Qué decide hacer Teresa? ¿Por qué?

## ¿Lo sabía Ud.?

Fachada de uno de los edificios que rodean la Plaza de San Martín en Lima, Perú.

- Lima, la capital de Perú, es una ciudad de contrastes. Junto a *(Next to)* edificios *(buildings)* muy modernos hay otros de arquitectura colonial. El 25% de la población es de origen indígena.
- La moneda *(currency)* que utilizan con más frecuencia los latinoamericanos cuando viajan fuera de su país es el dólar norteamericano. Esto se debe a que *(is due to the fact that)* es fácil cambiar dólares en la mayoría de los principales bancos de los países hispanoamericanos.

- ¿En qué ciudades de su país hay edificios de arquitectura colonial?
- ¿Se puede cambiar dinero de otros países en los bancos de los Estados Unidos?

See the *¿Cómo se dice...?* Web site for activities on authentic cultural material: http://spanish.college.hmco.com/students

# Pronunciación

## A The Spanish j

The Spanish **j** sounds somewhat like the *h* in the English word *hit*. It is never pronounced like the English *j* in *John* or *James*. Listen to your instructor and repeat the following words.

| | | |
|---|---|---|
| **J**ulia | de**j**ar | emba**j**ada |
| pasa**j**e | **j**abón | via**j**ero |
| tar**j**eta | ob**j**eto | **j**ueves |

## B The Spanish g (before e or i)

When followed by **e** or **i**, the Spanish **g** sounds like the Spanish **j** mentioned above. Listen to your instructor and repeat the following words.

| | | |
|---|---|---|
| **G**erardo | inteli**g**ente | a**g**ente |
| a**g**encia | **g**eneral | **G**enaro |
| re**g**istro | Ar**g**entina | in**g**eniero |

## C The Spanish h

The Spanish **h** is always silent. Listen to your instructor and repeat the following words.

| | | |
|---|---|---|
| **h**ay | **H**ilda | **h**abitación |
| **H**onduras | **h**ermano | **h**asta |
| a**h**ora | **h**otel | **h**ija |

# Estructuras

## 1 Present indicative of e:i stem-changing verbs *(Presente de indicativo de los verbos que cambian en la raíz **e:i**)*

| **servir** *to serve* | |
|---|---|
| sirvo | servimos |
| sirves | servís |
| sirve | sirven |

- Some **-ir** verbs undergo a special stem change in the present indicative. For these verbs, when **e** is the last stem vowel and it is stressed, it changes to **i.**

  —¿Qué **sirven** Uds. en sus fiestas? *"What do you serve at your parties?*
  —**Servimos** champán. *"We serve champagne."*

- Note that the stem vowel is not stressed in the **nosotros(-as)** and **vosotros(-as)** verb forms; therefore, the **e** does not change to **i.**
- Other verbs that undergo this change:[1]

  **conseguir** *to get, to obtain* **pedir** *to ask for, to request, to order*
  **decir** *to say, to tell* **seguir** *to follow, to continue*

- The verb **decir** undergoes the same change, but in addition it has an irregular first-person singular form: **yo digo.**
- Note that in the present tense **seguir** and **conseguir** drop the **u** before **a** or **o: yo sigo, yo consigo.**

## práctica

**A.** Form complete sentences by combining the words in the three columns in sequence, starting with A. Use each subject and each verb at least once.

| A | B | C |
|---|---|---|
| yo | decir | la comida |
| nosotros | servir | habitaciones |
| Ana y Eva | pedir | que necesitamos cheques de viajero |
| mis padres | conseguir | jabón y toalla |
| tú | seguir | al botones |
| el empleado | | un cuarto con baño privado |
| | | la llave del cuarto |
| | | la cena |

[1]For a complete list of stem-changing verbs, see Appendix B.

**B.** Complete the following dialogues, using the verbs given. Then act them out with a partner, adding a sentence or two to each dialogue.

1. decir
   —¿Tú ________ que el hotel es caro?
   —Sí, yo ________ que es caro, pero Carmen ________ que es barato.
2. servir
   —¿Qué ________ Uds. en sus fiestas?
   —________ entremeses y refrescos. ¿Qué ________ tú?
   —Yo ________ sándwiches y cerveza.
3. pedir
   —¿Qué ________ Uds. cuando van a un restaurante mexicano?
   —Yo ________ tacos y Ernesto ________ enchiladas.
4. conseguir
   —Yo no ________ trabajo.
   —Tú no ________ trabajo porque no hablas dos idiomas.

**C.** With a partner, take turns asking each other two things: what you order when you go to ethnic restaurants and what you serve to eat and drink at your parties.

**SUMMARY OF THE PRESENT INDICATIVE OF STEM-CHANGING VERBS**

| e:ie | o:ue | | e:i |
|---|---|---|---|
| cerrar | almorzar | morir | conseguir |
| comenzar | contar | mostrar | decir |
| empezar | costar | poder | pedir |
| entender | dormir | recordar | seguir |
| pensar | encontrar | volar | servir |
| perder | llover | volver | |
| preferir | | | |
| querer | | | |

Add to this list as you learn other stem-changing verbs.

## 2 Affirmative and negative expressions *(Expresiones afirmativas y negativas)*

| *Affirmative* | *Negative* |
|---|---|
| **algo** *something, anything* | **nada** *nothing, not anything* |
| **alguien** *someone, somebody, anyone* | **nadie** *nobody, no one, not anyone* |
| **alguno(-a), algún** *any, some* | **ninguno(-a), ningún** *no, none, not any* |
| **siempre** *always* | **nunca, jamás** *never* |
| **también** *also, too* | **tampoco** *neither, not either* |
| **o... o** *either . . . or* | **ni... ni** *neither . . . nor* |

| | |
|---|---|
| —¿Necesita Ud. **algo** más?<br>—No, no necesito **nada** más. | *"Do you need anything else?"*<br>*"No, I don't need anything else."* |
| —¿Tienes **algunos** amigos peruanos?<br>—No, no tengo **ningún** amigo peruano. | *"Do you have any Peruvian friends?"*<br>*"No, I don't have any Peruvian friends."* |
| —¿Hay **alguien** en tu cuarto?<br>—No, no hay **nadie**. | *"Is there anybody in your room?"*<br>*"No, there's no one."* |
| —¿Quieres café o Coca-Cola?<br>—Yo no bebo **ni** café **ni** Coca-Cola. | *"Do you want coffee or Coke?"*<br>*"I don't drink either coffee or Coke."* |

**ATENCIÓN** Note that **alguno(-a)** may be used in the plural forms, but **ninguno(-a)** is not pluralized.

**ATENCIÓN** **No** is never used as an adjective, as it sometimes is in English *(No person could do all that.)*.

- **Alguno** and **ninguno** drop the **-o** before a masculine singular noun: ***algún*** **niño**, ***ningún*** **niño**; but ***alguna*** **niña**, ***ninguna*** **niña**.
- Spanish sentences frequently use a double negative form to express a degree of negation: the adverb **no** is placed before the verb and the second negative word either follows the verb or appears at the end of the sentence. If, however, the negative word precedes the verb, **no** is never used.

| | |
|---|---|
| No hablo español **nunca**.<br>*or:* **Nunca** hablo español. | *I never speak Spanish.* |
| No compro **nada nunca**.<br>*or:* **Nunca** compro **nada**. | *I never buy anything.* |

- Note that Spanish often uses several negatives in one sentence.

—Yo **no** quiero **nada tampoco**. *I don't want anything either.*

## práctica

**A.** Your friend Oscar always gets the facts wrong when he talks about other people. Set him straight!

MODELO: Ana necesita algo.
*Ana no necesita nada.*

1. Raquel siempre viaja en el verano.
2. Ana va con Raquel, y Jorge va con ella también.
3. Siempre piden habitaciones dobles.
4. Siempre compran algo cuando viajan.
5. Siempre compran algunos objetos de oro.
6. Cenan en la pensión o en una cafetería.
7. Siempre hay alguien en su casa.

8. El esposo de Luisa nunca habla con nadie.
9. Carlos nunca averigua nada.
10. Elsa siempre pide información.

B. Answer these personal questions negatively, using the expressions you have just learned.

1. ¿Quiere Ud. viajar a Bolivia o a Perú?
2. ¿Tiene Ud. algunos amigos en Perú?
3. Yo no hablo portugués. ¿Y Ud.?
4. ¿Siempre viaja Ud. en invierno?
5. ¿Siempre viaja Ud. con alguien?
6. ¿Compra Ud. algo cuando va de vacaciones?

C. With a partner, write a list of complaints frequently heard on campus. Use the expressions you have just learned.

MODELO: *Nunca podemos comer nada en la cafetería.*

## 3 Verbs with irregular first-person forms *(Verbos irregulares en la primera persona)*

■ The following verbs are irregular in the first-person singular of the present tense.

| *Verb* | *yo form* | *Regular forms* |
|---|---|---|
| **salir** *(to go out)* | **salgo** | sales, sale, salimos, salís, salen |
| **hacer** *(to do, make)* | **hago** | haces, hace, hacemos, hacéis, hacen |
| **poner** *(to put, place)* | **pongo** | pones, pone, ponemos, ponéis, ponen |
| **traer** *(to bring)* | **traigo** | traes, trae, traemos, traéis, traen |
| **conducir** *(to drive; to conduct)* | **conduzco** | conduces, conduce, conducimos, conducís, conducen |
| **traducir** *(to translate)* | **traduzco** | traduces, traduce, traducimos, traducís, traducen |
| **conocer** *(to know)* | **conozco** | conoces, conoce, conocemos, conocéis, conocen |
| **caber** *(to fit)* | **quepo** | cabes, cabe, cabemos, cabéis, caben |
| **ver** *(to see)* | **veo** | ves, ve, vemos, veis, ven |
| **saber** *(to know)* | **sé** | sabes, sabe, sabemos, sabéis, saben |

## práctica

**A.** Your classmate is traveling to Peru. Here is a list of questions you want to ask in order to help him or her prepare for the trip.

1. ¿Conoces Perú? ¿Sabes a qué distancia está de los Estados Unidos?
2. ¿Sabes a cómo está el cambio de moneda?
3. ¿Haces la reservación del hotel antes de salir de viaje?
4. ¿Dónde pones el pasaporte?
5. El día del viaje, ¿sales de casa con tiempo? ¿Conduces tu coche para ir al aeropuerto?
6. ¿Traes muchas cosas para tu familia?

**B.** Read this paragraph about Anabel's preparations for her trip to Bolivia and then rewrite it as if you were Anabel, starting with **Yo...** .

Anabel sale para Bolivia esta noche. Va con su amiga Susana. Conduce al banco para comprar cheques de viajero, regresa a su casa, pone todos los documentos en su bolso de mano y después hace las maletas *(packs)*. Como sabe que hay mucho tráfico, sale de su casa temprano para ir al aeropuerto. Cuando llega al aeropuerto, ve que Susana está allí.

## 4 Saber vs. conocer

Spanish has two verbs that mean *to know,* **saber** and **conocer.**

- When *to know* means *to know something by heart, to know how to do something,* or *to know a fact,* **saber** is used.

| | |
|---|---|
| No **sé** dónde está la piscina. | *I don't know where the pool is.* |
| Juan **sabe** hablar ruso. | *Juan knows how to speak Russian.* |
| Ellos **saben** que ella es profesora. | *They know that she's a professor.* |

- When *to know* means *to be familiar with* or *to be acquainted with a person, a thing,* or *a place,* it is translated as **conocer.**

| | |
|---|---|
| Nosotros **conocemos** al empleado. | *We know the clerk.* |
| Elisa **conoce** las novelas de García Márquez. | *Elisa knows (is acquainted with) García Márquez's novels.* |
| ¿**Conoces** Canadá? | *Do you know (have you been to) Canada?* |

## práctica

**A.** Complete the following dialogues, using **saber** or **conocer** as appropriate. Then act them out with a partner.

1. —Yo ________ al abuelo de Olga.
   —¿Tú ________ dónde vive?
   —No, pero ________ su número de teléfono.
2. —Tú ________ Brasil, ¿no?
   —Sí, pero no ________ hablar portugués.

3. —¿Tú ________ los poemas de Bécquer?
   —Sí, ________ muchos de memoria *(by heart)*.
4. —¿________ tú qué hora es?
   —Sí, son las ocho.
5. —Jorge conduce muy mal.
   —Sí, no ________ conducir muy bien.

B. Interview a classmate, using the following questions. When you have finished, switch roles.

1. ¿Cuántos idiomas sabes hablar? ¿Cuáles son?
2. ¿Conoces a los padres de tu mejor amigo(-a)?
3. ¿Sabes dónde viven?
4. ¿Qué sabes hacer?
5. ¿Sabes tocar *(play)* el piano? ¿la guitarra? ¿el violín?
6. ¿Sabes preparar sangría?
7. ¿Conoces un buen restaurante? ¿Dónde está?
8. ¿Conoces a un actor famoso? ¿Quién es? ¿Cómo es?

## 5 Direct object pronouns *(Pronombres usados como complemento directo)*

### A. The direct object

■ In addition to a subject, most sentences have an object that directly receives the action of the verb.

Ellos compran el libro.
S. V. D.O.

In the preceding sentence, the subject (**Ellos**) performs the action, while **el libro,** the direct object, directly receives the action of the verb. The direct object of a sentence may be either a person or a thing.

■ The direct object can be easily identified as the answer to the questions *whom?* and *what?* about what the subject is doing.

| | |
|---|---|
| Ellos compran **el libro.** | What are they buying? |
| Pepe visita **a su primo.** | Whom is Pepe visiting? |

■ Direct object pronouns may be used in place of the direct object.

### B. Forms of the direct object pronouns

| Singular | | Plural | |
|---|---|---|---|
| **me** | *me* | **nos** | *us* |
| **te** | *you* (fam.) | **os** | *you* (fam.) |
| **lo** | *you* (form., masc.)<br>*him, it* (masc.) | **los** | *you* (form., masc.)<br>*them* (masc.) |
| **la** | *you* (form., fem.)<br>*her, it* (fem.) | **las** | *you* (form., fem.)<br>*them* (fem.) |

| | |
|---|---|
| —¿Tiene **la llave**? | *"Do you have the key?"* |
| —Sí, **la** tengo. | *"Yes, I have it."* |
| —¿Compra Ud. **los pasajes**? | *"Are you buying the tickets?"* |
| —Sí, **los** compro. | *"Yes, I'm buying them."* |

## C. Position of direct object pronouns

■ In Spanish, object pronouns are normally placed before a conjugated verb.

| D.O. | D.O. |
|---|---|
| Ellos sirven **la cena.** | *They serve dinner.* |
| Ellos **la** sirven. | *They serve it.* |

■ In negative sentences, the **no** must precede the object pronoun.

| D.O. | D.O. |
|---|---|
| Ellos sirven **la cena.** | *They serve dinner.* |
| Ellos **la** sirven. | *They serve it.* |
| Ellos **no la** sirven. | *They don't serve it.* |

■ When an infinitive is used with a conjugated verb, the direct object pronoun may either be attached to the infinitive or be placed before the conjugated verb. The same principle applies with the present participle in progressive constructions.

Puedo firmar**lo.**
**Lo** puedo firmar. } *I can sign it.*

Estoy leyendo**lo.**
**Lo** estoy leyendo. } *I am reading it.*

**ATENCIÓN** When a direct object pronoun is attached to a present participle (**leyéndolo, firmándola**), an accent mark is added to maintain the correct stress.

## práctica

**A.** Complete the following dialogue, using the appropriate direct object pronouns. Then act it out with a partner.

JULIO —¿Tú me puedes llevar a casa hoy?
DELIA —Sí, puedo llevar ____te____ a las tres.
JULIO —¡Ah! Necesito la maleta de mamá. ¿Tú ____la____ tienes?
DELIA —Sí, yo ____la____ tengo. ¿Tú quieres llevar ____la____ a México?
JULIO —Sí. También necesito comprar cheques de viajero...
DELIA —Podemos comprar ____los____ esta tarde.
JULIO —Rosa y yo tenemos que estar en el aeropuerto a las ocho de la noche. ¿Tú ____nos____ puedes llevar?
DELIA —Sí, yo ____los____ puedo llevar...
JULIO —¡Ah! Las sobrinas de Rosa quieren ir al aeropuerto con nosotros. ¿Tú ____las____ puedes traer a mi casa a las siete?
DELIA —¡No! ¡Yo no tengo un servicio de taxi!

**B.** You and your friends are planning a party. Volunteer to do the following tasks yourself.

> **Modelo:** ¿Quién invita a las chicas?
> *Yo las invito.*

1. ¿Quién llama a los muchachos?
2. ¿Quién compra las bebidas?
3. ¿Quién va a traer los discos compactos?
4. ¿Quién consigue el equipo estereofónico?
5. ¿Quién trae a mi compañera?
6. ¿Quién prepara *(is preparing)* los entremeses?
7. ¿Quién va a traer a Luis?
8. ¿Quién lleva a las chicas a su casa?

**C.** You and some friends will be traveling in Mexico shortly. Answer another friend's questions about your arrangements. Use direct object pronouns in your answers.

1. ¿Tus amigos te van a llamar esta noche?
2. ¿Tienen Uds. reservaciones para el hotel?
3. ¿Vas a comprar cheques de viajero?
4. ¿Tienes tu tarjeta de crédito?
5. ¿Llevas tu cámara fotográfica?
6. ¿Van a visitar Uds. las ruinas de Teotihuacán?
7. ¿Quién los va a llevar a Uds.[1] al aeropuerto?
8. ¿Me llevan con Uds. a México?

## 6 Weather expressions *(Expresiones para describir el tiempo)*

- In the following expressions, Spanish uses the verb **hacer,** *to make,* followed by a noun.

| | |
|---|---|
| **Hace** (mucho) frío. | *It is (very) cold.* |
| **Hace** (mucho) calor. | *It is (very) hot.* |
| **Hace** (mucho) viento. | *It is (very) windy.* |
| **Hace** sol. | *It is sunny.* |

- To ask about the weather, say, **"¿Qué tiempo hace?"** *(What's the weather like?).*

> —**¿Qué tiempo hace** hoy? — *"What's the weather like today?"*
> —**Hace** buen (mal) tiempo. — *"The weather is good (bad)."*

[1]A **Uds.** is needed for clarification because **los** could also be *them.*

■ The following words used to describe the weather do not combine with **hacer;** they are impersonal verbs used only in the infinitive, present participle, past participle, and third-person singular forms of all tenses.

| | |
|---|---|
| **llover (o:ue)** *to rain* | **Llueve.** *It is raining (It rains).* |
| **lloviznar** *to drizzle* | **Llovizna.** *It is drizzling (It drizzles).* |
| **nevar (e:ie)** *to snow* | **Nieva.** *It is snowing (It snows).* |

■ Other weather-related words are **lluvia** *(rain)* and **niebla** *(fog).*

| | |
|---|---|
| —¿**Hace** mucho **frío** en Buenos Aires? | *"Is it very cold in Buenos Aires?"* |
| —Sí, pero nunca **nieva.** | *"Yes, but it never snows."* |
| —¿Vas a volar hoy a San Francisco? | *"Are you going to fly to San Francisco today?"* |
| —No, porque **hay niebla.** | *"No, because it's foggy.*[1]*"* |

## práctica

**A.** Study the words in the following list, then complete the dialogues.

**el paraguas** *umbrella*
**el impermeable** *raincoat*
**el sombrero** *hat*
**el abrigo** *coat*
**el suéter** *sweater*

1. —¿Necesitas un paraguas?
   —Sí, porque en Oregón ________ mucho.
2. —¿No necesitas un abrigo?
   —No, porque ________.
3. —¿Quieres un impermeable?
   —No, gracias, apenas *(hardly)* ________.
4. —¿Por qué no quieres llevar el suéter?
   —¡Porque ________!
5. —¿Vas a llevar el sombrero?
   —Sí, porque ________.
6. —¿Necesitas un suéter y un abrigo?
   —Sí, porque ________.
7. —¿Un impermeable? ¿Por qué? ¿Llueve? ¿Llovizna?
   —No, pero ________.
8. —¡Qué lluvia! Necesito un ________ y un ________.

[1]**hay niebla** = *it's foggy*

**B.** Say what the weather will be like in different locations at different times of the year.

1. Portland, Oregón—el 2 de enero
2. Anchorage, Alaska—el 25 de diciembre
3. Phoenix, Arizona—el 13 de agosto
4. Londres *(London)*—el 5 de febrero
5. Chicago—el 6 de marzo

**C.** A visiting professor from Panama is planning a weekend visit to your hometown. What questions is he or she likely to ask about the weather there and what clothes to bring? How will you respond? Act out the scene with a partner. Say at least five lines each.

**D.** You and a classmate are in charge of preparing the weather report for a local T.V. station. Discuss the weather in your area today.

Sol

Nublado

Cubierto

Posibilidad de lluvia

Lluvia

Tormenta

Nieve

# ¡A ver cuánto aprendió!

INTERNET

See the *¿Cómo se dice...?* Web site for additional grammar and vocabulary practice: http://spanish.college.hmco.com/students

## ¡Repase el vocabulario!

Choose the word or phrase that best completes each sentence.

1. En el aeropuerto debo mostrar...
   a. el registro. b. el baño. c. el pasaporte.
2. Quiero una habitación...
   a. en la oficina de turismo. b. con vista a la calle. c. en el taxi.
3. Ellos leen...
   a. la piscina. b. el anuncio. c. el piso.
4. Debes pasar por la aduana...
   a. con el restaurante. b. con el piso. c. con las maletas.
5. Voy a comprar algo para...
   a. mis padres. b. la aduana. c. la capital.
6. El botones va a llevar...
   a. el interés. b. la plata. c. las maletas.

7. ¿Dónde puedo tomar...
   a. el aire acondicionado? b. el ascensor? c. la tarjeta de turista?
8. Sirven la cena...
   a. a las nueve de la mañana. b. a las tres de la tarde.
   c. a las nueve de la noche.
9. En el verano hay pocos cuartos...
   a. libres. b. favoritos. c. situados.
10. En el Hilton una habitación con vista a la calle cuesta ciento cincuenta dólares...
   a. por año. b. por mes. c. por día.
11. No tengo reservación, pero estoy en...
   a. el centro. b. la lista de espera. c. el cuarto.
12. La habitación no es barata; es...
   a. cara. b. libre. c. sencilla.
13. Ada dice que el hotel tiene...
   a. lugares de interés. b. servicio de habitación. c. embajada.
14. El baño tiene ducha y...
   a. elevador. b. escalera. c. bañadera.
15. En el baño no hay...
   a. inodoro. b. jabón. c. lavabo.
16. El empleado acaba de...
   a. ofrecer. b. llegar. c. ser.

## Entrevista

With a partner, interview each other by asking the following questions.

1. ¿Cuántas maletas llevas cuando viajas?
2. ¿Llevas cheques de viajero cuando viajas?
3. ¿Siempre llevas tu cámara fotográfica cuando viajas?
4. ¿Qué lugares de interés hay en la ciudad donde vives?
5. ¿A qué hora sirven el desayuno en la cafetería de la universidad?
6. ¿Quieres llevarme a almorzar?
7. ¿Quieres comprar una cámara de video?
8. ¿Prefieres objetos de oro o de plata?
9. ¿Hay alguien en tu cuarto ahora?
10. ¿Tu cuarto tiene baño privado?
11. ¿Usas impermeable cuando llueve?
12. ¿Sabes qué tiempo va a hacer mañana?

## Situaciones

What would you say in the following situations? What might the other person say? Act out the scenes with a partner. Take turns playing each role.

1. You have just checked into a hotel. You want to know what time they serve breakfast and whether they have room service.
2. Your friend is going to Alaska in February. Tell him or her what kind of weather to expect.
3. You are talking to the clerk at a tourist office. You need a list of hotels and boarding houses and a list of places of interest right away.
4. You work at an airport tourist office. Some tourists want to get downtown, and you know that they can take either a taxi or a bus.
5. You are a hotel clerk. Someone calls to reserve a single room with a private bathroom, but it is July, and you don't have any. Tell the person you can put his or her name on the waiting list.

## ¿Qué pasa aquí? *(What is happening here?)*

In groups of three or four, look at the illustration and make up a story about the people you see. Give them names and say where they are coming from and where they are going. Where are they going to stay? What places of interest are they going to visit?

## Para escribir

Complete the following dialogues.

1. *Carlos va a Tijuana.*

CARLOS —¿Dónde está tu pasaporte?
ROBERTO —________________________________________
CARLOS —¡Sí, lo necesitas! ¿No vas a ir a México?
ROBERTO —________________________________________
CARLOS —¿Tijuana? ¿Y para eso *(that)* necesitas todas esas maletas?
ROBERTO —________________________________________
CARLOS —¡No! ¡No puedo llevarlas al coche!

2. *En el hotel*

TURISTA —¿Tienen habitaciones?
EMPLEADO —________________________________________
TURISTA —No, interior.
EMPLEADO —________________________________________
TURISTA —¡Cien dólares por día! ¿Aceptan cheques de viajero?
EMPLEADO —________________________________________

# En la vida real

## Discusión

**CD-ROM**

**Do the interactive exercises on the CD-ROM for additional practice.**

Four or five students (or more, according to class size) will pretend to own hotels and will make up signs describing accommodations and prices. The rest of the class will discuss the similarities and differences and will decide in pairs or individually where they would like to stay. At the end of this activity each student will explain his or her choice.

A follow-up activity: After staying at the hotel people will have encountered one or more of the following problems:

(no) hay
- **agua caliente** *hot water*
- **cucarachas** *cockroaches*
- **frazadas, cobijas** *blankets*
- **sábanas limpias** *clean sheets*

**no funciona** *(it's not working)*
- **el aire acondicionado** *air conditioning*
- **el ascensor, el elevador** *elevator*
- **la calefacción** *heater*

Prepare a list of complaints on a card and drop it in the "suggestion box" (the instructor's desk).

## ¿Dónde hospedarse? *(Where shall we stay?)*

Imagine it's the month of August. Say whether these people are going to stay at the **Aloha Puerto Sol** hotel or at the **Atlanterra Sol** hotel. Give reasons for your choice, according to the information provided in the following ads. You should also indicate how much each group will have to pay. Start out by saying, **"Se van a hospedar en... porque..."**

1. La familia Salcedo: el papá, la mamá y dos niños. Jorgito tiene diez años y Alicia tiene ocho. No tienen mucho dinero.
2. Gustavo y Carolina, que son recién casados *(newlyweds)*. Desean ver un espectáculo y bailar. Tienen mucho dinero.
3. Teresa, Raquel y Rebeca, tres muchachas españolas que están viajando juntas. Les gusta jugar *(They like to play)* al tenis y bailar.

**ESTANCIAS EN EL HOTEL ALOHA PUERTO SOL******

LE OFRECEMOS:

- Alojamiento en régimen de habitación y desayuno.
- Todas las habitaciones son mini-suites.
- Mini-bar.
- Cesta de fruta en la habitación.
- Botella de vino en la habitación.
- Entrada al Aquapark con 50% de descuento.
- Entrada gratis al Zoo de Fuengirola.
- Programa completo de deportes y animación para adultos y niños (Mini-Club).
- Espectáculos - actuaciones.

**ALOHA PUERTO SOL H.D.**

| Precio por persona y día en habitación doble-habitación y desayuno | | | | | | |
|---|---|---|---|---|---|---|
| 01/05 - 15/07 01/10 - 31/10 | 01/09 - 30/09 | 16/07 - 31/06 | SUPL. M.P. | SUPL. P.C SOBRE M.P. | SUPL. INDIV. | DESCUENT 3ª PERSON |
| 3.165 | 4.060 | 4.455 | 1.340 | 610 | 1.310 | 15% |
| **Código 048** | | | IVA NO INCLUIDO | | | |

**ESTANCIAS EN EL HOTEL ATLANTERRA SOL******

LE OFRECEMOS:

- Régimen de habitación y desayuno. Habitación doble.
- Cesta de fruta en la habitación.
- Botella de vino en la habitación.
- 1 hora de tenis gratis.
- 1 copa gratis en la discoteca.
- Programa completo de deportes y animación para niños (Mini-Club) y adultos.
- Espectáculos - actuaciones.
- Salida de la habitación a las 14 horas.
- Condiciones especiales en nuestro restaurante grill «Oasis»
- Oferta novios 10%.

**ATLANTERRA SOL H.D.**

| | Precio por persona y día en habitación doble-habitación y desayuno | | | | | |
|---|---|---|---|---|---|---|
| | 01/10 - 31/10 | 16/07 al 30/09 | SUPL. M.P. | SUPL. PC. SOBRE M/P. | SUPL. INDIV. | DESCUENT 3ª PERSON |
| | 4.970 | 6.495 | 1.490 | 1.320 | 2.295 | 15% |
| Desc. niños 2 - 15 años | 1º 50% 2º 35% | 1º 35% 2º 35% | IVA NO INCLUIDO | | | |
| **Código 054** | | | | | | |

## De viaje *(Traveling)*

Get together with a couple of your classmates and plan a trip to a Spanish-speaking country. Visit a travel agency to obtain brochures of the country you are going to visit. Find out about hotels, rates of exchange, places of interest, and so on. Discuss how and when you will be leaving, how much spending money you'll bring, what cities and special sites you intend to visit, and what you will need to take with you.

Take this test. When you have finished, check your answers in the answer key provided in Appendix E. Then use a red pen to correct any mistakes you may have made. Are you ready?

## Lección 4

### A. The personal *a*

Form sentences, using the elements provided. Include the personal **a** when necessary.

1. yo / llevar / prima / a / la universidad
2. nosotros / llevar / los refrescos / a / la fiesta
3. ellos / invitar / Julio / y / su novia
4. nosotros / tener / cuatro primos

### B. Contractions

Complete the following sentences, using the Spanish equivalent of the words in parentheses.

1. Necesito llamar ________. *(Mr. Estrada)*
2. Yo vengo ________. *(from the club)*
3. ¿Tú vienes ________? *(from the terrace)*
4. Eduardo lleva ________ a la fiesta. *(the girls)*
5. El vaso es ________. *(Mr. Soto's)*

### C. Expressions with *tener*

Write the following sentences in Spanish.

1. My classmates are in a hurry.
2. I'm not hungry, but I'm very thirsty.
3. Are you hot? I'm cold!
4. My friends are sleepy.
5. We are not scared.
6. You are right, Miss Peña. Mary is thirty years old.

### D. Present indicative of the irregular verbs *ir, dar,* and *estar*

Complete the following sentences, using the present indicative of **ir, dar,** or **estar,** as appropriate.

1. Yo no ________ al baile con mis compañeros.
2. Nosotros ________ una fiesta aquí esta noche.
3. Mi hermana ________ en su casa.
4. ¿Dónde ________ el champán?
5. Las chicas ________ a la fiesta con sus amigos.
6. Tus primos no ________ mucho dinero.
7. Yo ________ cansado.
8. ¿Adónde ________ tus primos?
9. ¿Dónde ________ tú?
10. Yo no ________ mi número de teléfono.

### E. *Ir a* + infinitive

Form sentences that tell what *is* or *is not* going to happen. Use the given elements.

MODELO: mi prima / dar / fiesta / el domingo
*Mi prima va a dar una fiesta el domingo.*

1. yo / no hablar / con mi mamá / hoy
2. mis hijos / estudiar / en España
3. mi amiga / leer / el libro
4. Uds. / traer / los discos compactos
5. tú / bailar / en la fiesta
6. nosotros / brindar / con sidra

### F. Present indicative of *e:ie* stem-changing verbs

Complete the following sentences, using the present indicative of the verbs in the list, as necessary.

| entender | cerrar | empezar | preferir |
|---|---|---|---|
| pensar | querer | perder | comenzar |

1. Mi primo no ________ beber café.
2. Nosotros no ________ la Lección 2.
3. Ella siempre ________ mucho dinero en Las Vegas.
4. ¿________ tú la ventana?
5. Las clases ________ hoy.
6. Nosotros ________ a bailar ahora.
7. Yo no ________ trabajar el domingo.
8. Luis y yo ________ beber refrescos.

### G. Just words . . .

Choose the word or phrase in parentheses that best completes each sentence.

1. (Invitamos, Brindamos, Bailamos) a nuestros compañeros a la fiesta.
2. Siempre (comemos, empezamos, estamos) doce uvas a la medianoche el día de fin de año.
3. Aquí no beben (sidra, entremeses, pollo).
4. Esta orquesta es muy buena. ¡Es (magnífica, cansada, feliz)!
5. ¡Feliz año (simpático, nuevo, guapo)!
6. No bebo (cocteles, refresco, Coca-Cola) porque yo no tomo bebidas alcohólicas.
7. Aquí todos (bailamos, brindamos, estamos) con champán.
8. Tengo todos los (primos, pollos, discos compactos) de Ricky Martin.

### H. Culture

Circle the correct answer, based on the **¿Lo sabía Ud.?** section.

1. En España y en Latinoamérica (existe, no existe) mucha separación entre las generaciones.
2. Además del cumpleaños muchos hispanos celebran su (baile, santo).
3. En algunos países hispanos (existe, no existe) edad mínima para comprar bebidas.
4. En español se dice ("¡Salud!", "¡Santo!") al brindar.

## Lección 5

### A. Comparative forms

Form sentences, using the elements provided. Use the comparative or the superlative, as necessary.

1. Alfredo / estudiante / más / inteligente / clase
2. la Lección 2 / menos / interesante / la Lección 7
3. mi novia / más / bonita / tu novia
4. Roberto / más / guapo / familia
5. el profesor / tener / menos / veinte estudiantes
6. Ana / tan / alta / Roberto

### B. Irregular comparative forms

Complete the following sentences, using regular or irregular comparative forms, as necessary.

1. California es ________ que Maine.
2. El profesor de español habla español ________ que los estudiantes.
3. Eva tiene "A" en español, Roberto tiene "B" y Marisa tiene "F". Eva es la ________ estudiante. Marisa es la ________ estudiante.
4. Yo tengo veinte años y Raquel tiene catorce años. Yo soy ________ que Raquel.
5. Rhode Island es ________ que California.

### C. Present indicative of *o:ue* stem-changing verbs

Complete the following sentences, using the present indicative of the verbs in the list, as necessary.

| recordar | almorzar | costar |
|---|---|---|
| contar | volver | poder |

1. ¿Cuánto ________ el libro?
2. Ellos no ________ ir hoy.
3. ¿________ Ud. cuál es su número de teléfono?
4. Yo ________ de uno a veinte en español.
5. Tengo hambre. ¿A qué hora ________ (nosotros)?
6. ¿Cuándo ________ tú a España?

### D. Present progressive

Complete the following sentences, using the present progressive of the verbs in the list, as necessary.

| pedir | comer | hablar |
|---|---|---|
| leer | decir | dormir |

1. Ella ________ que nosotros necesitamos más dinero.
2. Yo ________ con mi abuela.
3. Nosotros ________ un libro.
4. ¿Qué ________ tú? ¿Entremeses?
5. Luis ________ en su cuarto *(room)*.
6. ¿Uds. ________ dinero?

**E. Uses of *ser* and *estar***

Form sentences, using the elements provided and the appropriate forms of **ser** or **estar.** Add the necessary connectors.

1. Elsa / mamá / Marta
2. Club Náutico / calle Siete
3. ¡Mmmm! / el pollo / delicioso
4. Roberto / de México / ahora / en California
5. cerveza / fría *(cold)*
6. escritorio / metal
7. hoy / lunes / mañana / martes
8. Elvira / médica
9. fiesta / casa / Alicia
10. orquesta / magnífica
11. ellos / cansados
12. Laura / mexicana

**F. Pronouns as objects of prepositions**

Complete the following sentences, using the Spanish equivalent of the words in parentheses.

1. La carta es para ________. *(me)*
2. Eduardo está hablando de ________. *(you, fam.)*
3. Hay dos libros para ________. *(them)*
4. Las fotografías son para ________. *(us)*
5. ¿Quieres almorzar ________? *(with me)*
6. Voy a dejar *(to leave)* el cuadro ________. *(with you, fam.)*

**G. Just words . . .**

Choose the word or phrase in parentheses that best completes each sentence.

1. El hijo de mi hija es mi (yerno, nieto, cuñado).
2. Vamos a ver (los cumpleaños, las pinturas, a la abuela) de Picasso en el museo.
3. Tengo que escribir muchas (medicinas, cartas, pensiones) este fin de semana.
4. ¿Quieres (extrañar, llover, almorzar) con él hoy?
5. ¿Tú (asistes, echas de menos, viajas) mucho a tu familia?
6. ¿No vamos a tener oportunidad de practicar el español? (¡Qué famoso!, ¡Qué lástima!, ¡Qué pequeño!)
7. Ellos quieren viajar en ómnibus; nunca (conducen su auto, comen en este restaurante, hablan francés) en Madrid.
8. ¿Quieres ver algunas (bebidas, fotos, cintas) de mi novia? ¡Es la chica más bonita del mundo!
9. Elba va a (mirar, asistir, viajar) a Madrid.
10. No es alto. Es de estatura (mayor, interesante, mediana).

### H. Culture

Read the following statements and circle **V** (Verdadero) or **F** (Falso), based on the **¿Lo sabía Ud.?** section.

**V F** 1. La Universidad de Salamanca es una de las más famosas del mundo.
**V F** 2. Sólo *(Only)* los españoles pueden estudiar en la Universidad de Salamanca.
**V F** 3. En el Museo del Prado sólo hay cuadros de pintores españoles.
**V F** 4. La mayoría de las universidades de los países hispanos no tienen residencias universitarias.
**V F** 5. En los países hispanos la fecha se escribe con el día antes del mes.

## Lección 6

### A. Present indicative of *e:i* stem-changing verbs

Give the Spanish equivalent of the following sentences.

1. At the Mexico Restaurant they serve dinner at nine.
2. She requests a room overlooking the street.
3. We follow the bellboy to the room.
4. Are you *(pl.)* getting reservations in December?
5. I'm saying (I say) that he must sign the register now.

### B. Affirmative and negative expressions

Change the following sentences to the affirmative.

1. Ellos no van a querer nada.
2. No hay nadie en el baño.
3. No tengo ningún objeto de oro y plata.
4. Ellos nunca pasan por la aduana.
5. Yo tampoco ceno a las nueve.
6. Jamás tiene las listas de los hoteles.
7. No puedes ir ni a la derecha ni a la izquierda.
8. Ellos nunca quieren nada tampoco.

### C. Verbs with irregular first-person forms

Complete the following sentences with the present indicative of the verbs in the list, as needed.

| traducir | hacer | conocer | saber | salir |
|---|---|---|---|---|
| poner | caber | ver | traer | conducir |

1. Yo ________ un Ford modelo 1998.
2. Yo no ________ dónde está el hotel.
3. Yo no ________ en este taxi. ¡Hay ocho personas!
4. Yo siempre ________ de la oficina a las cinco de la tarde.
5. Yo ________ las lecciones del inglés al portugués.
6. Yo no ________ los pasaportes. ¿Dónde están?

7. Yo no ________ nada los domingos.
8. Yo no ________ las llaves allí.
9. Yo no ________ Lima.
10. Yo ________ a mi amigo al aeropuerto.

**D. *Saber* vs. *conocer***

Complete the following sentences with **saber** or **conocer.**

1. Yo ________ que él no quiere ir.
2. Ester no ________ a mi sobrina, pero ella ________ dónde vive.
3. Peter ________ España, pero él no ________ hablar español.
4. Ellos no ________ los poemas de memoria *(by heart).*

**E. Direct object pronouns**

Complete the following sentences with the Spanish equivalent of the words in parentheses.

1. ¿El libro? No quiero COMPRAR LO. Es muy caro. *(to buy it)*
2. Yo TE LLAMO más tarde, Anita. *(call you)*
3. ¿La cena? Ellos LAS SIRVAN a las siete. *(serve it)*
4. ¿Los pasaportes? Rita LOS TIENE *(has them)*
5. Mamá no ME LLEVA al baile. *(take me)*
6. ¿Las toallas? Yo no LAS NECESITO *(need them)*
7. Yo tengo cheques de viajero, pero ellos no LOS ACCEPTAN *(accept them)*
8. Yo no puedo LLEVARTE, Sr. Vega. *(to take you)* LLEVARLO
9. Ellos quieren las cámaras fotográficas pero yo no LAS TENGO. *(have them)*
10. Nosotros no podemos LLAMARLA TE, Srta. Roca. *(to call you)*

**F. Weather expressions**

Complete the following sentences appropriately.

1. Necesito un paraguas. ________ mucho.
2. ¿No te vas a poner el abrigo? ¡Brrr! ¡________________!
3. ¡No necesito abrigo! ¡Hace ________!
4. En Alaska ________ mucho en el invierno.
5. Necesitas el sombrero. Hoy ________________.
6. No quiero vivir en Oregón porque allí llueve mucho, y no me gusta la ________.

**G. Just words . . .**

Choose the correct response to each question or statement.

1. ¿Son caras las habitaciones en los hoteles del centro?
   a. No, son de oro y de plata. b. No, son baratas.
   c. No, están en el segundo piso.

2. ¿Dónde vas a conseguir la lista de hoteles?
   a. En la oficina de turismo. b. En el baño. c. En un restaurante.

3. ¿Qué documentos debo mostrar?
   a. Veinte dólares. b. El pasaporte. c. El ascensor.

4. ¿A cómo está el cambio de moneda?
   a. No sé; voy a comprarlo. b. No sé; voy a visitarlo.
   c. No sé; voy a averiguarlo.
5. ¿El baño tiene ducha?
   a. Sí, y desayuno. b. Sí, y bañadera. c. Sí, y elevador.
6. Necesitamos una habitación doble y dos habitaciones sencillas.
   a. No tenemos ningún cuarto libre.
   b. Hay pocas habitaciones modernas. c. No hay piscina.
7. ¿Dónde trabaja el botones?
   a. En el autobús. b. En la aduana. c. En el hotel.
8. El cuarto con vista a la calle es muy caro.
   a. ¿Quiere una habitación interior?
   b. El ascensor está a la izquierda.
   c. No hay muchas oficinas de turismo por aquí.
9. ¿Qué desea, señorita?
   a. Una habitación sencilla con baño privado.
   b. El ómnibus está a la derecha. c. No hay objetos de oro.
10. ¿No puedes ir a México?
    a. No, voy a confirmar la información.
    b. No, voy a cancelar las reservaciones.
    c. No soy de México; soy de Guatemala.
11. ¿Tienen jabón?
    a. Están en la embajada norteamericana.
    b. Sí, tenemos uno con vista a la calle.
    c. Sí, pero no tenemos toallas.
12. ¿Están Uds. en la lista de espera?
    a. Tengo una lista de los lugares de interés.
    b. El botones tiene la lista.
    c. No, nosotros tenemos reservaciones.

### H. Culture

Circle the correct answer, based on the **¿Lo sabía Ud.?** section.

1. Lima, la capital de (Chile, Perú), es una ciudad de contrastes.
2. El (35%, 25%) de la población de Lima es de origen indígena.
3. La moneda más usada por los latinoamericanos cuando viajan es el (dólar, peso).
4. Es (fácil, difícil) cambiar dólares en los bancos hispanoamericanos.

# 3. España (II)

España

- España es un país que se distingue en la pintura y en la música. Algunos de los pintores más famosos del mundo son españoles: el Greco, Velázquez, Picasso, Miró y Dalí. En la música Andrés Segovia y Pablo Casals, entre otros, tienen fama internacional.
- Entre los deportes *(sports)* más populares de España están el fútbol, el ciclismo, el baloncesto *(basketball)* y, en el País Vasco, el jai alai.
- El día siete de julio se celebra en Pamplona la fiesta de San Fermín. Ese día sueltan los toros *(turn the bulls loose)* y la gente corre delante de *(in front of)* ellos hasta llegar a la plaza de toros para la corrida.

Saboreando *(tasting)* unas tapas en un bar de Málaga. Las tapas son pequeñas porciones de diferentes comidas típicas de España. Generalmente las tapas se sirven en los bares por la tarde.

*¿Cuáles son algunas comidas típicas de su país?*

Juan Carlos I de Borbón, rey *(king)* de España, aparece aquí con la Reina Sofía y con el primer ministro de gobierno, el líder José María Aznar.

*¿Quién es el presidente (o primer ministro) de su país?*

La Fundación Joan Miró está en el Parque de Montjuïc de Barcelona, junto a un edificio diseñado por el arquitecto catalán Josep Lluís Sert. Aquí está el Centro de Estudio de Artes Contemporáneas, establecido por Miró. La fundación contiene muchas de las pinturas y esculturas del gran artista.

*¿Quiénes son sus pintores favoritos?*

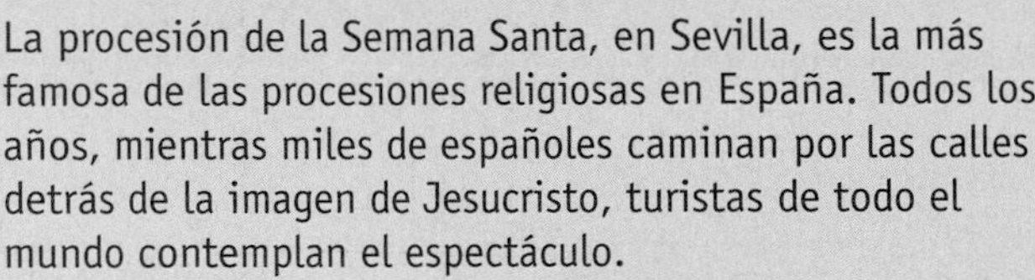

La procesión de la Semana Santa, en Sevilla, es la más famosa de las procesiones religiosas en España. Todos los años, mientras miles de españoles caminan por las calles detrás de la imagen de Jesucristo, turistas de todo el mundo contemplan el espectáculo.

*¿Qué fiestas religiosas se celebran en su país?*

Enrique Iglesias es uno de los cantantes españoles más famosos del mundo. Iglesias ha vendido *(has sold)* más de cien millones de discos, y ha recibido el premio Grammy como el mejor cantante de música popular en español.

*¿Conoce Ud. alguna canción en español? ¿Cuál es?*

Una pareja come paella, un plato típico de España, preparado con arroz *(rice)* y mariscos *(shellfish)* y otras carnes. La preparación de la paella varía de región a región, pero la más famosa es la paella valenciana.

*¿Cuáles son sus platos favoritos?*

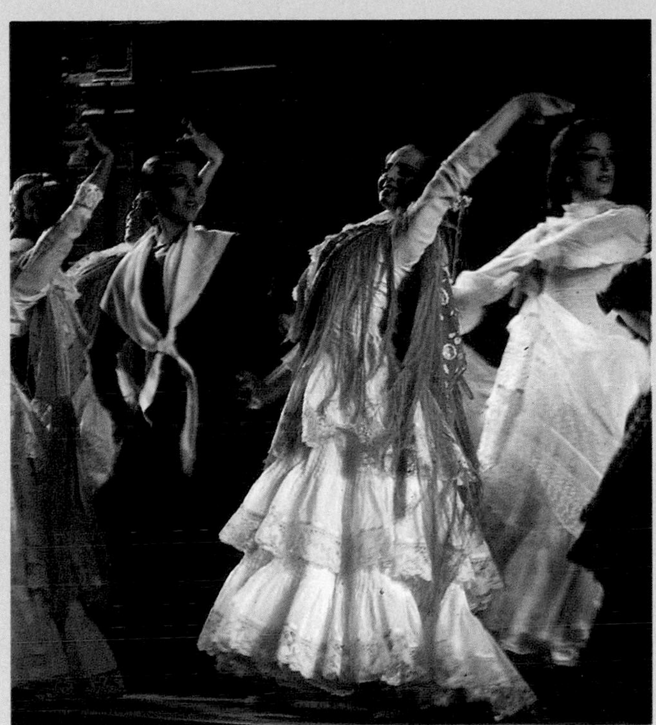

El Ballet Real aparece aquí en los jardines del Generalife, en Granada. El repertorio del Ballet Real incluye bailes clásicos y folklóricos. Aquí vemos una representación del baile flamenco, típico del sur de España.

*¿Qué tipo de baile prefiere Ud.: clásico, moderno o folklórico?*

La corrida de toros tiene orígenes antiquísimos y es uno de los espectáculos más populares de España. Las corridas generalmente tienen lugar *(take place)* los domingos por la tarde en estadios especiales llamados plazas de toros, de las cuales hay más de 400 en España.

*¿Quiere Ud. ver una corrida de toros algún día?*

TELEINFORME

VIDEO

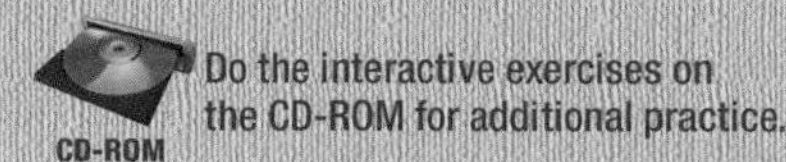
CD-ROM
Do the interactive exercises on
the CD-ROM for additional practice.

## Preparación

**¿Cuánto saben Uds. ya?** After reading **Panorama hispánico 3**, get together in groups of three or four students and answer the following questions with the appropriate information.

1. ¿Cuáles son los deportes más populares de España?
2. ¿Qué son las tapas y cuándo se comen?
3. Durante la primavera, ¿qué fiesta religiosa se celebra en España con procesiones?
4. ¿Cuál es un plato típico de España?
5. ¿Qué baile es típico del sur de España?
6. ¿Cuál es uno de los espectáculos más populares de España?

## Comprensión

A. **España: País de contrastes.** Read the following statements. After watching the video, circle **V** (**Verdadero**) or **F** (**Falso**), according to what you understood. If the statement is false, correct it.

V F 1. España forma parte de la Península Ibérica.
V F 2. El acueducto, un símbolo de la presencia romana en España, está en Sevilla.
V F 3. La invasión de los musulmanes fue decisiva en la historia de España.
V F 4. En Sevilla, Córdoba y Granada hay muchos ejemplos del arte islámico.
V F 5. El Monasterio del Escorial está cerca de Ávila.

B. **Sevilla.** Select the word or phrase that best completes each statement according to what you understood in the video.

1. Sevilla es la principal ciudad de (España, Andalucía).
2. (La Giralda, La Torre del Oro) es parte de una mezquita *(mosque)* demolida.
3. (La Torre del Oro, La Catedral de Sevilla) es un edificio de la época musulmana.
4. (La Giralda, El Alcázar) representa la fusión de las civilizaciones musulmana y cristiana.
5. La Plaza de España fue construida para (las Olimpiadas, Exposición Iberoamericana).
6. Se cree que el flamenco fue traído *(was brought)* por (los gitanos, los musulmanes).

## Ampliación

A. **Madrid y Sevilla.** Review the video segment about Madrid *(Panorama hispánico 2)* and compare it to the segment on Sevilla *(Panorama hispánico 3)*. Work in groups of three or four students to make a list of comparisons and contrasts between what you have learned about these two Spanish cities. Share your observations with the rest of the class.

B. **Dos culturas.** With a partner, describe a typical dance or custom from your area, town, state, or country that might compare to *el flamenco de Andalucía*. Try to research the custom's origin and its importance to the region's culture. Share your observations with the rest of the class.

# Hablando de las vacaciones

Lección 7

## OBJECTIVES

### Pronunciation

The Spanish **ll** and **ñ**

### Structure

Demonstrative adjectives and pronouns • Indirect object pronouns • Constructions with **gustar** • Time expressions with **hacer** • Preterit of regular verbs

### Communication

You will learn vocabulary related to travel.

# Hablando de las vacaciones

*Teresa llegó ayer de su viaje a Perú y ahora está hablando por teléfono con su amiga Silvia. Hace media hora que las chicas están charlando y Teresa le está contando de su viaje.*

TERESA —Me gustó mucho la capital, pero me gustó más Machu Picchu.

SILVIA —¡Y no me mandaste una tarjeta postal!

TERESA —Te compré dos, pero no las mandé. Oye, tengo que devolverte la maleta y el bolso de mano que me prestaste.

SILVIA —No hay apuro. ¿Llevaste mucho equipaje?

TERESA —Sí, llevé tres maletas. Pagué exceso de equipaje.

SILVIA —¿Cuánto te costó el pasaje? ¿Viajaste en primera clase?

TERESA —¿Estás loca? Viajé en clase turista. ¡Y me costó tres mil quinientos pesos![1] Ida y vuelta, claro…

SILVIA —¿Qué tal el vuelo?

TERESA —Un poco largo… Y como el avión salió con dos horas de retraso, llegamos muy tarde.

SILVIA —¿Te pasó algo interesante en Lima?

TERESA —Bueno… en la agencia de viajes donde compré el pasaje para Machu Picchu, conocí a un muchacho[2] muy simpático.

SILVIA —¿Viajó contigo? Tienes que contarme todo lo que pasó.

TERESA —Sí, viajé con él en avión a Cuzco, donde almorzamos juntos. Después, conversamos durante todo el viaje en tren a Machu Picchu.

SILVIA —No sé por qué tus vacaciones siempre son magníficas y mis vacaciones son tan aburridas.

TERESA —Pues la próxima vez tenemos que viajar juntas.

SILVIA —Bueno, pero sólo si vamos en tren o en barco. A mí no me gusta viajar en avión.

TERESA —Bueno, viajamos en tren. Oye, este sábado voy al cine con Cecilia, ¿quieres ir con nosotras?

SILVIA —¿Quién es Cecilia?

TERESA —Es la chica que te presenté en la biblioteca el mes pasado.

SILVIA —Ah, ésa… ya recuerdo. Sí, vamos juntas.

TERESA —¿Quieres ir a almorzar conmigo ahora?

SILVIA —No, gracias, ya almorcé.

TERESA —Bueno, entonces nos vemos mañana.

---

[1]Mexican currency.

[2]Note that **muchacho**(**-a**) can be used familiarly to refer to men and women under thirty.

# Vocabulario

## Nombres

**la agencia de viajes** travel agency
**el avión** plane
**el barco** boat, ship
**el bolso de mano** carry-on bag
**el cine** movie theater, movies
**la clase turista** tourist class
**el equipaje** luggage
**la hora** hour
**el pasaje, el billete** *(Spain)* ticket (for plane, train, or bus)
____ **de ida** one-way ticket
____ **de ida y vuelta** round-trip ticket
____ **de primera clase** first-class ticket
**el retraso, atraso** delay
**la tarjeta** card
____ **postal** postcard
**el tren** train
**la vez** time (occasion)
**el vuelo** flight

## Verbos

**conocer** to meet (for the first time)
**contar (o:ue)** to tell
**devolver (o:ue)** to return (something)
**gustar** to like, to be pleasing to
**mandar, enviar** to send
**pagar** to pay
**pasar** to happen
**presentar** to introduce
prestar to lend

## Adjetivos

**juntos(-as)** together
**largo(-a)** long
**loco(-a)** crazy
**pasado(-a)** last
**próximo(-a)** next

## Otras palabras y expresiones

**ayer** yesterday
**bueno, bien** okay, fine
**claro, por supuesto** of course
**como** since
**de** about
**después** then
**durante** during
**ése(-a)** that one
**el mes pasado** last month
**exceso de equipaje** excess baggage
**la próxima vez** next time
**llegar tarde**[1] to be late
**media hora** half an hour
**No hay apuro., No hay prisa.** There's no hurry.
**primera clase** first class
**pues** then
**¿Qué tal...?** How was (is) . . . ?
**sólo** only
**tarde** late
**todo** all
**todo el viaje** the whole trip
**todo lo que pasó** everything that happened
**ya** now

[1]**llegar temprano** to be early

## Vocabulario adicional

### En el aeropuerto

### De viaje *(traveling)*

| | | |
|---|---|---|
| **el (la) agente de viajes** | travel agent | El **agente de viajes** me vendió los pasajes. |
| **¡Buen viaje!** | Have a nice trip! | ¡Adiós, Marisa! **¡Buen viaje!** |
| **la entrada** | entrance | ¿Dónde está la **entrada** al aeropuerto? |
| **la salida** | exit | Aquella puerta no es la entrada; es la **salida.** |
| **tener... de retraso (atraso)** | to be . . . behind schedule | El avión **tiene dos horas de retraso.** |

## ¡Conversemos!

Answer the following questions, basing your answers on the dialogue.

1. ¿Hace una hora que Teresa y Silvia hablan por teléfono?
2. ¿De qué le está contando Teresa a su amiga?
3. ¿Qué le gustó más a Teresa, Machu Picchu o Lima?
4. ¿Qué le prestó Silvia a Teresa para el viaje?
5. ¿Pagó Teresa exceso de equipaje? ¿Por qué?
6. ¿Cuánto le costó a Teresa el pasaje?
7. ¿Viajó Teresa a Cuzco en avión o en tren?

8. ¿Con cuántas horas de retraso salió el avión?
9. ¿Las vacaciones de Teresa son magníficas o aburridas?
10. ¿Cómo van a viajar Teresa y Silvia la próxima vez?
11. ¿Adónde va Teresa este sábado? ¿Con quiénes va?
12. ¿Cuál de las chicas ya almorzó?

## ¿Lo sabía Ud.?

- **Cuzco,** situado a más de diez mil pies de altura en los Andes peruanos, es la antigua capital del imperio de los incas. Hoy día, la ciudad es un gran centro turístico y artístico.
- **Machu Picchu,** conocida también como "la ciudad perdida de los incas", está situada en la cordillera de los Andes a unos ciento diez kilómetros al noroeste *(northwest)* de Cuzco. El imperio de los incas se extendió desde el sur *(south)* de Colombia hasta el norte de Chile y Argentina.

Mercado de artesanías cerca de Cuzco, Perú.

- ¿Qué lugares turísticos hay en su ciudad?
- ¿Qué cordillera de este país es una continuación de la Cordillera de los Andes?
- ¿Qué civilizaciones indígenas existieron en este país?

INTERNET

See the *¿Cómo se dice...?* Web site for activities on authentic cultural material: http://spanish.college.hmco.com/students

# Pronunciación

## A The Spanish ll

STUDENT AUDIO

In most countries, the Spanish **ll** has a sound similar to the *y* in the English word *yes*. Listen to your instructor and repeat the following words.

| calle | cuchillo | llave | botella |
|---|---|---|---|
| llevar | llegar | pollo | platillo |

## B The Spanish ñ

The Spanish ñ is similar to the *ny* in the English word *canyon*. Listen to your instructor and repeat the following words.

| | | | |
|---|---|---|---|
| español | niño | mañana | España |
| señor | señorita | otoño | año |

# Estructuras

## 1 Demonstrative adjectives and pronouns *(Los adjetivos y los pronombres demostrativos)*

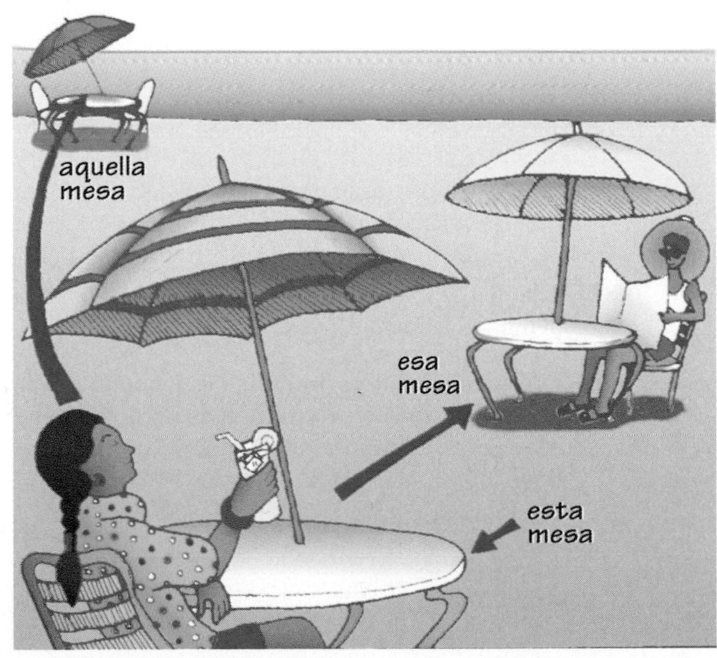

## A. Demonstrative adjectives

■ Demonstrative adjectives point out persons or things. Like all other adjectives, they agree in gender and number with the nouns they modify. The forms of the demonstrative adjectives are as follows.

| *Masculine* | | *Feminine* | | |
|---|---|---|---|---|
| ***Singular*** | ***Plural*** | ***Singular*** | ***Plural*** | |
| este | estos | esta | estas | *this, these* |
| ese | esos | esa | esas | *that, those* |
| aquel | aquellos | aquella | aquellas | *that, those* (at a distance in space or time) |

—¿Qué necesitas? — *"What do you need?"*
—Necesito **esta** pluma, **ese** cuaderno y **aquellos** libros. — *"I need this pen, that notebook, and those books* (over there)."

## B. Demonstrative pronouns

■ The forms of the demonstrative pronouns are as follows.

| *Masculine* | | *Feminine* | | *Neuter* | |
|---|---|---|---|---|---|
| ***Singular*** | ***Plural*** | ***Singular*** | ***Plural*** | | |
| éste | éstos | ésta | éstas | esto | *this* (one), *these* |
| ése | ésos | ésa | ésas | eso | *that* (one), *those* |
| aquél | aquéllos | aquélla | aquéllas | aquello | *that* (one), *those* (at a distance) |

—¿Quieres este jabón o **ése**? — *"Do you want this soap or that one?"*

—No quiero ni **éste** ni **ése**; quiero **aquél.** — *"I don't want this one or that one; I want that one over there."*

■ The masculine and feminine demonstrative pronouns are the same as the demonstrative adjectives, except that they have a written accent.

■ Each demonstrative pronoun has a neuter form. They are **esto, eso,** and **aquello.** The neuter forms, which do not change in number or gender, are used to refer to situations, ideas, and nonspecific objects or things, equivalent to the English *this, that matter; this, that business;* and *this, that stuff.*

—¿Entiendes **eso**? — *"Do you understand that?"*
—No, no lo entiendo. — *"No, I don't understand it."*

—¿Qué es **esto**? — *"What's this?"*
—No sé... — *"I don't know . . ."*

## práctica

**A.** Change the demonstrative adjectives according to the gender and number of the nouns, to talk about what is needed.

1. Yo necesito *esta* lista, ________ mesas, ________ reloj y ________ cuadros.
2. Eva necesita *ese* escritorio, ________ silla, ________ libros y ________ llaves.
3. Nosotros necesitamos *aquella* maleta, ________ billete, ________ toallas y ________ bolsos de mano.

**B.** Complete the following sentences according to the cue given.

1. Firmo este registro y ________ *(that one over there)*.
2. Quiero estos lápices y ________ *(those)*.
3. Necesito esta llave y ________ *(that one over there)*.
4. Voy a comprar esta toalla y ________ *(those)*.
5. No quiero esas maletas; quiero ________ *(these)*.
6. No voy a comer en ese restaurante. Voy a comer en ________ *(this one)*.

**C.** With a partner, use demonstrative adjectives to describe people or objects that are at varying distances from you.

1. sus cuadernos
2. la pizarra
3. las ventanas
4. la puerta
5. los coches en la calle
6. las chicas que están en la cafetería
7. los libros del profesor
8. su pluma (o lápiz)

## 2 Indirect object pronouns *(Pronombres usados como complemento indirecto)*

- In addition to a subject and a direct object, a sentence may have an indirect object.

| | |
|---|---|
| Él **te** da **el libro.** | *He gives you the book.* |
| I.O. D.O. | I.O. D.O. |

- An indirect object describes *to whom* or *for whom* an action is done. An indirect object pronoun can be used in place of an indirect object. In Spanish, the indirect object pronoun includes the meaning *to* or *for:* **Yo *les* mando los libros (a los estudiantes).**
- The forms of the indirect object pronouns are as follows. Notice that the indirect object pronouns are the same as the direct object pronouns, except in the third person.

| ***Singular*** | | ***Plural*** | |
|---|---|---|---|
| **me** | *(to, for) me* | **nos** | *(to, for) us* |
| **te** | *(to, for) you* (fam.) | **os** | *(to, for) you* (fam.) |
| **le** | *(to, for) you* (form.)<br>*(to, for) him*<br>*(to, for) her* | **les** | *(to, for) you* (form.)<br>*(to, for) them* (masc., fem.) |

- Indirect object pronouns are usually placed in front of the conjugated verb.

| | |
|---|---|
| —¿Qué **te** dice tu papá en la tarjeta? | *"What does your Dad say to you in the postcard?"* |
| —**Me** dice que viene por unos días. | *"He tells me (says to me) that he is coming for a few days."* |
| —En qué idioma **les** hablan sus padres a ustedes? | *"In what language do your parents speak to you?"* |
| —Ellos **nos** hablan en español. | *"They speak to us in Spanish."* |

- In sentences with a conjugated verb followed by an infinitive, the indirect object pronoun may either be placed in front of the conjugated verb or be attached to the infinitive.

**Le** quiero dar dinero.<br>Quiero dar**le** dinero. } *I want to give him money.*

- When used in sentences with the present progressive, an indirect object pronoun may either be placed in front of the conjugated verb or be attached to the present participle.

**Nos** está diciendo que viene hoy.<br>Está diciéndo**nos**[1] que viene hoy. } *He is telling us that he is coming today.*

**ATENCIÓN** The indirect object pronouns **le** and **les** sometimes require clarification when the person to whom they refer is not specified. Spanish provides clarification (or emphasis) by using the preposition **a** + *personal pronoun or noun*.

| | |
|---|---|
| **Le** doy el pasaje. | *I am giving the ticket . . .* (to him? to her? to you?) |
| *but:* **Le** doy el pasaje **a ella.** | *I am giving the ticket* to her. |

Note, however, that the prepositional phrase is optional, while the indirect object pronoun must always be used.

| | |
|---|---|
| **Le** traigo un libro **a Roberto**. | *I am bringing a book to Roberto.* |
| **¿Les** vas a dar el dinero **a ellas?** | *Are you going to give the money to them?* |

[1]When an indirect object pronoun is attached to a present participle, an accent mark is added to maintain the correct stress.

## práctica

**A.** You are in an airport waiting for a friend to arrive and you overhear some people making the following comments. Complete their sentences with the appropriate indirect object pronoun.

1. ________ dan los billetes. (a nosotros)
2. ________ doy el bolso de mano. (a ellos)
3. ________ doy la maleta. (a él)
4. ________ doy los cheques de viajero. (a ella)
5. ________ traigo la tarjeta de embarque. (a Uds.)
6. ________ piden el pasaporte. (a ella)
7. ________ traigo el equipaje. (a ti)
8. ________ traen el periódico. (a él)
9. ________ decimos "gracias". (a ellos)
10. ________ dan las bebidas. (a mí)

**B.** Add the appropriate indirect object pronouns to the following dialogues, and then act them out with a partner.

1. —¿ ________ vas a prestar tus maletas a David?
   —No, porque él nunca ________ devuelve nada.
   —Pero él ________ presta sus libros a ti...
2. —¿ ________ vas a escribir una carta a tus padres, Rosita?
   —No, voy a mandar ________ una tarjeta postal.
3. —¿Su hermana ________ va a traer los cheques de viajero esta tarde, señorita Paz?
   —Sí, y yo ________ voy a dar mil dólares a ella.
4. —¿Qué ________ vas a traer a Sergio y a mí, tía Isabel?
   —________ voy a traer dos cámaras fotográficas.
   —¿Y a Elsa?
   —A ella voy a traer ________ una cámara de video.

**C.** The following people are going on a trip and need certain items. Say who is going to give, bring, or buy the things they need.

MODELO: Oscar necesita un mapa.
*El papá de Oscar le va a traer (comprar, dar) el mapa.*

| | | |
|---|---|---|
| tu mamá | el amigo de... | mi hermano |
| nuestros amigos | el papá de... | la abuela de... |
| los chicos | el novio de... | su esposo(-a) |

1. Yo necesito las maletas.
2. Teresa necesita cheques de viajero.
3. Tú necesitas un bolso de mano.
4. Ana y yo necesitamos una tarjeta de crédito.
5. Carlos necesita una cámara de video.
6. Los chicos necesitan una cámara fotográfica.
7. Olga y Pedro necesitan dinero.
8. Ud. necesita una tarjeta postal.

**D.** You are going on a trip to Miami to visit your aunt and uncle. Discuss with a classmate what you are doing now and what you are going to do once you get there.

1. ¿Les estás escribiendo a tus tíos de la Florida?
2. ¿Qué les estás diciendo?
3. ¿Qué les vas a llevar a tus tíos?
4. ¿Tu papá te va a dar su cámara fotográfica?
5. ¿Nos vas a escribir desde *(from)* Miami?
6. ¿Me vas a dejar la llave de tu casa?
7. ¿Qué les vas a traer a tus padres?
8. ¿Qué me vas a traer a mí?

**E.** You are going on a trip. Say what you are going to bring the following people as souvenirs.

1. a tu mamá
2. a tus hermanos
3. a mí *(use* tú *form)*
4. a tu mejor amigo(-a)
5. a Carlos y a mí

## 3 Constructions with gustar *(Construcciones con **gustar**)*

■ The verb **gustar** means *to like* (literally, *to be pleasing to*). **Gustar** is always used with an indirect object pronoun (**me** in the following example).

| | |
|---|---|
| **Me gusta** tu casa.<br>I.O. V. S. | *I like your house.*<br>S. V. D.O. |
| | *Your house is pleasing to me.*<br>S. V. I.O. |

■ The two most commonly used forms of **gustar** are the third-person singular form, **gusta,** used if the subject is singular or if **gustar** is followed by one or more infinitives; and the third-person plural form, **gustan,** used if the subject is plural.

***Indirect object pronouns***

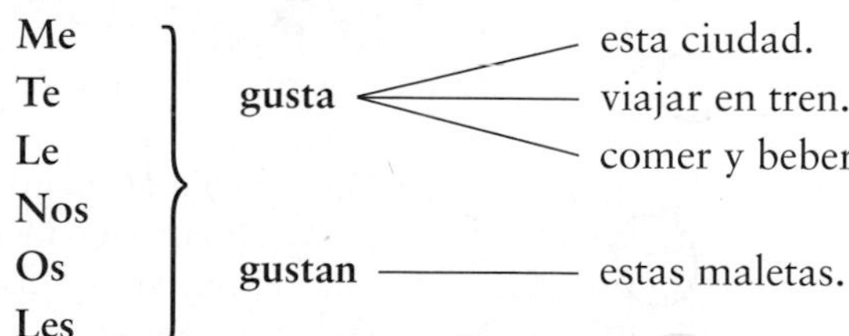

- Note that the verb **gustar** agrees with the *subject* of the sentence—that is, with the person or thing being liked.

| | |
|---|---|
| Me gusta **Lima.** | *I like Lima.* |
| No me gust**an los vuelos** largos. | *I don't like long flights.* |

**ATENCIÓN** When what is liked is an activity, **gustar** is followed by the infinitive.

| | |
|---|---|
| Me gust**a hablar** por teléfono. | *I like to talk (talking) on the phone.* |

- The person who does the liking is the indirect object.

**Me** gustan los cuadros de Picasso.
I.O.

| | |
|---|---|
| —¿**Te** gusta San Diego? | *"Do you like San Diego?"* |
| —Sí, **me** gusta mucho San Diego, pero **me** gusta más San Francisco. | *"Yes, I like San Diego very much, but I like San Francisco better."* |
| —**A Eva le** gusta Santa Bárbara y **a nosotros nos** gusta Reno. | *"Eva likes Santa Barbara and we like Reno."* |

**ATENCIÓN** Note that the words **mucho** and **más** *(better)* immediately follow **gustar.**

- The preposition **a** + *noun or pronoun* may be used to emphasize or specify the name of the person referred to by the indirect object pronoun.

| | |
|---|---|
| **A Eva** (**A ella**) le gusta el pollo y **a mí** me gusta la ensalada. | *Eva (She) likes chicken and I like salad.* |

## práctica

A. Rewrite the following sentences, using constructions with **gustar.**

MODELO: Yo prefiero San Diego.
*A mí me gusta más San Diego.*

1. Yo prefiero las ciudades grandes.
2. ¿Tú prefieres el bolso de mano azul?
3. Nosotros preferimos viajar en barco.
4. Marcelo prefiere los hoteles pequeños.
5. Ellos prefieren pasar las vacaciones en México.
6. ¿Ud. prefiere viajar en tren o en avión?
7. Adela prefiere los asientos de ventanilla.
8. ¿Uds. prefieren la comida italiana?

**B.** Interview a classmate to find out what the following members of his or her family like and don't like to do on weekends. When you have finished, switch roles.

MODELO: —A tu hermana, ¿qué le gusta hacer? ¿Qué no le gusta hacer?
—*A mi hermana le gusta ir a bailar. No le gusta trabajar.*

1. A ti
2. A tus hermanos
3. A tu padre
4. A Uds.
5. A tus primos

**C.** Interview a classmate, using the following questions. When you have finished, switch roles.

1. ¿Dónde te gusta pasar tus vacaciones?
2. ¿Te gustan más las ciudades grandes o las ciudades pequeñas?
3. ¿Te gusta más viajar en tren o en avión?
4. ¿Qué les gusta hacer a tus amigos los fines de semana?
5. ¿A Uds. les gusta bailar? ¿cantar?
6. ¿A tu mejor amiga le gustan las canciones de Enrique Iglesias?
7. ¿Qué estación del año te gusta más?
8. ¿Qué te gusta hacer cuando llueve?

**D.** With a classmate, prepare four questions to ask your instructor about his or her likes and dislikes.

**E.** Compare your likes and dislikes with those of two classmates. Consider your tastes in food, music, weekend activities, classes, and travel.

## 4 Time expressions with **hacer** *(Expresiones de tiempo con el verbo hacer)*

- English uses the present perfect progressive or the present perfect tense to express how long something has been going on.

*I* ***have been living*** *here* ***for*** *twenty years.*

- Spanish uses the following construction.

**Hace** + *length of time* + **que** + *verb* (in the present tense)
Hace veinte años que vivo aquí.

| | |
|---|---|
| —**¿Cuánto tiempo hace que** Ud. estudia español? | *"How long have you been studying Spanish?"* |
| —**Hace** tres meses **que** estudio español. | *"I have been studying Spanish for three months."* |
| —¿Tienes mucha hambre? | *"Are you very hungry?"* |
| —¡Sí! **Hace** ocho horas **que** no como. | *"Yes! I haven't eaten for eight hours."* |

**ATENCIÓN** To ask how long something has been going on, use the expression **¿Cuánto tiempo hace que...?**

## práctica

**A.** Tell how long each action depicted below has been going on. Use **hace... que** and the length of time specified.

1. veinte minutos

2. tres años

3. una hora

4. dos horas

5. siete horas

6. quince días

**B.** Interview a classmate, using the following questions and two questions of your own. When you have finished, switch roles.

1. ¿Cuánto tiempo hace que vives en la misma *(same)* casa?
2. ¿Cuánto tiempo hace que estudias aquí?

3. ¿Cuánto tiempo hace que trabajas en esta ciudad?
4. ¿Cuánto tiempo hace que hablas español?
5. ¿Cuánto tiempo hace que no comes?
6. ¿Cuánto tiempo hace que no ves a tus padres?
7. ¿Cuánto tiempo hace que conoces a tu mejor amigo(-a)?
8. ¿Cuánto tiempo hace que no tienes vacaciones?

C. In groups of three, prepare six questions to ask your instructor, using time expressions with **hacer.** You may want to use the verb **enseñar** *(to teach)* in your questions.

## 5 Preterit of regular verbs *(Pretérito de verbos regulares)*

- Spanish has two simple past tenses: the preterit and the imperfect. (The imperfect tense will be studied in **Lección 10.**) The preterit tense is used to refer to actions or states that the speaker views as completed in the past.
- The preterit of regular verbs is formed as follows. Note that the endings for the -**er** and -**ir** verbs are the same.

| **-ar** *verbs* | **-er** *verbs* | **-ir** *verbs* |
|---|---|---|
| **tomar** *to take* | **comer** *to eat* | **escribir** *to write* |
| tom**é** | com**í** | escrib**í** |
| tom**aste** | com**iste** | escrib**iste** |
| tom**ó** | com**ió** | escrib**ió** |
| tom**amos** | com**imos** | escrib**imos** |
| tom**asteis** | com**isteis** | escrib**isteis** |
| tom**aron** | com**ieron** | escrib**ieron** |

—¿**Hablaste** con Silvia ayer?
—Sí, **comimos** juntas en la cafetería.
—¿Le **escribió** Roberto?
—Sí, **recibió** una tarjeta de él ayer.

*"Did you speak with Silvia yesterday?"*
*"Yes, we ate together in the cafeteria."*
*"Did Roberto write to her?"*
*"Yes, she received a card from him yesterday."*

- The first-person plural of -**ar** and -**ir** verbs is identical to the present tense forms.

—¿A qué hora salieron Uds.?
—**Salimos** de casa a las seis y no **llegamos** hasta las siete.

*"What time did you leave?"*
*"We left home at six, and we didn't arrive until seven."*

- Verbs ending in -**gar,** -**car,** and -**zar** change **g** to **gu, c** to **qu,** and **z** to **c** before -**é** in the first-person singular of the preterit: **pagar** → **pagué; buscar** *(to look for)* → **busqué; empezar** → **empecé.**

—¿A qué hora **llegaste** al hospital?
—**Llegué** a las ocho y **empecé** a trabajar.

*"What time did you arrive at the hospital?"*
*"I arrived at eight and I started to work."*

- Certain **-er** and **-ir** verbs with the stem ending in a vowel change **i** to **y** in the third-person singular and plural endings: **leer** → **leyó, leyeron; creer** → **creyó, creyeron.**

  Él lo **leyó** en el periódico, pero no lo **creyó.**

- Verbs of the **-ar** and **-er** groups that are stem-changing in the present indicative are regular in the preterit.

  Rosa **volvió** a las seis y **cerró** las puertas. — *Rosa returned at six o'clock and closed the doors.*

- Spanish has no equivalent for the English word *did* used as an auxiliary verb in questions and negative sentences.

  —¿Encontraste el billete? — *"Did you find the ticket?"*
  —No lo busqué. — *"I didn't look for it."*

## práctica

**A.** Complete the following dialogues, using the verbs given. Then act them out with a partner.

1. hablar / hablar / llamar / charlar
   —¿Tú ________ por teléfono con tus suegros ayer?
   —Sí, ________ con ellos. Los ________ por la mañana y ________ hasta las once.
2. volver / volver / volver / volver
   —¿A qué hora ________ Uds.?
   —Yo ________ a las cuatro y Mario ________ a las seis. ¿A qué hora ________ tú?
   —A las siete.
3. recibir / mandar / recibir
   —¿________ (tú) las tarjetas que yo te ________?
   —No, no las ________.
4. llegar / llegar / comenzar
   —¿A qué hora ________ Ud., señorita?
   —________ a las nueve y ________ a trabajar a las nueve y media.
5. cerrar / cerrar / abrir
   —¿ ________ Uds. las puertas?
   —Sí, ________ las puertas y ________ las ventanas.

**B.** Say what you and your friends did yesterday.

1. ¿Qué comió Ud. ayer?
2. ¿Qué bebió Ud.?
3. ¿Estudiaron Uds. español anoche *(last night)?*
4. ¿A qué hora salió Ud. de su casa?
5. ¿A qué hora llegó Ud. a su primera clase?
6. ¿Trabajaron ayer sus amigos?
7. ¿Dónde almorzó su mejor amigo(-a)?
8. ¿A qué hora volvió Ud. a su casa?
9. ¿Leyó el periódico?
10. ¿A qué hora cenó Ud.?

C. With a partner, use the verbs listed to ask each other what you did yesterday and last night (**anoche**).

MODELO: —¿Dónde almorzaste ayer?
—*Almorcé en la cafetería.*

| | | |
|---|---|---|
| almorzar | leer | practicar |
| cenar | llegar | salir |
| cerrar | mandar | trabajar |
| conversar | mirar | ver |
| devolver | pagar | buscar |
| escribir | | |

# ¡A ver cuánto aprendió!

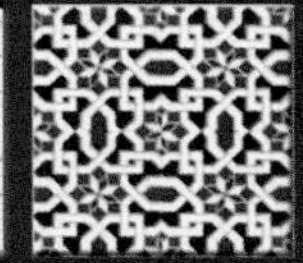

## ¡Repase el vocabulario!

INTERNET

See the *¿Cómo se dice...?* Web site for additional grammar and vocabulary practice: http://spanish.college.hmco.com/students

Complete the following sentences with words from the lesson vocabulary.

1. No me gusta viajar en la ________ de fumar.
2. No es la entrada; es la ________.
3. Le voy a ________ a Teresa las maletas que me prestó.
4. ¿Quiere un ________ de ventanilla o de pasillo?
5. Le tengo que dar la tarjeta de ________ a la ________ de vuelo.
6. Si vas a tomar el ________ a las ocho, tienes que estar en el aeropuerto a las siete.
7. Como Ana y Elsa viajan ________, conversan durante ________ el viaje.
8. —¿Qué ________ el vuelo?
   —Un ________ largo.
9. Los viajeros llegaron tarde; llegaron con dos horas de ________.
10. —Roberto, ¿le vas a prestar mil dólares para ir a Las Vegas?
    —¡¿Estás ________?!
11. Yo les deseé ________ viaje a los turistas.
12. Compré un pasaje de ida y ________.
13. Le voy a enviar una ________ postal.
14. ¿Tienes seis maletas? ¡Vas a pagar exceso de ________!
15. Elsa, te quiero ________ a mi amigo Roberto Fuentes.

## Entrevista

With a partner, interview each other, using the following questions.

1. ¿Adónde te gusta ir cuando tienes vacaciones?
2. ¿Te gusta más viajar en avión o en tren? ¿Por qué?
3. ¿Viajas en primera clase o en clase turista?
4. Cuando viajas, ¿les mandas tarjetas postales a tus amigos?

5. ¿Llevas mucho equipaje cuando viajas?
6. ¿Conociste a alguien interesante en tus vacaciones? (¿A quién?)
7. ¿Tus vacaciones son magníficas o aburridas?
8. ¿Adónde vas a ir de vacaciones la próxima vez? ¿Vas a ir con tu familia?
9. Cuando viajas, ¿les traes algo a tus amigos?
10. ¿Viajaste el verano pasado? ¿Adónde?

## Situaciones

What would you say in the following situations? What might the other person say? Act out the scenes with a partner. Take turns playing each role.

1. You are checking in for a flight at the airport. The airline representative wants to know how many suitcases you have. You are not sure whether you can take your carry-on bag on the plane.
2. You are seeing a friend off at the airport.
3. A friend has borrowed your suitcase. You want to know when he or she plans to return it to you, because you are going on a trip. Arrange to see your friend tomorrow at noon.
4. You are in a travel agency. You want to buy a round-trip ticket to Bogotá. Ask for a seat assignment.

## Para escribir

Write a short composition about the people in the photo. Tell who they are, what their relationship to each other is, where they went last summer, what they did, and also what they plan to do next summer.

# En la vida real

## En una agencia de viajes

**CD-ROM**

Do the interactive exercises on the CD-ROM for additional practice.

You and a classmate will play the roles of a travel agent and a tourist. Discuss the following.

- ticket prices according to destination and different kinds of transportation
- prices for first class or tourist class, one-way or round-trip
- flight schedules
- seat reservations
- how much luggage can be taken

## Planes para un viaje

You are helping some friends plan a trip. With a classmate, study the ad and answer your friends' questions.

**Caribe** Asómese al paraíso . . .

**SALIDAS EN AVION LINEA REGULAR DE IBERIA, DIRECTO A SANTO DOMINGO, TODOS LOS JUEVES Y VIERNES**

| PRECIOS POR PERSONA EN HABITACION DOBLE Y REGIMEN DE MEDIA PENSION | | |
|---|---|---|
| TEMPORADAS | 7 NOCHES | 14 NOCHES |
| Mayo y 1 al 21 de Junio | **114.900** | **137.800** |
| 22 al 30 de Junio | **125.900** | **148.800** |
| Julio y Septiembre | **137.500** | **165.000** |
| Agosto | **142.900** | **176.400** |
| Octubre | **131.500** | **159.000** |
| Noviembre y Diciembre (1 al 12) | **132.900** | **161.800** |

Suplemento Habitación Individual: Consultar al efectuar la reserva.
**LOS PRECIOS INCLUYEN**: Avión línea regular clase turista ida y vuelta. Traslados aeropuerto/hotel/aeropuerto. Estancia en habitación doble en régimen de Media Pensión (Hotel Bávaro Casino).

**OFERTA VALIDA PARA SALIDAS Y REGRESOS DESDE MADRID.**

1. ¿A qué país vamos a viajar?
2. ¿En qué clase viajamos?
3. ¿En qué hotel vamos a estar?
4. Queremos viajar en julio. ¿Cuánto tenemos que pagar (en pesetas) por una semana? ¿Y por dos semanas?
5. ¿El precio incluye el traslado *(transportation)* del aeropuerto al hotel y del hotel al aeropuerto?

6. ¿De qué ciudad salen los vuelos?
7. ¿Qué días de la semana salen los vuelos?

## ¿Adónde vamos?

You and a friend have won a radio contest. The prize is $5,000 to spend on a dream vacation. With a classmate, decide where you will go, how long you will be away, where you will stay, and what you will need to take with you.

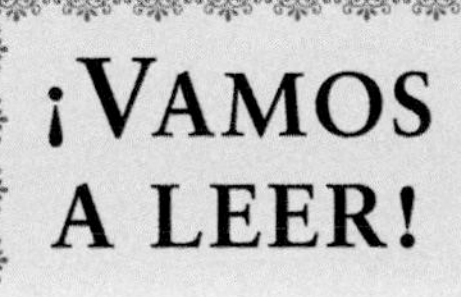


### Antes de leer

As you read Teresa's letter, find the answers to the following questions.

1. ¿Son buenas amigas Teresa y Ángela? ¿Cómo lo sabe Ud.?
2. ¿Teresa está de vacaciones todavía?
3. ¿Qué dice Teresa de las ruinas de Machu Picchu?
4. ¿A quién le mandó Teresa tarjetas postales?
5. ¿Cómo se llama el muchacho a quien Teresa conoció en Lima? ¿De dónde es?
6. ¿De qué conversaron Teresa y el muchacho?
7. ¿Qué dice Teresa de los peruanos?
8. ¿Adónde la llevaron los amigos de su padre?
9. ¿Qué le recomienda Teresa a Ángela?
10. ¿Adónde va a ir Teresa? ¿Por qué?

## *Una carta de Teresa*

12 de septiembre de 2002

Querida Ángela:

Hace mucho tiempo que no te escribo, pero siempre pienso en ti. Ya estoy de vuelta° de mi viaje a Perú. Me gustó todo, pero especialmente Machu Picchu, las famosas ruinas de los incas, que son muy interesantes. Ya sé que no te mandé tarjetas postales, pero tampoco le mandé ninguna a nadie.

**estoy...** *I'm back*

En Lima conocí a un muchacho argentino muy simpático y muy educado. Se llama José Luis Vera Vierci. Conversamos mucho, de todo tema° imaginable. Me mandó una tarjeta desde Buenos Aires, donde él vive.

*topic*

Los peruanos son encantadores.° Me trataron° muy bien. Los amigos de mi padre me llevaron a muchos lugares, especialmente al teatro, al cine y... ¡a restaurantes! La comida es muy buena, tan buena que aumenté° dos kilos.

*charming / they treated*

*I gained*

Bueno, para tus próximas vacaciones, te recomiendo una visita a Perú. Y ahora te dejo porque voy a ir a cenar con mis padres. Hoy es el cumpleaños de papá.

Te extraño mucho. Saludos a Sandra y a Marcelo.

Un abrazo,

*Teresa*

## Díganos

Answer the following questions, based on your own thoughts and feelings.

1. ¿Cuánto tiempo hace que Ud. no le escribe a su mejor amigo(-a)?
2. ¿A quién le manda Ud. tarjetas postales cuando va de vacaciones?
3. ¿Qué lugares interesantes visitó Ud. el verano pasado?
4. ¿Conoció Ud. a alguien simpático(-a) durante sus vacaciones?
5. Cuando Ud. conversa con sus amigos, ¿de qué temas hablan Uds.?
6. Cuando Ud. visita a sus amigos, ¿adónde lo (la) llevan?
7. ¿Qué me recomienda Ud. para mis próximas vacaciones?
8. ¿Cuándo es el cumpleaños de su papá? ¿Y de su mamá?

# ASÍ SOMOS

VIDEO

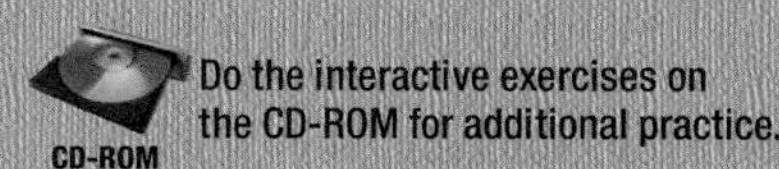
CD-ROM
Do the interactive exercises on the CD-ROM for additional practice.

NARRADORA —¿Qué países conoce Ud.?

ÁNGELA —Conozco Estados Unidos,... Perú, Venezuela, Ecuador,... México. Em... Conozco Europa, pues conozco Francia, Italia, España, Canadá.

## Preparación

A. **Vamos a viajar.** With a partner, answer the following questions based on your own information. You will hear answers to these same questions when you watch the video. After viewing the video, compare your answers with those you hear.

1. ¿A Ud. le gusta viajar?
2. ¿Qué países conoce Ud.?
3. ¿Qué lugar le gustó más?
4. ¿Cómo pasó Ud. las vacaciones este año?

B. **Durante las vacaciones.** List the different activities you might do while on a summer vacation and while on a winter vacation. Share the lists with the rest of the class.

## Comprensión

A. **¿Verdadero o falso?** Read the following statements. Circle **V** (**Verdadero**) or **F** (**Falso**) according to what you understood from the video. If a statement is false, correct it.

V F 1. A Tamara le encanta viajar.
V F 2. Pablo piensa que viajar es muy interesante.
V F 3. A Pablo y a Juan les gusta viajar.
V F 4. A Ángela le gusta mucho viajar.
V F 5. A Gustavo le gusta viajar bastante.

B. **¿Qué países conocen estas personas?** Select the word or phrase that best completes each statement, according to what you understood from the video.

1. Ángela conoce (Europa, Asia).
2. Gustavo vivió en (Brasil, Estados Unidos).
3. Leonardo (conoce, no conoce) algunos países de Europa.
4. Tamara (conoce, no conoce) muchos países.

C. **¿Quién lo dijo?** Match each statement with the name of the person who said it.

| | A | B |
|---|---|---|
| _____ | 1. Buenos Aires es una ciudad increíble. | a. Pablo |
| _____ | 2. Me fascinó el Medio Oriente. | b. Leonardo |
| _____ | 3. Me gustaron los Estados Unidos y Canadá. | c. Ángela |
| _____ | 4. De todos los países, me gusta el mío, España. | d. Gustavo |

D. **¿Verdadero o falso?** Read the following statements. Circle **V** (**Verdadero**) or **F** (**Falso**) according to what you understood from the video. If a statement is false, correct it.

V F 1. Tamara pasó *(spent)* sus vacaciones en Puerto Rico.
V F 2. John visitó a sus parientes *(relatives)* en los Estados Unidos.
V F 3. La casa de Zaida está en Bogotá, Colombia.
V F 4. Pablo pasó sus vacaciones con sus amigos.

E. **Entrevista** ***(Interview)***. Watch the video segment called *Entrevista* at the end of Lesson 7. Answer the following questions according to what you understood from the interview.

1. ¿Qué profesión tiene Manuel Ticó?
2. ¿Cuál es su nacionalidad?
3. ¿Qué oportunidades tiene él en su trabajo?
4. ¿Cuáles son los países que conoce Manuel?
5. ¿A Manuel le gusta su trabajo?
6. ¿Tiene él una rutina en su trabajo?

## Ampliación

A. **¿Adónde quiere viajar?** With a partner, make a list of the countries you have visited and the countries you would like to visit. Share the list with the rest of the class and determine which countries have been visited the most and which countries students would most like to visit.

B. **De vacaciones.** Interview a classmate about a memorable vacation he or she has had. Include information about where you went, what activities you enjoyed, and what you learned on this vacation. Then exchange roles.

# En un restaurante cubano

Lección
8

## OBJECTIVES

### Pronunciation

The Spanish **l**, **r**, **rr**, and **z**

### Structure

Direct and indirect object pronouns used together • Preterit of **ser**, **ir**, and **dar** • Preterit of **e:i** and **o:u** stem-changing verbs • Uses of **por** and **para** • Ordinal numbers

### Communication

You will learn vocabulary related to restaurant menus, ordering meals at a restaurant, and paying the bill.

# En un restaurante cubano

*Hoy es el primero de diciembre. Es el aniversario de bodas de Lidia y Jorge Torres y para celebrarlo van a cenar a uno de los mejores restaurantes de Miami. Ahora llegan al restaurante El Caribe.*

LIDIA —¡Qué sorpresa! ¡Éste es un restaurante muy elegante!
JORGE —Y la comida es excelente.
MOZO —Por aquí, por favor. Aquí está el menú.
LIDIA —Gracias. *(Lee el menú.)*

PARA LA CENA

(Todos los platos de la lista se sirven con la sopa del día y ensalada.)

| | | | |
|---|---|---|---|
| ***Pescados y mariscos*** | | | |
| Langosta | **$18.00** | Trucha | **$11.50** |
| Salmón | **$14.50** | Camarones | **$11.00** |
| ***Carne*** | | | |
| Albóndigas | **$ 6.00** | Pavo relleno | **$10.00** |
| Bistec | **$12.00** | Pollo frito | **$ 8.50** |
| Cordero | **$13.00** | Arroz con pollo | **$ 6.00** |
| Lechón asado | **$17.00** | | |

JORGE —¿Por qué no pides un filete? Aquí preparan unos filetes muy ricos. ¿O langosta?
LIDIA —No, anoche fui a la cena de los Ruiz y sirvieron langosta.
MOZO —Les recomiendo la especialidad de la casa: lechón asado y arroz con frijoles negros. De postre, helado, flan o torta helada.
JORGE —Yo quiero lechón asado y arroz con frijoles negros. ¿Y tú?
LIDIA —Yo quiero sopa, camarones y arroz.
JORGE —Para tomar tráiganos un vermut y después media botella de vino tinto.
MOZO —Muy bien, señor. *(Anota el pedido.)*

*Antes de cenar, Lidia y Jorge toman vermut y conversan.*

LIDIA —¿Tus padres fueron a la fiesta que dio Eva ayer?
JORGE —Sí, fue en el club Los Violines.
LIDIA —¿Le dieron el regalo que compraron para ella en México?
JORGE —¿La pulsera? Sí, se la dieron. Le encantó.
LIDIA —¿Te la enseñaron antes de dársela?
JORGE —Sí, me la enseñaron cuando fui por ellos anteayer por la tarde.
LIDIA —La consiguieron a muy buen precio en una tienda muy elegante.

*Después de comer, Lidia y Jorge beben café. Jorge pide la cuenta, la paga, le deja una buena propina al mozo y salen. Tienen entradas para ir a ver una comedia y, como llueve a cántaros y el teatro queda lejos, toman un taxi.*

JORGE —Feliz aniversario, mi amor. *(Le da un beso.)*
LIDIA —*(Lo abraza.)* Feliz aniversario, querido.

# Vocabulario

## Cognados

**el aniversario** anniversary
**la comedia** comedy
**cubano(-a)** Cuban
**elegante** elegant
**la especialidad** specialty
**excelente** excellent
**la lista** list, menu
**el menú** menu
**el salmón** salmon
**la sorpresa** surprise
**el teatro** theater
**el vermut** vermouth

## Nombres

**las albóndigas** meatballs
**el amor** love
**el arroz** rice
**el arroz con pollo** chicken and rice
**el beso** kiss
**el bistec** steak
**la botella** bottle
**los camarones** shrimp
**la carne** meat
**la comida** food, meal
**el cordero** lamb
**la cuenta** bill
**la entrada, el boleto** ticket (i.e., for a show)
**el filete** tenderloin steak
**el flan** caramel custard
**los frijoles** beans
**el helado** ice cream[1]
**la langosta** lobster
**el lechón** pork
**los mariscos** shellfish
**el mozo, camarero**[2] waiter
**el pavo** turkey
**el pedido** order
**el pescado** fish
**el plato** dish
**el postre** dessert
**el precio** price
**la propina** tip
**la pulsera** bracelet
**el regalo** present, gift
**la sopa** soup[1]
**la tienda** store
**la torta helada** ice cream cake
**la trucha** trout

## Verbos

**abrazar** to hug
**anotar** to write down
**dejar** to leave (behind)
**encantar**[3] to love, to like very much
**pedir (e:i)** to order
**quedar** to be located
**recomendar (e:ie)** to recommend
**tomar** to drink

## Adjetivos

**asado(-a)** roasted
**frito(-a)** fried
**helado(-a)** iced, ice cold
**medio(-a)** half
**relleno(-a)** stuffed
**rico(-a), sabroso(-a)** tasty, delicious
**tinto** red (wine)

## Otras palabras y expresiones

**aniversario de bodas** wedding anniversary
**anoche** last night
**anteayer** the day before yesterday
**de postre** for dessert
**después de** after
**lejos** far
**llover (o:ue) a cántaros** to rain cats and dogs, to pour down raining
**mi amor** my love, my darling
**por aquí** this way
**¡Qué sorpresa!** What a surprise!
**querido(-a)** dear, darling
**se sirven** are served
**tráiganos** bring us

---

[1]In Spanish, the verb **tomar** is used often with **helado** and **sopa.**
[2]**La camarera** means waitress.
[3]**Encantar** uses the same structure as **gustar: Le encantó** la pulsera.

## Vocabulario adicional

**ESPECIALIDAD EN CARNES Y MARISCOS**

### Menú

PARA EL ALMUERZO

| | | | |
|---|---|---|---|
| Sándwich de pollo | $3.50 | Papas fritas *(French fries)* | $1.00 |
| Sándwich de jamón y queso *(ham and cheese)* | $2.50 | Tortilla a la española *(Omelette)* | $2.50 |
| Sándwich de huevo *(egg)* | $1.50 | Tortilla mexicana | $ .50 |
| Sopa del día | $2.00 | Frijoles | $1.75 |
| Ensalada | $3.50 | Arroz | $1.80 |
| Hamburguesa[1] | $2.50 | Arroz con frijoles negros | $2.00 |

PARA LA CENA

(Todos los platos de la lista se sirven con la sopa del día y ensalada.)

***Pescados y mariscos***

| | | | |
|---|---|---|---|
| Langosta | $18.00 | Trucha | $11.50 |
| Salmón | $14.50 | Camarones | $11.00 |

***Carne***

| | | | |
|---|---|---|---|
| Albóndigas | $ 6.00 | Pavo relleno | $10.00 |
| Bistec | $12.00 | Pollo frito | $ 8.50 |
| Cordero | $13.00 | Arroz con pollo | $ 6.00 |
| Lechón asado | $17.00 | | |

POSTRES

| | | | |
|---|---|---|---|
| Arroz con leche *(Rice pudding)* | $2.00 | Helado | $1.50 |
| | | Frutas[1] | $1.25 |
| Torta de chocolate[1] | $2.50 | Queso | $3.00 |
| Flan con crema | $2.50 | | |

BEBIDAS

| | | | |
|---|---|---|---|
| Agua mineral | $1.00 | Café | $ .80 |
| Cerveza | $3.00 | Té[1] | $ .80 |
| Champán | $6.00 | Chocolate caliente *(Hot chocolate)* | $1.20 |
| Vino blanco | $3.50 | | |
| Vino tinto | $3.50 | Jugo de frutas *(Fruit juice)* | $1.50 |
| Vermut | $3.50 | | |
| | | Leche fría *(Cold milk)* | $1.20 |

[1]All these words are cognates, so you can guess what they mean.

## Para poner la mesa *(To set the table)*

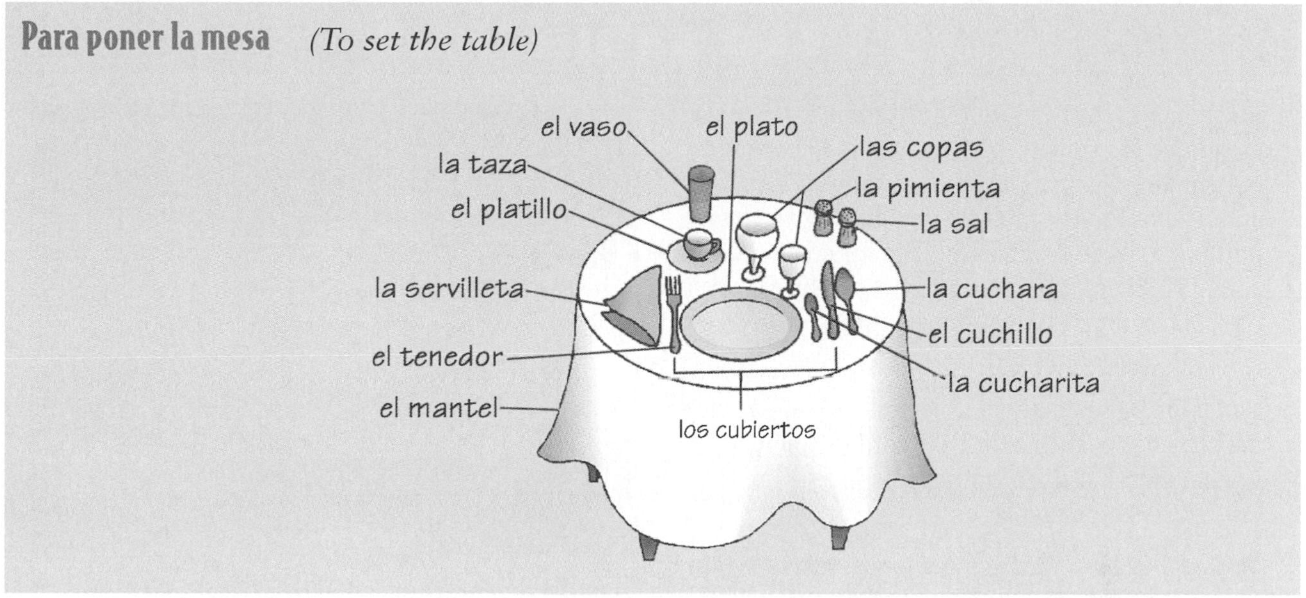


## ¡Conversemos!

Answer the following questions, basing your answers on the dialogue.

1. ¿Cuándo es el aniversario de bodas de Lidia y Jorge?
2. ¿Qué dice Lidia del restaurante? ¿Y qué dice Jorge de la comida?
3. ¿Cuál es la especialidad de la casa?
4. ¿Qué pide Lidia? ¿Qué pide Jorge?
5. ¿Qué beben Lidia y Jorge?
6. ¿Adónde fueron los padres de Jorge ayer?
7. ¿Qué regalo compraron para Eva?
8. ¿Cuándo le enseñaron la pulsera a Jorge?
9. ¿La consiguieron a buen precio?
10. ¿Qué deja Jorge para el mozo?
11. ¿Qué dicen Jorge y Lidia al salir del restaurante?
12. ¿Por qué tienen que tomar un taxi para ir al teatro?

## ¿Lo sabía Ud.?

■ La ciudad de Miami en el estado de la Florida es uno de los centros turísticos más importantes del mundo. Cientos de miles de turistas latinoamericanos la visitan todos los años. Más de un millón de hispanos viven en Miami, en su mayoría cubanos. El español se usa tanto en Miami que en muchos lugares hay letreros *(signs)* que dicen *"English spoken here."*

■ En los países de habla hispana, el café se sirve después del postre, nunca durante la comida. Generalmente es café tipo expreso, y se sirve en tazas muy pequeñas.

■ Después de comer, los hispanos generalmente se quedan sentados *(remain seated)* alrededor de la mesa y conversan. A esto se le llama "hacer la sobremesa."

■ En los países de habla hispana, la propina que generalmente se ofrece en los restaurantes es del 10%, pero hay variación según el país y el tipo de restaurante. Con frecuencia la propina está incluida en la cuenta.

- ¿En qué otras ciudades de los Estados Unidos hay muchas personas de origen latinoamericano?

Cubanos en un café de la Pequeña Habana en Miami, Florida.

- ¿Se bebe mucho café en este país? ¿Qué tipo de café es muy popular ahora?
- Generalmente, ¿cuánto se deja de propina en este país?

INTERNET

See the *¿Cómo se dice...?* Web site for activities on authentic cultural material: http://spanish.college.hmco.com/students

# Pronunciación

##  A The Spanish l

STUDENT AUDIO

The Spanish **l** is pronounced like the *l* in the English word *lean.* The tip of the tongue must touch the palate. Listen to your instructor and repeat the following words.

| | | |
|---|---|---|
| langosta | Silvia | sólo |
| loco | helado | filete |
| capital | él | plato |

## B The Spanish r

The Spanish **r** sounds something like the *dd* in the English word *ladder.* Listen to your instructor and repeat the following words.

| | | |
|---|---|---|
| teatro | hora | tarde |
| dejar | Teresa | cordero |
| frijoles | primero | postre |

## C The Spanish rr (spelled r at the beginning of words and rr between vowels)

The Spanish **rr** is a strong trill. Listen to your instructor and pronounce the following words.

| | | |
|---|---|---|
| aburrido | Rosa | Reyes |
| rico | arroz | Roberto |
| recomendar | Raúl | relleno |

## D Thc Spanish z

In Latin America the Spanish **z** is pronounced like the *ss* in the English word *pressing*. In Spain it is pronounced like the *th* in thc English word *think*. Avoid using the buzzing sound of the English *z* in the words *zoo* and *zebra*. Listen to your instructor and repeat the following words.

| | | |
|---|---|---|
| pizarra | vez | Pérez |
| Zulema | zoológico | taza |
| lápiz | mozo | azul |

## 1 Direct and indirect object pronouns used together *(Pronombres de complemento directo e indirecto usados juntos)*

- When an indirect object pronoun and a direct object pronoun are used together, the indirect object pronoun always comes first.

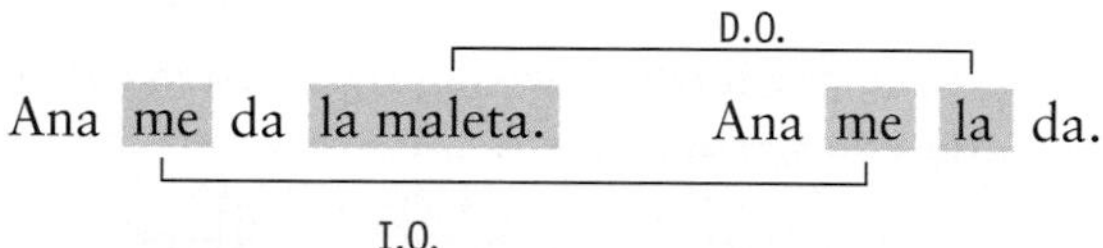

D.O.
Ana me da la maleta.
Ana me la da.
I.O.


- With an infinitive, the pronouns can either be placed before the conjugated verb or be attached to the infinitive.

I.O. D.O.

Ana **me** **la** va a dar.

Ana va a **dármela.**[1]

- With the present progressive, the pronouns can either be placed before the conjugated verb or be attached to the gerund.

I.O. D.O.

Ella **te** **lo** está diciendo.

Ella está **diciéndotelo.**[1]

- If both pronouns begin with **l,** the indirect object pronoun (**le** or **les**) is changed to **se.**

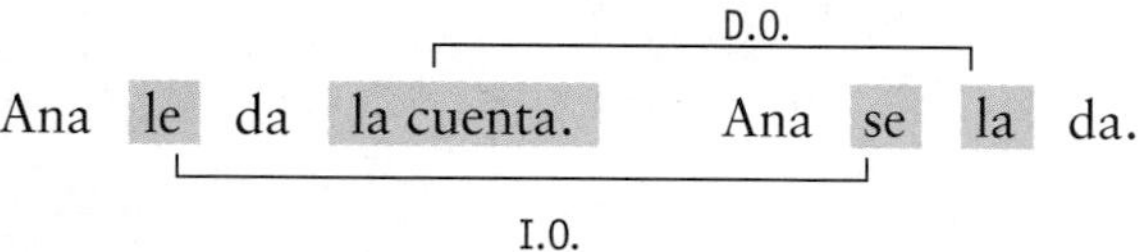

D.O.
Ana le da la cuenta.
Ana se la da.
I.O.


For clarification, it is sometimes necessary to add **a él, a ella, a Ud., a Uds., a ellos,** or **a ellas.**

—¿A quién le da la cuenta Ana?
—**Se la** da **a él.**

[1]Note the use of the written accent, which follows the rules for accentuation. See Appendix A.

## práctica

**A.** Complete the following dialogues, using direct and indirect object pronouns. Then act them out with a partner, adding a sentence or two to each dialogue.

1. —¿*Le* dejaste *la propina* al mozo?
   —Sí, ________ ________ dejé en la mesa.
2. —¿*Me* compraste *las entradas* para el teatro?
   —No, no ________ ________ compré. Lo siento.
3. —¿El mozo *te* sirvió *el café*?
   —Sí, ________ ________ sirvió.
4. —¿*Le* vas a dar *la pulsera* a tu madre?
   —Sí, ________ ________ voy a dar mañana.
5. —¿*Nos* va a traer *los postres* ahora?
   —Sí, ________ ________ voy a traer ahora.
6. —¿El mozo *les* va a traer a Uds. *la cuenta*?
   —Sí, va a traér ________ en seguida.

**B.** You have a friend who is always willing to help others. Explain how, using the information provided.

> MODELO: *Yo* necesito *una maleta.* (comprar)
> *Mi amigo* ***me la*** *compra.*

1. *Yo* necesito *dos tarjetas postales.* (comprar)
2. *Tú* necesitas *los discos compactos.* (traer)
3. *Nosotros* queremos *frutas.* (servir)
4. *Elsa* necesita *un bolso de mano.* (prestar)
5. *Mis hermanos* necesitan *dinero.* (dar)
6. *Mi prima* necesita *las maletas.* (traer)
7. *Ud.* necesita *la cinta.* (enviar)
8. *Yo* quiero *los libros.* (dar)

**C.** You are in a bad mood, and people keep asking you to do things you don't want to do. Tell them you can't do the favors they are requesting.

> MODELO: —¿Puedes trae*rme el menú*?
> *—No, no puedo traér**telo**.*

1. —¿Puedes trae*rme las servilletas?*
2. —¿Puedes dar*le el mantel* a Julio?
3. —¿Puedes compra*rle el regalo* a mamá?
4. —¿Puedes presta*rme los cubiertos?*
5. —¿Puedes trae*rnos el helado?*
6. —¿Puedes dar*le las cucharas* a Luisa?

**D.** Now repeat Exercise C, following the model below.

> MODELO: —¿Puedes trae*rme el menú?*
> *—No, no* ***te lo*** *puedo traer.*

**E.** Interview a classmate, using the following questions and two questions of your own. When you have finished, switch roles.

1. Cuando tú necesitas dinero, ¿a quién se lo pides?
2. Cuando tú les pides dinero a tus padres, ¿te lo dan?
3. Si yo necesito tu libro de español, ¿me lo prestas?
4. Si Uds. no entienden algo, ¿se lo preguntan a su profesor(-a)?
5. Si tú y yo somos amigos(-as) y yo necesito tu coche, ¿tú me lo prestas?
6. Necesito tu pluma. ¿Puedes prestármela?
7. Necesito cheques de viajero. ¿Tú me los puedes conseguir?
8. Yo no tengo el número de teléfono del profesor (de la profesora). ¿Tú se lo puedes pedir?

## 2 Preterit of ser, ir, and dar *(Pretérito de los verbos **ser, ir** y **dar**)*

■ The preterit forms of **ser, ir,** and **dar** are irregular.

| **ser** *to be* | **ir** *to go* | **dar** *to give* |
|---|---|---|
| fui | fui | di |
| fuiste | fuiste | diste |
| fue | fue | dio |
| fuimos | fuimos | dimos |
| fuisteis | fuisteis | disteis |
| fueron | fueron | dieron |

■ Note that **ser** and **ir** have identical forms in the preterit.

—Ayer **fue** el cumpleaños de Lucía, ¿no?
*"Yesterday was Lucía's birthday, right?"*

—Sí, Ana y yo **fuimos** a su casa y le **dimos** los regalos.
*"Yes, Ana and I went to her house and gave her the presents."*

—¿**Fuiste** a la fiesta que **dio** Sara?
*"Did you go to the party that Sara gave?"*

—Sí, **fui. Fue** la mejor fiesta del año.
*"Yes, I went. It was the best party of the year."*

### práctica

**A.** Complete the following dialogues, using the preterit of **ser, ir,** or **dar** as appropriate. Then act them out with a partner, adding a sentence or two to each dialogue.

1. —¿Adónde ________ tú ayer?
   —________ a la tienda. Compré una pulsera de oro y se la ________ a mi esposa.
2. —¿ ________ Uds. a casa de tía Eva ayer?
   —Sí, ________ y le ________ el libro que tú mandaste para ella.
3. —¿Uds. ________ estudiantes del Dr. Paz?
   —Carlos ________ su estudiante, pero Raquel y yo ________ estudiantes de la Dra. Guerra.

4. —¿A quién le ________ (tú) la botella de vino tinto?
   —Se la ________ a Jorge.
5. —¿Adónde ________ Uds. anoche?
   — ________ al teatro. Los padres de Dora nos ________ las entradas.

**B.** Interview a classmate, using the following questions. When you have finished, switch roles.

1. ¿Quién fue tu profesor(-a) favorito(-a) el año pasado?
2. ¿Fuiste a la cafetería ayer? ¿A qué hora?
3. ¿Adónde fuiste el sábado pasado? ¿Con quién fuiste?
4. ¿Tus amigos fueron a visitarte?
5. ¿Dieron tus amigos una fiesta para celebrar tu cumpleaños?
6. ¿Diste una fiesta el viernes pasado? ¿Alguien dio una fiesta el sábado?

## 3 Preterit of **e:i** and **o:u** stem-changing verbs *(Pretérito de los verbos que cambian en la raíz:* ***e:i*** *y* ***o:u****)*

- Verbs of the **-ir** conjugation that have a stem change in the present tense change **e** to **i** and **o** to **u** in the third-person singular and plural of the preterit.[1]

| **preferir** *to prefer* | | **dormir** *to sleep* | |
|---|---|---|---|
| preferí | preferimos | dormí | dormimos |
| preferiste | preferisteis | dormiste | dormisteis |
| prefirió | prefirieron | durmió | durmieron |

- Other verbs that follow the same pattern:

| | |
|---|---|
| pedir | seguir |
| mentir *(to lie)* | conseguir |
| servir | morir |
| repetir *(to repeat)* | |

—¿Cómo **durmieron** Uds. anoche?
—Nosotros **dormimos** bien, pero Paco no **durmió** muy bien.

*"How did you sleep last night?"*
*"We slept well, but Paco didn't sleep very well."*

—¿Qué **pidieron** ellos?
—Raúl **pidió** camarones y Rosa **pidió** langosta.

*"What did they order?"*
*"Raúl ordered shrimp and Rosa ordered lobster."*

—Beba dice que Ada salió con tu novio.
—Te **mintió.**

*"Beba says that Ada went out with your boyfriend."*
*"She lied to you."*

[1]Remember that the **-ar** and **-er** stem-changing verbs are regular in the preterit: **él cerró, ellos volvieron.** Exceptions are **poder** and **querer,** which are explained in **Lección 9.**

## práctica

**A.** Find out what Andrés did yesterday by adding the correct form of the missing verbs.

1. Yo ________ (ir) a visitar a mi padre y le ________ (pedir) dinero.
2. ________ (Conseguir) entradas para el teatro.
3. ________ (Salir) con otra chica y le ________ (mentir) a mi novia.
4. Nosotros ________ (ir) a un restaurante y yo ________ (pedir) cordero asado; ella ________ (pedir) langosta.
5. Yo ________ (volver) a mi casa y ________ (dormir) dos horas.
6. Mis padres me ________ (invitar) a una fiesta pero yo ________ (preferir) no ir.
7. Por la noche, yo ________ (dar) una fiesta y ________ (servir) ponche.

**B.** Now, using the information above, prepare questions to ask your classmates about what Andrés did.

## 4 Uses of **por** and **para** *(Usos de **por** y **para**)*

### A. Uses of *por*

The preposition **por** is used to express the following concepts.

- motion or approximate location *(through, around, along, by)*

| | |
|---|---|
| Luis salió **por** la ventana. | *Luis went out through the window.* |
| Enrique va **por** la calle Juárez. | *Enrique is going down Juárez Street.* |
| Gustavo pasó **por** el hotel. | *Gustavo went by the hotel.* |

- cause or motive of an action *(because of, on account of, on behalf of)*

| | |
|---|---|
| Llegamos tarde **por** la lluvia. | *We were late because of the rain.* |
| Lo hago **por** ellos. | *I do it on their behalf.* |

- means, manner, unit of measure *(by, for, per)*

| | |
|---|---|
| Siempre viajamos **por** tren. | *We always travel by train.* |
| Van a 100 kilómetros **por** hora. | *They're going 100 kilometers per hour.* |

- *in exchange for*

| | |
|---|---|
| Te doy 50 dólares **por** esa cámara. | *I'll give you 50 dollars for that camera.* |

- period of time during which an action takes place *(during, in, for)*

| | |
|---|---|
| Ella trabaja **por** la mañana. | *She works in the morning.* |
| Va a estar aquí **por** dos meses. | *He's going to be here for two months.* |

- *in search of, for*

| | |
|---|---|
| Voy a venir **por** ti a las siete. | *I'll come by for you at seven.* |

## práctica

Interview a classmate, using the following questions. When you have finished, switch roles.

1. ¿Tienes una clase por la mañana? ¿Y por la noche?
2. Antes de ir a clase, ¿vas por tus amigos? ¿Alguien viene por ti?
3. ¿Cuánto pagaste por tu libro de español?
4. ¿Pasaste por mi casa anoche?
5. Si tú pierdes la llave de tu casa, ¿entras por la ventana?
6. ¿Tus padres hacen mucho por ti?
7. ¿Tú les escribes a tus padres o prefieres llamarlos por teléfono?
8. ¿Prefieres viajar por tren o por avión? ¿Por qué?

### B. Uses of *para*

The preposition **para** is used to express the following concepts.

- destination

| | |
|---|---|
| Quiero un pasaje **para** Montevideo. | *I want a ticket for Montevideo.* |
| ¿A qué hora hay vuelos **para** Buenos Aires? | *What time are the flights to Buenos Aires?* |

- goal for a point in the future (*by* or *for* a certain time)

| | |
|---|---|
| Quiero el dinero **para** el sábado. | *I want the money for Saturday.* |
| Debo estar allí **para** el mes de noviembre. | *I must be there by the month of November.* |

- whom or what something is for

| | |
|---|---|
| Compré una mesa **para** mi cuarto. | *I bought a table for my room.* |
| Compramos los libros **para** Fernando. | *We bought the books for Fernando.* |

- *in order to*

| | |
|---|---|
| Necesito mil dólares **para** pagar el viaje. | *I need a thousand dollars in order to pay for the trip.* |
| Vamos al teatro **para** celebrar nuestro aniversario de bodas. | *We are going to the theater (in order) to celebrate our wedding anniversary.* |

- objective or goal

| | |
|---|---|
| Mi novio estudia **para** médico. | *My boyfriend is studying to be a doctor.* |

SI USTED NECESITA
¡¡CREDITO!!
Gustosamente se lo damos!
Flores, Arreglos, Regalos

## práctica

**A.** Look at the illustrations and describe what is happening, using **por** or **para.**

1. Fuimos ________ a Miami.
2. Daniel salió ________. 
3. La torta es ________. 
4. Luisa va a estar en Orlando ________. 
5. Jorge pagó ________ el vino. 
6. Eva sale mañana ________. 

**B.** Imagine that you and your partner are planning a trip to Spain. Take turns answering the following questions.

1. ¿Cuánto dinero necesitan Uds. para pagar el viaje?
2. ¿Van a pedirles dinero a sus padres para el viaje?
3. ¿Para qué día quieren los pasajes?
4. ¿A qué hora sale el avión para Madrid?
5. ¿Por cuánto tiempo piensan estar en Madrid?
6. ¿Van a traer regalos para su familia?
7. ¿Van Uds. a España para practicar el español?
8. John estudia para profesor de español y quiere visitar Madrid. ¿Puede ir con Uds.?

**C.** Complete the following description of a trip to Paraguay, using **por** or **para.**

Robert y yo salimos ________ Asunción la semana próxima. Vamos a viajar ________ avión. Tenemos pasajes ________ el sábado ________ la mañana. Pagamos tres mil dólares ________ los billetes, pero como pensamos pasar ________ Caracas y ________ Lima, donde vamos a estar ________ unos días, no es muy caro. Mañana ________ la tarde vamos a Bloomingdale's ________ comprar algunos regalos ________ nuestros amigos paraguayos. Desde Lima, vamos a llamar ________ teléfono a nuestros amigos en Asunción, y ellos van a ir al aeropuerto ________ nosotros.

D. Plan a trip to a Hispanic country with a classmate. Using the paragraph in Exercise C as a model, describe your travel plans.

## 5 Ordinal numbers (*Números ordinales)*

| | | | |
|---|---|---|---|
| **primero(-a)**[1] | *first* | **sexto(-a)** | *sixth* |
| **segundo(-a)**[1] | *second* | **séptimo(-a)** | *seventh* |
| **tercero(-a)**[1] | *third* | **octavo(-a)** | *eighth* |
| **cuarto(-a)** | *fourth* | **noveno(-a)** | *ninth* |
| **quinto(-a)** | *fifth* | **décimo(-a)** | *tenth* |

■ Ordinal numbers agree in gender and number with the nouns they modify.

el segundo **chico** la segunda **chica**
los primeros **días** las primeras **semanas**

■ Ordinal numbers are seldom used after **décimo** *(tenth)*.

**ATENCIÓN** The ordinal numbers **primero** and **tercero** drop the final **-o** before masculine singular nouns.

el **primer**[2] día el **tercer**[3] año

### práctica

A. Supply the ordinal numbers that correspond to the following cardinal numbers.

1. cuatro
2. diez
3. uno
4. siete
5. dos
6. ocho
7. tres
8. nueve
9. cinco
10. seis

B. Imagine that the whole class is staying at a hotel in Miami. Your classmates were assigned rooms on different floors. With a partner, take turns saying who is on what floor.

---

[1]abbreviated 1°, 2°, 3°, and so on
[2]abbreviated 1[er]
[3]abbreviated 3[er]

# ¡A ver cuánto aprendió!

INTERNET

See the *¿Cómo se dice...?* Web site for additional grammar and vocabulary practice: http://spanish.college.hmco.com/students

## ¡Repase el vocabulario!

Match each question in column A with the answers in column B, and then read them aloud.

| A | B |
|---|---|
| 1. ¿Qué celebran hoy? | a. Flan con helado. |
| 2. ¿Está rico el pavo relleno? | b. Sí, quiero pedirlos, pero son muy caros. |
| 3. ¿Cuál es la especialidad de la casa? | c. El pedido. |
| 4. ¿Qué bebidas prefieres? | d. Lechón asado con arroz y frijoles negros. |
| 5. ¿Qué quieres de postre? | e. Sí, a cántaros. |
| 6. ¿Vas a pedir agua mineral? | f. Hamburguesas. |
| 7. ¿Qué está anotando el mozo? | g. Sí, me encanta. |
| 8. ¿Quieres bistec? | h. Ocho dólares. |
| 9. ¿Adónde vamos esta noche? | i. Sí, está muy sabroso. |
| 10. ¿Está lloviendo? | j. Ana. |
| 11. ¿No quieres camarones? | k. Sí, una botella. |
| 12. ¿Cuánto vas a dejar de propina? | l. No, prefiero té. |
| 13. ¿Qué venden en McDonald's? | m. Al teatro. |
| 14. ¿Quién paga la cuenta? | n. Su aniversario de bodas. |
| 15. ¿Quieres café? | o. Sí, quiero comer carne. |
| 16. ¿Te gusta la pulsera? | p. Vermut o vino tinto. |

## Entrevista

You and a classmate are at the El Caribe Restaurant. Look at the menu on page 190 and ask each other the following questions.

1. ¿Qué vas a pedir?
2. ¿Prefieres carne o pescado?
3. ¿Qué me recomiendas para comer?
4. ¿Qué prefieres tomar: vino blanco, champán o agua mineral?
5. ¿Qué quieres de postre: arroz con leche, torta o flan con crema?
6. ¿Cuánto es la cuenta?
7. ¿Cuánto vas a dejar de propina?
8. ¿Qué vas a hacer después de cenar?

## Situaciones

What would you say in the following situations? What might the other person say? Act out the scenes with a partner. Take turns playing each role.

1. You are at a restaurant, and you are very hungry. Ask to see the menu; order a first and second course and something to drink while you wait for your food. Then tell the waiter what you want for dessert.
2. You are a waiter or waitress. Recommend two or three main dishes and a dessert to your customers. Ask them if they want coffee or tea.
3. You are cooking a gourmet dinner. Ask your roommate to set the table. Name the utensils and other items you want.
4. You are hosting a party at your home. Some of your guests have brought children. Offer a selection of beverages.

## Para escribir

Write a dialogue between a waiter or waitress and a customer. Include the following exchanges.

- asking for a menu
- ordering the food, drink(s), and dessert
- asking for the check

# En la vida real

CD-ROM

Do the interactive exercises on the CD-ROM for additional practice.

## ¿Qué les servimos?

You and a classmate are hosting a special weekend for some foreign students. Discuss the breakfast, lunch, and dinner menus you will be preparing, taking into account your guests' different preferences.

- María Inés Soto is a vegetarian.
- Juan Carlos Reyes loves meat and dairy products.
- Isabel Peña is on a diet.
- Francisco Rojas is extremely thin and wants to gain weight.
- Raquel Arias loves seafood.

Some additional words and phrases that you might include:

**el chorizo** *sausage* } **con huevos** *with eggs*
**el tocino** *bacon* }
**el cereal** *cereal*
**la mantequilla** *butter*
**la mermelada** *jam*
**el pan** *bread*
**el panqueque** *pancake*
**el yogur** *yogurt*
**las zanahorias** *carrots*

## ¡Vamos a cenar!

You and a classmate have received a $40.00 gift coupon to eat dinner at the El Caribe Restaurant. Select what you are going to have, including drinks and dessert. And don't forget to leave a tip!

## ¡Buen provecho!

You and a friend have decided to go out to dinner tonight. Read the following ads for Hispanic restaurants in Miami, and answer the questions on the next page.

1. Ud. y un amigo quieren comer pescado. ¿A qué restaurante pueden ir?
2. Si quieren hacer reservaciones en ese restaurante, ¿a qué número deben llamar?
3. ¿Cuál es la especialidad del restaurante Las Redes?
4. ¿Por qué es famoso el restaurante Segovia?
5. ¿Cuándo hay música en el restaurante Segovia?
6. ¿Cuánto cuesta el almuerzo allí?
7. ¿Qué comidas típicas cubanas sirven en el restaurante La Carreta?
8. Si quieren dar un banquete, ¿a qué restaurante deben ir?
9. ¿En qué calle está El Bodegón Castilla?
10. ¿Cree Ud. que en El Bodegón Castilla sirven comida cubana o española?

PANORAMA HISPÁNICO

# 4. México

México

- Con más de veintitrés millones de habitantes en el área metropolitana, la Ciudad de México es el centro urbano más grande del mundo. Fundada por los aztecas en el año 1325, es también la capital más antigua de América.
- El turismo es una de las principales fuentes de ingreso *(sources of income)* de la economía mexicana. Cancún, Acapulco, Puerto Vallarta, Ixtapa, Mazatlán y otros centros turísticos reciben millones de visitantes todos los años, principalmente de los Estados Unidos.
- La comida mexicana es muy conocida *(well known)* en los Estados Unidos. Muchos de los alimentos típicos mexicanos, como los frijoles y las tortillas de maíz, son de origen indígena. Los platos más populares son las enchiladas, el guacamole, los tamales y los tacos.
- Antes de la conquista de México por parte de los españoles, existían allí numerosas culturas indígenas, las de los aztecas, los mayas, los toltecas y los mixtecas, entre otras. Aún hoy existen grandes concentraciones de indígenas en las regiones de Yucatán, Chiapas y Oaxaca.

En muchos lugares de México es posible visitar ruinas muy bien conservadas, como por ejemplo las pirámides, que son un elemento muy importante de la arquitectura prehispánica. Ésta es la Pirámide del Mago en Uxmal, una antigua ciudad maya en la península de Yucatán. Está formada por cinco templos construidos uno encima *(on top)* del otro.

*¿Qué culturas indígenas existen en su país?*

La península de Yucatán es famosa no sólo por sus ruinas mayas sino *(but)* también por sus playas *(beaches)* de aguas cálidas *(warm)* y cristalinas. A cien kilómetros de Cancún está Akumal, un centro turístico de belleza *(beauty)* inigualable.

*¿Qué centros turísticos hay en el estado donde Ud. vive?*

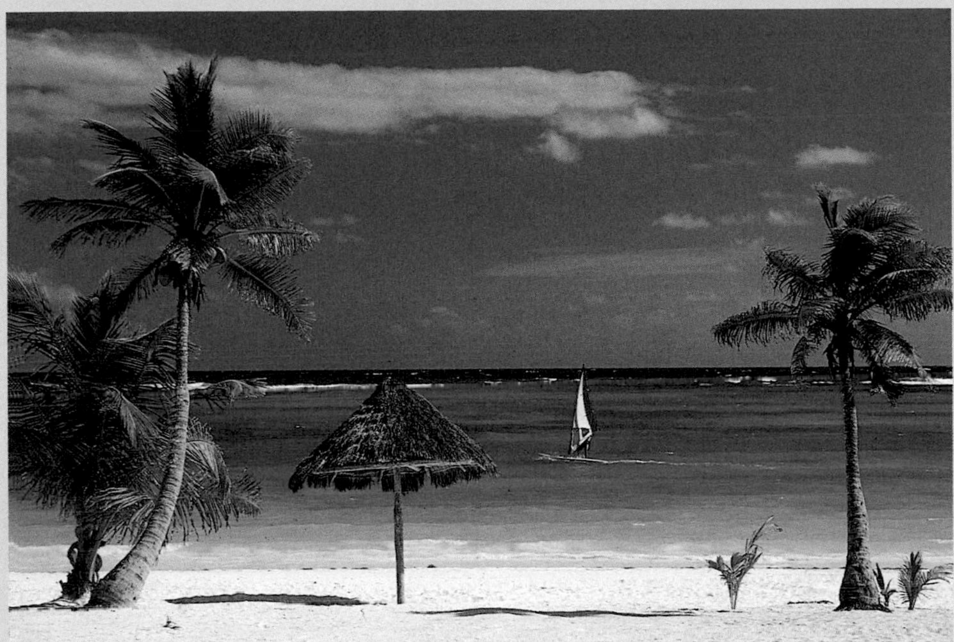

El mercado del pueblo de Tlacolula, en el estado de Oaxaca, es uno de los más famosos de México. Allí los indígenas de la región venden productos agrícolas y también objetos de artesanía, como vasijas de barro *(clay pots)* y sarapes. Lo más popular de la artesanía de Oaxaca es la cerámica negra.

*¿Le gustan a Ud. los objetos de artesanía?*

Este mural del famoso artista mexicano Diego Rivera presenta la historia y las costumbres de la civilización totoneca. El mural está en el Palacio Nacional, construido en el lugar donde antes estaba el palacio del emperador azteca Moctezuma. Otros murales famosos de Rivera están en el Ministerio de Educación y en la Universidad Nacional Autónoma de México, ambos *(both)* en la Ciudad de México.

*¿Conoce Ud. otros pintores mexicanos? ¿Cuáles?*

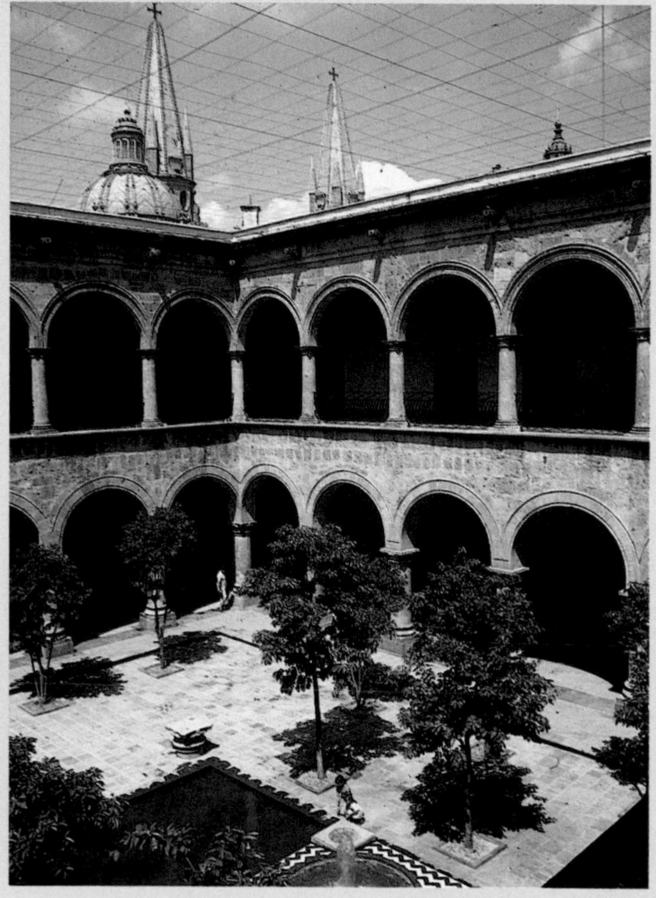

Guadalajara, capital del estado de Jalisco, con más de cinco millones de habitantes, es la segunda ciudad de México en población. La ciudad tiene una rica tradición cultural. En ella se mezclan magníficos ejemplos de la arquitectura y el arte español coloniales con modernas avenidas y edificios contemporáneos. Aquí vemos el patio del Museo del Estado, famoso por sus magníficas pinturas de José Clemente Orozco.

*¿Cuál es la capital del estado donde Ud. vive?*

El Ballet Folklórico de México le ofrece al público espectáculos llenos *(full)* de arte y color. El ballet actúa *(performs)* los miércoles y los domingos en el Palacio de Bellas Artes de la Ciudad de México. Sus danzas y trajes típicos son de una gran belleza *(beauty)*.

*¿A Ud. le gusta bailar? ¿Por qué o por qué no?*

El primero y el dos de noviembre se celebra en México el Día de los Muertos *(Dead)*. En la foto, una mujer reza *(prays)* en el Cementerio de Patzcuaro, en el estado de Michoacán. Los habitantes del pueblo llevan comida a las tumbas de sus familiares y se quedan *(they stay)* allí toda la noche. Miles de velas *(candles)* y flores de papel adornan el cementerio, creando un espectáculo inolvidable.

*¿Existe un equivalente al Día de los Muertos en su país?*

Estatua de Cuauhtémoc, último emperador azteca, que fue vencido *(defeated)* por Hernán Cortés en 1521. Cuauhtémoc simboliza el orgullo *(pride)* del pueblo *(people, nation)* mexicano.

*¿Qué estatuas importantes hay en su ciudad?*

El Paseo de la Reforma en la Ciudad de México. En este paseo hay numerosos monumentos impresionantes, entre ellos la estatua del rey Carlos IV de España, el espléndido monumento a Cristóbal Colón *(Christopher Columbus)* y el del Ángel de la Independencia, que vemos en la foto.

*¿Qué monumentos históricos hay en la ciudad de Washington, D.C.?*

TELEINFORME

VIDEO

CD-ROM
Do the interactive exercises on the CD-ROM for additional practice.

## Preparación

**¿Cuánto saben Uds. ya?** After reading **Panorama hispánico 4,** get together in groups of three or four students and answer the following questions.

1. ¿Cuál es el centro urbano más grande del mundo?
2. ¿Cuál es la capital más antigua de América?
3. ¿Cuántos millones de habitantes viven en la Ciudad de México?
4. ¿Cuáles son algunos de los centros turísticos de México?
5. ¿De qué estado mexicano es Guadalajara la capital?
6. ¿Cómo es la arquitectura de Guadalajara?
7. ¿Cuándo se celebra el Día de los Muertos?
8. ¿Cómo se celebra el Día de los Muertos en México?

## Comprensión

**A. La Ciudad de México, Cuernavaca y Teotihuacán.** Read the following statements. After watching the video, circle **V** (**Verdadero**) or **F** (**Falso**), according to what you understood. If the statement is false, correct it.

V F 1. Otro nombre para la Ciudad de México es "el D.F.".
V F 2. No hay metro en la Ciudad de México.
V F 3. La Catedral Metropolitana fue construida *(was built)* sobre templos aztecas.
V F 4. El clima de Cuernavaca es como el de la Ciudad de México.
V F 5. Teotihuacán fue una gran ciudad precolombina.

**B. Guadalajara.** Select the word or phrase that best completes each statement according to what you understood in the video.

1. Guadalajara fue fundada en (1542, 1452).
2. La población de Guadalajara es (menor, mayor) que la población de la Ciudad de México.
3. Guadalajara es la capital de (la República Mexicana, Jalisco).
4. La Catedral de Guadalajara tiene dos (plazas, torres) doradas *(golden)*.

**C. Yucatán.** Select the word or phrase that best completes each statement according to what you understood from the video.

1. La península de Yucatán fue el centro de la civilización (maya, azteca).
2. Cancún está en (Jalisco, la península de Yucatán).
3. Chichén Itzá es una (ciudad, civilización) antigua.
4. Los mayas realizaron descubrimientos importantes en (la ingeniería, la geografía).

## Ampliación

A. **Dos culturas.** With a partner, make a list of counterparts you can find in your local area, city, state, or country for each of the following items.

1. México, D.F.
2. Guadalajara
3. Cancún
4. Teotihuacán
5. Chichén Itzá

B. **Quiero visitar...** Interview a partner to determine which of the Mexican cities in the video segment he/she would like to visit. Use the following questions as a guide.

1. ¿Te gusta la Ciudad de México? ¿Guadalajara? ¿Cancún?
2. ¿Qué lugares quieres visitar? ¿Por qué?
3. ¿Cuáles son algunos de los monumentos que quieres ir a ver?
4. ¿Qué actividades te interesan?

Lección 9

# Un día muy ocupado

## OBJECTIVES

### Pronunciation

La entonación

### Structure

Reflexive constructions • Some uses of the definite article • Possessive pronouns • Irregular preterits • Formation of adverbs

### Communication

You will learn vocabulary related to household chores and the hairdresser.

# Un día muy ocupado

*Aunque hoy es sábado, Mirta e Isabel se levantaron temprano para terminar de limpiar el apartamento. Esta noche, las dos chicas están invitadas a un concierto en la Casa de Cultura Paraguaya. Isabel está un poco cansada porque anoche se acostó tarde.*

MIRTA —¿Por qué viniste tan tarde anoche? ¿Dónde estuviste?

ISABEL —En la tienda. Tuve que comprar un regalo para Eva porque mañana es su cumpleaños. Bueno, ¿empezamos a limpiar?

MIRTA —Sí, yo voy a barrer la cocina y le voy a pasar la aspiradora a la alfombra.

ISABEL —Entonces yo voy a limpiar el baño. Después voy a cocinar y a planchar mi vestido rojo. Me lo voy a poner esta noche.

MIRTA —Yo no sé qué ponerme.

ISABEL —¿Por qué no te pones el vestido azul? Es muy bonito.

MIRTA —No, me lo probé ayer y no me queda bien. ¡Ah! ¿Dónde está la palita?

ISABEL —En la terraza. ¡Ay! Necesito bañar al perro, ducharme y vestirme... ¡y tengo turno en la peluquería a las tres!

MIRTA —Yo quiero lavarme la cabeza y no me acordé de comprar champú. ¿Puedo usar el tuyo?

ISABEL —Sí, está en el botiquín.

MIRTA —Gracias. Yo no pude ir a la farmacia ayer.

*Cuando llegó a la peluquería, Isabel le pidió una revista al peluquero y se sentó a esperar su turno.*

ISABEL —*(Al peluquero)* Quiero corte, lavado y peinado.

PELUQUERO —Tiene el pelo muy lacio. ¿No quiere una permanente?

ISABEL —No, cuando quiero rizos, uso el rizador. ¡Ay, tengo el pelo muy largo!

PELUQUERO —Últimamente está de moda el pelo corto. *(Le corta el pelo y, cuando termina, Isabel se mira en el espejo.)*

ISABEL —¡Muy bien! Ahora quiero pedir turno para mi amiga para la semana próxima.

PELUQUERO —¿El miércoles, primero de febrero, a las nueve y media? Generalmente hay menos gente por la mañana.

ISABEL —Está bien. Mi amiga se llama Mirta Ortega.

*Isabel deja la cartera en el mostrador. El peluquero la llama.*

PELUQUERO —¡Señorita! ¿Esta cartera es suya?

ISABEL —Sí, es mía. Gracias.

# Vocabulario

## Cognados

**el apartamento** apartment
**el champú** shampoo
**el concierto** concert
**la cultura** culture
**la farmacia** pharmacy, drugstore
**generalmente** generally
**paraguayo(-a)** Paraguayan
**el permanente**[1] permanent (wave)
**el turno** turn

## Nombres

**la alfombra** rug, carpet
**la aspiradora** vacuum cleaner
**el botiquín** medicine cabinet
**la cartera, el bolso, la bolsa** purse, handbag
**la cocina** kitchen
**el corte** haircut, cut
**el espejo** mirror
**la gente**[2] people
**el lavado** shampoo, wash
**el mostrador** counter
**la palita, el recogedor** dustpan
**el peinado** hairdo, hairstyle
**el pelo** hair
**la peluquería, el salón de belleza** salon, beauty parlor
**el (la) peluquero(-a)** hairdresser, beautician
**el perro** dog
**la revista** magazine
**el rizador** curling iron
**el rizo** curl
**la semana** week
**el turno, la cita** appointment
**el vestido** dress

## Verbos

**acordarse (o:ue)**[3] to remember
**acostarse (o:ue)** to go to bed
**bañar(se)** to bathe (oneself)
**barrer** to sweep
**cocinar** to cook
**cortar(se)** to cut (oneself)
**ducharse** to take a shower
**esperar** to wait (for)
**lavar(se)** to wash (oneself)
**levantarse** to get up
**limpiar(se)** to clean (oneself)
**llamarse** to be called
**planchar** to iron
**ponerse** to put on
**probarse (o:ue)** to try on
**quedar** to fit
**sentarse (e:ie)** to sit down
**terminar** to finish
**usar** to use, to wear
**vestirse (e:i)** to get dressed

## Adjetivos

**corto(-a)** short
**lacio** straight (hair)

## Otras palabras y expresiones

**aunque** although
**bueno** well, okay
**cortarse el pelo** to get a haircut
**estar de moda** to be in style
**estar invitado(-a)** to be invited
**lavarse la cabeza** to wash one's hair
**pasar la aspiradora** to vacuum
**pedir (e:i) turno, cita** to make an appointment
**temprano** early
**últimamente** lately

---

[1]In many countries, ***la* permanente** is used.
[2]**Gente** is used in the singular in Spanish.
[3]**Acordarse** is always used with a reflexive pronoun.

## Vocabulario adicional

### En la barbería

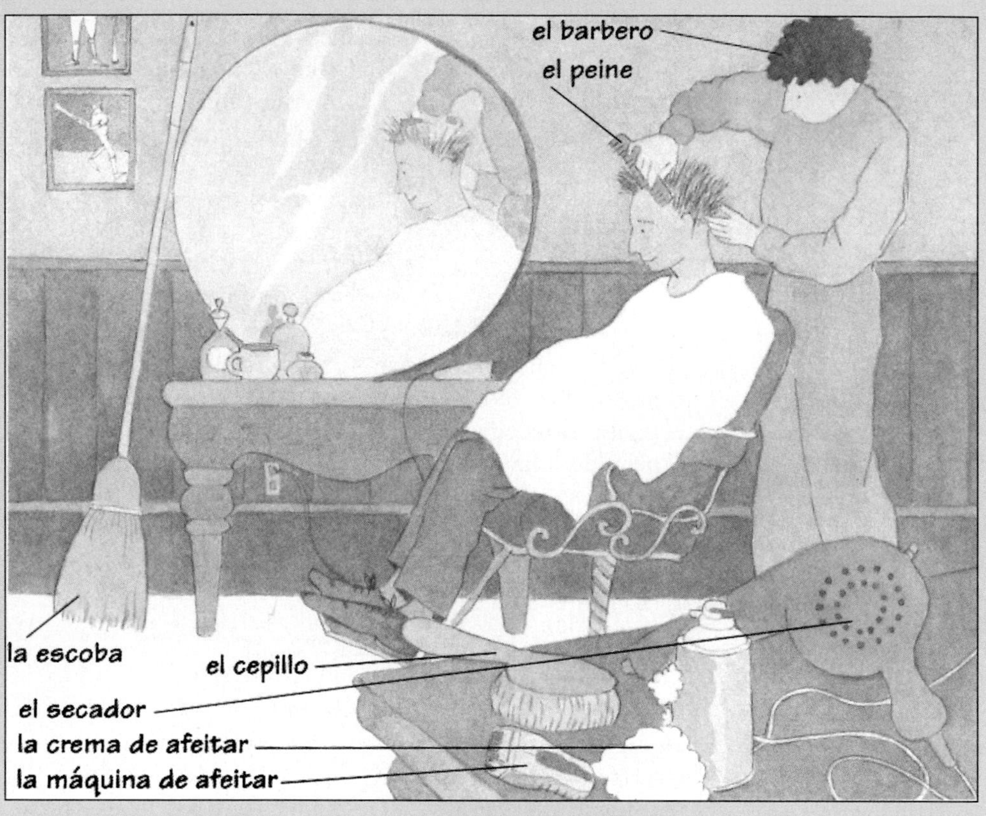


### Verbos útiles

**ensuciar(se)** to get (oneself) dirty — El niño **se ensució** las manos.
**olvidarse (de)** to forget — **Me olvidé de** pedir turno en la peluquería.
**peinar(se)** to comb or style one's hair — **Me voy a peinar** antes de salir.
**regalar** to give (as a gift) — María me **regaló** un vestido verde.

## ¡Conversemos!

Answer the following questions, basing your answers on the dialogues.

1. ¿Para qué se levantaron temprano hoy Mirta e Isabel?
2. ¿Qué van a hacer las chicas esta noche?
3. ¿Quién le va a pasar la aspiradora a la alfombra?
4. ¿Qué va a planchar Isabel? ¿Para qué?
5. ¿Quién celebra su cumpleaños mañana?

6. ¿Sabe Mirta qué ponerse esta noche?
7. ¿Por qué no se pone Mirta el vestido azul?
8. ¿Qué tiene que hacer Isabel antes de ir a la peluquería?
9. ¿Por qué no quiere Isabel una permanente?
10. ¿Dónde dejó Isabel la cartera?
11. ¿Qué le pregunta el peluquero a Isabel?
12. ¿Por qué es mejor ir a la peluquería por la mañana?

## ¿Lo sabía Ud.?

**Asunción** es la capital de Paraguay. La ciudad fue fundada en el año 1537. Allí se ve un contraste muy grande entre los edificios muy modernos y las casas coloniales. No muchos turistas visitan esta encantadora *(charming)* ciudad, pero los que lo hacen hablan muy bien de la hospitalidad de los paraguayos.

**Paraguay** tiene más o menos el tamaño *(size)* de California. Su moneda es el **guaraní,** que es de valor bastante estable. El idioma oficial es el español, pero los paraguayos hablan también el guaraní, un idioma indígena que aún se conserva y que se enseña en las escuelas. Alrededor *(Around)* del ochenta y uno por ciento de la población sabe leer y escribir.

- ¿Sabe Ud. cuándo fue fundada la ciudad donde Ud. vive?
- ¿El dólar es de valor estable o no?
- ¿Qué idiomas indígenas se hablan en este país?
- ¿Qué por ciento de la población de este país sabe leer y escribir?

Edificios modernos junto a casas viejas en Asunción, Paraguay.

INTERNET

See the *¿Cómo se dice...?* Web site for activities on authentic cultural material: http://spanish.college.hmco.com/students

# Pronunciación

## La entonación

Intonation refers to the variations in the pitch of your voice when you are talking. Intonation patterns in Spanish are different from those in English. Note the following regarding Spanish intonation.

1. For normal statements, the pitch generally rises on the first stressed syllable.

Yo compré el regalo para Elena.

2. For questions eliciting information, the pitch is highest on the stressed syllable of the interrogative pronoun.

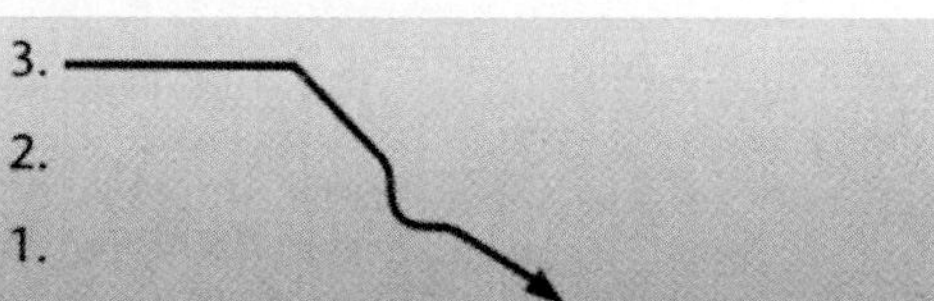


¿Cómo está tu mamá?

3. For questions that can be answered with **sí** or **no,** the pitch is generally highest on the last stressed syllable.

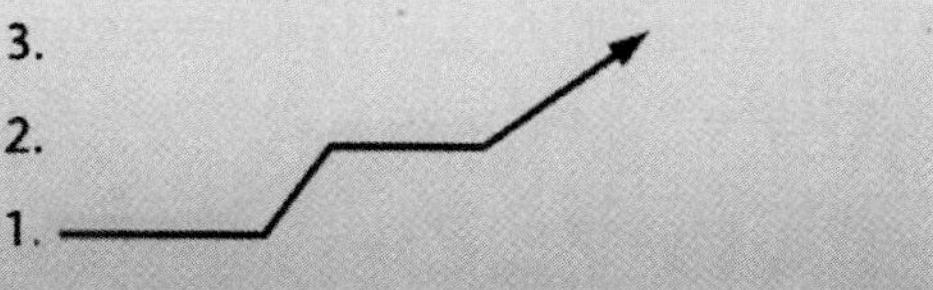


¿Fuiste al mercado ayer?

4. In exclamations, the pitch is highest on the first stressed syllable.

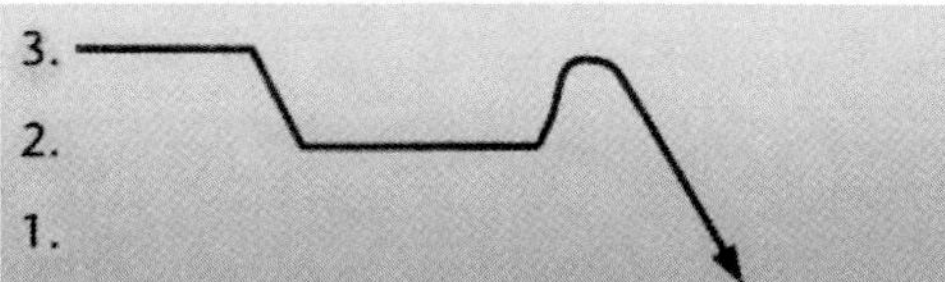


¡Qué bonita es esa alfombra!

Listen to your instructor and repeat the following sentences, imitating closely your instructor's intonation.

1. Marta no trabajó anoche.
2. ¿Dónde vive tu hermano?
3. ¿Le diste el dinero a Ramona?
4. ¡Qué delgado es ese muchacho!
5. ¿Vas a ir a la peluquería?
6. ¿Quién puede llevarte?

## 1 Reflexive constructions *(Construcciones reflexivas)*

### A. Reflexive pronouns

| ***Subjects*** | ***Reflexive pronouns*** | |
|---|---|---|
| yo | **me** | *myself, to (for) myself* |
| tú | **te** | *yourself, to (for) yourself* (**tú** form) |
| nosotros(-as) | **nos** | *ourselves, to (for) ourselves* |
| vosotros(-as) | **os** | *yourselves, to (for) yourselves* (**vosotros** form) |
| Ud. | **se** | *yourself, to (for) yourself* (**Ud.** form) |
| Uds. | **se** | *yourselves, to (for) yourselves* (**Uds.** form) |
| él | **se** | *himself, to (for) himself* |
| ella | **se** | *herself, to (for) herself* |
| | **se** | *itself, to (for) itself* |
| ellos, ellas | **se** | *themselves, to (for) themselves* |

- Reflexive pronouns are used whenever the direct or indirect object is the same as the subject of the sentence.
- Note that except for **se,** the reflexive pronouns have the same forms as the direct and indirect object pronouns.
- The third-person singular and plural **se** is invariable.
- Reflexive pronouns are positioned in the sentence in the same manner as object pronouns. They are placed in front of a conjugated verb: **Yo *me* levanto;** or they may be attached to an infinitive or to a present participle: **Yo voy a levantar*me*. Yo estoy levantándo*me*.**

## B. Reflexive verbs

■ Many verbs can be made reflexive in Spanish, that is, they can be made to act upon the subject, by the use of a reflexive pronoun.

| **lavarse** | *to wash oneself* |
|---|---|
| Yo **me lavo** | *I wash (myself)* |
| Tú **te lavas** | *You wash (yourself)* (**tú** form) |
| Ud. **se lava** | *You wash (yourself)* (**Ud.** form) |
| Él **se lava** | *He washes (himself)* |
| Ella **se lava** | *She washes (herself)* |
| Nosotros(-as) **nos lavamos** | *We wash (ourselves)* |
| Vosotros(-as) **os laváis** | *You wash (yourselves)* (**vosotros** form) |
| Uds. **se lavan** | *You wash (yourselves)* (**Uds.** form) |
| Ellos **se lavan** | *They* (masc.) *wash (themselves)* |
| Ellas **se lavan** | *They* (fem.) *wash (themselves)* |

Julia baña al perro.

Julia se baña.

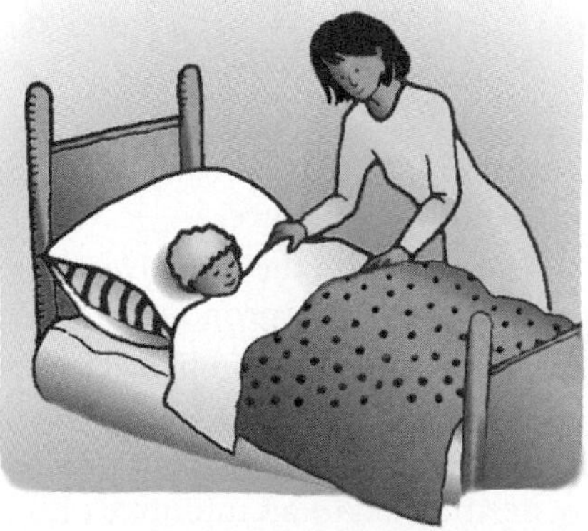

Elsa acuesta a su hijo a las siete.

Elsa se acuesta a las diez.

- In addition to the verbs included in the vocabulary list, the following verbs are commonly used in reflexive constructions.

**afeitarse** *to shave*
**despertarse (e:ie)** *to wake up*
**desvestirse (e:i)** *to get undressed*
**preocuparse (por)** *to worry (about)*
**sentirse (e:ie)** *to feel* (mood or physical condition)

| | |
|---|---|
| —¿A qué hora **se acuestan** Uds.? | *"What time do you go to bed?"* |
| —Yo **me acuesto** a las diez y Ana **se acuesta** a las doce. | *"I go to bed at ten and Ana goes to bed at twelve."* |
| —¿Cómo te sientes? | *"How do you feel?"* |
| —Me siento bien, gracias. | *"I feel fine, thank you."* |

**ATENCIÓN** The Spanish reflexives are seldom translated using the reflexive pronouns in English: **Yo me acuesto** = *I go to bed.*

- The following verbs have different meanings when they are used with reflexive pronouns.

| | |
|---|---|
| **acostar (o:ue)** *to put to bed* | **acostarse** *to go to bed* |
| **dormir (o:ue)** *to sleep* | **dormirse** *to fall asleep* |
| **ir** *to go* | **irse** *to go away, leave* |
| **levantar** *to raise, lift* | **levantarse** *to get up* |
| **llamar** *to call* | **llamarse** *to be called* |
| **poner** *to put, place* | **ponerse** *to put on* |
| **probar (o:ue)** *to try; to taste* | **probarse** *to try on* |
| **quitar** *to take away* | **quitarse** *to take off* |

| | |
|---|---|
| —¿Te vas a **acostar**? | *"Are you going to go to bed?"* |
| —Sí, pero primero voy a **acostar** a los niños. | *"Yes, but first, I'm going to put the children to bed."* |

## práctica

**A.** Say what you and your relatives normally do by adding the correct form of the missing verbs.

1. Mi tía siempre ________ (despertarse) tarde.
2. Yo ________ (levantarse) muy temprano.
3. Mi padre ________ (afeitarse) en el baño.
4. Nosotros ________ (bañarse) por la mañana.
5. Mi hermana ________ (lavarse) la cabeza todos los días.
6. Mis primos ________ (vestirse) en diez minutos.
7. Yo ________ (desvestirse) y ________ (acostarse).
8. Mi mamá ________ (preocuparse) mucho cuando yo llego tarde.

**B.** Say what these people are doing.

1. María ________ bien.

2. Los estudiantes ________ en la clase.

3. Juan le ________ el dinero al niño.

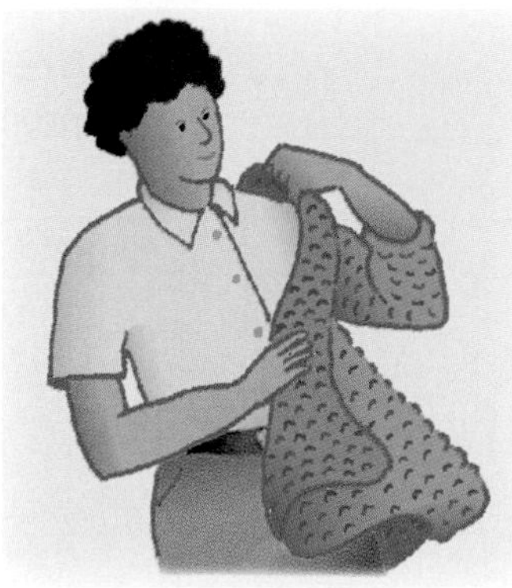

4. Pepito ________ el suéter.

5. Yo ________ la ________ en la clase.

6. Yo ________ a las seis.

7. Rosa ________ el ________ en la ________.

8. Rosa ________ el ________.

9. Sergio ________ a Eva.

10. El muchacho ________ Sergio ________.

C. Interview a classmate, using the following questions and two questions of your own. When you have finished, switch roles.

1. ¿A qué hora te levantas tú generalmente? ¿y los sábados?
2. ¿A qué hora te levantaste hoy?
3. ¿A qué hora te acuestas?
4. ¿A qué hora te acostaste anoche?
5. ¿Puedes bañarte y vestirte en diez minutos?
6. ¿Te lavas la cabeza cuando te bañas?
7. ¿Te miras en el espejo para peinarte?
8. ¿Te acordaste de traer el libro de español?
9. ¿Cómo se llama tu mejor amigo(-a)?
10. ¿Se preocupan tus padres por ti?

D. With a partner, take turns saying what these people do according to the time and the circumstances.

1. A las seis de la mañana, yo ________.
2. En el baño, Carlos ________ con champú.
3. Antes de salir, tú te bañas y te ________.
4. En la tienda, antes de comprar un vestido, Rocío ________.
5. Cuando hace mucho frío, nosotros ________.
6. Frente al espejo, mi hermana ________.
7. Mi papá ________ con una máquina de afeitar.
8. Cuando yo vuelvo a mi casa muy tarde, mis padres ________.
9. En la clase, cuando están aburridos, los estudiantes ________.
10. A las once de la noche, Uds. ________.

**Summary of Personal Pronouns**

| *Subject* | *Direct object* | *Indirect object* | *Reflexive* | *Object of prepositions* |
|---|---|---|---|---|
| yo | me | me | me | mí |
| tú | te | te | te | ti |
| usted *(fem.)* | la | le | se | usted |
| usted *(masc.)* | lo | | | usted |
| él | lo | | | él |
| ella | la | | | ella |
| nosotros(-as) | nos | nos | nos | nosotros(-as) |
| vosotros(-as) | os | os | os | vosotros(-as) |
| ustedes *(fem.)* | las | les | se | ustedes |
| ustedes *(masc.)* | los | | | ustedes |
| ellos | los | | | ellos |
| ellas | las | | | ellas |

## 2 Some uses of the definite article *(Algunos usos del artículo definido)*

The definite article has the following uses in Spanish.

- The possessive adjective is often replaced by the definite article. An indirect object pronoun or a reflexive pronoun (if the subject performs the action upon himself or herself) usually indicates who the possessor is. Note the use of the definite article in Spanish in the following specific situations indicating possession.
- With parts of the body

| | |
|---|---|
| Voy a cortar**le el pelo.** | *I'm going to cut his hair.* |
| **Me** lavé **las manos.** | *I washed my hands.* |

- With articles of clothing and personal belongings

| | |
|---|---|
| **¿Te** quitaste **el vestido?** | *Did you take off your dress?* |
| Ellos **se** quitaron **el suéter.** | *They took off their sweaters.* |

**ATENCIÓN** The number of the subject and verb generally does not affect the number of the thing possessed. Spanish uses the singular to indicate that each person has only one of any particular object.

| | |
|---|---|
| Ellas se quitaron **el vestido.** (Each one has one dress.) | *They took off their dresses.* |
| *but:* Ellas se quitaron **los zapatos.** (Each one has two shoes.) | *They took off their shoes.* |

- The definite article is used with abstract and generic nouns.

| | |
|---|---|
| Me gusta **el té,** pero prefiero **el café.** | *I like tea, but I prefer coffee.* |
| **Las madres** siempre se preocupan por sus hijos. | *Mothers always worry about their children.* |
| **La educación** es muy importante. | *Education is very important.* |

- The definite article is used with certain nouns, including **cárcel** *(jail),* **iglesia** *(church),* and **escuela** when they are preceded by a preposition.

| | |
|---|---|
| —¿Vas a **la iglesia** los viernes? | *"Do you go to church on Fridays?"* |
| —No, voy a **la escuela.** | *"No, I go to school."* |

- Remember that the definite article is also used with days of the week, when indicating titles in indirect address, and when telling time.

| | |
|---|---|
| **El Sr. Vega** viene **el sábado** a **las tres** de la tarde. | *Mr. Vega is coming on Saturday at three o'clock in the afternoon.* |

## práctica

**A.** Interview a classmate, using the following questions. When you have finished, switch roles.

1. ¿Qué te gusta más, el pavo relleno o el arroz con pollo?
2. ¿Qué les gusta más a tus padres, el café o el té?
3. ¿Te gustan los rizos o prefieres el pelo lacio?
4. ¿Quién te corta el pelo?
5. ¿Con qué champú te lavas la cabeza?
6. ¿Te quitas los zapatos cuando llegas a tu casa?
7. ¿Te gustan los idiomas extranjeros *(foreign)*?
8. ¿Te gusta más el francés o el español?
9. ¿Vas a la iglesia los domingos?
10. ¿Qué es más importante para ti, el amor o el dinero?

**B.** Supply the Spanish equivalent of the words in parentheses. Then act out the dialogues with a partner.

1. —¿Qué están haciendo ________ Paz y ________ Díaz? *(Miss / Mrs.)*
   —Se están poniendo ________. *(their dresses)*
2. —¿Te ensuciaste ________, Paquito? *(your hands)*
   —Sí, pero ________. *(I washed them)*

3. —________ son más inteligentes que ________. *(Women / men)*
   —________ siempre dicen eso. *(Women)*
4. —¿Él está en ________? *(school)*
   —Sí, pero su hermano está en ________. *(jail)*
5. —¿Qué dice ________ Peña? *(Dr.)*
   —Ella dice que ________ es muy importante. *(education)*

## 3 Possessive pronouns *(Pronombres posesivos)*

| ***Singular*** | | ***Plural*** | | |
|---|---|---|---|---|
| ***Masculine*** | ***Feminine*** | ***Masculine*** | ***Feminine*** | |
| el mío | la mía | los míos | las mías | *mine* |
| el tuyo | la tuya | los tuyos | las tuyas | *yours* (fam.) |
| el suyo | la suya | los suyos | las suyas | *yours* (form.) / *his* / *hers* |
| el nuestro | la nuestra | los nuestros | las nuestras | *ours* |
| el vuestro | la vuestra | los vuestros | las vuestras | *yours* (fam.) |
| el suyo | la suya | los suyos | las suyas | *yours* (form.) / *theirs* |

■ In Spanish, possessive pronouns agree in gender and number with the thing possessed. They are generally used with the definite article.

| | |
|---|---|
| —Aquí están **mis maletas.** ¿Dónde están **las tuyas?** | *"Here are my suitcases. Where are yours?"* |
| —**Las mías** están en mi cuarto. | *"Mine are in my room."* |
| —**Nuestro profesor** es de Colombia. | *"Our professor is from Colombia."* |
| —**El nuestro** es de Venezuela. | *"Ours is from Venezuela."* |
| —**Mi apartamento** está en la calle Palma. | *"My apartment is on Palma Street."* |
| —**El mío** está en la calle Estrella. | *"Mine is on Estrella Street."* |

**ATENCIÓN** After the verb **ser,** the definite article is frequently omitted.

| | |
|---|---|
| —¿Estos billetes son **suyos,** señor? | *"Are these tickets yours, sir?"* |
| —No, no son **míos.** | *"No, they're not mine."* |

■ Because the third-person forms of the possessive pronouns (**el suyo, la suya, los suyos, las suyas**) can be ambiguous, they can be replaced by the pronouns on the next page for clarification.

| | | |
|---|---|---|
| el de<br>la de<br>los de<br>las de | Ud.<br>él<br>ella<br>Uds.<br>ellos<br>ellas | el [libro] de él<br>el **de él**<br><br>Es **suyo.** *(unclarified)*<br>Es **el de él.** *(clarified)* |

—Estas maletas son de Eva y de Jorge, ¿no?
—Bueno, la maleta azul es **de ella** y la maleta marrón es **de él.**

*"These suitcases are Eva's and Jorge's, aren't they?"*
*"Well, the blue suitcase is hers, and the brown suitcase is his."*

—¿El espejo es **de Uds.?**
—No, es **de ellos.**

*"Is the mirror yours?"*
*"No, it's theirs."*

## práctica

**A.** Provide the correct possessive pronoun for each subject.

MODELO: Yo tengo una tarjeta postal. Es...
*Yo tengo una tarjeta postal. Es mía.*

1. Mario tiene una revista. Es...
2. Nosotros tenemos dos entradas. Son...
3. Tú tienes un espejo. Es...
4. Inés tiene dos pinturas. Son...
5. Yo tengo dos casas. Son...
6. Ud. tiene un perro. Es...
7. Ellas tienen los vestidos. Son...
8. Paco tiene una botella de vino. Es...

**B.** Complete the following dialogue using the correct possessive pronoun.

1. —Mis entradas están aquí. ¿Dónde están ________, Anita? *(yours)*
   —________ están en mi cuarto, pero Pedro no tiene ________. *(Mine / his)*
2. —Yo no tengo maletas, pero Ana me va a prestar una de ________. *(hers)*
   —O yo puedo prestarte una de ________. *(mine)*
   —¡Pero tú vas a necesitar todas ________! *(yours)*
   —Yo tengo tres maletas...
3. —Mis hijos están en Lima. ¿Dónde están ________, señor Fuentes? *(yours)*
   —________ están en Arequipa. *(Mine)*

**C.** With a partner, make comparisons between the objects and people described and those in your own experience. Use appropriate possessive pronouns when asking each other questions.

MODELO: —El hermano de Teresa tiene quince años. ¿Y el tuyo?
*—El mío tiene dieciocho.*

1. Los mejores amigos de Rosa son de Cuba.
2. El apartamento de Ana tiene cuatro cuartos.

3. Los padres de Ramiro viven en San Diego.
4. El cumpleaños de Jorge es en septiembre.
5. Las maletas de Alina son verdes.
6. La hermana de Rafael es muy bonita.
7. El idioma de Hans es alemán.
8. Las primas de Enrique son uruguayas.

Now, with your partner, compare other aspects of your lives, such as your room or apartment, relatives, classes, car, tapes, jobs, and so on.

## 4 Irregular preterits *(Pretéritos irregulares)*

- The following Spanish verbs are irregular in the preterit.

| | |
|---|---|
| **tener:** | tuve, tuviste, tuvo, tuvimos, tuvisteis, tuvieron |
| **estar:** | estuve, estuviste, estuvo, estuvimos, estuvisteis, estuvieron |
| **poder:** | pude, pudiste, pudo, pudimos, pudisteis, pudieron |
| **poner:** | puse, pusiste, puso, pusimos, pusisteis, pusieron |
| **saber:** | supe, supiste, supo, supimos, supisteis, supieron |
| **hacer:** | hice, hiciste, hizo,[1] hicimos, hicisteis, hicieron |
| **venir:** | vine, viniste, vino, vinimos, vinisteis, vinieron |
| **querer:** | quise, quisiste, quiso, quisimos, quisisteis, quisieron |
| **decir:** | dije, dijiste, dijo, dijimos, dijisteis, dijeron[2] |
| **traer:** | traje, trajiste, trajo, trajimos, trajisteis, trajeron[2] |
| **conducir:** | conduje, condujiste, condujo, condujimos, condujisteis, condujeron[2] |
| **traducir:** | traduje, tradujiste, tradujo, tradujimos, tradujisteis, tradujeron[2] |

| | |
|---|---|
| —¿Por qué no **viniste** anoche? | *"Why didn't you come last night?"* |
| —No **pude; tuve** que trabajar. Y tú, ¿qué **hiciste**? | *"I wasn't able to; I had to work. And you, what did you do?"* |
| —Yo **estuve** en casa toda la noche. | *"I was home all night."* |
| —¿Qué me **trajeron** Uds.? | *"What did you bring me?"* |
| —Te **trajimos** una cartera. | *"We brought you a purse."* |
| —¿Dónde la **pusieron?** | *"Where did you put it?"* |
| —La **pusimos** en tu cuarto. | *"We put it in your room."* |

**ATENCIÓN** The preterit of **hay** (impersonal form of **haber**) is **hubo** *(there was, there were).*

| | |
|---|---|
| Anoche **hubo** un concierto. | *Last night there was a concert.* |

---

[1]Note that in the third-person singular form, **c** changes to **z** in order to maintain the soft sound.
[2]Note that in the third-person plural ending of these verbs, the **i** is omitted.

## práctica

**A.** Elsa and David are arguing. Complete their dialogue, using the preterit of the verbs given. Then act it out with a partner.

ELSA —¿Dónde ________ (estar) (tú) anoche?
¡ ________ (Venir) muy tarde!
DAVID —¡Te lo ________ (decir)! ________ (Estar) en casa de mamá.
________ (Tener) que hablar con papá. No te llamé porque no
________ (poder).
ELSA —¿No ________ (poder) o no ________ (querer)?
DAVID —Bueno. ¿Dónde ________ (poner) tú las cartas que yo
________ (traducir) ayer en la oficina?
ELSA —¡Tú no ________ (traer) ninguna carta!
DAVID —No... los empleados las ________ (traer) cuando ________
(venir) ayer.
ELSA —Ellos no me ________ (decir) nada. ¡Son unos idiotas!

**B.** Answer the following questions about yourself and your friends.

1. ¿Qué tuvo que hacer ayer?
2. ¿Qué hicieron sus amigos ayer?
3. ¿Dónde estuvieron Uds. anoche?
4. ¿Hubo una fiesta en su casa ayer?
5. ¿Uds. tuvieron que limpiar la casa?
6. ¿Vino a clase la semana pasada?
7. ¿Pudo venir Ud. temprano a la universidad ayer?
8. ¿Condujo su coche ayer?

**C.** Read what the following people typically do. Then, using your imagination, say what everyone did differently yesterday.

1. Yo estoy en mi casa por la mañana.
2. Tú vienes a la universidad a las diez de la mañana.
3. Paquito hace la tarea por la tarde.
4. Julio tiene que trabajar en el hospital.
5. Nosotros traemos a nuestros hijos a la escuela.
6. Ellos traducen las lecciones al inglés.
7. María se pone el vestido azul.
8. Yo conduzco mi coche.

**D.** In groups of three, prepare some questions for your instructor about what he or she did yesterday, last night, or last week. Use irregular preterit forms in your questions.

## 5 Formation of adverbs *(La formación de los adverbios)*

- Most Spanish adverbs are formed by adding **-mente** (the equivalent of the English *-ly*) to the adjective.

| | | | |
|---|---|---|---|
| especial | *special* | especial**mente** | *especially* |
| reciente | *recent* | reciente**mente** | *recently* |
| general | *general* | general**mente** | *generally* |

- Adjectives ending in **-o** change the **-o** to **-a** before adding **-mente.**

| | | | |
|---|---|---|---|
| lento | *slow* | lent**amente** | *slowly* |
| rápido | *rapid* | rápid**amente** | *rapidly* |
| desafortunado | *unfortunate* | desafortunad**amente** | *unfortunately* |

- If two or more adverbs are used together, both change the **-o** to **-a,** but only the last adverb takes the **-mente** ending.

—Habló clara y **lentamente.** *He spoke clearly and slowly.*

- If the adjective has an accent, the adverb retains it.

fácil **fácilmente**

### práctica

**A.** Change the following adjectives to adverbs.

1. fácil
2. feliz
3. claro *(clear)*
4. raro *(rare)*
5. necesario
6. frecuente *(frequent)*
7. triste
8. trágico *(tragic)*
9. alegre *(merry)*
10. desgraciado

**B.** Complete the following sentences with appropriate adverbs.

1. Ellos hablaron ________ y ________.
2. Mis padres vienen a verme ________.
3. Jaime llegó ________.
4. El muchacho me habló ________.
5. ________ me levanto a las siete.
6. Los muchachos cantan ________.
7. ________ no tengo dinero.
8. Compré esa máquina de afeitar ________ para ti.
9. ________ no pude ir a México con ellos.

**C.** Interview a classmate, using the following questions and two of your own. Include adverbs in your responses. When you have finished, switch roles.

1. ¿A qué hora te levantas tú?
2. ¿Tú y tu familia van de compras juntos?
3. ¿Tú ves a tus abuelos a menudo *(often)*?
4. ¿Vas al teatro a menudo?
5. ¿Tú tienes mucho dinero?

**D.** With a partner, discuss what you frequently do, rarely do, and what, unfortunately, you can't do.

# ¡A ver cuánto aprendió!

**INTERNET**

See the *¿Cómo se dice...?* Web site for additional grammar and vocabulary practice: http://spanish.college.hmco.com/students

## ¡Repase el vocabulario!

Say whether the following statements are logical or not. If they're not logical, give a statement that is.

1. El perro limpió el apartamento.
2. No puedo afeitarme porque no tengo escoba.
3. Elvira lee una revista en la peluquería.
4. Tengo el pelo muy lacio. Necesito un rizador.
5. Generalmente pongo el recogedor en el botiquín.
6. Tengo que ir a la tienda porque necesito corte, lavado y peinado.
7. No estoy haciendo nada. Estoy muy ocupado.
8. Ahora podemos comer porque yo ya cociné. Preparé cordero y arroz.
9. No quiero una permanente porque no me gustan los rizos.
10. Una semana tiene diez días.
11. Me voy. El peluquero no terminó de cortarme el pelo.
12. Nunca me olvido de nada. Siempre me acuerdo de todo.
13. El peluquero me cortó el pelo.
14. Necesito el secador para planchar mi vestido.
15. Generalmente hay menos gente en la peluquería por la mañana.

## Entrevista

With a partner, interview each other by asking the following questions.

1. ¿Te gusta el pelo corto o el pelo largo?
2. ¿Vas a pedir turno en la peluquería? ¿Para cuándo?
3. ¿Te lavas la cabeza todos los días?
4. ¿Crees que está de moda el pelo corto o el pelo largo?
5. ¿Estás invitado(-a) a alguna fiesta el sábado?
6. ¿Tienes algo que ponerte para ir a una fiesta?
7. ¿Qué le vas a regalar a tu mejor amigo(-a) para su cumpleaños?
8. ¿Barres la cocina o le pasas la aspiradora?
9. ¿Sabes cocinar?
10. ¿Siempre limpias la cocina cuando la ensucias?
11. ¿Por quién te preocupas tú a veces *(sometimes)*?
12. Generalmente ¿a qué hora te acuestas?

## Situaciones

What would you say in the following situations? What might the other person say?

1. You are at home. Ask your younger brother if he bathed and combed his hair. Also ask if he cleaned his room. Tell him he has to sweep the kitchen.
2. Someone asks about your schedule. Tell him or her what time you generally go to bed and get up. Also say how long it takes you to bathe and get dressed.

3. You are at the beauty parlor (barbershop). Tell the hairdresser (barber) what you want done. Then make an appointment for next month.

## Para escribir

Write a composition about your daily routine. Say what you do from the time you wake up until the time you go to bed.

# En la vida real

CD-ROM

Do the interactive exercises on the CD-ROM for additional practice.

## ¡Vamos a la peluquería!

Carefully read the following ads for two hair salons, and then answer the questions that follow.

**PELUQUERÍA ANABEL**

*Especiales de esta semana*

Permanentes de . . . . . . . . . . . .$35 a $50
Tinte . . . . . . . . . . . . . . . . . . . . .$15
Manicura . . . . . . . . . . . . . . . . $7
Corte . . . . . . . . . . . . . . . . . . . . .$8
Corte, lavado y peinado . . . . . .$20

Abierto de martes a sábado
Martes a viernes de 9 a 5
Sábados de 8 a 6

**Avenida Paz #28 Teléfono 287–3574**

*Si presenta este anuncio Ud. recibe un 10% de descuento.*

*Salón de belleza La Época*

- Expertos peluqueros y barberos
- Especialidad en permanentes
- Tenemos los mejores equipos y los precios más bajos para hombres y mujeres.

**Abierto de lunes a sábado de 9 a 5**
**Calle Bolívar No. 439**

**Para pedir su turno llame al teléfono 287–2308**

*Martes precios especiales para mayores de 50 años.*

1. En la peluquería Anabel, ¿cuál es el precio mínimo de una permanente?
2. Si Ud. quiere cortarse el pelo el lunes, ¿a qué peluquería puede ir?
3. Su hermano desea afeitarse y cortarse el pelo. ¿Puede ir a la peluquería Anabel? ¿Por qué sí o por qué no?
4. ¿Adónde puede ir? ¿Por qué?
5. ¿Por qué es importante tener el anuncio de la peluquería Anabel?
6. ¿Cuánto hay que pagar por un tinte y por un corte de pelo?
7. Mi abuela tiene 58 años. ¿Por qué debe ir a la peluquería La Época y qué día debe ir?
8. ¿A qué teléfono debe llamar ella para pedir turno?
9. ¿Cuál es la especialidad del salón de belleza La Época?
10. ¿Cuál es la dirección de la peluquería Anabel?

## Una visita importante

With a classmate, act out a scene involving two roommates who are expecting a visitor. Discuss what you have to do in order to get the house (apartment) and yourselves ready for your guest, and divide up the chores that must be done.

## ¿Qué es?

The class will be divided into two teams. Your instructor will give each student an item from the vocabulary list in this lesson to draw on the board. The other members of the team must try to guess what is being drawn. If they guess within one minute, they get a point.

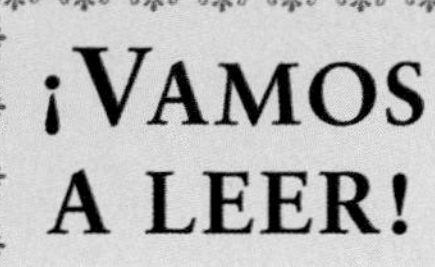


## Antes de leer

A. Before you read the fable of the hare and the tortoise (**la liebre y la tortuga**), think about things you already know that may be useful to you as you read. For example, what characteristics are typically associated with hares and tortoises? What is the purpose of a fable? With the answers to these questions in mind, make a brief list of vocabulary you might expect to encounter in the reading.

B. As you read the fable, find the answers to the following questions.

1. ¿Por qué se burla continuamente la liebre de la tortuga?
2. ¿Qué le hace la tortuga a la liebre en presencia de los otros animales?
3. ¿Cómo responde la liebre?
4. ¿A quién nombran *(name)* juez de la carrera?
5. Durante la carrera, ¿qué hace la liebre? ¿Y la tortuga?
6. ¿Cómo termina la carrera?
7. ¿Cuál es la moraleja *(moral)* de la fábula?

# *La liebre y la tortuga*

(FÁBULA DE ESOPO°) — *Aesop*

Una liebre° se burla° continuamente de una tortuga,° porque la pobre tortuga es muy lenta. — *hare / makes fun / tortoise*

La tortuga no quiere hacer caso de° las burlas de la liebre, pero un día, harta° de oírlas, decide desafiar° a la liebre, en presencia de los otros animales, a tener una carrera.° — **hacer...** *to pay attention to*; *fed up / to challenge*; *race*

—¡Qué idea! —dice la liebre—. Tú sabes muy bien que las tortugas no pueden ganar° ninguna carrera... — *win*

—¡Ésa es tu opinión! ¿Estás lista° para comenzar? — *ready*

Los animales nombran juez° al zorro° y empieza la carrera. En dos segundos, la liebre desaparece. La tortuga empieza a caminar° con su lentitud de siempre. — *judge / fox*; *to walk*

Al rato, la liebre se detiene° para esperar a la tortuga. Espera y espera hasta que empieza a tener sueño. — *stops*

—Puedo dormir una siesta° y continuar la carrera más tarde —piensa la liebre. Y se duerme, tranquila y feliz, en la verde hierba.° — *nap*; *grass*

Mientras tanto,° la tortuga sigue caminando lentamente pero sin parar° y pasa a la liebre, que continúa durmiendo. — **Mientras...** *Meanwhile* / **sin...** *without stopping*

Lenta y paciente, la tortuga gana la carrera. La liebre, avergonzada,° se queda donde está sin mirar a los animales que aclaman° a la tortuga victoriosa. — *ashamed*; *are applauding*

Moraleja: *Con perseverancia se gana a veces° la carrera.* — **a...** *sometimes*

## Díganos

Answer the following questions, based on your own thoughts and experiences.

1. ¿Ud. se burla de alguien a veces? ¿Por qué?
2. ¿De qué o de quién está harto(-a) Ud.?
3. ¿Ud. se identifica con la liebre o con la tortuga? ¿Por qué?

# ASÍ SOMOS

VIDEO

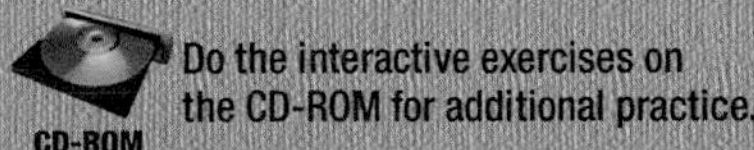
CD-ROM
Do the interactive exercises on the CD-ROM for additional practice.

NARRADORA —¿Cómo es su rutina diaria?

ZAIDA —Mi rutina diaria comienza entre seis y siete de la mañana de acuerdo a la hora en que tenga clase. Eh... me levanto a las seis y media, tomo una ducha *(I take a shower)*, me visto para ir a la universidad. Tengo clase de siete a cuatro de la tarde todos los días. Y almuerzo a las once de la mañana...

## Preparación

**A. Su rutina diaria.** Answer the following questions based on your own information. You will hear answers to some of these questions when you watch the video. After viewing the video, compare your answers with those you hear.

1. ¿Cómo es su rutina diaria?
2. ¿A qué hora se levanta?
3. ¿A qué hora desayuna? ¿A qué hora almuerza? ¿A qué hora cena?
4. ¿A qué hora se acuesta?
5. ¿Quién hace los trabajos de la casa? ¿Qué día los hace?

**B. Mis quehaceres favoritos.** Make a list of the household chores you know in Spanish. Then rate them in order of your preference, from your favorite chore to your least favorite chore. Share your list with the class.

## Comprensión

**A. ¿Verdadero o falso?** Read the following statements. Circle **V** (**Verdadero**) or **F** (**Falso**) according to what you understood from the video. If a statement is false, correct it.

V F 1. Por lo regular *(As a rule)* Pedro hace ejercicio por la mañana.
V F 2. Pedro come con sus amigos en la universidad.
V F 3. Pedro y sus amigos juegan futbolito *(soccer)* o billar *(billiards)* por la tarde.
V F 4. Zaida se levanta muy tarde.
V F 5. Zaida tiene clase sólo por la mañana.
V F 6. Zaida va al gimnasio por la tarde.
V F 7. Juan se levanta temprano.
V F 8. Juan duerme una siestecita *(little nap)* por la tarde.
V F 9. Juan sale con su novia o con sus amigos después de cenar *(after having dinner)*.
V F 10. Anselmo no tiene hijos.
V F 11. Anselmo sale de casa a las siete y media.
V F 12. Anselmo llega a la oficina a las nueve.

**B. ¿Quién lo dijo?** Match each statement with the name of the person who said it.

| A | B |
|---|---|
| _____ 1. Una vez a la semana hacemos la limpieza general de toda la casa. | a. Zaida |
| _____ 2. Una señora y mi madre hacen los trabajos de la casa. | b. Gustavo |
| _____ 3. Mis compañeras y yo nos turnamos *(take turns)* para limpiar la casa. | c. Otmara |
| _____ 4. Tengo una señora que nos limpia la casa. | d. Ángela |
| _____ 5. Todos ayudamos y cooperamos en la casa. | e. Juan |

## Ampliación

**A. La rutina diaria.** With a partner, compare your daily routine on a school day with your daily routine on a weekend day. Share your observations with the class.

**B. Los quehaceres de la casa.** Make a list of all the household chores you know in Spanish. Then, make a schedule for when each chore needs to be done and assign a person to do them. Share your schedule with the class.

Take this test. When you have finished, check your answers in the answer key provided in Appendix E. Then use a red pen to correct any mistakes you may have made. Are you ready?

## Lección 7

### A. Demonstrative adjectives and pronouns

Give the Spanish equivalent of the following.

1. these postcards and those (over there)
2. that suitcase and this one
3. these travel agencies and those (over there)
4. this plane and that one (over there)
5. this boat and that one
6. these letters and those

### B. Indirect object pronouns

Rewrite the following sentences, using indirect object pronouns to replace the words in italics.

1. Ella trae la lista *para ellos*.
2. Yo voy a preparar un sándwich *para ti*.
3. Él trae el equipaje *para Ud*.
4. Ana va a comprar las tarjetas postales *para mí*.
5. El agente de viajes trae los pasajes *para nosotros*.
6. Traen los cheques de viajeros *para ellas*.

### C. Constructions with *gustar*

Write the following sentences in Spanish.

1. I don't like that travel agency.
2. He likes the aisle seat.
3. Do you like this carry-on bag?
4. We don't like to travel by plane.
5. Do they like their hotel?

### D. Time expressions with *hacer*

Form sentences with the elements provided, using the expression **hace... que** to report how long an event has been going on. Follow the model.

> MODELO: una hora / nosotros / trabajar
> *Hace una hora que nosotros trabajamos.*

1. dos días / yo / no dormir
2. un mes / tú / no llamarme
3. media hora / nosotros / estar aquí
4. un año / ellos / vivir / España
5. doce horas / mi hija / no comer

### E. Preterit of regular verbs

Rewrite the following sentences so that instead of describing things that *are going to happen*, they describe things that *already happened*.

1. Mañana Luisa y yo vamos a comprar los billetes. (ayer)
2. La semana próxima yo voy a viajar. (la semana pasada)
3. Hoy ella va a presentarme a sus padres. (ayer)
4. ¿No van a pagar Uds. los pasajes hoy? (ayer)
5. Esta tarde ellos van a abrir las ventanas. (al mediodía)
6. Nosotros vamos a comer en la cafetería. (el lunes)
7. ¿Vas a empezar a estudiar mañana? (esta mañana)
8. Yo voy a prestarle las maletas. (ayer)

### F. Just words . . .

Complete the following sentences, using appropriate words or phrases from the vocabulary list in Lección 7.

1. Voy a la agencia de ________ para comprar el pasaje.
2. ¿Uds. van a volar a México mañana? ¡ ________!
3. No puedo comprar un pasaje de primera clase. Tengo que viajar en clase ________.
4. Voy a Buenos Aires, pero no vuelvo. Quiero un pasaje de ________.
5. ¡Son las cuatro! El avión tiene tres horas de ________.
6. Mañana te voy a ________ el bolso de mano que me prestaste.
7. La ________ vez tenemos que viajar juntas.
8. Aquí está la entrada y ahí está la ________.
9. No tengo valijas; sólo un bolso de ________.
10. A Eva y a Luisa les gusta viajar ________.
11. Llevé cinco maletas y pagué ________ de equipaje.
12. Puedo ir de California a Arizona en avión, en coche, en tren o en ómnibus, pero no en ________.

### G. Culture

Answer the following questions, based on the **¿Lo sabía Ud.?** section.

1. ¿A qué altura está situada Cuzco?
2. ¿De qué civilización es Cuzco la antigua capital?
3. ¿Qué es la ciudad de Cuzco hoy día?
4. ¿Cómo se conoce a Machu Picchu?
5. ¿Cuánto se extendió el imperio de los incas?

## Lección 8

### A. Direct and indirect object pronouns used together

Answer the following questions, using the cues provided, substituting direct object pronouns for the italicized words, and making any necessary changes.

1. ¿Cuándo le van a mandar *el pasaje* a Jorge? (mañana)
2. ¿Quién te va a comprar *las entradas*? (Elsa)

3. ¿Quién les va a traducir *las cartas* a Uds.? (Luis)
4. ¿Cuándo me vas a traer *el lechón*? (esta tarde)
5. ¿Quién le va a dar *la pulsera* a Ud.? (la profesora)

**B. Preterit of *ir*, *ser*, and *dar***

Change the following sentences according to the new subjects.

1. Yo fui al restaurante y comí pavo asado. (Nosotros)
2. Ud. no fue mi profesor el año pasado. (Él)
3. ¿Ud. le dio la botella, señora? (Tú, querido)
4. ¿Quién pidió el bistec? ¿Fuiste tú, Tere? (Ud., señorita)
5. Ella no le dio el flan a Pedro. (Nosotras)
6. Ellos fueron al teatro. (Yo)
7. Nosotros no le dimos la cuenta. (Yo)
8. ¿Fueron ellos al restaurante anoche? (tú)
9. Carlos y yo fuimos a la fiesta la semana pasada. (Ellos)
10. ¿Fueron Uds. sus estudiantes el año pasado? (Raúl y Eva)
11. Nosotros te dimos la propina. (Yo)
12. Ella nos dio una torta helada. (Ellos)

**C. Preterit of *e:i* and *o:u* stem-changing verbs**

Complete the following sentences, using the preterit tense of the verbs listed below, as needed.

| mentir | pedir | dormir | repetir |
|---|---|---|---|
| seguir | morir | conseguir | servir |

1. ¿________ ellos en el hotel el jueves?
2. Los chicos ________ a sus padres a la tienda.
3. Nosotros ________ sándwiches de jamón y queso.
4. Ella me ________. No tiene veinte años; tiene diez y siete.
5. ¿No ________ Ud. el dinero para ir de vacaciones?
6. ¿Qué le ________ los niños a Santa Claus?
7. El hombre ________ en un accidente.
8. Ella me ________ la pregunta *(question)*.

**D. Uses of *por* and *para***

Complete the following sentences with **por** or **para,** as needed.

Ayer fui a la agencia de viajes ________ comprar un pasaje ________ Madrid. Pagué setecientos dólares ________ el pasaje, pero eso no es demasido caro. Quería *(I wanted)* el pasaje ________ el sábado, pero no pude conseguirlo. El avión sale el domingo ________ la mañana. ________ la tarde fui otra vez al centro ________ comprar un regalo ________ mi hermano, porque mañana es su aniversario de bodas. Llamé a mi padre ________ teléfono ________ decirle que no podía *(I wasn't able)* ir ________ él hasta las siete. Caminé *(I walked)* ________ el centro y pasé ________ la casa de Julia, que estudia ________ dentista. Julia me deseó buen viaje.

### E. Ordinal numbers

Complete the following sentences.

1. Marzo es el ________ mes del año.
2. Mayo es el ________ mes del año.
3. Abril es el ________ mes del año.
4. El ________ mes del año es octubre.
5. Agosto es el ________ mes del año.
6. Enero es el ________ mes del año.

### F. Just words . . .

Match each question in column A with the best response in column B. Use each response once.

| A | B |
|---|---|
| 1. ¿Qué quieres de postre? | a. No, prefiero cordero. |
| 2. ¿Quieres café? | b. Sí, con champán. |
| 3. ¿Quieres albóndigas? | c. No, agua mineral. |
| 4. ¿Cuánto vas a dejar de propina? | d. Los frijoles son muy buenos aquí. |
| 5. ¿Qué vas a pedir? | e. Es una sorpresa... |
| 6. ¿Cómo está la comida? | f. No, prefiero jugo de frutas. Hace mucho calor. |
| 7. ¿Qué vas a anotar? | g. No, no me gusta el pescado. |
| 8. ¿Qué me recomiendas? | h. No sé. ¿Quieres ver el menú? |
| 9. ¿Quieres salmón? | i. Sí, con crema, por favor. |
| 10. ¿Qué sirven en este restaurante? | j. No, la pimienta. |
| 11. ¿Vas a beber cerveza? | k. Sí, traigan las copas. |
| 12. ¿Quieres chocolate caliente? | l. Sí, ¿dónde están las tazas, los platitos y las cucharitas? |
| 13. ¿Vamos a celebrar nuestro aniversario? | m. Cinco dólares. |
| 14. ¿Van al teatro? | n. Creo que es pescado y mariscos. |
| 15. ¿Qué me vas a traer? | o. El pedido. |
| 16. ¿Vamos a tomar vermut? | p. Sí, porque voy a poner la mesa. |
| 17. ¿Cuál es la especialidad de la casa? | q. La cuenta. |
| 18. ¿Quieres la sal? | r. No, al cine. |
| 19. ¿No vas a servir el té? | s. Arroz con leche o flan. |
| 20. ¿Necesitas el mantel y las servilletas? | t. Está rica. |

### G. Culture

Circle the correct answer, based on the **¿Lo sabía Ud.?** section.

1. Cientos de miles de turistas (franceses, latinoamericanos, españoles) visitan Miami todos los años.
2. Más de un millón de hispanos viven en Miami, en su mayoría (cubanos, mexicanos, uruguayos).
3. En los países de habla hispana, el café se sirve (después del, antes del, durante el) postre.

4. Después de comer, los hispanos generalmente "hacen la (comida, cena, sobremesa)".
5. En los restaurantes hispanos, la propina es del (10%, 25%, 15%).

## Lección 9

### A. Reflexive constructions

Rewrite each sentence according to the new cue. Follow the model.

MODELO: Yo *me despierto* a las nueve. (levantarse)
*Yo me levanto a las nueve.*

1. *La gente* se viste muy bien. (Tú)
2. Ellos *se bañan* todos los días. (afeitarse)
3. *Nosotros* nos acostamos a las once. (Ellos)
4. ¿*Tú* no te preocupas por tus hijos? (Ud.)
5. Yo *me pruebo* el vestido. (ponerse)
6. *Nosotros* nos sentamos aquí. (Juan)
7. *Ella* se lava la cabeza todos los días. (Tú)
8. Yo no *me peiné*. (cortarse el pelo)
9. *Ellos* no se acordaron de eso. (Yo)
10. *Yo* me fui. (Uds.)
11. ¿Cómo se llama *ella*? (tú)
12. *Los niños* no se despertaron hasta las diez. (Daniel)

### B. Some uses of the definite article

Form sentences with the elements given, adding the necessary connectors. Use verbs in the present tense. Follow the model.

MODELO: yo / ponerse / vestido
*Yo me pongo el vestido.*

1. ¿ / tú / quitarse / suéter / ?
2. el barbero / cortarme / pelo
3. la peluquera / lavarme / cabeza
4. Uds. / no lavarse / manos
5. nosotros / preferir / té
6. madres / preocuparse / por / sus hijos
7. comunicación / ser / lo más importante

### C. Possessive pronouns

Give the Spanish equivalent of the pronouns in parentheses.

1. El espejo de Nora está en la mesa. ________ está en mi cuarto. *(Mine)*
2. Mis revistas están aquí. ¿Dónde están ________, Sr. Vega? *(yours)*
3. Ellos van a enviar sus cartas hoy. ¿Cuándo vamos a enviar ________? *(ours)*
4. No tengo maletas. ¿Puedes prestarme ________, Anita? *(yours)*
5. Aquí están los regalos de Jorge. ¿Dónde están ________? *(ours)*
6. Enrique necesita tu cuaderno, Eva. ________ está en la universidad. *(His)*

**D. Irregular preterits**

Give the Spanish equivalent of the verbs in parentheses.

1. Ellos ________ que ir al teatro. *(had)*
2. ¿Dónde ________ Uds. anoche? *(were)*
3. Yo lo ________ al italiano. *(translated)*
4. Yo no ________ ir a la peluquería. *(was able)*
5. ¿Dónde ________ tú la aspiradora? *(put)*
6. Anoche ________ una fiesta. *(there was)*
7. Él no ________ las maletas. *(packed)*
8. Mi abuelo no ________ ayer. *(came)*
9. Ellos ________ nada. *(didn't say)*
10. Ella me ________ un secador. *(brought)*

**E. Formation of adverbs**

Give the Spanish equivalent of the adverbs in parentheses.

1. Me gustan esas alfombras, ________ la azul. *(especially)*
2. Yo ________ voy a conciertos. *(frequently)*
3. El profesor habló ________ y ________. *(slowly and clearly)*
4. Vino a verme ________. *(recently)*
5. ________ voy a la peluquería los sábados. *(Generally)*
6. ________ no voy al teatro. *(Unfortunately)*

**F. Just words . . .**

Complete the following sentences, using the appropriate words and phrases from the vocabulary list in **Lección 9.**

1. Necesito la ________ para barrer la cocina.
2. Voy a pedir turno en la peluquería para corte, ________ y ________.
3. Prefiero el pelo largo porque el pelo corto no está de ________.
4. ¿Por qué no le pasas la ________ a la alfombra?
5. Siempre como en restaurantes porque no me gusta ________.
6. Tengo que comprar ________ para lavarme la cabeza.
7. No tiene rizos; tiene el pelo muy ________.
8. No le di el dinero para comprar la ________ *Time.*
9. No puedo peinarme porque no tengo ________.
10. Voy a afeitarme. ¿Dónde está la ________ de ________?
11. Es el cumpleaños de Jorge. Tengo que comprarle un ________.

**G. Culture**

Read the following statements and circle **V** (**Verdadero**) or **F** (**Falso**), based on the **¿Lo sabía Ud.?** section.

V F 1. Montevideo es la capital de Paraguay.
V F 2. Paraguay es más o menos del tamaño *(size)* de California.
V F 3. Muchos turistas visitan Paraguay.
V F 4. En Paraguay hablan dos idiomas: el español y el italiano.
V F 5. La mayoría de los paraguayos saben leer y escribir.

Lección 10

# Las vacaciones de Silvia

## OBJECTIVES

### Pronunciation

Pronunciation in context

### Structure

**Hace** meaning *ago* • The imperfect • The preterit contrasted with the imperfect • Verbs that change meaning in the preterit

### Communication

You will learn vocabulary related to leisure activities.

# Las vacaciones de Silvia

Córdoba, Argentina
12 de febrero del 2002

Querida Victoria:

¡Estaba equivocada! Creí que no me iba a gustar ir de vacaciones con mis padres y que me iba a aburrir y, sin embargo, me estoy divirtiendo mucho.

Llegamos a Córdoba hace una semana. Al día siguiente de llegar fuimos a acampar junto al Río de los Sauces. Papá y mi hermano armaron las tiendas de campaña y todos dormimos profundamente en nuestras bolsas de dormir. ¡Hice de todo! Nadé, fui de pesca con Miguel Ángel (no pesqué nada, a pesar de que tenía una caña de pescar nueva), monté a caballo y en bicicleta.

Anoche unos amigos chilenos dieron una fiesta. Yo no quería ir, pero papá me convenció y fui. Allí conocí a Gustavo, un muchacho de Santiago. ¡Bailé toda la noche con él!

¿Y a ti cómo te fue en Buenos Aires? ¿Fuiste de compras? ¿Te quedaste en casa de tus tíos? Espero que sí, porque los hoteles en Buenos Aires cuestan un ojo de la cara. Yo me hospedé en uno hace tres meses y me costó una fortuna...

El próximo año tienes que venir con nosotros. ¡En serio! Pensamos ir a Bariloche y alquilar una cabaña. Miguel Ángel dice que te va a enseñar a esquiar (cuando éramos niños íbamos a Bariloche todos los años y él aprendió a esquiar muy bien).

Bueno, me voy porque mamá me dijo que Gustavo me estaba esperando. ¡Vamos a planear otra fiesta!

Un abrazo,

Silvia

P.D. En este viaje aprendí a apreciar la naturaleza, el campo y..., ¡a los muchachos chilenos!

# Vocabulario

## Cognados

**la bicicleta** bicycle
**chileno(-a)** Chilean
**la fortuna** fortune

## Nombres

**el abrazo** hug
**el caballo** horse
**la cabaña** cabin
**el campo** country
**la caña de pescar** fishing rod
**la naturaleza** nature
**el (la) niño(-a)** child
**el río** river
**el saco (la bolsa) de dormir** sleeping bag
**el sauce** (weeping) willow
**la tienda de campaña** tent

## Verbos

**aburrirse** to be bored
**acampar** to camp
**alquilar** to rent
**apreciar** to appreciate
**armar** to pitch (a tent)
**convencer** to convince
**divertirse (e:ie)** to have a good time, to enjoy oneself
**enseñar**[1] to teach
**esquiar** to ski
**hospedarse (en)** to stay (at a hotel)
**nadar** to swim
**pescar** to fish, to catch a fish
**planear** to plan
**quedarse** to stay, to remain

## Otras palabras y expresiones

**a pesar de (que)** in spite of, despite
**al día siguiente** the next day
**¿Cómo te fue?** How did it go for you?
**costar un ojo de la cara** to cost an arm and a leg
**de todo** everything
**en serio** seriously
**Espero que sí.** I hope so.
**estar equivocado(-a)** to be wrong
**ir de compras** to go shopping
**ir de pesca** to go fishing
**ir de vacaciones** to go on vacation
**junto a** near, next to
**montar a caballo** to ride a horse
**montar en bicicleta** to ride a bicycle
**profundamente** soundly
**sin embargo** however, nevertheless
**toda la noche** all night long

[1]**Enseñar** takes the preposition a when followed by an infinitive: **Me enseñó *a* esquiar.**

# Vocabulario adicional

## Actividades al aire libre *(Outdoor activities)*

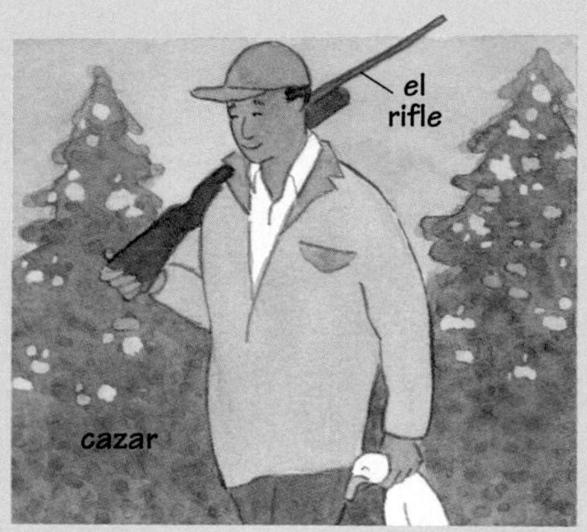

---

[1]Present tense: **juego, juegas, juega, jugamos, jugáis, juegan**

## Términos geográficos

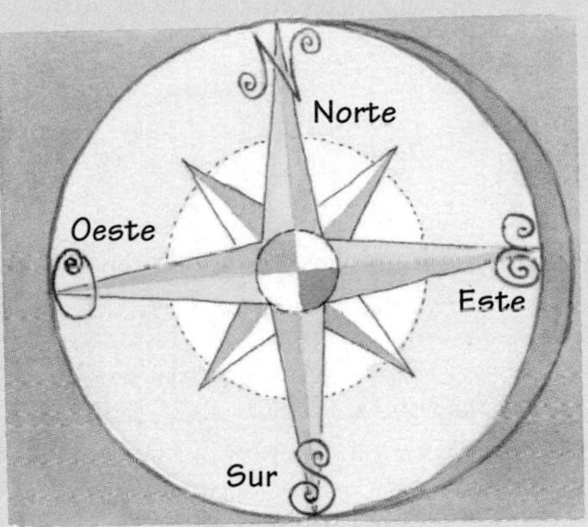


# ¡Conversemos!

Answer the following questions, basing your answers on Silvia's letter to Victoria.

1. ¿Con quiénes fue Silvia de vacaciones? ¿Se está divirtiendo?
2. ¿Cuánto tiempo hace que llegaron?
3. ¿Adónde fueron al día siguiente de llegar?
4. ¿Quiénes armaron las tiendas de campaña? ¿Dónde durmieron todos? ¿Cómo durmieron?
5. ¿Con quién fue de pesca Silvia? ¿Pescó algo?
6. Silvia no quería ir a la fiesta. ¿Por qué fue?
7. ¿A quién conoció allí?
8. ¿Qué hizo Silvia en la fiesta?
9. Según *(According to)* Silvia, ¿son caros o baratos los hoteles en Buenos Aires? (¿Cómo lo sabe usted?)

10. ¿Qué planes tiene Silvia para el año próximo?
11. ¿Adónde iban Silvia y Miguel Ángel cuando eran niños?
12. ¿Qué le dijo a Silvia su mamá?
13. ¿Qué van a hacer Silvia y Gustavo?
14. ¿Qué aprendió Silvia en este viaje?

## ¿Lo sabía Ud.?

- Mar del Plata (Argentina), Viña del Mar (Chile) y Punta del Este (Uruguay) están entre *(among)* las playas más hermosas e importantes de la América del Sur. Estas ciudades son centros turísticos internacionales.
- Mucha gente va a Chile y al sur de Argentina (Bariloche) para esquiar durante junio, julio y agosto, que son los meses de invierno en el hemisferio sur *(southern)*.

- ¿Qué ciudades de este país son centros turísticos internacionales?
- ¿Qué centros de esquí importantes hay en este país?

WWW INTERNET See the *¿Cómo se dice...?* Web site for activities on authentic cultural material: http://spanish.college.hmco.com/students

Vista de Mar del Plata y del océano Atlántico. Mar del Plata está a unos 400 kilómetros de Buenos Aires.

# Pronunciación

STUDENT AUDIO

In this lesson, there are some new words or phrases that may be challenging to pronounce. For further pronunciation practice of Spanish sounds, listen to your instructor and repeat the following words and phrases.

1. ¡Estaba **equivocada**!
2. Aprendí a **apreciar** la naturaleza.
3. Creí que me iba a **aburrir** y, sin embargo, me estoy **divirtiendo** mucho.
4. Monté a **caballo** y en **bicicleta.**
5. No **pesqué** nada, a pesar de que tenía una **caña de pescar** nueva.

# Estructuras

## 1 Hace... meaning *ago* (*Hace... como equivalente de* ago)

- In sentences using the preterit and in some cases the imperfect, **hace** + *period of time* is the equivalent of the English *ago*. When **hace** is placed at the beginning of the sentence, the construction is as follows.

> **Hace** + *period of time* + **que**
> **Hace** + dos años + **que** la conocí.

| | |
|---|---|
| —¿Cuánto tiempo hace que conociste a tu novia? | *"How long ago did you meet your girlfriend?"* |
| —**Hace tres años que** la conocí. | *"I met her three years ago."* |
| —**Hace diez años que** ellos vinieron a los Estados Unidos. ¿Y tú? | *"They came to the United States ten years ago. And you?"* |
| —Yo llegué **hace cuatro años.** | *"I arrived four years ago."* |

**ATENCIÓN** Note that it is also possible to say: **Yo llegué hace cuatro años.**

## práctica

**A.** Say how long ago everything happened, according to the information provided.

1. Armamos la tienda de campaña a las dos. Son las cinco.
2. Ellos fueron a esquiar en agosto. Estamos en diciembre.
3. Tú montaste a caballo el lunes. Hoy es viernes.
4. Empecé a nadar a las diez. Son las diez y cuarto.
5. Yo alquilé la cabaña el quince de julio. Hoy es el treinta de julio.
6. Carlos compró el saco de dormir en 1998. Estamos en el año 200_.

**B.** With a partner, take turns asking each other how long ago you did each of the following things.

1. ir a la playa
2. ir al dentista
3. comprar tu coche
4. ir de compras
5. ir al teatro
6. empezar a estudiar español
7. ver a tus padres
8. ir de vacaciones
9. llamar a tu mejor amigo(-a)
10. levantarte

## 2 The imperfect *(El imperfecto de indicativo)*

There are two simple past tenses in the Spanish indicative: the preterit, which you studied in **Lecciones 7**, **8**, and **9**, and the imperfect.

### A. Regular forms

■ To form the regular imperfect, add the following endings to the verb stem.

| **-ar *verbs*** | | **-er *and* -ir *verbs*** | | | |
|---|---|---|---|---|---|
| **hablar** | | **comer** | | **vivir** | |
| habl- | **aba** | com- | **ía** | viv- | **ía** |
| habl- | **abas** | com- | **ías** | viv- | **ías** |
| habl- | **aba** | com- | **ía** | viv- | **ía** |
| habl- | **ábamos** | com- | **íamos** | viv- | **íamos** |
| habl- | **abais** | com- | **íais** | viv- | **íais** |
| habl- | **aban** | com- | **ían** | viv- | **ían** |

■ Note that the endings of the **-er** and **-ir** verbs are the same, and that there is a written accent on the first **í** of the endings of the **-er** and **-ir** verbs.

■ The Spanish imperfect tense is equivalent to three English forms.

Yo **vivía** en Santiago.
{ *I used to live in Santiago.*
*I was living in Santiago.*
*I lived in Santiago.*

- The imperfect is used to refer to habitual or repeated actions in the past, with no reference to when they began or ended.

| | |
|---|---|
| —¿Tú **asistías** a la universidad cuando **vivías** en Cuba? | *"Did you attend the university when you were living in Cuba?"* |
| —No, **trabajaba** cuando **vivía** en Cuba. | *"No, I worked when I was living in Cuba."* |

- The imperfect is also used to refer to actions, events, or conditions that the speaker views as *in the process of* happening in the past, again with no reference to when they began or ended.

| | |
|---|---|
| —**Veníamos** para casa cuando vimos a Raúl. | *We were coming home when we saw Raúl.* |

## B. Irregular forms

- Only three verbs are irregular in the imperfect tense: **ser, ver,** and **ir.**

| ser | ver | ir |
|---|---|---|
| era | veía | iba |
| eras | veías | ibas |
| era | veía | iba |
| éramos | veíamos | íbamos |
| erais | veíais | ibais |
| eran | veían | iban |

| | |
|---|---|
| —¿**Ibas** mucho a casa de tus abuelos cuando **eras** niño? | *"Did you often go to your grandparents' house when you were a child?"* |
| —Sí, los **veía** todos los sábados. | *"Yes, I used to see them every Saturday."* |
| —¿Adónde **iban** Uds. de vacaciones cuando eran niños? | *"Where did you go on vacation when you were children?"* |
| —**Íbamos** a la playa o a las montañas. | *"We used to go to the beach or to the mountains."* |

## práctica

**A.** Ten years ago María wrote this composition about herself and her family. Rewrite her composition, using the imperfect tense.

Mi familia y yo vivimos en Buenos Aires. Mi padre trabaja para la compañía Sandoval y mi madre enseña en la universidad. Es una profesora excelente. Mis hermanos y yo asistimos a la escuela. Generalmente pasamos las vacaciones en Mar del Plata. Allí nadamos, pescamos y tomamos el sol. Como a mi padre le gusta ir a las montañas para esquiar, en invierno vamos a Bariloche. Mis abuelos viven en Rosario y no los vemos mucho, pero siempre les escribimos.

B. Now write a paragraph about your own childhood, using Exercise A as a model.

C. Interview a classmate, using the following questions and two of your own. When you have finished, switch roles.

1. ¿Dónde vivías tú cuando eras niño(-a)?
2. ¿A qué escuela asistías?
3. ¿Te gustaba estudiar?
4. ¿Eras buen estudiante?
5. ¿Adónde iban tú y tu familia de vacaciones?
6. ¿Qué les gustaba hacer?
7. ¿Preferías pasar las vacaciones en el campo o en la ciudad?
8. ¿Te divertías mucho o te aburrías?
9. ¿Veías mucho a tus abuelos?
10. ¿Vivías cerca de tus abuelos?

D. Compare your teenage years with those of a classmate by taking turns completing the following sentences.

1. Cuando yo era adolescente...
2. Mi familia y yo siempre...
3. Mis abuelos...
4. Mi mejor amigo(-a)...
5. Frecuentemente nosotros...
6. Cuando yo tenía dieciséis años...
7. En la escuela yo...
8. Todos los fines de semana, mis amigos y yo...
9. En el verano...
10. Cuando yo quería salir con mis amigos, mis padres...

## 3 The preterit contrasted with the imperfect *(El pretérito contrastado con el imperfecto)*

■ The difference between the preterit and the imperfect can be visualized in the following way.

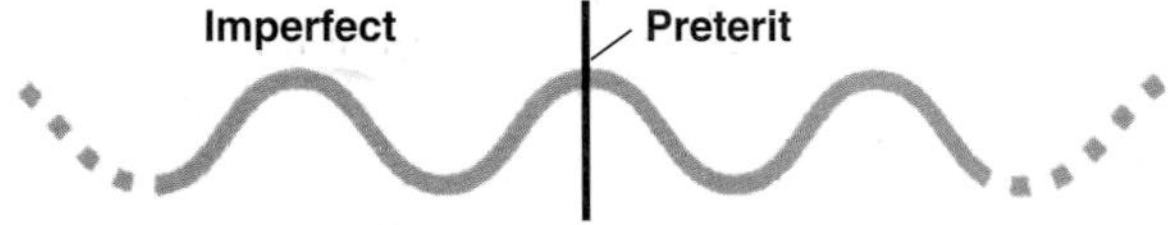


The wavy line representing the imperfect shows an action or event taking place over a period of time in the past. There is no reference to when the action began or ended. The vertical line representing the preterit shows an action or event as completed in the past.

In many instances, the choice between the preterit and the imperfect depends on how the speaker views the action or event. The following table summarizes some of the most important uses of both tenses.

| Preterit | Imperfect |
|---|---|
| 1. Reports past actions that the speaker views as finished and completed.<br>Yo **estuve** allí el año pasado.<br>Ayer **compré** una caña de pescar. | 1. Describes past actions in the process of happening, with no reference to their beginning or end.<br>**Iba** a la biblioteca cuando lo vi. |
| | 2. Refers to repeated or habitual actions or events: *used to . . .*<br>Cuando **era** niña **iba**[1] de vacaciones a Montevideo. |
| 2. Sums up a condition or state viewed as a whole (and no longer in effect).<br>Me **sentí** mal todo el día. | 3. Describes a physical, mental, or emotional state or condition in the past.<br>Me **sentía** muy mal. |
| | 4. Expresses time in the past.<br>**Eran** las ocho de la noche cuando llegaron a su casa. |
| | 5. Is generally used in indirect discourse.<br>Me dijo que no **sabía** apreciar la naturaleza. |
| | 6. Describes age in the past.<br>Cuando **tenía** veinte años, vivía en Chile. |
| | 7. Describes or sets the stage in the past.<br>**Hacía** frío y **llovía**. |

| | |
|---|---|
| —¿Qué **te dijo** Nora anoche? | *"What did Nora tell you last night?"* |
| —**Me dijo** que le **gustaba** esquiar. | *"She told me that she liked to ski."* |
| —¿Qué hora **era** cuando **llegaste** a tu casa? | *"What time was it when you got home?"* |
| —**Eran** las cuatro. | *"It was four o'clock."* |
| —¿Por qué no te **quedaste** en el club? | *"Why didn't you stay at the club?"* |
| —Porque no me **sentía** bien. | *"Because I wasn't feeling well."* |

[1]Note that this use of the imperfect also corresponds to the English *would* used to describe a repeated action in the past: *When I was a child, I used to go to Montevideo on vacation. = When I was a child, **I would** go to Montevideo on vacation.*

## práctica

**A.** Write the Spanish equivalent of the following sentences, paying special attention to the use of the preterit or the imperfect in each situation.

***Preterit***

1. I *went* to the lake last year. *(Narrates an action as a completed whole.)*
2. I *was* sick all day long. *(Sums up a condition or state viewed as a whole.)*

***Imperfect***

1. I *was going* to the lake when I saw Mary. *(Describes an action in progress.)*
2. I always *used to be* sick. *(Describes what used to happen.)*
3. I *was* cold.
   They *were* very happy here. *(A physical, mental, or emotional state or condition in the past.)*
4. He said he *wanted* a sleeping bag. *(Indirect discourse.)*
5. It *was* six o'clock in the morning. *(Time in the past.)*
6. My niece *was* five years old. *(Age in the past.)*
7. My boyfriend *was* tall and handsome. *(Description in the past.)*

**B.** Complete the following dialogues. Then act them out with a partner.

1. —¿Cuántos años ________ (tener) tú cuando ________ (venir) a vivir a Caracas?
   —________ (Tener) doce años.
2. —¿Qué te ________ (decir) el instructor ayer?
   —Me ________ (decir) que yo ________ (necesitar) practicar más.
3. —¿Qué tiempo ________ (hacer) cuando Uds. ________ (salir) de casa esta mañana?
   —________ (Hacer) frío y ________ (nevar).
4. —¿Adónde ________ (ir) Uds. de vacaciones cuando ________ (ser) niños?
   —Siempre ________ (ir) a la playa, pero un verano mis padres ________ (decidir) alquilar una cabaña en las montañas y ésas ________ (ser) nuestras mejores vacaciones.
5. —¿Qué hora ________ (ser) cuando tú ________ (llegar) a casa ayer?
   —________ (Ser) las ocho.
   —¿________ (Ir) a la tienda?
   —Sí, ________ (ir) con Nora. Cuando nosotras ________ (ir) a la tienda, ________ (ver) un accidente en la calle.
   —¿________ (Morir) alguien?
   —No, por suerte no ________ (morir) nadie.

C. This interview takes place in Buenos Aires. Play the role of a reporter interviewing a famous star.

—____________________________________________________

—Yo nací *(I was born)*[1] en Sevilla, y no te digo cuándo.

—____________________________________________________

—Yo tenía diez años cuando nos fuimos a vivir a Madrid.

—____________________________________________________

—¿Cuando era niña? Era fea y un poco gorda.

—____________________________________________________

—Sí, tenía un perro que se llamaba Chispita.

—____________________________________________________

—Cuando era niña me gustaban las actividades al aire libre. Me gustaba nadar, montar a caballo y escalar montañas.

—____________________________________________________

—Estudié en la Escuela de Arte Dramático.

—____________________________________________________

—Empecé a trabajar en televisión en 1995.

—____________________________________________________

—Vine a Buenos Aires en el año 1999.

—____________________________________________________

—Sí, el año pasado estuve en París y trabajé en un club nocturno.

—____________________________________________________

—Estuve allí por tres meses.

—____________________________________________________

—No, no pienso volver a España por ahora.

D. Interview a classmate, using the following questions and two of your own. When you have finished, switch roles.

1. ¿Cuántos años tenías cuando aprendiste a nadar?
2. ¿Adónde ibas de vacaciones?
3. ¿Te divertías durante el verano?
4. ¿Te gustaba acampar?
5. ¿Qué te gustaba hacer cuando eras niño(-a)?
6. ¿Cómo era tu primer(-a) novio(-a)?
7. ¿Qué hiciste ayer?
8. ¿A qué hora te levantaste esta mañana?
9. ¿Qué tiempo hacía cuando saliste de tu casa?
10. ¿Qué hora era cuando llegaste a la universidad?
11. ¿Tomaste una clase de inglés el año pasado?
12. ¿Quién fue tu profesor(-a)?

E. In groups of four or five, prepare 8 to 10 questions to ask your instructor about his or her life as a teenager.

[1]**Nacer** is a regular verb in the preterit.

## 4 Verbs that change meaning in the preterit *(Verbos que cambian de significado en el pretérito)*

■ Some Spanish verbs change meaning when they are used in the preterit. Note the usage of the verbs in the following examples.

**conocer:** conocí (preterit) — *I met*
conocía (imperfect) — *I knew (was acquainted or familiar with)*

Anoche **conocí** a una chica muy simpática. *(met her for the first time)*
Yo no **conocía** la ciudad. *(I wasn't familiar with the city.)*

**saber:** supe (preterit) — *I found out, I learned*
sabía (imperfect) — *I knew*

Lo **supe** cuando él me lo dijo. *(I found it out.)*
Yo no **sabía** que te gustaba esquiar. *(I wasn't aware of it.)*

**no querer:** no quise (preterit) — *I refused*
no quería (imperfect) — *I didn't want*

Raúl **no quiso** ir. *(didn't want to and refused)*
Rita **no quería** ir, pero después decidió ir. *(didn't want to at the time)*

—¿Tú **conocías** al cuñado de Carmen? — *"Did you know Carmen's brother-in-law?"*
—No, lo **conocí** anoche. — *"No, I met him last night."*

—¿**Sabías** que teníamos una fiesta? — *"Did you know that we were having a party?"*
—No, lo **supe** esta mañana. — *"No, I found (it) out this morning."*

—¿Y Roberto? ¿No vino? — *"And Roberto? Didn't he come?"*
—No, **no quiso** venir. — *"No, he refused to come."*

## práctica

**A.** Interview a classmate, using the following questions and at least two of your own.

1. ¿Conocías tú al profesor (a la profesora) antes de empezar esta clase?
2. ¿Cuándo lo (la) conociste?
3. ¿Sabías tú la nacionalidad del profesor (de la profesora)?
4. ¿Cuándo la supiste?
5. Yo no quería venir a clase hoy. ¿Y tú?
6. Tú no viniste al concierto anoche. ¿No pudiste o no quisiste?

**B.** Act out the following scene from a soap opera (**telenovela**) with a partner, providing the missing verbs.

ADRIÁN —¿Tú ________ que Rosaura estaba embarazada *(pregnant)*?
SARA —No, lo ________ anoche.
ADRIÁN —¡Qué horrible! Dicen que su esposo es un idiota. Los padres de ella no ________ ir a la boda *(wedding)*. Ese día se fueron a Europa.
SARA —Pero, ¿dónde ________ Rosaura a Lorenzo?
ADRIÁN —En una fiesta. Rosaura no ________ ir, pero Olga la llevó.
SARA —¿Olga ________ a Lorenzo?
ADRIÁN —Sí, Olga es la ex esposa de Lorenzo...

# ¡A ver cuánto aprendió!

INTERNET

See the *¿Cómo se dice...?* Web site for additional grammar and vocabulary practice: http://spanish.college.hmco.com/students

## ¡Repase el vocabulario!

Say whether the following statements are logical or not. If a statement is not logical, give one that is.

1. El caballo se hospedó en el hotel.
2. Compré un traje de baño para ir a la playa.
3. Lo pasé muy bien en México. Me divertí mucho.
4. Es muy barato; cuesta un ojo de la cara.
5. Alquilé el campo para ir de pesca.
6. Van a escalar el mar.
7. Viven en el campo porque no les gusta la ciudad.
8. Jugamos al tenis en la cabaña.
9. Ella no sabe esquiar. Yo le voy a enseñar.
10. Está en la playa tomando la nieve.
11. Viven en Nueva York porque les gusta el oeste de los Estados Unidos.
12. Voy a comprar una bicicleta para montar a caballo.
13. Papá armó la tienda de campaña.
14. Voy a poner al salvavidas en la mochila.
15. Durmió muy mal; durmió profundamente toda la noche.
16. Nunca tiene razón; siempre está equivocado.

## Entrevista

With a partner, take turns interviewing each other, using the following questions.

1. ¿Acampaste el fin de semana pasado?
2. ¿Te gustaba ir a las montañas cuando eras niño(-a)?
3. Cuando eras niño(-a), ¿preferías montar a caballo o en bicicleta?
4. ¿Quieres ir a cazar conmigo?
5. ¿Fuiste de pesca el verano pasado?

6. ¿Fuiste de compras el sábado pasado?
7. ¿Prefieres jugar al golf o al tenis?
8. ¿Prefieres nadar o tomar el sol?
9. ¿Prefieres vivir cerca del mar o cerca de un lago?
10. Cuando vas de vacaciones, ¿prefieres quedarte en la casa de un(-a) amigo(-a) o prefieres hospedarte en un hotel?
11. Los hoteles de tu ciudad, ¿cuestan un ojo de la cara?
12. La última vez *(The last time)* que fuiste de vacaciones, ¿cómo te fue?

## Situaciones

What would you say in the following situations? What might the other person say? Act out the scenes with a partner. Take turns playing each role.

1. On your vacation, you learned how to swim and ride a horse, and you caught a trout. Someone asks whether you had a good time. Say what you did.
2. A friend invites you to go camping. You don't have a tent or a sleeping bag, and you want to know what else you will need.
3. You are trying to convince a friend to go camping. Tell him or her how much fun it can be.

## ¿Qué pasa aquí?

In groups of three or four, look at the following photo and make up a story about the people you see. Say who they are, their professions, how long they have been on vacation, what they did yesterday, and so on.

## Para escribir

Tomás and Víctor are very good friends, but their tastes differ: Tomás likes the outdoors, while Víctor prefers city life. Using your imagination, write an account of how each of them spent his vacation last summer.

# En la vida real

CD-ROM

Do the interactive exercises on the CD-ROM for additional practice.

## Nuestras vacaciones

You and a classmate are going on a vacation. Make plans for the trip, including activities and things you might need to take with you. Then tell a group of classmates about your plans.

## Viajes a México

Ángela and Elena went to Ixtapa on vacation, and Alberto and Julio went to Playa Blanca on the Pacific coast of Mexico. The four went with Club Méditerranée. Read the ad below and answer the following questions.

**Conozca el nuevo y sensacional modo de disfrutar las vacaciones "al estilo de CLUB MEDITERRANEE" con**

**Dos fabulosas excursiones especiales para viajeros sofisticados y exigentes, amantes del sol, el mar ¡y la buena vida!**

| IT3AM1VB770 CLUB MEDITERRANEE | | IT3AM1VB771 CLUB MEDITERRANEE | |
|---|---|---|---|
| **Ixtapa** | | **Playa Blanca** | |
| ZIHUATANEJO | | (COSTA CAREYES) | |
| **PLAN 1** - 4 días/3 noches | | **PLAN 1** - 4 días/3 noches | |
| Salidas: los Jueves | | Salidas: los Domingos | |
| ADULTO | MENOR | ADULTO | MENOR |
| $ 16,300.00 | $ 12,100.00 | $ 19,550.00 | $ 15,500.00 |
| NOCHE ADICIONAL $ 1,640.00 | | NOCHE ADICIONAL $ 1,150.00 | |
| **PLAN 2** - 5 días/4 noches | | **PLAN 2** - 5 días/4 noches | |
| Salidas: los Domingos | | Salidas: los Jueves | |
| ADULTO | MENOR | ADULTO | MENOR |
| $ 20,250.00 | $ 13,250.00 | $ 24,650.00 | $ 16,850.00 |
| NOCHE ADICIONAL $ 1,640.00 | | NOCHE ADICIONAL $ 1,150.00 | |

**NOTA:** Estos precios incluyen tarifa aérea especial saliendo desde México, D.F. también operamos con tarifa especial saliendo desde Guadalajara, Monterrey y otros destinos. Favor de consultar estas tarifas en cualquiera de nuestras oficinas.

**Utilice la Tarjeta American Express y disfrute los siguientes beneficios:**

- Membresía por un año del Club Mediterranée.
- Seguro de vida contra accidentes por $ 1,000,000.00 durante el transporte aéreo.

1. ¿Cómo son las excursiones en los Viajes Bojorquez?
2. ¿Para qué tipo de viajeros son?

3. Las chicas viajaron con el plan 1 a Ixtapa. ¿Qué día salieron y cuántas noches estuvieron en Ixtapa?
4. ¿Cuánto pagaron por el viaje?
5. Las chicas usaron la tarjeta American Express para pagar el viaje. ¿Qué beneficios recibieron?
6. Los muchachos viajaron con el plan 2 y estuvieron en Playa Blanca por cinco noches. ¿Cuánto les costó el viaje?

## El viaje de fin de curso

Imagine that your class is planning a field trip. One group of students would like to do outdoor activities such as camping, fishing, and swimming. Another group would prefer a visit to a large city and stay in hotels, visit museums, see films, etc. After preparing for a discussion, each group must try to convince the other to agree to its plan.

# 5. América central

- Costa Rica es el país con el mayor ingreso *(income)* por persona, y con el más alto nivel de educación de Centroamérica. Es un país democrático y no tiene ejército *(army)*. A Costa Rica la llaman "la Suiza *(Switzerland)* de América" por su tradición pacifista. Uno de sus presidentes, Oscar Arias, recibió el Premio Nóbel de la Paz.
- El Salvador es el país más pequeño de Centroamérica, pero es el más densamente poblado. Más de seis millones de habitantes viven en un área aproximadamente del tamaño del estado de Massachusetts. Nicaragua, en comparación, es cinco veces más grande que El Salvador, pero tiene una población de sólo unos 4, 8 millones de habitantes.
- El canal de Panamá es actualmente la única vía de comunicación que conecta los dos grandes océanos. Ahorra *(It saves)* 16.000 kilómetros de travesía *(voyage)* para los barcos que ya no *(no longer)* tienen que pasar por el Cabo de Hornos.

Nicaragua se siente orgullosa *(proud)* de su poeta nacional Rubén Darío, creador y líder del modernismo, un movimiento literario que comenzó a fines del siglo XIX. En la foto aparece una de las muchas estatuas del gran poeta que hay en Managua, la capital del país.

*¿Qué poetas norteamericanos puede nombrar Ud.?*

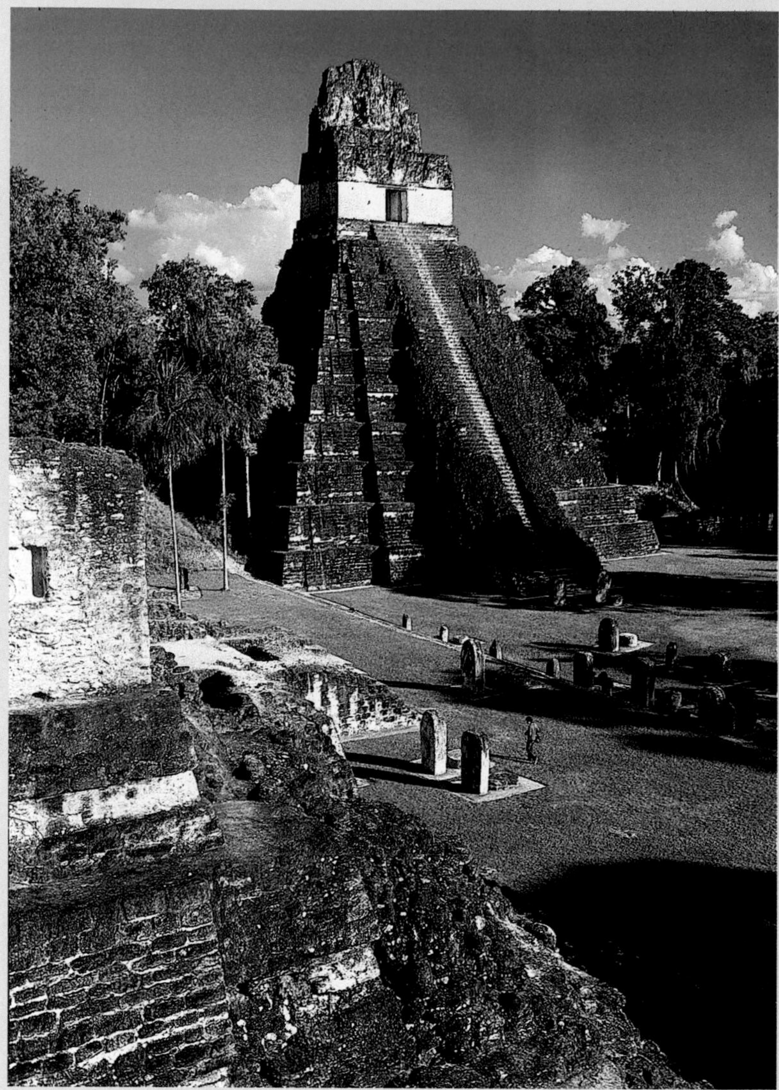

Tikal, situada en un bosque *(forest)* tropical al noroeste de Guatemala, es la ciudad más grande y más antigua de la civilización maya. En esta ciudad vivían unas 80.000 personas. Aquí se ve el Templo del Gran Jaguar, el edificio más alto y más importante de Tikal.

*¿Cuáles son algunas de las ciudades más antiguas de su país?*

El cultivo del banano *(banana tree)* es una de las principales fuentes *(sources)* de ingreso de los países centroamericanos. El banano se cultiva en Panamá, Costa Rica, El Salvador, Honduras, Nicaragua y Guatemala. En la foto, un agricultor verifica el tamaño de las bananas en una hacienda de El Salvador.

*¿Qué frutas se cultivan en la región donde Ud. vive?*

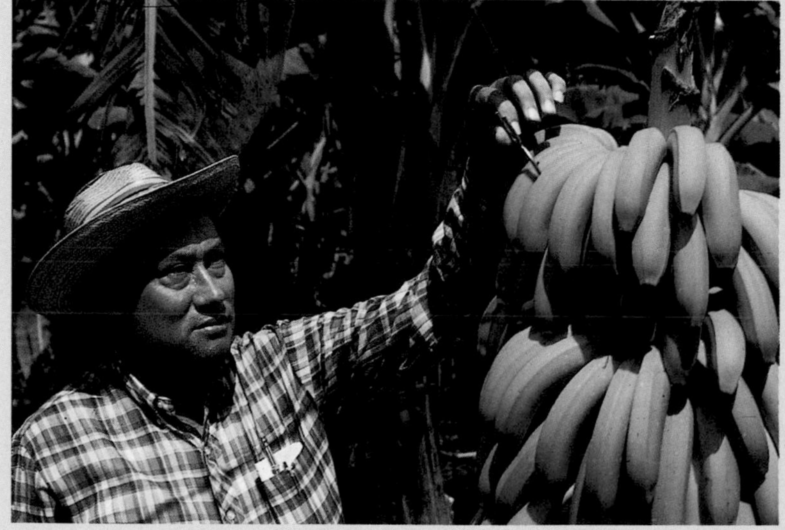

Estudiantes de la Universidad Nacional Autónoma de Honduras se dirigen a sus clases. Esta universidad, que está en Tegucigalpa, la capital de Honduras, es el centro educativo más importante del país.

*¿Cuál es la universidad más importante del estado donde Ud. vive?*

Guatemala es la ciudad más grande y más importante del país centroamericano del mismo nombre. La mayor parte de la ciudad es moderna, pues fue reconstruida después de una serie de terremotos *(earthquakes)* ocurridos en 1917–1918. En sus calles se mezclan las construcciones antiguas, como la Universidad de San Carlos, la Catedral y el Conservatorio Nacional de Música, y edificios modernos como la Ciudad Olímpica y el Palacio Nacional.

*¿Cuáles son los edificios más antiguos de su ciudad?*

Costa Rica es el país centroamericano que más se preocupa por proteger la naturaleza y la ecología. Son famosos sus parques nacionales y algunos de sus jardines, como el Jardín Botánico de Lankester, que aparece en la foto. Este jardín contiene numerosas especies de orquídeas y otras plantas tropicales.

*¿Cuáles son los principales parques nacionales de su país?*

La construcción del canal de Panamá por parte de los Estados Unidos duró *(lasted)* siete años y se terminó en el año 1914.

*¿Puede Ud. identificar otros canales famosos?*

TELEINFORME

VIDEO

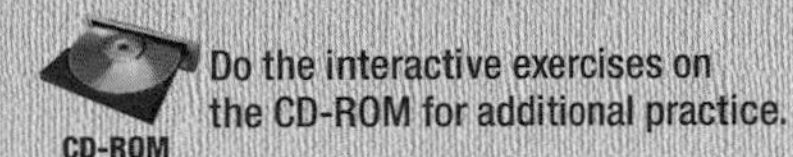
CD-ROM
Do the interactive exercises on the CD-ROM for additional practice.

## Preparación

**¿Cuánto saben Uds. ya?** After reading **Panorama hispánico 5,** get together in groups of three or four students and answer the following questions.

1. ¿Cuál es la única vía *(route)* de comunicación que conecta el océano Pacífico con el océano Atlántico?
2. ¿Cómo es la educación en Costa Rica?
3. ¿Cómo llaman a Costa Rica y por qué?
4. ¿Dónde se cultiva el banano *(banana tree)*?
5. ¿Qué protegen en Costa Rica?

## Comprensión

**A. Panamá.** Read the following statements. After watching the video, circle **V (Verdadero)** or **F (Falso)**, according to what you understood. If a statement is false, correct it.

V F 1. Hay bosques lluviosos en Panamá.
V F 2. En Panamá viven civilizaciones indígenas.
V F 3. La ciudad de Panamá está en la costa del Atlántico.
V F 4. La ciudad de Panamá no es una ciudad moderna.
V F 5. La ciudad de Panamá fue el centro del imperio español en América por muchos años.
V F 6. La ciudad de Panamá tiene muchos ejemplos de arquitectura colonial española.

**B. Las carretas *(oxcarts)* costarricenses.** Select the appropriate word or phrase that best completes each statement according to what you understood in the video.

1. Se usan las carretas en las (calles, fincas) de Costa Rica.
2. Las carretas están hechas *(made)* de (madera, plástico).
3. Las carretas tienen dos (ruedas, flores) grandes.
4. Lo más típico de las carretas es que usan (muchos, pocos) colores llamativos *(bright)*.

**C. El Jardín Botánico de Lankester.** Select the word or phrase that best completes each statement, according to what you understood.

1. La orquídea es (un pájaro, una flor) tropical.
2. En el Jardín Botánico de Lankester hay más de (80, 800) variedades de orquídeas.
3. En los jardines de Lankester hay más de (100, 150) géneros de pájaros.
4. El hombre que fundó *(founded)* el Jardín de Lankester era (costarricense, inglés, estadounidense).
5. Hoy día (la universidad, la presidencia) de Costa Rica mantiene el jardín.
6. Costa Rica tiene excelentes programas para proteger (las carretas, la naturaleza).

## Ampliación

A. **Una entrevista.** You and a partner are going to conduct a series of interviews. Make a list of three questions for each of the following people:

1. a una persona de la ciudad de Panamá
2. al artesano costarricense que pinta *(paints)* las carretas
3. al administrador del Jardín Botánico de Lankester

B. **Dos culturas.** With a partner, describe a special place or typical handicraft from your area that might compare to "El Jardín Botánico de Lankester" or "las carretas costarricenses."

# Haciendo diligencias

Lección 11

## OBJECTIVES

### Pronunciation

Pronunciation in context

### Structure

The subjunctive mood • The subjunctive with verbs of volition • The subjunctive with verbs of emotion

### Communication

You will learn vocabulary related to everyday activities and running errands.

# Haciendo diligencias

*En una casa de la calle Ponce en San Juan, Puerto Rico, vive la familia Vargas. Sergio está muy cansado hoy y quiere quedarse en la cama hasta tarde porque hoy tiene el día libre. Su mamá quiere que haga varias diligencias, de modo que el pobre muchacho tiene que levantarse en cuanto suena el despertador a las siete de la mañana.*

*A las nueve llega a la tintorería, que queda cerca de su casa.*

SERGIO —Vengo a recoger esta ropa. Aquí está el comprobante. *(Piensa)* Ojalá que estén listos mis pantalones.

EMPLEADA —*(Lee)* Un abrigo de mujer y un pantalón. *(A Sergio)* Un momento, por favor. *(Al rato vuelve.)* Los pantalones son rosados, ¿verdad?

SERGIO —¡Eran blancos cuando los traje...!

*A las diez, Sergio está en el departamento de fotografía de la tienda La Francia.*

SERGIO —Hace una semana que traje un rollo de película en colores. Espero que esté listo.

EMPLEADA —A ver... ¿Sergio Vargas...? Sí, las fotos salieron muy bien.

SERGIO —¿Y cuánto cobran por revelar un rollo de película?

EMPLEADA —Seis dólares, señor.

SERGIO —Muy bien. *(Mira las fotografías.)* ¿Quién es esta señora? ¡Estas fotos no son mías!

*A las once, Sergio estaciona su motocicleta frente al banco.*

SERGIO —Quiero depositar este cheque, que está a nombre de mi madre. ¿Es necesario que lo firme ella?

EMPLEADA —Si lo va a depositar en la cuenta corriente de ella, no.

SERGIO —Muy bien, eso es lo que quiero hacer. También quiero sacar doscientos dólares de mi cuenta de ahorros.

EMPLEADA —Llene esta tarjeta, por favor.

SERGIO —Necesito que me dé el saldo de mi cuenta de ahorros.

EMPLEADA —Sólo tiene veinte dólares. Lo siento, señor Vargas, pero no tiene suficiente dinero.

*Cuando Sergio sale del banco, no encuentra su motocicleta.*

SERGIO —*(Grita)* ¡Ay, no! ¡Alguien me robó la motocicleta!

SEÑORA —El muchacho que se llevó su motocicleta dijo que Ud. era su hermano...

SERGIO —¡Yo soy hijo único!

SEÑORA —*(Piensa)* Se parecen mucho. Me sorprende que no sean hermanos.

SERGIO —*(Mientras camina hacia la estación de policía)* ¡El próximo martes trece no salgo de casa!

# Vocabulario

## Cognados

**el banco** bank
**el cheque** check
**el departamento** department, section
**la motocicleta, la moto** motorcycle
**suficiente** sufficient, enough

## Nombres

**la cama** bed
**el comprobante** claim check
**la cuenta** account
**la cuenta corriente** checking account
**la cuenta de ahorros** savings account
**el despertador** alarm clock
**la diligencia** errand
**la estación de policía** police station
**el pantalón, los pantalones** pants, trousers
**el rollo de película** roll of film
**la ropa**[1] clothes, clothing
**el saldo** balance
**la tintorería** dry cleaner

## Verbos

**caminar** to walk
**cobrar** to charge
**depositar** to deposit
**esperar** to hope
**estacionar, aparcar, parquear** to park
**gritar** to scream
**llenar** to fill out
**llevarse** to take (away)
**parecerse (yo me parezco)** to look like
**recoger** to pick up
**revelar** to develop (film)
**robar** to steal
**sacar** to take out, to withdraw
**sonar (o:ue)** to ring
**sorprender** to surprise

## Adjetivos

**libre** off, free
**listo(-a)** ready
**pobre** poor

## Otras palabras y expresiones

**a ver** let's see
**al rato** a while later
**de modo que, de manera que** so
**en cuanto, tan pronto como** as soon as
**frente a** in front of
**hacer diligencias** to run errands
**hacia** toward
**hijo(-a) único(-a)** only child
**Llene...** Fill out . . .
**mientras** while
**ojalá** I hope, God grant
**quedarse en la cama hasta tarde** to sleep late
**suena el despertador** the alarm goes off
**¿verdad?** right?, true?

---

[1]**Ropa** is always used in the singular.

## Vocabulario adicional
### En el banco

**a plazos** on installments — Compré el coche **a plazos.**
**ahorrar** to save — Tienes que **ahorrar** más dinero.
**al contado** in cash — No voy a comprarlo a plazos; voy a comprarlo **al contado.**
**fechar** to date (a check, a letter, etc.) — Tiene que firmar y **fechar** el cheque.
**gratis** free of charge — No cuesta nada; es **gratis.**
**pedir prestado(-a)** to borrow — Voy a **pedirle prestados** doscientos dólares a Juan.
**pedir un préstamo** to apply for a loan — Voy al banco para **pedir un préstamo** de cinco mil dólares.

## ¡Conversemos!

Answer the following questions, basing your answers on the dialogues.

1. ¿Qué quiere hacer Sergio hoy? ¿Por qué?
2. ¿Qué pasa en cuanto suena el despertador?
3. ¿Por qué no puede quedarse en la cama hoy?
4. ¿Dónde estaban los pantalones de Sergio?
5. ¿De qué color eran los pantalones de Sergio? Y ahora, ¿de qué color son?
6. ¿A qué departamento de la tienda La Francia va Sergio?

7. Las fotos que él quería revelar, ¿son en colores o en blanco y negro?
8. ¿Puede sacar Sergio doscientos dólares de su cuenta de ahorros? ¿Por qué o por qué no?
9. ¿Cuál es el saldo de su cuenta de ahorros?
10. ¿Por qué grita Sergio "¡Ay, no!"?
11. ¿Sergio tiene hermanos? ¿Cómo lo sabe Ud.?
12. ¿Qué dice Sergio mientras camina a la estación de policía?

## ¿Lo sabía Ud.?

■ Puerto Rico es una de las Antillas Mayores. Es un Estado Libre Asociado a los Estados Unidos, y sus lenguas oficiales son el español y el inglés. Su capital es San Juan.

Los indios llamaban a la isla de Puerto Rico "Borinquén", y hoy en día muchos de sus habitantes todavía usan el nombre "Borinquén". En vez de *(Instead of)* decir que son "puertorriqueños" dicen que son "boricuas" o "borinqueños".

■ Cada nación latinoamericana tiene un banco central encargado de *(in charge of)* emitir el dinero y de controlar la actividad de los bancos comerciales. En algunos países hay también sucursales *(branches)* de bancos extranjeros. El uso del cheque no es tan común en América Latina como en los Estados Unidos, pero muchos bancos tienen sus propias *(own)* tarjetas de crédito.

- ¿Cuál es el estado de este país que está formado por un grupo de islas?
- En este país, ¿qué institución está encargada de emitir el dinero?

See the *¿Cómo se dice...?* Web site for activities on authentic cultural material: http://spanish.college.hmco.com/students

La Puerta de San Juan, en el Viejo San Juan, parte antigua de la capital de Puerto Rico.

# Pronunciación

In this lesson, there are some new words or phrases that may be challenging to pronounce. For further pronunciation practice of Spanish sounds, listen to your instructor and repeat the following words and phrases.

1. Su mamá quiere que haga varias **diligencias.**
2. Sergio quiere **quedarse en la cama hasta tarde.**
3. ¿Cuánto cobran por **revelar un rollo de película?**
4. Quiero **sacar** doscientos dólares de mi **cuenta de ahorros.**
5. Cuando Sergio sale del banco, no encuentra su **motocicleta.**

# Estructuras

## 1 The subjunctive mood *(El modo subjuntivo)*

### A. Introduction to the subjunctive

Until now, you have been using verbs in the indicative mood. The indicative is used to express factual, definite events. By contrast, the subjunctive is used to reflect the speaker's feelings or attitudes toward events, or when the speaker views events as uncertain, unreal, or hypothetical.

- The Spanish subjunctive is most often used in subordinate or dependent clauses.

- The subjunctive is also used in English, although not as often as in Spanish. Consider the following sentence:

  *I suggest that he **arrive** tomorrow.*

The expression that requires the use of the subjunctive is in the main clause, *I suggest*. The subjunctive appears in the subordinate clause, *that he **arrive** tomorrow*. The subjunctive is used because the action of arriving is not real; it is only what is *suggested* that he do.

## B. Present subjunctive forms of regular verbs

- To form the present subjunctive, add the following endings to the stem of the first-person singular of the present indicative after dropping the **o.**

| -ar *verbs* | -er *verbs* | -ir *verbs* |
|---|---|---|
| habl **-e** | com **-a** | viv **-a** |
| habl **-es** | com **-as** | viv **-as** |
| habl **-e** | com **-a** | viv **-a** |
| habl **-emos** | com **-amos** | viv **-amos** |
| habl **-éis** | com **-áis** | viv **-áis** |
| habl **-en** | com **-an** | viv **-an** |

- Note that the endings for **-er** and **-ir** verbs are identical.
- The following table shows how to form the first-person singular of the present subjunctive. The stem is the same for all persons.

| *Verb* | *First-person singular present indicative* | *Subjunctive stem* | *First-person singular present subjunctive* |
|---|---|---|---|
| camin**ar** | camino | camin- | **camine** |
| aprend**er** | aprendo | aprend- | **aprenda** |
| escrib**ir** | escribo | escrib- | **escriba** |
| dec**ir** | digo | dig- | **diga** |
| hac**er** | hago | hag- | **haga** |
| tra**er** | traigo | traig- | **traiga** |
| sac**ar** | saco | sac- | **saque**[1] |
| lleg**ar** | llego | lleg- | **llegue**[1] |
| empez**ar** | empiezo | empiez- | **empiece**[1] |

## práctica

Give the present subjunctive of the following verbs.

1. *yo:* solicitar, recibir, traer, decir, caminar, comer, ver
2. *tú:* escribir, cobrar, decidir, regresar, venir, barrer, aparcar
3. *él:* gritar, hacer, mandar, salir, anotar, esperar
4. *nosotros:* cocinar, depositar, leer, poner, pagar
5. *ellos:* caminar, deber, robar, conocer, vender, salir, empezar

[1]Remember that in verbs ending in **-gar, -car,** and **-zar, g** changes to **gu, c** changes to **qu,** and **z** changes to **c** before **e.**

## C. Subjunctive forms of stem-changing verbs

- Verbs that end in **-ar** and **-er** undergo the same stem changes in the present subjunctive as in the present indicative.

| **recomendar (e:ie)** *to recommend* | | **recordar (o:ue)** *to remember* | |
|---|---|---|---|
| recomiende | recomend**emos** | recuerde | record**emos** |
| recomiendes | recomend**éis** | recuerdes | record**éis** |
| recomiende | recomiend**en** | recuerde | recuerd**en** |

| **entender (e:ie)** *to understand* | | **devolver (o:ue)** *to return (something)* | |
|---|---|---|---|
| entienda | entend**amos** | devuelva | devolv**amos** |
| entiendas | entend**áis** | devuelvas | devolv**áis** |
| entienda | entiend**an** | devuelva | devuelv**an** |

- In stem-changing verbs that end in **-ir**, the unstressed **e** changes to **i** and the unstressed **o** changes to **u** in the first- and second-person plural (**nosotros** and **vosotros**) forms. The other persons follow the same pattern as the indicative.

| **mentir (e:ie)** *to lie* | | **dormir (o:ue)** *to sleep* | |
|---|---|---|---|
| mienta | m**i**nt**amos** | duerma | d**u**rm**amos** |
| mientas | m**i**nt**áis** | duermas | d**u**rm**áis** |
| mienta | mient**an** | duerma | duerm**an** |

## D. Verbs that are irregular in the subjunctive

- The following verbs are irregular in the subjunctive.

| **dar** | **estar** | **saber** | **ser** | **ir** |
|---|---|---|---|---|
| dé | esté | sepa | sea | vaya |
| des | estés | sepas | seas | vayas |
| dé | esté | sepa | sea | vaya |
| demos | estemos | sepamos | seamos | vayamos |
| deis | estéis | sepáis | seáis | vayáis |
| den | estén | sepan | sean | vayan |

**ATENCIÓN** The subjunctive of **hay** (impersonal form of **haber**) is **haya.**

## práctica

Give the present subjunctive of the following verbs.

1. *yo:* dormir, mentir, recomendar, dar, pensar, ir
2. *tú:* volver, estar, ser, preferir, recordar, morir, ver, pedir

3. *él:* cerrar, saber, perder, probar, dar, servir, seguir
4. *nosotros:* sentir, ir, dar, dormir, perder, cerrar, saber, ser
5. *ellos:* estar, ser, recordar, saber, encontrar, repetir

## E. Uses of the subjunctive

There are four main concepts that call for the use of the subjunctive in Spanish:

- Volition: demands, wishes, advice, persuasion, and other attempts to impose will

| | |
|---|---|
| Ella **quiere** que yo estacione aquí. | *She wants me to park here.* |
| Te **aconsejo** que no **vayas** a ese banco. | *I advise you not to go to that bank.* |
| Les **ruego** que no se **vayan.** | *I beg you not to leave.* |

- Emotion: pity, joy, fear, surprise, hope, and so on

| | |
|---|---|
| **Espero** que **lleguen** temprano. | *I hope they arrive early.* |
| **Siento** que no **puedas** venir a clase. | *I'm sorry you can't come to class.* |
| Me **sorprende** que no **vayas** al concierto. | *It surprises me that you're not going to the concert.* |

- Doubt, disbelief, denial, uncertainty, and negated facts

| | |
|---|---|
| **Dudo** que **paguen** la cuenta. | *I doubt they'll pay the bill.* |
| **No creo** que ella **sea** una idiota. | *I don't think she's an idiot.* |
| **No es verdad** que Antonio **sea** instructor de tenis. | *It isn't true that Antonio is a tennis instructor.* |

- Unreality, indefiniteness, and nonexistence

| | |
|---|---|
| ¿**Hay alguien** que **esté** libre hoy? | *Is there anyone who's free today?* |
| **No hay nadie** que **tenga** el comprobante. | *There's nobody that has his or her claim check.* |

Bienvenido
a la era
del dinero
electrónico
servibanca
Su dinero electronico

## 2 The subjunctive with verbs of volition *(El subjuntivo con verbos que indican voluntad o deseo)*

- All impositions of will, as well as indirect or implied commands, require the subjunctive in subordinate clauses. The subject in the main clause must be different from the subject in the subordinate clause.
- Note the sentence structure for this use of the subjunctive in Spanish.

| Él **quiere** | que yo **estudie.** |
|---|---|
| *He wants* | *me to study.* |
| main clause | subordinate clause |

| | |
|---|---|
| —¿Quiere que le **dé** el número de mi cuenta? | *"Do you want me to give you my account number?"* |
| —Sí, y también necesito que **firme** la tarjeta. | *"Yes, and I also need you to sign the card."* |
| —Roberto quiere que tú **vayas** a la fiesta. | *"Robert wants you to go to the party."* |
| —Sí, pero yo no quiero ir. | *"Yes, but I don't want to go."* |

**ATENCIÓN** Notice that the infinitive is used after a verb of volition if there is no change of subject: **Yo no quiero *ir*.**

- Some verbs of volition are:

**aconsejar** *to advise*
**desear** *to want*
**mandar** *to order*
**necesitar** *to need*
**pedir** (e:i) *to ask for, request*
**querer** (e:ie) *to want*
**recomendar** (e:ie) *to recommend*
**rogar** (o:ue) *to beg, plead*
**sugerir** (e:ie) *to suggest*

## práctica

**A.** Tell the following people that you want them to do something other than what they'd like to do.

MODELO: Yo quiero lavarme la cabeza ahora. (más tarde)
*Yo te sugiero que te laves la cabeza más tarde.*

1. Nosotros necesitamos comprar una motocicleta. (un coche)
2. Yo quiero probarme el vestido aquí. (tu cuarto)
3. Ella quiere abrir una cuenta corriente. (una cuenta de ahorros)
4. Ellos quieren ir al banco hoy. (mañana)
5. Esteban quiere dar una fiesta el viernes. (el sábado)
6. Mi hermano quiere ser profesor de francés. (de inglés)
7. Anita y yo queremos venir mañana. (el lunes)
8. Uds. necesitan ir al campo en bicicleta. (en auto)
9. Alicia quiere pagar la cuenta este mes. (el mes próximo)
10. Nosotros queremos hacer la sopa. (ensalada)

**B.** Describe what the following people want each person to do, using the present subjunctive.

Anita

MODELO: *La mamá de Anita quiere que ella* ***estudie.***

1. Tito

2. Julia

3. Beto

4. Los estudiantes

5. Hugo

C. Your friends are always coming to you with their problems. Tell them what you suggest, recommend, or advise for each situation.

MODELO: Mañana tengo un examen. ¿Qué me aconsejas que haga?
*Te aconsejo que estudies mucho.*

1. Yo no puedo lavar mis pantalones en casa. ¿Adónde me sugieres que los lleve?
2. Un Porsche es muy caro para mí. ¿Qué coche me recomiendas que compre?
3. A mi hermano le regalaron mil dólares. ¿Qué le sugieres que haga con el dinero?
4. Mi prima no tiene suficiente dinero para ir al teatro. ¿Le aconsejas que se lo pida prestado a su papá o a su novio?
5. Alguien nos robó las maletas. ¿Adónde nos aconsejas que vayamos?
6. Tengo hambre. ¿Qué me recomiendas que coma?
7. Mi tía está enferma. ¿Qué le aconsejas que haga?
8. Los chicos ensuciaron la alfombra. ¿Qué les sugieres que hagan?
9. A mi hermana no le gusta cocinar. ¿Qué le sugieres que haga?
10. Mañana es el cumpleaños de mi padre. ¿Qué me sugieres que le regale?

D. With a classmate, look at the list of errands that must be done tomorrow. Then take turns saying what you want each other to do, and give different reasons why you can't do it.

MODELO: Comprar la medicina para Ernesto.
Yo quiero que tú compres la medicina para Ernesto.
*Yo no puedo comprarla porque tengo que estudiar.*

1. Llevar los pantalones a la tintorería.
2. Llevar a revelar el rollo de película.
3. Depositar el cheque en el banco.
4. Llevar la motocicleta al taller de mecánica.
5. Comprar las bebidas para la fiesta.
6. Llevar los discos compactos a casa de Ana.
7. Alquilar un video.
8. Comprar los billetes para la excursión.
9. Recoger las entradas para el concierto.
10. Pedirle prestada la grabadora a Rosita.
11. Ir a la oficina de turismo para pedir la lista de hoteles.
12. Comprar el regalo para Eva.
13. Devolverle las maletas a Luis.

**E.** Discuss with a classmate things that important people in your lives (parents, relatives, friends, professors, etc.) want you to do. List at least five things, and then compare your results with the rest of the class.

**F.** Write two or three problems on a slip of paper. Then, form a small group with two or three classmates. Switch slips within the group and take turns offering solutions to each other's problems.

## 3 The subjunctive with verbs of emotion *(El subjuntivo con verbos de emoción)*

- In Spanish, the subjunctive is always used in subordinate clauses when the verb in the main clause expresses any kind of emotion, such as fear, joy, pity, hope, pleasure, surprise, anger, regret, sorrow, likes and dislikes, and so forth.

| | |
|---|---|
| —**Siento** que Julia no **venga** hoy. | *"I'm sorry that Julia is not coming today."* |
| —**Espero** que **pueda** venir mañana. | *"I hope she can come tomorrow."* |
| —Ramón no tiene dinero para comprar un coche. | *"Ramón doesn't have money to buy a car."* |
| —Ojalá que **consiga** un préstamo. | *"I hope that he obtains a loan."* |

**ATENCIÓN** **Ojalá** is always followed by the subjunctive.

**Tus envíos pueden ser cobrados en:**

bancapromex BITAL Woolworth

Elektra Centrales TELECOMM TELEGRAFOS

- If there is no change of subject, the infinitive is used instead of the subjunctive.

| | |
|---|---|
| Me alegro de estar aquí.<br>(**Yo** me alegro—**yo** estoy aquí.) | *I'm glad to be here.* |

- Some verbs and expressions that express emotion are:

**alegrarse (de)** *to be glad*
**esperar** *to hope*
**sentir (e:ie)** *to be sorry, to regret*
**sorprender** *to surprise*
**temer** *to fear*
**es una lástima** *it's a pity*
**ojalá** *I hope*

## práctica

**A.** You are talking to a classmate. Say whether you are glad (**Me alegro de que...**) or sorry (**Siento que...**) about what is happening to your classmate and his or her family.

MODELO: Estoy enferma.
*Siento que estés enferma.*

1. Yo quiero salir, pero tengo que quedarme en casa.
2. Mi hermano y yo no nos sentimos bien.
3. Mi mamá estaba enferma, pero ahora está mejor.
4. Mi hijo es muy inteligente.
5. Mi hermana sabe cocinar muy bien.
6. No hay suficiente dinero en mi cuenta corriente.
7. Mis padres van a Buenos Aires.
8. Mis profesores me dan muchos problemas.

Now, tell your classmate about three things that are going on in your life. He or she should react appropriately.

B. Use your imagination to complete the sentence in parentheses, according to the situation described in the first sentence.

MODELO: Mi hermano quiere depositar un cheque que está a nombre de nuestra madre. (Espero que...)
*Espero que no tenga problemas para depositarlo.*

1. Elsa quiere sacar mil dólares de su cuenta de ahorros. (Temo que...)
2. Quiero comprar una motocicleta, pero no tengo suficiente dinero. (Es una lástima que...)
3. Vamos a ir a la tintorería para recoger mis pantalones. (Espero que...)
4. Hoy no puedo ir con Uds. porque tengo que hacer muchas diligencias. (Siento que...)
5. Ellos van a pedir un préstamo en el banco. (Ojalá que...)
6. Carlitos tiene solamente seis años y tiene cien mil dólares en el banco. (Me sorprende que...)

C. Complete the following sentences to express how you feel, using the infinitive or the subjunctive as appropriate.

1. Yo me alegro mucho de...
2. Yo me alegro mucho de que mis amigos...
3. Yo temo no...
4. Yo temo que mi papá [mamá, hijo(-a)] no...
5. Yo siento...
6. Yo siento que el profesor (la profesora, los profesores)...
7. Yo espero...
8. Yo espero que mis padres (Ud.)...
9. Ojalá que...
10. Es una lástima que...

# ¡A ver cuánto aprendió!

INTERNET

See the *¿Cómo se dice...?* Web site for additional grammar and vocabulary practice: http://spanish.college.hmco.com/students

## ¡Repase el vocabulario!

Complete the following sentences with the appropriate words; then read them aloud.

1. Quiero comprar ________ nueva, especialmente unos pantalones.
2. ¿Cuánto ________ Uds. por ________ un rollo de película en colores?
3. Voy a ________ mil dólares de mi cuenta de ahorros y los voy a ________ en mi cuenta corriente.
4. Necesita el ________ para recoger los pantalones.
5. ¡________ Julio! ¡Los muchachos se llevaron su motocicleta y nunca se la devolvieron!
6. A ver... No puedo verte esta semana, de ________ que tienes que venir la semana próxima.

7. Llegó Antonio y al ________ llegó Luis.
8. Anita caminó ________ mí y me dio un beso.
9. ¿Lo vas a comprar al ________ o a plazos?
10. Tengo mi ________ de cheques, pero no quiero pagar con un cheque; quiero pagar en ________.
11. Si quieres asistir a la universidad, tienes que empezar a ________ dinero.
12. Tienes tu libreta de ________ contigo, ¿verdad? ¿O la dejaste en casa?
13. Para sacar dinero, siempre uso el ________ automático.
14. No me desperté porque no sonó el ________.
15. Mi hermano es alto y de ojos azules, como tú. Uds. se ________ mucho.
16. Hoy no trabajo. Tengo el día ________.

## Entrevista

With a partner, interview each other by asking the following questions.

1. ¿En qué calle y en qué ciudad vives?
2. ¿Tienes hermanos o eres hijo(-a) único(-a)?
3. ¿Te pareces más a tu mamá o a tu papá?
4. ¿Te gusta levantarte temprano o quedarte en la cama hasta tarde?
5. ¿Hiciste algunas diligencias ayer? (¿Cuáles?)
6. ¿Lavas tu ropa en casa o la llevas a la tintorería?
7. ¿Estás ahorrando dinero para comprar algo especial? (¿Qué?)
8. ¿Prefieres que te regalen un coche o una motocicleta? (¿Por qué?)
9. ¿Prefieres tomar fotografías en colores o en blanco y negro?
10. La última *(last)* vez que tomaste fotos, ¿las fotos salieron bien?
11. ¿Vives cerca o lejos de la universidad?
12. ¿Trabajas los sábados o tienes los sábados libres?

## Situaciones

What would you say in the following situations? What might the other person say? Act out the scenes with a partner. Take turns playing each role.

1. You are at the dry cleaner and you want to pick up your pants. You are upset because they are not ready. You want to know when they are going to be ready.
2. You are in the photo section of a large department store. Find out how much they charge to develop black-and-white and color film. Ask about the rolls of film you brought in last week for developing.
3. You are at the bank. You want to withdraw money from your savings account and deposit it in your checking account, but you're not sure what you have to do.

## Para escribir

Write a short composition about the people in the photo on page 267. Describe what the employees and the customers do and want to do. Include as many banking transactions as possible.

# En la vida real

CD-ROM

Do the interactive exercises on the CD-ROM for additional practice.

## Mis diligencias

Have a conversation with a classmate about the errands you have run lately, including those that did not go as planned.

Here are some words and expressions you may want to include:

**mala suerte** *bad luck*
**todo me fue mal** *everything went wrong (for me)*
**todo el día** *all day long*
**el taller de mecánica** *mechanic's shop*

## ¿Qué dice tu horóscopo?

Read the following horoscopes, and then compare your own horoscope with those of your classmates. Try to find a classmate for each sign of the zodiac by asking, **¿De qué signo eres?** *(What's your sign?)*. Offer each other suggestions on how to fulfill your horoscopes.

CAPRICORNIO

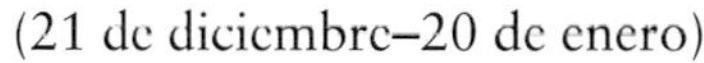

(21 de diciembre–20 de enero)
Tú eres, como siempre, ¡superpráctico! Debes recordar, sin embargo *(however)*, que a veces es bueno ser impulsivo. Si recibes una invitación interesante... ¿por qué no aceptarla?

ACUARIO

(21 de enero–19 de febrero)
Si quieres progresar en tus estudios o en tu profesión, no debes dejar para mañana lo que puedes hacer hoy. Alguien muy importante te está observando.

PISCIS

(20 de febrero–20 de marzo)
Más que nunca, Cupido va a ser parte de tu vida *(life)* este año. Probablemente va a querer que estés preparado para cualquier cosa *(anything)*, incluso una boda.

ARIES

(21 de marzo–20 de abril)
¡Siempre empiezas proyectos con mucho entusiasmo pero casi nunca los terminas! Tienes que hacer lo posible por aprender a ser perseverante. Este año va a ser muy importante para ti.

TAURO

(21 de abril–20 de mayo)
Buena oportunidad para mejorar *(improve)* las finanzas. Un nuevo empleo... una beca *(scholarship)*... Pero tienes que hacer tu parte y aceptar nuevas responsabilidades.

**GÉMINIS**

(21 de mayo–20 de junio)
¡Tienes que salir de la rutina! ¿Por qué no tomas una clase o das una fiesta? Hay muchas personas que quieren ser tus amigos... pero tú no les das la oportunidad.

**CÁNCER**

(21 de junio–20 de julio)
Muy pronto vas a tener que tomar una decisión muy importante. Debes pensar en todas las posibilidades antes de decidir lo que vas a hacer. Hay alguien que está esperando ansiosamente *(anxiously)* tu decisión.

**LEO**

(21 de julio–20 de agosto)
Pronto vas a recibir noticias *(news)* de alguien que hace mucho que no ves. También debes tratar de llamar o de escribirles a aquellas personas que son parte de tu pasado.

**VIRGO**

(21 de agosto–20 de septiembre)
Como siempre, estás trabajando demasiado. No debes sentirte culpable *(guilty)* si decides tomarte unas vacaciones o simplemente ir al cine o al teatro con tus amigos. Esta semana vas a tener muchas oportunidades de divertirte y debes aprovecharlas *(take advantage of them)*.

**LIBRA**

(21 de septiembre–20 de octubre)
Tú eres generalmente una persona muy equilibrada, pero últimamente le estás dando más importancia a tu trabajo y a tus proyectos que a tu familia. Tienes que pasar más tiempo con tu familia.

**ESCORPIÓN**

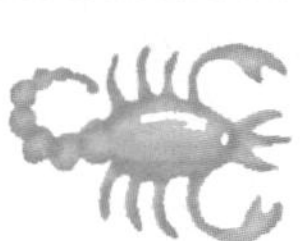

(21 de octubre–20 de noviembre)
Éstos son los momentos indicados para tomar decisiones importantes. Es muy posible que hagas un viaje muy largo, probablemente al extranjero *(abroad)*.

**SAGITARIO**

(21 de noviembre–20 de diciembre)
Hay una persona que está secretamente enamorada de *(in love with)* ti. Muy pronto vas a saber quién es. Debes aceptar las invitaciones de tus amigos porque vas a conocer a esa persona en una fiesta o en un picnic.

## Tenemos algunas quejas... *(We have some complaints)*

Get ready to complain and to respond to complaints about different commercial establishments. The class will be divided into two groups owning different businesses. Group A owns a restaurant, a hotel, and a travel agency. Group B owns a bank, a beauty salon, and a maid service. Before the two groups express their complaints to each other about bad service, each group should decide on the types of concerns and problems that they'll present.

## Antes de leer

**A.** Before you read the fable, look at the illustration. Is the milkmaid happy or sad? What is she thinking about? Why? Now make a list of situations in which the saying "Don't count your chickens before they hatch" would apply.

**B.** As you read the fable, find the answers to the following questions.

1. ¿Adónde va la lechera?
2. ¿Qué lleva en la cabeza?
3. ¿En qué va pensando?
4. ¿Qué es lo primero que va a comprar con el dinero que obtenga?
5. ¿En qué se van a convertir los huevos?
6. ¿Qué va a hacer con el dinero que obtenga de la venta de los pollitos?
7. ¿Qué le va a pedir a su padre que haga?
8. Cuando su padre venda el cochino, ¿qué va a comprar con el dinero de esa venta?
9. ¿Qué pasa cuando la lechera tropieza?
10. ¿Por qué pierde lo único que tenía?
11. ¿Cuál es la moraleja de la fábula?

# La lechera
# (Fábula de origen oriental)

Una lechera° va al mercado, llevando un cántaro° en la cabeza. Va muy contenta, pensando en el dinero que va a ganar con la venta° de la leche.

"Con el dinero que obtenga, voy a comprar un canasto° de huevos que, en el verano, se van a convertir en° pollitos que me van a rodear cantando *pío, pío.*"

Entusiasmada con esta idea, la lechera piensa que, cuando venda los pollos va a tener suficiente dinero para comprar un cochino.°

"En cuanto el cochino engorde le voy a pedir a mi padre que lo lleve al mercado y que lo venda. Con el dinero que le den, voy a comprar una vaca° y un ternero.°"

Tan contenta va la lechera con estos pensamientos° que no se fija en una piedra° que hay en el camino y tropieza.° El cántaro se le cae° de la cabeza y se rompe, derramando° toda la leche. ¡Adiós leche, dinero, pollos, cochino, vaca y ternero!

¡Pobre lechera! Por estar haciendo castillos en el aire, perdió lo único que realmente tenía.

Quiero que recuerdes, lector,° esta moraleja: "No anheles° impaciente el bien futuro; mira que ni el presente está seguro".

milkmaid / jug
sale
basket
**se...** are going to turn into
pig
cow
calf
thoughts
stone / she trips / falls
spilling
reader / **No...** Don't yearn

## Díganos

Answer the following questions, based on your own thoughts and experiences.

1. ¿Hace Ud. "castillos en el aire" a veces?
2. ¿Qué animales domésticos tenía Ud. cuando era niño(-a)? ¿Perros? ¿Gatos *(cats)*? ¿Caballos? ¿Loros *(Parrots)*? ¿Conejillos de Indias *(Guinea pigs)*?
3. ¿Recuerda Ud. una circunstancia en que Ud. sufrió una desilusión *(disappointment)*?
4. ¿Qué significado tiene para Ud. la moraleja de esta fábula?

## ASÍ SOMOS

VIDEO

CD-ROM

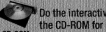

Do the interactive exercises on the CD-ROM for additional practice.

NARRADORA —Cuando Ud. va de compras, ¿prefiere pagar con cheque, con tarjeta de crédito o en efectivo?

JUAN —Cuando voy de compras siempre pago en efectivo porque no tengo tarjeta de crédito y no tengo cheque.

## Preparación

**A. Las diligencias.** Answer the following questions about who runs the errands in your family. You will hear answers to some of these questions when you watch the video. After viewing the video, compare your answers with those you hear.

1. ¿Quién hace las diligencias en su familia?
2. ¿Quién lleva la ropa a la tintorería *(dry cleaner)*?
3. ¿Quién lava la ropa?
4. ¿Quién va al banco?
5. ¿Quién lleva el carro al taller de mecánica *(mechanic's shop)*?
6. ¿Quién hace las compras?
7. ¿Quién va al correo?

**B. Vamos al banco.** With a partner, answer the following questions about your banking habits. You will hear answers to some of these questions when you watch the video. After viewing the video, compare your answers with those you hear.

1. ¿Cuándo va Ud. al banco?
2. ¿Usa Ud. el cajero automático frecuentemente?
3. Cuando Ud. va de compras, ¿prefiere pagar con cheque, con tarjeta de crédito o en efectivo?
4. ¿Cuántas tarjetas de crédito tiene Ud.?

## Comprensión

**A. Las diligencias.** Select the word or phrase that best completes each statement, according to what you understood.

1. (El papá, La mamá) de Juan se ocupa de *(takes charge of)* los aspectos financieros.
2. La casa es la responsabilidad de (Olga, Ricardo).
3. (Olga, Ricardo) lleva a los niños a la escuela.
4. En la casa de Tamara (todos, la mamá y el papá) comparten *(share)* las tareas del hogar *(household chores)*.

**B. El banco.** Answer the following questions according to what you understood from the video.

1. ¿Qué hace Víctor en el banco?
2. ¿Va Tamara al banco con mucha frecuencia?
3. ¿Qué hace Tamara cuando va al banco?
4. ¿Con qué frecuencia deposita Gustavo dinero en el banco?

C. **¿Quién lo dijo?** Match each statement with the name of the person who said it. More than one statement may correspond with one person.

| | A | B |
|---|---|---|
| _____ | 1. Me permite flexibilidad en los retiros *(withdrawals)* de dinero. | a. Tamara |
| _____ | 2. No tengo tarjeta de crédito. | b. John |
| _____ | 3. El cajero automático: sí lo uso con bastante frecuencia. | c. Juan |
| _____ | 4. Lo uso solamente en emergencias. | |

D. **¿Verdadero o falso?** Read the following statements. Circle **V** (**Verdadero**) or **F** (**Falso**) according to what you understood from the video. If a statement is false, correct it.

V F 1. Víctor nunca usa tarjeta de crédito.
V F 2. Víctor paga en efectivo cuando es una compra pequeña *(small)*.
V F 3. Cuando va de compras, Juan siempre paga en efectivo.
V F 4. Gustavo dice que las tarjetas de crédito no son seguras *(safe)*.
V F 5. Paola prefiere usar la tarjeta de crédito porque sus papás *(parents)* pagan la cuenta *(bill)*.
V F 6. Gustavo prefiere pagar en efectivo.
V F 7. Gustavo tiene cuatro tarjetas de crédito.
V F 8. Tamara tiene muchas tarjetas de crédito.
V F 9. Tamara dice que las tarjetas son difíciles de obtener *(to get)*.

## Ampliación

A. **Mis diligencias.** Make a list of errands you need to do this week. Then in groups of three or four, compare your lists. Determine who has the most errands and who has the least errands to do.

B. **Mis asuntos financieros.** Interview a classmate about his or her weekly expenses and banking habits. Use the following questions as a guide.

1. En una semana, ¿cuánto dinero gastas?
2. ¿Cuánto dinero necesitas para las siguientes cosas?
   - comida
   - transporte *(transportation)*
   - gastos de la casa *(household expenses)*
   - gastos personales *(personal expenses)*
3. ¿Tienes cuenta de ahorros o cuenta corriente?
4. ¿Cómo se llama tu banco?
5. ¿Dónde está tu banco?
6. ¿Usas el cajero automático con mucha frecuencia?

Lección 12

# Pidiendo información

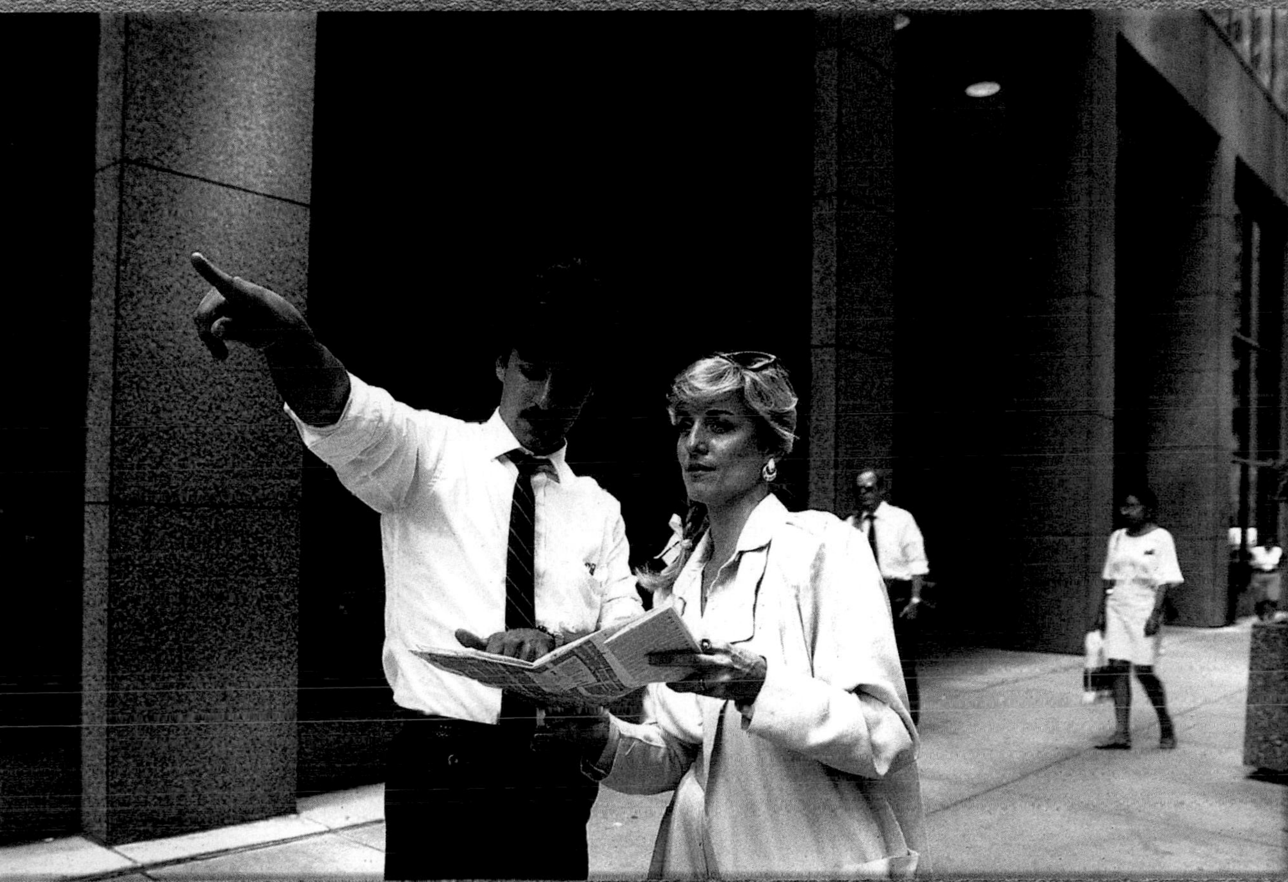

## OBJECTIVES

### Pronunciation

Pronunciation in context

### Structure

The **Ud.** and **Uds.** commands • The relative pronouns **que** and **quien** • The subjunctive to express doubt, disbelief, and denial

### Communication

You will learn vocabulary related to asking for directions and postal services.

# Pidiendo información

*Julia, una chica de Honduras, llegó a Madrid hace una semana. Con sus amigos españoles visitó el Parque del Retiro, el Palacio Real y las antiguas ciudades de Segovia, Ávila y Toledo. En cada lugar compró un montón de tarjetas postales para enviárselas a sus padres y a sus amigos. Hoy decidió ir al correo para enviar las tarjetas, y recoger un paquete y un giro postal.*

JULIA —*(Piensa)* Dudo que el correo esté abierto a esta hora. Creo que abren a las nueve. *(A un señor que está parado en la esquina)* Dígame, señor, ¿dónde queda la oficina de correos?

SR. GÓMEZ —Está a cinco manzanas de aquí, en la Plaza de La Cibeles.

JULIA —Es que... soy extranjera y no conozco las calles. ¿Puede decirme cómo llegar allí?

SR. GÓMEZ —¡Ah!, siga derecho por esta calle hasta llegar a la Plaza de Colón.

JULIA —¿Cuántas cuadras?

SR. GÓMEZ —Dos. Después doble a la derecha al llegar al semáforo, en la calle Alcalá.

JULIA —¿La oficina de correos está en esa calle?

SR. GÓMEZ —Sí, allí mismo. Es un edificio antiguo y está frente a la estación del metro.

*En el correo, Julia habla con el empleado que está en la ventanilla de información.*

JULIA —Vengo a recoger un paquete y un giro postal. Me llamo Julia Reyes.

EMPLEADO —¿Tiene un documento de identidad?

JULIA —Mi pasaporte... pero lo dejé en el hotel.

EMPLEADO —No creo que se los den sin identificación.

JULIA —Bueno, vuelvo esta tarde. ¿Dónde puedo comprar sellos?

EMPLEADO —Vaya a la ventanilla número dos, a la izquierda.

*En la ventanilla número dos, Julia le pide al empleado los sellos que necesita.*

JULIA —Quiero enviar estas tarjetas postales por vía aérea y una carta certificada a Honduras.

EMPLEADO —Son diez euros[1], señorita.

JULIA —¿Puede decirme cómo llegar desde aquí a El[2] Corte Inglés?

EMPLEADO —Salga por la puerta principal, cruce la Plaza de La Cibeles y camine por la Gran Vía hasta llegar a la Plaza Callao. El Corte Inglés está al lado de la plaza.

---

[1]The Spanish currency as of 2002.

[2]Note that **a** and **el** do not contract to form **al** since **El** is part of the store name.

*En El Corte Inglés, Julia se encuentra con su amiga Pilar, con quien va a ir de compras.*

JULIA —Creía que no ibas a estar aquí.
PILAR —Oye, guapa, no es cierto que los españoles siempre lleguemos tarde. A veces somos puntuales.

*Las chicas suben al tercer piso, donde está el departamento de ropa para señoras.*

# Vocabulario

## Cognados

**el documento** document
**la estación** station
**el palacio** palace
**el parque** park
**puntual** punctual

## Nombres

**el departamento de (ropa para) señoras (damas)** women's department
**el documento de identidad (identificación)** I.D.
**el edificio** building
**el (la) español(-a)** Spaniard
**la esquina** corner
**el (la) extranjero(-a)** foreigner
**el giro postal** money order
**la manzana**[1] *(Spain)*, **la cuadra** *(Sp. Am.)* city block
**el metro, el subterráneo** subway
**la oficina de correos, el correo** post office
**el paquete** package, parcel
**la puerta principal** main exit (door)
**el sello, la estampilla, el timbre** *(Mex.)* stamp
**el semáforo** traffic light
**la ventanilla** window (of a car or booth, as in a bank or post office)

## Verbos

**cruzar** to cross
**doblar** to turn, to bend
**dudar** to doubt
**encontrarse (con) (o:ue)** to meet
**subir** to go up, to climb

## Adjetivos

**abierto(-a)** open
**antiguo(-a), viejo(-a)**[2] old
**certificado(-a)** registered, certified
**parado(-a)** standing
**real** royal

---

[1]In Spanish America, **manzana** is used to refer to a block of buildings, not to the distance between streets.
[2]When referring to people, use **viejo,** not **antiguo.**

## Otras palabras y expresiones

**a veces** sometimes
**al lado de** next to
**allí mismo** right there
**cada** each
**derecho** straight (ahead)
**desde** from
**es que...** the fact is . . .
**está a... de aquí** it is . . . from here
**frente a** across from
**hasta llegar** until you get
**No es cierto. (No es verdad.)** It's not true.
**por vía aérea** by airmail
**quien(-es)** who, whom
**sin** without
**un montón de** a pile of

# Vocabulario adicional

## El correo

## La computadora

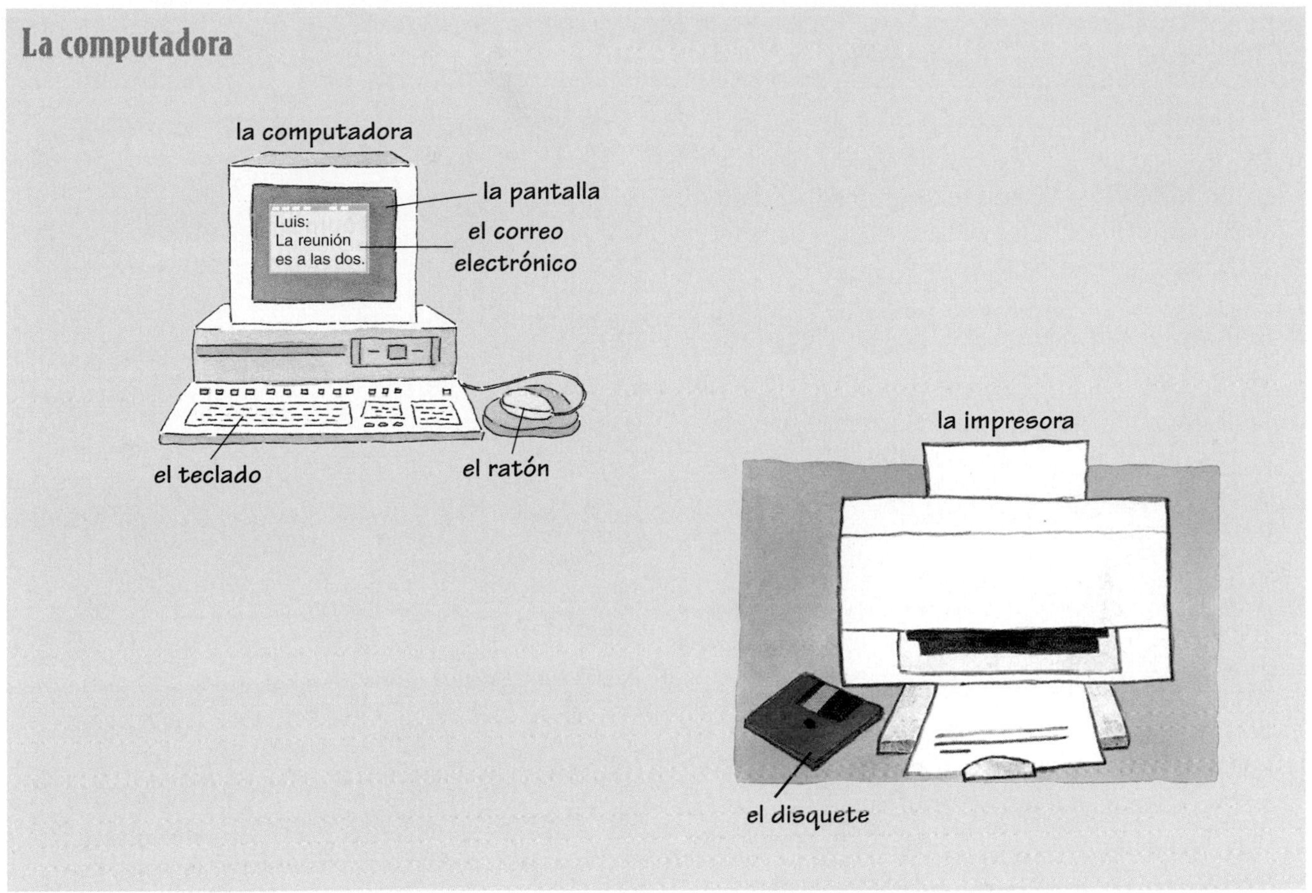


# ¡Conversemos!

Answer the following questions, basing your answers on the dialogues.

1. ¿Cuánto tiempo hace que Julia está en Madrid?
2. ¿Qué lugares visitó con sus amigos españoles?
3. ¿A quién le pregunta dónde queda la oficina de correos?
4. En la calle Alcalá, ¿Julia debe doblar a la izquierda o a la derecha?
5. ¿Cómo es el edificio de correos y dónde está?
6. ¿Por qué no puede Julia recoger el paquete y el giro postal?
7. ¿En qué ventanilla puede comprar sellos?
8. ¿Cómo va a enviar las tarjetas postales Julia?
9. ¿Por dónde sale Julia del correo y qué cruza?
10. ¿A qué tienda va Julia y con quién se encuentra allí?
11. ¿Qué dice Pilar de los españoles?
12. ¿En qué piso está el departamento de ropa para señoras?

# ¿Lo sabía Ud.?

■ Situada en la parte central de la península Ibérica, Madrid es la capital de España. Su población de más de seis millones de habitantes y su importancia cultural y económica la hacen la principal ciudad española.

Una de las calles principales de la ciudad es la Gran Vía, donde hay muchas tiendas elegantes y cafés al aire libre.

■ El correo de Madrid, o el Palacio de Comunicaciones, es un edificio monumental. Está frente a la hermosa fuente *(fountain)* de La Cibeles, que, para muchos, es el símbolo de Madrid.

■ El Palacio Real, situado frente a la Plaza de Oriente, fue la antigua residencia de los reyes de España. Está considerado uno de los mejores edificios de su tipo en Europa.

■ El metro de Madrid es un sistema de transporte muy eficiente y barato. Es el medio *(means)* de transportación que usa la mayoría de los madrileños. También hay un metro en Barcelona.

■ Segovia es un punto de atracción turístico. Entre sus muchos lugares de interés están el Alcázar, un castillo fortaleza *(fortress)*, y el famoso acueducto romano.

■ El uso del "Internet" o la "Red," como se llama en español, es cada día más popular en el mundo hispano, y muchos países tienen su propia página *(home page)*.

- ¿Qué población tiene la capital de este país?
- ¿Cuál es el "símbolo" de Nueva York?
- ¿En qué ciudades de este país hay metro?

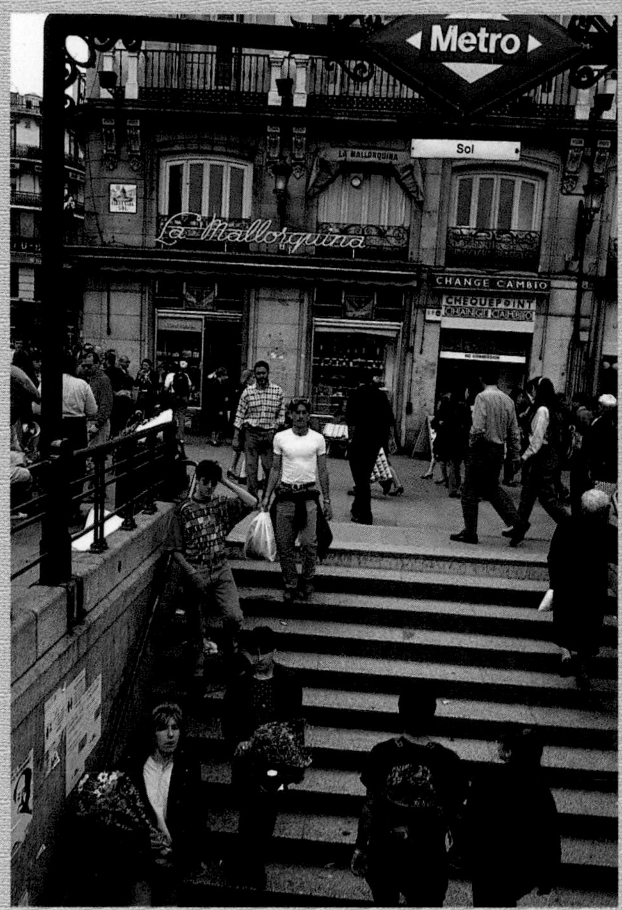


Entrada del metro en La Puerta del Sol, Madrid, España.

See the *¿Cómo se dice...?* Web site for activities on authentic cultural material: http://spanish.college.hmco.com/students

# Pronunciación

STUDENT AUDIO

In this lesson, there are some new words or phrases that may be challenging to pronounce. For further pronunciation practice of Spanish sounds, listen to your instructor and repeat the following words and phrases.

1. Es que... soy **extranjera** y no conozco las calles.
2. Doble a la derecha al llegar al **semáforo.**
3. ¿La oficina de **correos** está en esa calle?
4. ¿Tiene un **documento de identidad?**
5. Quiero enviar estas tarjetas postales **por vía aérea.**

# Estructuras

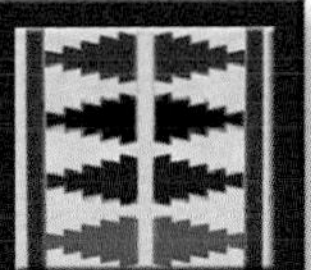

## 1 The Ud. and Uds. commands *(Formas del imperativo para Ud. y Uds.)*

The command forms for **Ud.** and **Uds.**[1] are identical to the corresponding present subjunctive forms.

### A. Regular forms

**Endings of the Formal Commands**

| | | Ud. | Uds. |
|---|---|---|---|
| **-ar** verbs | cantar | cant **-e** | cant **-en** |
| **-er** verbs | beber | beb **-a** | beb **-an** |
| **-ir** verbs | vivir | viv **-a** | viv **-an** |

—¿Cuándo volvemos? — *"When do we return?"*
—**Vuelvan** mañana y **traigan** los documentos. — *"Come back tomorrow and bring the documents."*

—¿Sigo derecho? — *"Do I keep going straight ahead?"*
—No, no **siga** derecho. **Doble** a la izquierda. — *"No, don't keep going straight ahead. Turn left."*

**ATENCIÓN** To give a negative **Ud./Uds.** command, place **no** in front of the verb: **No siga** derecho.

[1]**Tú** commands will be studied in **Lección 13.**

## B. Irregular forms

■ The command forms of the following verbs are irregular.

| | dar | estar | ser | ir |
|---|---|---|---|---|
| Ud. | dé | esté | sea | vaya |
| Uds. | den | estén | sean | vayan |

—¿Adónde tengo que ir? *"Where do I have to go?"*
—**Vaya** a la ventanilla número dos. *"Go to window number two."*

—¿A qué hora tenemos que estar aquí? *"At what time do we have to be here?"*
—**Estén** aquí a las ocho. ¡**Sean** puntuales! *"Be here at eight. Be punctual!"*

## práctica

**A.** What commands would these people give?

1. *El profesor a los estudiantes:*

venir a clase temprano
abrir el libro
ir a la pizarra
hacer los ejercicios
cerrar el libro
hablar solamente español
no hablar inglés en la clase

2. *La directora a la secretaria:*

estar en la oficina a las ocho
traer las cartas
traducir los documentos
llevar las cartas al correo
comprar estampillas
llamar por teléfono al Sr. Paz
conseguir la dirección del Banco de Ponce
no volver hasta las tres

**B.** María Ester, a girl from Colombia, has decided to visit a few places of interest in Madrid, but doesn't know how to get to them. Using the map below, can you help her?

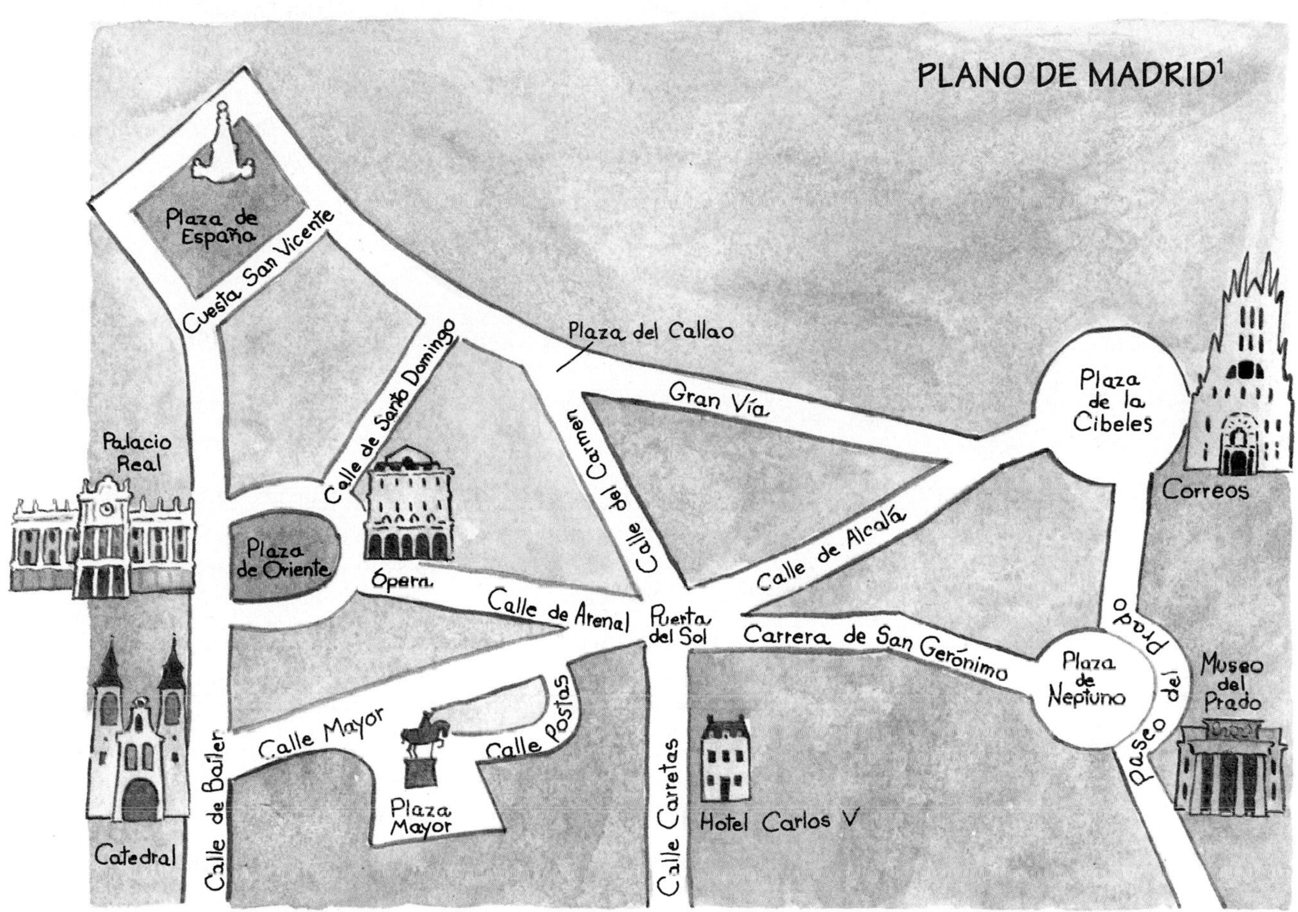


¿Cómo voy...

1. del hotel Carlos V al Museo del Prado?
2. del Museo del Prado a la Plaza Mayor?
3. de la Plaza Mayor al Palacio Real y la Catedral?
4. de la Plaza de Oriente a la Plaza de España?
5. de la Plaza de España a la Puerta del Sol?
6. de la Puerta del Sol a Correos?

[1]This is a simplified version of an actual map of Madrid.

## C. Position of object pronouns with direct commands

■ In all direct *affirmative* commands, the object pronouns are placed *after* the verb and attached to it.

| **Ud.** *form* | | **Uds.** *form* | |
|---|---|---|---|
| Hága**lo**. | *Do it.* | Cómpren**lo**. | *Buy it.* |
| Díga**les**. | *Tell them.* | Dígan**le**. | *Tell him/her.* |
| Tráiga**nosla**. | *Bring it to us.* | Tráigan**selo**. | *Bring it to him/her.* |
| Quéde**se**. | *Stay.* | Quéden**se**. | *Stay.* |

**ATENCIÓN** Note the use of the written accent, which follows the rules for accentuation. See Appendix A.

■ In all *negative* commands, the pronouns are placed *in front of the verb.*

| **Ud.** *form* | | **Uds.** *form* | |
|---|---|---|---|
| No **lo** haga. | *Don't do it.* | No **lo** hagan. | *Don't do it.* |
| No **le** hable. | *Don't speak to him/her.* | No **le** hablen. | *Don't speak to him/her.* |
| No **se lo** dé. | *Don't give it to him/her.* | No **se lo** den. | *Don't give it to him/her.* |

■ Remember that when an indirect and a direct object pronoun are used together in the same sentence, the indirect object always precedes the direct object.

## práctica

**A.** Using the direct commands, tell your younger brothers to do the following.

1. Levantarse a las siete, bañarse y vestirse.
2. Hacer unos sándwiches y ponerlos en el refrigerador.
3. Escribirle una carta a la abuela y echarla al correo.
4. Mandarle un paquete a Teresa.
5. Llamar a la Dra. Peña, pero no llamarla antes de las tres.
6. Comprarle el regalo a mamá, pero no dárselo hoy.
7. Decirle a Marta que la fiesta es mañana, pero no decírselo a Raúl.
8. No acostarse muy tarde.

**B.** You are having dinner at a fancy restaurant. Tell the waiter what you want or don't want him to do.

> MODELO: ¿Le traigo el menú?
> *Sí, tráigamelo, por favor. (No, no me lo traiga.)*

1. ¿Le traigo la lista de vinos?
2. ¿Le sirvo la ensalada primero?
3. ¿Le pongo pimienta a la ensalada?

4. ¿Abro la botella de vino ahora?
5. ¿Le traigo una tortilla a la española?
6. ¿Le sirvo el café ahora?
7. ¿Le traigo la cuenta ahora?

C. With a partner, take turns telling a group of people what to do about the items given.

MODELO: las estampillas
*Cómprenlas.*

1. el paquete
2. el giro postal
3. los documentos
4. las cartas
5. el regalo
6. los pantalones
7. la cuenta corriente
8. el registro

D. With a partner, take turns playing the roles of a tourist who is planning a trip to an exotic location and a travel agent. The tourist should name a destination and ask whether he or she should bring along certain items. The agent should say whether each article would or would not be appropriate. List five or six items each. Follow the models.

MODELO: —¿Debo llevar las tarjetas postales?
—*No, no las lleve. Cómprelas allí.*

—¿Debo llevar mi tienda de campaña?
—*Sí, llévela. No hay hoteles.*

## 2 The relative pronouns que and quien *(Los pronombres relativos que y quien)*

Relative pronouns are used to combine two sentences that have a common element, usually a noun or a pronoun.

### A. The relative pronoun *que*

¿Dónde está **el paquete**? Trajiste **el paquete.**

common element

¿Dónde está el paquete **que** trajiste?

R.P.

**La chica** se llama Rosa. **La chica** vino esta mañana.

common element

La chica **que** vino esta mañana se llama Rosa.

R.P.

- Note that the relative pronoun **que** not only helps to combine the two sentences in each example, but also replaces the nouns **el paquete** and **la chica** in the second sentences.
- The relative pronoun **que** is invariable and is used for both persons and things. It is the Spanish equivalent of *that*, *which*, and *who*. Unlike its English equivalent, the Spanish **que** is never omitted.

| | |
|---|---|
| —¿Para quién es el libro **que** compraste? | *"For whom is the book that you bought?"* |
| —Es para la señora **que** enseña español. | *"It is for the woman who teaches Spanish."* |

## B. The relative pronoun *quien*

| | |
|---|---|
| —¿La muchacha **con quien** hablabas es americana? | *"Is the girl with whom you were talking an American?"* |
| —No, es extranjera. | *"No, she's a foreigner."* |
| —¿Quiénes son esos señores? | *"Who are those gentlemen?"* |
| —Son los señores **de quienes** te habló José. | *"They are the gentlemen about whom José spoke to you."* |

- The relative pronoun **quien** is used only with persons.
- The plural of **quien** is **quienes. Quien** does not change for gender.
- **Quien** is generally used after prepositions, i.e., **con quien, de quienes.**
- **Quien** is the Spanish equivalent of *whom* and *that*.

## práctica

**A.** Complete the following dialogues, using **que, quien,** or **quienes.** Then act them out with a partner.

1. —¿Quién es el señor ________ trajo las cartas?
   —Es el papá de Marisa, la chica con ________ trabajo.
2. —¿Dónde están las estampillas ________ compré ayer?
   —En tu escritorio.
3. —Las chicas con ________ salimos anoche llamaron esta mañana.
   —¿Qué dijeron?
   —Que nos van a traer los libros ________ necesitamos.
4. —¿Con quién vas al museo?
   —Con María Luisa, la chica de ________ te hablé.
5. —¿Ella es la muchacha ________ trabaja contigo?
   —No, es la chica con ________ estudio.

**B.** Interview a classmate, using the following questions. When you have finished, switch roles.

1. ¿Cómo se llama la persona a quien más admiras?
2. ¿Cómo se llama el profesor o la profesora que enseña tu clase favorita?
3. ¿Quiénes son las personas que viven contigo?

4. ¿Cómo se llaman las personas con quienes vas a salir el sábado?
5. ¿Quién es la persona que más te quiere?
6. ¿Cuál es la comida que más te gusta?
7. ¿Cuál es el color que más te gusta?
8. ¿Dónde está el banco en el que tienes tu cuenta corriente? (¿Y tu cuenta de ahorros?)

## 3 The subjunctive to express doubt, disbelief, and denial *(Uso del subjuntivo para expresar duda, incredulidad y negación)*

### A. Doubt

■ In Spanish, the subjunctive is always used in a subordinate clause when the verb of the main clause expresses doubt or uncertainty.

| | |
|---|---|
| —Vamos al correo. | *"Let's go to the post office."* |
| —**Dudo** que **esté** abierto a esta hora. | *"I doubt that it's open at this time."* |
| —Estoy seguro de que abren a las ocho. | *"I'm sure that they open at eight."* |

**ATENCIÓN** When *no doubt* is expressed and the speaker is certain of the reality (**Estoy seguro[-a], No dudo**), the indicative is used: **Estoy seguro** de que **abren** a las ocho.

### B. Disbelief

■ The verb **creer** is followed by the subjunctive in negative sentences, where it expresses disbelief.

| | |
|---|---|
| —¿Uds. van a ir de compras hoy? | *"Are you going to go shopping today?"* |
| —No..., **no creo** que **tengamos** tiempo... | *"No..., I don't think we'll have time..."* |
| —Yo creo que pueden ir, si salen temprano. | *"I think you can go if you leave early."* |

**ATENCIÓN** **Creer** is followed by the indicative when it expresses belief or conviction: **Yo creo** que **pueden** ir.

### C. Denial

■ When the main clause expresses denial of what is said in the subordinate clause, the subjunctive is used.

| | |
|---|---|
| —¡Tú siempre llegas tarde! | *"You always arrive late!"* |
| —**No es verdad** que siempre **llegue** tarde. No niego que a veces llego un poco tarde, pero a veces soy puntual. | *"It's not true that I always arrive late. I don't deny that sometimes I arrive a little late, but sometimes I'm punctual."* |

**ATENCIÓN** When the main clause does *not* deny, but rather confirms what is said in the subordinate clause, the indicative is used: **No niego** que a veces **llego** un poco tarde.

## práctica

**A.** Say whether the following statements are true or not. If a statement is false, correct it.

MODELO: Nosotros celebramos la independencia de Chile.
*No es verdad que nosotros celebremos la independencia de Chile; celebramos la independencia de los Estados Unidos.*

1. Texas es más grande que Maine.
2. Hace más calor en Alaska que en Arizona.
3. Buenos Aires es la capital de Chile.
4. México está al norte de los Estados Unidos.
5. El 25 de diciembre celebramos la independencia de nuestro país.
6. El presidente del país puede ser extranjero.
7. Necesitamos un documento de identidad para comprar estampillas.
8. Revelan rollos de película en el correo.
9. Echamos las cartas en el buzón.
10. Podemos comprar un giro postal en el correo.

**B.** You and a friend are spending the weekend in a very small town. Your friend wants to know about things to do, places to go, and so on. Answer, expressing belief or disbelief, doubt or certainty.

1. ¿Tú crees que hay habitaciones libres en el hotel?
2. ¿Tú crees que un cuarto cuesta menos de cien dólares la noche?
3. ¿Tú crees que aceptan cheques de viajero en el hotel?
4. ¿Tú crees que hay un aeropuerto aquí?
5. ¿Podemos alquilar un coche?
6. Son las siete; ¿tú crees que el correo está abierto?
7. Vamos al centro. Quiero ir a una tienda elegante.
8. Tengo el pelo muy largo. Dicen que aquí hay peluquerías excelentes.
9. Quiero ir a cenar a un restaurante francés.
10. ¿Tú crees que vamos a volver aquí algún día?

**C.** Complete the following sentences logically, using the subjunctive or the indicative as appropriate.

1. Yo dudo que en mi cuenta de ahorros…
2. Estoy seguro(-a) de que el banco…
3. No creo que la oficina de correos…
4. Estoy seguro(-a) de que la estación del metro…
5. No es verdad que yo…
6. Yo no niego que mis padres…
7. Creo que los sellos…
8. No dudo que allí mismo…

# ¡A ver cuánto aprendió!

INTERNET

See the *¿Cómo se dice...?* Web site for additional grammar and vocabulary practice: http://spanish.college.hmco.com/students

## ¡Repase el vocabulario!

Complete the following sentences with words from the lesson vocabulary.

1. Tengo que bajar porque el departamento de señoras no está ________; está ________.
2. No estamos sentados; estamos ________.
3. Hoy vamos a visitar el ________ del Retiro y el ________ Real.
4. Dígame, ¿la ________ del metro está en la calle Alcalá?
5. Mis padres me van a mandar un ________ postal porque necesito dinero.
6. Recibí un ________ de tarjetas de Navidad el año pasado.
7. Le voy a decir al secretario que ponga las cartas certificadas en mi ________.
8. Mandé el paquete por vía ________ y ________.
9. Está allí ________, en la esquina. Va a ________ la calle.
10. Los colores del ________ son rojo, amarillo y verde.
11. Primero voy a estudiar y después voy a ________ con Carlos en la tienda.
12. En ________ lugar que visitamos, compramos tarjetas.
13. La oficina está arriba. Dudo que ellos puedan ________ hasta el décimo piso.
14. Elsa le va a preguntar al cartero dónde queda la ________ de correos.
15. Para ir al banco no debe seguir derecho. Debe ________ a la izquierda.

## Entrevista

With a partner, interview each other by asking the following questions.

1. ¿Sabes dónde queda la oficina de correos?
2. ¿Es verdad que abren el correo a las siete de la mañana?
3. ¿A cuántas cuadras de tu casa queda el correo?
4. ¿Qué queda frente a tu casa? ¿Al lado de tu casa?
5. ¿Cómo puedo ir de aquí a tu casa?
6. Para ir a la cafetería, ¿debo seguir derecho o doblar a la izquierda o a la derecha?
7. ¿Prefieres los edificios antiguos o modernos?
8. ¿Hay metro en la ciudad donde vives?
9. ¿Hay muchos extranjeros en la ciudad donde vives?
10. ¿Tienes pasaporte?
11. ¿Crees que los norteamericanos son puntuales?
12. ¿Es verdad que tú siempre llegas tarde a clase?

## Situaciones

What would you say in the following situations? What might the other person say? Act out the scenes with a partner. Take turns playing each role.

1. You are in Madrid, and you want to know where the post office is located. You are a foreigner and you don't know your way around. Ask someone on the street for help.

2. A foreigner asks you for directions to a post office in your town. Explain to him or her how to get to the nearest one.
3. You are at the post office. You want to send some letters by airmail, buy some stamps, and find out how much it costs to send a registered letter to the United States. You also want to know if there is a package for you.

## Para escribir

You are an advice columnist for a Spanish newspaper. How would you respond to the following letters? Use command forms to give your advice in writing.

1. Tengo 18 años y quiero vivir sola *(alone)* en un apartamento, pero mis padres no quieren que me vaya de la casa. ¿Qué me sugiere que haga?
   *Ansiosa de libertad*
2. Pienso viajar a París este verano y tengo un amigo que quiere ir conmigo. Yo no quiero ofenderlo, pero no deseo ir con él porque es muy aburrido y siempre está cansado. ¿Qué puedo hacer?
   *Un viajero*
3. Tengo un novio que es muy bueno, pero no es muy interesante. El sábado pasado fui a una fiesta y conocí a un hombre extraordinario y muy guapo que me invitó a salir. ¿Debo aceptar su invitación o no? ¿Qué me aconseja que haga?
   *Indecisa*
4. Tenemos unos vecinos *(neighbors)* que tienen cinco hijos; los niños son terribles y lo rompen *(break)* todo. Planeamos dar una fiesta muy elegante para celebrar el fin de año y queremos invitarlos pero ellos siempre llevan a sus hijos a todas partes *(everywhere)*. ¿Cómo les pedimos que no traigan a sus hijos a la fiesta?
   *Entre la espada y la pared*[1]

# En la vida real

CD-ROM

Do the interactive exercises on the CD-ROM for additional practice.

## ¿Cómo voy...?

With a classmate, figure out how to give a new student the following directions:

***Within the university***

¿Cómo voy de la clase de español...
1. a la biblioteca?
2. al edificio de administración?
3. a la cafetería?
4. al baño?

***Outside the university***

¿Cómo voy de la universidad...
1. al restaurante McDonald's?
2. a la oficina de correos?
3. a la gasolinera *(gas station)*?
4. a tu casa o apartamento?

---

[1] *Between a rock and a hard place (lit., between the sword and the wall)*

## Señales de tráfico *(Traffic signs)*

You are traveling in Spain and see the following signs. What do they mean?

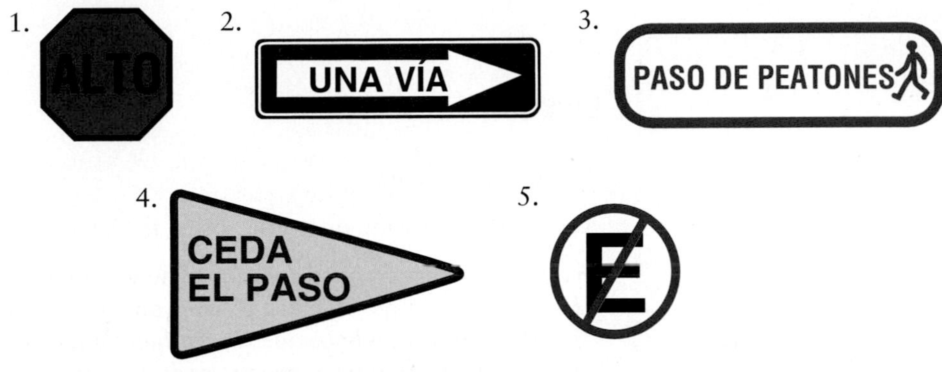


a. Yield
b. No parking
c. Stop
d. One way
e. Pedestrian crossing

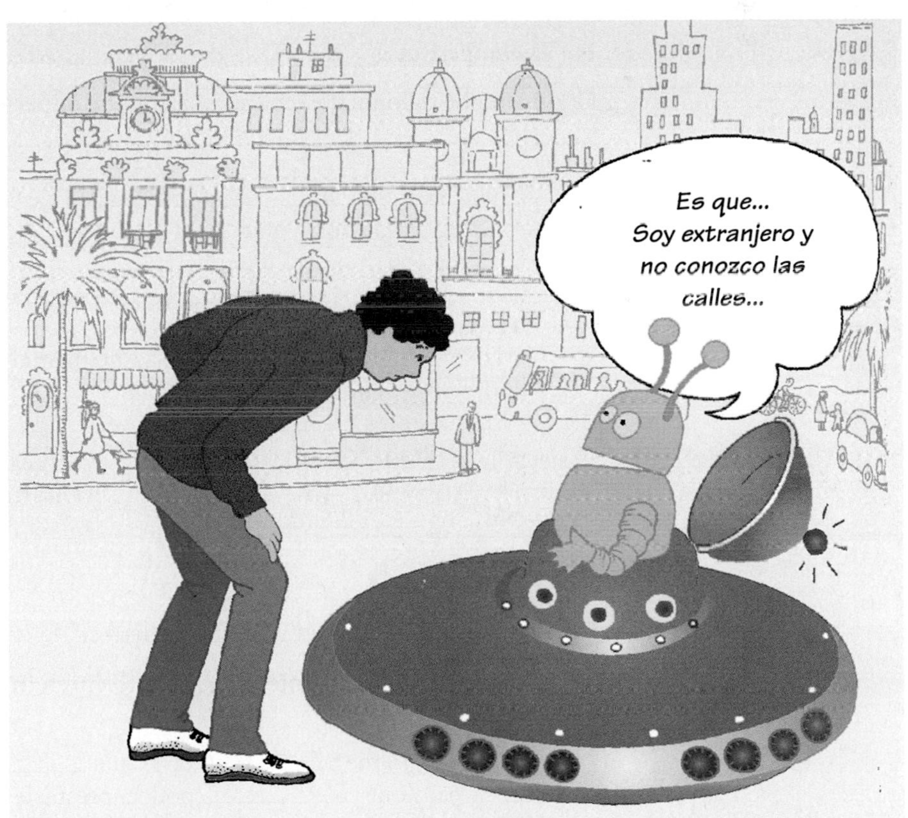

Es que...
Soy extranjero y
no conozco las
calles...


## Nuestra casa es su casa

You and your roommate are going away for a couple of weeks and are letting friends from out of town stay in your apartment. With your roommate (a classmate), prepare a list of (1) recommendations of fun things to do in town, including instructions for how to get to them; (2) household chores or errands they should do in your absence.

Take this test. When you have finished, check your answers in the answer key provided for this section in Appendix E. Then use a red pen to correct any mistakes you may have made. Are you ready?

## Lección 10

### A. Hace... meaning *ago*

Answer the following questions, using the cues provided.

1. ¿Cuánto tiempo hace que conociste a tu mejor amigo(-a)? (cuatro años)
2. ¿Cuánto tiempo hace que tú y tus amigos fueron a acampar? (seis meses)
3. ¿Cuánto tiempo hace que tú y tu familia fueron a la playa? (tres días)
4. ¿Cuánto tiempo hace que tus padres volvieron del campo? (una semana)
5. ¿Cuánto tiempo hace que llegaste a tu casa? (quince minutos)

### B. The imperfect

Complete the following exchanges, using the imperfect of the verbs in the list.

costar (1)   vivir (3)   hospedarse (1)   ser (4)   ir (2)   ver (1)

1. —¿Qué hora ________ cuando tú llegaste a casa?
   —________ las dos y media.
2. —¿Dónde ________ tú cuando ________ chico?
   —Yo ________ en Lima, pero todos los años mi familia y yo ________ de vacaciones a Buenos Aires.
   —¿Tú ________ a tus abuelos frecuentemente?
   —No, porque ellos ________ en Chile.
3. —¿En qué hotel ________ Julio cuando ________ a California?
   —En el Hilton.
   —¿Es verdad que ________ un ojo de la cara?
   —No, no ________ muy caro.

### C. The preterit contrasted with the imperfect

Complete the following sentences, using the preterit or the imperfect of the verbs in parentheses.

1. Anoche Sergio me ________ (decir) que ________ (necesitar) una bolsa de dormir pero que tú ________ (poder) prestarle tu tienda de campaña.
2. Ayer Carlos y yo ________ (comprar) una caña de pescar. Cuando nosotros ________ (ser) niños, ________ (ir) de pesca con nuestros amigos.
3. Cuando yo ________ (tener) diez años, mi familia y yo ________ (venir) a los Estados Unidos a vivir. Nosotros ________ (hablar) inglés y español.
4. —¿Cómo te ________ (ir) anoche, en la fiesta de Margarita?
   —No muy bien. (Yo) ________ (tener) que irme a las diez porque me ________ (doler) mucho la cabeza.
5. Cuando Amalia ________ (ir) a la biblioteca, ________ (ver) un accidente en la calle Quinta. Dos personas ________ (morir).

### D. Verbs that change meaning in the preterit

Answer the following questions, using the cues provided.

1. ¿Dónde conoció Beto a Marisa? (en la universidad)
2. ¿Marisa conocía a la hermana de Beto? (sí)
3. ¿Tú querías venir a clase hoy? (no)
4. ¿Uds. sabían que hoy había examen? (no)
5. David se quedó en su casa hoy. ¿No quiso venir? (no)

### E. Just words . . .

Match each question in column A with the best response in column B.

| A | B |
|---|---|
| 1. ¿Qué actividades al aire libre te gustan? | a. Tomo el sol. |
| 2. ¿Fueron en coche? | b. No, alquilamos una cabaña. |
| 3. ¿Se divirtieron en la fiesta? | c. Profundamente. |
| 4. ¿Marcelo es chileno? | d. Sí, pero estaba equivocada. |
| 5. ¿Acamparon? | e. No, pero Eva me convenció y fui. |
| 6. ¿El Amazonas es un lago? | f. Sí, es de Santiago. |
| 7. ¿Qué país está al oeste de Argentina? | g. ¡Espero que sí! |
| 8. ¿Qué haces en la playa? | h. Me dio un abrazo. |
| 9. ¿Tú dijiste que él planeaba trabajar toda la noche? | i. No, en bicicleta. |
| 10. ¿Cómo dormiste? | j. Al tenis. |
| 11. ¿Qué hizo Luis cuando te vio? | k. No, pero yo le voy a enseñar. |
| 12. ¿Tú no querías ir a esquiar? | l. ¡No! ¡Es un río! |
| 13. ¿El niño sabe nadar? | m. Montar a caballo y escalar montañas. |
| 14. ¿Tus padres te van a prestar el dinero? | n. Chile. |
| 15. ¿A qué juegan? | o. Sí, lo pasamos muy bien. |

### F. Culture

Answer the following questions based on the **¿Lo sabía Ud.?** section.

1. ¿Qué ciudades sudamericanas son centros turísticos internacionales?
2. ¿A dónde va mucha gente en junio, julio y agosto para esquiar?
3. ¿Cuáles son los meses de invierno en el hemisferio sur?

## Lección 11

### A. The subjunctive mood

Give the present subjunctive of the following verbs, according to each subject.

1. estar: nosotros
2. caminar: tú
3. sacar: yo
4. parecerse: ella
5. dar: ellos
6. saber: tú
7. recoger: nosotros
8. ser: ustedes
9. ir: usted
10. recibir: él

**B. The subjunctive with verbs of volition**

Complete the following exchanges, using the infinitive or the present subjunctive of the verbs in parentheses.

1. —¿Tú quieres ________ (depositar) el dinero en el banco?
   —Sí, mi esposa quiere que (yo) ________ (abrir) una cuenta de ahorros.
2. —¿Qué me aconsejas que ________ (hacer)?
   —Yo te sugiero que ________ (estar) aquí a las dos.
3. —¿Tienes que hacer diligencias?
   —Sí, mi madre quiere que ________ (ir) a la tintorería y al banco.
4. —Yo les recomiendo que ________ (pagar) a plazos.
   —No, nosotros queremos ________ (pagar) al contado.
5. —Yo te sugiero que ________ (traer) tu talonario de cheques.
   —Sí, y también necesito ________ (llenar) la tarjeta.

**C. The subjunctive with verbs of emotion**

Rewrite the following sentences, according to the new beginnings.

1. Ellos tienen los pantalones de Oscar.
   Me alegro de que ellos...
2. Julio estaciona el coche cerca del banco.
   Espero que Julio...
3. Tú sabes el saldo de mi cuenta corriente.
   Me sorprende que tú...
4. Ada está en la estación de policía.
   Temo que Ada...
5. Nosotros no podemos traer los comprobantes.
   Es una lástima que nosotros...
6. Ellos van al banco.
   Ojalá que ellos...

**D. Just words . . .**

Give the word or phrase that is equivalent to each of the following.

1. estacionar
2. moto
3. se usa para dormir
4. que no tiene hermanos
5. no levantarse temprano
6. lo que se hace con un rollo de película
7. en cuanto
8. de modo que
9. pantalones, vestidos, etc.
10. que no tiene dinero
11. escribir la fecha
12. que no cuesta nada

**E. Culture**

Read the following statements and circle **V** (**Verdadero**) or **F** (**Falso**), based on the **¿Lo sabía Ud.?** section.

V F 1. Puerto Rico es una de las Antillas Menores.
V F 2. Las lenguas oficiales de Puerto Rico son el español y el inglés.
V F 3. La capital de Puerto Rico es San José.

V F 4. Los puertorriqueños también se llaman "boricuas".
V F 5. En Latinoamérica no existen sucursales de bancos extranjeros.
V F 6. El uso del cheque es mucho más común en América Latina que en los Estados Unidos.

## Lección 12

### A. The *Ud.* and *Uds.* commands

Complete the following sentences, using the Spanish equivalent of the words in parentheses.

1. ________ en la oficina de correos a las ocho, señoras. *(Be)*
2. Necesito el paquete. ________ esta tarde, señorita. *(Bring it to me)*
3. ________ por la puerta principal, señoritas. *(Go out)*
4. ¿Las estampillas? ________ esta tarde, señora. *(Give them to him)*
5. ________ a la ventanilla número cuatro, señoras. *(Go)*
6. ________ aquí, señor López. *(Stay)*
7. Necesitamos el giro postal. ________ mañana, señorita Paz. *(Send it to us)*
8. ¿Los libros? ________ allí mismo, señor. *(Put them)*

### B. The relative pronouns *que* and *quien*

Rewrite the following, using **que, quien,** or **quienes.**

1. Ésta es la señora. La señora vino ayer.
2. Éstos son los niños. Yo te hablé de los niños.
3. Ésa es la profesora. Nosotros compramos los libros para la profesora.

### C. The subjunctive to express doubt, disbelief, and denial

Complete the following sentences, using the present subjunctive or the present indicative of the verbs in parentheses.

1. Yo no creo que ella ________ (ser) española.
2. Dudo que el departamento de ropa para damas ________ (estar) en el segundo piso.
3. No es verdad que ustedes ________ (necesitar) documentos de identidad.
4. Creo que Quito ________ (estar) a cien kilómetros de aquí.
5. Estoy seguro de que ellos ________ (encontrarse) en el restaurante.
6. Es verdad que yo ________ (visitar) a mis tíos a veces.
7. No dudo que tú ________ (poder) mandar las cartas por vía aérea.
8. Yo no niego que Elena ________ (ser) la novia de mi hermano.

### D. Just words . . .

Complete the following sentences using vocabulary learned in **Lección 12.**

1. Teresa vive al ________ de mi casa.
2. ¿Doblo o sigo ________?
3. Marina necesita dinero. Le voy a mandar un ________ postal.
4. ¿Vas a tomar el ________ para ir al centro?

5. La ventana está ________ . ¿Puedes cerrarla, por favor?
6. No puedes ________ la calle porque el ________ está en rojo.
7. Tenemos que ________. El apartamento de Susana está arriba, en el segundo piso.
8. Está ________ en la esquina, leyendo.
9. ¿Es un edificio ________ o moderno?
10. El Palacio Real está a cinco ________ de aquí, ________ al parque.
11. Yo veía a mis abuelos ________ día.
12. Yo nunca llego tarde; soy muy ________.
13. Compré un ________ de tarjetas postales.
14. Tengo que ________ una carta al correo. ¿Hay un ________ en la esquina de tu casa?
15. Escriba con ________ de molde.

### E. Culture

Complete the following, based on the **¿Lo sabía Ud.?** section.

1. Madrid está situada en la parte ________ de la Península Ibérica.
2. Una de las calles principales de Madrid es la Gran ________.
3. El Palacio de Comunicaciones está frente a la hermosa ________ de La Cibeles.
4. El Palacio Real fue la antigua residencia de los ________ de España.
5. El medio de transportación que usa la mayoría de los madrileños es el ________.
6. En Segovia está el famoso ________ romano.

# 6. El caribe

Cuba

Rep. Dominicana

Puerto Rico

- El Viejo San Juan, fundado en 1521, es uno de los barrios coloniales mejor conservados de las Américas. El barrio está casi totalmente rodeado de murallas de piedra *(stone walls)* construidas por los españoles.
- Puerto Rico es una de las áreas más densamente pobladas del mundo. Con una extensión de unos nueve mil kilómetros cuadrados, tiene una población de cerca de *(around)* cuatro millones de habitantes.
- La isla donde se encuentra la República Dominicana fue descubierta en 1492 durante el primer viaje de Colón al Nuevo Mundo. Colón le dio a la isla el nombre de La Española. La parte occidental *(western)* está ocupada por la República de Haití, donde se hablan francés y francés criollo *(creole)*.
- La Habana, capital de Cuba, con más de dos millones de habitantes, es la ciudad más grande del Caribe. Antes de la revolución de Castro en 1958, era uno de los mayores centros de atracción turística del Caribe para los norteamericanos. Hoy el gobierno cubano trata de atraer a turistas de Europa y de Latinoamérica.

Puerto Rico tiene numerosas playas de arena *(sand)* blanca y fina como la Playa de las Croabas. Miles de turistas visitan estas playas todos los años, especialmente en el invierno.

*¿A Ud. le gusta ir a la playa?*

La sección antigua de La Habana, Cuba, se distingue por los numerosos edificios coloniales que aún conserva. "La Habana Vieja", como se conoce la parte antigua de la ciudad, fue declarada por la UNESCO *Monumento de la humanidad*, y se caracteriza por sus calles estrechas *(narrow)*, sus casas de tipo colonial y sus monumentos históricos. La Catedral de La Habana, que aparece en la foto, es uno de los edificios más característicos de la arquitectura colonial española.

*¿Hay edificios de tipo colonial en la ciudad donde Ud. vive?*

La fortaleza *(fortress)* del Morro está situada a la entrada de la bahía *(Bay)* de San Juan, en Puerto Rico. Los españoles la construyeron en el siglo XVI para defender la isla de los ataques de los piratas. Hoy el Morro es un monumento nacional y constituye una importante atracción turística.

*¿Qué monumentos históricos se encuentran donde Ud. vive?*

El béisbol es el deporte más popular en los países del Caribe. De sus equipos *(teams)* locales, como éste de Puerto Rico, han salido algunos de los mejores jugadores *(players)* de las Grandes Ligas de los Estados Unidos. El béisbol es también un deporte popular en Nicaragua, Panamá, Venezuela y México.

*¿Puede Ud. nombrar algunos jugadores de béisbol hispanos de las Grandes Ligas?*

La Catedral de Santa María la Menor en Santo Domingo, capital de la República Dominicana, fue la primera catedral fundada en América. Diego Colón, hijo de Cristóbal Colón, inició su construcción en 1514. La catedral se terminó de construir en 1540. Se dice que aquí están enterrados *(buried)* los restos de Cristóbal Colón.

*¿En qué fecha se conmemora la llegada* (arrival) *de Colón al Nuevo Mundo?*

La Universidad de La Habana, la más antigua de la isla de Cuba, fue establecida en 1728. La universidad tiene dos sedes *(campuses)*: la antigua está en el centro de la ciudad, y la moderna se encuentra en las afueras *(outskirts)* de la ciudad.

*¿Cuál es la universidad más antigua de su país?*

El clima tropical del Caribe ofrece condiciones ideales para el cultivo de una gran variedad de frutas: el mango, la papaya, la banana y la guayaba, entre muchas otras. En la foto, un puesto de frutas en el Viejo San Juan muestra esta gran variedad.

*¿Puede Ud. identificar las frutas que aparecen en la foto?*

Do the interactive exercises on the CD-ROM for additional practice.

## Preparación

**¿Cuánto saben Uds. ya?** After reading **Panorama hispánico 6**, get together in groups of three or four students and answer the following questions.

1. ¿Por qué van muchos turistas a Puerto Rico?
2. ¿Quiénes construyeron la fortaleza del Morro y para qué?
3. ¿Cuál es la ciudad más grande del Caribe?
4. ¿Cómo se llama la parte antigua de la ciudad de La Habana?
5. ¿Cuál es la universidad más antigua de Cuba y cuántas sedes *(campuses)* tiene?
6. ¿Qué nombre le dio Colón a la isla donde se encuentra la República Dominicana?
7. ¿Cuál es el deporte más popular en las islas del Caribe?
8. ¿Cuál fue la primera catedral fundada en América?

## Comprensión

**A. San Juan, Puerto Rico.** Complete the following statements with the appropriate words according to what you understood.

1. San Juan está en el ______ del país.
2. San Juan fue fundada por ______.
3. El Castillo de San Cristóbal y El Morro son dos ______ coloniales del Viejo San Juan.
4. Las ______ del Viejo San Juan son estrechas *(narrow)*.
5. Los turistas visitan las playas de Puerto Rico para jugar al ______, practicar ______ y descansar.

**B. La Habana, Cuba.** Select the word or phrase that best completes each statement, according to what you understood.

1. Cuba está situada en la entrada del (Mar Caribe, Golfo de México).
2. A Cuba la llaman "(el Oro, la Perla) de las Antillas".
3. Una (quinta, tercera) parte de la población cubana vive en La Habana.
4. La Catedral queda en (el Morro, La Habana Vieja).
5. Los (españoles, ingleses) construyeron fortalezas en La Habana.
6. (Muchos, Muy pocos) estudiantes toman clases en la Universidad de la Habana.

**C. Santo Domingo, República Dominicana.** Read the following statements. After watching the video, circle **V** (**Verdadero**) or **F** (**Falso**), according to what you understood. If a statement is false, correct it.

V F 1. La capital de la República Dominicana es Santo Domingo.
V F 2. Santo Domingo es la ciudad más antigua de las Américas.
V F 3. Diego, el hermano de Cristóbal Colón, vivió en el Alcázar de Colón.
V F 4. Cada doce de agosto celebran en Santo Domingo el Día de Colón.
V F 5. Santa María la Menor es una catedral muy antigua.

## Ampliación

A. **Dos culturas.** With a partner, prepare some questions that you would like to ask a Cuban, a Puerto Rican, or a Dominican living in the U.S. about similarities and differences between life in this country and life in their homeland.

B. **Las islas del Caribe.** In small groups, discuss the similarities and differences you see between the three Caribbean islands featured in this video module. Share your observations with the class.

# Se alquila un apartamento

Lección 13

## OBJECTIVES

### Pronunciation

Pronunciation in context

### Structure

The familiar commands (**tú**) • **¿Qué?** and **¿cuál?** used with **ser** • The subjunctive to express indefiniteness and nonexistence

### Communication

You will learn vocabulary related to renting an apartment, the various parts of a house, and home furnishings.

# Se alquila un apartamento

*David y su esposa Lucía son colombianos y están estudiando en la Universidad Nacional Autónoma de México. Viven en una pensión, pero quieren mudarse a un apartamento que esté más cerca de la universidad.*

LUCÍA —David, en el periódico anuncian un apartamento que está en un buen barrio[1] y tiene dos dormitorios.

DAVID —¡A ver! Dame el periódico. *(Lee el anuncio.)*

*Anuncios clasificados*

*Se alquila:* apartamento amueblado: dos recámaras, sala, comedor, cocina y cuarto de baño. Calefacción central, aire acondicionado. Colonia 1. Para obtener más información, llame al teléfono 481-3520 de 1 a 5 de la tarde. Alquiler: $1.200.

LUCÍA —Podemos llamar para verlo.

DAVID —No sé... Es muy caro para nosotros, Lucía. Además, necesitamos un apartamento que tenga garaje...

*Al día siguiente, en cuanto vuelven de la universidad, David y Lucía van a ver el apartamento.*

LUCÍA —¡Me encantan los muebles y las cortinas!

DAVID —Con el sueldo que nosotros ganamos no vamos a poder pagar el alquiler.

LUCÍA —Entonces, en vez de trabajar medio día podemos trabajar tiempo completo.

DAVID —¡Estás loca! No hay nadie que pueda trabajar tiempo completo y al mismo tiempo estudiar en la universidad.

LUCÍA —¡No seas tan pesimista, David!

DAVID —No soy pesimista; soy realista. Además, vamos a necesitar dinero para comprar mantas, sábanas, fundas y utensilios de cocina.

[1]The word **colonia** is also used in Mexico.

LUCÍA —*(No le hace caso y va a la cocina.)* David, ven a la cocina. Mira, tiene refrigerador, microondas, lavaplatos, una cocina nueva... y un fregadero grande.
DAVID —No podemos tomar una decisión hasta ver otros apartamentos.
LUCÍA —Pero David, no vamos a encontrar ningún otro apartamento que sea tan bueno como éste.
DAVID —Tal vez no... pero no podemos pagar el alquiler de este apartamento.
LUCÍA —Oye, ¿y si ganamos la lotería?
DAVID —Hazme un favor, no digas tonterías. ¡Vámonos!
LUCÍA —*(Bromeando)* ¡Aguafiestas!
DAVID —Es que... tú te casaste con un hombre pobre, mi amor...

# Vocabulario

## Cognados

**clasificado(-a)** classified
**colombiano(-a)** Colombian
**la decisión** decision
**el favor** favor
**el garaje** garage
**la lotería** lottery
**el refrigerador** refrigerator
**el utensilio** utensil

## Nombres

**el (la) aguafiestas** spoilsport
**el alquiler** rent
**el barrio** neighborhood
**la calefacción central**[1] central heating
**la cocina** stove, kitchen
**el comedor** dining room
**la cortina** curtain
**el dormitorio, la recámara** bedroom
**el fregadero** kitchen sink
**la funda** pillowcase
**el lavaplatos** dishwasher
**la manta, la frazada, la cobija** blanket
**el (horno de) microondas** microwave (oven)
**los muebles** furniture
**el periódico, el diario** newspaper
**la sábana** sheet
**la sala** living room
**el sueldo, el salario** salary

## Verbos

**anunciar** to announce
**bromear** to kid
**casarse (con)** to marry, to get married
**ganar** to earn, to win
**mudarse** to move (from one house or place to another)

## Adjetivos

**amueblado(-a)** furnished
**mismo(-a)** same
**pobre** poor

[1]**poner (prender) la calefacción (el aire acondicionado)** to turn on the heat (the air conditioning)

### Otras palabras y expresiones

**además** besides
**al mismo tiempo** at the same time
**decir tonterías** to talk nonsense
**en vez de** instead of
**hacer caso** to pay attention
**medio día** half a day, part time
**se alquila** for rent
**tal vez** maybe, perhaps
**tiempo completo** full time
**tomar una decisión** to make a decision
**¡Vámonos!** Let's go!

## Vocabulario adicional

### El salón de estar

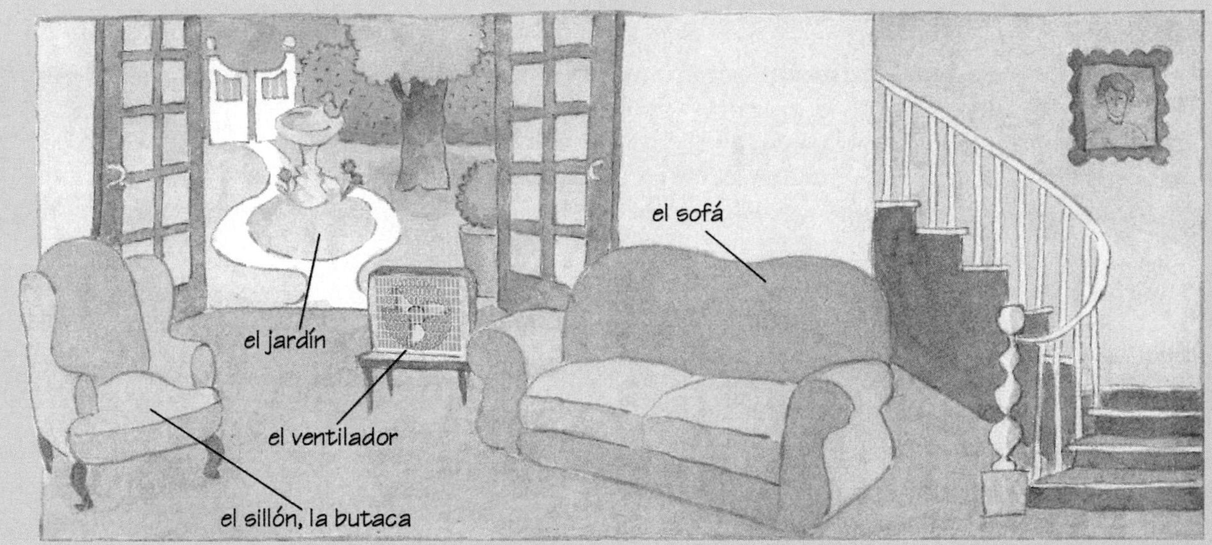


### El dormitorio

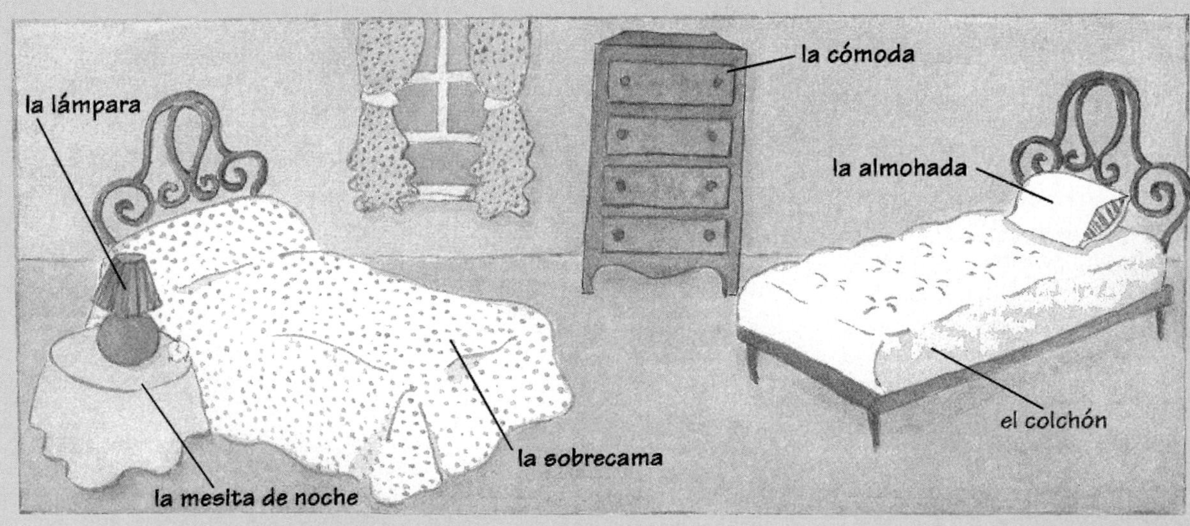

## Aparatos electrodomésticos y batería de cocina *(Home appliances and cookware)*

# ¡Conversemos!

Answer the following questions, basing your answers on the dialogue.

1. ¿David y Lucía estudian en su país?
2. ¿Por qué quieren mudarse?
3. Si ellos alquilan el apartamento que anuncian en el periódico, ¿van a tener que comprar muebles? ¿Por qué?
4. ¿Cómo describen el apartamento en el anuncio?
5. ¿Qué quiere Lucía que haga David?
6. ¿Cree usted que David y Lucía tienen automóvil? ¿Cómo lo sabe usted?
7. ¿Qué hacen al día siguiente en cuanto vuelven de la universidad?
8. ¿Le gustan a Lucía los muebles y las cortinas del apartamento?
9. ¿Por qué le dice David a Lucía que está loca?
10. ¿Qué tiene la cocina del apartamento?
11. ¿Qué le dice Lucía a David del apartamento?
12. ¿Por qué no quiere David alquilar el apartamento?
13. Cuando Lucía habla de ganar la lotería, ¿qué le dice David?
14. ¿Lucía se casó con un hombre que tiene mucho dinero?

## ¿Lo sabía Ud.?

■ En las grandes ciudades españolas y latinoamericanas, la mayoría de la gente vive en apartamentos, que en España se llaman "pisos." Los apartamentos se alquilan o se compran. Muchos edificios tienen oficinas o tiendas en la planta baja y apartamentos en los otros pisos.

■ La palabra "barrio" tiene una connotación negativa en muchos lugares de los Estados Unidos, pero en los países hispanos equivale simplemente al inglés *neighborhood*.

■ La Universidad Nacional Autónoma de México está situada en la parte sur de la Ciudad de México. Es la principal universidad del país, y es una de las más grandes del mundo. Unos 400.000 estudiantes asisten a la UNAM.

- En la ciudad donde usted vive, ¿la mayoría de la gente vive en casas o en apartamentos?
- ¿Le gusta a usted el barrio donde vive?
- ¿Puede usted nombrar algunas de las universidades más importantes del país?

See the *¿Cómo se dice...?* Web site for activities on authentic cultural material: http://spanish.college.hmco.com/students

Mural del pintor mexicano David Alfaro Siqueiros en el edificio de la Administración de la Universidad de México.

## Pronunciación

In this lesson, there are some new words or phrases that may be challenging to pronounce. For further pronunciation practice of Spanish sounds, listen to your instructor and repeat the following words and phrases.

1. Quieren **mudarse** a un apartamento.
2. Se alquila apartamento **amueblado.**

3. ¡Me encantan los **muebles** y las **cortinas**!
4. Tiene **refrigerador** y un **fregadero** grande.
5. **Hazme** un favor, no digas **tonterías.**

## 1 The familiar commands (tú) *(Las formas imperativas de* ***tú****)*

Unlike other commands in Spanish, the familiar affirmative command does not use the subjunctive.

### A. *Tú* commands[1]

- The affirmative command form for **tú** has exactly the same form as the third-person singular form of the present indicative.

| Verb | Present Indicative | Familiar Command (tú)[1] |
|---|---|---|
| hablar | él habla | **habla** (tú) |
| comer | él come | **come** (tú) |
| abrir | él abre | **abre** (tú) |
| cerrar | él cierra | **cierra** (tú) |
| volver | él vuelve | **vuelve** (tú) |

—Teresa, **trae** las frazadas. *"Teresa, bring the blankets."*
—**Espera** un momento. Estoy ocupada. *"Wait a moment. I'm busy."*

—Me voy. *"I'm leaving."*
—**Vuelve** temprano y **cierra** la puerta. *"Return early and close the door."*

- Spanish has eight irregular **tú** command forms.

| | | | | | |
|---|---|---|---|---|---|
| decir | **di** | poner | **pon** | tener | **ten** |
| hacer | **haz** | salir | **sal** | venir | **ven** |
| ir | **ve** | ser | **sé** | | |

—Carlitos, **ven** aquí; **hazme** un favor. **Ve** a la casa de Rita y **dile** que la fiesta es hoy. *"Carlitos, come here. Do me a favor. Go to Rita's house and tell her the party is today."*

—¿Dónde pongo el ventilador? *"Where shall I put the fan?"*
—**Ponlo** en la mesa. *"Put it on the table."*

[1]The affirmative command form for **vosotros** is formed by changing the final **r** of the infinitive to **d:** hablar → **hablad,** comer → **comed,** vivir → **vivid.**

### B. Negative forms

- The negative **tú**[1] commands use the corresponding forms of the present subjunctive.

| | |
|---|---|
| hablar | no **hables** tú |
| vender | no **vendas** tú |
| decir | no **digas** tú |

—¿Voy con Julia? — *"Shall I go with Julia?"*
—No, no **vayas** con ella. — *"No, don't go with her."*

—¿Pongo las sábanas aquí? — *"Do I put the sheets here?"*
—No, no las **pongas** aquí. — *"No, don't put them here."*

**ATENCIÓN** Object and reflexive pronouns are positioned with familiar commands just as they are with the formal commands.

| | |
|---|---|
| Pon**lo** aquí. | *Put it here.* |
| No **lo** pongas allí. | *Don't put it there.* |
| Vénde**nosla.** | *Sell it to us.* |
| No **nos la** vendas. | *Don't sell it to us.* |

## práctica

**A.** Play the role of an older sibling giving instructions to a younger brother or sister, using the cues provided.

1. levantarse temprano
2. estudiar y no hablar por teléfono con sus amigos
3. hacer la tarea y no mirar televisión
4. escribirle una carta a la abuela
5. bañar al perro
6. ir al mercado *(market)* y comprar frutas
7. recoger la ropa de la tintorería
8. llamar por teléfono a Carlos y decirle que traiga los discos compactos
9. lavar el mantel y las servilletas pero no lavar las sábanas
10. limpiar su cuarto
11. poner la mesa
12. barrer la cocina pero no pasarle la aspiradora a la alfombra

**B.** Juana always has a hard time deciding what to do. Give her some suggestions, using the cues provided.

MODELO: No sé qué clase tomar. (francés)
*Toma una clase de francés.*

1. No sé adónde ir esta noche. (cine)
2. No sé con quién salir. (Mauricio)
3. No sé qué hacer mañana. (ir de compras)

[1]The negative **vosotros** commands also use the present subjunctive: **no habléis.**

4. No sé qué comprar. (un traje de baño)
5. No sé qué regalarle a papá. (una cámara fotográfica)
6. No sé qué comprarle a mamá (un vestido)
7. No sé qué hacer para comer. (sopa y pollo)
8. No sé qué decirle a Jorge. (que te lleve al baile)
9. No sé en qué banco poner mi dinero. (en el Banco de América)
10. No sé qué hacer con mi pelo. (cortártelo)

C. Say two commands, one affirmative and one negative, that the following people would be likely to give.

1. una madre a su hijo de quince años
2. un(-a) estudiante a su compañero(-a) de cuarto
3. una muchacha a su novio
4. una médica a una niña
5. un profesor a un estudiante

D. With a partner, play the role of roommates. Imagine that you are both telling a third roommate, who is very lazy, what to do and what not to do.

E. Lucía and David are moving into their new apartment and some friends are helping them. Based on the illustration, what does Lucía tell each person to do? Use familiar commands.

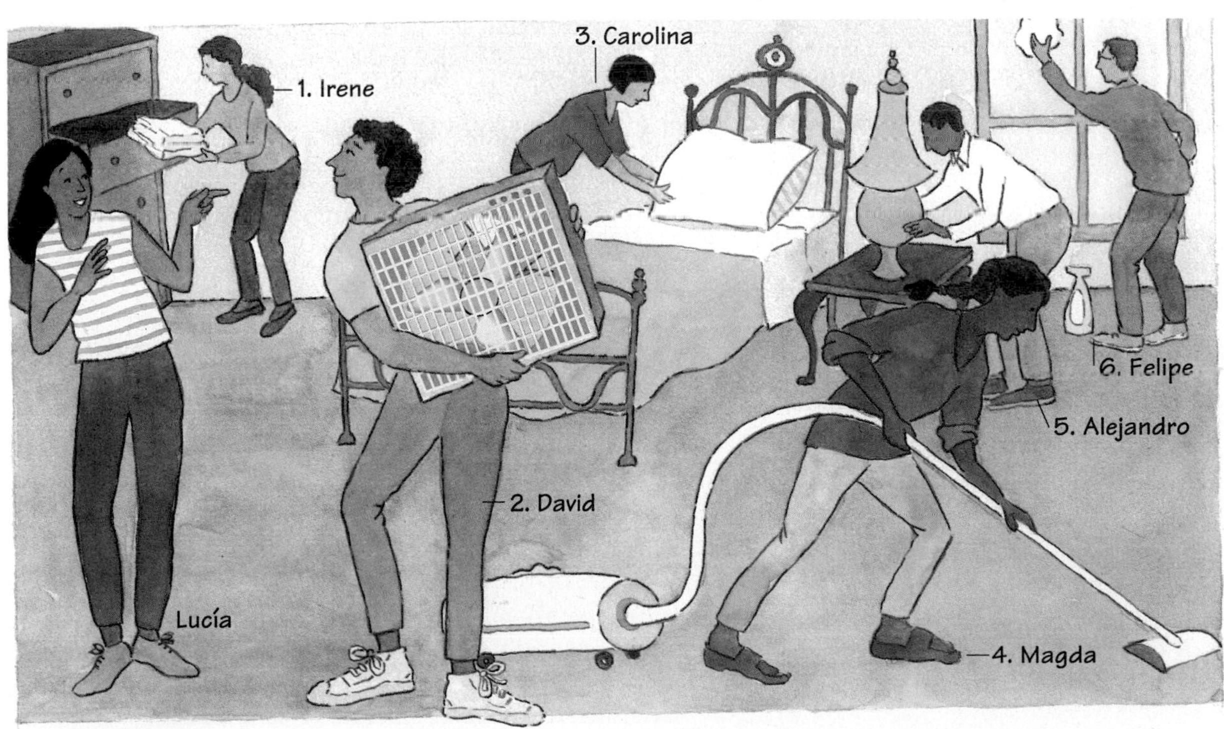

## 2 ¿Qué? and ¿cuál? used with ser *(Qué y cuál usados con el verbo ser)*

- *What* translates as **¿qué?** when it is used as the subject of the verb and it asks for a definition.

| | |
|---|---|
| —¿**Qué** es una enchilada? | *"What is an enchilada?"* |
| —Es un plato mexicano. | *"It's a Mexican dish."* |

- *What* translates as **¿cuál?** when it is used as the subject of a verb and it asks for a choice. **Cuál** conveys the idea of selection from among several or many available objects, ideas, and so on.

| | |
|---|---|
| —¿**Cuál** es su número de teléfono? | *"What is your phone number?"* |
| —792–4856. | *"792–4856."* |

### práctica

**A.** Write the questions you would ask to get the following information. Use **qué** or **cuál**, as needed.

1. —________________________________________
   —Mi apellido es Velázquez.
   —________________________________________
   —Calle Rosales, número 420.
   —________________________________________
   —835–2192.
2. —¿Quiere una sangría?
   —________________________________________
   — Es una bebida que se hace con frutas y vino tinto. ¿Quiere comer una paella?
   —________________________________________
   —Es un plato español que se prepara con arroz, pollo y mariscos.

**B.** With a partner, ask each other the following questions.

1. ¿Cuál es la fecha de tu cumpleaños?
2. ¿Cuál es tu color favorito?
3. ¿Cuál es la estación del año que más te gusta?

4. ¿Cuál es tu programa de televisión favorito?
5. ¿Cuál es el título de tu libro favorito?
6. ¿Cuál es la ciudad más grande de tu estado?

## 3 The subjunctive to express indefiniteness and nonexistence *(El subjuntivo para expresar lo indefinido y lo inexistente)*

- The subjunctive is always used when the subordinate clause refers to someone or something that is indefinite, unspecified, or nonexistent.

| | |
|---|---|
| Necesitan **un apartamento** que **esté** cerca de la universidad. | *They need an apartment that is close to the university.* |
| En la oficina necesitan a **alguien** que **sepa** español. | *At the office they need someone who knows Spanish.* |
| Busco **un empleado** que **hable** inglés. | *I'm looking for an employee who speaks English.* |
| ¡No hay **nadie** que **pueda** trabajar tiempo completo! | *There's nobody who can work full time!* |

- If the subordinate clause refers to existent, definite, or specific persons or things, the indicative is used instead of the subjunctive.

| | |
|---|---|
| Viven en **un apartamento** que **está** cerca de la universidad. | *They live in an apartment that is near the university.* |
| En la oficina hay **alguien** que **sabe** español. | *At the office there is someone who knows Spanish.* |
| Busco **al empleado** que **habla** inglés. | *I'm looking for the employee who speaks English.* |
| Hay **alguien** que **puede** trabajar tiempo completo. | *There's someone who can work full time.* |

### práctica

**A.** Indicate that there is nobody in your class to whom the circumstances below apply. Follow the model.

MODELO: En mi clase...
...hay una chica que baila flamenco.
*En mi clase no hay nadie que baile flamenco.*

En mi clase...

1. ...hay dos chicas que son de Paraguay.
2. ...hay un muchacho que conduce un Mercedes Benz.
3. ...hay un muchacho que habla francés.
4. ...hay tres estudiantes que tienen solamente quince años.
5. ...hay una chica que sabe tocar el violín.
6. ...hay dos muchachos que dan fiestas todos los sábados.
7. ...hay una chica que va a Europa todos los veranos.
8. ...hay dos muchachas que vienen a la universidad los domingos.
9. ...hay tres estudiantes que siempre están ocupados.
10. ...hay una chica que sale de su casa a las cinco de la mañana.

**B.** With a partner, play the roles of a newcomer to Mexico City and a helpful long-time resident who is able to offer solutions to all of the newcomer's needs. Follow the model.

> **Modelo:** una casa – tener piscina
> —*Quiero (Necesito, Busco) una casa que tenga piscina.*
> —*En mi barrio hay una casa que tiene piscina.*

1. una casa – tener tres dormitorios
2. una casa – estar cerca de la universidad
3. una casa – no costar un ojo de la cara
4. un coche – tener aire acondicionado
5. muebles – ser baratos
6. un empleo – pagar bien
7. alguien – ayudarme a mudarme
8. un restaurante – servir hamburguesas

**C.** A friend of yours is planning to move to your city or town and wants some information about it. Answer his or her questions as completely as possible.

1. ¿Hay alguna casa en un buen barrio que sea barata?
2. ¿Hay alguna casa que tenga piscina?
3. ¿Hay algún apartamento que esté cerca del centro?
4. Yo necesito una secretaria. ¿Conoces a alguien que sepa hablar alemán y japonés?
5. A mí me gusta la comida argentina. ¿Hay algún restaurante que sirva comida argentina?
6. A mis padres les gusta la comida mexicana. ¿Hay algún restaurante que sirva comida mexicana?

**D.** Complete the following sentences logically, using the subjunctive or indicative as appropriate.

1. Necesitamos un apartamento que…
2. En mi barrio no hay ninguna casa que…
3. Alquilan un apartamento que…
4. Rosa tiene una criada *(maid)* que…
5. Busco a alguien que…
6. En esta clase no hay nadie que…
7. Mi novio(-a) necesita un empleo que…
8. ¿Hay alguien aquí que…?

**E.** The students want to know more about each other. The members of the class will take turns asking whether there is anybody there who speaks German, vacations in a foreign country, needs a new apartment, etc.

# ¡A ver cuánto aprendió!

INTERNET

See the *¿Cómo se dice...?* Web site for additional grammar and vocabulary practice: http://spanish.college.hmco.com/students

## ¡Repase el vocabulario!

Choose the best answer for each of the following questions.

1. ¿Es de Bogotá?
   a. Sí, es uruguayo.
   b. Sí, es chileno.
   c. Sí, es colombiano.
2. ¿Dónde vas a poner el sofá?
   a. En el comedor.
   b. En la sala.
   c. En la secadora.
3. ¿Por qué estás enojado con tu hermano?
   a. Porque no me hace caso.
   b. Porque es de estatura mediana.
   c. Porque tiene refrigerador.
4. ¿Para qué quieres la frazada?
   a. Para ponerla en la cacerola.
   b. Para ponerla en la cama.
   c. Para decir tonterías.
5. ¿Por qué no puedes alquilar ese apartamento?
   a. Porque no gano suficiente dinero.
   b. Porque se alquila.
   c. Porque tengo que pagar exceso de equipaje.
6. ¿Para dónde son las cortinas?
   a. Para aquella butaca.
   b. Para aquella ventana.
   c. Para aquel jardín.
7. ¿Por qué no te gusta Emilio?
   a. Porque es muy simpático.
   b. Porque trabaja tiempo completo.
   c. Porque es un aguafiestas.
8. ¿Qué vas a poner en la sala en vez del sofá?
   a. Un asiento de ventanilla.
   b. Una escalera.
   c. Una butaca.
9. ¿Es un apartamento amueblado?
   a. Sí, pero no tiene lavaplatos.
   b. Sí, pero no tiene tienda de campaña.
   c. Sí, pero no tiene barrio.

10. ¿Qué necesitas para el dormitorio?
    a. Una caña de pescar.
    b. Un rizador y un secador.
    c. Una cama y una mesita de noche.
11. ¿Qué aparatos electrodomésticos necesitas para la cocina?
    a. Una licuadora y una tostadora.
    b. Una lavadora y una secadora.
    c. Una butaca y una cómoda.
12. ¿Qué necesitas para freír *(fry)* el pollo?
    a. La cafetera.
    b. La sartén.
    c. La plancha.

## Entrevista

With a partner, interview each other using the following questions.

1. ¿Tu casa tiene calefacción central y aire acondicionado?
2. ¿Qué muebles tienes en tu dormitorio? ¿Y en tu sala?
3. ¿Te vas a mudar a otra ciudad?
4. ¿Prefieres alquilar un apartamento o comprar una casa? ¿Por qué?
5. ¿Prefieres una casa que tenga garaje para tres coches o una casa que tenga piscina?
6. ¿Trabajas tiempo completo o medio día?
7. ¿Dices tonterías a veces?
8. ¿Juegas a la lotería?
9. ¿Eres un(-a) aguafiestas a veces?
10. ¿Con quién te casaste? (Si eres soltero[-a], ¿con quién quieres casarte?)
11. ¿Cuál es el apellido de tu mejor amigo(-a)?
12. ¿Prefieres un amigo que sea muy inteligente o un amigo que tenga mucho dinero?

## Situaciones

What would you say in the following situations? What might the other person say? Act out the scenes with a partner. Take turns playing each role.

1. You are talking to a real estate agent. You are looking for a house that is in a good neighborhood, with at least five bedrooms, air conditioning, and a three-car garage.
2. You are describing the house or apartment where you live to a friend.
3. You and your friend are going to share an apartment. Describe one you have just seen, telling him or her why you should take the apartment. Your friend doesn't think it's a good idea.

## Para escribir

Write a composition describing the house of your dreams *(sueños)*. Include the following information:

- location
- kind of neighborhood
- what type of rooms you want
- number of bedrooms and bathrooms
- backyard (patio)
- color scheme
- furniture you would have in each room
- conveniences

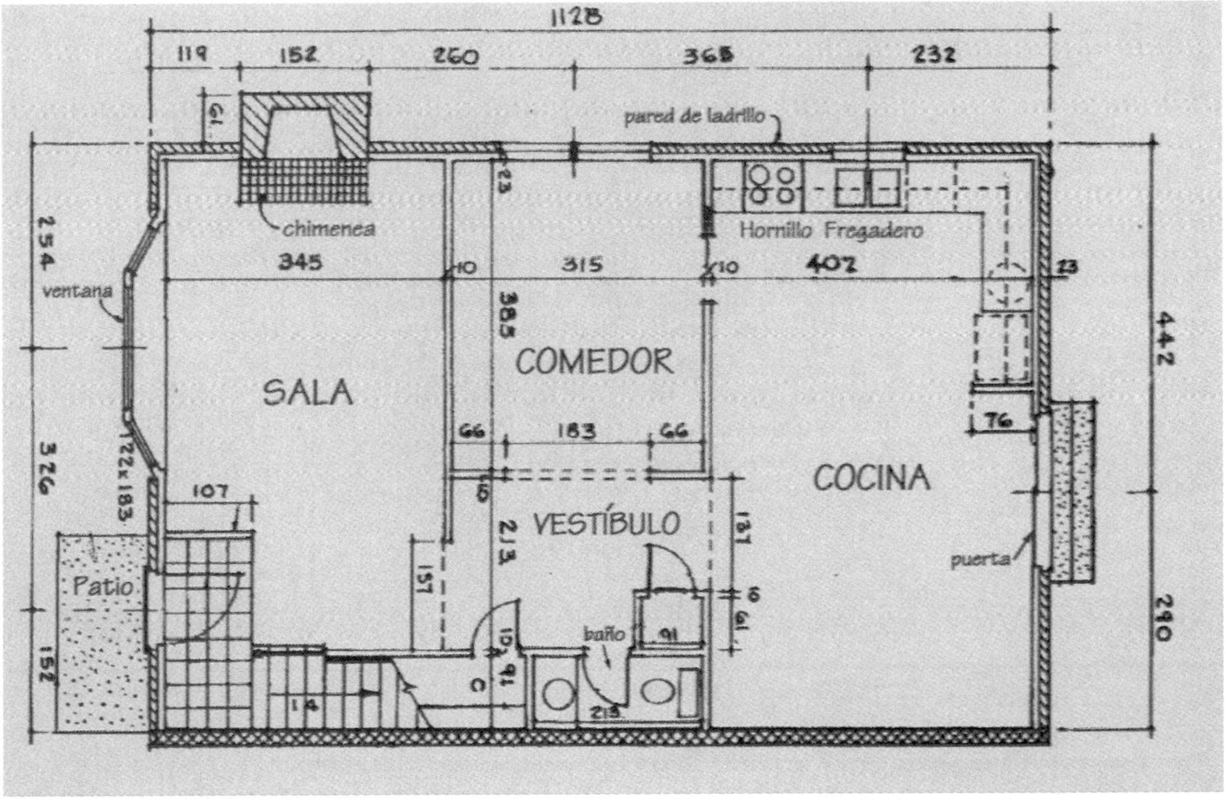

# En la vida real

**CD-ROM**

Do the interactive exercises on the CD-ROM for additional practice.

## Mi pareja ideal

Pair up with a classmate to write personal ads designed to help you find your ideal mate. Your description of the type of person you are looking for (use **Busco...** or **Quiero conocer a...**) should include physical characteristics, personality, age, economic status, and favorite activities. Don't forget to describe yourselves, as well.

## Casas y apartamentos

Imagine that you and several classmates own a real estate agency. Prepare ads for the following types of houses.

1. A very expensive house in a good neighborhood.
2. A small house in a student neighborhood.
3. Two different types of apartment for rent.

## En busca de apartamento

Some friends of yours want to buy an apartment in or near Barcelona. Help them by using the information provided in the ads below to answer their questions.

Veranee todo el año en Barcelona. Vista panoramica, por encima capa polución ciudad, 135 m. sobre el nivel del mar

**APARTAMENTOS**

**(JUNTO AL PARQUE GUINARDO)**

Calle Dr. Cadevall, 1-3 Barcelona (entrada por Avda. V.de Montserrat y calle Fco. Alegre)
Gran calidad, estar-comedor, 2 ó 3 dorm., cocina, baño, calef. ind., terraza, antena colectiva, y parabólica, 70 a 90 m². A partir de ptas. 7.000.000

*Información: MANSUR, S.A. De 5.30 a 8.30 h. tarde*
*Tel. 257-53-45. Con financiación de Caja Postal*

**TORREDEMBARRA**

Apartamentos 2 habitaciones, salón comedor, cocina, baño completo con instalación para lavadora. Situados en el centro del pueblo.
Avda. Catalunya 11.
**Precio: 4.000.000 pesetas**
Vd. puede ser propietario con 1 millón de pesetas más 3 milliones de hipoteca (a 15 años)
Vea apartamento de muestra y compruebe su calidad.

***Información en la misma obra laborable de 10 a 14 h. y de 16.30 a 20 hs. Excepto lunes y martes***

1. ¿Hay algún apartamento que esté cerca de la ciudad de Barcelona? ¿Cuál? ¿Cuántos dormitorios tiene? ¿Tiene piscina? ¿Cuál es el número de teléfono?
2. ¿Hay algún apartamento que quede cerca de la playa? ¿Cuál es la dirección? ¿Los apartamentos son grandes o pequeños? ¿Se puede estacionar allí?
3. ¿Hay algún apartamento que quede cerca de un parque? ¿Qué parque? ¿A qué hora se puede ver? ¿Cuánto cuesta el más barato?
4. ¿Hay algún apartamento donde se pueda poner una lavadora? ¿Cuánto tiempo hay para pagar la hipoteca *(mortgage)*? ¿Se puede ver cualquier *(any)* día de la semana? ¿Cuánto cuesta?

## Antes de leer

A. The title of this selection is "The major's calf." Taking into account that this **tradición** is about someone who constantly makes bets on everything, what do you think will happen? Is this selection going to be serious or humorous?

B. As you read the selection, find the answers to the following questions.

1. ¿A quién le escribe Juan Echerry?
2. ¿Quién es don Pedro Uriondo? ¿Cómo es?
3. ¿Qué manía tiene don Pedro Uriondo? ¿Siempre pierde las apuestas o siempre las gana?
4. ¿Qué le aconseja Juan Echerry a su amigo?
5. ¿Qué dice Domingo Echizarraga de don Pedro Uriondo?
6. ¿Cuándo sale de regreso para el Cuzco? ¿Qué lleva?
7. Según don Pedro Uriondo, ¿a qué se debía la cojera del comandante?
8. ¿Qué apuesta le hizo Uriondo a Echizarraga?
9. ¿Cuánto dinero le apostó?
10. ¿Quién ganó la apuesta? ¿Por qué?
11. ¿Cuál era la apuesta entre el capitán Uriondo y Juan Echerry?
12. ¿Cuánto dinero habían apostado?

# *La pantorrilla del comandante*

RICARDO PALMA (PERÚ: 1833–1919)

Ricardo Palma nació en Lima y comenzó su carrera literaria escribiendo obras de teatro y poesía, pero su gloria como escritor se debe principalmente a sus "tradiciones". Este género, creado por Palma, no tiene equivalente exacto en la literatura europea.

Aunque *(Although)* es difícil definir las **tradiciones,** podemos decir que son relatos breves *(short stories)* escritos con humor e ironía, y en los cuales hay una mezcla *(blend)* de lo real y lo imaginario.

I

Fragmento de carta de Juan Echerry al segundo comandante del batallón Gerona.

Cuzco, 3 de diciembre de 1822

Mi querido amigo: Aprovecho para escribirte la oportunidad de ir el capitán don Pedro Uriondo con cartas del virrey para el general Valdés.

Uriondo es el español más simpático que madre andaluza[1] trajo al mundo, pero tiene la manía° de proponer apuestas° por todo y sobre todo, ¡y siempre las

bad habit / bets

[1]from Andalucía, a region in Southern Spain

gana! Hermano, te ruego que no le aceptes ninguna apuesta y que les adviertas° lo mismo a tus amigos. Uriondo se jacta° de que jamás pierde una apuesta, y dice la verdad. De modo que te aconsejo que abras los ojos y tengas mucho cuidado.

warn
se... brags

Tu amigo,

Juan Echerry

II

Carta de Domingo Echizarraga a Juan Echerry.

Sama, 28 de diciembre de 1822

Mi inolvidable camarada: Te doy las gracias por haberme proporcionado la amistad° del capitán Uriondo. El muchacho vale en oro lo que pesa° y ya es el favorito de la oficialidad. Mañana sale de regreso para el Cuzco con cartas del general para el virrey.

friendship / weighs

En cuanto a sus laureles como ganador° de apuestas, digamos que van marchitos°. Dijo esta mañana que mi cojera° dependía, no del balazo° que me dieron, sino de un lunar° que, según él afirmaba, tenía yo en la pierna° izquierda. Yo que conozco mi agujereado° cuerpo, y que sé que no tengo lunares, me empecé a reír. Uriondo apostó seis onzas a que me convencía de la existencia del lunar. Aceptarle era robarle el dinero, y me negué°, pero él insistió tercamente en su afirmación. Intervinieron varios oficiales, diciéndome todos:

winner
withered / limp / shot
mole / leg
full of holes
me... I refused

—¡Vamos, comandante, gánese ese dinero que le cae de las nubes!

Me convencieron. Enseñé la pierna y todos vieron que en ella no había ningún lunar. Uriondo se puso rojo y tuvo que confesar que estaba equivocado°. Insistió en darme las seis onzas.

wrong

Contra tu consejo tuve la debilidad de aceptarle una apuesta a tu amigo, quedándome más que la ganancia de las seis onzas, la gloria de ser el primero en vencer° al que tú considerabas invencible. ¡Que Dios te guarde de un balazo y a mí... lo mismo!

defeat

Domingo Echizarraga

III

Carta de Juan Echerry al segundo comandante del Gerona.

Cuzco, 10 de enero de 1823

Compañero: ¡Me arruinaste!

El capitán Uriondo había apostado° conmigo treinta onzas a que te hacía enseñar la pantorrilla el día de los Inocentes.[1]

había... had bet

Desde ayer hay, por culpa tuya, treinta onzas menos en el bolsillo° de tu amigo, que te perdona° la desobediencia a su consejo.

pocket
forgives

Juan Echerry

[1]El día de los Inocentes se celebra el 28 de diciembre y es similar a *April Fool's Day.*

## Díganos

Answer the following questions, based on your own thoughts and experiences.

1. ¿Hace usted apuestas a veces?
2. ¿Qué cosas le aconseja usted a su mejor amigo(-a)? ¿Su amigo(-a) sigue sus consejos?
3. ¿Cree usted que su mejor amigo(-a) vale en oro lo que pesa? ¿Por qué?
4. ¿Hace usted bromas *(practical jokes)* el primero de abril?
5. ¿Se pone usted rojo(-a) a veces? ¿Es usted una persona tímida?
6. ¿Perdona usted fácilmente o le es difícil perdonar?

# ASÍ SOMOS

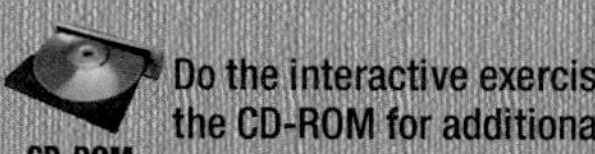


Do the interactive exercises on the CD-ROM for additional practice.

NARRADORA —¿Cómo es su casa?

MARÍA —Mi casa está en el centro de... del pueblo y posee dos pisos. En la parte superior *(upper level)* tiene dos habitaciones en las que dormimos mi hermano y yo, uno en cada una y una salita de estar *(small sitting room)*. En el primer piso se encuentra la cocina, el salón *(living room)* y la habitación de mis padres y un baño. Y bueno, arriba también otro baño. Y después está el bajo, que es donde está la bodega *(cellar)* y el garaje.

## Preparación

A. **¿Dónde vive Ud.?** Answer the following questions about where you live. You will hear answers to some of these questions when you watch the video. After viewing the video, compare your answers with those you hear.

1. ¿Vive Ud. en una casa o en un apartamento?
2. ¿Dónde vive la mayoría *(majority)* de los estudiantes de la universidad?
3. ¿Cómo es su casa?
4. ¿Cómo es la casa de su familia?
5. ¿Cómo es la casa de sus sueños *(dream house)*?

B. **¿Cómo es su personalidad?** With a partner, answer the following questions about the different personalities of people you know. You will hear answers to some of these questions when you watch the video. After viewing the video, compare your answers with those you hear.

1. ¿Cómo es su personalidad?
2. ¿Cómo es la personalidad de su madre? ¿De su padre?

3. ¿Cómo es la personalidad de su mejor amigo(-a)?
4. ¿Cómo es la personalidad de su profesor(-a)?

## Comprensión

**A. ¿Dónde viven?** As the people in the video describe where they live, circle **D** (**Departamento**) if they live in an apartment or **C** (**Casa**) if they live in a house, according to what you understand.

| | | |
|---|---|---|
| D | C | 1. Alejandro |
| D | C | 2. Leonardo |
| D | C | 3. Otmara |
| D | C | 4. Miriam |
| D | C | 5. María |
| D | C | 6. Jaime |
| D | C | 7. Pedro |

**B. ¿Quién lo dijo?** Match each statement with the name of the person who said it.

**A**

_____ 1. Mi casa tiene seis habitaciones *(rooms)*, una mini-alberca *(swimming pool)* y una cochera *(garage)* para seis coches.

_____ 2. Tenemos sala-comedor pequeñita, cocinita, dos recámaras *(bedrooms)* y un baño y medio *(half bath)*.

_____ 3. Mi casa es un "chalet".

_____ 4. Mi casa tiene cinco salas, tres comedores, una piscina y cinco garajes.

_____ 5. Mi apartamento tiene dos pisos *(stories)* y un altillo *(attic)*.

_____ 6. En el primer piso se encuentran la cocina, el salón *(living room)*, la habitación de mis padres y un baño.

**B**

a. Alejandro
b. Jaime
c. María
d. Pedro
e. Yolanda
f. Leonardo

**C. Mi personalidad.** Answer the following questions, according to what you understood.

1. ¿Milka es optimista o pesimista? ¿Es idealista o realista?
2. ¿Leonardo ve lo negativo o lo positivo de la vida?
3. ¿Pedro es nervioso o muy tranquilo?
4. ¿Alejandro es una persona alegre o triste?
5. ¿Es Jaime un poco tímido o muy tímido?
6. ¿Otmara es optimista o pesimista?
7. ¿Cómo ve la vida Otmara?

D. **¿Verdadero o falso?** Read the following statements. Circle **V** (**Verdadero**) or **F** (**Falso**) according to what you understood from the video. If a statement is false, correct it.

**V F** 1. El señor Velasco Pérez es de México.
**V F** 2. El señor Velasco Pérez trabaja en bienes raíces *(real estate)*.
**V F** 3. En la oficina del señor Velasco Pérez administran propiedades *(manage properties)*.
**V F** 4. En la oficina hacen negocios *(do business)* sólo con mexicanos.
**V F** 5. La oficina está en la mejor área de Guadalajara.
**V F** 6. Las propiedades que venden allí son las más baratas *(the least expensive)* de la ciudad.
**V F** 7. Los apartamentos que venden allí son muy pequeños.

## Ampliación

A. **¿Cómo es mi casa?** Take turns interviewing a classmate about his or her present living situation. Then compare your living situations with each other. Use the following questions as a guide.

1. ¿Dónde vives?
2. ¿Cómo es tu casa o apartamento?
3. ¿Es grande o pequeño(-a)? ¿Cuántas habitaciones *(rooms)* hay? ¿Cuáles son?
4. ¿Cómo es tu habitación?
5. ¿Cuáles son los muebles que tienes en tu casa o en tu habitación?

B. **La casa de mis sueños** *(My dream house)*. With a partner, describe your dream house or apartment. Be sure to include information about the number of rooms, different types of rooms, and other important features.

Lección 14

# Una cita

## OBJECTIVES

### Pronunciation

Pronunciation in context

### Structure

The subjunctive or indicative after certain conjunctions • First-person plural commands • Constructions with **se**

### Communication

You will learn vocabulary related to shopping for groceries and typical weekend activities.

## Otras palabras y expresiones

**a menos que** unless
**ahora que lo pienso** now that I think about it
**antes de que** before
**¡caramba!** gee!
**con tal (de) que** provided that
**De acuerdo.** Okay.
**de vez en cuando** from time to time
**poner una película** to show a movie
**ponerse a dieta** to go on a diet
**tener ganas de** to feel like (doing something)
**tomar algo**[1] to have something to drink
**¡Yo invito!** My treat!

# Vocabulario adicional

## Cosas del supermercado

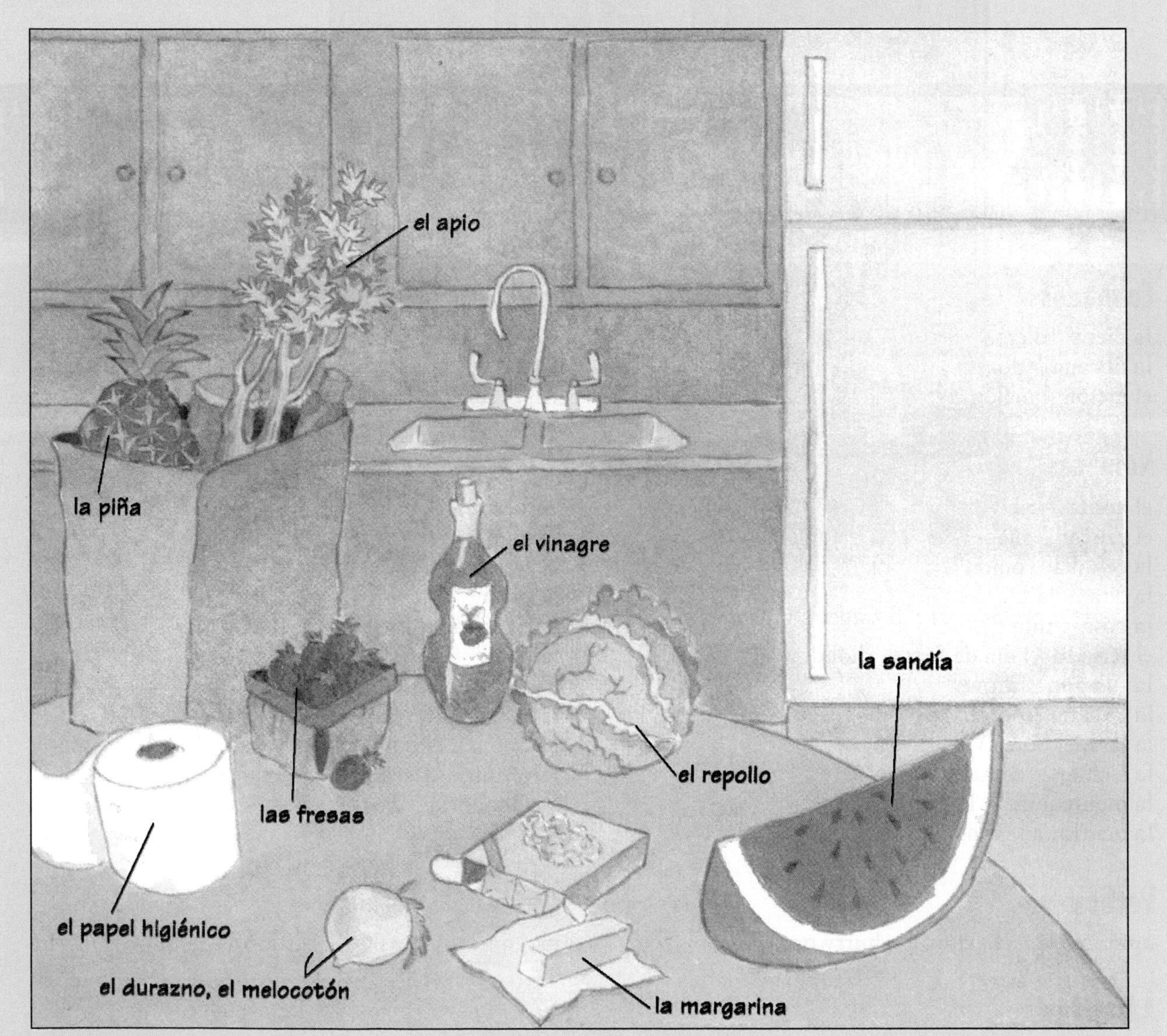


[1]**comer algo** = to have something to eat

### Las diversiones

| | |
|---|---|
| **el circo** circus | Los niños querían ir al **circo** pero no tenían dinero. |
| **la montaña rusa** roller coaster | La **montaña rusa** de Disneylandia es la mejor de todas. |
| **el parque de diversiones** amusement park | Six Flags es mi **parque de diversiones** favorito. |
| **el zoológico** zoo | En ese **zoológico** hay muchos animales de África. |

## ¡Conversemos!

Answer the following questions, basing your answers on the dialogue.

1. ¿Con quiénes tienen una cita Oscar y Jorge?
2. ¿Qué está leyendo Oscar? ¿Para qué?
3. ¿Qué película ponen hoy en el cine Rex?
4. ¿Qué dice el periódico de la película *Amor prohibido*?
5. ¿Qué le pregunta Oscar a Jorge?
6. ¿A dónde quiere ir Oscar cuando termine la película?
7. ¿A qué hora se abre el supermercado?
8. Según Oscar, ¿qué necesitan comprar?
9. ¿Cuántas latas de frijoles compran los muchachos?
10. ¿Qué frutas necesitan para la ensalada?
11. ¿Por qué dice Oscar que van a tener que ponerse a dieta?
12. ¿Por qué tienen que apurarse los muchachos?

Supermercado
ECONO-FACUNDO
Abierto todo los días de 7:30 am a 7:00 pm. Los viernes abrimos hasta las 9:00 pm y los domingos hasta las 5:00 pm.
Ext. Avenida Roosevelt
Hato Rey, P.R. 00918
Tel. 756-7474

## ¿Lo sabía Ud.?

Aunque hoy en día hay un gran número de supermercados en los países hispanos, muchas personas prefieren comprar en los mercados al aire libre o en las tiendas pequeñas que generalmente se especializan en uno o dos productos. Por ejemplo, se vende **carne** en la **carnicería, frutas** en la **frutería, verduras** en la **verdulería** y **pan** en la **panadería.**

En España, Cuba, México y Argentina, entre otros países, la producción de películas tiene gran importancia. Algunos directores iberoamericanos famosos son Víctor Érice (España), Tomás Gutiérrez Alea (Cuba), Jaime Humberto Hermosillo (México) y Eduardo Mignogna (Argentina).

Las películas norteamericanas son muy populares en el mundo hispánico. Generalmente tienen subtítulos en español o están dobladas *(dubbed)*. Muchos de los títulos en español son completamente diferentes a los del inglés. Por ejemplo, la película *Chicken Run* se llama ***Evasión en la granja;*** *Where the Heart Is* se llama ***La fuerza del amor.***

- ¿Hay en su ciudad pequeñas tiendas que se especializan en dos o más productos?
- ¿Pasan películas extranjeras en los cines de su ciudad? ¿Están dobladas o tienen subtítulos?
- ¿Tiene gran importancia la producción de películas en su país?

See the *¿Cómo se dice...?* Web site for activities on authentic cultural material: http://spanish.college.hmco.com/students

Comprando frutas y vegetales en un mercado de aire libre.

# Pronunciación

STUDENT AUDIO

In this lesson, there are some new words or phrases that may be challenging to pronounce. For further pronunciation practice of Spanish sounds, listen to your instructor and repeat the following words and phrases.

1. Tienen una cita con dos amigas **venezolanas.**
2. Oscar está leyendo **la guía de espectáculos.**
3. **Apurémonos** porque tenemos que limpiar el apartamento.
4. **Llamémoslas** para preguntarles si quieren ir al cine.
5. Comamos **perros calientes y hamburguesas** de vez en cuando.

# Estructuras

## 1 The subjunctive or indicative after certain conjunctions
*(El subjuntivo o el indicativo después de ciertas conjunciones)*

### A. Conjunctions that are always followed by the subjunctive

- Some conjunctions, by their very meaning, imply uncertainty or condition. They are, therefore, always followed by the subjunctive. Here are some of them.

**en caso de que** *in case*
**sin que** *without*
**con tal (de) que** *provided that*
**a menos que** *unless*
**para que** *in order that*
**antes de que** *before*

—Voy a ir al cine **con tal que** los chicos **vayan** conmigo.
—Llámelos **antes de que salgan.**

*"I'm going to go to the movies provided the boys go with me."*
*"Call them before they leave."*

—No me van a dar el préstamo **a menos que** ella **firme** la carta.
—Yo puedo firmarla **en caso de que** ella no **quiera** hacerlo.

*"They're not going to give me the loan unless she signs the letter."*
*"I can sign it in case she doesn't want to do it."*

—Te voy a dar dinero **para que vayas** al mercado.
—Voy a salir **sin que** los chicos me **vean,** porque siempre quieren ir conmigo.

*"I'm going to give you money so that you can go to the market."*
*"I'm going to leave without the boys seeing me, because they always want to go with me."*

## B. Conjunctions that are followed by the subjunctive or indicative

■ The subjunctive follows certain conjunctions when the main clause refers to the future or is a command. Some of these conjunctions are:

**cuando** *when* | **tan pronto como, en cuanto** *as soon as*
**hasta que** *until*

—¿Lo van a esperar? *"Are you going to wait for him?"*
—Sí, **hasta que llegue.** *"Yes, until he arrives."*
—**En cuanto llegue,** díganle que me llame. *"As soon as he arrives, tell him to call me."*

■ If there is no indication of a future action, the conjunction of time is followed by the indicative.

—¿Siempre lo esperan? *"Do you always wait for him?"*
—Sí, **hasta que llega.** *"Yes, until he arrives."*

## práctica

**A.** Complete the following dialogue between two friends who are expecting a houseguest, using **con tal que, sin que, en caso de que, a menos que, para que,** and **antes de que** and the verbs given. Then act it out with a partner adding two original lines.

—Tenemos que limpiar el apartamento ________ (llegar) él.
—Yo voy a preparar unos sándwiches ________ (tener) hambre.
—Sí, ¿y por qué no compras unos refrescos ________ (poder) tomar algo en cuanto llegue?
—Bueno, pero yo no puedo ir al supermercado ________ tú me ________ (dar) el dinero.
—Está bien. Yo te voy a dar el dinero ________ tú me lo ________ (devolver) mañana.
—Vale. Voy ahora mismo. Voy a salir ________ me ________ (ver) Paquito porque va a querer ir conmigo.
—________________________________________
—________________________________________

**B.** Compare what the people mentioned usually do to what they are going to do.

1. Todos los días yo llamo a mi amiga en cuanto llego a casa.
   Mañana,...
2. Generalmente esperamos al profesor hasta que llega.
   El próximo viernes,...
3. Todos los meses, tan pronto como recibimos el sueldo, lo depositamos en el banco.
   El mes próximo,...
4. Cuando Uds. van a verla, siempre le llevan un regalo.
   La semana próxima,...
5. Ud. se lo dice a ellos cuando los ve.
   Dígaselo a ellos...

C. Give the Spanish equivalent of the words in parentheses.

1. —Vamos a almorzar ______ . *(as soon as they arrive)*
   —Voy a preparar la ensalada ______ en seguida. *(so that we can eat)*
2. —Siempre le doy un beso a mi hijo ______ . *(when I see him)*
   —Yo no veo al mío muy frecuentemente.
3. —Tenemos que salir de la casa ______ . *(without the children seeing us)*
   —No podemos hacer eso ______ por la ventana. *(unless we leave)*
4. —Tengo que limpiar el apartamento ______ . *(before my friends arrive)*
   —¿Por qué no esperas ______ ? *(until I come back)*
   —Puedo esperarte ______ antes de las dos. *(provided that you be here)*

## 2 First-person plural commands *(El imperativo de la primera persona del plural)*

- The first-person plural of an affirmative command *(let's + verb)* may be expressed in two different ways:
- by using the first-person plural of the present subjunctive

| | |
|---|---|
| **Compremos** carne y pescado. | *Let's buy meat and fish.* |

- by using the expression **vamos a** + *infinitive*

| | |
|---|---|
| **Vamos a comprar** carne y pescado. | *Let's buy meat and fish.* |

- The verb **ir** does not use the subjunctive for the first-person plural affirmative command.

| | |
|---|---|
| **Vamos** al cine. | *Let's go to the movies.* |

- For the negative command, the subjunctive is used.

| | |
|---|---|
| **No vayamos** al cine. | *Let's not go to the movies.* |

- In all direct affirmative commands, the object pronouns are attached to the verb. An accent must be used to maintain the original stress.

| | |
|---|---|
| Llamémos**lo.** | *Let's call him.* |
| Escribámos**les.** | *Let's write to them.* |

- If the pronouns **nos** or **se** are attached to the verb, the final **-s** of the verb is dropped before adding the pronoun.

| | |
|---|---|
| Vámo**nos.** | *Let's leave.* |
| Sentémo**nos** aquí. | *Let's sit here.* |
| Vistámo**nos** ahora. | *Let's get dressed now.* |
| Démo**selo** a los niños. | *Let's give it to the children.* |
| Digámo**selo** a ella. | *Let's tell (it to) her.* |

- In direct negative commands, the object pronouns are placed in front of the verb.

| | |
|---|---|
| No **lo** hagamos. | *Let's not do it.* |
| No **nos** vistamos ahora. | *Let's not get dressed now.* |
| No **nos** vayamos todavía. | *Let's not leave yet.* |

## práctica

**A.** You and a classmate are going to a restaurant. Take turns asking each other what you should do and responding with first-person plural commands.

*Antes de ir:*

1. ¿A qué restaurante vamos?
2. ¿Hacemos reservaciones?
3. ¿Llevamos el coche o tomamos un taxi?

*En el restaurante:*

1. ¿Dónde nos sentamos?
2. ¿Qué pedimos para comer?
3. ¿Qué tomamos?
4. ¿Qué comemos de postre?
5. ¿Pedimos algo más?
6. ¿Cuánto le dejamos de propina al mozo?
7. ¿Adónde vamos ahora?
8. ¿Invitamos a alguien?

**B.** With a partner, play the roles of two friends who are planning a weekend together, but who can't agree on anything. One makes a suggestion and the other suggests something else, giving a reason for his or her refusal. Give at least eight suggestions.

MODELO: —Vamos a la playa.
—*No, no vayamos a la playa. No hace mucho sol. Vamos al campo.*

## 3 Constructions with se *(Construcciones con* **se***)*

■ In Spanish the pronoun **se** + *the third-person singular or plural form of the verb* is used as an impersonal construction. It is equivalent to the English passive voice, in which the person doing the action is not specified. It is also equivalent to English constructions that use the impersonal subjects *one, they, people,* and *you* (indefinite). The impersonal construction is widely used in Spanish.

Se habla español en Chile. { *Spanish is spoken in Chile.* / *They speak Spanish in Chile.* }

—¿A qué hora **se abren** los supermercados? *"What time do the supermarkets open?"*
—**Se abren** a las nueve de la mañana. *"They open at nine A.M."*

| | |
|---|---|
| —**Se dice** que el tomate es una verdura. | *"It's said that the tomato is a vegetable."* |
| —Sí, **se dice,** pero en realidad es una fruta. | *"Yes, it's said, but it's really a fruit."* |

■ The impersonal **se** is often used in ads, instructions, or directions.

FOR SALE

NO SMOKING

EXIT TO THE RIGHT

## práctica

A. In groups of three, draw signs with the following information on them.

1. No parking
2. Exit to the left
3. Spanish spoken here
4. No littering (*to litter:* **tirar basura**)
5. No crossing
6. No swimming
7. Cars for sale

B. With a classmate, act out a scene between a tourist in Madrid and a resident of the city who responds to the tourist's questions about the city. Use constructions with **se** in your conversation.

El turista necesita saber…

1. …el horario *(schedule)* de los bancos, del correo y de las tiendas.
2. …qué idiomas habla la gente.
3. …qué y dónde comen.
4. …si venden objetos de oro y de plata.
5. …dónde alquilan coches.

# ¡A ver cuánto aprendió!

**INTERNET**

See the *¿Cómo se dice…?* Web site for additional grammar and vocabulary practice: http://spanish.college.hmco.com/students

## ¡Repase el vocabulario!

Select the response that best answers each question.

1. ¿Vas a hacer una ensalada de frutas?
   a. Sí, necesito una lata de frijoles.
   b. Sí, necesito dos latas de salsa de tomate.
   c. Sí, necesito naranjas.

2. ¿Qué te gustó más en el parque de diversiones?
   a. El supermercado.
   b. La montaña rusa.
   c. El feriado.

3. ¿Qué película pasan hoy?
   a. Sí, las películas fueron nominadas.
   b. No sé, no tengo la guía de espectáculos.
   c. Pasan por el cine.

4. A ver… ¿qué verduras necesitamos?
   a. Agua y vinagre.
   b. Pescado y pollo.
   c. Lechuga, repollo y zanahorias.

5. ¿Vas a ponerle mantequilla al pan?
   a. No, azúcar.
   b. No, margarina.
   c. No, repollo.

6. ¿Adónde vas a llevar a los niños para que se diviertan?
   a. Al mercado.
   b. A la biblioteca.
   c. Al circo.

7. ¿No tienes una cita con Juan Carlos?
   a. Sí, pero no puedo ir porque él es famoso.
   b. Sí, pero no tengo ganas de ir.
   c. Sí, pero el supermercado no se abre hasta las diez.

8. ¿Qué vas a usar para hacer el jugo?
   a. Huevos.
   b. Toronjas.
   c. Aceite.

9. ¿Ves a tus amigos?
   a. Sí, tengo que apurarme.
   b. Sí, de vez en cuando.
   c. Sí, tengo que darme prisa.
10. Dicen que esa película es fantástica.
    a. Sí, fue nominada como la mejor.
    b. Sí, a mí tampoco me gustó.
    c. Sí, ganó la licencia para conducir.
11. Mi hermano quiere ver los elefantes.
    a. Llévalo al parque de diversiones.
    b. Llévalo al zoológico.
    c. Llévalo a la playa.
12. ¿Tienes ganas de tomar algo?
    a. Sí, pescado.
    b. Sí, carne.
    c. Sí, una copa de vino blanco.

## Entrevista

With a partner, take turns interviewing each other, using the following questions.

1. ¿Sabes a qué hora se abre y se cierra el mercado los domingos?
2. ¿Te preocupas cuando alguien viene a comer a tu casa? ¿Por qué o por qué no?
3. ¿Cuántas docenas de huevos compras para un mes?
4. ¿Qué frutas y qué verduras te gustan más? ¿Qué verdura no te gusta?
5. ¿Prefieres comer carne, pescado o pollo?
6. Los fines de semana, ¿prefieres ir al cine o a bailar?
7. Cuando vas al cine, ¿prefieres ir a la primera función o a la última?
8. ¿Te gusta ir a tomar algo cuando termina la función? ¿Adónde vas?
9. ¿Sabes qué películas están nominadas para el Óscar?
10. ¿Qué película tienes ganas de ver?
11. ¿Aceptas una cita con una persona a quien no conoces?
12. ¿Qué te gusta hacer cuando es feriado?

## Situaciones

What would you say in the following situations? What would the other person say? Act out the scenes with a partner. Take turns playing each role.

1. Tell a group of friends you are going to meet them at the amusement park.
2. You and your roommate are having a party tonight, and he or she is about to go to the grocery store. Discuss the items you will need for a fruit salad.
3. Invite a friend to go see a movie with you this weekend and tell her or him it's your treat. Discuss possible movies and times, and make plans to do something afterwards.
4. Tell a friend what you are going to do as soon as you get home.

## Para escribir

Write a dialogue in which you and a friend make plans for the weekend.

# En la vida real

## Discusión

**CD-ROM**

**Do the interactive exercises on the CD-ROM for additional practice.**

With a classmate, discuss a movie or a T.V. show you have both seen and summarize the plot. Say whether you liked it or not and why.

Here are some words and phrases you might want to use:

**actor** *actor*
**actriz** *actress*

**(la) película**
- **de acción**
- **de ciencia ficción**
- **cómica**
- **dramática**
- **de guerra** *(war)*
- **de horror**
- **de misterio**
- **policíaca**

## De la cocina a la mesa

You and a classmate are planning a dinner party. One of you has found a recipe (**receta**) for enchiladas, and the other, a recipe for flan. Read your recipe silently, and then tell your partner how to prepare the dish, without looking at the recipe. After your classmate does the same, read each other's recipes to see if your descriptions left out any of the steps. Here are some words you might want to use:

**calentar** (**e:ie**) to heat up, warm up
**cubrir** to cover
**cucharada** spoonful
**cucharadita** teaspoonful
**derretir** (**e:i**) to melt
**enfriar** to cool (down)
**freír** (**e:í**) to fry
**libra** pound
**mojar** to dip
**rallado**(**-a**) grated
**revolver** (**o:ue**) to stir

ENCHILADAS

Ingredientes:

1 docena de tortillas de maíz
1 lata de salsa de enchilada
1/4 taza de aceite
1 libra de queso rallado
1 cebolla grande, rallada

Preparación:

Caliente la salsa en una sartén. En otra sartén caliente las tortillas en el aceite, sin freírlas. Sáquelas del aceite y mójelas en la salsa. Póngalas en un plato, y cúbralas con queso y cebolla. Enrolle las tortillas como tubos y cúbralas con el resto del queso. Póngalas en el horno a 325 grados por cinco minutos.

**FLAN**

Ingredientes:

*Para el flan*
2 tazas de leche evaporada
4 huevos
8 cucharadas de azúcar
1 cucharadita de vainilla

*Para el caramelo*
3 cucharadas de azúcar

**Preparación:** En el molde donde va a hacer el flan, ponga a derretir al fuego tres cucharadas de azúcar. Después de unos minutos el azúcar va a tener un color dorado. Mueva el molde para cubrirlo todo con el caramelo y déjelo enfriar.

Bata los huevos. Añada el azúcar, la leche y la vainilla y revuélvalo bien. Pongalo todo en el molde y cocínelo a Baño María[1] en el horno a 350 grados por una hora. (Para saber si ya está cocinado, introduzca un cuchillo en el flan y si sale limpio, ya está listo.)

Sáquelo del horno y déjelo enfriar. Póngalo en el refrigerador. Antes de servirlo, voltee el molde en un plato.

[1]Double boiler

# 7. América del sur (I)

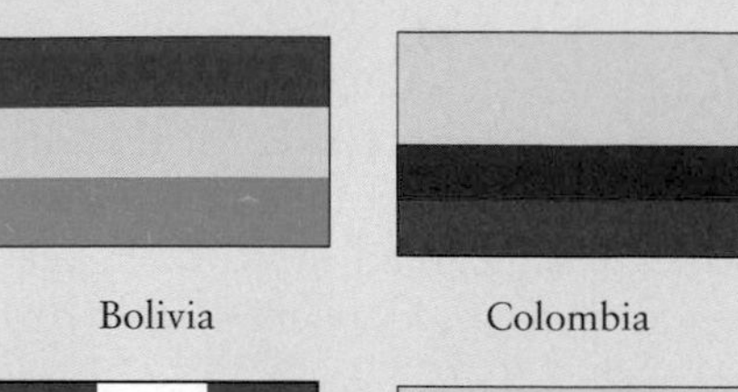

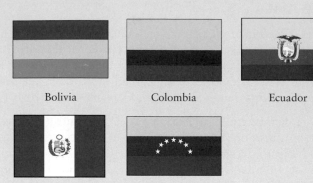

Bolivia Colombia

Ecuador

Perú

Venezuela

- La cuenca *(basin)* del Amazonas, que ocupa partes de Perú, Ecuador, Colombia, Brasil y Venezuela, es la más grande del mundo. El río Amazonas tiene más de 1.000 tributarios.
- Bolivia tiene dos capitales. Sucre es la capital histórica y sede *(seat)* del poder *(power)* judicial. La Paz es la capital administrativa y está situada a más de diez mil pies de altura. La ciudad se encuentra al pie del nevado *(snow-covered)* Illimani, que alcanza *(reaches)* una altura de más de veinte mil pies.
- Las islas Galápagos, situadas en el océano Pacífico frente a las costas de Ecuador, se consideran una de las zonas ecológicas mejor conservadas. Las distintas especies de plantas y animales que allí se encuentran son exclusivas de las islas y no tienen similaridad con las especies del continente.
- Caracas, la capital de Venezuela, es el lugar de nacimiento de Simón Bolívar, el Libertador de América. Bolívar luchó *(fought)* por la independencia de Colombia, Venezuela, Ecuador, Perú y Bolivia.

Este brazalete de oro, usado en ritos funerarios preincaicos, se encuentra en el Museo del Oro en Lima, Perú. En el museo existe una gran variedad de piezas precolombinas de oro y de plata con piedras preciosas. Esta colección es un ejemplo del talento artístico y de los conocimientos técnicos de las culturas indígenas que habitaban el continente antes de la llegada de Colón.

*¿Cuáles son algunos museos famosos de su país? ¿Dónde están?*

La Avenida Doce de Octubre es una de las principales de Quito, la capital de Ecuador. Esta ciudad, situada al pie del volcán Pichincha, goza de *(enjoys)* un clima primaveral todo el año por estar a una altura de 9.250 pies sobre el nivel del mar.

*¿Dónde hay volcanes en su país?*

En los llanos orientales *(eastern plains)* de Colombia, la ganadería *(livestock)* es la principal fuente de ingresos. Estos "llaneros" llevan una manada *(herd)* de caballos a los corrales de una hacienda en el departamento de Meta, situado al sureste de Colombia.

*¿Qué región de su país es conocida por la importancia de la ganadería?*

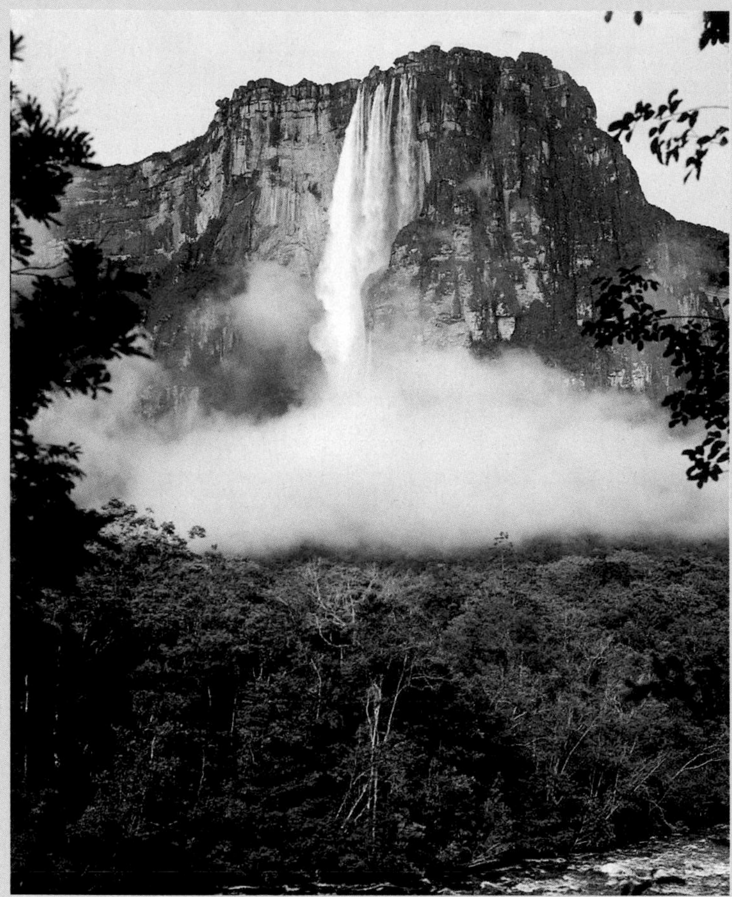

El Salto Ángel *(Angel Falls)*, localizado en el Parque Nacional de Canaima en Venezuela, es el más alto del mundo, con una altura de unos 3.200 pies. Las cataratas *(falls)* se llaman Ángel en honor al piloto norteamericano Jimmy Angel, que fue el primero en aterrizar *(land)* allí en 1937.

*¿Qué cataratas de los Estados Unidos y Canadá son famosas en todo el mundo?*

Entrada del metro en la estación de Sabana Grande en Caracas, Venezuela. Se comenzó a construir el metro de Caracas en los años 70.

*¿Hay un metro en la ciudad donde Ud. vive?*

Esta vista es de una de las típicas calles coloniales de Cartagena de Indias en la costa norte de Colombia. Durante la conquista y el período colonial, la parte antigua de la ciudad estaba completamente amurallada *(walled in)* para dar protección contra los ataques de piratas ingleses y franceses.

*¿En qué ciudades de su país se ve la influencia de otras culturas?*

En el centro de Lima hay dos grandes plazas: la Plaza de Armas y la Plaza de San Martín. La Plaza de San Martín, que aparece en la foto, se llama así en honor a José de San Martín, considerado héroe nacional por haber liberado Perú, además de Argentina y Chile, del dominio español.

*¿Cuáles son algunos lugares o monumentos norteamericanos nombrados en honor a héroes nacionales?*

Las islas Galápagos deben su nombre a sus tortugas gigantes, llamadas galápagos, que pesan unos 280 kilos y viven unos 250 años. Las Galápagos se hicieron famosas por los estudios sobre la evolución de las especies que hizo en ellas el naturalista británico Charles Darwin. El gobierno ecuatoriano estableció el Parque Nacional de las Islas Galápagos en 1959.

*¿Cuáles son algunos de los lugares de Norteamérica que tienen interés especial para los naturalistas?*

Una manada de alpacas pace *(grazes)* en las montañas de Bolivia. La alpaca pertenece a la familia de las llamas, especie relacionada con los camellos, que habita la región de los Andes. La llama se usa principalmente como animal de transporte mientras que la lana *(wool)* de la alpaca se utiliza para hacer alfombras y diferentes artículos de ropa.

*¿En qué países de Sudamérica se pueden encontrar llamas y alpacas?*

VIDEO

CD-ROM

Do the interactive exercises on the CD-ROM for additional practice.

## Preparación

**¿Cuánto saben Uds. ya?** After reading **Panorama hispánico 7**, get together in groups of three or four students and answer the following questions.

1. ¿En qué países está la cuenca *(basin)* del río Amazonas?
2. ¿Cuál es la capital de Ecuador? ¿Y de Venezuela?
3. ¿Cuáles son las dos capitales de Bolivia?
4. ¿Cómo se llaman las cataratas *(waterfalls)* más altas del mundo?
5. ¿Quién fue José de San Martín?

## Comprensión

**A. Santa Fe de Bogotá, Colombia.** Select the word or phrase that best completes each statement, according to what you understood.

1. El nombre completo (de la capital, del barrio histórico) de Colombia es Santa Fe de Bogotá.
2. En el barrio de la Candelaria hay muchas casas de estilo (moderno, colonial) con hermosos balcones.
3. La ciudad es una mezcla de lo antiguo y (lo tropical, lo moderno).
4. En el Museo del Oro hay (cientos, miles) de piezas de oro prehispánicas.
5. Desde *(from)* (el cerro, los rascacielos [*skyscrapers*]) de Monserrate se ve una bonita vista de Bogotá.

**B. Ecoturismo en Venezuela.** Read the following statements. After watching the video, circle **V** (**Verdadero**) or **F** (**Falso**), according to what you understood. If a statement is false, correct it.

V F 1. Hay variedad de regiones geográficas en Venezuela.
V F 2. Venezuela está a más de seis horas de Miami por avión.
V F 3. En los llanos *(plains)* de Maracaibo trabajan vaqueros *(cowboys)*.
V F 4. El ecoturismo no atrae a muchos turistas a Venezuela.
V F 5. El gobierno de Venezuela considera que la protección de la naturaleza es muy importante.

**C. Ecuador.** Select the word or phrase that best completes each statement, according to what you understood.

1. La geografía de Ecuador es muy ________.
2. Pichincha y Cayambe son dos ________ cerca de Quito.
3. El Panecillo está al pie del barrio ________ de Quito.
4. Quito fue fundada sobre las ruinas de una ciudad ________.
5. "La mitad del mundo" es un ________ que marca el lugar por donde pasa la línea que separa los hemisferios norte y sur.
6. La Plaza de los Ponchos es un famoso ________ donde los otavaleños venden su artesanía.

## Ampliación

**A. ¿Adónde vamos?** Divide the class into three groups: one group prefers to travel to Colombia, the second group prefers to travel to Venezuela, and the third group prefers to travel to Ecuador. Each group should list the reasons for their choice of travel destination. Share the results with the rest of the class.

**B. Dos culturas.** In pairs, discuss what you observed about ecotourism in Venezuela and what you know about ecotourism in your local area, state, or country. What are the benefits and attractions of ecotourism? Share your observations with the rest of the class.

# De compras

Lección 15

## OBJECTIVES

### Pronunciation
Pronunciation in context

### Structure
The past participle • The present perfect • The past perfect (pluperfect)

### Communication
You will learn vocabulary related to clothing and shopping.

# De compras

ANITA —Esta mañana he abierto el armario y he llegado a la conclusión de que ni tú ni yo tenemos nada que ponernos. ¡Tenemos que ir de compras hoy mismo! ¡Mira este anuncio!

HUGO —Gerardo me ha pedido que lo ayude... Además, yo tengo ropa...

ANITA —¡Vieja y pasada de moda! Y ayer tú me dijiste que necesitabas cambiar las botas que habías comprado en El Corte Inglés porque son muy anchas... ¡Y tienes que comprarte zapatos!

*Anita ha convencido a su esposo y ahora están en El Corte Inglés, una tienda por departamentos que está en el centro de Madrid. Hugo sube por*

---

[1]Sign of the euro, the Spanish currency as of 2002.

*la escalera mecánica hasta el primer piso, donde está el departamento de ropa para caballeros. Anita se queda en la planta baja, donde está el departamento de ropa para señoras. Allí se encuentra con su amiga Tere.*[1]

ANITA —¿Qué tal? Aprovechando las rebajas, ¿no? Dime Tere, ¿cuánto cuesta esa blusa de seda?
TERE —Cincuenta y seis euros. ¿Qué talla usas?
ANITA —Uso talla treinta y ocho.[2] Voy a probármela.
TERE —Espera, ¿no te gusta esta falda? Combina muy bien con la blusa y es talla mediana. Pruébatela. El probador está a la izquierda.
ANITA —*(Desde el probador)* Tere, hazme un favor. Tráeme una falda talla treinta y seis.
TERE —Espera... Lo siento, no hay tallas más pequeñas. ¿Por qué no te pruebas este suéter?
ANITA —No... no me gusta...

*Anita compró la blusa, pero no compró la falda porque le quedaba grande y era demasiado cara. Después fue a la zapatería porque necesitaba comprar un par de sandalias rojas para combinar con un bolso rojo que Hugo le había regalado.*

*En el departamento de ropa para caballeros, Hugo compró dos camisetas y un chaleco. Ahora está en la zapatería.*

HUGO —Quiero cambiar estas botas.
DEPENDIENTE —Muy bien, señor. ¿Qué número calza?
HUGO —Calzo el cuarenta y cuatro.[3]
DEPENDIENTE —En seguida vuelvo. *(Al rato)* Pruébese éstas.
HUGO —Éstas son un poco estrechas. Me aprietan...
DEPENDIENTE —*(Le prueba otro par.)* ¿Qué tal éstas?
HUGO —Éstas me quedan bien. Me las llevo. ¿Puede envolvérmelas, por favor?

*Hugo, Anita y Tere se encuentran a la salida.*

ANITA —Hugo, llévanos a comer. ¡Estamos muertas de hambre!
HUGO —¡Yo también! Esperadme[4] aquí. Yo voy por el coche.
ANITA —¿Has estado en el restaurante Villa Alegre alguna vez?
TERE —Sí, es muy bueno. Vamos a ése.

*Cuando Anita y Hugo llegan a su casa, ella ve las compras de su esposo.*

ANITA —¡Un chaleco y dos camisetas! ¿Esto es todo lo que has comprado? ¡Ay! ¿Qué voy a hacer yo contigo?
HUGO —Bueno, puedes regalarme un traje para mi cumpleaños...

---

[1]nickname for Teresa
[2]equivalent to an American size 10
[3]equivalent to an American size 11
[4]Hugo is a Spaniard, so he uses the **vosotros** form here.

# Vocabulario

## Cognados

**el centro** center
**la conclusión** conclusion
**importado(-a)** imported
**el par** pair
**la sandalia** sandal
**el suéter** sweater

## Nombres

**el algodón** cotton
**el armario, el ropero** wardrobe, closet
**la blusa** blouse
**la bota** boot
**la camisa** shirt
**la camiseta** T-shirt
**el chaleco** vest
**la chaqueta** jacket
**la compra** purchase
**el cuero** leather
**el departamento de (ropa para) caballeros** men's department
**el (la) dependiente(-a)** store clerk
**la escalera mecánica** escalator
**la falda** skirt
**la ganga** bargain
**el hilo, el lino** linen
**la lana** wool
**el número** size (of shoes)
**la planta baja** ground floor
**el probador** fitting room
**la rebaja, la liquidación** sale
**la seda** silk
**la talla, la medida** size
**la tienda por departamentos, el almacén** department store
**el traje** suit
**la zapatería** shoe department, shoe store
**el zapato** shoe

## Verbos

**apretar (e:ie)** to be tight
**aprovechar** to take advantage of
**ayudar** to help, assist
**calzar** to take (a certain size in shoes)
**cambiar** to exchange, change
**envolver (o:ue)** to wrap
**llevarse** to take (buy)
**rebajar** to mark down

## Adjetivos

**ancho(-a)** wide
**estrecho(-a)** narrow
**mediano(-a)** medium
**verdadero(-a)** real

### Otras palabras y expresiones

**alguna vez** ever
**de compras** shopping
**En seguida vuelvo.** I'll be right back.
**estar muerto(-a) de hambre** to be starving
**¿Esto es todo lo que has comprado?** Is this all you've bought?
**hacer juego, combinar** to match, go together
**hoy mismo** this very day
**me aprietan** they feel tight (on me)
**no tener nada que ponerse** not to have anything to wear
**pasado(-a) de moda** out of style
**quedarle grande (chico) a uno** to be too big (small) on someone

## Vocabulario adicional

### Mirando vidrieras *(window shopping)*

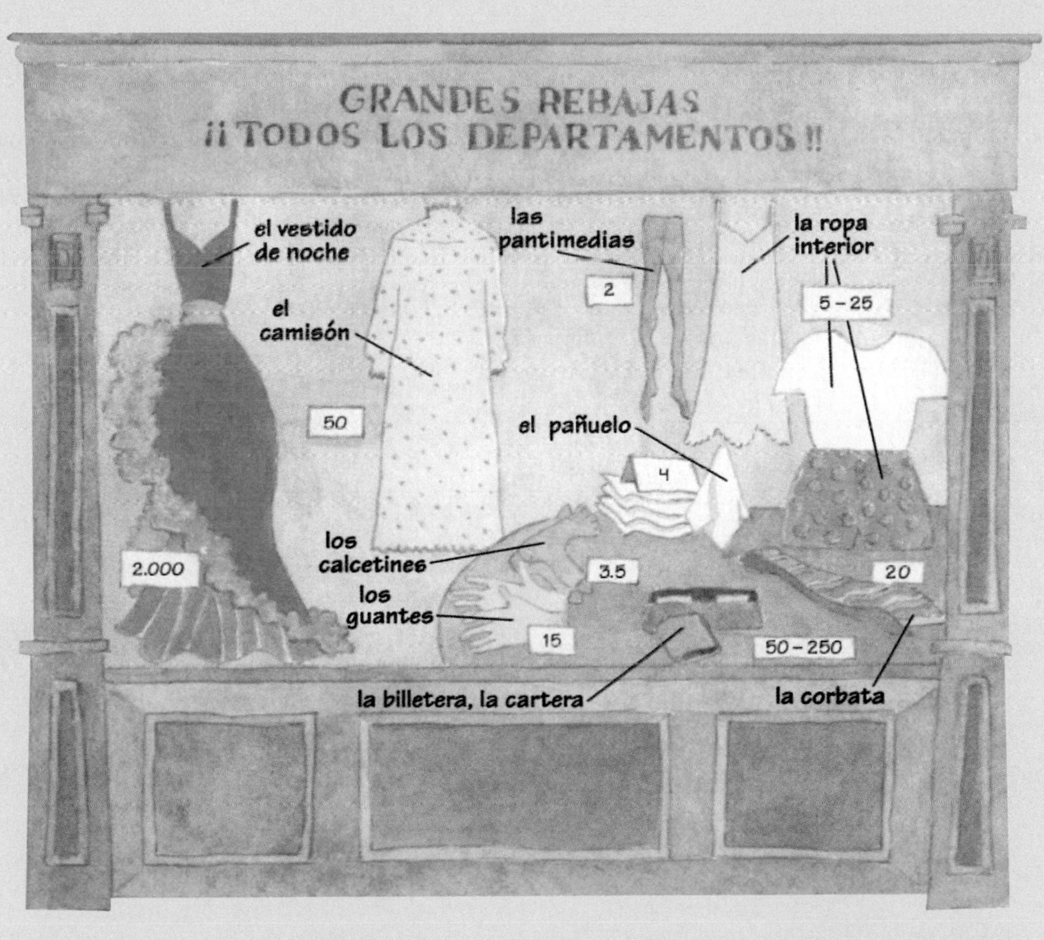

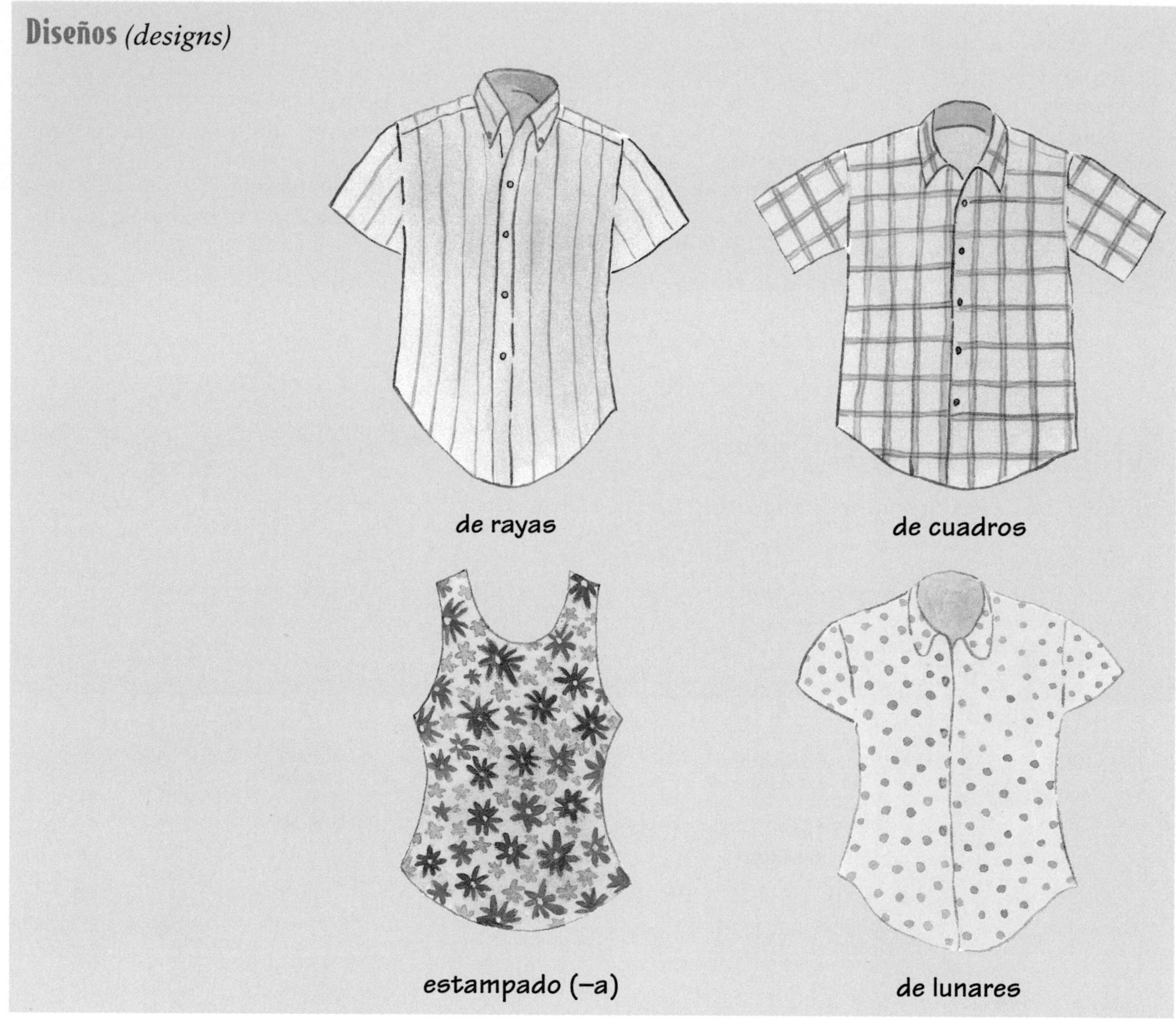


## ¡Conversemos!

Answer the following questions, basing your answers on the dialogues.

1. ¿Qué van a hacer Anita y Hugo hoy? ¿Por qué?
2. ¿Qué tienen el viernes y el sábado en El Corte Inglés?
3. ¿Cuántas horas va a estar abierta la tienda?
4. ¿Qué tipo de ropa para mujer aparece *(appears)* en el anuncio? ¿Y para hombre?
5. Según Anita, ¿cómo es la ropa de Hugo?
6. ¿A qué tienda van? ¿Dónde está?
7. ¿Dónde se queda Anita y con quién se encuentra allí?

8. ¿Qué se prueba Anita y dónde va para probársela?
9. ¿Por qué no compró Anita la falda?
10. ¿Qué compró Hugo y adónde fue después? ¿Qué hizo allí?
11. ¿Qué van a hacer Hugo, Anita y Tere después de encontrarse a la salida? ¿Por qué?
12. ¿Qué quiere Hugo que Anita le regale para su cumpleaños?

## ¿Lo sabía Ud.?

- Lo que en los Estados Unidos es el primer piso es la planta baja en los países hispanos. Entonces el primer piso en España, por ejemplo, corresponde al segundo piso en los Estados Unidos.
- En las ciudades hispanas hay excelentes tiendas donde se puede comprar ropa hecha *(ready-to-wear)*, pero muchas personas prefieren utilizar los servicios de un sastre *(tailor)* o de una modista *(dressmaker)*.
- Aunque ahora hay muchos grandes almacenes, todavía existen en los países hispanos muchas tiendas pequeñas especializadas en un solo producto. Por ejemplo, se vende **perfume** en la **perfumería, joyas** *(jewelry)* en la **joyería** y **relojes** en la **relojería.**
- Actualmente *(Nowadays)*, los dependientes de las tiendas a menudo tutean *(use the **tú** form of address)* a los clientes en España.
- En España y en Latinoamérica, muchas personas tienen sobrenombres *(nicknames)*; por ejemplo: Teresa: **Tere;** Enrique: **Quique;** Roberto o Alberto: **Beto;** Francisco: **Paco;** María Teresa: **Marité;** Antonia: **Toña;** Dolores: **Lola;** José: **Pepe;** Luis: **Lucho;** Manuel: **Manolo.**

- ¿Dónde prefiere comprar ropa la mayoría de los norteamericanos?
- En su país, ¿la mayoría de las tiendas especializadas están en centros comerciales *(malls)* o en edificios independientes?
- ¿Qué sobrenombres son comunes en su país?

Una joyería elegante en la Ciudad de México.

See the *¿Cómo se dice...?* Web site for activities on authentic cultural material: http://spanish.college.hmco.com/students

# Pronunciación

STUDENT AUDIO

In this lesson, there are some new words or phrases that may be challenging to pronounce. For further pronunciation practice of Spanish sounds, listen to your instructor and repeat the following words and phrases.

1. He llegado a **la conclusión** de que ni tú ni yo tenemos **nada que ponernos.**
2. Hugo sube por **la escalera mecánica** hasta el primer piso.
3. **Tráeme** una falda **talla** treinta y seis.
4. ¿Puede **envolvérmelas** por favor?
5. Puedes regalarme un **traje** para mi cumpleaños.

# Estructuras

## 1 The past participle *(El participio pasado)*

### A. Forms of the past participle

| Past Participle Endings | | |
|---|---|---|
| -ar *verbs* | -er *verbs* | -ir *verbs* |
| habl-**ado** *(spoken)* | com-**ido** *(eaten)* | decid-**ido** *(decided)* |

■ The following verbs have irregular past participles.

| | | |
|---|---|---|
| abrir | **abierto** | *opened* |
| cubrir | **cubierto** | *covered* |
| decir | **dicho** | *said* |
| hacer | **hecho** | *done* |
| escribir | **escrito** | *written* |
| morir | **muerto** | *died* |
| poner | **puesto** | *put* |
| romper | **roto** | *broken* |
| ver | **visto** | *seen* |
| volver | **vuelto** | *returned* (somewhere) |
| devolver | **devuelto** | *returned* (something) |
| envolver | **envuelto** | *wrapped* |

**ATENCIÓN** Verbs ending in **-er** and **-ir** whose stem ends in a strong vowel require an accent mark on the **i** of the **-ido** ending.

| | | |
|---|---|---|
| creer | **creído** | *believed* |
| leer | **leído** | *read* |
| oír[1] | **oído** | *heard* |
| traer | **traído** | *brought* |

## práctica

Supply the past participle of each of the following verbs.

1. tener
2. traer
3. cerrar
4. decir
5. aprovechar
6. apretar
7. cortar
8. volver
9. romper
10. cubrir
11. cambiar
12. sentir
13. entrar
14. salir
15. hacer
16. poner
17. abrir
18. escribir
19. ver
20. aceptar
21. devolver
22. leer
23. dar
24. sacar

### B. Past participles used as adjectives

■ In Spanish, most past participles may be used as adjectives. As such, they agree in number and gender with the nouns they modify.

| | |
|---|---|
| La peluquería está **abierta** hoy. | *The beauty parlor is open today.* |
| El restaurante está **abierto** hoy. | *The restaurant is open today.* |
| Las peluquerías están **abiertas** hoy. | *The beauty parlors are open today.* |
| Le mandé dos cartas **escritas** en inglés. | *I sent him two letters written in English.* |
| No dejen los libros **abiertos**. | *Don't leave the books open.* |

[1]Present tense: **oigo, oyes, oye, oímos, oís, oyen.**

## práctica

**A.** You are very efficient. When a friend asks whether you did something, you say it is already done.

MODELO: ¿Ya pusiste la mesa?
*Sí, ya está puesta.*

1. ¿Ya cerraste la puerta?
2. ¿Ya abriste las ventanas?
3. ¿Ya hiciste la ensalada?
4. ¿Ya envolviste el regalo?
5. ¿Ya escribiste las cartas?
6. ¿Ya pagaste la cuenta?
7. ¿Ya cubriste los muebles?
8. ¿Ya lavaste la blusa?

**B.** Act out the following dialogues with a partner, providing the missing adjectives (past participle form) of the verbs listed.

| | |
|---|---|
| abrir | servir |
| cerrar | traducir |
| escribir | usar |
| hacer | envolver |
| poner | |

1. —¿Dónde fueron ________ las sandalias?
   —En México.
2. —Oye, ¿está ________ la puerta?
   —Sí, pero las ventanas están ________.
   —Pues ábrelas, porque hace mucho calor.
3. —¿Ya podemos comer?
   —Sí, la mesa ya está ________ y la comida está ________.
4. —¿Aquí se vende ropa ________?
   —Sí, este vestido de noche es ________.
5. —¿Esos libros están ________ en español?
   —Sí, pero también están ________ al inglés y al francés.
6. —¿Ya compraste los regalos?
   —Sí, y ya están ________.

## 2 The present perfect *(El pretérito perfecto)*

■ The present perfect tense is formed by using the present indicative of the auxiliary verb **haber** with the past participle of the verb that expresses the action or state. This tense is equivalent to the English present perfect *(have + past participle*, as in *I have spoken.)*.

**Present indicative of haber**

| | |
|---|---|
| he | hemos |
| has | habéis |
| ha | han |

**Formation of the Present Perfect Tense**

| | hablar | tener | venir |
|---|---|---|---|
| yo | **he** hablado | **he** tenido | **he** venido |
| tú | **has** hablado | **has** tenido | **has** venido |
| Ud. / él / ella | **ha** hablado | **ha** tenido | **ha** venido |
| nosotros(-as) | **hemos** hablado | **hemos** tenido | **hemos** venido |
| vosotros(-as) | **habéis** hablado | **habéis** tenido | **habéis** venido |
| Uds. / ellos / ellas | **han** hablado | **han** tenido | **han** venido |

—¿**Has pagado** más de cien dólares por una blusa alguna vez? — *"Have you ever paid more than one hundred dollars for a blouse?"*
—No, nunca **he pagado** tanto dinero. — *"No, I've never paid that much money."*

—¿**Has visto** a Teresa? — *"Have you seen Teresa?"*
—No, no la **he visto.** — *"No, I haven't seen her."*

■ Note that when the past participle is part of a perfect tense, it is invariable. The past participle only changes in form when it is used as an adjective.

Ella ha escrit**o** la cart**a.** — *She has written the letter.*
La cart**a** está escrit**a.** — *The letter is written.*

■ In the Spanish present perfect tense the auxiliary verb **haber** can never be separated from the past participle as it can in English.

Yo nunca **he estado** en Lima. — *I have never been in Lima.*

■ Remember that when reflexive or object pronouns are used with compound tenses, the pronouns are placed immediately before the auxiliary verb.

**Le** ha dado mucho dinero a su hijo. — *He has given a lot of money to his son.*
María y José **se** han ido. — *María and José have left.*

## práctica

**A.** Look at the following illustrations and describe what these people have done today, using the present perfect.

1. Tú

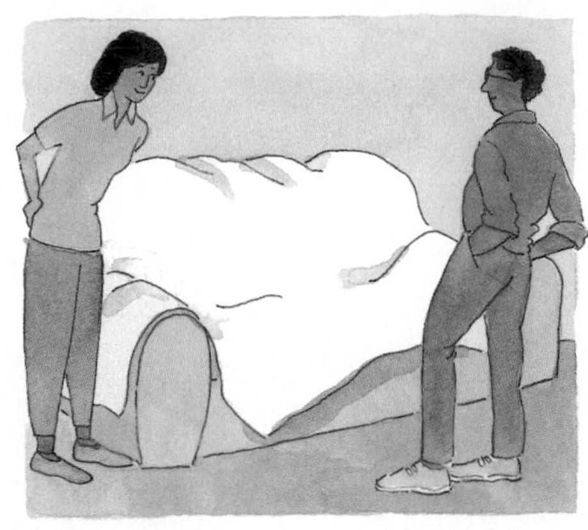

2. Tú y yo

3. Los chicos

4. Yo

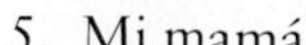

5. Mi mamá

6. Uds.

B. With a partner, take turns asking each other what you have done lately.

MODELO: ir al cine / con quién
—¿Has ido al cine últimamente?
—Sí, he ido.
—¿Con quién?
—Con mi novio(-a).

1. comprar ropa / qué
2. ver alguna película / cuál
3. dar alguna fiesta / dónde
4. mandar algún mensaje electrónico / a quién
5. tomar algún examen / en qué clase
6. visitar algún lugar interesante / cuál
7. escribir alguna carta / a quién
8. poner dinero en el banco / en cuál
9. leer un libro / cuál
10. recibir algún regalo / de quién

C. With a partner, discuss five things that you or your family and friends have never done and five things you have done many times. Compare your own experiences with those of your partner.

MODELO: —*Yo nunca he estado en España.*
—*Yo tampoco he estado en España.*
*(Yo he estado en España dos veces.)*

ASINCA
DESDE 1945
FABRICA ARTICULOS PIEL
Los Mejores precios y todo tipo de Complementos
Ctra. PALMA-ALCUDIA (Esq.Ctra.Manacor) INCA-Tel 971 50 12 50

## 3 The past perfect (pluperfect) *(El pluscuamperfecto)*

- The past perfect tense is formed by using the imperfect tense of the auxiliary verb **haber** with the past participle of the verb that expresses the action or state.
- This tense is equivalent to the English past perfect *(had + past participle*, as in *I had spoken.)*. Generally, the past perfect tense expresses an action that had taken place before another action in the past.

| ***Imperfect of* haber** | |
|---|---|
| había | habíamos |
| habías | habíais |
| había | habían |

**Formation of the Past Perfect Tense**

| | **estudiar** | **beber** | **ir** |
|---|---|---|---|
| yo | **había** estudiado | **había** bebido | **había** ido |
| tú | **habías** estudiado | **habías** bebido | **habías** ido |
| Ud. / él / ella | **había** estudiado | **había** bebido | **había** ido |
| nosotros(-as) | **habíamos** estudiado | **habíamos** bebido | **habíamos** ido |
| vosotros(-as) | **habíais** estudiado | **habíais** bebido | **habíais** ido |
| Uds. / ellos / ellas | **habían** estudiado | **habían** bebido | **habían** ido |

—¿No hablaste con Teresa? *"Didn't you speak with Teresa?"*
—No, cuando yo llegué, ella ya **se había ido.** *"No, when I arrived, she had already left."*

### práctica

**A.** One of your brothers is never around when there is work to be done. Say what had already been done by the time he got home last night.

MODELO: nosotros / lavar los platos
*Cuando él llegó, nosotros ya habíamos lavado los platos.*

1. yo / barrer la cocina
2. los chicos / pasarle la aspiradora a la alfombra
3. Roberto y yo / hacer la comida
4. Elsa / planchar la ropa
5. tú / limpiar el refrigerador
6. Carmen y Elena / bañar al perro
7. Anita / poner la mesa
8. Raúl y Carlos / comprar las bebidas
9. Mirta / lavar las sábanas
10. Raúl y yo / envolver los regalos

B. Interview a classmate, using the following questions. When you have finished, switch roles.

1. Cuando llegaste a tu casa anoche, ¿las otras personas ya habían cenado?
2. A las once de la noche, ¿ya te habías acostado?
3. Cuando te levantaste esta mañana, ¿alguien te había preparado el desayuno?
4. Cuando yo llegué a clase, ¿ya habías llegado tú?
5. Cuando llegaste a clase hoy, ¿ya habías hecho todos los ejercicios de esta lección?
6. ¿Ya habías tomado español antes de tomar esta clase?

C. Complete the following sentences logically, using the pluperfect tense.

1. Antes de venir a esta universidad, yo nunca...
2. Antes de tomar esta clase, mis compañeros y yo nunca...
3. Hasta el año pasado, mis amigos y yo siempre...
4. Hasta el semestre pasado, los estudiantes de esta clase nunca...
5. Hasta que yo cumplí dieciséis años, yo nunca...
6. Hasta el verano pasado, mi familia y yo siempre...

# ¡A ver cuánto aprendió!

INTERNET

See the *¿Cómo se dice...?* Web site for additional grammar and vocabulary practice: http://spanish.college.hmco.com/students

## ¡Repase el vocabulario!

Choose the correct word or phrase to complete each statement.

1. Puede probarse (la ganga, el chaleco, el armario) en el probador.
2. Mi bolso (hace juego, está muerto de hambre, va de compras) con mis sandalias.
3. Yo calzo el número siete y estos zapatos son número diez. (Me aprietan mucho. Me quedan grandes. Me quedan bien.)
4. Necesito un par de (calcetines, tallas, escaleras mecánicas).
5. Pagué solamente treinta dólares por el vestido de lino. Hoy hubo una gran (bota, liquidación, billetera) en la tienda París.
6. Estos pantalones me quedan un poco chicos, pero no los he devuelto todavía porque (me gustan mucho, son muy estrechos, no me quedan bien).
7. Hace frío. Ponte (la chaqueta, las sandalias, el pañuelo) de lana.
8. Mi ropa es vieja y está pasada de (cuero, compra, moda).
9. ¿Qué medida (usa, vuela, camina) Ud.?
10. El traje tiene que hacer juego con (la corbata, la ropa interior, el camisón).
11. Puse el dinero en (la billetera, la lana, el algodón).
12. No hay ropa en mi ropero. No tengo nada que (ponerme, bañarme, afeitarme).
13. ¿Usa Ud. talla grande, chica o (abierta, ancha, mediana)?
14. Pues yo me quedo en la (seda, taza, planta baja).
15. Compré una falda estampada y una falda (de lunares, muy sabrosa, enfadada).

## Entrevista

With a partner, interview each other by asking the following questions.

1. ¿Prefieres camisas (blusas) de rayas o de cuadros?
2. ¿Qué talla de camisa (blusa) usas?
3. ¿Qué número calzas?
4. ¿Te aprietan los zapatos que llevas puestos?
5. Cuando compras un par de zapatos, ¿te los llevas puestos?
6. ¿Dónde has comprado esa falda (chaqueta, camisa)?
7. ¿Tu camisa (blusa) y tus pantalones siempre hacen juego?
8. ¿Cuál es la tienda que más te gusta? ¿Por qué te gusta?
9. ¿Prefieres comprar cuando hay una liquidación? ¿Por qué?
10. ¿Qué ropa prefieres?
11. ¿Tienes mucha ropa o no tienes nada que ponerte?
12. ¿Prefieres usar la escalera o la escalera mecánica?

## Situaciones

What would you say in the following situations? What would the other person say? Act out the scenes with a partner. Take turns playing each role.

1. You are shopping in a large department store. You need a pair of gloves, a white shirt, and a blue tie. You also saw a brown suit in the window that you liked, and you want to know how much it costs.
2. You are a clerk. A customer is admiring a pink blouse. Ask her what size she wears, and tell her the fitting room is on the left.
3. A clerk at a shoe store wants to sell you a pair of boots. The ones he is showing you are too expensive and too tight on you.
4. Tell your friend that you haven't eaten yet, that you are starving, and that you want to have something to eat.

## Para escribir

Write a dialogue between yourself and a clerk at a department store. You should mention what size you wear, what colors you like, and whether or not something fits you. Describe different things you want to buy.

# En la vida real

**CD-ROM**

Do the interactive exercises on the CD-ROM for additional practice.

## Haciendo las maletas

You and a classmate are going on vacation. You are going to Hawaii in August and she or he is going to Colorado in December. Help each other select the type of clothes you will need for the trip, according to the different activities you are planning.

Here are some other words and phrases you may want to use in addition to the lesson vocabulary:

**los bluejeans, los vaqueros** *jeans*
**la bufanda** *scarf*
**de rayón** *made of rayon*
**los pantalones cortos** *shorts*

## ¡De compras!

Help a friend of yours who is shopping at El Corte Inglés in Madrid. Answer her questions, using the information provided in the ad.

Ahora en El Corte Inglés, Rebajas sobre Rebajas. Todo cuesta mucho menos.
SEÑORAS
• Vestidos lisos y estampados, en poliéster-algodón 95€
• Pareos estampados, en distintos dibujos y colores 15€
CABALLEROS
• Pantalones de sport y de vestir, lisos y fantasía, en poliéster-lana y poliéster-algodón 59€
• Mocasines en piel de búfalo, con piso de suela 150€
JÓVENES
• Para ellas, bañadores y bikinis, lisos y fantasía 85€
• Para ellos, bañadores, lisos y estampados 45€
NIÑOS
• Camisetas para niños y niñas, lisas y estampadas 10€
• Playeros en distintos colores, todas las tallas 12€
MENAJE
• Batería de cocina ocho piezas, en acero vitrificado, tres colores 150€
TEXTILES
• Mantelería de seis servicios estampada, acabada en festón 35€
MUEBLES
• Sillón cromado, con asiento y respaldo en piel 25€
LAS REBAJAS
DE EL CORTE INGLÉS


1. ¿En qué mes son las rebajas?
2. Tengo una hija de nueve años. ¿Qué puedo comprarle?
3. Mi esposo necesita zapatos. ¿Qué tipo de zapatos venden y cuánto cuestan?
4. No tengo nada que ponerme. ¿Qué puedo comprar para mí?
5. Pensamos ir a la playa. ¿Qué puedo comprar para mí y para mis hijos?
6. Es el cumpleaños de mi padre. ¿Qué puedo regalarle? ¿Cuánto me va a costar?
7. ¿Para cuántas personas son los manteles?
8. ¿Cuánto cuesta el sillón?

## La última moda

Stage a fashion show in class. A few students will play the role of runway models, and other students will describe the clothes and shoes the models are wearing. The rest of the class will be customers and will ask the price and size of the clothes and shoes the models are wearing.

### Antes de leer

A. As you read the selection, keep in mind that the author criticizes the lack of punctuality. Think about the problems that are caused by not being punctual and how this affects other people.

B. As you read the selection, find the answers to the following questions.

1. ¿Por qué dice el autor que "después de almorzar" es algo demasiado elástico?
2. ¿Tiene el amigo del autor una hora exacta para almorzar?
3. ¿A qué hora dice el señor que va a estar en el café sin falta?
4. ¿Qué sucede al día siguiente a las ocho?
5. ¿Qué piensa el amigo del autor sobre la puntualidad?
6. ¿Por qué es una buena idea acudir puntualmente a una cita?

JULIO CAMBA (ESPAÑA)(1882–1962)

Julio Camba, escritor de estilo satírico y humorístico, publicó numerosos artículos en los cuales da sus impresiones sobre la vida y la cultura de los distintos países que visitó.

El artículo que ofrecemos a continuación pertenece al libro de ensayos *La rana viajera*. Otros libros del autor son *Alemania*, *Londres*, *Aventuras de una peseta*, *Lúculo o el arte de comer*, *La ciudad automática*, *Mis páginas mejores*, y otros.

# *El tiempo y el espacio (Adaptado)*

Tengo algo urgente que discutir con un amigo. Por supuesto el amigo dice que hoy no puede ser.

—¿Mañana...?

—Muy bien. ¿A qué hora?

—A cualquier hora. Después de almorzar, por ejemplo...

Yo digo que eso no es una hora. "Después de almorzar" es algo demasiado° vago, demasiado elástico.

—¿A qué hora almuerza usted? —pregunto.

—A la hora de almorzar.

—Pero ¿qué hora es la hora de almorzar para usted? ¿El mediodía? ¿La una de la tarde? ¿Las dos...?

—Más o menos... —dice mi amigo—. Yo almuerzo de una a dos. A veces a las tres... De todos modos° a las cuatro siempre estoy libre.°

—Entonces, ¿a las cuatro?

—Sí, claro que, si llego unos minutos tarde —añade°— usted me puede esperar, ¿verdad? Quien dice a las cuatro, dice a las cuatro y media. En fin, de cuatro a cinco yo estoy sin falta° en el café.

Yo quiero ser exacto.

—¿A las cinco?

—Muy bien. A las cinco... Es decir, de cinco a cinco y media... Uno no es un tren, ¡qué diablo°!

—Pues podemos decir a las cinco y media —propongo yo. Entonces mi amigo tiene una idea brillante.

—¿Por qué no decimos a la hora del aperitivo? —sugiere.

Finalmente, decidimos reunirnos de siete a ocho. Al día siguiente son las ocho, y claro está, mi amigo no viene. Llega a las ocho y media echando el bofe° y no me encuentra.

—No es justo —exclama días después al encontrarnos en la calle—. Me hace usted fijar una hora, me hace usted correr, y no me espera ni diez minutos. Yo llego a las ocho y media en punto°, y usted no está esperándome.

Y lo más curioso es que la indignación de mi amigo es auténtica. Para él, la puntualidad es algo completamente absurdo.

Pero —digo yo— una cita es una cosa que tiene que estar tan limitada en el tiempo como en el espacio.

De despreciar° el tiempo, podemos despreciar también el espacio. Y de respetar el espacio, ¿por qué no considerar también el tiempo?

too

**De...** Anyway / free

he adds

**sin...** without fail

**qué...** what the heck

**echando...** out of breath

**en...** on the dot

If we scorn

—Pero con esa precisión, con esa exactitud°, la vida es imposible —opina mi amigo.

° accuracy

—¿Cómo explicarle que esa exactitud y esa precisión sirven, al contrario, para simplificar la vida? ¿Cómo convencerle de que, llegando puntualmente a las citas uno ahorra mucho tiempo para hacer otras cosas?

## Díganos

Answer the following questions, based on your own thoughts and experiences.

1. ¿Es Ud. puntual o generalmente llega tarde?
2. Si Ud. tiene una cita y la persona llega tarde, ¿cúanto tiempo la espera?
3. Para Ud. ¿la puntualidad es importante o algo absurdo?
4. ¿Está Ud. de acuerdo con el autor o con el amigo del autor? ¿Por qué?

# ASÍ SOMOS

Do the interactive exercises on the CD-ROM for additional practice.

NARRADORA —¿Qué estilo *(style)* de ropa usa Ud. para ir a clase?

LEONARDO —Normal... o sea, jeans, una camiseta, zapatos y una chaqueta de jeans también.

NARRADORA —¿Cómo se viste Ud. cuando tiene una cita *(date)*?

LEONARDO —Dependiendo de la cita también, pero regularmente con pantalón y camisa y a veces corbata.

## Preparación

A. **¿Cómo se viste...?** Answer the following questions about the clothes you wear to go to school. You will hear answers to some of these questions when you watch the video. After viewing the video, compare your answers with those you hear.

1. ¿Qué estilo *(style)* de ropa usa Ud. para ir a clase?
2. ¿Qué estilo de zapatos usa Ud. para ir a clase?
3. ¿Qué estilo de ropa usa su profesor(-a) para ir a clase?
4. ¿Cómo se viste Ud. cuando tiene una cita?
5. ¿Cómo se viste Ud. cuando está en casa?

**B. La ropa de moda.** With a partner, answer the following questions about the latest styles of clothing. You will hear answers to some of these questions when you watch the video. After viewing the video, compare your answers with those you hear.

1. ¿Qué estilo de ropa está de moda ahora?
2. ¿Qué estilo de ropa no está de moda ahora?
3. ¿Qué estilo de ropa le gusta a Ud.?
4. ¿Qué estilo de ropa no le gusta a Ud.?
5. ¿Compra Ud. la ropa en los grandes almacenes o en las boutiques?
6. ¿Compra Ud. los zapatos en los grandes almacenes o en las boutiques?

## Comprensión

**A. ¿Cómo se visten?** Answer the following questions according to what you understood from the video.

1. Para ir a clase, ¿Paola usa falda o jeans?
2. ¿Leonardo usa camisas o camisetas?
3. ¿Se viste María de una manera *(manner)* informal o formal?
4. ¿Lleva Juan uniforme o ropa casual para ir a clase?
5. A Miriam, ¿le gusta más usar jeans o usar faldas?
6. ¿La mayoría *(majority)* de los estudiantes entrevistados usa ropa formal o ropa informal para ir a clase?

**B. ¿Quién lo dijo?** Match each statement with the name of the person who said it.

| | | |
|---|---|---|
| _____ | 1. Utilizo *(I use)* traje *(suit)*, corbata y una buena colonia *(cologne)*. | a. Juan |
| _____ | 2. Utilizo los zapatos bien embolados *(polished)*. | b. Paola |
| _____ | 3. Me visto con saco y camisa sport. | c. Otmara |
| _____ | 4. Uso pantalón y camisa y a veces corbata. | d. Jaime |
| _____ | 5. No me gusta vestirme muy sofisticado. | e. Leonardo |
| _____ | 6. Uso pantalones de tela o una falda. | f. Pedro |
| _____ | 7. Casi siempre me gusta ponerme minifaldas, zapatos altos y blusas. | |

**C. La moda de hoy.** Read the following statements. Circle **V** (**Verdadero**) or **F** (**Falso**) according to what you understood from the video. If a statement is false, correct it.

**V F** 1. En Bogotá usan camisas de lana *(wool)* o sacos.
**V F** 2. En España la gente va bien arreglada *(dressed up)* para ir a una cita o a una fiesta.
**V F** 3. En España está de moda ir a clase con ropa formal.
**V F** 4. Juan dice que los pantalones de mezclilla también se llaman "jeans".
**V F** 5. Alejandro dice que los jeans y las playeras están de moda.
**V F** 6. En el país de Otmara hace mucho frío.

D. **De compras.** Answer the following questions, according to what you understood.

1. ¿Hay muchos almacenes grandes en Nicaragua?
2. ¿Compra Juan ropa en los grandes almacenes o en las boutiques?
3. ¿Miriam prefiere comprar ropa en un almacén o en una boutique?
4. ¿En Colombia hay muchos o pocos centros comerciales?
5. ¿Cómo es la calidad de la ropa en los centros comerciales de Colombia?
6. Para una ocasión especial, ¿Otmara compra en un almacén o en una boutique?
7. ¿Otmara compra ropa de diario *(everyday)* en un almacén o en una boutique?
8. Para Alejandro, ¿es importante el precio de la ropa?

E. **Entrevista.** Read the following statements. After watching the video, circle **V** (**Verdadero**) or **F** (**Falso**), according to what you understood. If a statement is false, correct it.

V F 1. En la tienda sólo venden jeans.
V F 2. Venden sólo una marca *(brand)* de jeans.
V F 3. A Jorge le gusta trabajar en la tienda.
V F 4. A Jorge no le gusta el ambiente de la tienda.
V F 5. Jorge hace amistad con algunos clientes.
V F 6. Los artículos más populares son los Levi's.

## Ampliación

A. **Vamos de compras.** Make a list in Spanish of the new clothes you would like to buy at the local shopping center. Then in groups of three or four, compare your lists.

B. **Mi ropa favorita.** Interview a classmate about his or her favorite clothes. Use the following questions as a guide.

1. ¿Cuál es tu ropa favorita?
2. ¿Qué ropa te gusta ponerte para salir?
3. ¿Cuál es tu ropa favorita para estar en casa?
4. ¿Qué ropa usas para ir a una fiesta?
5. ¿Cómo te vistes para ir a clase?

Take this test. When you have finished, check your answers in the answer key provided for this section in Appendix E. Then use a red pen to correct any mistakes you may have made. Are you ready?

## Lección 13

### A. The familiar commands *(tú)*

Give the Spanish equivalent of the words in parentheses.

1. ________ , Paco. ¿Pusiste los platos en el fregadero? *(Tell me)*
2. ________ el trabajo y luego ________ la cocina, Ana. *(Do / clean)*
3. ________ de mi recámara, Carlos. *(Leave)*
4. ________ con ella y ________ las cortinas para el cuarto, Pepe. *(Go / buy)*
5. ¿Los libros? ________ en la mesa, querida. *(Put them)*
6. ________ conmigo. *(Come)*
7. ________ buena y ________ las sábanas y la frazada, Anita. *(Be / bring me)*
8. ________ paciencia. ________ unos minutos más. *(Have / Wait for me)*
9. ________ la casa si no tiene aire acondicionado, Luis. *(Don't buy)*
10. ¿El té? todavía *(yet)*, Petrona. *(Don't serve it.)*
11. ________ , querido. *(Don't go away)*
12. ________ a las seis y ________ hasta las once. *(Get up / work)*

### B. *Qué* and *cuál* used with *ser*

Supply the questions that elicited the following responses, beginning with **qué** or **cuál**, as needed.

1. Mi número de teléfono es 862–4031.
2. El apellido de mi madre es Lovera.
3. Un pasaporte es un documento que necesitamos para viajar a un país extranjero.
4. Las lecciones que necesitamos son la once y la doce.
5. Su dirección es calle Universidad, número treinta.
6. La paella es un plato hecho *(made)* con pollo, arroz y mariscos.

### C. The subjunctive to express indefiniteness and nonexistence

Complete the following sentences, using the present subjunctive or the present indicative of the verbs given in parentheses.

1. ¿Hay alguien aquí que ________ (saber) hablar español?
2. Vivo en una casa que ________ (tener) cinco dormitorios.
3. No conozco a nadie que ________ (ser) colombiano.
4. ¿Ud. quiere una casa que ________ (tener) piscina?
5. Necesito un empleado que ________ (trabajar) tiempo completo.
6. Aquí hay una chica que ________ (hablar) francés, pero no hay nadie que ________ (hablar) ruso.

**D. Just words . . .**

Match the questions in column A with the appropriate responses in column B. Use each response once.

| A | B |
|---|---|
| 1. ¿Tienes frío? | a. No, pero tiene terraza. |
| 2. ¿Por qué es tan cara la casa? | b. No, uso el fregadero. |
| 3. ¿Por qué necesitas un garaje tan grande? | c. No, necesito una cafetera. |
| 4. ¿Cuánto va a costar el refrigerador? | d. Porque era más cómodo. |
| 5. ¿La casa tiene jardín? | e. La semana próxima. |
| 6. ¿Dónde lo leíste? | f. Está en un buen barrio. |
| 7. ¿Necesitas una tostadora? | g. Una cómoda y una butaca. |
| 8. ¿Tienes lavaplatos? | h. No, tiempo completo. |
| 9. ¿Cuándo se mudan? | i. En el periódico. |
| 10. ¿Tienen dinero? | j. Sí, pero no tenemos fundas. |
| 11. ¿Por qué compraste este sofá en vez del otro? | k. ¡Tengo tres coches! |
| 12. ¿Vas a trabajar medio día? | l. Póngalo en la sala. |
| 13. ¿Qué muebles necesitas? | m. Sí, pon la calefacción, por favor. |
| 14. ¿Dónde pongo el sofá? | n. Sí, ganaron la lotería. |
| 15. ¿Tienen almohadas? | o. Quinientos dólares. |
| 16. ¿Dónde vas a poner el pollo? | p. En el microondas. |

**E. Culture**

Read the following statements and circle **V** (**Verdadero**) or **F** (**Falso**) based on the **¿Lo sabía Ud.?** section.

V F 1. En España llaman "pisos" a los apartamentos.
V F 2. En los países latinos muchos edificios tienen oficinas o tiendas en la planta baja.
V F 3. La palabra "barrio" tiene una connotación negativa en los países de habla hispana.
V F 4. La Universidad Nacional Autónoma de México es la menos importante del país.
V F 5. Unos 400.000 estudiantes asisten a la UNAM.

## Lección 14

**A. The subjunctive or indicative after certain conjunctions**

Give the Spanish equivalent of the verbs in parentheses.

1. Tan pronto como Marta ________ a casa, le voy a dar las entradas. *(arrives)*
2. Voy a esperarlos hasta que ________. *(they return)*
3. Cuando ellos ________ a trabajar, siempre dejan las ventanas abiertas. *(go)*
4. Cuando lo ________, dile que somos seis. *(see)*

5. Vamos antes de que ________ la lámpara que te gusta. *(they sell)*
6. Ella va a ir al parque con tal que tú ________ con ella. *(go)*
7. No puedo sacar el sillón de la casa sin que ellos me ________. *(see)*
8. En caso de que ella ________ otras frutas, yo puedo traérselas. *(needs)*
9. No puedo comprar las verduras a menos que tú me ________ el dinero. *(give)*
10. Voy a llamar a Raúl para que nos ________ al cine. *(takes)*

**B. First-person plural commands**

Answer the following questions, using appropriate command forms and the cues provided.

1. ¿Adónde vamos? (al supermercado)
2. ¿A qué hora vamos? (a las dos)
3. ¿Qué compramos? (frutas y vegetales)
4. ¿A quién le pedimos el dinero? (a mamá)
5. ¿Adónde vamos después? ¿Al teatro? (no, al cine)
6. ¿A qué hora volvemos a casa? (a las siete)
7. ¿A qué hora nos acostamos esta noche? (a las once)
8. ¿A qué hora nos levantamos mañana? (a las seis)

**C. Constructions with *se***

Form questions with the elements given, adding the necessary connectors. Follow the model.

MODELO: a qué hora / abrir / las tiendas
*¿A qué hora se abren las tiendas?*

1. qué idioma / hablar / Chile
2. a qué hora / cerrar / las cafeterías
3. a qué hora / abrir / el supermercado
4. dónde / vender / aceite
5. por dónde / subir / segundo piso

**D. Just words . . .**

Complete the following sentences, using words learned in **Lección 14.**

1. ¿Tú le pones crema y ________ al café?
2. Quiero una ________ de salsa de tomate y una de frijoles.
3. ¿Compraste mantequilla o ________? A mí me gusta el pan con mantequilla.
4. No quiero zanahorias; no me gustan las ________.
5. ¿Te vas a ________ a dieta?
6. Tengo una ________ con Rosalía. Vamos a ir al cine.
7. ¿Qué ________ ponen en el cine Rex?
8. El 4 de julio es ________; no tenemos que trabajar.
9. Voy a comprar una ________ de huevos.
10. Necesitamos papel ________ para el baño.
11. Fuimos al parque de ________ el sábado pasado.
12. A él le gustan mucho los animales. Lo voy a llevar al ________.

### E. Culture

Read the following statements and circle **V** (**Verdadero**) or **F** (**Falso**) based on the **¿Lo sabía Ud.?** section.

V F 1. En los países hispanos no existen los supermercados.
V F 2. En los países hispanos muchas personas prefieren comprar en tiendas pequeñas especializadas, como carnicerías y panaderías.
V F 3. La producción de películas no tiene gran importancia en los países hispanos.
V F 4. Las películas norteamericanas no son populares en el mundo hispano.
V F 5. Las películas norteamericanas que se ven en el mundo hispano generalmente están dobladas o tienen subtítulos en español.

## Lección 15

### A. The past participle

Give the Spanish equivalent of the following past participles.

1. written
2. opened
3. seen
4. done
5. broken
6. gone
7. spoken
8. eaten
9. drunk
10. received

### B. Past participles used as adjectives

Give the Spanish equivalent of the words in parentheses.

1. Los espejos están ________. *(broken)*
2. ¿Están ________ las puertas de la tienda? *(open)*
3. El hombre estaba ________. *(dead)*
4. El departamento de señoras está ________. *(closed)*
5. Estas sandalias fueron ________ aquí. *(made)*

### C. The present perfect

Complete the sentences with the present perfect tense of the verbs in the list, as needed.

| decir | usar | comer |
|---|---|---|
| quedarse | hacer | envolver |

1. ¿Tú nunca ________ esa falda?
2. Él me ________ los zapatos.
3. Ellos me ________ que no tienen nada que hacer.
4. Nosotros ________ demasiado.
5. Yo ________ en la planta baja.
6. ¿Uds. no ________ el trabajo todavía?

### D. The past perfect (pluperfect)

Complete the following sentences with the past perfect tense of the verbs in parentheses.

1. Cuando yo llegué, la liquidación ya ________ (terminar).
2. Elsa dijo que ellos ________ (ir) al departamento de ropa para caballeros.
3. El dependiente me ________ (decir) que la cartera costaba cincuenta dólares.
4. Yo ya ________ (abrir) la puerta del probador.
5. Nosotros todavía no ________ (comprar) la camisa.
6. ¿Tú le ________ (preguntar) qué talla usaba?

### E. Just words . . .

Choose the appropriate answer to each of the following questions.

1. ¿Qué número calza Ud.?
   a. Talla mediana.
   b. El treinta y seis.
   c. No tengo pantimedias.
2. ¿Quiere las botas negras y el bolso azul?
   a. No, no hacen juego.
   b. En seguida vuelvo.
   c. No, me gusta la ropa interior.
3. ¿Puedo probarme estos zapatos?
   a. Sí, pero antes tiene que ponerse calcetines.
   b. Sí, pero necesita esta corbata.
   c. Sí, pero necesita ponerse estos guantes.
4. ¿Va a llevar este par de zapatos?
   a. No, me quedan muy bien.
   b. No, están en la zapatería.
   c. No, me aprietan un poco.
5. ¿Dónde pusiste el traje?
   a. ¡En la billetera, por supuesto!
   b. ¡En el ropero, por supuesto!
   c. ¡En la rebaja, por supuesto!
6. ¿Tiene frío, señora?
   a. Sí, tráigame el pañuelo.
   b. Sí, tráigame las sandalias.
   c. Sí, tráigame la chaqueta.
7. ¿Quieres comer algo?
   a. Sí, estoy muerta de hambre.
   b. Sí, me gusta este vestido.
   c. Sí, quiero esa camisa y esa blusa.
8. ¿Cómo subieron al tercer piso?
   a. Nos encontramos en la planta baja.
   b. Por la escalera mecánica.
   c. Compramos ropa.

### F. Culture

Circle the correct answer, based on the **¿Lo sabía Ud.?** section.

1. El primer piso en España corresponde (a la planta baja, al segundo piso) en los Estados Unidos.
2. En las ciudades hispanas muchas mujeres prefieren (comprar ropa hecha, utilizar los servicios de una modista).
3. En los países hispanos (existen, no existen) grandes almacenes de ropa.
4. En España los dependientes de las tiendas (a veces, nunca) tutean a los clientes.

Lección 16

# Las carreras

## OBJECTIVES

### Pronunciation

Pronunciation in context

### Structure

The future • The conditional • The future perfect and the conditional perfect

### Communication

You will learn vocabulary related to college activities and careers.

# Las carreras

Los Ángeles, California
24 de agosto del 2002

Estimado Sergio:

Te diré que no te he escrito antes porque no he tenido tiempo. Mañana estaré también muy ocupado porque tendré que matricularme para las clases de otoño. Pienso tomar administración de empresas, sociología y psicología. Mi consejero me ha sugerido que tome una clase de química o de física pero, como sabes, nunca me han gustado las ciencias. ¡Prefiero la literatura!

Me gustaría mucho ir a Buenos Aires en diciembre, pero tengo exámenes finales hasta el 20 y tengo que sacar buenas notas. Debo mantener un promedio de "A" porque tengo una beca.

¿Por qué no vienes tú a Los Ángeles? Podríamos ir a Disneylandia y visitar San Diego, mi ciudad favorita. Tienes que venir antes del año 2004 porque para entonces ya me habré graduado. ¡Trataré de conseguir un trabajo antes, porque la vida de estudiante es vida de pobre!

Escríbeme pronto. Un abrazo de tu amigo,

Daniel

P.D.[1] ¡Saludos a tu hermana!

---

Buenos Aires, Argentina
15 de septiembre del 2002

Estimado Daniel:

¡Gracias por la invitación! De haber sabido que ibas a invitarme a Los Ángeles, no habría gastado tanto dinero en mi viaje a Río de Janeiro y habría ahorrado dinero para el pasaje.

Yo también estoy muy ocupado. La carrera de abogado no es fácil, y todos los profesores de la Facultad de Derecho creen que sus clases son lo único que debería importarnos.

Mi hermana Amalia (le di tus saludos) está estudiando periodismo y se pasa la vida haciendo investigación y escribiendo informes. Yo supongo que algún día será una periodista magnífica.

[1]Post Data: post scriptum

¿Te acuerdas de José Luis? Está estudiando ingeniería y probablemente el año próximo irá a los Estados Unidos para tomar unos cursos especiales. ¡Yo haría lo mismo! De haber seguido los consejos de su padre, ya habría terminado la carrera de médico.

¿Y tú? ¿Cuál es tu especialización? Yo pensé que tu asignatura favorita era la contabilidad...

Bueno, me voy porque Marcos me invitó a un partido de fútbol. Es en el estadio de Boca y juega nuestro equipo. ¡Chau!

Afectuosamente,

Sergio

P.D. Saludos de Amalia.

**Titulaciones Oficiales**

**Ingenierías:**

- Informática
- Industrial

**Licenciaturas:**

- Administración y Dirección de Empresas
- Derecho
- Periodismo
- Publicidad y Relaciones Públicas
- Comunicación Audiovisual
- Lenguas Aplicadas a la Comunicación y al Marketing
- Lenguas Aplicadas a las Actividades Empresariales
- Filología Inglesa

# Vocabulario

### Cognados

**afectuosamente** affectionately
**la ciencia** science
**especial** special
**el estadio** stadium
**la física** physics
**la literatura** literature
**probablemente** probably
**la psicología** psychology
**la sociología** sociology

## Nombres

**la administración de empresas** business administration
**la asignatura, la materia** (school) subject
**la beca** scholarship
**la carrera** university studies, career
**el (la) consejero(-a)** advisor
**el consejo** advice
**la contabilidad** accounting
**el curso** course, class
**el equipo** team
**la especialización** major (field of study)
**el examen final** final exam
**la facultad de derecho** law school
**el fútbol** soccer
**el informe** paper, report
**la ingeniería** engineering
**la investigación** research
**la nota** grade
**el partido** game
**el periodismo** journalism
**el (la) periodista** journalist
**el promedio** grade point average
**la química** chemistry
**el tiempo** time
**la vida** life

## Verbos

**gastar** to spend (i.e., money)
**graduarse**[1] to graduate
**importar** to matter
**mantener** to maintain *(conj. like* **tener***)*
**matricularse** to register
**sacar** to get, to receive (a grade)
**suponer** to suppose *(conj. like* **poner***)*
**tratar (de)** to try

## Adjetivo

**estimado(-a)** dear

## Otras palabras y expresiones

**como** as
**de haber seguido** had he followed
**lo único**[2] the only thing
**para entonces** by then
**pronto** soon
**Saludos a...** Say hello to

# Vocabulario adicional

## Profesiones y oficios *(trades)*[3]

**el (la) bibliotecario(-a)** librarian

**el (la) carpintero(-a)** carpenter

**el (la) cocinero(-a)** cook, chef

---

[1]Present tense: **me gradúo, te gradúas, se gradúa, nos graduamos, os graduáis, se gradúan**
[2]Lo + *adjective* is equivalent to *the + adjective + thing:* **lo importante** = *the important thing;* **lo bueno** = *the good thing*
[3]For an extensive list of professions and trades, see Appendix F.

**el (la) contador(-a)** accountant

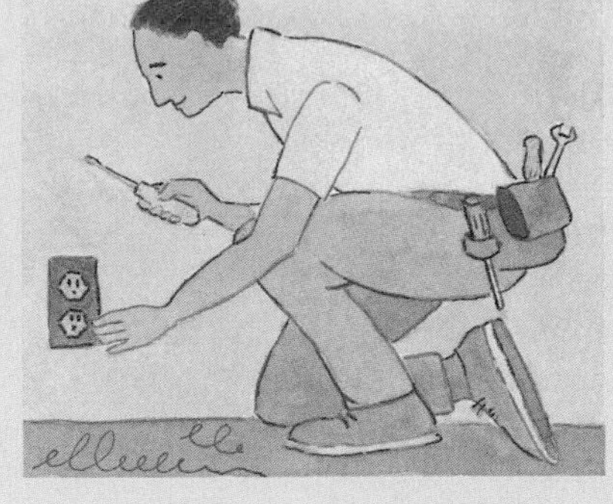

**el (la) electricista** electrician

**el hombre (la mujer) de negocios** businessman (woman)

**el (la) ingeniero(-a)** engineer

**el (la) plomero(-a)** plumber

**el (la) programador(-a)** programmer

**el (la) psicólogo(-a)** psychologist

**el (la) vendedor(-a)** salesperson

## Para hablar de los estudios

| | |
|---|---|
| **aprobar (o:ue)** to pass (an exam or course) | **Aprobé** el examen. |
| **entregar** to turn in, deliver | ¿**Entregaste** la tarea? |
| **el examen parcial (de mitad de curso)** midterm exam | Tengo dos **exámenes parciales.** |
| **el horario** schedule | Tengo un buen **horario** este semestre. |
| **el laboratorio** laboratory | Trabajo en el **laboratorio** de lenguas. |
| **las matemáticas** mathematics | Mi profesor de **matemáticas** es el profesor Trujillo. |
| **la matrícula** registration, tuition | Tengo que pagar la **matrícula.** |
| **quedar suspendido(-a)** to fail (an exam or course) | Eva **quedó suspendida** en química. |
| **el requisito** requirement | Yo he tomado todos los **requisitos** generales. |
| **el trimestre** quarter, trimester | Este **trimestre** tengo una clase de física. |

# ¡Conversemos!

Answer the following questions, basing your answers on the letters.

1. ¿Daniel estará ocupado mañana? ¿Qué tendrá que hacer?
2. ¿Qué asignaturas piensa tomar Daniel?

3. ¿Qué le ha sugerido su consejero? ¿Por qué no quiere él seguir su consejo?
4. ¿Adónde le gustaría ir a Daniel? ¿Podrá ir? ¿Por qué?
5. ¿Qué promedio debe mantener Daniel? ¿Por qué?
6. ¿Para qué año se habrá graduado Daniel?
7. ¿Qué habría hecho Sergio de haber sabido que Daniel lo iba a invitar a Los Ángeles?
8. Según Sergio, ¿qué creen todos los profesores de la Facultad de Derecho?
9. ¿Qué dice Sergio que Amalia será algún día?
10. ¿Adónde irá José Luis el año próximo? ¿Qué va a hacer allí?
11. De haber seguido los consejos de su padre, ¿qué carrera habría estudiado José Luis?
12. ¿Para qué van a ir Sergio y Marcos al estadio de Boca?

## ¿Lo sabía Ud.?

■ En la mayoría de las universidades hispanas no existe el concepto de "*major*" usado en los Estados Unidos. Los estudiantes españoles y latinoamericanos toman muy pocas clases optativas *(electives)*, ya que la mayoría comienza a especializarse a partir de su primer año en la universidad.

■ En España y en Latinoamérica, las universidades se dividen en "facultades", donde los estudiantes toman clases directamente relacionadas con su especialización (por ejemplo, la Facultad de Medicina, la Facultad de Ingeniería, la Facultad de Arquitectura, etc.). No existen requisitos generales, pues éstos se toman en la escuela secundaria.

■ En lugar de letras, el sistema de calificaciones *(grading system)* en las universidades hispanas usa números. Por lo general, se califica asignando notas de 1 a 5 en Hispanoamérica y de 1 a 10 en España. Una nota de 3 o de 6 es normalmente la nota mínima para aprobar una clase o un examen.

- ¿Cuáles son algunos de los requisitos generales que se toman en las universidades de su país?

Estudiantes de la Facultad de Derecho en Lima, Perú.

- En su país, ¿cuál es la nota mínima para aprobar una clase o un examen?

See the *¿Cómo se dice...?* Web site for activities on authentic cultural material: http://spanish.college.hmco.com/students

# Pronunciación

In this lesson, there are some new words or phrases that may be challenging to pronounce. For further pronunciation practice of Spanish sounds, listen to your instructor and repeat the following words and phrases.

1. Pienso tomar **administración de empresas.**
2. Me ha sugerido que tome una clase de **química** o de **física.**
3. Para entonces ya **me habré graduado.**
4. **Habría ahorrado** dinero para el pasaje.
5. ¿Cuál es tu **especialización**?

# Estructuras

## 1 The future *(El futuro)*

■ Most Spanish verbs are regular in the future tense. The infinitive serves as the stem of almost all of them, and the endings are the same for all three conjugations.

**The Future Tense**

| *Infinitive* | | *Stem* | *Ending* | |
|---|---|---|---|---|
| trabajar | yo | trabajar- | é | trabajaré |
| aprender | tú | aprender- | ás | aprenderás |
| escribir | Ud. | escribir- | á | escribirá |
| hablar | él | hablar- | á | hablará |
| decidir | ella | decidir- | á | decidirá |
| dar | nosotros(-as) | dar- | emos | dar**emos** |
| ir | vosotros(-as) | ir- | éis | ir**éis** |
| caminar | Uds. | caminar- | án | caminar**án** |
| perder | ellos | perder | án | perder**án** |
| recibir | ellas | recibir- | án | recibir**án** |

**ATENCIÓN** Note that all the endings, except the one for the **nosotros** form, have written accents.

| | |
|---|---|
| —¿Qué clases **tomarás** el año próximo? | *"What classes will you take next year?"* |
| —No sé. Lo **decidiré** cuando hable con mi consejero. | *"I don't know. I'll decide when I talk with my advisor."* |

■ The English equivalent of the Spanish future is *will* or *shall + a verb*. As you have already learned, Spanish also uses the construction **ir a** + *infinitive* or *the present tense with a time expression* to express future action, very much like the English present tense or the expression *going to*.

| | |
|---|---|
| **Vamos a ir** al estadio esta noche.<br>*or:* **Iremos** al estadio esta noche. | *We're going (We'll go) to the stadium tonight.* |
| Anita **toma** el examen mañana.<br>*or:* Anita **tomará** el examen mañana. | *Anita is taking (will take) the exam tomorrow.* |

**ATENCIÓN** The Spanish future is *not* used to express willingness, as is the English future. In Spanish this is expressed with the verb **querer**.

**¿Quieres** llamar a Tomás? — *Will you call Tomás?*

■ A small number of verbs are irregular in the future. These verbs use a modified form of the infinitive as a stem, but have the same endings as the regular verbs.

**Irregular Future Stems**

| *Infinitive* | *Modified form (Stem)* | *First-person singular* |
|---|---|---|
| decir | dir- | **diré** |
| hacer | har- | **haré** |
| querer | querr- | **querré** |
| saber | sabr- | **sabré** |
| poder | podr- | **podré** |
| caber | cabr- | **cabré** |
| poner | pondr- | **pondré** |
| venir | vendr- | **vendré** |
| tener | tendr- | **tendré** |
| salir | saldr- | **saldré** |
| valer[1] | valdr- | **valdré** |

—¿Qué les **dirás** a tus padres? — *"What will you tell your parents?"*
—Les **diré** que no **podremos** venir en enero y que **vendremos** en febrero. — *"I will tell them that we won't be able to come in January and that we will come in February."*

**ATENCIÓN** The future of **hay** (impersonal form of **haber**) is **habrá.**

**¿Habrá** una fiesta? — *Will there be a party?*

## práctica

**A.** Say what the following people will do after classes are over, using the future tense.

1. Jorge / ir de vacaciones / México
2. Marta y yo / salir para Colombia / julio

[1]*to be worth*

3. Mis padres / venir / a visitarme / agosto
4. Ana / tener que / trabajar / verano
5. Yo / tomar / una clase / francés
6. Uds. / poner / alfombra nueva / casa
7. Tú / viajar / por Latinoamérica
8. Ud. / pasar / dos semanas / Sevilla

**B.** You and a friend will be attending a special program in Spain next year. Take turns answering these questions about your trip.

1. ¿A qué ciudad irán?
2. ¿Cuándo saldrán de viaje?
3. ¿Viajarán en barco o en avión?
4. ¿Cuánto tiempo estarán estudiando?
5. ¿Podrán visitar muchas ciudades?
6. ¿Qué lugares visitarán?
7. ¿Les enviarán tarjetas postales a sus amigos?
8. ¿Cuánto dinero necesitarán para el viaje?
9. ¿Se lo pedirán a sus padres?
10. ¿Cuándo volverán?

**C.** Now, use the questions in Exercise B as a model to ask a classmate about his or her upcoming study-travel plans.

**D.** Say what the following people will do in each situation.

1. Los estudiantes tienen que escribir un informe para su clase de sociología.
2. Jorge no tiene dinero para pagar la matrícula.
3. Ud. y yo tenemos un examen mañana.
4. Antonio y Luis no saben qué clases pueden tomar.
5. Yo tengo un examen de matemáticas y no tengo calculadora.
6. Los muchachos tienen mucha hambre.

**E.** With a partner, write predictions about five of your classmates and what will happen to them in the future. Compare your predictions to those of other groups.

MODELO: *Dentro de cinco años, John será periodista y trabajará para el periódico* Los Angeles Times.

## 2 The conditional *(El condicional)*

- The conditional tense in Spanish is equivalent to the conditional in English, expressed by *should* or *would + a verb.*[1] Like the future tense, the conditional uses the infinitive as the stem and has only one set of endings for all three conjugations.

**The Conditional Tense**

| *Infinitive* | | *Stem* | *Ending* | |
|---|---|---|---|---|
| trabajar | yo | trabajar- | **ía** | trabaj**aría** |
| aprender | tú | aprender- | **ías** | aprender**ías** |
| escribir | Ud. | escribir- | **ía** | escribir**ía** |
| ir | él | ir- | **ía** | ir**ía** |
| ser | ella | ser- | **ía** | ser**ía** |
| dar | nosotros(-as) | dar- | **íamos** | dar**íamos** |
| hablar | vosotros(-as) | hablar- | **íais** | hablar**íais** |
| servir | Uds. | servir- | **ían** | servir**ían** |
| estar | ellos | estar- | **ían** | estar**ían** |
| preferir | ellas | preferir- | **ían** | preferir**ían** |

- All of the conditional endings have written accents.

—Él dijo que **tomaría** esta clase. *"He said that he would take this class."*

—Sí, y también dijo que **hablaría** con una consejera. *"Yes, and he also said that he would speak with an advisor."*

- The conditional is also used as the future of a past action. The future states what *will* happen; the conditional states what *would* happen.

| ***Future*** (states what *will* happen) | ***Conditional*** (states what *would* happen) |
|---|---|
| Él **dice** que **estará** aquí mañana. | Él **dijo** que **estaría** aquí mañana. |
| *He says that he will be here tomorrow.* | *He said that he would be here tomorrow.* |

[1]The conditional is never used in Spanish as an equivalent of *used to.*
Cuando era pequeño siempre **iba a la playa.** *When I was little I would always go to the beach.*

- The verbs that have irregular stems in the future tense are also irregular in the conditional. The endings are the same as those for regular verbs.

| Irregular Conditional Stems | | |
|---|---|---|
| ***Infinitive*** | ***Modified form (Stem)*** | ***First-person singular*** |
| decir | dir- | **diría** |
| hacer | har- | **haría** |
| querer | querr- | **querría** |
| saber | sabr- | **sabría** |
| poder | podr- | **podría** |
| caber | cabr- | **cabría** |
| poner | pondr- | **pondría** |
| venir | vendr- | **vendría** |
| tener | tendr- | **tendría** |
| salir | saldr- | **saldría** |
| valer | valdr- | **valdría** |

—¿A qué hora te dijo que **vendría**? *"What time did he tell you he would come?"*

—Dijo que **saldría** de casa a las dos. *"He said he would leave home at two."*

**ATENCIÓN** The conditional of **hay** (impersonal form of **haber**) is **habría.**

Dijo que **habría** un examen mañana. *He said there would be an exam tomorrow.*

## práctica

**A.** Nobody would do the things that Carlos does. With a partner, take turns saying what the following people would do instead.

MODELO: Carlos come en la cafetería. (yo)
*Yo no comería en la cafetería; comería en mi casa.*

Carlos...

1. se levanta a las cinco. (Uds.)
2. estudia por la mañana. (Ana y Luis)
3. viene a la universidad en ómnibus. (nosotros)
4. toma clases de alemán. (yo)
5. se baña por la noche. (Elsa)
6. se acuesta a las nueve de la noche. (Ud.)
7. va a las montañas los fines de semana. (ellos)
8. sale con Margarita. (tú)

**B.** Interview a classmate, using the following questions.

1. ¿Qué harías con mil dólares?
2. ¿Adónde irías de vacaciones? ¿En qué mes saldrías de vacaciones? ¿Por qué?
3. ¿Qué te gustaría hacer hoy?

4. ¿Dónde te gustaría almorzar mañana?
5. ¿Preferirías ver un partido de fútbol o un partido de fútbol americano?
6. ¿Qué asignaturas te gustaría tomar el semestre (trimestre) próximo?
7. ¿Preferirías un apartamento en la planta baja o en el séptimo piso? ¿Por qué?
8. Vamos a tener una fiesta. ¿Qué podrías traer?

C. Describe what you would do in the following situations, using the conditional.

1. Su amigo(-a) le pide consejos sobre la carrera que debe seguir.
2. Su equipo de fútbol americano favorito juega hoy.
3. Un compañero quiere que Ud. lo ayude con su informe.
4. Sus amigos lo (la) invitan a ir al cine esta noche y Ud. tiene que trabajar mañana.
5. Una persona muy antipática lo (la) invita a salir.
6. Usted tiene que estar en la universidad a las siete de la mañana.
7. Usted tiene una beca y necesita mantener un buen promedio.
8. Ud. va a matricularse y no sabe qué asignaturas debe tomar.

D. With a partner, take turns telling each other what you would do if you won a million dollars in the lottery. Say at least five things each, and then compare your responses with those of other classmates.

## 3 The future perfect and the conditional perfect *(El futuro perfecto y el condicional perfecto)*

### A. The future perfect

■ The future perfect in Spanish corresponds closely in formation and meaning to the same tense in English. The Spanish future perfect is formed with the future tense of the auxiliary verb **haber** + *the past participle* of the main verb.

***Future tense of* haber**

| | |
|---|---|
| habré | habremos |
| habrás | habréis |
| habrá | habrán |

**Formation of the Future Perfect Tense**

| | | |
|---|---|---|
| yo | **habré terminado** | *I will have finished* |
| tú | **habrás vuelto** | *you will have returned* |
| Ud. / él / ella | **habrá comido** | *you (he, she) will have eaten* |
| nosotros(-as) | **habremos escrito** | *we will have written* |
| vosotros(-as) | **habréis dicho** | *you* (fam.) *will have said* |
| Uds. / ellos / ellas | **habrán salido** | *you (they) will have left* |

■ Like its English equivalent, the future perfect is used to indicate an action that will have taken place by a certain time in the future.

—¿Tus padres estarán aquí para el dos de junio? — *"Will your parents be here by June second?"*
—Sí, para esa fecha ya **habrán vuelto** de Madrid. — *"Yes, by that date they will have returned from Madrid."*

## práctica

A. Complete the following dialogues, using the future perfect forms of the verbs listed. Then act them out with a partner.

acostarse
cenar
limpiar
salir
terminar (2)
volver (2)

1. —Esta noche a las once voy a llamar a Quique.
   —¿Estás loco(-a)? Para esa hora él ya ________. Llámalo mañana a las siete.
   —Para esa hora ya ________ de su casa.
2. —¿Uds. ________ de México para el 4 de julio?
   —No, no ________ todavía. Vamos a estar allí hasta agosto.
3. —Tú y yo podemos salir para España el 12 de diciembre porque ya estaremos de vacaciones.
   —Bueno, tú ________ las clases para entonces, pero yo no las ________ todavía.
4. —No podemos traer a mis amigos esta noche porque la casa está muy sucia *(dirty)*.
   —No te preocupes. Para cuando Uds. vengan, las chicas ya la ________.
5. —¿Quieres cenar con nosotros hoy?
   —Gracias, pero para cuando yo vuelva, Uds. ya ________.

B. With your partner, discuss things that you will or will not have done by the following times.

1. para las once de la noche
2. para mañana a las cinco de la mañana
3. para mañana a las seis de la tarde
4. para el sábado próximo
5. para junio del año próximo
6. para el año 2008

## B. The conditional perfect

■ The conditional perfect is formed with the conditional tense of the auxiliary verb **haber** + *the past participle* of the main verb.

| *Conditional tense of* **haber** | |
|---|---|
| habría | habríamos |
| habrías | habríais |
| habría | habrían |

**Formation of the Conditional Perfect Tense**

| | | |
|---|---|---|
| yo | **habría vuelto** | *I would have returned* |
| tú | **habrías comido** | *you would have eaten* |
| Ud. / él / ella | **habría salido** | *you (he, she) would have left* |
| nosotros(-as) | **habríamos estudiado** | *we would have studied* |
| vosotros(-as) | **habríais hecho** | *you* (fam.) *would have done* |
| Uds. / ellos / ellas | **habrían muerto** | *you (they) would have died* |

■ Like the English conditional perfect, the Spanish conditional perfect is used to indicate an action that would have taken place but didn't.

| | |
|---|---|
| —Yo me matriculé ayer. | *"I registered yesterday."* |
| —Yo **me habría matriculado** la semana pasada. | *"I would have registered last week."* |

## práctica

**A.** Last summer, my family, a friend, and I took a trip to New York. Based on what I tell you about our trip, say what you and each member of your family would have done differently, if anything.

MODELO: Mi padre llevó tres maletas.
*Mi padre habría llevado una maleta.*

1. Nosotros fuimos a Nueva York.
2. Viajamos en tren.
3. Yo me senté en la sección de no fumar.
4. Mi mamá preparó sándwiches para el viaje.
5. Mi amigo y yo bebimos refrescos en el café del tren.
6. En Nueva York, mi amigo se quedó en casa de su abuelo.
7. Nosotros nos quedamos en un hotel.
8. Mis padres fueron a ver una comedia musical.
9. Yo fui a bailar.
10. Nosotros visitamos el Museo de Arte Moderno.
11. Mi amigo visitó la Estatua de la Libertad.
12. Estuvimos en Nueva York por dos semanas.

**B.** You and your family had unannounced guests last Saturday. You were not prepared! Say what you and other members of your family would have done, had you known that they were coming.

MODELO: mi mamá
*Mi mamá habría limpiado la casa.*

1. yo
2. mi papá
3. mi hermana y yo
4. mis hermanos
5. mis padres
6. mi mamá y yo

**Summary of the Tenses of the Indicative**

| ***Simple Tenses*** | | | |
|---|---|---|---|
| | -ar | -er | -ir |
| *Presente* | hablo | como | vivo |
| *Pretérito* | hablé | comí | viví |
| *Imperfecto* | hablaba | comía | vivía |
| *Futuro* | hablaré | comeré | viviré |
| *Condicional* | hablaría | comería | viviría |
| ***Compound Tenses*** | | | |
| *Pretérito perfecto* | **he** hablado | **he** comido | **he** vivido |
| *Pretérito pluscuamperfecto* | **había** hablado | **había** comido | **había** vivido |
| *Futuro perfecto* | **habré** hablado | **habré** comido | **habré** vivido |
| *Condicional perfecto* | **habría** hablado | **habría** comido | **habría** vivido |

# ¡A ver cuánto aprendió!

INTERNET

See the *¿Cómo se dice...?* Web site for additional grammar and vocabulary practice: http://spanish.college.hmco.com/students

## ¡Repase el vocabulario!

Complete the following sentences with the missing words; then read them aloud.

1. Como Fernando sacó una "F" en física, quedó ________ en esa asignatura.
2. Estoy tomando una clase de administración de ________.
3. Voy a ________ de no gastar mucho dinero.
4. Quiere ser abogado. Estudia en la Facultad de ________.
5. Tengo que preparar un ________ para mi clase de literatura.
6. Fue elegido *(chosen)* el mejor ________ porque vendió cien casas en un año.

7. Voy a hablar con mi ________ para que me diga qué clases debo tomar.
8. ¿Quieres jugar al ________ esta tarde?
9. Tengo que ________ un promedio alto o pierdo la beca.
10. Para Juan, lo ________ importante es el fútbol.
11. Escribe para la revista *Time*. Es ________.
12. Para ser ________ tienes que estudiar en la Facultad de Ingeniería.
13. ¿Cuál es tu ________? ¿Matemáticas o contabilidad?
14. Mañana tengo un examen de ________ de curso.
15. Mi papá es un hombre de ________.
16. El ________ de ese restaurante cocina muy bien.

## Entrevista

Use the following questions to interview a classmate.

1. ¿Estarás muy ocupado(-a) mañana? ¿Qué tendrás que hacer?
2. ¿Tendrás que matricularte pronto? ¿Qué clases piensas tomar?
3. ¿Has hablado con tu consejero(-a) últimamente?
4. ¿Cuál es tu asignatura favorita? ¿Cuál es tu especialización?
5. ¿Tú preferirías ser bibliotecario(-a), contador(-a), abogado(-a) o psicólogo(-a)? ¿O preferirías tener alguna otra profesión? ¿Cuál?
6. Al terminar este semestre, ¿ya habrás tomado todos los requisitos?
7. ¿Qué promedio mantienes en tus clases? ¿Apruebas todos los cursos?
8. ¿Tú te habrás graduado para el año 2006?
9. ¿Tú podrías venir a la universidad los domingos?
10. ¿Qué harás tú el verano próximo? ¿Adónde te gustaría viajar?
11. ¿Tratarás de tomar otras clases de español?
12. De haber sabido lo que sabes ahora acerca *(about)* del español, ¿lo habrías estudiado cuando eras niño(-a)?
13. ¿Cuándo crees tú que el profesor (la profesora) nos dará el próximo examen?
14. Para las once de la noche, ¿ya te habrás acostado?
15. Mañana a las nueve, ¿ya habrás salido de tu casa?

## Situaciones

What would you say in the following situations? What might the other person say? Act out the scenes with a partner. Take turns playing each role.

1. A freshman asks you what courses to take. Find out something about his or her interests and plans, and make some appropriate course recommendations. Be sure to mention some of your school's requirements.
2. You are talking with a friend about classes you like, classes you don't like, and the reasons why.
3. You have just graduated, and one of your parents has taken you out for a celebration dinner. You haven't done everything they had hoped you would do in college, but you are pleased with your decisions. Discuss your plans for the future.

## ¿Qué pasa aquí?

In groups of three or four, make up a story about the people in the photo. Say who they are, what subjects they are taking, their majors, their grade point averages, when they will graduate, and so forth.

## Para escribir

Write a composition about your college activities. Include the following information:

- your major
- classes you are taking this semester
- classes you took last semester
- classes you like and classes you don't like
- your extracurricular activities
- your career plans

# En la vida real

CD-ROM

Do the interactive exercises on the CD-ROM for additional practice.

## El primer empleo

With a classmate, play the roles of a recent college graduate who is applying for a job and a prospective employer. The interviewer wants to know about the applicant's college courses and activities and how they are relevant to the job.

Here is a list that might help you answer the interviewer's questions:

*Lista de materias*

Administración de empresas
Alemán
Álgebra
Antropología
Arte
Astronomía
Biología
Cálculo
Ciencias económicas
Ciencias políticas
Contabilidad
Drama
Educación física
Electrónica
Español
Estadística
Física
Francés
Geología
Geometría
Historia
Humanidades
Informática *(Computer Science)*
Inglés
Literatura
Matemáticas
Música
Química
Relaciones públicas
Ruso
Sociología
Telecomunicaciones

## Necesitamos trabajo...

Some friends of yours are looking for jobs. Help them by answering their questions about the classified ads below.

1. ¿Qué empresa necesita secretario(-a)?
2. Si deseo trabajar de secretario(-a) en la compañía Optim, ¿qué idioma necesito hablar?
3. ¿En qué ciudad está el laboratorio farmacéutico?
4. ¿Qué experiencia mínima debo tener si solicito el puesto de director de servicio extranjero?
5. ¿Para solicitar qué empleos necesito mandar una foto?
6. ¿Qué edad debo tener para trabajar en la empresa financiera?
7. ¿Qué debo enviar a la empresa financiera antes del día 20 de noviembre?

IMPORTANTE
LABORATORIO
FARMACEUTICO
NACIONAL
BUSCA
**TECNICO**
Capacitado para crear y dirigir una linea de productos OTC

- Se requiere persona con experiencia en este campo.
- Condiciones a convenir.

*Interesados escribir adjuntando curriculum a GISPERT PUBLICIDAD, c. Balmes, 1008007-Barcelona, indicando en el sobre la Ref.ª 21 210*

**EMPRESA FINANCIERA**
**PRECISA**
**DIRECTOR DE SERVICIO EXTRANJERO**

**SE REQUIERE:**
- Capacidad de organización y gestión.
- Edad: entre 35 y 45 años.
- Perfecto dominio del idioma inglés y conocimientos de otros idiomas.
- Experiencia mínima de 3 años en el servicio de extranjero.
- Titulado en Ciencias Económicas o Empresariales.

**SE OFRECE:**
- Incorporación inmediata.
- Remuneración a convenir, de acuerdo con la experiencia y conocimientos aportados por el candidato.
- Proceso de selección con garantía de absoluta reserva en los datos aportados.

**Los candidatos enviarán "curriculum vitae" antes del día 20 de noviembre, acompañado de fotografía, dirección y teléfono al Apartado 1.540 de Vigo.**

*(Oferta INEM nº 2.971 OR.)*

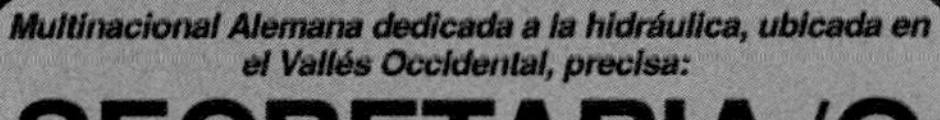

Multinacional Alemana dedicada a la hidráulica, ubicada en el Vallés Occidental, precisa:


**SECRETARIA/O**
DPTO. COMPRAS

SE REQUIERE:
- Dominio del idioma alemán a nivel conversación.
- Experiencia Administrativa en área de Compras.
- Facilidad de trato con proveedores.
- Edad 22-37 años.

Condiciones económicas según aptitudes.
Interesadas escribir historial a:

OPTIM

*OPTIM*
*C. Estació, n.º 9, 1.º, 1.ª*
*08814 PALAU DE PLEGAMANS*
*Indicar ref. 2.475.*

# 8. América del sur (II)

Argentina

Chile

Paraguay

Uruguay

- Buenos Aires, la capital de Argentina, tiene una población de alrededor de doce millones de habitantes, y su área metropolitana es una de las más extensas del mundo. Su sistema de metro, "el subterráneo", es el más antiguo de Latinoamérica.
- Uruguay es el país de habla hispana más pequeño de la América del Sur. El 45% de la población del país está concentrado en Montevideo, la capital. Muy cerca de esta ciudad está la playa de Punta del Este, de fama internacional.
- La represa *(dam)* de Itaipú, entre Brasil y Paraguay, es la represa hidroeléctrica más grande del mundo y fue construida por los gobiernos de Brasil y Paraguay.
- Paraguay es conocido por sus joyas de oro y de plata, sus objetos de madera tallada *(carved wood)* y sus encajes *(laces)* de "ñandutí". Estos encajes son hechos a mano, y para hacerlos, se utilizan más de cien diseños diferentes.
- La isla de Pascua, situada en el océano Pacífico, pertenece a Chile y es famosa por las gigantescas estatuas de piedra que se encuentran allí.

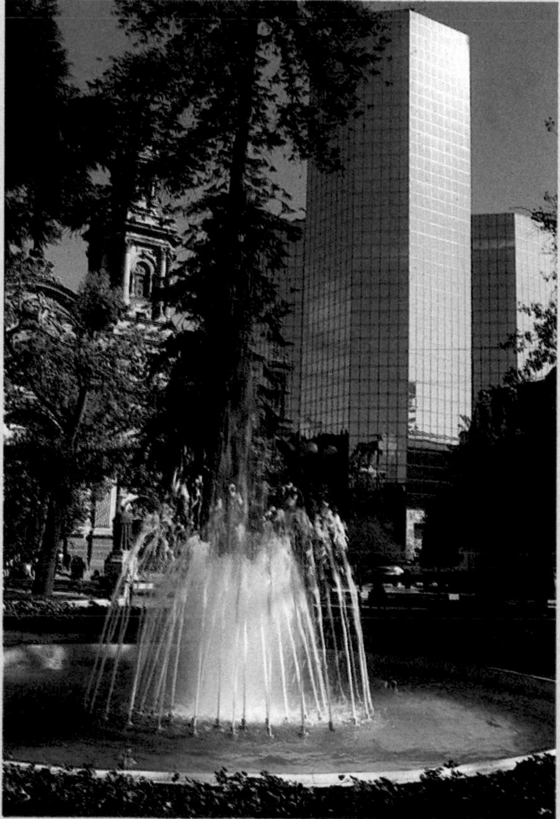

El centro de Santiago, capital de Chile, se distingue por el contraste de modernos rascacielos y edificios coloniales como la Casa Colorada, residencia del primer presidente de la República; el Palacio de la Moneda, palacio presidencial actual, y la catedral, construida en 1780.

*¿Cómo se llama, en español, la residencia del presidente de los Estados Unidos?*

Una pareja baila el tango, el baile típico de Argentina. El tango se hizo *(became)* popular en Latinoamérica a principios del siglo XX y fue introducido en los Estados Unidos alrededor de 1912.

*¿Conoce Ud. algunos otros bailes típicos latinoamericanos? ¿Cuáles?*

El gaucho argentino, inmortalizado en la literatura y en la música popular argentinas, es hoy día más una leyenda que un personaje real. Una de las costumbres de los gauchos que persiste es la del rodeo, como se ve en la foto.

*¿En qué son similares los vaqueros norteamericanos y los gauchos argentinos?*

Vista panorámica del puerto de Asunción, la capital de Paraguay. En esta ciudad se mezclan armoniosamente la arquitectura colonial y la moderna. Aquí se ve la Plaza de los Héroes y, al fondo, el río Paraguay, que sirve como vía de comunicación con el océano Atlántico.

*¿Cuáles son algunos de los puertos principales de su país?*

Vista del Obelisco y de la avenida Nueve de Julio, en Buenos Aires. La avenida Nueve de Julio es una de las más anchas del mundo y lleva este nombre para conmemorar la fecha de la independencia de Argentina.

*¿Le gusta a Ud. la idea de vivir en una gran ciudad como Buenos Aires? ¿Por qué o por qué no?*

Las cataratas *(falls)* de Iguazú, formadas por los ríos Iguazú y Paraná, están situadas en el punto de unión entre Argentina, Brasil y Paraguay. Se consideran las cataratas más anchas y caudalosas *(abundant)* del mundo, y de ahí su nombre, que en el idioma guaraní significa "agua grande".

*¿Son exclusivamente de los Estados Unidos las cataratas del Niágara?*

Punta del Este, en Uruguay, es uno de los centros turísticos más importantes de la América del Sur. Es, además, sede *(site)* de competencias de veleros *(sailboats)*, de carreras *(races)* de automóviles y de torneos *(tournaments)* de tenis, de golf y de polo.

*¿Vive Ud. cerca de algún centro turístico importante?*

# TELEINFORME

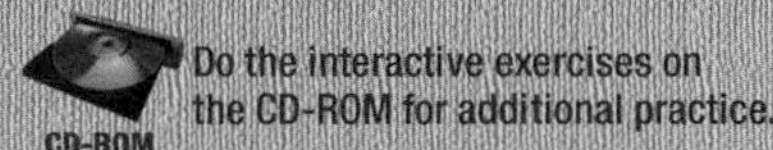


Do the interactive exercises on the CD-ROM for additional practice.

## Preparación

**¿Cuánto saben Uds. ya?** After reading **Panorama hispánico 8**, get together in groups of three or four students and answer the following questions.

1. ¿Cuál es la capital de Argentina? ¿Y de Chile?
2. ¿Cuál es la población de Buenos Aires?
3. ¿Qué monumento importante está en la avenida Nueve de Julio?
4. ¿Dónde está situada la represa *(dam)* de Itaipú?
5. ¿Qué ríos forman las cataratas *(waterfalls)* de Iguazú?
6. ¿Qué significa la palabra guaraní *Iguazú*?

## Comprensión

**A. Buenos Aires, Argentina.** Complete the following statements according to what you understood.

1. Buenos Aires ha sido llamada "el ________ de Suramérica."
2. Los inmigrantes de Buenos Aires son ingleses, ________, griegos, ________, españoles y, sobre todo, ________.
3. La Avenida Nueve de Julio es una de las avenidas más ________ del mundo.
4. Muchos ________ se establecieron en el barrio de La Boca.
5. El género musical más conocido *(famous)* de Argentina es ________.

**B. Paraguay.** Read the following statements. After watching the video, circle **V (Verdadero)** or **F (Falso)**, according to what you understood. If a statement is false, correct it.

V F 1. La película *La misión* fue filmada en Paraguay.
V F 2. La capital de Paraguay es Montevideo.
V F 3. Paraguay significa "aguas que corren hacia el mar".
V F 4. El río Paraguay divide el país en cuatro regiones.
V F 5. Paraguay tiene varias salidas al mar.
V F 6. Itaipú es la planta hidroeléctrica más grande del mundo.
V F 7. Las cataratas *(waterfalls)* de Iguazú están cerca de la frontera *(border)* de Paraguay con Brasil.

**C. La Patagonia.** Select the word or phrase that best completes each statement, according to what you understood.

1. La Patagonia es (un país, una región).
2. La Patagonia está en el extremo (sur, norte) de Suramérica.
3. El punto más alto de los Andes mide *(measures)* (6.600, 660) metros de altura.
4. Chile y (Brasil, Argentina) son países del Cono Sur.
5. Ushuaia, cerca de la Antártida, es la (región, ciudad) más meridional *(southernmost)* del mundo.

## Ampliación

A. **Otros países, otras culturas.** With a partner, discuss in Spanish what aspect of each place (Buenos Aires, Paraguay, or La Patagonia) appealed to you and why. Share your observations with the rest of the class.

B. **Dos culturas.** With a partner, make a list of counterparts you can find in your local area, city, state, or country for each of the following items.

1. Buenos Aires
2. el barrio de La Boca
3. la represa Itaipú
4. las cataratas de Iguazú
5. los Andes
6. La Patagonia

Lección 17

# Problemas médicos

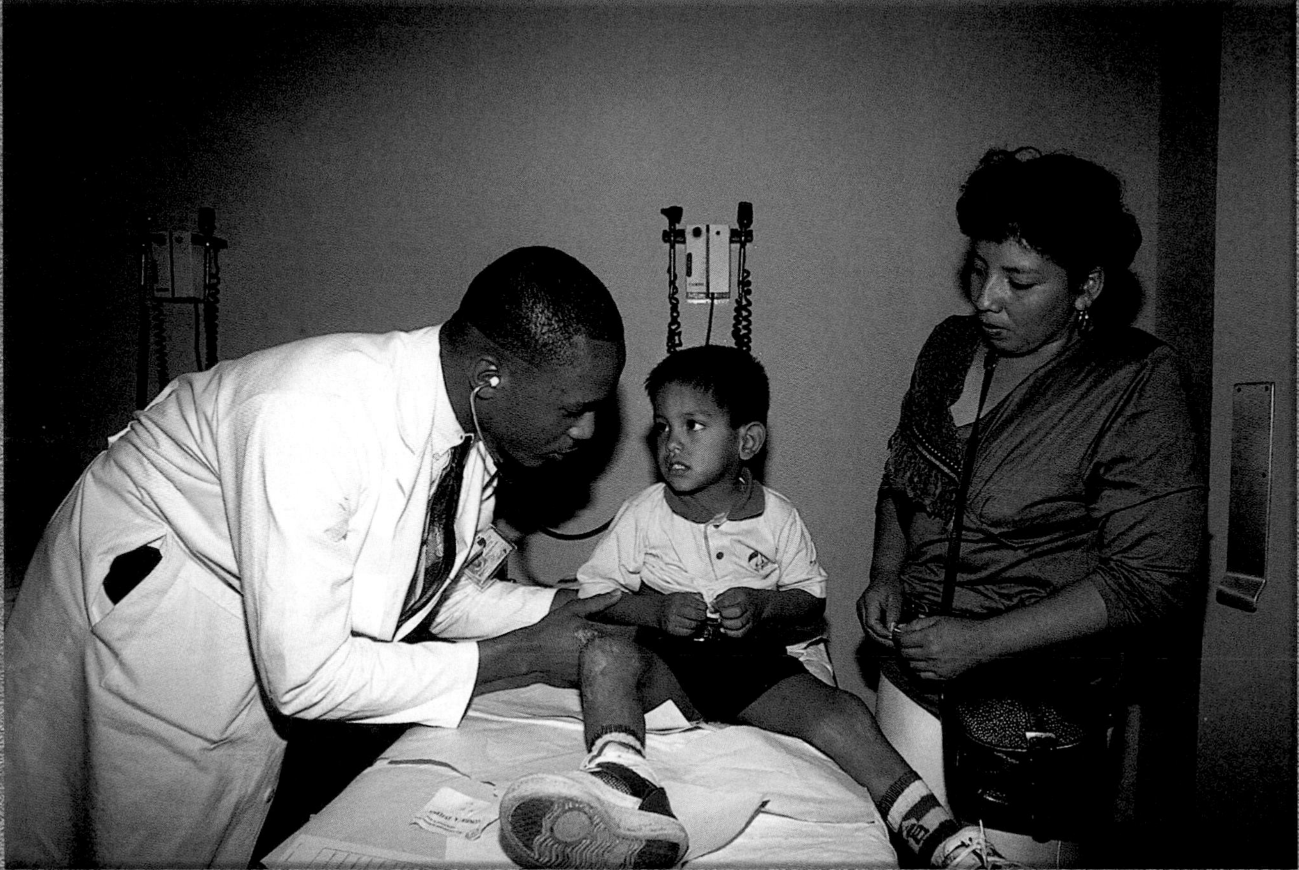

## OBJECTIVES

### Pronunciation

Pronunciation in context

### Structure

The imperfect subjunctive • Uses of some prepositions after certain verbs • The present perfect subjunctive

### Communication

You will learn vocabulary related to medical emergencies and visits to the doctor's office.

# Problemas médicos

*Mirta y su esposo se encuentran en un restaurante para almorzar. Ella no se siente muy bien hoy.*

MIRTA —No sé qué me pasa. Tengo fiebre y me duele mucho la cabeza.[1] Ya tomé cuatro aspirinas.
HÉCTOR —Te dije que fueras al médico para que te hiciera un buen chequeo. Espero que ya hayas llamado al doctor Valdivia.
MIRTA —Él está de vacaciones. Teresa me sugirió que viera a la doctora Vargas. Tengo una cita para esta tarde.

*Más tarde, en el consultorio de la doctora Vargas.*

DOCTORA —Tiene una temperatura de ciento dos grados. ¿Cuánto tiempo hace que tiene esos dolores de cabeza?
MIRTA —Una semana. Tengo tos y me duele la garganta. ¿Cree que tengo catarro o gripe?
DOCTORA —Tiene gripe. Voy a recetarle un antibiótico. ¿Es Ud. alérgica a alguna medicina?
MIRTA —Sí. Soy alérgica a la penicilina.
DOCTORA —¿Está Ud. embarazada?
MIRTA —No, doctora.
DOCTORA —Tome estas pastillas cuatro veces al día. Empiece a tomarlas hoy mismo. Aquí tiene la receta.

*En la sala de emergencia del mismo hospital. Oscar tuvo un accidente y lo trajeron al hospital en una ambulancia. Ahora está hablando con un médico.*

MÉDICO —¿Qué le pasó?
OSCAR —Me atropelló un coche. Me duele mucho la pierna. Creo que me la rompí.
MÉDICO —Sí, temo que se la haya roto. Vamos a hacerle unas radiografías. Veo que también tiene una herida en el brazo. Voy a llamar a la enfermera.

*Con la enfermera*

ENFERMERA —El doctor me dijo que le desinfectara y le vendara la herida para evitar una infección. ¿Cuándo fue la última vez que le pusieron una inyección antitetánica?
OSCAR —Hace dos años.

*La enfermera lleva a Oscar a la sala de rayos X. Oscar tiene la pierna rota y el médico se la enyesa.*

MÉDICO —¿Hay alguien que pueda venir a buscarlo?
OSCAR —Sí, voy a llamar a mi compañero de cuarto, pero no creo que haya llegado a casa todavía.

---

[1]Note that definite articles, rather than possessive adjectives, are used in Spanish with parts of the body.

# Vocabulario

## Cognados

**el accidente** accident
**alérgico(-a)** allergic
**la ambulancia** ambulance
**el antibiótico** antibiotic
**la aspirina** aspirin
**la emergencia** emergency
**la infección** infection
**la inyección** injection, shot
**la medicina** medicine
**la penicilina** penicillin
**la temperatura** temperature

## Nombres

**el brazo** arm
**la cabeza** head
**el catarro, resfriado, resfrío** cold
**el chequeo, examen** checkup
**el (la) compañero(-a) de cuarto** roommate
**el consultorio** doctor's office
**el dolor** pain
**— de cabeza** headache
**la fiebre** fever
**la garganta** throat
**el grado** degree
**la gripe** flu
**la herida** wound
**la inyección antitetánica** tetanus shot
**la pastilla** pill
**la pierna** leg
**la radiografía** X-ray
**la receta** prescription
**la sala de emergencia** emergency room
**la sala de rayos X** X-ray room
**la tos** cough

## Verbos

**atropellar** to run over, hit someone (i.e., with a car)
**buscar** to pick up, to get
**desinfectar** to disinfect
**doler**[1] **(o:ue)** to hurt, to ache
**enyesar** to put in a cast
**evitar** to avoid
**recetar** to prescribe
**romper(se), quebrar(se) (e:ie)** to break
**vendar** to bandage

## Adjetivos

**embarazada** pregnant
**médico(-a)** medical

## Otras palabras y expresiones

**al día** a day
**hacer una radiografía** to take an X-ray
**poner una inyección** to give an injection, a shot
**todavía** yet
**la última vez** the last time

[1]**Doler** has the same structure as **gustar: Me duele la cabeza.**

## Vocabulario adicional

### El cuerpo

1. el pelo, el cabello
2. el ojo
3. la nariz
4. los dientes
5. la lengua
6. la boca
7. la oreja
8. el oído

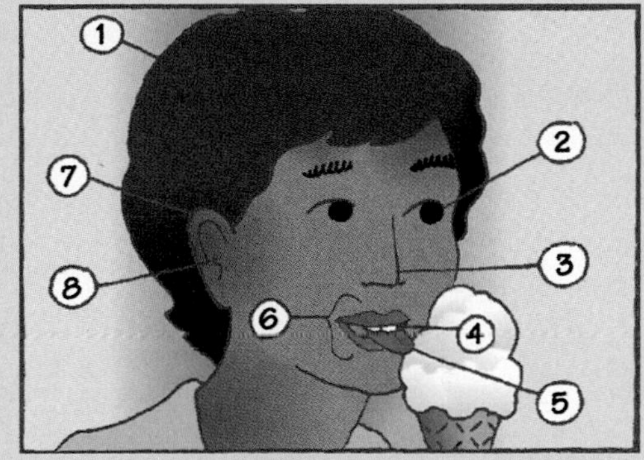

9. la cabeza
10. la cara
11. el pecho
12. el estómago
13. la mano
14. la rodilla
15. el tobillo
16. el dedo del pie
17. el pie

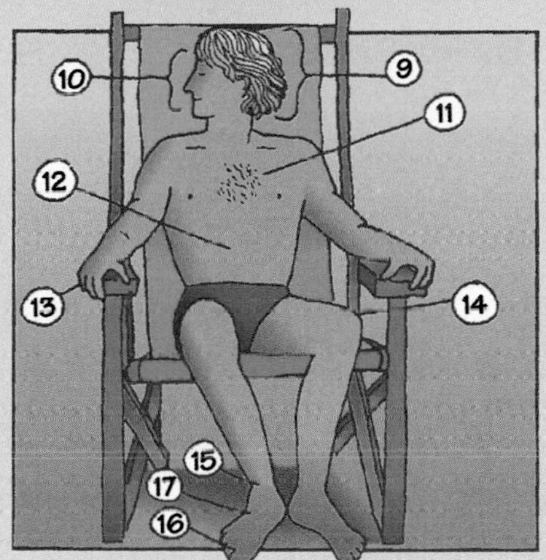

18. el cuello
19. la espalda
20. el dedo

## ¡Conversemos!

Answer the following questions, basing your answers on the dialogues.

1. ¿Dónde se encuentran Mirta y su esposo, y por qué están allí?
2. ¿Qué problemas tiene Mirta?
3. ¿Qué espera Héctor que haya hecho Mirta?
4. ¿Qué le sugirió Teresa a Mirta?
5. ¿Por qué no le receta la doctora penicilina a Mirta?
6. ¿Cuántas veces al día tiene que tomar Mirta las pastillas?
7. ¿Qué le pasó a Oscar y dónde está ahora?
8. ¿Qué clase *(kind)* de accidente tuvo Oscar?
9. ¿Qué le dijo el médico a la enfermera?
10. ¿Cree Ud. que la enfermera le va a poner una inyección antitetánica a Oscar? ¿Por qué o por qué no?
11. ¿Adónde lleva la enfermera a Oscar y para qué?
12. ¿Qué le hace el médico a Oscar? ¿Por qué?

## ¿Lo sabía Ud.?

■ En la mayoría de los países de habla hispana, los hospitales son gratis *(free)* y subvencionados *(subsidized)* por el gobierno. Hay clínicas privadas para la gente de mejor posición económica que no quiere ir a un hospital público.

■ Especialmente en las grandes ciudades hispanas, la medicina está muy adelantada *(advanced)*, pero en muchos pueblos *(towns)* remotos no hay médicos ni hospitales. En ese caso, mucha gente recurre a *(turn to)* los servicios de un curandero *(healer)*. Muchas mujeres tienen sus bebés con la ayuda de una partera *(midwife)*.

■ En España y en algunos países latinoamericanos, las farmacias venden principalmente medicinas. En algunos países hispanos es posible comprar ciertas medicinas —como la penicilina —sin tener receta médica.

- En este país, ¿los hospitales son gratis?
- La mayoría de las mujeres de este país, ¿tienen su bebé en un hospital o en su casa, con la ayuda de una partera?
- ¿En este país se pueden comprar antibióticos sin receta médica?

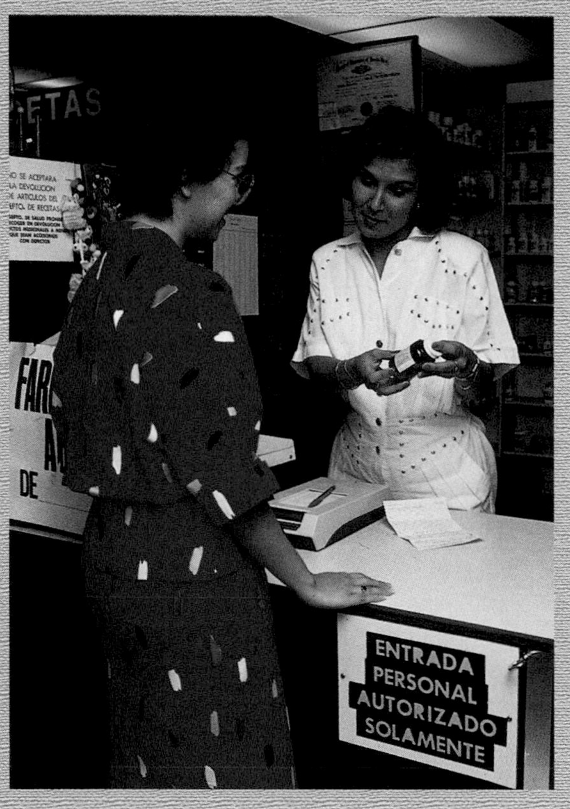


Comprando medicinas en una farmacia de Humacao, Puerto Rico.

See the *¿Cómo se dice...?* Web site for activities on authentic cultural material: http://spanish.college.hmco.com/students

## Pronunciación

In this lesson, there are some new words or phrases that may be challenging to pronounce. For further pronunciation practice of Spanish sounds, listen to your instructor and repeat the following words and phrases.

1. ¿Es Ud. **alérgica** a alguna medicina?
2. Tuvo un accidente y lo trajeron al hospital en una **ambulancia.**
3. Veo que también tiene una **herida** en el brazo.
4. Me dijo que le **desinfectara** y le **vendara** la herida.
5. ¿Cuándo fue la última vez que le pusieron una **inyección antitetánica**?

## 1 The imperfect subjunctive *(El imperfecto de subjuntivo)*

### A. Forms

- To form the imperfect subjunctive of all Spanish verbs—regular and irregular—drop the **-ron** ending of the third-person plural of the preterit and add the following endings to the stem.[1]

**Imperfect Subjunctive Endings**

| -ra *form* | |
|---|---|
| -ra | ´-ramos |
| -ras | -rais |
| -ra | -ran |

**Forms of the Imperfect Subjunctive**

| *Verb* | *Third-person plural preterit* | *Stem* | *First-person singular imperfect subjunctive* |
|---|---|---|---|
| hablar | habla**ron** | habla- | **hablara** |
| aprender | aprendie**ron** | aprendie- | **aprendiera** |
| vivir | vivie**ron** | vivie- | **viviera** |
| dejar | deja**ron** | deja- | **dejara** |
| ir | fue**ron** | fue- | **fuera** |
| saber | supie**ron** | supie- | **supiera** |
| decir | dije**ron** | dije- | **dijera** |
| poner | pusie**ron** | pusie- | **pusiera** |
| pedir | pidie**ron** | pidie- | **pidiera** |
| estar | estuvie**ron** | estuvie- | **estuviera** |

**ATENCIÓN** The **nosotros** form of the imperfect subjunctive always takes an accent on the vowel that precedes the **-ra** ending.

[1]A second form of the imperfect subjunctive ends in **-se** rather than **-ra: hablase, hablases, hablase, hablásemos, hablaseis, hablasen.** The two forms are interchangeable, but the **-ra** form is more commonly used.

## práctica

Give the imperfect subjunctive forms of the following verbs.

1. yo: ganar, volver, pedir, decir, recibir
2. tú: ser, dormir, querer, dar, conocer
3. él: ir, estar, poner, conducir, servir
4. nosotros: saber, poder, regresar, conseguir, hacer
5. ellos: tener, recetar, comenzar, seguir, mentir

### B. Uses

■ The imperfect subjunctive is used in a subordinate clause when the verb of the main clause is in the past and calls for the subjunctive.

| | |
|---|---|
| —¿Qué te dijo el médico? | *"What did the doctor tell you?"* |
| —Me dijo que **comiera** menos. | *"He told me to eat less."* |
| —Yo esperaba que el profesor me **diera** una "A". | *"I was hoping that the professor would give me an A."* |
| —Bueno, yo te sugerí que **estudiaras** más. | *"Well, I suggested that you study more."* |

■ When the verb of the main clause is in the present, but the subordinate clause refers to the past, the imperfect subjunctive is used.

| | |
|---|---|
| —Es una lástima que no **fueras** al teatro ayer. | *"It's a pity that you didn't go to the theater yesterday."* |
| —No me sentía bien. | *"I wasn't feeling well."* |

## práctica

**A.** Complete the following dialogues, using the imperfect subjunctive of the verbs given. Then act them out with a partner.

1. —¿Qué te dijo Roberto?
   —Me dijo que ________ (ir) al médico para que me ________ (hacer) un chequeo y me recomendó que ________ (ver) al Dr. Salgado.
2. —No fui al hospital porque no tenía coche.
   —¿Por qué no le pediste a alguien que te ________ (llevar)?
   —No había nadie que ________ (poder) llevarme a esa hora.
   —Pues yo te dije que me ________ (llamar) si me necesitabas.
3. —¿Fuiste al médico?
   —Sí, y me dijo que ________ (tomar) estas pastillas para el dolor de garganta y me sugirió que no ________ (hablar) mucho.
4. —¿Le dieron el trabajo a Sandra?
   —No, porque necesitaban una enfermera que ________ (saber) español.
   —Yo le dije que ________ (estudiar) español, pero no me hizo caso.

5. —Siento que tú no ________ (poder) venir a mi casa ayer.
—No me sentía bien... Yo le pedí a Ramón que te ________ (llamar) por teléfono y te ________ (decir) que yo estaba enferma.
—Pues yo esperaba que tú ________ (venir) con los niños.

**B.** Describe all the things your parents did and did not want you to do at college, using the cues provided and the imperfect subjunctive.

Mis padres querían que yo...

1. *escribirles* todas las semanas
2. *llamarlos* por teléfono los domingos
3. *tomar* varias clases el primer semestre
4. *estudiar* mucho
5. *abrir* una cuenta corriente en el banco
6. *hacer* la tarea todos los días
7. *levantarme* temprano
8. *visitarlos* en las vacaciones

Mis padres no querían que yo...

1. *vivir* lejos de la universidad
2. *ir* a muchas fiestas
3. *comer* hamburguesas todos los días
4. *gastar* mucho
5. *pedirles* dinero extra todos los meses
6. *conducir* muy rápido
7. *olvidarme* de tomar la medicina
8. *acostarme* muy tarde

**C.** Compare your childhood and adolescence to those of a classmate by completing the following sentences.

1. Cuando yo era chico(-a), mis padres esperaban que yo...
2. Cuando yo era niño(-a), mi mamá no me permitía que...
3. Cuando yo estaba en la escuela primaria, mis maestros *(teachers)* querían que yo...
4. Cuando yo tenía diez años, quería que mis amigos...
5. Cuando yo estaba en la escuela secundaria, no quería que mi papá...
6. Cuando yo tenía dieciséis años, esperaba que mis padres...

## 2 Uses of some prepositions after certain verbs *(Usos de algunas preposiciones con ciertos verbos)*

In Spanish, some verbs are used with prepositions that have no equivalent to or are different from the ones used in English. The prepositions used most often are **a, de, con,** and **en.**

■ The preposition **a**

**aprender a** *to learn (how)*
**asistir a** *to attend*
**ayudar a** *to help*
**empezar** (**comenzar**) **a** *to begin, to start*
**enseñar a** *to teach*
**invitar a** *to invite*
**ir a** *to go*
**venir a** *to come*

| | |
|---|---|
| —¿**Fuiste a** estudiar con Rafael? | *"Did you go to study with Rafael?"* |
| —Sí, **empezamos a** estudiar para el examen final. | *"Yes, we started to study for the final exam."* |
| —Yo quiero **aprender a** bailar bailes latinoamericanos. | *"I want to learn how to dance Latin American dances."* |
| —Yo te puedo **enseñar a** bailar. | *"I can teach you how to dance."* |

■ The preposition **de**

**acordarse de** *to remember*
**alegrarse de** *to be glad*
**enamorarse de** *to fall in love with*
**olvidarse de** *to forget*

| | |
|---|---|
| —No te **olvides de** llamar al médico. | *"Don't forget to call the doctor."* |
| —Bueno..., y tú, **acuérdate de** tomar las pastillas. | *"Okay . . . , and you, remember to take your pills."* |

■ The preposition **con**

**casarse con** *to marry, to get married to*
**comprometerse con** *to get engaged to*
**soñar** (**o:ue**) **con** *to dream about (of)*

| | |
|---|---|
| —Teresa **se comprometió con** Antonio. | *"Teresa got engaged to Antonio."* |
| —Debe estar muy contenta. Siempre **soñó con casarse con** él. | *"She must be very happy. She always dreamed of marrying him."* |

■ The preposition **en**

**fijarse en** *to notice*
**insistir en** *to insist on*
**pensar en** *to think about*

| | |
|---|---|
| —¿**En** que estás **pensando**? | *"What are you thinking about?"* |
| —Estoy **pensando en** la fiesta de Beatriz. Ella **insistió en** invitar a Pablo y él siempre causa problemas... | *"I am thinking about Beatriz's party. She insisted on inviting Pablo and he always causes problems . . ."* |

## práctica

**A.** Complete the following dialogues with the Spanish equivalent of the words in parentheses. Then act them out with a partner.

1. —¿________ pedir la receta, Anita? *(Did you remember)*
—Sí, pero ________ dejarla en la farmacia. *(I forgot)*

2. —¿Ángel te dijo que le dolía el estómago?
   —Sí, él ________ que lo llevara a la sala de emergencia. *(he insisted on)*
3. —¿Dónde ________ poner inyecciones tu mamá? *(did learn)*
   —En Cuba. Y también le ________ hacer radiografías. *(they taught)*
4. —Luis ________ Raquel, pero ella nunca ________ él. *(fell in love with / noticed)*
   —No, ella ________ Ernesto. *(married)*
5. —¡Hola, Luisa! ________ verte. *(I'm glad)*
   —¡Hola! Vengo a ________ ir al cine. *(to invite you)*
   —Ay, no puedo porque tengo que ________ la conferencia *(lecture)* de la Dra. Ruiz. *(to attend)*

**B.** With a partner, take turns asking and answering questions about the people in the following situations.

1. 

2. 

3. 

4. 

5. 

6. 

**C.** With a partner discuss the following:

1. things you would like to learn to do or can teach others to do
2. what time you start to work and to study
3. what you always (never) remember to do and what you always (never) forget to do
4. what you dream about doing
5. what you insist on doing

## 3 The present perfect subjunctive *(El pretérito perfecto de subjuntivo)*

■ The present perfect subjunctive is formed with the present subjunctive of the auxiliary verb **haber** + *the past participle* of the main verb.

| ***Present subjunctive of* haber** | |
|---|---|
| haya | hayamos |
| hayas | hayáis |
| haya | hayan |

| Formation of the Present Perfect Subjunctive | |
|---|---|
| yo | **haya cambiado** |
| tú | **hayas temido** |
| Ud. / él / ella | **haya salido** |
| nosotros(-as) | **hayamos hecho** |
| vosotros(-as) | **hayáis puesto** |
| Uds. / ellos / ellas | **hayan visto** |

■ The present perfect subjunctive is used in the same way as the present perfect tense in English, but only in sentences that require the subjunctive in the subordinate clause. It is used to describe events that have ended prior to the time indicated in the main clause.

—Me alegro de que **hayas venido.** — *"I'm glad you have come."*
—Es una lástima que papá no **haya podido** venir conmigo. — *"It is a pity that Dad has not been able to come with me."*

—¿Hay alguien aquí que **haya estado** en Guadalajara? — *"Is there anyone here who has been in Guadalajara?"*
—No, no hay nadie que **haya viajado** a México. — *"No, there's no one who has travelled to Mexico."*

### práctica

**A.** Complete the following dialogues, using the present perfect subjunctive forms of the verbs listed. Then act them out with a partner.

morir    tener    tomar    poner    decir    llevar    ir

1. —Rafael se cortó la rodilla. Espero que el médico le ________ una inyección antitetánica.
   —Yo dudo que él ________ al médico.
2. —¿Ana ha traído las pastillas?
   —No creo que ella ________ tiempo de ir a la farmacia.

3. —Ha habido un accidente en la calle Lima.
   —Ojalá que no ________ nadie.
4. —¿Tú dices que Marta está embarazada?
   —No es verdad que yo ________ eso.
5. —Yo creo que Alberto se ha roto una pierna.
   —Espero que sus hermanos lo ________ a la sala de emergencia.
6. —Mamá no cree que nosotros ________ la medicina.
   —Es que Uds. nunca hacen lo que ella les dice.

**B.** Express your own feelings and those of the people mentioned, using the present perfect subjunctive.

1. Yo espero que el médico...
2. Ojalá que mis padres...
3. Es una lástima que la enfermera...
4. Mis padres no creen que yo...
5. No es verdad que mis amigos...
6. Me alegro mucho de que Ud....
7. Yo siento que mi compañero de cuarto...
8. Mi profesor siente que los estudiantes...

**C.** With a partner, prepare two questions to ask your classmates about their life experiences and what they have done. Use the present perfect subjunctive and always begin with **"¿Hay alguien aquí que...?"**

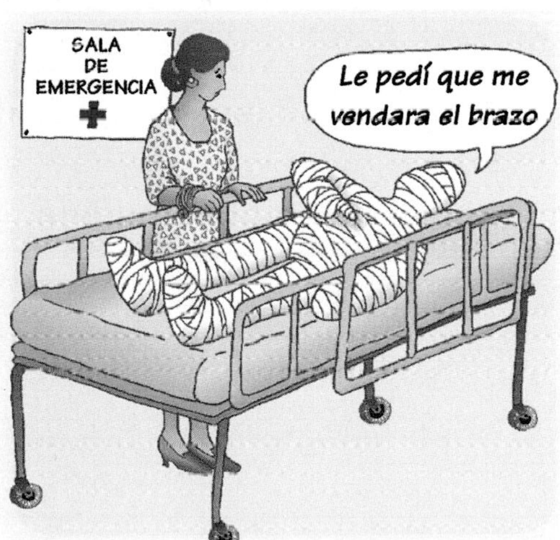

# ¡A ver cuánto aprendió!

**INTERNET**

See the *¿Cómo se dice...?* Web site for additional grammar and vocabulary practice: http://spanish.college.hmco.com/students

## ¡Repase el vocabulario!

**A.** Say whether the following statements are logical or not. If a statement is not logical, give one that is.

1. En serio, los muchachos vinieron a esquiar en una ambulancia.
2. Cuando tengo dolor de estómago voy al médico.
3. Si necesito una radiografía voy al aeropuerto.

4. Me vendaron la herida.
5. Tiene fiebre. Tiene una temperatura de ciento tres grados.
6. Algunas personas son alérgicas a la penicilina.
7. Las orejas sirven para planchar.
8. La aspirina es un antibiótico.
9. La lengua está en la boca.
10. La rodilla es parte de la cara.
11. Tenemos treinta dedos.
12. Necesitamos la nariz para caminar.
13. Para hacerle una radiografía, debemos ir a la sala de rayos X.
14. Roberto está embarazado.
15. Está enferma. Debe ir al consultorio del médico.
16. Cada vez que tengo dolor de cabeza tomo dos aspirinas.
17. Lo atropelló una bolsa de dormir en el mar.
18. Fuimos de pesca a la sala de emergencia y nos divertimos mucho.

**B.** Name all the parts of the body numbered below.

## Entrevista

With a partner, interview each other by asking the following questions.

1. ¿Cómo te sientes hoy?
2. ¿Te duelen los oídos? (¿la garganta?)
3. ¿Qué haces cuando te duele la cabeza?

4. Si te duele el estómago, ¿qué tomas?
5. ¿Cuándo fue la última vez que te hicieron un chequeo?
6. ¿Eres alérgico a alguna medicina? (¿A cuál?)
7. ¿Te hicieron radiografías del pecho alguna vez?
8. ¿Te han puesto una inyección antitetánica alguna vez? (¿Cuándo?)
9. ¿Qué medicina tomas cuando tienes tos?
10. ¿Has tenido un accidente alguna vez? (¿Cuándo?)
11. ¿Te has roto una pierna (un brazo) alguna vez?
12. ¿Vas al médico frecuentemente?

## Situaciones

What would you say in the following situations? What might the other person say? Act out the scenes with a partner. Take turns playing each role.

1. A friend wants you to go to the store with him or her. You can't go, for the following reasons: you've just taken two aspirins because you have a headache, your little brother cut his hand and you have to disinfect the wound.
2. You have had an accident and are in the emergency room, talking to the doctor. You need something for the pain.
3. You are at the doctor's office because you started having headaches three days ago. The doctor wants to know whether you are allergic to any medications.

## Para escribir

Write a note to your instructor, explaining that you cannot take an exam because you are sick. Describe your symptoms.

# En la vida real

## Llenando una hoja clínica

CD-ROM

Do the interactive exercises on the CD-ROM for additional practice.

With a partner, play the role of a health care worker who is taking the history of a new patient. Refer to the list of words and phrases on pages 416–417. Be as thorough as possible in obtaining both personal information (such as date of birth, family history, childhood experiences, education, and marital status) and medical data (including illnesses, accidents, and surgeries, and how long ago the patient had them; allergies; and any general pains the patient is currently suffering) for the patient's permanent file. Write down his or her responses. When you have finished, switch roles with your partner.

Here are some words and phrases you might want to use:

**la amigdalitis** *tonsilitis*
**la apendicitis** *appendicitis*
**el asma** *asthma*
**la bronquitis** *bronchitis*
**las enfermedades de la niñez** *childhood diseases*
**el mareo** *dizziness, dizzy spell*
**nacer** *to be born*
**la operación** *surgery*
**las paperas** *mumps*
**la presión arterial** *blood pressure*
**la pulmonía** *pneumonia*
**el sarampión** *measles*
**la varicela** *chicken pox*

## Buenos consejos

What advice from this list would you give to the people below?

**Buenos consejos para conservar la salud**[1]

| Debe | No debe |
|---|---|
| ✔ comer más vegetales y frutas | ✘ fumar |
| ✔ dormir lo suficiente | ✘ consumir mucho alcohol |
| ✔ visitar al médico periódicamente | ✘ consumir mucha sal o azúcar |
| ✔ hacer ejercicio | ✘ usar drogas |
| ✔ consumir menos calorías | ✘ comer mucha grasa |
| ✔ aprender a relajarse | ✘ trabajar en exceso |
| ✔ evitar la tensión (*stress*) | |
| ✔ pensar positivamente | |
| ✔ tener una dieta balanceada | |
| ✔ controlar su peso (*weight*) | |

1. El Sr. Vega toma diez cervezas todos los días.
2. La Srta. Díaz está siempre sentada, mirando la televisión.
3. Elsa come muchos dulces *(sweets)*.
4. El Dr. Álvarez trabaja catorce horas cada día.
5. La Sra. Carreras duerme sólo cuatro horas cada noche.
6. Estela se preocupa constantemente por todo.
7. Adela siempre come papas fritas, hamburguesas, mantequilla, pollo frito, etc.
8. Hace cinco años que Carlos no va a ver a su médico.
9. La dieta de Eduardo es de 5.000 calorías al día.
10. Raúl pesa *(weighs)* 300 libras *(pounds)*.
11. Raquel solamente come carne y pastas.
12. A Jorge le gustan mucho los cigarrillos.

---

[1]*health*

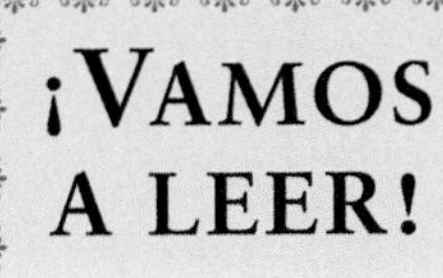

# ¡VAMOS A LEER!

## Antes de leer

A. Reading a poem is different from reading a story or an essay. The poet often uses words in original ways to express his or her feelings. Visualizing the words or images in a poem will help you better understand the feelings or message the poet is conveying. Think about the following words from the poems you are going to read. What feelings do they convey?

| | |
|---|---|
| **arte** *art* | **carbón** *coal* |
| **monte** *mountains* | **pena** *sorrow* |
| **joya** *jewel* | **esclavo** *slave* |
| **diamante** *diamond* | **oscuro** *dark* |
| **luz** *light* | **sol** *sun* |

B. As you read the introduction to Martí, and the poems, answer the following questions.

1. ¿En que año nació *(was born)* el poeta?
2. ¿Dónde y en qué año murió?
3. ¿Cuáles son los temas principales de la poesía de Martí?
4. ¿De dónde viene el poeta y adónde va?
5. ¿Cómo se describe el poeta?
6. ¿Qué es más importante para el poeta: la amistad *(friendship)* o el amor?
7. ¿Con qué compara Martí a un amigo sincero?
8. ¿Qué dice el poeta del diamante?
9. Teniendo en cuenta la biografía de Martí, ¿por qué cree Ud. que él dice que es hijo de un pueblo esclavo?
10. ¿Cómo dice Martí que quiere salir del mundo?
11. Según el poeta, ¿cómo mueren los traidores?
12. ¿Cómo dice Martí que morirá él y por qué?

JOSÉ MARTÍ
(CUBA: 1853–1895)

José Martí dedicó su vida y su obra a la independencia de Cuba, donde murió en el campo de batalla° en 1895. Es famoso no sólo como poeta y ensayista, sino también como orador.

**campo...** *battlefield*

Los poemas de Martí se caracterizan por la melodía, el ritmo y el uso de frases cortas, con las que expresa ideas muy profundas. Sus temas principales son la libertad, la justicia, la independencia de su patria y la defensa de los pobres y de los oprimidos.

**De *Versos sencillos***

**I**

Yo vengo de todas partes°,
y hacia todas partes voy:
arte soy entre las artes,
y en los montes, monte soy.

**todas...** *everywhere*

Si dicen que del joyero
tome la joya mejor
tomo a un amigo sincero
y pongo a un lado el amor.

Todo es hermoso y constante,
todo es música y razón,° *reason*
y todo, como el diamante,
antes que luz es carbón.

Oculto° en mi pecho bravo *I hide*
la pena que me lo hiere°: *hurts*
el hijo de un pueblo° esclavo *people*
vive por él, calla° y muere. *is silent*

### XXIII

Yo quiero salir del mundo
por la puerta natural:
en un carro° de hojas° verdes *carriage / leaves*
a morir me han de llevar°. **han...** *will take*

No me pongan en lo oscuro
a morir como un traidor:
¡yo soy bueno, y como bueno
moriré de cara al sol!

## Díganos

Answer the following questions based on your own thoughts and experiences.

1. ¿Le gusta a Ud. la poesía?
2. ¿Quién es su poeta favorito(-a)?
3. ¿Conoce Ud. otros poetas hispanos? ¿Cuáles?
4. ¿Cuál es la "mejor joya" para Ud.?
5. Para Martí todo es hermoso y constante, ¿cree Ud. lo mismo?

VIDEO CD-ROM Do the interactive exercises on the CD-ROM for additional practice.

NARRADORA —¿Cuándo fue la última vez que Ud. visitó al médico?

MIRIAM —La última vez que fui al médico fue porque tuve una infección del estómago. Eh... Bueno, fui a la playa y no sé qué fue lo que comí, a lo mejor pescado *(fish)* o algo así y me cayó mal *(it made me sick)* y estuve muy mal, muy delicada del estómago.

## Preparación

A. **Mente sana en cuerpo sano.** Answer the following questions about your healthy habits. You will hear answers to some of these questions when you watch the video. After viewing the video, compare your answers with those you hear.

1. ¿Qué hace Ud. para conservar la salud?
2. ¿Cuándo fue la última vez que Ud. visitó al médico?
3. ¿Qué tipo de comida come Ud.?
4. ¿Qué tipo de ejercicio o deporte practica Ud.?

B. **La asistencia médica.** With a partner, answer the following questions about the state of healthcare in your country. You will hear answers to some of these questions when you watch the video. After viewing the video, compare your answers with those you hear.

1. ¿Qué tipo de asistencia médica hay en su país?
2. ¿Qué opina Ud. de la asistencia médica en su país?
3. ¿Cómo son los médicos?
4. ¿Cómo son los hospitales?

## Comprensión

A. **Para conservar la salud.** Select the word or phrase that best completes each statement.

1. Alejandro hace mucho (ejercicio, alimentos).
2. Otmara no come (frutas, carnes rojas).
3. Juan no (consume drogas, toma mucha agua).
4. Miriam sale a (caminar, comer) en los parques.
5. El doctor Brambilla habla de (las reglas universales, los aspectos sociales) de la salud.

**B. ¿Quién lo dijo?** Match each statement with the name of the person who said it.

| | | |
|---|---|---|
| _____ 1. | Tuve hepatitis A y me hicieron exámenes médicos. | a. Miriam |
| _____ 2. | Tuve un examen de la vista y me pusieron lentes *(eyeglasses)*. | b. Jaime |
| _____ 3. | Tuve una infección del estómago. | c. Otmara |
| _____ 4. | Tuve amigdalitis *(tonsilitis)* y el médico me dio tratamiento *(treatment)*. | d. Alejandro |

**C. ¿Verdadero o falso?** Read the following statements. Circle **V (Verdadero)** or **F (Falso)** according to what you understood from the video. If a statement is false, correct it.

**V F** 1. La gente trabajadora no recibe asistencia médica en El Salvador.
**V F** 2. En el país de Otmara, el Seguro Social es para la gente que trabaja.
**V F** 3. En el país de Otmara, el Seguro Social no incluye las medicinas.
**V F** 4. En el país de María, sólo las personas que trabajan tienen Seguridad Social.

**D. ¿Qué opinan?** Select the word or phrase that best completes each statement.

1. Según Leonardo, los hospitales de su país son muy (buenos, malos).
2. Según Juan, la gente pobre necesita (comida, asistencia médica) en Nicaragua.
3. Según la doctora González, la preparación de los médicos en su país es (mala, buena).
4. En la clínica donde trabaja la doctora, hay carencia *(shortages)* de (médicos, medicinas).

**E. Entrevista.** Select the word or phrase that best completes each statement.

1. En la clínica de la Dra. González ofrecen (veinte, veintiún, treinta) servicios.
2. La Dra. González menciona los servicios en especialidades como (cardiología, hematología).
3. El (gabinete [*room*] de rayos equis [*X-ray*], servicio de farmacia) es importante en la evaluación de los pacientes *(patients)*.
4. En la clínica tienen un gabinete de (ultrasonido, servicio de psiquiatría).

## Ampliación

**A. Para conservar mejor la salud.** Make a list in Spanish of the things you need to do to get in better shape. Assign deadlines by which to accomplish the items on your list. Then in groups of three or four, compare your lists. Determine who has the healthiest lifestyle now, and who will have the healthiest lifestyle after accomplishing their lists.

**B. Cuando fui al médico...** Interview a classmate about the last time he or she visited the doctor's office. Use the following questions as a guide.

1. ¿Cuándo fue la última vez que visitaste al médico?
2. ¿Por qué fuiste al médico?
3. ¿Fuiste a la sala de emergencia, al consultorio del médico o a una clínica?
4. ¿Qué tipo de tratamiento te dio el médico?

Lección 18

# ¡Este coche no sirve!

## OBJECTIVES

### Pronunciation

Pronunciation in context

### Structure

The pluperfect subjunctive • *If* clauses • Summary of the uses of the subjunctive

### Communication

You will learn vocabulary related to automobiles, including going to a service station and dealing with road emergencies.

# ¡Este coche no sirve!

*Gloria y Julio, una pareja de recién casados, están de vacaciones en Costa Rica. Ahora están en la carretera, camino a San José.*

GLORIA —Julio, ¡estás manejando muy rápido! La velocidad máxima es de noventa kilómetros por hora. ¡Si te ve un policía, te va a poner una multa!

JULIO —No te preocupes. ¿Dónde estamos? ¿Tú tienes el mapa?

GLORIA —Está en el portaguantes pero, según ese letrero, estamos a cuarenta kilómetros de San José.

JULIO —¿Hay una gasolinera cerca? El tanque está casi vacío.

GLORIA —Es una lástima que no hayas llenado el tanque antes...

JULIO —Si me lo hubieras dicho antes, lo habría hecho.

GLORIA —¡Hablas como si yo tuviera la culpa!

JULIO —*(Bromeando)* ¿Y a quién voy a culpar? Mira, allí hay una estación de servicio...

*Julio para en la estación de servicio para comprar gasolina.*

JULIO —*(Al empleado)* Llene el tanque, por favor. Además, ¿podría revisar el aceite y las llantas?

EMPLEADO —Sí, señor.

JULIO —Ayer tuve un pinchazo y cuando fui al taller, el mecánico me dijo que necesitaba neumáticos nuevos.

EMPLEADO —Sí, si yo fuera usted, los cambiaría... y también compraría un acumulador nuevo.

GLORIA —¡Ay, Julio! El mecánico también te dijo que arreglaras los frenos e instalaras una bomba de agua nueva.

JULIO —Haremos todo eso en San José, si es necesario.

GLORIA —¿No dijiste que también cambiarías el filtro del aceite y que comprarías limpiaparabrisas nuevos?

JULIO —Si yo hubiera sabido que íbamos a tener tantos problemas, habría comprado un coche nuevo antes de salir de viaje.

GLORIA —Sí, porque vamos a gastar una fortuna en arreglos.

JULIO —¡Y ayer el motor estaba haciendo un ruido extraño...!

*Cuando Julio trata de arrancar, el coche no funciona.*

JULIO —¡Ay, no! Tendremos que llamar una grúa para remolcar el coche hasta San José.

GLORIA —No vale la pena. Yo lo dejaría aquí.

JULIO —¡Estoy de acuerdo contigo! Si yo pudiera, compraría un coche nuevo ahora mismo.

# Vocabulario

## Cognados

**el filtro** filter
**la gasolina** gasoline
**el kilómetro** kilometer
**el mecánico** mechanic
**el motor** motor, engine
**necesario(-a)** necessary
**el tanque** tank

## Nombres

**el acumulador, la batería** battery
**el arreglo** repair
**la bomba de agua** water pump
**el camino** road
**la carretera** highway
**la culpa** blame, fault
**el freno** brake
**la gasolinera, la estación de servicio** gas (service) station
**la grúa, el remolcador** tow truck
**el letrero** sign
**el limpiaparabrisas** windshield wiper
**la multa** fine, ticket
**el neumático, la llanta, la goma** tire
**la pareja** couple (people)
**el policía** police officer
**el portaguantes, la guantera** glove compartment
**los recién casados** newlyweds
**el ruido** noise
**el taller (de mecánica)** repair shop
**la velocidad** speed

## Verbos

**arrancar** to start (a car)
**arreglar** to repair, to fix
**culpar** to blame
**funcionar** to work, to function
**instalar** to install
**parar** to stop
**remolcar** to tow
**revisar, chequear** to check

## Adjetivos

**extraño(-a)** strange
**vacío(-a)** empty

## Otras palabras y expresiones

**ahora mismo** right now
**camino a...** on the way to . . .
**casi** almost
**como si** as if
**estar de acuerdo** to agree
**no sirve** it's no good
**(no) vale la pena** it's (not) worth the trouble
**poner (dar) una multa** to give a ticket (fine)
**rápido** fast, rapidly
**salir de viaje** to leave on a trip
**según** according to
**tener la culpa** to be one's fault
**tener un pinchazo** to have a flat tire
**velocidad máxima** speed limit

## Vocabulario adicional

### En el taller de mecánica

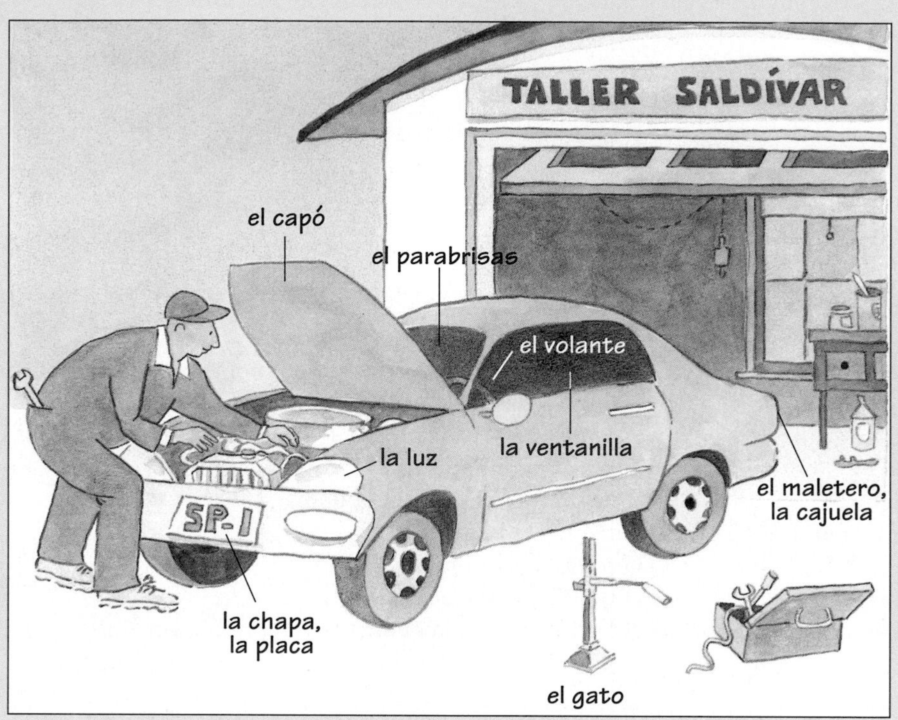


### Para hablar del coche

| | | |
|---|---|---|
| **automático(-a)** | automatic | Yo prefiero un coche **automático.** |
| **la autopista** | freeway, highway | En California hay muchas **autopistas.** |
| **la bocina** | horn | Aquí está prohibido tocar la **bocina.** |
| **la bolsa de aire** | air bag | Este coche tiene dos **bolsas de aire.** |
| **el carburador** | carburetor | El mecánico revisó el **carburador.** |
| **de cambios mecánicos** | standard shift | No sé conducir un coche **de cambios mecánicos.** |
| **descompuesto(-a)** | out of order, not working | No pude usar el coche porque estaba **descompuesto.** |
| **lleno(-a)** | full | El tanque está **lleno.** |
| **la milla** | mile | La velocidad máxima es de 65 **millas** por hora. |
| **la pieza de repuesto** | spare part | ¿Se venden **piezas de repuesto** aquí? |
| **el teléfono celular** | cellular phone | Tengo un **teléfono celular** en el coche. |

## ¡Conversemos!

Answer the following questions, basing your answers on the dialogue.

1. ¿Quiénes están en la carretera y adónde van?
2. ¿Cuál es la velocidad máxima en la carretera?
3. Julio está manejando muy rápido. ¿Qué va a pasar si un policía lo ve?

4. Según el letrero, ¿a qué distancia están Julio y Gloria de San José?
5. ¿Por qué necesitan ir a una gasolinera?
6. ¿Tiene el tanque mucha gasolina?
7. ¿Qué cosas hace el empleado de la gasolinera?
8. ¿Qué le pasó al coche de Julio ayer y qué le dijo el mecánico que necesitaba?
9. ¿Está de acuerdo el empleado con el mecánico?
10. ¿Qué otros problemas tiene el coche?
11. ¿Cree Gloria que va a costar mucho dinero arreglar el coche?
12. ¿Qué haría Julio si pudiera?

## ¿Lo sabía Ud.?

■ En las grandes ciudades como Madrid, Caracas, la Ciudad de México y Buenos Aires, hay muchísimos automóviles y autobuses, lo cual *(which)* está causando graves problemas de contaminación del aire *(smog)*. Sin embargo, en muchas zonas rurales de los países hispanos, particularmente en Hispanoamérica, hay muy pocos automóviles, ya que no hay carreteras, o las que existen están en muy malas condiciones.

■ En la mayoría de los países hispanos, la gasolina y los automóviles son mucho más caros que en los Estados Unidos. Por esta razón es muy popular la motocicleta, especialmente entre la gente joven.

■ En los países hispanos, se usa el sistema métrico decimal. Un kilómetro equivale a 0,6 millas; un galón equivale a 3,8 litros.

- ¿En qué ciudades de este país hay mucha contaminación del aire?
- ¿Qué medio de transporte prefiere usar la gente joven en la ciudad donde Ud. vive?

See the *¿Cómo se dice...?* Web site for activities on authentic cultural material: http://spanish.college.hmco.com/students

Congestión de tráfico en San José, Costa Rica.

# Pronunciación

In this lesson, there are some new words or phrases that may be challenging to pronounce. For further pronunciation practice of Spanish sounds, listen to your instructor and repeat the following words and phrases.

1. La **velocidad máxima** es de noventa kilómetros por hora.
2. Si me lo **hubieras dicho** antes, lo **habría hecho.**
3. El **mecánico** me dijo que necesitaba **neumáticos** nuevos.
4. Dijiste que comprarías **limpiaparabrisas** nuevos.
5. Tendremos que llamar una **grúa** para **remolcar** el coche.

# Estructuras

## 1 The pluperfect subjunctive *(El pluscuamperfecto de subjuntivo)*

- The pluperfect subjunctive is formed with the imperfect subjunctive of the auxiliary verb **haber** + *the past participle* of the main verb. It is used in the same way that the past perfect is used in English, but only in sentences in which the main clause calls for the subjunctive.

| *Imperfect subjunctive of* **haber** | |
|---|---|
| hubiera | hubiéramos |
| hubieras | hubierais |
| hubiera | hubieran |

| **Formation of the Pluperfect Subjunctive** | |
|---|---|
| yo | **hubiera hablado** |
| tú | **hubieras comido** |
| Ud. / él / ella | **hubiera vivido** |
| nosotros(-as) | **hubiéramos visto** |
| vosotros(-as) | **hubierais hecho** |
| Uds. / ellos / ellas | **hubieran vuelto** |

| | |
|---|---|
| —Yo me alegré de que ellos **hubieran vendido** el coche. | *"I was glad that they had sold the car."* |
| —Sí, porque no servía para nada. | *"Yes, because it was no good."* |
| —¿No había nadie que **hubiera visto** esa película? | *"Wasn't there anybody who had seen that movie?"* |
| —Sí, Eva la había visto ya. | *"Yes, Eva had already seen it."* |

## práctica

**A.** Say what your mother had expected everyone in the family to do by the time she got home yesterday.

MODELO: Aída / planchar la ropa
*Mamá esperaba que Aída **hubiera planchado** la ropa.*

Mamá esperaba que...

1. yo / hacer la comida
2. Quique / lavar el coche
3. nosotros / llevar a Raulito a la escuela
4. tú / escribirle a tío Carlos
5. Uds. / devolver los libros a la biblioteca
6. Eva y Luis / comprar la batería
7. Irma / poner la mesa
8. Eva y yo / pasarle la aspiradora a la alfombra
9. Daniel / llevar el coche al taller
10. Jorge y yo / cambiar las llantas

**B.** Say that you doubted that the following things had occurred.

MODELO: Carlos / venir muy tarde
*Yo dudaba que Carlos hubiera venido muy tarde.*

1. Pepe / arreglar los frenos
2. tú / salir de viaje
3. mis amigos / poder cambiar el filtro
4. el policía / ponerles una multa
5. nosotros / tener la culpa
6. el mecánico / conseguir las piezas de repuesto
7. Uds. / venir ayer
8. Irma / comprar un coche con bolsas de aire

**C.** With a partner, take turns deciding how the people mentioned reacted to the following. Always use the pluperfect subjunctive.

MODELO: Yo había comprado un coche nuevo. (Mis padres)
*Mis padres se alegraron de (lamentaron) que yo hubiera comprado un coche nuevo.*

1. Los recién casados se habían ido a Costa Rica. (La madre del muchacho)
2. El mecánico había revisado el coche. (Tú)
3. Ella había conducido el coche a cien millas por hora. (El esposo de Elsa)
4. Carlos había tenido que llamar una grúa. (Yo)

5. Nosotros habíamos decidido no arreglar el coche. (El mécanico)
6. El policía le había puesto una multa a mi hermano. (Mis padres)
7. Ellos habían llevado el coche al taller de mecánica. (Nosotros)
8. Tú habías cambiado la llanta. (Tu amigo)

## 2 *If* clauses (*Cláusulas con* ***si***)

- In Spanish, the imperfect subjunctive is used in *if* clauses when a contrary-to-fact statement is made.

| | |
|---|---|
| —Si **tuviera** dinero, compraría la batería hoy. | *"If I had money, I would buy the battery today."* |
| —Usa tu tarjeta de crédito... | *"Use your credit card..."* |

- Note that the imperfect subjunctive is used in the *if* clause and the conditional is used in the main clause. When a statement expresses a contrary-to-fact situation in the past, the pluperfect subjunctive is used in the *if* clause and the conditional perfect is used in the main clause.

| | |
|---|---|
| —No pude comprar el coche. | *"I wasn't able to buy the car."* |
| —**Si hubieras ahorrado** tu dinero, habrías podido comprarlo. | *"If you had saved your money, you would have been able to buy it."* |

- The imperfect subjunctive is also used in *if* clauses that express an unlikely fact, or simply the Spanish equivalent of the English *if . . . were to . . .*

| | |
|---|---|
| —**Si** Raúl me **invitara** a salir con él, aceptaría. | *"If Raúl were to ask me to go out with him, I would accept."* |
| —No creo que te invite... | *"I don't think he'll ask you . . . "* |

- The imperfect subjunctive is also used after the expression **como si** *(as if)*.

| | |
|---|---|
| —Pepe se compró otro coche. | *"Pepe bought himself another car."* |
| —Ese hombre gasta dinero **como si fuera** millonario. | *"That man spends money as if he were a millionaire."* |

- When an *if* clause refers to something that is possible or likely to happen, the indicative is used.

| | |
|---|---|
| —¿Me vas a comprar los zapatos? | *"Are you going to buy me the shoes?"* |
| —Si **tengo** dinero, te los compro. | *"If I have money, I'll buy them for you."* |

**ATENCIÓN** The present subjunctive is *never* used in an *if* clause.

## práctica

**A.** Interview a classmate, using the following questions.

1. Si tuvieras un pinchazo, ¿tratarías de cambiar la llanta?
2. ¿Qué harías si los frenos de tu coche no funcionaran?
3. ¿Qué haces si tu coche no arranca?
4. Si tu coche hubiera estado descompuesto, ¿cómo habrías venido a la universidad hoy?
5. Si el tanque de tu coche estuviera casi vacío, ¿a qué gasolinera irías?
6. Si no quieres que te pongan una multa, ¿a qué velocidad debes manejar en la autopista?
7. Si el arreglo de tu coche costara mil dólares, ¿podrías pagarlo?
8. ¿Qué harías si alguien te dejara una fortuna?
9. ¿Qué harías si tuvieras que comprar un coche nuevo?
10. Si tu mejor amigo(-a) quiere usar tu coche, ¿se lo prestas?

**B.** Say what the following people are going to do, would do, or would have done according to each situation.

MODELO: María quiere comprar ropa, pero no tiene dinero.
*Si María tuviera dinero compraría ropa.*

1. Yo no estudié mucho el semestre pasado y mi promedio fue de "C".
2. Teresa quiere ir al cine, pero no tiene tiempo.
3. Nosotros necesitamos comprar un coche nuevo. Es posible que tengamos suficiente dinero.
4. Juan quiere que yo le dé la dirección de Pedro, pero yo no la sé.
5. Mi madre quería que yo fuera contador, pero no me gustaban las matemáticas.
6. Tú quieres estudiar para programador(-a), pero no tienes computadora. Es posible que tus padres te regalen una.
7. Yo habría llevado a Marta al estadio, pero tuve que trabajar.
8. Nosotros habríamos hablado con el profesor, pero él no estaba en la universidad hoy.

**C.** With a partner, take turns asking each other what you would do or what would happen if the following were true.

MODELO: tener mucho dinero
—¿Qué harías tú si tuvieras mucho dinero?
*—Si yo tuviera mucho dinero, compraría mucha ropa.*

1. necesitar dinero
2. perder tus tarjetas de crédito
3. tener más tiempo libre
4. enseñar esta clase
5. querer aprender otro idioma
6. poder viajar a cualquier país
7. dar una gran fiesta
8. estar cansado(-a)
9. no sentirse bien
10. llover a cántaros

## 3 Summary of the uses of the subjunctive *(Resumen de los usos del subjuntivo)*

- **Use the subjunctive . . .**

  a. After verbs of volition (when there is change of subject).

  **Yo** quiero que **él salga.**

  b. After verbs of emotion (when there is change of subject).

  **Me alegro** de que **tú estés** aquí.

- **Use the infinitive . . .**

  a. After verbs of volition (when there is no change of subject).

  **Yo** quiero **salir.**

  b. After verbs of emotion (when there is no change of subject).

  **Me alegro** de **estar** aquí.

- **Use the subjunctive . . .**

  a. To express doubt, denial, and disbelief.

  **Dudo** que **pueda** venir.
  **Niego** que él **esté** aquí.
  **No creo** que él **vaya** con Eva.

  b. To refer to the indefinite or non-existent.

  **Busco** una casa que **sea** cómoda.
  **No había nadie** que lo **supiera.**

  c. With certain conjunctions when referring to a future action.[1]

  Lo **llamaré** cuando **llegue.**

  d. In an *if* clause, to refer to something contrary-to-fact or to something impossible or very improbable.

  Si **pudiera,** iría.
  Si el presidente me **invitara** a la Casa Blanca, yo aceptaría.

- **Use the indicative . . .**

  a. When there is no doubt, denial, or disbelief.

  **No dudo** que **puede** venir.
  **No niego** que él **está** aquí.
  **Creo** que él **va** con Eva.

  b. To refer to something specific.

  **Tengo** una casa que **es** cómoda.
  **Había alguien** que lo **sabía.**

  c. With certain conjunctions when there is no indication of future action.

  Lo **llamo** cuando **llego.**

  d. In an *if* clause, when not referring to anything that is contrary-to-fact, impossible, or very improbable.

  Si **puedo,** iré.
  Si Juan me **invita** a su casa, aceptaré.

### práctica

**A.** Complete the following dialogue, using the subjunctive, indicative, or infinitive of the verbs given, and act it out with a partner.

—¿Qué vas a hacer cuando ________ (llegar) a tu casa?
—Yo quiero ________ (estudiar) para el examen, pero mi mamá quiere que yo ________ (llevar) el coche al taller de mecánica.
—No creo que ________ (valer) la pena arreglar ese coche, porque no sirve.
—Es verdad, pero dudo que nosotros ________ (poder) comprar uno nuevo.

[1]The subjunctive is always used after the conjunctions **con tal que, sin que, en caso de que, a menos que, para que,** and **antes de que,** which by their very meaning imply uncertainty or condition: **Puedo salir sin que los chicos me vean, a menos que estén en la sala.**

—Yo espero ________ (poder) comprar uno el mes próximo.
—Yo conozco a una chica que ________ (querer) vender su coche. Si tú ________ (querer) verlo, podemos ir mañana a su casa.
—Si ________ (poder) iría, pero tengo que trabajar.

B. With a partner, take turns asking each other the following questions.

1. ¿A quién llamarías tú si tu coche no arrancara?
2. Tengo que arreglar mi coche. ¿A qué taller me recomiendas que lo lleve?
3. Si tú vas a comprar un coche, ¿prefieres uno que sea automático o de cambios mecánicos?
4. ¿Es cierto que tú tienes un teléfono celular en tu auto?
5. ¿Tú crees que es una buena idea aumentar *(to increase)* la velocidad máxima en la autopista?
6. ¿Esperas que tus padres te regalen un coche para tu cumpleaños?
7. ¿Tú podrías comprar una casa sin que tus padres te ayudaran?
8. ¿Es verdad que tú gastas dinero como si fueras millonario(-a)?
9. ¿Tú tratas de llegar a la clase antes de que llegue el profesor?
10. ¿Qué vas a hacer hoy tan pronto como llegues a tu casa?

C. Complete the following, according to your own thoughts and experience regarding college and family life.

1. Mis profesores quieren que yo...
2. Mis padres me aconsejan que...
3. Mi mejor amigo me sugirió que...
4. Yo habría sacado una "A" si...
5. Yo voy a llamar a mi amigo(-a) en cuanto...
6. Yo no tendría que pagar la matrícula si...
7. Yo no creo que mi profesor(-a) de español...
8. En mi clase de español no hay nadie que...
9. Yo dudo que mis amigos...
10. El verano próximo, yo espero...

# ¡A ver cuánto aprendió!

**INTERNET**

See the *¿Cómo se dice...?* Web site for additional grammar and vocabulary practice: http://spanish.college.hmco.com/students

## ¡Repase el vocabulario!

Circle the word or phrase that best completes each sentence.

1. Tuve un pinchazo. Tendré que cambiar (el acumulador, el neumático, la bomba de agua).
2. Voy a llevar el coche al taller porque está (sabroso, sentado, descompuesto).
3. Tendrá que llenar el tanque porque está casi (preocupado, extraño, vacío).
4. Te van a poner una multa porque estás (manejando muy rápido, mirando las luces, abriendo el maletero).

5. No pude parar porque (los frenos no funcionaban, no tenía limpiaparabrisas, tenía las manos en el volante).
6. Iba (autopista, carretera, camino) a Quito cuando tuvimos un accidente.
7. Vino (una ambulancia, una chapa, una grúa) para remolcar el coche.
8. Los recién (cansados, casados, cazados) salieron de viaje ayer.
9. Según (ese letrero, esa ventanilla, ese gato), estamos a cien kilómetros de San José.
10. Pondré los mapas en el (arreglo, aceite, portaguantes).
11. Gasté una fortuna en el (ruido, arreglo, taller) del coche.
12. No vale la (pareja, chapa, pena) arreglar el coche.
13. Cuando él tiene problemas con el coche, siempre (gasta, para, culpa) al mecánico.
14. Ella dice que necesitamos un coche nuevo porque el nuestro no sirve, pero yo no estoy de (extraño, acuerdo, ruido).
15. Levantó (el maletero, el capó, la ventanilla) para revisar el motor.
16. Mi coche tiene (bomba, bolsas, bocina) de aire.

## Entrevista

With a partner, interview each other by asking the following questions.

1. ¿Tendrás que ir a la gasolinera mañana?
2. ¿Está lleno o vacío el tanque de tu coche?
3. ¿Necesita tu coche un acumulador nuevo?
4. ¿Cuándo piensas comprar neumáticos nuevos para tu coche?
5. ¿Tienes que cambiar el filtro de aceite de tu coche?
6. ¿Cuál es el número de la chapa de tu coche?
7. ¿Cuántas millas hay de tu casa a la universidad?
8. Generalmente ¿a qué velocidad manejas en la autopista?
9. ¿Te gustaría manejar un Mercedes Benz?
10. ¿Qué harías si tu coche no funcionara bien?

## Situaciones

What would you say in the following situations? What might the other person say? Act out the scenes with a partner. Take turns playing each role.

1. You have a flat tire, and you think the brakes on your car are out of order. You want your mechanic to check them.
2. Tell a tourist that he or she can buy gasoline at the service station located at the next corner.
3. You are a police officer, and you have stopped a motorist. The car doesn't have a license plate, and the lights aren't working. Ask to see the motorist's driver's license.
4. Your car won't start, and you're going to need a tow truck. Someone passes by as you fiddle with the ignition.
5. Your friend bought a car that was a lemon, and then spent three thousand dollars to have it fixed. Say what you would have done in this situation.

## ¿Qué pasa aquí?

In groups of three or four, look at the cartoon and write a dialogue between the mechanic and the driver.

## Para escribir

What if **Romeo** and **Julieta** were living now? Write an account of what their circumstances would be and what they would be doing. In our story, of course, they *don't* die! Start out with: **Romeo y Julieta vivirían en...**

# En la vida real

**CD-ROM**

Do the interactive exercises on the CD-ROM for additional practice.

## ¡Nos vamos!

You and a classmate are planning to drive to Mexico. Working together, make a list of everything you need to do before you leave. Make sure you include things you need to do to get the car and yourselves ready.

## Comprando coche

What questions would you ask before buying a car? Carefully read the following brochure and identify the questions that would cover these topics:

1. la condición del coche (dos preguntas)
2. la garantía
3. las reparaciones (dos preguntas)
4. la inspección del estado
5. el precio de reventa *(resale)*

Cuando vaya a
comprar un automóvil,
¡pregunte!

Ciertas preguntas le ahorrarán dinero.
Determine primero qué automóvil necesita y cuánto dinero puede invertir.
Consulte por lo menos con tres comerciantes de automóviles antes de decidir a cuál le comprará.

Pregunte a cada comerciante:
–¿Qué garantía tiene el automóvil?
–Si el automóvil se descompone, ¿quién va a componerlo?
–¿El automóvil será aprobado en la inspección del Estado?
–¿Qué precio de reventa tendrá el automóvil cuando Ud. quiera venderlo?
–¿Está el automóvil en perfectas condiciones?
–¿Le dejarán probar el automóvil antes de entregárselo?
–Si el automóvil necesita ser reparado, ¿quién pagará la reparación?

Recuerde hacer estas preguntas y ahorrará mucho dinero.

Asegúrese de que el vendedor no lo engañe. Muchos vendedores tratarán de engañarlo para hacer la venta.

**¡PREGUNTE EL PRECIO!**

Hágale saber al vendedor que Ud. ya conoce los precios de otros competidores.

Recuerde que los vendedores a veces pueden cambiar el precio. No cierre el trato si el precio que le ofrecen no le parece correcto o justo.

**RECUERDE, ES SU DINERO.**

## En la agencia de seguros

With a classmate, play the roles of an insurance agent and a student who wants to purchase an auto insurance policy (**un seguro de automóvil**). The agent wants to determine the overall condition of the car, whether the student is a conscientious driver, and how much the car is worth. The student is anxious to make a good impression.

Take this test. When you have finished, check your answers in the answer key provided for this section in Appendix E. Then use a red pen to correct any mistakes you have made. Are you ready?

## Lección 16

### A. The future

Rewrite the following sentences using the future tense.

1. Le *vamos a decir* la verdad.
2. ¿Qué *van a hacer* Uds.?
3. No *van a querer* ir.
4. Lo *voy a saber* mañana.
5. No *van a poder* venir.
6. ¿Adónde *vamos a ir*?
7. ¿Dónde lo *vas a poner*?
8. Nosotros *vamos a venir* con él.
9. *Voy a tener* que trabajar.
10. *Vamos a salir* mañana.

### B. The conditional

Rewrite the following sentences to say what the people named *would* do, using the conditional tense.

1. Yo *voy* a México.
2. Nosotros les *escribimos*.
3. ¿Tú se lo *dices*?
4. Ellos *hablan* con Ana.
5. ¿Ud. lo *pone* en el banco?
6. ¿Uds. *vienen* el domingo?
7. Julio *pide* ensalada.
8. Nosotros lo *hacemos* hoy.
9. Tú no *sales* con ella.
10. Ella *no camina*; *va* en coche.

### C. The future perfect

Complete the following sentences, using the future perfect of the verbs listed.

comer
terminar
escribir
volver
decir

1. Para mañana, el consejero me ________ qué clases tomar.
2. Para las cuatro de la tarde, ellos ________ a casa.
3. Para junio, yo ________ las clases.
4. Para las dos, nosotros ya ________ el postre.
5. ¿Tú ________ todas las cartas para las cinco de la tarde?

**D. The conditional perfect**

Complete the following, using the Spanish equivalent of the words in parentheses.

1. Yo ________ más para el examen. (would have studied)
2. Julio me ________ con el informe. (would have helped)
3. Luis y yo ________ al partido de fútbol. (would have gone)
4. Mis padres ________ la matrícula. (would have paid)
5. ¿Qué ________, Anita? (would you have done)

**E. Just words . . .**

Match the questions in column A with the answers in column B.

| | A | | B |
|---|---|---|---|
| 1. | ¿Adónde vas? | a. | Sí, porque juega nuestro equipo. |
| 2. | ¿Qué materias estás tomando? | b. | El año próximo. |
| 3. | ¿Quién es tu consejero? | c. | No, es plomero. |
| 4. | ¿Asiste a la Facultad de Derecho? | d. | Al laboratorio. |
| | | e. | Sí, para pagar la matrícula. |
| 5. | ¿Qué tienes que escribir? | f. | Física, química y sociología. |
| 6. | ¿Qué nota sacaste? | g. | No, quedé suspendido. |
| 7. | ¿Es periodista? | h. | El Dr. Peña. |
| 8. | ¿Necesitas dinero? | i. | Un informe para mi clase de biología. |
| 9. | ¿Aprobaste el examen? | j. | Sí, quiere ser abogado. |
| 10. | ¿Es carpintero? | k. | Una "B". |
| 11. | ¿Vamos al estadio hoy? | l. | Sí, trabaja para el *Times*. |
| 12. | ¿Cuándo te gradúas? | | |

**F. Culture**

Circle the correct answer, based on the **¿Lo sabía Ud.?** section.

1. En las universidades hispanas no (entrega, existe, queda) el concepto de "*major*" usado en los Estados Unidos.
2. La mayoría de los estudiantes comienzan a (matricularse, graduarse, especializarse) a partir de su primer año en la universidad.
3. En España, las universidades se dividen en (facultades, carreras, administraciones).
4. Los estudiantes toman clases relacionadas con su (consejero, equipo, especialización).
5. Una nota de (1 a 4, 3 a 6, 2 a 5) es la mínima para aprobar una clase.

## Lección 17

### A. The imperfect subjunctive

Rewrite the following sentences with the new beginnings.

1. Quiere que vaya con ellos.
   Quería...
2. Les digo que no se preocupen.
   Les dije...
3. Me alegro de que el doctor te vea hoy.
   Me alegré...
4. Temo que me ponga una inyección.
   Temí...
5. Necesito una enfermera que sepa español.
   Necesitaba...
6. No creo que tengan que desinfectarme la herida.
   No creí...
7. ¿Hay alguien que pueda recetar penicilina?
   ¿Había...?
8. Me alegro de que te sientas bien.
   Me alegré...
9. No es verdad que necesitemos una ambulancia.
   No era verdad...
10. No creo que esté embarazada.
    No creía...

### B. Uses of some prepositions after certain verbs

Complete the following sentences, using the verbs listed and the appropriate prepositions.

| insistir | comprometerse | olvidarse |
|---|---|---|
| venir | enamorarse | soñar |

1. Yo nunca ________ traer mis libros a clase.
2. Julio y Estrella ________ casarse el año que viene.
3. El profesor ________ que todos los estudiantes hagan los ejercicios.
4. Nosotros ________ verla cinco días a la semana.
5. Adela ________ Pepe en la fiesta de anoche.
6. Yo ________ mi novia la primera vez que la vi.

### C. The present perfect subjunctive

Complete these sentences with the present perfect subjunctive form of the verbs in parentheses.

1. Es una lástima que los enfermeros no ________ (encontrar) las radiografías.
2. Pedro, me alegro de que (tú) ________ (ir) a la sala de emergencias.
3. ¿Hay alguien que ________ (comprar) el antibiótico?
4. Los padres de Clara esperan que la médica ________ (enyesarle) la pierna.
5. No creo que Ud. ________ (romperse) el brazo, señor.
6. No es verdad que nosotros ________ (volver) al hospital.

### D. Just words . . .

Choose the word or phrase in parentheses that best completes each of the following sentences.

1. Ella es alérgica a la (radiografía, penicilina, clase).
2. Comemos con (los oídos, los dientes, el pecho).
3. Hablamos con (la espalda, los dedos, la lengua).
4. Vemos con (los ojos, la boca, las orejas).
5. Caminamos con (las manos, el cuello, los pies).
6. Me desinfectaron (el dolor, la herida, la receta).
7. ¿Te (rompiste, atropellaste, evitaste) el brazo alguna vez?
8. Me dolía mucho (la pierna, el pelo, el consultorio).
9. Le vendé (el tobillo, el pelo, el catarro).
10. Tenía ciento tres (fiebre, gripe, grados) de temperatura.
11. ¿Cuándo fue la última vez que le (cortaron, quebraron, pusieron) una inyección antitetánica?
12. ¿Por qué tomaste aspirinas? ¿Tenías (dolor de cabeza, tos, frío)?
13. ¿Tienes Alka Seltzer? Es para (el pecho, el estómago, los dedos de los pies).
14. Va a tener un niño. Está (cansada, enferma, embarazada).
15. Raúl no se siente bien. El médico dice que tiene (pastillas, gripe, recetas).

### E. Culture

Answer the following questions, based on the **¿Lo sabía Ud.?** section.

1. ¿Quién subvenciona *(subsidizes)* los hospitales en los países de habla hispana?
2. ¿Adónde va la gente que no quiere ir a un hospital público?
3. ¿Qué clase de servicios médicos hay en muchos pueblos remotos?
4. ¿Quién ayuda a algunas mujeres hispanas cuando van a tener un bebé?
5. ¿Es posible comprar ciertas *(certain)* medicinas en algunos países hispanos sin tener receta?

## Lección 18

### A. The pluperfect subjunctive

Give the Spanish equivalent of the words in parentheses.

1. No había nadie que ________ el accidente. *(had seen)*
2. Yo me alegré de que ellos no ________ un pinchazo. *(had had)*
3. Ellos no creían que nosotros ________ la gasolina. *(had paid)*
4. Yo temía que ________ la pierna, Anita. *(you had broken)*
5. Ellos se alegraron de que yo ________. *(had returned)*

### B. *If* clauses

Complete the following sentences, using the present indicative, the imperfect subjunctive, or the pluperfect subjunctive, as needed.

1. Si yo ________ (tener) tiempo, iré a buscarte.
2. Nosotros iríamos con ellos si ________ (poder).
3. Si ellos ________ (ir) a la biblioteca, habrían encontrado el libro.
4. Si Uds. ________ (querer) ir con nosotros, podemos llevarlos.
5. Tú habrías hablado con ella si la ________ (ver).
6. Antonio gasta dinero como si ________ (ser) rico.

### C. Summary of the uses of the subjunctive

Complete the following sentences, using the verbs in parentheses in the appropriate tense of the subjunctive or the indicative.

1. Yo quería que ellos ________ una batería nueva. *(install)*
2. Espero que ellos ________ hablar con el mecánico. *(can)*
3. Dile que me ________ si quiere ir. *(call)*
4. Yo no creo que nosotros ________ ir al partido, pero creo que ________ ir al cine. *(can / can)*
5. ¿Hay alguien aquí que ________ administración de empresas? *(has taken)*
6. Voy a ayudar a mi mamá cuando ________ a casa. *(arrive)*
7. Le di dinero para que ________ pagar la multa. *(could)*
8. No es verdad que su coche no ________ bueno. *(is)*

### D. Just words . . .

Complete the following sentences, using words learned in **Lección 18**.

1. ¿Cuál es la ________ máxima en la carretera?
2. Adela y Fernando son ________ casados.
3. No pude parar porque los ________ estaban descompuestos.
4. ¿Tienes tu licencia de ________?
5. Fuimos a la estación de ________.
6. Está lloviendo, y el ________ de mi coche no funciona. ¡No veo nada!
7. ¿Está lleno o ________ el tanque?
8. Voy a poner las maletas en el ________.
9. Mi coche no arranca; la grúa lo va a ________.
10. Un sinónimo de "batería" es ________.
11. Yo pongo los mapas en la ________ del coche.
12. No es mi ________ que el coche no tenga gasolina.
13. Yo no arreglaría el coche. ¡No ________ la pena!
14. Mis padres van a salir de ________ el 15 de junio.
15. No estoy de ________ contigo; no creo que debamos comprar un coche nuevo.

### E. Culture

Circle the correct answer, based on the **¿Lo sabía Ud.?** section.

1. Madrid, Buenos Aires y México tienen graves problemas de (asimilación, contaminación, introducción) del aire.
2. En zonas rurales de Hispanoamérica, las carreteras están en muy (buenas, medianas, malas) condiciones.
3. La gasolina es más (cara, barata, libre) en la mayoría de los países hispanos.
4. La gente joven usa más (el camión, la motocicleta, la bicicleta).
5. Un kilómetro equivale a (0,7; 0,6; 0,5) millas.

# 9. Las minorías hispanas en los Estados Unidos

Estados Unidos

- Muchas de las estrellas *(stars)* de cine y de televisión en los Estados Unidos son de ascendencia hispana: Rita Moreno, Ricardo Montalbán, Charlie Sheen, Emilio Estévez, Edward James Olmos, María Conchita Alonso, Linda Ronstadt, Andy García y Rosie Pérez, entre muchos otros.
- En la ciudad de Nueva York hay más de dos millones de hispanos, la mayoría de los cuales son puertorriqueños. Otros grupos hispanos concentrados en Nueva York son los dominicanos, los centroamericanos y los cubanos.
- La minoría hispana más numerosa en los Estados Unidos es la de origen mexicano, que se concentra principalmente en los estados de Tejas, Colorado, Nuevo México, Arizona y California.
- Más de medio millón de cubanos viven en Miami, donde ejercen una gran influencia cultural y económica. Hace cuatro décadas, cuando los cubanos empezaron a llegar a Miami, la ciudad era fundamentalmente un centro turístico. Hoy Miami es un centro industrial y comercial de primer orden, y el puente que une la economía de los Estados Unidos con la de América Latina y aun la de España.

Para las muchachas latinoamericanas, tiene mucha importancia la celebración de los quince años. En México la fiesta recibe el nombre de "quinceañera"; en otros países se llama la celebración de "los quince". Las familias latinas en los Estados Unidos, generalmente siguen la tradición con un baile y una comida especial.

*¿Qué cumpleaños es muy importante para muchas chicas norteamericanas?*

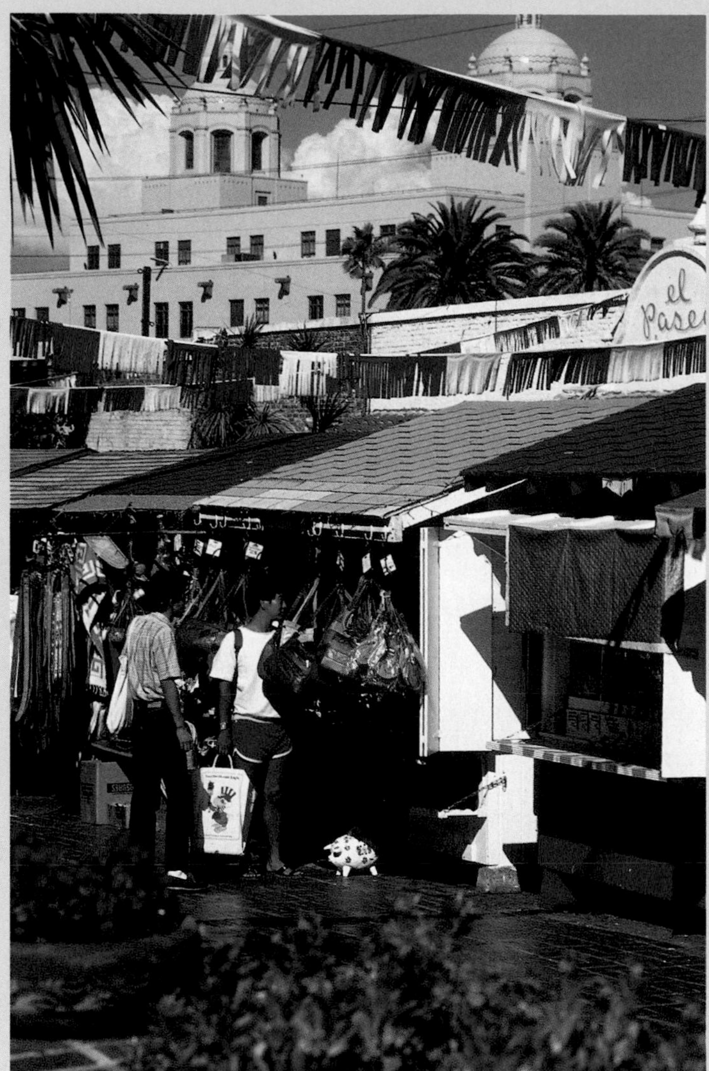

La calle Olvera, con sus aceras adoquinadas *(tiled sidewalks)*, sus piñatas, sus mariachis y sus puestos de artesanía mexicana es un trozo *(piece)* del viejo México en el corazón de Los Ángeles. Aquí se ve el edificio Ávila, construido de adobe y considerado el más antiguo de los edificios existentes en Los Ángeles.

*¿Puede Ud. describir lo que ve en esta foto?*

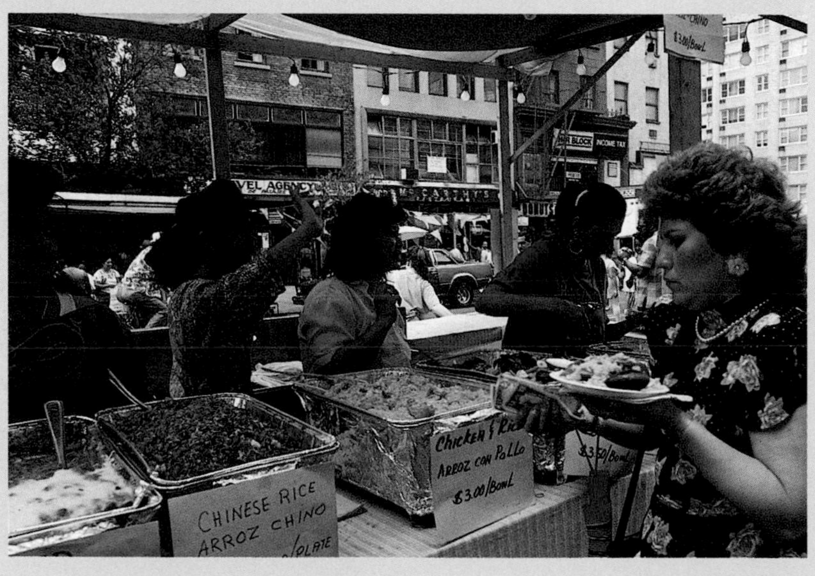


Uno de los grupos minoritarios más numerosos en la ciudad de Nueva York es el de los puertorriqueños. Aquí se ve un festival hispano en la calle 14 de Manhattan, el centro de Nueva York.

*¿Cuál es el grupo minoritario más numeroso en su ciudad?*

La cantante cubana Gloria Estefan es una de las más populares de los Estados Unidos. Gloria canta y compone canciones en español y en inglés. Recientemente su nombre fue añadido *(was added)* al famoso *Walk of Fame* de Hollywood.

*¿Cuál es su cantante favorito?*

La actriz Jennifer López, de origen puertorriqueño, se ha convertido en una de las actrices y cantantes latinas más populares. Ella interpretó el papel *(role)* de *Selena*, la trágicamente desaparecida cantante de la música *"Tex-Mex"*, en la película del mismo nombre. Jennifer López ya había participado en varias películas, entre ellas *My Family*, *U Turn*, *Money Train* y *The Cell*.

*¿Cuál es su actriz favorita?*

Edward James Olmos, nacido en Los Ángeles, de padres mexicanos, es uno de los actores hispanos más conocidos en los Estados Unidos. Entre sus películas están *Stand and Deliver*, *My Family* y *Selena*, donde representa el papel del padre de la famosa cantante de origen mexicano.

*¿Cuál es su actor favorito?*

No hay duda de que en la ciudad de San Antonio, Tejas, la cultura mexicana es la predominante. En la foto, una familia come en el restaurante mexicano "Mi tierra".

*¿Cuál es su restaurante mexicano favorito?*

Ileana Ros-Lehtinen, cubana de nacimiento, es una muestra del poder político de los hispanos en los Estados Unidos. Educadora de profesión, y ya con una maestría de Ciencias en Lideratura Educacional y una candidatura al doctorado, se decidió por la política. Fue Representante a la Cámara y Senadora de la Florida y, desde 1989, es Representante al Congreso de los Estados Unidos. Ileana Ros fue la primera mujer hispana elegida para esta posición.

*¿Puede Ud. nombrar otros políticos hispanos? ¿Cuáles?*

TELEINFORME

VIDEO

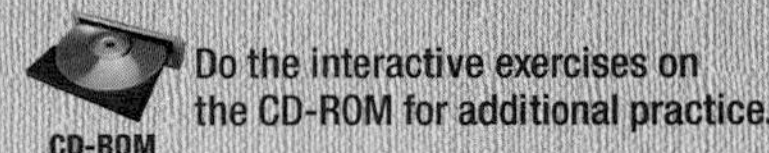
CD-ROM
Do the interactive exercises on the CD-ROM for additional practice.

## Preparación

**¿Cuánto saben Uds. ya?** After reading **Panorama hispánico 9** get together in groups of three or four students and answer the following questions.

1. ¿En qué estados vive la mayoría de las personas de origen mexicano?
2. ¿De dónde son los hispanos que viven en Nueva York?
3. ¿Dónde vive la mayor parte de los cubanos?
4. ¿En qué ciudad está la calle Olvera?
5. ¿Qué se ve en la calle Olvera?
6. ¿Cuál es uno de los edificios *(buildings)* más antiguos de la ciudad de Los Ángeles?

## Comprensión

**A. La calle Olvera, Los Ángeles.** Select the word or phrase that best completes each statement, according to what you understood.

1. La calle Olvera es una de las calles más _______ de Los Ángeles.
2. En el mercado mexicano venden _______ típicas.
3. El Cinco de Mayo es una _______ mexicoamericana.
4. Algunos ejemplos de la comida mexicana son _______, _______ y _______.
5. Los fines de semana hay _______, _______ y presentaciones de baile en la calle Olvera.

**B. El desfile puertorriqueño de Nueva York.** Read the following statements. After watching the video, circle **V** (**Verdadero**) or **F** (**Falso**), according to what you understood. If a statement is false, correct it.

V F 1. La bandera *(flag)* puertorriqueña fue creada en Puerto Rico.
V F 2. La bandera puertorriqueña ondeó por primera vez en Puerto Rico en el año 1902.
V F 3. Puerto Rico es un Estado Libre Asociado *(Commonwealth)* de los Estados Unidos.
V F 4. El desfile puertorriqueño se inició en el año 1957.
V F 5. Muy pocas personas asisten al desfile puertorriqueño.
V F 6. Algunos políticos participan en el desfile puertorriqueño de Nueva York.

## Ampliación

**A. Celebraciones hispanas.** With a partner, discuss in Spanish what you would like to see and do if you went to a festival on Olvera Street in Los Angeles or the Puerto Rican Day celebration in New York City.

**B. Dos culturas.** After viewing all the video modules, what have you learned about the Hispanic world and its people that you did not know before? Discuss this in Spanish with a partner.

# Appendix A Spanish Sounds

## Vowels

There are five distinct vowels in Spanish: **a**, **e**, **i**, **o**, and **u**. Each vowel has only one basic, constant sound. The pronunciation of each vowel is constant, clear, and brief. The length of the sound is practically the same whether it is produced in a stressed or unstressed syllable.[1]

While producing the sounds of the English stressed vowels that most closely resemble the Spanish ones, the speaker changes the position of the tongue, lips, and lower jaw, so that the vowel actually starts as one sound and then glides into another. In Spanish, however, the tongue, lips, and jaw keep a constant position during the production of the sound.

**English:** ban*a*na **Spanish:** banana

The stress falls on the same vowel and syllable in both Spanish and English, but the English stressed *a* is longer than the Spanish stressed **a**.

**English:** ban*a*na **Spanish:** banana

Note also that the English stressed *a* has a sound different from the other *a*'s in the word, while the Spanish **a** sound remains constant.

a The Spanish **a** sounds similar to the English *a* in the word *father.*

| alta | casa | palma | Ana |
|---|---|---|---|
| cama | Panamá | alma | apagar |

e The Spanish **e** is pronounced like the English *e* in the word *eight.*

| mes | entre | este | deje |
|---|---|---|---|
| ese | encender | teme | prender |

i The Spanish **i** has a sound similar to the English *ee* in the word *see.*

fin ir sí sin dividir Trini difícil

o The Spanish **o** is similar to the English *o* in the word *no,* but without the glide.

| toco | como | poco | roto |
|---|---|---|---|
| corto | corro | solo | loco |

u The Spanish **u** is pronounced like the English *oo* sound in the word *shoot* or the *ue* sound in the word *Sue.*

| su | Lulú | Úrsula | cultura |
|---|---|---|---|
| un | luna | sucursal | Uruguay |

### Diphthongs and Triphthongs

When unstressed **i** or **u** falls next to another vowel in a syllable, it unites with that vowel to form what is called a *diphthong.* Both vowels are pronounced as one syllable. Their sounds do not change; they are only pronounced more rapidly and with a glide. For example:

| tr**ai**ga | Lid**ia** | tr**ei**nta | s**ie**te | **oi**go | ad**ió**s |
|---|---|---|---|---|---|
| **Au**rora | ag**ua** | b**ue**no | antig**uo** | c**iu**dad | L**ui**s |

[1]In a stressed syllable, the prominence of the vowel is indicated by its loudness.

A triphthong is the union of three vowels: a stressed vowel between two unstressed ones (**i** or **u**) in the same syllable. For example: Parag**uay**, estud**iéi**s.

NOTE: Stressed **i** and **u** do not form diphthongs with other vowels, except in the combinations **iu** and **ui.** For example: **rí**-o, sa-**bí**-ais.

In syllabication, diphthongs and triphthongs are considered a single vowel; their components cannot be separated.

## Consonants

**p** Spanish **p** is pronounced in a manner similar to the English *p* sound, but without the puff of air that follows after the English sound is produced.

| | | | | |
|---|---|---|---|---|
| pesca | pude | puedo | parte | papá |
| postre | piña | puente | Paco | |

**k** The Spanish **k** sound, represented by the letters **k, c** before **a, o, u** or a consonant, and **qu,** is similar to the English *k* sound, but without the puff of air.

| | | | | | |
|---|---|---|---|---|---|
| casa | comer | cuna | clima | acción | que |
| quinto | queso | aunque | kiosko | kilómetro | |

**t** Spanish **t** is produced by touching the back of the upper front teeth with the tip of the tongue. It has no puff of air as in the English *t*.

| | | | | |
|---|---|---|---|---|
| todo | antes | corto | Guatemala | diente |
| resto | tonto | roto | tanque | |

**d** The Spanish consonant **d** has two different sounds depending on its position. At the beginning of an utterance and after **n** or **l,** the tip of the tongue presses the back of the upper front teeth.

| | | | | |
|---|---|---|---|---|
| día | doma | dice | dolor | dar |
| anda | Aldo | caldo | el deseo | un domicilio |

In all other positions the sound of **d** is similar to the *th* sound in the English word *they*, but softer.

| | | | | |
|---|---|---|---|---|
| medida | todo | nada | nadie | medio |
| puedo | moda | queda | nudo | |

**g** The Spanish consonant **g** is similar to the English *g* sound in the word *guy* except before **e** or **i.**

| | | | | | |
|---|---|---|---|---|---|
| goma | glotón | gallo | gloria | lago | alga |
| gorrión | garra | guerra | angustia | algo | Dagoberto |

**j** The Spanish sound **j** (or **g** before **e** and **i**) is similar to a strongly exaggerated English *h* sound.

| | | | | |
|---|---|---|---|---|
| gemir | juez | jarro | gitano | agente |
| juego | giro | bajo | gente | |

**b, v** There is no difference in sound between Spanish **b** and **v.** Both letters are pronounced alike. At the beginning of an utterance or after **m** or **n, b** and **v** have a sound identical to the English *b* sound in the word *boy.*

| | | | | |
|---|---|---|---|---|
| vivir | beber | vamos | barco | enviar |
| hambre | batea | bueno | vestido | |

When pronounced between vowels, the Spanish **b** and **v** sound is produced by bringing the lips together but not closing them, so that some air may pass through.

| | | | |
|---|---|---|---|
| sábado | autobús | yo voy | su barco |

**y, ll** In most countries, Spanish **ll** and **y** have a sound similar to the English *y* sound in the word *yes*.

| | | | |
|---|---|---|---|
| el llavero | trayecto | su yunta | milla |
| oye | el yeso | mayo | yema |
| un yelmo | trayectoria | llama | bella |

NOTE: When it stands alone or is at the end of a word, Spanish **y** is pronounced like the vowel **i.**

| | | | | |
|---|---|---|---|---|
| rey | hoy | y | doy | buey |
| muy | voy | estoy | soy | |

**r** The sound of Spanish **r** is similar to the English *dd* sound in the word *ladder*.

| | | | | |
|---|---|---|---|---|
| crema | aroma | cara | arena | aro |
| harina | toro | oro | eres | portero |

**rr** Spanish **rr** and also **r** in an initial position and after **n, l,** or **s** are pronounced with a very strong trill. This trill is produced by bringing the tip of the tongue near the alveolar ridge and letting it vibrate freely while the air passes through the mouth.

| | | | | |
|---|---|---|---|---|
| rama | carro | Israel | cierra | roto |
| perro | alrededor | rizo | corre | Enrique |

**s** Spanish **s** is represented in most of the Spanish world by the letters **s, z,** and **c** before **e** or **i.** The sound is very similar to the English sibilant *s* in the word *sink*.

| | | | |
|---|---|---|---|
| sale | sitio | presidente | signo |
| salsa | seda | suma | vaso |
| sobrino | ciudad | cima | canción |
| zapato | zarza | cerveza | centro |

**h** The letter **h** is silent in Spanish.

| | | | |
|---|---|---|---|
| hoy | hora | hilo | ahora |
| humor | huevo | horror | almohada |

**ch** Spanish **ch** is pronounced like the English *ch* in the word *chief*.

| | | | |
|---|---|---|---|
| hecho | chico | coche | Chile |
| mucho | muchacho | salchicha | |

**f** Spanish **f** is identical in sound to the English *f*.

| | | | |
|---|---|---|---|
| difícil | feo | fuego | forma |
| fácil | fecha | foto | fueron |

**l** Spanish **l** is similar to the English *l* in the word *let*.

| | | | | |
|---|---|---|---|---|
| dolor | lata | ángel | lago | sueldo |
| los | pelo | lana | general | fácil |

**m** Spanish **m** is pronounced like the English *m* in the word *mother*.

| | | | |
|---|---|---|---|
| mano | moda | mucho | muy |
| mismo | tampoco | multa | cómoda |

**n** In most cases, Spanish **n** has a sound similar to the English *n*.

| | | | |
|---|---|---|---|
| nada | nunca | ninguno | norte |
| entra | tiene | sienta | |

The sound of Spanish **n** is often affected by the sounds that occur around it. When it appears before **b**, **v**, or **p**, it is pronounced like an **m**.

| | | |
|---|---|---|
| tan bueno | toman vino | sin poder |
| un pobre | comen peras | siguen bebiendo |

**ñ** Spanish **ñ** is similar to the English *ny* sound in the word *canyon*.

| | | | |
|---|---|---|---|
| señor | otoño | ñoño | uña |
| leña | dueño | niños | años |

**x** Spanish **x** has two pronunciations depending on its position. Between vowels the sound is similar to English *ks*.

| | | | |
|---|---|---|---|
| examen | exacto | boxeo | éxito |
| oxidar | oxígeno | existencia | |

When it occurs before a consonant, Spanish **x** sounds like *s*.

| | | | |
|---|---|---|---|
| expresión | explicar | extraer | excusa |
| expreso | exquisito | extremo | |

NOTE: When **x** appears in **México** or in other words of Mexican origin, it is pronounced like the Spanish letter **j**.

# Rhythm

Rhythm is the variation of sound intensity that we usually associate with music. Spanish and English each regulate these variations in speech differently, because they have different patterns of syllable length. In Spanish the length of the stressed and unstressed syllables remains almost the same, while the English stressed syllables are considerably longer than unstressed ones. Pronounce the following Spanish words, enunciating each syllable clearly.

| | | |
|---|---|---|
| es-tu-dian-te | bue-no | Úr-su-la |
| com-po-si-ción | di-fí-cil | ki-ló-me-tro |
| po-li-cí-a | Pa-ra-guay | |

Because the length of the Spanish syllables remains constant, the greater the number of syllables in a given word or phrase, the longer the phrase will be.

# Linking

In spoken Spanish, the different words in a phrase or a sentence are not pronounced as isolated elements but are combined together. This is called *linking*.

| | | |
|---|---|---|
| Pepe come pan. | ⇨ | Pe-pe-co-me-pan |
| Tomás toma leche. | | To-más-to-ma-le-che |
| Luis tiene la llave. | | Luis-tie-ne-la-lla-ve |
| La mano de Roberto. | | La-ma-no-de-Ro-ber-to |

- The final consonant of a word is pronounced together with the initial vowel of the following word.

| | | |
|---|---|---|
| Carlos anda | ⇨ | Car-lo-san-da |
| un ángel | | u-nán-gel |
| el otoño | | e-lo-to-ño |
| unos estudios interesantes | | u-no-ses-tu-dio-sin-te-re-san-tes |

- A diphthong is formed between the final vowel of a word and the initial vowel of the following word. A triphthong is formed when there is a combination of three vowels (see rules for the formation of diphthongs and triphthongs on pages 459–460).

| | | |
|---|---|---|
| su hermana | | suher-ma-na |
| tu escopeta | | tues-co-pe-ta |
| Roberto y Luis |  | Ro-ber-toy-Luis |
| negocio importante | | ne-go-cioim-por-tan-te |
| lluvia y nieve | | llu-viay-nie-ve |
| ardua empresa | | ar-duaem-pre-sa |

- When the final vowel of a word and the initial vowel of the following word are identical, they are pronounced slightly longer than one vowel.

| | |
|---|---|
| Ana alcanza | A-n*a*l-can-za |
| lo olvido | l*o*l-vi-do |
| tiene eso | tie-n*e*-so |
| Ada atiende | Ad*a*-tien-de |

The same rule applies when two identical vowels appear within a word.

| | |
|---|---|
| crees | cr*e*s |
| Teherán | T*e*-rán |
| coordinación | c*o*r-di-na-ción |

- When the final consonant of a word and the initial consonant of the following word are the same, they are pronounced as one consonant with slightly longer than normal duration.

| | |
|---|---|
| el lado | e-*l*a-do |
| Carlos salta | Car-lo-*s*al-ta |
| tienes sed | tie-ne-*s*ed |

## Intonation

Intonation is the rise and fall of pitch in the delivery of a phrase or a sentence. In general, Spanish pitch tends to change less than English, giving the impression that the language is less emphatic.

As a rule, the intonation for normal statements in Spanish starts in a low tone, rises to a higher one on the first stressed syllable, maintains that tone until the last stressed syllable, and then goes back to the initial low tone, with still another drop at the very end.

| | |
|---|---|
| Tu amigo viene mañana. | José come pan. |
| Ada está en casa. | Carlos toma café. |

## Syllable Formation in Spanish

General rules for dividing words into syllables:

### Vowels

- A vowel or a vowel combination can constitute a syllable.

a-lum-no     a-bue-la     Eu-ro-pa

- Diphthongs and triphthongs are considered single vowels and cannot be divided.

bai-le     puen-te     Dia-na     es-tu-diáis     an-ti-guo

- Two strong vowels (**a, e, o**) do not form a diphthong and are separated into two syllables.

  em-ple-ar  vol-te-ar  lo-a

- A written accent on a weak vowel (**i** or **u**) breaks the diphthong, separating the vowels into two syllables.

  trí-o  dú-o  Ma-rí-a

### Consonants

- A single consonant forms a syllable with the vowel that follows it.

  po-der  ma-no  mi-nu-to

  NOTE: Spanish **ch, ll,** and **rr** are considered single consonants: **a-ma-ri-llo, co-che, pe-rro.**

- When two consonants appear between two vowels, they are separated into two syllables.

  al-fa-be-to  cam-pe-ón  me-ter-se  mo-les-tia

  EXCEPTION: When a consonant cluster composed of **b, c, d, f, g, p,** or **t** with **l** or **r** appears between two vowels, the cluster joins the following vowel: **so-bre, o-tros, ca-ble, te-lé-gra-fo.**

- When three consonants appear between two vowels, only the last one goes with the following vowel.

  ins-pec-tor  trans-por-te  trans-for-mar

  EXCEPTION: When there is a cluster of three consonants in the combinations described in rule 2, the first consonant joins the preceding vowel and the cluster joins the following vowel: **es-cri-bir, ex-tran-je-ro, im-plo-rar, es-tre-cho.**

## Accentuation

In Spanish, all words are stressed according to specific rules. Words that do not follow the rules must have a written accent to indicate the change of stress. The basic rules for accentuation are as follows.

- Words ending in a vowel, **n,** or **s** are stressed on the next-to-last syllable.

  | | | | |
  |---|---|---|---|
  | **hi**-jo | **ca**-lle | **me**-sa | fa-**mo**-sos |
  | flo-**re**-cen | **pla**-ya | **ve**-ces | |

- Words ending in a consonant, except **n** or **s,** are stressed on the last syllable.

  ma-**yor**  a-**mor**  tro-pi-**cal**  na-**riz**  re-**loj**  co-rre-**dor**

- All words that do not follow these rules must have the written accent.

  | | | | |
  |---|---|---|---|
  | ca-**fé** | **lá**-piz | **mú**-si-ca | sa-**lón** |
  | **án**-gel | **lí**-qui-do | fran-**cés** | **Víc**-tor |
  | sim-**pá**-ti-co | rin-**cón** | a-**zú**-car | de-**mó**-cra-ta |
  | sa-**lió** | **dé**-bil | e-**xá**-me-nes | |

- Pronouns and adverbs of interrogation and exclamation have a written accent to distinguish them from relative pronouns.

  | | |
  |---|---|
  | ¿**Qué** comes? | *What are you eating?* |
  | La pera que él no comió. | *The pear that he did not eat.* |

| | |
|---|---|
| **¿Quién** está ahí? | *Who is there?* |
| El hombre a quien tú llamaste. | *The man whom you called.* |
| **¿Dónde** está él? | *Where is he?* |
| En el lugar donde trabaja. | *At the place where he works.* |

- Words that have the same spelling but different meanings take a written accent to differentiate one from the other.

| | | | | | | | |
|---|---|---|---|---|---|---|---|
| el | *the* | él | *he, him* | te | *you* | té | *tea* |
| mi | *my* | mí | *me* | si | *if* | sí | *yes* |
| tu | *your* | tú | *you* | mas | *but* | más | *more* |

# Appendix B Verbs

## Regular Verbs

### Model -ar, -er, -ir verbs

INFINITIVE

| | | |
|---|---|---|
| amar *(to love)* | comer *(to eat)* | vivir *(to live)* |

PRESENT PARTICIPLE

| | | |
|---|---|---|
| amando *(loving)* | comiendo *(eating)* | viviendo *(living)* |

PAST PARTICIPLE

| | | |
|---|---|---|
| amado *(loved)* | comido *(eaten)* | vivido *(lived)* |

**SIMPLE TENSES**

*Indicative Mood*

PRESENT

| *(I love)* | | *(I eat)* | | *(I live)* | |
|---|---|---|---|---|---|
| amo | amamos | como | comemos | vivo | vivimos |
| amas | amáis | comes | coméis | vives | vivís |
| ama | aman | come | comen | vive | viven |

IMPERFECT

| *(I used to love)* | | *(I used to eat)* | | *(I used to live)* | |
|---|---|---|---|---|---|
| amaba | amábamos | comía | comíamos | vivía | vivíamos |
| amabas | amabais | comías | comíais | vivías | vivíais |
| amaba | amaban | comía | comían | vivía | vivían |

PRETERIT

| *(I loved)* | | *(I ate)* | | *(I lived)* | |
|---|---|---|---|---|---|
| amé | amamos | comí | comimos | viví | vivimos |
| amaste | amasteis | comiste | comisteis | viviste | vivisteis |
| amó | amaron | comió | comieron | vivió | vivieron |

FUTURE

| *(I will love)* | | *(I will eat)* | | *(I will live)* | |
|---|---|---|---|---|---|
| amaré | amaremos | comeré | comeremos | viviré | viviremos |
| amarás | amaréis | comerás | comeréis | vivirás | viviréis |
| amará | amarán | comerá | comerán | vivirá | vivirán |

### CONDITIONAL

| *(I would love)* | | *(I would eat)* | | *(I would live)* | |
|---|---|---|---|---|---|
| amaría | amaríamos | comería | comeríamos | viviría | viviríamos |
| amarías | amaríais | comerías | comeríais | vivirías | viviríais |
| amaría | amarían | comería | comerían | viviría | vivirían |

## *Subjunctive Mood*

### PRESENT

| *([that] I [may] love)* | | *([that] I [may] eat)* | | *([that] I [may] live)* | |
|---|---|---|---|---|---|
| ame | amemos | coma | comamos | viva | vivamos |
| ames | améis | comas | comáis | vivas | viváis |
| ame | amen | coma | coman | viva | vivan |

### IMPERFECT (two forms: -ra, -se)

| *([that] I [might] love)* | *([that] I [might] eat)* | *([that] I [might] live)* |
|---|---|---|
| amara(-ase) | comiera(-iese) | viviera(-iese) |
| amaras(-ases) | comieras(-ieses) | vivieras(-ieses) |
| amara(-ase) | comiera(-iese) | viviera(-iese) |
| amáramos(-ásemos) | comiéramos(-iésemos) | viviéramos(-iésemos) |
| amarais(-aseis) | comierais(-ieseis) | vivierais(-ieseis) |
| amaran(-asen) | comieran(-iesen) | vivieran(-iesen) |

## *Imperative Mood*

| *(love)* | *(eat)* | *(live)* |
|---|---|---|
| ama (tú) | come (tú) | vive (tú) |
| ame (Ud.) | coma (Ud.) | viva (Ud.) |
| amemos (nosotros) | comamos (nosotros) | vivamos (nosotros) |
| amad (vosotros) | comed (vosotros) | vivid (vosotros) |
| amen (Uds.) | coman (Uds.) | vivan (Uds.) |

## COMPOUND TENSES

### PERFECT INFINITIVE

| | | |
|---|---|---|
| haber amado | haber comido | haber vivido |

### PERFECT PARTICIPLE

| | | |
|---|---|---|
| habiendo amado | habiendo comido | habiendo vivido |

## *Indicative Mood*

### PRESENT PERFECT

| *(I have loved)* | *(I have eaten)* | *(I have lived)* |
|---|---|---|
| he amado | he comido | he vivido |
| has amado | has comido | has vivido |
| ha amado | ha comido | ha vivido |
| hemos amado | hemos comido | hemos vivido |
| habéis amado | habéis comido | habéis vivido |
| han amado | han comido | han vivido |

### PLUPERFECT

| *(I had loved)* | *(I had eaten)* | *(I had lived)* |
|---|---|---|
| había amado | había comido | había vivido |
| habías amado | habías comido | habías vivido |
| había amado | había comido | había vivido |
| habíamos amado | habíamos comido | habíamos vivido |
| habíais amado | habíais comido | habíais vivido |
| habían amado | habían comido | habían vivido |

### FUTURE PERFECT

| *(I will have loved)* | *(I will have eaten)* | *(I will have lived)* |
|---|---|---|
| habré amado | habré comido | habré vivido |
| habrás amado | habrás comido | habrás vivido |
| habrá amado | habrá comido | habrá vivido |
| habremos amado | habremos comido | habremos vivido |
| habréis amado | habréis comido | habréis vivido |
| habrán amado | habrán comido | habrán vivido |

### CONDITIONAL PERFECT

| *(I would have loved)* | *(I would have eaten)* | *(I would have lived)* |
|---|---|---|
| habría amado | habría comido | habría vivido |
| habrías amado | habrías comido | habrías vivido |
| habría amado | habría comido | habría vivido |
| habríamos amado | habríamos comido | habríamos vivido |
| habríais amado | habríais comido | habríais vivido |
| habrían amado | habrían comido | habrían vivido |

## *Subjunctive Mood*

### PRESENT PERFECT

| *([that] I [may] have loved)* | *([that] I [may] have eaten)* | *([that] I [may] have lived)* |
|---|---|---|
| haya amado | haya comido | haya vivido |
| hayas amado | hayas comido | hayas vivido |
| haya amado | haya comido | haya vivido |
| hayamos amado | hayamos comido | hayamos vivido |
| hayáis amado | hayáis comido | hayáis vivido |
| hayan amado | hayan comido | hayan vivido |

### PLUPERFECT (two forms: -ra, -se)

| *([that] I [might] have loved)* | *([that] I [might] have eaten)* | *([that] I [might] have lived)* |
|---|---|---|
| hubiera(-iese) amado | hubiera(-iese) comido | hubiera(-iese) vivido |
| hubieras(-ieses) amado | hubieras(-ieses) comido | hubieras(-ieses) vivido |
| hubiera(-iese) amado | hubiera(-iese) comido | hubiera(-iese) vivido |
| hubiéramos(-iésemos) amado | hubiéramos(-iésemos) comido | hubiéramos(-iésemos) vivido |
| hubierais(-ieseis) amado | hubierais(-ieseis) comido | hubierais(-ieseis) vivido |
| hubieran(-iesen) amado | hubieran(-iesen) comido | hubieran(-iesen) vivido |

# Stem-Changing Verbs

## The -ar and -er stem-changing verbs

Stem-changing verbs are those that have a spelling change in the root of the verb. Stem-changing verbs that end in **-ar** and **-er** change the stressed vowel **e** to **ie,** and the stressed **o** to **ue.** These changes occur in all persons, except the first- and second-persons plural, of the present indicative, present subjunctive, and imperative.

| Infinitive | Indicative | Imperative | Subjunctive |
|---|---|---|---|
| **cerrar** | cierro | —— | cierre |
| *(to close)* | cierras | cierra | cierres |
| | cierra | cierre | cierre |
| | cerramos | cerremos | cerremos |
| | cerráis | cerrad | cerréis |
| | cierran | cierren | cierren |
| **perder** | pierdo | —— | pierda |
| *(to lose)* | pierdes | pierde | pierdas |
| | pierde | pierda | pierda |
| | perdemos | perdamos | perdamos |
| | perdéis | perded | perdáis |
| | pierden | pierdan | pierdan |
| **contar** | cuento | —— | cuente |
| *(to count;* | cuentas | cuenta | cuentes |
| *to tell)* | cuenta | cuente | cuente |
| | contamos | contemos | contemos |
| | contáis | contad | contéis |
| | cuentan | cuenten | cuenten |
| **volver** | vuelvo | —— | vuelva |
| *(to return)* | vuelves | vuelve | vuelvas |
| | vuelve | vuelva | vuelva |
| | volvemos | volvamos | volvamos |
| | volvéis | volved | volváis |
| | vuelven | vuelvan | vuelvan |

Verbs that follow the same pattern:

| | | | |
|---|---|---|---|
| acordarse | *to remember* | entender | *to understand* |
| acostar(se) | *to go to bed* | extender | *to stretch* |
| almorzar | *to have lunch* | llover | *to rain* |
| atravesar | *to go through* | mover | *to move* |
| cocer | *to cook* | mostrar | *to show* |
| colgar | *to hang* | negar | *to deny* |
| comenzar | *to begin* | nevar | *to snow* |
| confesar | *to confess* | pensar | *to think; to plan* |
| costar | *to cost* | probar | *to prove; to taste* |
| demostrar | *to demonstrate, show* | recordar | *to remember* |
| | | rogar | *to beg* |
| despertar(se) | *to wake up* | sentar(se) | *to sit down* |
| empezar | *to begin* | soler | *to be in the habit of* |
| encender | *to light; to turn on* | soñar | *to dream* |
| encontrar | *to find* | torcer | *to twist* |

## The -ir stem-changing verbs

There are two types of stem-changing verbs that end in **-ir:** one type changes stressed **e** to **ie** in some tenses and to **i** in others, and stressed **o** to **ue** or **u;** the second type changes stressed **e** to **i** only in all the irregular tenses.

### Type I: -ir: e > ie or i / o > ue or u

These changes occur as follows.

*Present Indicative:* All persons except the first- and second-persons plural change **e** to **ie** and **o** to **ue.** *Preterit:* Third-person singular and plural changes **e** to **i** and **o** to **u.** *Present Subjunctive:* All persons change **e** to **i** and **o** to **u.** *Imperfect Subjunctive:* All persons change **e** to **i** and **o** to **u.** *Imperative:* All persons except the first- and second-persons plural change **e** to **ie** and **o** to **ue;** first-person plural changes **e** to **i** and **o** to **u.** *Present Participle:* This form changes **e** to **i** and **o** to **u.**

| Infinitive | Indicative | | Imperative | Subjunctive | |
|---|---|---|---|---|---|
| | **PRESENT** | **PRETERIT** | | **PRESENT** | **IMPERFECT** |
| sentir *(to feel)* | siento | sentí | | sienta | sintiera(-iese) |
| | sientes | sentiste | siente | sientas | sintieras |
| **PRESENT PARTICIPLE** | siente | sintió | sienta | sienta | sintiera |
| sintiendo | sentimos | sentimos | sintamos | sintamos | sintiéramos |
| | sentís | sentisteis | sentid | sintáis | sintierais |
| | sienten | sintieron | sientan | sientan | sintieran |
| dormir *(to sleep)* | duermo | dormí | | duerma | durmiera(-iese) |
| | duermes | dormiste | duerme | duermas | durmieras |
| **PRESENT PARTICIPLE** | duerme | durmió | duerma | duerma | durmiera |
| durmiendo | dormimos | dormimos | durmamos | durmamos | durmiéramos |
| | dormís | dormisteis | dormid | durmáis | durmierais |
| | duermen | durmieron | duerman | duerman | durmieran |

Other verbs that follow the same pattern:

| | | | |
|---|---|---|---|
| advertir | *to warm* | herir | *to wound, hurt* |
| arrepentirse | *to repent* | mentir | *to lie* |
| consentir | *to consent; to pamper* | morir | *to die* |
| convertir(se) | *to turn into* | preferir | *to prefer* |
| discernir | *to discern* | referir | *to refer* |
| divertir(se) | *to amuse oneself* | sugerir | *to suggest* |

### Type II: -ir: e > i

The verbs in the second category are irregular in the same tenses as those of the first type. The only difference is that they have only one change: **e > i** in all irregular persons.

| Infinitive | Indicative | | Imperative | Subjunctive | |
|---|---|---|---|---|---|
| pedir *(to ask for, request)* | PRESENT | PRETERIT | | PRESENT | IMPERFECT |
| | pido | pedí | | pida | pidiera(-iese) |
| **PRESENT** | pides | pediste | pide | pidas | pidieras |
| **PARTICIPLE** | pide | pidió | pida | pida | pidiera |
| p*i*diendo | pedimos | pedimos | pidamos | pidamos | pidiéramos |
| | pedís | pedisteis | pedid | pidáis | pidierais |
| | piden | pidieron | pidan | pidan | pidieran |

Verbs that follow this pattern:

| | | | |
|---|---|---|---|
| concebir | *to conceive* | repetir | *to repeat* |
| competir | *to compete* | reñir | *to fight* |
| despedir(se) | *to say good-bye* | seguir | *to follow* |
| elegir | *to choose* | servir | *to serve* |
| impedir | *to prevent* | vestir(se) | *to dress* |
| perseguir | *to pursue* | | |

# Orthographic-Changing Verbs

Some verbs undergo a change in the spelling of the stem in some tenses in order to maintain the sound of the final consonant. The most common ones are those with the consonants **g** and **c**. Remember that **g** and **c** in front of **e** or **i** have a soft sound, and in front of **a**, **o**, or **u** have a hard sound. In order to keep the soft sound in front of **a**, **o**, or **u**, **g** and **c** change to **j** and **z**, respectively. In order to keep the hard sound of **g** or **c** in front of **e** and **i**, **u** is added to the **g** (**gu**) and the **c** changes to **qu**. The most important verbs that are regular in all the tenses but change in spelling are the following.

1. Verbs ending in **-gar** change **g** to **gu** before **e** in the first person of the preterit and in all persons of the present subjunctive.

   **pagar** *to pay*
   *Preterit:* pa**gu**é, pagaste, pagó, etc.
   *Pres. Subj.:* pa**gu**e, pa**gu**es, pa**gu**e, pa**gu**emos, pa**gu**éis, pa**gu**en
   Verbs that follow the same pattern: **colgar, llegar, navegar, negar, regar, rogar, jugar.**

2. Verbs ending in **-ger** or **-gir** change **g** to **j** before **o** and **a** in the first person of the present indicative and in all the persons of the present subjunctive.

   **proteger** *to protect*
   *Pres. Ind.:* prote**j**o, proteges, protege, etc.
   *Pres. Subj.:* prote**j**a, prote**j**as, prote**j**a, prote**j**amos, prote**j**áis, prote**j**an
   Verbs that follow the same pattern: **coger, corregir, dirigir, elegir, escoger, exigir, recoger.**

3. Verbs ending in **-guar** change **gu** to **gü** before **e** in the first person of the preterit and in all persons of the present subjunctive.

   **averiguar** *to find out*
   *Preterit:* averi**gü**é, averiguaste, averiguó, etc.
   *Pres. Subj.:* averi**gü**e, averi**gü**es, averi**gü**e, averi**gü**emos, averi**gü**éis, averi**gü**en
   The verb **apaciguar** follows the same pattern.

4. Verbs ending in **-guir** change **gu** to **g** before **o** and **a** in the first person of the present indicative and in all persons of the present subjunctive.

**conseguir** *to get*
*Pres. Ind.:* consigo, consigues, consigue, etc.
*Pres. Subj.:* consiga, consigas, consiga, consigamos, consigáis, consigan
Verbs that follow the same pattern: **distinguir, perseguir, proseguir, seguir.**

5. Verbs ending in **-car** change **c** to **qu** before **e** in the first person of the preterit and in all persons of the present subjunctive.

**tocar** *to touch; to play (a musical instrument)*
*Preterit:* toqué, tocaste, tocó, etc.
*Pres. Subj.:* toque, toques, toque, toquemos, toquéis, toquen
Verbs that follow the same pattern: **atacar, buscar, comunicar, explicar, indicar, pescar, sacar.**

6. Verbs ending in **-cer** or **-cir** preceded by a consonant change **c** to **z** before **o** and **a** in the first person of the present indicative and in all persons of the present subjunctive.

**torcer** *to twist*
*Pres. Ind.:* tuerzo, tuerces, tuerce, etc.
*Pres. Subj.:* tuerza, tuerzas, tuerza, torzamos, torzáis, tuerzan
Verbs that follow the same pattern: **convencer, esparcir, vencer.**

7. Verbs ending in **-cer** or **-cir** preceded by a vowel change **c** to **zc** before **o** and **a** in the first person of the present indicative and in all persons of the present subjunctive.

**conocer** *to know, be acquainted with*
*Pres. Ind.:* conozco, conoces, conoce, etc.
*Pres. Subj.:* conozca, conozcas, conozca, conozcamos, conozcáis, conozcan
Verbs that follow the same pattern: **agradecer, aparecer, carecer, entristecer** *(to sadden),* **establecer, lucir, nacer, obedecer, ofrecer, padecer, parecer, pertenecer, reconocer, relucir.**

8. Verbs ending in **-zar** change **z** to **c** before **e** in the first person of the preterit and in all persons of the present subjunctive.

**rezar** *to pray*
*Preterit:* recé, rezaste, rezó, etc.
*Pres. Subj.:* rece, reces, rece, recemos, recéis, recen
Verbs that follow the same pattern: **abrazar, alcanzar, almorzar, comenzar, cruzar, empezar, forzar, gozar.**

9. Verbs ending in **-eer** change the unstressed **i** to **y** between vowels in the third-persons singular and plural of the preterit, in all persons of the imperfect subjunctive, and in the present participle.

**creer** *to believe*
*Pres. Part:* creyendo
*Preterit:* creí, creíste, creyó, creímos, creísteis, creyeron
*Imp. Subj.:* creyera(-ese), creyeras, creyera, creyéramos, creyerais, creyeran
*Past Part.:* creído
Verbs that follow the same pattern: **leer, poseer.**

10. Verbs ending in **-uir** change the unstressed **i** to **y** between vowels (except **-quir,** which has the silent **u**) in the following tenses and persons.

**huir** *to escape, flee*
*Pres. Part.:* huyendo
*Pres. Ind.:* huyo, huyes, huye, huimos, huís, huyen
*Preterit:* huí, huiste, huyó, huimos, huisteis, huyeron
*Imperative:* huye, huya, huyamos, huid, huyan

*Pres. Subj.:* huya, huyas, huya, huyamos, huyáis, huyan
*Imp. Subj.:* huyera(-ese), huyeras, huyera, huyéramos, huyerais, huyeran
Verbs that follow the same pattern: **atribuir, concluir, constituir, construir, contribuir, destituir, destruir, disminuir, distribuir, excluir, incluir, influir, instruir, restituir, sustituir.**

**11.** Verbs ending in **-eír** lose the **e** in the third-person singular and plural of the preterit, in all persons of the imperfect subjunctive, and in the present participle.

**reír** *to laugh*
*Pres Ind.:* río, ríes, ríe, reímos, reís, ríen
*Preterit:* reí, reíste, rio, reímos, reísteis, rieron
*Pres. Subj.:* ría, rías, ría, riamos, riáis, rían
*Imp. Subj.:* riera(-ese), rieras, riera, riéramos, rierais, rieran
*Pres. Part.:* riendo
Verbs that follow the same pattern: **freír, sonreír.**

**12.** Verbs ending in **-iar** add a written accent to the **i,** except in the first- and second-persons plural of the present indicative and subjunctive.

**fiar**(se) *to trust*
*Pres. Ind.:* (me) fío, (te) fías, (se) fía, (nos) fiamos, (os) fiáis, (se) fían
*Pres. Subj.:* (me) fíe, (te) fíes, (se) fíe, (nos) fiemos, (os) fiéis, (se) fíen
Verbs that follow the same pattern: **ampliar, criar, desviar, enfriar, enviar, guiar, telegrafiar, vaciar, variar.**

**13.** Verbs ending in **-uar** (except **-guar**) add a written accent to the **u,** except in the first- and second-persons plural of the present indicative and subjunctive.

**actuar** *to act*
*Pres. Ind.:* actúo, actúas, actúa, actuamos, actuáis, actúan
*Pres. Subj.:* actúe, actúes, actúe, actuemos, actuéis, actúen
Verbs that follow the same pattern: **acentuar, continuar, efectuar, exceptuar, graduar, habituar, insinuar, situar.**

**14.** Verbs ending in **-ñir** lose the **i** of the diphthongs **ie** and **ió** in the third person singular and plural of the preterit and all persons of the imperfect subjunctive. They also change the **e** of the stem to **i** in the same persons in the present indicative and present subjunctive.

**teñir** *to dye*
*Pres. Ind.:* tiño, tiñes, tiñe, teñimos, teñís, tiñen
*Preterit:* teñí, teñiste, tiñó, teñimos, teñisteis, tiñeron
*Pres. Subj.:* tiña, tiñas, tiña, tiñamos, tiñáis, tiñan
*Imp. Subj.:* tiñera(-ese), tiñeras, tiñera, tiñéramos, tiñerais, tiñeran
Verbs that follow the same pattern: **ceñir, constreñir, desteñir, estreñir, reñir.**

# Some Common Irregular Verbs

Only those tenses with irregular forms are given below.

**adquirir** *to acquire*
*Pres. Ind.:* adquiero, adquieres, adquiere, adquirimos, adquirís, adquieren
*Pres. Subj.:* adquiera, adquieras, adquiera, adquiramos, adquiráis, adquieran
*Imperative:* adquiere, adquiera, adquiramos, adquirid, adquieran

**andar** *to walk*
*Preterit:* anduve, anduviste, anduvo, anduvimos, anduvisteis, anduvieron
*Imp. Subj.:* anduviera (anduviese), anduvieras, anduviera, anduviéramos, anduvierais, anduvieran

**avergonzarse** *to be ashamed, to be embarrassed*
*Pres. Ind.:* me avergüenzo, te avergüenzas, se avergüenza, nos avergonzamos, os avergonzáis, se avergüenzan
*Pres. Subj:* me avergüence, te avergüences, se avergüence, nos avergoncemos, os avergoncéis, se avergüencen
*Imperative:* avergüénzate, avergüéncese, avergoncémonos, avergonzaos, avergüéncense

**caber** *to fit, to have enough room*
*Pres. Ind.:* quepo, cabes, cabe cabemos, cabéis, caben
*Preterit:* cupe, cupiste, cupo, cupimos, cupisteis, cupieron
*Future:* cabré, cabrás, cabrá, cabremos, cabréis, cabrán
*Conditional:* cabría, cabrías, cabría, cabríamos, cabríais, cabrían
*Imperative:* cabe, quepa, quepamos, cabed, quepan
*Pres. Subj.:* quepa, quepas, quepa, quepamos, quepáis, quepan
*Imp. Subj.:* cupiera (cupiese), cupieras, cupiera, cupiéramos, cupierais, cupieran

**caer** *to fall*
*Pres. Ind.:* caigo, caes, cae, caemos, caéis, caen
*Preterit:* caí, caíste, cayó, caímos, caísteis, cayeron
*Imperative:* cae, caiga, caigamos, caed, caigan
*Pres. Subj.:* caiga, caigas, caiga, caigamos, caigáis, caigan
*Imp. Subj.:* cayera (cayese), cayeras, cayera, cayéramos, cayerais, cayeran
*Past Part.:* caído

**conducir** *to guide, to drive*
*Pres. Ind.:* conduzco, conduces, conduce, conducimos, conducís, conducen
*Preterit:* conduje, condujiste, condujo, condujimos, condujisteis, condujeron
*Imperative:* conduce, conduzca, conduzcamos, conducid, conduzcan
*Pres. Subj.:* conduzca, conduzcas, conduzca, conduzcamos, conduzcáis, conduzcan
*Imp. Subj.:* condujera (condujese), condujeras, condujera, condujéramos, condujerais, condujeran
(All verbs ending in **-ducir** follow this pattern.)

**convenir** *to agree (see* **venir***)*

**dar** *to give*
*Pres. Ind.:* doy, das, da, damos, dais, dan
*Preterit:* di, diste, dio, dimos, disteis, dieron
*Imperative:* da, dé, demos, dad, den
*Pres. Subj.:* dé, des, dé, demos, deis, den
*Imp. Subj.:* diera (diese), dieras, diera, diéramos, dierais, dieran

**decir** *to say, tell*
*Pres. Ind.:* digo, dices, dice, decimos, decís, dicen
*Preterit:* dije, dijiste, dijo, dijimos, dijisteis, dijeron
*Future:* diré, dirás, dirá, diremos, diréis, dirán
*Conditional:* diría, dirías, diría, diríamos, diríais, dirían
*Imperative:* di, diga, digamos, decid, digan
*Pres. Subj.:* diga, digas, diga, digamos, digáis, digan
*Imp. Subj.:* dijera (dijese), dijeras, dijera, dijéramos, dijerais, dijeran
*Pres. Part.:* diciendo
*Past Part.:* dicho

**detener** *to stop; to hold; to arrest (see* **tener***)*

**entretener** *to entertain, amuse (see* **tener***)*

**errar** *to err; to miss*
*Pres. Ind.:* yerro, yerras, yerra, erramos, erráis, yerran
*Imperative:* yerra, yerre, erremos, errad, yerren
*Pres. Subj.:* yerre, yerres, yerre, erremos, erréis, yerren

**estar** *to be*
*Pres. Ind.:* estoy, estás, está, estamos, estáis, están
*Preterit:* estuve, estuviste, estuvo, estuvimos, estuvisteis, estuvieron
*Imperative:* está, esté, estemos, estad, estén
*Pres. Subj.:* esté, estés, esté, estemos, estéis, estén
*Imp. Subj.:* estuviera (estuviese), estuvieras, estuviera, estuviéramos, estuvierais, estuvieran

**haber** *to have*
*Pres. Ind.:* he, has, ha, hemos, habéis, han
*Preterit:* hube, hubiste, hubo, hubimos, hubisteis, hubieron
*Future:* habré, habrás, habrá, habremos, habréis, habrán
*Conditional:* habría, habrías, habría, habríamos, habríais, habrían
*Pres. Subj.:* haya, hayas, haya, hayamos, hayáis, hayan
*Imp. Subj.:* hubiera (hubiese), hubieras, hubiera, hubiéramos, hubierais, hubieran

**hacer** *to do, to make*
*Pres. Ind.:* hago, haces, hace, hacemos, hacéis, hacen
*Preterit:* hice, hiciste, hizo, hicimos, hicisteis, hicieron
*Future:* haré, harás, hará, haremos, haréis, harán
*Imperative:* haz, haga, hagamos, haced, hagan
*Pres. Subj.:* haga, hagas, haga, hagamos, hagáis, hagan
*Imp. Subj.:* hiciera (hiciese), hicieras, hiciera, hiciéramos, hicierais, hicieran
*Past Part.:* hecho

**imponer** *to impose; to depose (see* **poner***)*

**ir** *to go*
*Pres. Ind.:* voy, vas, va, vamos, vais, van
*Imp. Ind.:* iba, ibas, iba, íbamos, ibais, iban
*Preterit:* fui, fuiste, fue, fuimos, fuisteis, fueron
*Imperative:* ve, vaya, vayamos, id, vayan
*Pres. Subj.:* vaya, vayas, vaya, vayamos, vayáis, vayan
*Imp. Subj.:* fuera (fuese), fueras, fuera, fuéramos, fuerais, fueran

**jugar** *to play*
*Pres. Ind.:* juego, juegas, juega, jugamos, jugáis, juegan
*Imperative:* juega, juegue, juguemos, jugad, jueguen
*Pres. Subj.:* juegue, juegues, juegue, juguemos, juguéis, jueguen

**obtener** *to obtain (see* **tener***)*

**oír** *to hear*
*Pres. Ind.:* oigo, oyes, oye, oímos, oís, oyen
*Preterit:* oí, oíste, oyó, oímos, oísteis, oyeron
*Imperative:* oye, oiga, oigamos, oíd, oigan
*Pres. Subj.:* oiga, oigas, oiga, oigamos, oigáis, oigan
*Imp. Subj.:* oyera (oyese), oyeras, oyera, oyéramos, oyerais, oyeran
*Pres. Part.:* oyendo
*Past Part.:* oído

**oler** *to smell*
*Pres. Ind.:* huelo, hueles, huele, olemos, oléis, huelen
*Imperative:* huele, huela, olamos, oled, huelan
*Pres. Subj.:* huela, huelas, huela, olamos, oláis, huelan

**poder** *to be able to*
*Preterit:* pude, pudiste, pudo, pudimos, pudisteis, pudieron
*Future:* podré, podrás, podrá, podremos, podréis, podrán

*Conditional:* podría, podrías, podría, podríamos, podríais, podrían
*Imperative:* puede, pueda, podamos, poded, puedan
*Pres. Subj.:* pueda, puedas, pueda, podamos, podáis, puedan
*Imp. Subj.:* pudiera (pudiese), pudieras, pudiera, pudiéramos, pudierais, pudieran
*Pres. Part.:* pudiendo

**poner** *to place, put*
*Pres. Ind.:* pongo, pones, pone, ponemos, ponéis, ponen
*Preterit:* puse, pusiste, puso, pusimos, pusisteis, pusieron
*Future:* pondré, pondrás, pondrá, pondremos, pondréis, pondrán
*Conditional:* pondría, pondrías, pondría, pondríamos, pondríais, pondrían
*Imperative:* pon, ponga, pongamos, poned, pongan
*Pres. Subj.:* ponga, pongas, ponga, pongamos, pongáis, pongan
*Imp. Subj.:* pusiera (pusiese), pusieras, pusiera, pusiéramos, pusierais, pusieran
*Past Part.:* puesto

**querer** *to want, wish; to like, love*
*Preterit:* quise, quisiste, quiso, quisimos, quisisteis, quisieron
*Future:* querré, querrás, querrá, querremos, querréis, querrán
*Conditional:* querría, querrías, querría, querríamos, querríais, querrían
*Imp. Subj.:* quisiera (quisiese), quisieras, quisiera, quisiéramos, quisierais, quisieran

**resolver** *to decide on, to solve*
*Past Part.:* resuelto

**saber** *to know*
*Pres. Ind.:* sé, sabes, sabe, sabemos, sabéis, saben
*Preterit:* supe, supiste, supo, supimos, supisteis, supieron
*Future:* sabré, sabrás, sabrá, sabremos, sabréis, sabrán
*Conditional:* sabría, sabrías, sabría, sabríamos, sabríais, sabrían
*Imperative:* sabe, sepa, sepamos, sabed, sepan
*Pres. Subj.:* sepa, sepas, sepa, sepamos, sepáis, sepan
*Imp. Subj.:* supiera (supiese), supieras, supiera, supiéramos, supierais, supieran

**salir** *to leave; to go out*
*Pres. Ind.:* salgo, sales, sale, salimos, salís, salen
*Future:* saldré, saldrás, saldrá, saldremos, saldréis, saldrán
*Conditional:* saldría, saldrías, saldría, saldríamos, saldríais, saldrían
*Imperative:* sal, salga, salgamos, salid, salgan
*Pres. Subj.:* salga, salgas, salga, salgamos, salgáis, salgan

**ser** *to be*
*Pres. Ind.:* soy, eres, es, somos, sois, son
*Imp. Ind.:* era, eras, era, éramos, erais, eran
*Preterit:* fui, fuiste, fue, fuimos, fuisteis, fueron
*Imperative:* sé, sea, seamos, sed, sean
*Pres. Subj.:* sea, seas, sea, seamos, seáis, sean
*Imp. Subj.:* fuera (fuese), fueras, fuera, fuéramos, fuerais, fueran

**suponer** *to assume, to suppose (see* **poner***)*

**tener** *to have*
*Pres. Ind.:* tengo, tienes, tiene, tenemos, tenéis, tienen
*Preterit:* tuve, tuviste, tuvo, tuvimos, tuvisteis, tuvieron
*Future:* tendré, tendrás, tendrá, tendremos, tendréis, tendrán
*Conditional:* tendría, tendrías, tendría, tendríamos, tendríais, tendrían
*Imperative:* ten, tenga, tengamos, tened, tengan
*Pres. Subj.:* tenga, tengas, tenga, tengamos, tengáis, tengan
*Imp. Subj.:* tuviera (tuviese), tuvieras, tuviera, tuviéramos, tuvierais, tuvieran

**traducir** *to translate (see* **conducir***)*

**traer** *to bring*
*Pres. Ind.:* traigo, traes, trae, traemos, traéis, traen
*Preterit:* traje, trajiste, trajo, trajimos, trajisteis, trajeron
*Imperative:* trae, traiga, traigamos, traed, traigan
*Pres. Subj.:* traiga, traigas, traiga, traigamos, traigáis, traigan
*Imp. Subj.:* trajera (trajese), trajeras, trajera, trajéramos, trajerais, trajeran
*Pres. Part.:* trayendo
*Past Part.:* traído

**valer** *to be worth*
*Pres. Ind.:* valgo, vales, vale, valemos, valéis, valen
*Future:* valdré, valdrás, valdrá, valdremos, valdréis, valdrán
*Conditional:* valdría, valdrías, valdría, valdríamos, valdríais, valdrían
*Imperative:* vale, valga, valgamos, valed, valgan
*Pres. Sub.:* valga, valgas, valga, valgamos, valgáis, valgan

**venir** *to come*
*Pres. Ind.:* vengo, vienes, viene, venimos, venís, vienen
*Preterit:* vine, viniste, vino, vinimos, vinisteis, vinieron
*Future:* vendré, vendrás, vendrá, vendremos, vendréis, vendrán
*Conditional:* vendría, vendrías, vendría, vendríamos, vendríais, vendrían
*Imperative:* ven, venga, vengamos, venid, vengan
*Pres. Subj.:* venga, vengas, venga, vengamos, vengáis, vengan
*Imp. Subj.:* viniera (viniese), vinieras, viniera, viniéramos, vinierais, vinieran
*Pres. Part.:* viniendo

**ver** *to see*
*Pres. Ind.:* veo, ves, ve, vemos, veis, ven
*Imp. Ind.:* veía, veías, veía, veíamos, veíais, veían
*Preterit:* vi, viste, vio, vimos, visteis, vieron
*Imperative:* ve, vea, veamos, ved, vean
*Pres. Subj.:* vea, veas, vea, veamos, veáis, vean
*Imp. Subj.:* viera (viese), vieras, viera, viéramos, vierais, vieran
*Past Part.:* visto

**volver** *to return*
*Past Part.:* vuelto

# Appendix C Glossary of Grammatical Terms

**adjective:** A word that is used to describe a noun: *tall* girl, *difficult* lesson.

**adverb:** A word that modifies a verb, an adjective, or another adverb. It answers the questions "How?" "When?" "Where?": She walked *slowly.* She'll be here *tomorrow.* She is *here.*

**agreement:** A term applied to changes in form that nouns cause in the words that surround them. In Spanish, verb forms agree with their subjects in person and number (**yo** habl**o**, **él** habl**a**, etc.). Spanish adjectives agree in gender and number with the noun they describe. Thus, a feminine plural noun requires a feminine plural ending in the adjective that describes it (cas**as** amarill**as**) and a masculine singular noun requires a masculine singular ending in the adjective (libr**o** negr**o**).

**auxiliary verb:** A verb that helps in the conjugation of another verb: I *have* finished. He *was* called. She *will* go. He *would* eat.

**command form:** The form of the verb used to give an order or a direction: *Go! Come* back! *Turn* to the right!

**conjugation:** The process by which the forms of the verb are presented in their different moods and tenses: I *am,* you *are,* he *is,* she *was,* we *were,* etc.

**contraction:** The combination of two or more words into one: *isn't, don't, can't.*

**definite article:** A word used before a noun indicating a definite person or thing: *the* woman, *the* money.

**demonstrative:** A word that refers to a definite person or object: *this, that, these, those.*

**diphthong:** A combination of two vowels forming one syllable. In Spanish, a diphthong is composed of one *strong* vowel (**a, e, o**) and one *weak* vowel (**u, i**) or two weak vowels: **ei, ua, ui.**

**exclamation:** A word used to express emotion: *How* strong! *What* beauty!

**gender:** A distinction of nouns, pronouns, and adjectives, based on whether they are masculine or feminine.

**indefinite article:** A word used before a noun that refers to an indefinite person or object: *a* child, *an* apple.

**infinitive:** The form of the verb generally preceded in English by the word *to* and showing no subject or number: *to do, to bring.*

**interrogative:** A word used in asking a question: *Who? What? Where?*

**main clause:** A group of words that includes a subject and a verb and by itself has complete meaning: *They saw me. I go now.*

**noun:** A word that names a person, place, or thing: *Ann, London, pencil.*

**number:** Refers to singular and plural: *chair, chairs.*

**object:** Generally a noun or a pronoun that is the receiver of the verb's action. A direct object answers the question *"What?"* or *"Whom?":* We know *her.* Take *it.* An indirect object answers the question *"To whom?"* or *"To what?":* Give *John* the money. Nouns and pronouns can also be objects of prepositions: The letter is *from Rick.* I'm thinking *about you.*

**past participle:** Past forms of a verb: *gone, worked, written.*

**person:** The form of the pronoun and of the verb that shows the person referred to: *I* (first-person singular), *you* (second-person singular), *she* (third-person singular), and so on.

**possessive:** A word that denotes ownership or possession: This is *our* house. The book isn't *mine.*

**preposition:** A word that introduces a noun or pronoun and indicates its function in the sentence: They were *with* us. She is *from* Nevada.

**present participle:** A verb form in English that ends in *-ing: eating, sleeping, working.* In Spanish, this form cannot be used as a noun or after a preposition.

**pronoun:** A word that is used to replace a noun: *she, them, us,* and so on. A **subject pronoun** refers to the person or thing spoken of: *They* work. An **object pro-**

**noun** receives the action of the verb: They arrested *us* (direct object pronoun). She spoke to *him* (indirect object pronoun). A pronoun can also be the object of a preposition: The children stayed with *us*.

**reflexive pronoun:** A pronoun that refers back to the subject: *myself, yourself, himself, herself, itself, ourselves,* and so on.

**subject:** The person, place, or thing spoken of: *Robert* works. *Our car* is new.

**subordinate clause:** A clause that has no complete meaning by itself but depends on a main clause: They knew *that I was here*.

**tense:** The group of forms in a verb that show the time in which the action of the verb takes place: *I go* (present indicative), *I'm going* (present progressive), *I went* (past), *I was going* (past progressive), *I will go* (future), *I would go* (conditional), *I have gone* (present perfect), *I had gone* (past perfect), *that I may go* (present subjunctive), and so on.

**verb:** A word that expresses an action or a state: We *sleep*. The baby *is* sick.

# Appendix D English Translations of Opening Passages

## Lección 1

*NICE TO MEET YOU!*

Good morning! My name is Juan Carlos Mirabal and I am from California. I'm a student at the University of California. And you? Where are you from?

Good afternoon! My name is Laura Estévez and I am from Arizona. What is your name? Are you a student? I'm a teacher.

Hello! My name is Maria Luisa Vargas Peña and I am from New Mexico. I'm a secretary. And my name is Marcos Fuentes and I'm from Texas. I'm a systems analyst. Are you students?

How is it going? My name is Marisa Barrios and I am Mexican. I'm a dentist. Are you American?

Good evening! My name is Rafael Hernández and I am from Texas. I'm a pilot. How are you (all)? Fine?

My name is Beatriz López and I am from Puerto Rico. I am a Spanish teacher. How are you? What's new?

See you later!
See you tomorrow!
See you Monday!
Good-Bye!
Bye!

## Lección 2

*THE FIRST DAY OF CLASSES*

MISS A. *(At the door)* Excuse me. Good morning, professor.
PROF. Good morning. Come in and have a seat, please.
MISS A. Thank you very much.
PROF. Miss Alba, (this is) Dr. Díaz.
MISS A. It's a pleasure, Dr. Díaz.
DR. D. The pleasure is mine, Miss Alba.
MISS A. Excuse me, professor, what time is it?
PROF. It's eleven thirty.
MISS A. At what time is the class today?
PROF. It's at three in the afternoon.

L. What's your address, Mario?
M. Ninety-eight Magnolia Street.
L. Oh, I also need Pedro's address. He is Rocío's friend, isn't he?
M. Yes. The address is one hundred seventy-five Olmos Avenue.
R. Mario, how many students are there in the class?
M. There are forty students.

S. Professor, how do you say *"de nada"* in English?
PROF. You say, "You're welcome."
S. What does "to return" mean?
PROF. It means *"regresar."*

L. Do you work, Daniel?
D. Yes, I work at a hospital. And you?
L. I don't work; I only study.
D. How many classes are you taking?
L. I'm taking five classes. Listen, are you taking French this semester?
D. No, because I already speak French. I'm taking a German class with Dr. Smith.
L. I don't speak French, but I speak a little Italian and Portuguese.

## Lección 3

*ON THE PHONE*

*Raquel, Pedro, Marisa, and Carmen are university students who live in Los Angeles, and are very good friends. Raquel wants to be a doctor, Pedro wants to be a lawyer, and Marisa and Carmen want to be teachers. Pedro is dark, tall, and very charming. The girls are intelligent and pretty. Raquel wishes to speak with Pedro.*

M. Yes?
R. Hello. Is Pedro there?
M. No, he's not. I'm sorry.
R. What time is he coming back?
M. At nine o'clock at night.
R. Then I will call later.
M. Very well. Good-bye.

*Carmen speaks with her friend Marisa.*

M. Hello.
C. Hello. Is Marisa there?
M. Yes, speaking . . . Carmen?
C. Yes. How's it going, Marisa?
M. Very well, thank you. What's new?
C. Nothing. Listen! Where do we eat tomorrow? In the cafeteria?
M. No, tomorrow I have to write a report and I must read several articles in the library.
C. I also have to study for an exam.
M. Then we shall see each other on Tuesday.

*Pedro speaks with Raquel.*

RO. Hello.
P. Hello. Is Raquel there?
RO. Yes. Who is speaking?
P. Pedro Morales.
RO. One moment, please.
RA. *(To Rosa)* Who is it?
RO. It's your friend Pedro.
RA. Hi, Pedro. How's it going?
P. Fine, and you?
RA. So-so.
P. Why? Love problems?
RA. No, financial problems. I need money!
P. So do I! Listen, are you working at the hospital tonight?
RA. No, today I am not working at night. On Mondays my boyfriend and I study at the library.
P. Are you coming to my house tomorrow?
RA. No, because tomorrow I have to go to another hospital to apply for work.
RO. *(To Raquel)* Listen. What is your friend Pedro like? Is he handsome?
RA. Yes, and very intelligent, but . . . he has a girlfriend.

## Lección 4

| AN INVITATION |
|---|
| You are invited to a *New Year's Eve* party |
| At the home (address) of *Adela Benavente* |
| Street: *18 de Julio* Number: *923* |
| City: *Montevideo* |
| The party starts at *9:00 P.M.* |

BEFORE THE PARTY

A. Many of my classmates are going to come to my party. Are you going to bring your cousin?
H. Yes, and I'm also going to bring some compact discs and the *empanadas* that my Mom is going to prepare.
A. And we are going to prepare chicken, hors-d'oeuvres, and potato salad. Everything is going to be delicious!
H. Oh, Adela, I'm hungry now!
A. Do you want a sandwich? And, if you're thirsty, there's soda pop, beer, and mineral water.
H. Yes, I want a sandwich and a soda pop . . . No . . . I prefer a glass of water. Listen, what time does the dance start at the club?
A. At eleven. Are you going to call Julio and Teresa?
H. Yes, because they plan to go to the club with us. Today is Teresa's birthday.
A. Oh, yea? How old is she?
H. I think she turns twenty today. She's giving a party on Saturday and we are invited.

*Adela and her friends have a very good time at the party. They all dance, talk, eat, and drink. Afterwards, they go to the Yacht Club to celebrate the arrival of the new year. Julio is not going because he's sick.*

*At the Yacht Club*

H. The band is great. Shall we dance, Adela?
A. Not now, Humberto. I'm a little tired and I'm very hot. Why don't we go to the terrace?
H. Good idea. I'm going to take the drinks. Do you want champagne, cider, or (a) cocktail?
A. To toast, a glass of champagne, please. Afterwards, sangria . . .
J. Don't you have grapes? In Spain we always eat twelve grapes at midnight on the 31st of December.
A. No, Javier. We don't have grapes. It's twelve o'clock!
E. Happy new year! Happy new year!

### Lección 5

*PLANS FOR A WEEKEND*

*Carol, a student from the United States, is in Spain. She attends the University of Salamanca and lives in a boarding house near the Plaza Mayor. She wants to learn to speak Spanish perfectly, and that is why she never misses the opportunity to practice the language. Now she is talking with two Spanish friends at a sidewalk cafe. They are eating sandwiches and drinking coffee.*

L. Hey, Carol, can you go with us to Madrid this weekend?
CL. No, I can't . . . I have to write a lot of letters: to my grandmother, to my uncle, to my brother . . .
L. You miss your family very much, don't you?
CL. Yes, . . . especially my older brother.
CN. What is your brother like? Blond? Dark?
CL. He's blond, slim, and medium height. He is studying medicine.
CN. Very interesting! When is he coming to Spain? In the summer?
CL. No, he's going to travel to Mexico with his wife and two daughters.
CN. Bah! He's married . . . What a pity! Don't you have another brother?
CL. No, I'm sorry. I have here a photograph of my nieces.
CN. *(She looks at the photo.)* These are your nieces? They're very pretty!
CL. They start attending school on September fifteenth.
L. Listen! Why don't you come to Madrid with us? It's more interesting than writing letters . . .
CL. Are you going by car?
L. No, we prefer to go by bus. It's as comfortable as the car, it doesn't cost much, and we don't have to drive.
CL. Good idea! I never drive in Madrid. And where do you plan to go?
CN. To the Prado Museum. They have there some of the most famous paintings in the world.
L. It's very interesting! And Madrid has some very good restaurants! We always have lunch at Casa Botín; as far as I'm concerned it's the best of all.
CL. Okay. Let's go to Madrid! . . . If it doesn't rain! Because if it rains, I will not go.
CN. No, dear, it isn't going to rain.
CL. When do we return?
L. Saturday night or Sunday.
CL. Oh, Luis, Marisol's party is tomorrow. Where is it?
L. It's at her house. Do you want to go with me?
CL. Yes, we (will) go with you.
L. Great! Be ready at nine.

### Lección 6

*A TRIP TO PERU*

*Teresa, a Mexican teacher, is going to spend her vacation in Peru. She has just arrived in Lima, where she's planning to spend a few days before going to Machu Picchu to visit the famous Incan ruins. Teresa shows her passport and then goes through customs. In the airport, Teresa sees gold and silver objects, and buys some for her family.*

*Teresa goes to the tourist office in order to get information.*

T. Good morning, sir. I don't know Lima. Do you have a list of hotels and boarding houses?
E. Yes, Miss. Here it is.

*Teresa reads an ad about Hotel Bolívar.*

**Hotel Bolívar**

The best hotel in Lima, located downtown and near many places of interest, is the favorite of thousands of tourists who visit our beautiful capital. We have ample rooms overlooking the street and interior ones. All the rooms have private bathrooms, air conditioning, and television. The hotel has two restaurants that offer international meals and room service. We accept credit cards and traveler's checks. To make reservations, call 285-3946.

T. I wish to go to the Hotel Bolívar. Where can I find a taxi?
E. Go to the second door on the right. There is also a bus that takes you downtown.

*At the Hotel Bolívar, Teresa asks for a room.*

T. I need a single room with a private bathroom, please.
E. We have one overlooking the street that costs 208 soles per day. There's also another interior one on the second floor for 130 new soles.
T. They are rather expensive. Don't you have any cheaper rooms?
E. No, there isn't any. There are few vacant rooms now.
T. I prefer the interior room. What is the exchange rate?
E. I don't know . . . I am going to find out. Please sign here.

*Teresa signs the register.*

T. I want to have dinner in my room. Until what time do they serve dinner?
E. They serve it until eleven.
T. Can someone take my suitcases to the room, please?
E. Yes, the bellhop will come to take them right away. Here's the key.

*Since it is warm, Teresa decides to go to the swimming pool.*

## Lección 7

SPEAKING OF VACATIONS

*Teresa arrived yesterday from her trip to Peru, and now she is talking on the phone with her friend Silvia. The girls have been talking for a half hour, and Teresa is telling her about her trip.*

T. I liked the capital very much, but I liked Machu Picchu better.
S. And you didn't send me a postcard!
T. I bought you two, but I didn't send them. Listen, I have to return (to you) the suitcase and the carry-on bag that you lent me.
S. There is no hurry. Did you take a lot of luggage?
T. Yes, I took three suitcases. I paid excess baggage fees.
S. How much did the plane ticket cost you? Did you travel first class?
T. Are you crazy? I traveled in tourist class. It cost me three thousand five hundred pesos! Round-trip, of course . . .
S. How was the flight?
T. A little long . . . And since the plane left two hours behind schedule, we arrived very late.
S. Did anything interesting happen to you in Lima?
T. Well . . . at the travel agency where I bought the ticket to Machu Picchu, I met a very charming young man.
S. Did he travel with you? You have to tell me everything that happened.
T. Yes, I traveled with him by plane to Cuzco, where we had lunch together. Then we talked during the entire train ride to Machu Picchu.
S. I don't know why your vacations are always great and my vacations are so boring.
T. Then next time we have to travel together.
S. Okay, but only if we go by train or by boat. I don't like to travel by plane.
T. Okay, we'll travel by train. Listen, this Saturday, I'm going to the movies with Cecilia. Do you want to go with us?
S. Who is Cecilia?
T. She is the girl that I introduced to you at the library last month.
S. Oh, that one . . . I remember now. Yes, let's go together.
T. Do you want to go have lunch with me now?
S. No, thanks, I already had lunch.
T. Okay, then I'll see you tomorrow.

## Lección 8

AT A CUBAN RESTAURANT

*Today is December first. It's Lidia and Jorge Torres's wedding anniversary and to celebrate it they are going to dinner at one of the best restaurants in Miami. Now they arrive at the El Caribe Restaurant.*

L. What a surprise! This is a very elegant restaurant!
J. And the food is excellent.
W. This way, please. Here is the menu.
L. Thanks. *(She reads the menu.)*

| FOR DINNER | | | |
|---|---|---|---|
| (All dishes are served with the soup of the day and salad.) | | | |
| *Fish and shellfish* | | | |
| Lobster | $18.00 | Trout | $11.50 |
| Salmon | $14.50 | Shrimp | $11.00 |
| *Meat* | | | |
| Meatballs | $ 6.00 | Stuffed turkey | $10.00 |
| Steak | $12.00 | Fried chicken | $ 8.50 |
| Lamb | $13.00 | Chicken & rice | $ 6.00 |
| Roast pork | $17.00 | | |

J. Why don't you order a tenderloin steak? They prepare some delicious steaks here. Or lobster?
L. No, last night I went to dinner at the Ruiz's, and they served lobster.
W. I recommend to you the specialty of the house: roast pork and rice with black beans. For dessert, ice cream, caramel custard, or ice cream cake.
J. I want roast pork and rice with black beans. And you?
L. I want soup, shrimp, and rice.
J. To drink, bring us a vermouth and then a half bottle of red wine.
W. Very well, sir. *(He writes down the order.)*

*Before eating dinner, Lidia and Jorge drink vermouth and talk.*

L. Did your parents go to the party that Eva gave yesterday?
J. Yes. It was at the Los Violines Club.
L. Did they give her the gift (that) they bought for her in Mexico?
J. The bracelet? Yes, they gave it to her. She loved it.
L. Did they show it to you before they gave it to her?
J. Yes, they showed it to me when I went for them the day before yesterday in the afternoon.
L. They got it at a very good price in a very elegant store.

*After eating, Lidia and Jorge drink coffee. Jorge asks for the bill, pays it, leaves the waiter a good tip and they leave. They have tickets to see a comedy and, since it is raining cats and dogs, and the theater is far, they take a taxi.*

J. Happy anniversary, my love. *(He gives her a kiss.)*
L. *(She hugs him.)* Happy anniversary, dear.

## Lección 9

### A Very Busy Day

*Although today is Saturday, Mirta and Isabel got up early to finish cleaning the apartment. Tonight, the two girls are invited to a concert at the House of Paraguayan Culture. Isabel is a little tired because last night she went to bed late.*

M. Why did you come (home) so late last night? Where were you?
I. At the store. I had to buy a present for Eva because tomorrow is her birthday. Well, shall we start cleaning?
M. Yes, I'm going to sweep the kitchen and I'm going to vacuum the rug.
I. Then I'm going to clean the bathroom. Later I'm going to cook and iron my red dress. I'm going to wear it tonight.
M. I don't know what to wear.
I. Why don't you wear your blue dress? It's very pretty.
M. No, I tried it on yesterday and it doesn't fit. Oh! Where's the dustpan?
I. On the terrace. Oh! I need to bathe the dog, shower, and get dressed . . . and I have an appointment at the hairdresser's at three!
M. I want to wash my hair and I didn't remember to buy shampoo. May I use yours?
I. Yes, it's in the medicine cabinet.
M. Thanks. I couldn't go to the pharmacy yesterday.

*When she arrived at the beauty parlor, Isabel asked the hairdresser for a magazine and sat down to wait for her turn.*

I. *(To the hairdresser)* I want a haircut, shampoo, and set.
P. You have very straight hair. Don't you want a perm?
I. No, when I want curls, I use the curling iron. Oh, my hair is very long!
P. Short hair is in style now. *(He cuts her hair and, when he finishes, Isabel looks at herself in the mirror.)*

I. Very good! Now I want to make an appointment for my friend for next week.
P. Wednesday, February first, at nine-thirty? Generally, there are fewer people in the morning.
I. That's fine. My friend's name is Mirta Ortega.

*Isabel leaves her purse on the counter. The hairdresser calls her.*

P. Miss! Is this purse yours?
I. Yes, it's mine. Thank you.

## Lección 10

*SILVIA'S VACATION* Córdoba, Argentina
February 12, 2002

Dear Victoria,

I was wrong! I thought I wasn't going to like going on vacation with my parents and that I was going to be bored; however, I am having a very good time.

We arrived in Cordoba one week ago. The day after we arrived, we went camping near Río de los Sauces. My Dad and my brother pitched the tents and we all slept soundly in our sleeping bags. I did everything! I swam, I went fishing with Miguel Ángel (I didn't catch anything, in spite of the fact that I had a new fishing rod), I rode on horseback, and I rode a bike.

Last night a few Chilean friends gave a party. I didn't want to go, but my Dad convinced me and I went. There I met Gustavo, a young man from Santiago. I danced with him all night.

And how did it go for you in Buenos Aires? Did you go shopping? Did you stay at your aunt and uncle's home? I hope so, because hotels in Buenos Aires cost an arm and a leg. I stayed in one three months ago and it cost me a fortune . . .

Next year you have to come with us. Seriously! We plan to go to Bariloche and rent a cabin. Miguel Ángel says he's going to teach you how to ski (when we were children we used to go to Bariloche every year and he learned to ski very well).

Okay, I'm leaving, because Mom told me that Gustavo was waiting for me. We're going to plan another party!

A hug,
Silvia

P.S. On this trip I learned to appreciate nature, the country, and . . . Chilean young men!

## Lección 11

*RUNNING ERRANDS*

*In a house on Ponce Street in San Juan, Puerto Rico, lives the Vargas family. Sergio is very tired today and wants to sleep late because today he has the day off. His mother wants him to run several errands, so the poor boy has to get up as soon as the alarm goes off at seven in the morning.*

*At nine, he arrives at the dry cleaner's that is (located) near his house.*

S. I'm here to pick up my clothes. Here's the claim check. *(Thinking)* I hope my trousers are ready.
E. *(Reads)* A woman's overcoat and a pair of trousers. *(To Sergio)* One moment, please. *(She comes back a while later.)* The pants are pink, right?
S. They were white when I brought them in . . . !

*At ten, Sergio is in the photo section of the La Francia store.*

S. I brought in a roll of color film a week ago. I hope it's ready.
E. Let's see . . . Sergio Vargas . . . ? Yes, the pictures came out very well.
S. And how much do you charge to develop a roll of film?
E. Six dollars, sir.
S. Very well. *(He looks at the photographs.)* But who is this lady? These pictures aren't mine!

*At eleven, Sergio parks his motorcycle in front of the bank.*

S. I want to deposit this check, which is in my mother's name. Is it necessary for her to sign it?
C. If you're going to deposit it in her checking account, no.
S. Very well, that's what I want to do. I also want to withdraw two hundred dollars from my savings account.
C. Fill out this card, please.
S. I need you to give me the balance of my savings account.
C. You only have twenty dollars. I'm sorry, Mr. Vargas, but you don't have enough money.

*When Sergio leaves the bank, he doesn't find his motorcycle.*

S. *(Screaming)* Oh no! Somebody stole my motorcycle!
L. The young man who took (away) your motorcycle said he was your brother . . .
S. I'm an only child!
L. *(Thinking)* They look a lot like each other. I'm surprised they're not brothers.
S. *(As he walks to the police station)* Next Tuesday the thirteenth I'm not leaving the house!

**Lección 12**

ASKING FOR INFORMATION

*Julia, a girl from Honduras, arrived in Madrid a week ago. With her Spanish friends she visited the Parque del Retiro, the Palacio Real, and the old cities of Segovia, Avila, and Toledo. At each place, she bought a pile of postcards to send to her parents and friends. Today she decided to go to the post office to send the postcards and to pick up a package and a money order.*

J. *(Thinking)* I doubt that the post office is open at this hour. I think it opens at nine. *(To a gentleman who is standing on the corner)* Tell me, sir, where is the post office located?
MR. G. It's five blocks from here, at the Plaza de La Cibeles.
J. The fact is . . . I'm a foreigner, and I don't know the streets. Can you tell me how to get there?
MR. G. Oh! Continue straight ahead on this street until you get to the Plaza de Colón.
J. How many blocks?
MR. G. Two. Then turn right when you get to the traffic light, on Alcalá Street.
J. Is the post office on that street?
MR. G. Yes, right there. It's an old building, and it's across from the subway station.

*At the post office, Julia speaks with the employee who is at the information window.*

J. I'm here to pick up a package and a money order. My name is Julia Reyes.
E. Do you have an I.D.?
J. My passport . . . but I left it at the hotel.
E. I don't think they'll give it to you without identification.
J. Fine, I'll come back this afternoon. Where can I buy stamps?
E. Go to window number two, to the left.

*At window number two, Julia asks the employee for the stamps she needs.*

J. I want to send these postcards by air mail and a registered letter to Honduras.
E. It's ten euros, miss.
J. Can you tell me how to get from here to El Corte Inglés?
E. Go out through the main door, cross the Plaza de La Cibeles and walk along the Gran Vía until you get to the Plaza Callao. El Corte Inglés is next to the plaza.

*At El Corte Inglés, Julia meets her friend Pilar, with whom she is going to go shopping.*

J. I thought you wouldn't be here.
P. Listen, girl, it's not true that Spaniards always arrive late. Sometimes we're punctual.

*The girls go up to the third floor, where the ladies' department is.*

**Lección 13**

APARTMENT FOR RENT

*David and his wife, Lucía, are Colombian and they are studying at the Universidad Nacional Autónoma de México. They live in a boarding house, but they want to move to an apartment which is closer to the university.*

L. David, in the newspaper they are advertising an apartment that's in a good neighborhood and has two bedrooms.
D. Let's see! Give me the newspaper. *(He reads the ad.)*

**Classified Ads**

*For rent:* furnished apartment: two bedrooms, living room, dining room, kitchen, and bathroom. Central heating, air conditioning. Colonia 1. For information, call 481-3520 from 1 to 5 in the afternoon. Rent: $1,200.

L. We can call to go see it.
D. I don't know . . . It's very expensive for us, Lucía. Besides, we need an apartment that has a garage . . .

*On the following day, as soon as they return from the university, David and Lucía go see the apartment.*

L. I love the furniture and the curtains!
D. With the salary we're earning, we're not going to be able to pay the rent.
L. Then, instead of working part time we can work full time.
D. You're crazy! There's nobody who can work full time and at the same time study at the university.
L. Don't be so pessimistic, David!
D. I'm not pessimistic; I'm realistic. Besides, we're going to need money to buy blankets, sheets, pillowcases, and kitchen utensils.
L. *(She doesn't pay attention to him and goes to the kitchen.)* David, come to the kitchen. Look, it has a refrigerator, a microwave oven, a dishwasher, a new stove . . . and a big sink.
D. We cannot make a decision until we see other apartments.
L. But David, we're not going to find any apartment that's as good as this one.
D. Perhaps not . . . but we can't pay the rent for this apartment.
L. Listen, and if we win the lottery?
D. Do me a favor. Don't talk nonsense. Let's go!
L. *(Kidding)* Spoilsport!
D. The fact is . . . you married a poor man, my love . . .

## Lección 14

A DATE

*Oscar and Jorge, two Cuban American students who live in Miami, have a date tonight with two Venezuelan friends: Elsa and Adela. The boys are going to fix dinner for them in their apartment. Now Oscar is reading the movie guide to see what movie is being shown.*

**REX Cinema**
**Last week**

**Forbidden Love**

With Verónica Montiel and Ricardo Mirabal. Nominated as the best movie of the year!

First show: 3:00 P.M.
Last show: 9:00 P.M.

O. Do you feel like seeing a good movie?
J. Yes, but let's not go to the first show because it's too early.
O. Okay, and when the movie ends, we can go to the Versailles cafeteria to have something to drink. My treat.
J. Good idea. But let's not stay too late because tomorrow we have to work.
O. No, man, tomorrow is a holiday.
J. That's true. I think the supermarket is (already) open. Let's go now to buy the things we need for the dinner.
O. Yes, the market opens at seven.

*At the supermarket.*

O. We need many things: butter, milk, a dozen eggs, bread, sugar . . .
J. Aren't we going to buy meat?
O. Yes, let's buy meat, fish, and chicken. Also oil, two cans of beans, and six (cans) of tomato sauce.
J. No, let's not buy so much tomato sauce, unless you want to eat Italian food for the rest of the month.
O. You're right. Let's see . . . we need apples, grapes, oranges, melon, grapefruit, and pears for the fruit salad . . .
J. Where are the vegetables? We have to buy lettuce, potatoes, carrots, onions, and tomatoes.
O. Gee! Now that I think about it, this is going to cost a fortune. We'll have to go on a diet.

J. OK. Let's go on a diet, provided that we can eat hot dogs and hamburgers from time to time.

O. Listen, let's hurry up because we have to clean the apartment and prepare dinner before the girls arrive.

J. Yes, but let's call them as soon as we get home to ask them if they want to go to the movies or if they prefer to go dancing.

**Lección 15**

*SHOPPING*

A. This morning I have opened the closet and I have come to the conclusion that neither you nor I have anything to wear. We have to go shopping today. Look at this advertisement!

> **El Corte Inglés**
>
> Grand sale—Friday and Saturday
> We have lowered our prices on all of our clothes. Take advantage of these great reductions.
> REAL BARGAINS
> Silk blouses—Cotton shirts—Imported leather jackets—Linen shirts—Wool suits
> Open from 9 A.M. to 9 P.M.

H. Gerardo has asked me to help him . . . Besides, I have clothes . . .

A. Old and out of style! And yesterday you told me that you needed to exchange the boots that you had bought in El Corte Inglés because they were too wide . . . And you have to buy shoes!

*Anita has convinced her husband and they are now in the Corte Inglés, a department store that is in downtown Madrid. Hugo takes the escalator up to the first floor, where the men's clothing department is. Anita stays on the ground floor, where the women's clothing department is. There she meets her friend Tere.*

A. How's it going? Taking advantage of the sales, right? Tell me, Tere, how much does that silk blouse cost?

T. Fifty-six euros. What size do you wear?

A. I wear size thirty-eight. I'm going to try it on.

T. Wait, don't you like this skirt? It goes very well with the blouse, and it's a medium. Try it on. The fitting room is to the left.

A. *(From the fitting room)* Tere, do me a favor. Bring me a size thirty-six skirt.

T. Wait . . . I'm sorry, there are no smaller sizes. Why don't you try on this sweater?

A. No . . . I don't like it . . .

*Anita bought the blouse, but she did not buy the skirt because it was too big on her and it was too expensive. Afterwards, she went to the shoe department because she needed to buy a pair of red sandals to match a red purse Hugo had given her.*

*In the men's clothing department, Hugo bought two T-shirts and a vest. Now he is in the shoe department.*

H. I wish to exchange these boots.

C. Very well, sir. What size do you take?

H. I take size forty-four.

C. I'll be right back. *(A little while later)* Try these.

H. These are a little narrow. They are tight . . .

C. *(He tries on another pair.)* How are these?

H. These fit well. I'll take them. Can you wrap them up, please?

*Hugo, Anita, and Tere meet at the exit.*

A. Hugo, take us out to eat. We are starving!

H. I am too! Wait for me here. I'll go get the car.

A. Have you ever been to the Villa Alegre Restaurant?

T. Yes, it is very good. Let's go to that one.

*When Anita and Hugo arrive at their home, she sees her husband's purchases.*

A. A vest and two T-shirts! Is that all that you have bought? Ah! What am I going to do with you?

H. Well, you can give me a suit for my birthday . . .

**Lección 16**

*CAREERS*

Los Angeles, California
August 24, 2002

Dear Sergio,

I want you to know that I haven't written to you before because I haven't had time. Tomorrow I will be very busy also because I will have to register for the fall classes. I plan to take business administration, sociology, and psychology. My advisor has suggested that I take chemistry or physics but, as you know, I have never liked science. I prefer literature!

I would very much like to go to Buenos Aires in December, but I have final exams until the twentieth and I have to get good grades. I must maintain an "A" average because I have a scholarship.

Why don't you come to Los Angeles? We could go to Disneyland and visit San Diego, my favorite city. You have to come before the year 2004 because by then I will have graduated. I will try to get a job before then, because the life of a student is a poor person's life!

Write soon. A hug from your friend,

Daniel

P.S. Say hi to your sister!

Buenos Aires, Argentina
September 15, 2002

Dear Daniel,

Thank you for the invitation! Had I known that you were going to invite me to Los Angeles, I wouldn't have spent so much money on my trip to Rio de Janeiro and I would have saved money for the ticket.

I'm very busy too. Studying to be a lawyer is not easy, and all the professors in law school think that their classes are the only thing that should matter to us.

My sister Amalia (I said hi to her for you) is studying journalism and spends her whole life doing research and writing reports. I suppose that some day she will be a great journalist.

Do you remember José Luis? He's studying engineering and probably next year he'll go to the United States to take some special courses. I would do the same thing! Had he followed his father's advice, he would have finished medical school.

And you? What's your major? I thought your favorite subject was accounting . . . Well, I'm leaving because Marcos invited me to a soccer game. It's at the Boca Stadium and our team is playing. Bye!

Affectionately,
Sergio

P.S. Amalia says hi.

**Lección 17**

*MEDICAL PROBLEMS*

*Mirta and her husband are in a restaurant to have lunch. She doesn't feel very well today.*

M. I don't know what's wrong. I have a fever and my head hurts a lot. I already took four aspirins.

H. I told you to go to the doctor so he could give you a good check up. I hope you have (already) called Dr. Valdivia.

M. He's on vacation. Teresa suggested that I see Dr. Vargas. I have an appointment for this afternoon.

*Later in Dr. Vargas' office.*

DR. You have a temperature of 102 degrees. How long have you had those headaches?

M. A week. I have a cough and my throat aches. Do you think I have a cold or the flu?

DR. Yes, you have the flu. I am going to prescribe an antibiotic for you. Are you allergic to any medication?

M. Yes. I am allergic to penicillin.

DR. Are you pregnant?

M. No, doctor.

DR. Take these pills four times a day. Start taking them this very day. Here is the prescription.

*In the emergency room of the same hospital. Oscar had an accident and they brought him to the hospital in an ambulance. Now he is talking with the doctor.*

M. What happened to you?

O. A car hit me. My leg hurts a lot. I think I broke it.

M. Yes, I'm afraid you may have broken it. We are going to take some X-rays. I see you also have a wound on your arm. I am going to call the nurse.

*With the nurse*

N. The doctor told me to disinfect and bandage your wound in order to avoid an infection. When was the last time you had (they gave you) a tetanus shot?

O. Two years ago.

*The nurse takes Oscar to the X-ray room. Oscar's leg is broken and the doctor puts it in a cast.*

M. Is there anybody who can come pick you up?

O. Yes, I'm going to call my roommate, but I don't think he's arrived home yet.

## Lección 18

*This Car Is No Good!*

*Gloria and Julio, a newlywed couple, are on vacation in Costa Rica. Now they're on the highway, on the way to San José.*

G. Julio, you're driving very fast! The speed limit is ninety kilometers per hour. If a police officer sees you, he's going to give you a ticket!

J. Don't worry. Where are we? Do you have the map?

G. It's in the glove compartment but, according to that sign, we are forty kilometers from San José.

J. Is there a gas station nearby? The tank is almost empty.

G. It's a pity that you didn't fill the tank before . . .

J. If you had told me (it) before, I would have done it.

G. You talk as if it were my fault!

J. *(Kidding)* And who am I going to blame? Look, there's a service station . . .

*Julio stops at the service station to buy gasoline.*

J. *(To the attendant)* Fill the tank, please. Also, could you check the oil and the tires?

A. Yes, sir.

J. Yesterday I had a flat, and when I went to the repair shop, the mechanic told me that I needed new tires.

A. Yes, if I were you, I would change them . . . and I would also buy a new battery.

G. Ah, Julio! The mechanic also told you to fix the brakes and install a new water pump.

J. We'll do all that in San José, if it's necessary.

G. Didn't you also say that you'd change the oil filter and that you'd buy new windshield wipers?

J. If I had known that we were going to have so many problems, I would have bought a new car before leaving on this trip.

G. Yes, because we're going to spend a fortune on repairs.

J. And yesterday, the motor was making a strange noise . . . !

*When Julio tries to start (it), the car doesn't work.*

J. Oh, no! We'll have to call a tow truck to tow the car to San José.

G. It's not worth it. I would leave it here.

J. I agree with you! If I could, I would buy a new car right now.

# Appendix E Answer Key to the Self-Tests

## Self-Test Lecciones 1–3

### Lección 1

**A.** 1. be-a-erre-i-o-ese
2. a-ce-o-ese-te-a 3. de-i-a-zeta
4. efe-e-erre-e-i griega-ere-a
5. ge-u-e-ve-a-ere-a
6. hache-e-ene-a-o
7. jota-i-eme-e-ene-e-zeta
8. ele-e-igriega-ve-a

**B.** 1. once 2. diecisiete (diez y siete) 3. treinta 4. veinte 5. quince 6. trece 7. veintiocho (veinte y ocho) 8. diecinueve (diez y nueve) 9. doce 10. catorce

**C.** 1. verde 2. anaranjado 3. amarillo 4. rosado 5. negro 6. morado 7. café (marrón) 8. rojo, blanco y azul

**D.** 1. domingo 2. miércoles 3. viernes 4. martes 5. sábado 6. jueves

**E.** 1. noviembre 2. marzo 3. julio 4. enero 5. mayo 6. septiembre 7. otoño 8. primavera

**F.** son / somos / eres / soy / es / es / son

**G.** 1. g 2. j 3. l 4. a 5. c 6. i 7. e 8. k 9. b 10. d 11. h 12. f

**H.** 1. María. 2. Sí. José María.

### Lección 2

**A.** 1. la 2. la 3. los 4. el 5. los 6. los 7. el 8. las 9. la 10. el

**B.** 1. unas 2. unos 3. una 4. unos 5. una 6. un 7. unos 8. un

**C.** 1. treinta y ocho 2. cien 3. noventa y uno 4. ochenta y cinco 5. setenta y dos 6. cincuenta y siete 7. cuarenta y seis 8. sesenta y tres

**D.** 1. La clase de español es a las diez y media de la mañana. 2. La clase de inglés es a la una y cuarto de la tarde. 3. La clase de literatura es a las nueve menos veinte de la noche.

**E.** 1. trabajas / trabajo / regresas 2. estudian / no estudiamos / toman 3. necesitan / necesita / necesita 4. Deseas / llamo 5. Hablan ustedes / no hablamos

**F.** 1. los estudiantes de la señorita Vega 2. el profesor de Amanda 3. los amigos de Paco

**G.** 1. avenida 2. dirección 3. dice 4. quiere 5. asiento 6. alemán / francés 7. Cuántos 8. permiso 9. solamente 10. poco

**H.** 1. las seis de la tarde 2. el inglés

### Lección 3

**A.** 1. la 2. la 3. los 4. la 5. la 6. las 7. el 8. las 9. los 10. la

**B.** 1. mi bolígrafo / mis libros 2. La casa de él / la casa de ella 3. Nuestra profesora 4. Nuestros amigos 5. tus lápices 6. El profesor de ellos / el profesor de ustedes

**C.** 1. ciento noventa y cinco
2. doscientos ochenta y seis
3. trescientos setenta y uno
4. cuatrocientos sesenta
5. quinientos cincuenta y tres
6. seiscientos cuarenta y cuatro
7. setecientos treinta y dos
8. ochocientos veintisiete
9. novecientos dieciocho
10. mil quinientos trece

**D.** 1. La chica es alta. 2. El escritorio es pequeño. 3. Las chicas son norteamericanas. 4. Es una mujer muy simpática. 5. Necesito las plumas rojas.

E. 1. aprendemos 2. comes 3. creo 4. leen 5. bebe 6. debe 7. venden 8. abro 9. reciben 10. escribimos

F. 1. m 2. f 3. i 4. k 5. b 6. o 7. a 8. d 9. h 10. c 11. n 12. e 13. g 14. l 15. j

G. 1. ¿Bueno? 2. Sí, son equivalentes.

# Self-Test Lecciones 4-6

### Lección 4

A. 1. Yo llevo a mi prima a la universidad. 2. Nosotros llevamos los refrescos a la fiesta. 3. Ellos invitan a Julio y a su novia. 4. Nosotros tenemos cuatro primos.

B. 1. al señor Estrada 2. del club 3. de la terraza 4. a las chicas (a las muchachas) 5. del señor Soto

C. 1. Mis compañeros de clase tienen prisa. 2. Yo no tengo hambre, pero tengo mucha sed. 3. ¿Tienes (Tiene Ud.) calor? ¡Yo tengo frío! 4. Mis amigos tienen sueño. 5. (Nosotros) no tenemos miedo. 6. (Ud.) tiene razón, Srta. Peña. Mary tiene treinta años.

D. 1. voy 2. damos 3. está 4. está 5. van 6. dan 7. estoy 8. van 9. estás 10. doy

E. 1. Yo no voy a hablar con mi mamá hoy. 2. Mis hijos van a estudiar en España. 3. Mi amiga va a leer el libro. 4. Uds. van a traer los discos compactos. 5. Tú vas a bailar en la fiesta. 6. Nosotros vamos a brindar con sidra.

F. 1. quiere (piensa) 2. entendemos (empezamos, comenzamos) 3. pierde 4. Cierras 5. empiezan (comienzan) 6. empezamos (comenzamos) 7. pienso (quiero) 8. preferimos (queremos, pensamos)

G. 1. Invitamos 2. comemos 3. sidra 4. magnífica 5. nuevo 6. cocteles 7. brindamos 8. discos compactos

H. 1. no existe 2. santo 3. no existe 4. ¡Salud!

### Lección 5

A. 1. Alfredo es el estudiante más inteligente de la clase. 2. La Lección 2 es menos interesante que la Lección 7. 3. Mi novia es más bonita que tu novia. 4. Roberto es el más guapo de la familia. 5. El profesor tiene menos de veinte estudiantes. 6. Ana es tan alta como Roberto.

B. 1. más grande 2. mejor 3. mejor / peor 4. mayor 5. más pequeño

C. 1. cuesta 2. pueden 3. Recuerda 4. cuento 5. almorzamos 6. vuelves

D. 1. está diciendo 2. estoy hablando 3. estamos leyendo 4. estás comiendo 5. está durmiendo 6. están pidiendo

E. 1. Elsa es la mamá de Marta. 2. El Club Náutico está en la calle Siete. 3. ¡Mmmm! el pollo está delicioso. 4. Roberto es de México y ahora está en California. 5. La cerveza está fría. 6. El escritorio es de metal. 7. Hoy es lunes y mañana es martes. 8. Elvira es médica. 9. La fiesta es en casa de Alicia. 10. La orquesta es magnífica. 11. Ellos están cansados. 12. Laura es mexicana.

F. 1. mí 2. ti 3. ellos 4. nosotros 5. conmigo 6. contigo

G. 1. nieto 2. las pinturas 3. cartas 4. almorzar 5. echas de menos 6. ¡Qué lástima! 7. conducen su auto 8. fotos 9. viajar 10. mediana

H. 1. V 2. F 3. F 4. V 5. V

### Lección 6

A. 1. En el restaurante México sirven la cena a las nueve. 2. Ella pide una habitación con vista a la calle. 3. (Nosotros) seguimos al botones a la habitación. 4. ¿Consiguen Uds. reservaciones en diciembre? 5. (Yo) digo que él debe firmar el registro ahora.

**B.** 1. Ellos van a querer algo. 2. Hay alguien en el baño. 3. Tengo algunos objetos de oro y de plata. 4. Ellos siempre pasan por la aduana. 5. Yo también ceno a las nueve. 6. Siempre tiene las listas de los hoteles. 7. Puedes ir o a la derecha o a la izquierda. 8. Ellos siempre quieren algo también.

**C.** 1. conduzco 2. sé 3. quepo 4. salgo 5. traduzco 6. veo 7. hago 8. pongo 9. conozco 10. traigo

**D.** 1. sé 2. conoce / sabe 3. conoce / sabe 4. saben

**E.** 1. comprarlo 2. te llamo 3. la sirven 4. los tiene 5. me lleva 6. las necesito 7. los aceptan 8. llevarlo 9. las tengo 10. llamarla

**F.** 1. Llueve 2. Hace mucho frío 3. calor 4. nieva 5. hace mucho sol 6. lluvia

**G.** 1. b 2. a 3. b 4. c 5. b 6. a 7. c 8. a 9. a 10. b 11. c 12. c

**H.** 1. Perú 2. 25% 3. dólar 4. fácil

# Self-Test Lecciones 7–9

### Lección 7

**A.** 1. estas tarjetas postales y aquéllas 2. esa maleta y ésta 3. estas agencias de viajes y aquéllas 4. este avión y aquél 5. este barco y ése 6. estas cartas y ésas

**B.** 1. Ella les trae la lista. 2. Yo te voy a preparar (voy a prepararte) un sándwich. 3. Él le trae el equipaje. 4. Ana me va a comprar (va a comprarme) las tarjetas postales. 5. El agente de viajes nos trae los pasajes. 6. Les traen los cheques de viajeros.

**C.** 1. No me gusta esa agencia de viajes. 2. A él le gusta el asiento de pasillo. 3. ¿Le (Te) gusta este bolso de mano? 4. No nos gusta viajar por avión. 5. ¿Les gusta (a ellos) su hotel?

**D.** 1. Hace dos días que yo no duermo. 2. Hace un mes que tú no me llamas. 3. Hace media hora que nosotros estamos aquí. 4. Hace un año que ellos viven en España. 5. Hace doce horas que mi hija no come.

**E.** 1. Ayer Luisa y yo compramos los billetes. 2. La semana pasada yo viajé. 3. Ayer ella me presentó a sus padres. 4. ¿No pagaron Uds. los pasajes ayer? 5. Al mediodía ellos abrieron las ventanas. 6. El lunes nosotros comimos en la cafetería. 7. ¿Empezaste a estudiar esta mañana? 8. Ayer yo le presté las maletas.

**F.** 1. viajes 2. Buen viaje 3. turista 4. ida 5. retraso 6. devolver 7. próxima 8. salida 9. mano 10. juntas 11. exceso 12. barco

**G.** 1. Cuzco está situada a más de diez mil pies de altura. 2. Es la antigua capital del imperio de los incas. 3. Es un gran centro turístico y artístico. 4. Se conoce como "la ciudad perdida de los incas". 5. Se extendió desde el sur de Colombia hasta el norte de Chile y Argentina.

### Lección 8

**A.** 1. Se lo van a mandar (Van a mandárselo) mañana. 2. Elsa me las va a comprar (va a comprármelas). 3. Luis nos las va a traducir (va a traducírnoslas). 4. Se (Te) lo voy a traer (voy a traérselo / traértelo) esta tarde. 5. La profesora me la va a dar (va a dármela).

**B.** 1. Nosotros fuimos al restaurante y comimos pavo asado. 2. Él no fue mi profesor el año pasado. 3. ¿Tú le diste la botella, querido? 4. ¿Quién pidió el bistec? ¿Fue Ud., señorita? 5. Nosotras no le dimos el flan a Pedro.

6. Yo fui al teatro. 7. Yo no le di la cuenta. 8. ¿Fuiste tú al restaurante anoche? 9. Ellos fueron a la fiesta la semana pasada. 10. ¿Raúl y Eva fueron mis estudiantes el año pasado? 11. Yo te di la propina. 12. Ellos nos dieron una torta helada.

C. 1. ¿Durmieron ellos en el hotel el jueves? 2. Los chicos siguieron a sus padres a la tienda. 3. Nosotros servimos / pedimos sándwiches de jamón y queso. 4. Ella me mintió. No tiene viente años; tiene diez y siete. 5. ¿No consiguió Ud. el dinero para ir de vacaciones? 6. ¿Qué le pidieron los niños a Santa Claus? 7. El hombre murió en un accidente. 8. Ella me repitió la pregunta.

D. para / para / por / para / por / Por / para / para / por / para / por / por / por / para

E. 1. tercer 2. quinto 3. cuarto 4. décimo 5. octavo 6. primer

F. 1. s 2. i 3. a 4. m 5. q 6. t 7. o 8. d 9. g 10. h 11. c 12. f 13. b 14. r 15. e 16. k 17. n 18. j 19. l 20. p

G. l. latinoamericanos 2. cubanos 3. después 4. sobremesa 5. 10%

### Lección 9

A. 1. Tú te vistes muy bien. 2. Ellos se afeitan todos los días. 3. Ellos se acuestan a las once. 4. ¿Ud. no se preocupa por sus hijos? 5. Yo me pongo el vestido. 6. Juan se sienta aquí. 7. Tú te lavas la cabeza todos los días. 8. Yo no me corté el pelo. 9. Yo no me acordé de eso. 10. Uds. se fueron. 11. ¿Cómo te llamas (tú)? 12. Daniel no se despertó hasta las diez.

B. 1. ¿Tú te quitas el suéter? 2. El barbero me corta el pelo. 3. La peluquera me lava la cabeza. 4. Uds. no se lavan las manos. 5. Nosotros preferimos el té. 6. Las madres se preocupan por sus hijos. 7. La comunicación es lo más importante.

C. 1. El mío 2. las suyas 3. las nuestras 4. las tuyas 5. los nuestros 6. El suyo

D. 1. tuvieron 2. estuvieron 3. traduje 4. pude 5. pusiste 6. hubo 7. hizo 8. vino 9. no dijeron 10. trajo

E. 1. especialmente 2. frecuentemente 3. lenta y claramente 4. recientemente 5. Generalmente 6. Desafortunadamente

F. 1. escoba 2. lavado / peinado 3. moda 4. aspiradora 5. cocinar 6. champú 7. lacio 8. revista 9. peine 10. máquina (crema) / afeitar 11. regalo

G. 1. F 2. V 3. F 4. F 5. V

## Self-Test Lecciones 10–12

### Lección 10

A. 1. Hace cuatro años que conocí a mi mejor amigo(-a). 2. Hace seis meses que mis amigos y yo fuimos a acampar. 3. Hace tres días que mi familia y yo fuimos a la playa. 4. Hace una semana que mis padres volvieron del campo. 5. Hace quince minutos que llegué a mi casa.

B. 1. era / Eran 2. vivías / eras / vivía / íbamos / veías / vivían 3. se hospedaba / iba / costaba / era

C. 1. dijo / necesitaba / podías 2. compramos / éramos / íbamos 3. tenía / vinimos / hablábamos 4. fue / Tuve / dolía 5. iba / vio murieron

D. 1. Beto conoció a Marisa en la universidad. 2. Sí, Marisa conocía a la hermana de Beto. 3. No, yo no quería venir a clase hoy. 4. No, nosotros no sabíamos que hoy había examen. 5. No, no quiso venir.

E. 1. m 2. i 3. o 4. f 5. b 6. l 7. n 8. a 9. d 10. c 11. h 12. e 13. k 14. g 15. j

F. 1. Punta del Este, Mar del Plata y Viña del Mar. 2. A Chile y a Bariloche. 3. Junio, julio y agosto.

**Lección 11**

A. 1. estemos 2. camines 3. saque 4. se parezca 5. den 6. sepas 7. recojamos 8. sean 9. vaya 10. reciba

B. 1. depositar / abra 2. haga / estés 3. vaya 4. paguen / pagar 5. traigas / llenar

C. 1. Me alegro de que ellos tengan los pantalones de Oscar. 2. Espero que Julio estacione el coche cerca del banco. 3. Me sorprende que tú sepas el saldo de mi cuenta corriente. 4. Temo que Ada esté en la estación de policía. 5. Es una lástima que nosotros no podamos traer los comprobantes. 6. Ojalá que ellos vayan al banco.

D. 1. aparcar, parquear 2. motocicleta 3. cama 4. hijo(-a) único(-a) 5. quedarse en la cama hasta tarde 6. revelar 7. tan pronto como 8. de manera que 9. ropa 10. pobre 11. fechar 12. gratis

E. 1. F 2. V 3. F 4. V 5. F 6. F

**Lección 12**

A. 1. Estén 2. Tráigamelo 3. Salgan 4. Déselas 5. Vayan 6. Quédese 7. Mándenoslo 8. Póngalos

B. 1. Ésta es la señora que vino ayer. 2. Éstos son los niños de quienes te hablé. 3. Ésa es la profesora para quien nosotros compramos los libros.

C. 1. sea 2. esté 3. necesiten 4. está 5. se encuentran 6. visito 7. puedes 8. es

D. 1. lado 2. derecho 3. giro 4. metro (subterráneo) 5. abierta 6. cruzar / semáforo 7. subir 8. parado(-a) 9. antiguo 10. cuadras (manzanas) / frente 11. cada 12. puntual 13. montón 14. echar / buzón 15. letra

E. 1. central 2. Vía 3. fuente 4. reyes 5. metro 6. acueducto

# Self-Test Lecciones 13–15

**Lección 13**

A. 1. Dime 2. Haz / limpia 3. Sal 4. Ve / compra 5. Ponlos 6. Ven 7. Sé / tráeme 8. Ten / Espérame 9. No compres 10. No lo sirvas 11. No te vayas 12. Levántate / trabaja

B. 1. ¿Cuál es su (tu) número de teléfono? 2. ¿Cuál es el apellido de su (tu) madre? 3. ¿Qué es un pasaporte? 4. ¿Cuáles son las lecciones que Uds. necesitan? 5. ¿Cuál es su (tu) dirección? 6. ¿Qué es la paella?

C. 1. sepa 2. tiene 3. sea 4. tenga 5. trabaje 6. habla / hable

D. 1. m 2. f 3. k 4. o 5. a 6. i 7. c 8. b 9. e 10. n 11. d 12. h 13. g 14. l 15. j 16. p

E. 1. V 2. V 3. F 4. F 5. V

**Lección 14**

A. 1. llegue 2. vuelvan (regresen) 3. van 4. veas 5. vendan 6. vayas 7. vean 8. necesite 9. des 10. lleve

B. 1. Vamos al supermercado. 2. Vamos a las dos. 3. Compremos frutas y vegetales. 4. Pidámoselo a mamá. 5. No, no vayamos al teatro. Vamos al cine. 6. Volvamos a las siete. 7. Acostémonos a las once. 8. Levantémonos a las seis.

C. 1. ¿Qué idioma se habla en Chile? 2. ¿A qué hora se cierran las cafeterías? 3. ¿A qué hora se abre el supermercado? 4. ¿Dónde se vende aceite? 5. ¿Por dónde se sube al segundo piso?

**D.** 1. azúcar 2. lata 3. margarina 4. verduras 5. poner 6. cita 7. película 8. feriado 9. docena 10. higiénico 11. diversiones 12. zoológico

**E.** 1. F 2. V 3. F 4. F 5. V

### Lección 15

**A.** 1. escrito 2. abierto 3. visto 4. hecho 5. roto 6. ido 7. hablado 8. comido 9. bebido (tomado) 10. recibido

**B.** 1. rotos 2. abiertas 3. muerto 4. cerrado 5. hechas

**C.** 1. has usado 2. ha envuelto 3. han dicho 4. hemos comido 5. me he quedado 6. han hecho

**D.** 1. había terminado 2. habían ido 3. había dicho 4. había abierto 5. habíamos comprado 6. habías preguntado

**E.** 1. b 2. a 3. a 4. c 5. b 6. c 7. a 8. b

**F.** 1. al segundo piso 2. utilizar los servicios de una modista 3. existen 4. a veces

## Self-Test Lecciones 16–18

### Lección 16

**A.** 1. Le diremos la verdad. 2. ¿Qué harán Uds.? 3. No querrán ir. 4. Lo sabré mañana. 5. No podrán venir. 6. ¿Adónde iremos? 7. ¿Dónde lo pondrás? 8. Nosotros vendremos con él. 9. Tendré que trabajar. 10. Saldremos mañana.

**B.** 1. Yo iría a México. 2. Nosotros les escribiríamos. 3. ¿Tú se lo dirías? 4. Ellos hablarían con Ana. 5. ¿Ud. lo pondría en el banco? 6. ¿Uds. vendrían el domingo? 7. Julio pediría ensalada. 8. Nosotros lo haríamos hoy. 9. Tú no saldrías con ella. 10. Ella no caminaría; iría en coche.

**C.** 1. habrá dicho 2. habrán vuelto 3. habré terminado 4. habremos comido 5. habrás escrito

**D.** 1. Yo habría estudiado y habría aprobado el examen. 2. Julio me habría ayudado con el informe. 3. Luis y yo habríamos ido al partido. 4. Mis padres habrían pagado la matrícula. 5. ¿Qué habrías hecho tú, Anita?

**E.** 1. d 2. f 3. h 4. j 5. i 6. k 7. l 8. e 9. g 10. c 11. a 12. b

**F.** 1. existe 2. especializarse 3. facultades 4. especialización 5. 3 ó 6

### Lección 17

**A.** 1. Quería que fuera con ellos. 2. Les dije que no se preocuparan. 3. Me alegré de que el doctor te viera hoy. 4. Temí que me pusiera una inyección. 5. Necesitaba una enfermera que supiera español. 6. No creí que tuvieran que desinfectarme la herida. 7. ¿Había alguien que pudiera escribir una receta para penicilina? 8. Me alegré de que te sintieras bien. 9. No era verdad que necesitáramos una ambulancia. 10. No creí que estuviera embarazada.

**B.** 1. me olvido de 2. sueñan con 3. insiste en 4. venimos a 5. se comprometió con 6. me enamoré de

**C.** 1. hayan encontrado 2. hayas ido 3. haya comprado 4. le haya enyesado 5. se haya roto

**D.** 1. penicilina 2. los dientes 3. la lengua 4. los ojos 5. los pies 6. la herida 7. rompiste 8. la pierna 9. el tobillo 10. grados 11. pusieron 12. dolor de cabeza 13. el estómago 14. embarazada 15. gripe

**E.** 1. El gobierno subvenciona los hospitales. 2. Van a las clínicas privadas. 3. En muchos pueblos remotos, la gente va a un curandero.

4. Las ayuda una partera. 5. Sí, se pueden comprar medicinas como la penicilina sin receta médica.

**Lección 18**

**A.** 1. hubiera visto 2. hubieran tenido 3. hubiéramos pagado 4. te hubieras roto (quebrado) 5. hubiera vuelto

**B.** 1. tengo 2. pudiéramos 3. hubieran ido 4. quieren 5. hubieras visto 6. fuera

**C.** 1. instalaran 2. puedan 3. llame 4. podamos / podemos 5. haya tomado 6. llegue 7. pudiera 8. sea

**D.** 1. velocidad 2. recién 3. frenos 4. conducir 5. servicio 6. limpiaparabrisas 7. vacío 8. maletero 9. remolcar 10. acumulador 11. guantera 12. culpa 13. vale 14. viaje 15. acuerdo

**E.** 1. contaminación 2. malas 3. cara 4. motocicleta 5. 0,6

# Appendix F Professions and Trades

accountant **contador(-a)**
actor **actor**
actress **actriz**
administrator **administrador(-a)**
agent **agente**
architect **arquitecto(-a)**
artisan **artesano(-a)**
artist **artista**
baker **panadero(-a)**
bank officer **empleado(-a) bancario(-a)**
bank teller **cajero(-a)**
banker **banquero(-a)**
barber **barbero(-a)**
bartender **barman, cantinero(-a)**
bill collector **cobrador(-a)**
bookkeeper **tenedor(-a) de libros**
brickmason (bricklayer) **albañil**
butcher **carnicero(-a)**
buyer **comprador(-a)**
camera operator **camarógrafo(-a)**
carpenter **carpintero(-a)**
cashier **cajero(-a)**
chiropractor **quiropráctico(-a)**
clerk **dependiente(-a)** *(store)*, **oficinista** *(office)*
computer operator **computista**
construction worker **obrero(-a) de la construcción**
constructor **constructor(-a)**
contractor **contratista**
cook **cocinero(-a)**
copilot **copiloto(-a)**
counselor **consejero(-a)**
dancer **bailarín(-ina)**
decorator **decorador(-a)**
dental hygienist **higienista dental**
dentist **dentista**
designer **diseñador(-a)**
detective **detective**
dietician **especialista en dietética**
diplomat **diplomático(-a)**
director **director(-a)**
dockworker **obrero(-a) portuario(-a)**
doctor **doctor(-a), médico(-a)**
draftsman **dibujante**
dressmaker **modista**
driver **conductor(-a)**
economist **economista**
editor **editor(-a)**
electrician **electricista**
engineer **ingeniero(-a)**
engineering technician **ingeniero(-a) técnico(-a)**
eye doctor **oculista**
farmer **agricultor(-a)**
fashion designer **diseñador(-a) de alta costura**
fire fighter **bombero(-a)**
fisherman **pescador(-a)**
flight attendant **auxiliar de vuelo**
foreman **capataz, encargado(-a)**
funeral director **empresario(-a) de pompas fúnebres**
garbage collector **basurero(-a)**
gardener **jardinero(-a)**
guard **guardia**
guide **guía**
hairdresser **peluquero(-a)**
home economist **economista doméstico(-a)**
housekeeper **mayordomo, ama de llaves**
inspector **inspector(-a)**
instructor **instructor(-a)**
insurance agent **agente de seguros**
interior designer **diseñador(-a) de interiores**
interpreter **intérprete**
investigator **investigador(-a)**
janitor **conserje**
jeweler **joyero(-a)**
journalist **periodista**
judge **juez(-a)**
lawyer **abogado(-a)**
librarian **bibliotecario(-a)**
machinist **maquinista**
maid **criada**
mail carrier **cartero(-a)**
manager **gerente**
mechanic **mecánico(-a)**
midwife **comadrón(-ona), partero(-a)**
miner **minero(-a)**
model **modelo**
musician **músico(-a)**
nurse **enfermero(-a)**
optician **óptico(-a)**
optometrist **optometrista**
painter **pintor(-a)**
paramedic **paramédico(-a)**
pharmacist **farmacéutico(-a)**
photographer **fotógrafo(-a)**
physical therapist **terapista físico(-a)**
physician **médico(-a)**
pilot **piloto** *(masc., fem.)*, **aviador(-a)**
plumber **plomero(-a)**
police officer **policía**
printer **impresor(-a)**
psychologist **psicólogo(-a)**
public relations agent **agente de relaciones públicas**
real estate agent **agente de bienes raíces**
receptionist **recepcionista**
reporter **reportero(-a), periodista**
sailor **marinero(-a)**
sales representative **vendedor(-a)**
scientist **científico(-a)**
secretary **secretario(-a)**
security guard **guardia**
social worker **trabajador(-a) social**
sociologist **sociólogo(-a)**
soldier **soldado, militar**
stenographer **estenógrafo(-a)**
stockbroker **bolsista**
student **estudiante**
supervisor **supervisor(-a)**
surgeon **cirujano(-a)**
systems analyst **analista de sistemas**
tailor **sastre**
taxi driver **chofer de taxi, taxista**
teacher **maestro(-a)** *(elem. school)*, **profesor(-a)** *(high school and college)*
technician **técnico(-a)**
telephone operator **telefonista**
television and radio announcer **locutor(-a)**
television and radio technician **técnico(-a) de radio y televisión**
teller **cajero(-a)**
therapist **terapista**
travel agent **agente de viajes**
truck driver **camionero(-a)**
typist **mecanógrafo(-a), dactilógrafo(-a)**

undertaker **director(-a) de pompas fúnebres**
veterinarian **veterinario(-a)**
waiter **mozo, camarero**
waitress **camarera**
watchmaker **relojero(-a)**
worker **obrero(-a)**
writer **escritor(-a)**

# Vocabulary

The Spanish-English vocabulary contains all active and passive vocabulary that appears in the student text. Active vocabulary includes words and expressions that appear in the vocabulary lists that follow the dialogues and in charts and word lists that are part of the grammar explanations. Passive vocabulary consists of words and expressions that are given an English gloss in photo captions, the **Panorama hispánico** and **¿Lo sabía Ud.?** sections, readings, exercises, activities, and authentic documents.

The English-Spanish Vocabulary contains only those words and expressions that are considered active.

The following abbreviations are used in the vocabularies:

| | | | | | |
|---|---|---|---|---|---|
| *abbr.* | abbreviation | *form.* | formal | *pl.* | plural |
| *adj.* | adjective | *i.o.* | indirect object | *prep.* | preposition |
| *adv.* | adverb | *inf.* | infinitive | *pron.* | pronoun |
| *aux.* | auxiliary | *lang.* | language | *p.p.* | past participle |
| *d.o.* | direct object | *m.* | masculine noun | *sing.* | singular |
| *f.* | feminine noun | *Mex.* | Mexico | *Sp.* | Spain |
| *fam.* | familiar | *obj.* | object | *Sp. Am.* | Spanish America |

## Spanish-English

### A

**a** at, to, 3; toward
  ____ **casa** home
  ¿____ **cómo está el cambio de moneda?** What is the exchange rate?, 6
  ____ **la derecha** to the right, 6
  ____ **la(s)...** at (*hour*), 2
  ____ **menos que** unless, 14
  ____ **menudo** often
  ____ **pesar de (que)** in spite of, despite, 10
  ____ **plazos** in installments, 11
  ¿____ **qué hora?** At what time?, 2
  ____ **sus órdenes** at your service
  ____ **(en) todas partes** everywhere
  ____ **veces** sometimes, 12
  ____ **ver** let's see, 11
**abajo** downstairs, 12
**abierto(-a)** (*p.p.* of **abrir** *and adj.*) open(ed), 12
**abogado(-a)** (*m., f.*) lawyer, 3
**abrazar** to hug, 8
**abrazo** (*m.*) hug, 10
**abrigo** (*m.*) overcoat, 11; coat
**abril** April, 1
**abrir** to open, 3
**abuela** (*f.*) grandmother, 5
**abuelo** (*m.*) grandfather, 5
**aburrido(-a)** bored, 4; boring, 7
**aburrirse** to be bored, 10
**acabado(-a)** finished
**acabar** to finish
  ____ **de** to have just, 6
**acampar** to camp, 10
**accidente** (*m.*) accident, 17
**acción** (*f.*) action
**aceite** (*m.*) oil, 14
**aceptar** to accept, 6
**acera** (*f.*) sidewalk
**aclamar** to applaud
**aconsejar** to advise, 11
**acordarse (o:ue) (de)** to remember, 9
**acostar (o:ue)** to put to bed, 9
  **acostarse** to go to bed, 9
**actividad** (*f.*) activity, 10
**actor** (*m.*) actor
**actriz** (*f.*) actress
**actualmente** nowadays
**actuar** to perform
**acumulador** (*m.*) battery, 18
**adelantado(-a)** advanced
**además** besides, 13
**adicional** additional
**adiós** good-bye, 1
**adjetivo** (*m.*) adjective
**administración de empresas** (*f.*) business administration, 16
**adónde** where? (*destination*), 4
**adoquinado(-a)** tiled
**aduana** (*f.*) customs, 6
**advertir (e:ie)** to warn
**aeropuerto** (*m.*) airport, 6
**afectuosamente** affectionately, 16
**afeitar(se)** to shave, 9
**afueras** (*f. pl.*) outskirts
**agencia de viajes** (*f.*) travel agency, 7
**agente** (*m., f.*) agent
  ____ **de viajes** (*m., f.*) travel agent, 7
**agosto** August, 1
**agua** (*f.*) water, 4
  ____ **caliente** (*f.*) hot water
  ____ **mineral** (*f.*) mineral water, 4

**aguafiestas** (*m., f.*) spoilsport, 13
**agujereado(-a)** full of holes
**ah** oh, 2
**ahora** now, 4
_____ **mismo** right now, 18
_____ **que lo pienso** now that I think about it, 14
**ahorrar** to save, 11
**ahorros** (*m. pl.*) savings, 11
**aire acondicionado** (*m.*) air conditioning, 6
**al** (*m. sing.*) (*contraction*) to the, 4
_____ **aire libre** outdoor, 10
_____ **contado** in cash, 11
_____ **día** a day, 17
_____ **día siguiente** the following day, 10
_____ **extranjero** abroad
_____ **lado de** next to, 12
_____ **medio día** at noon, 4
_____ **mismo tiempo** at the same time, 13
_____ **rato** a while later, 11
**albóndiga** (*f.*) meatball, 8
**alcanzar** to achieve, to reach
**aldea** (*f.*) small town
**alegrarse (de)** to be glad, 11
**alegre** merry
**alemán** (*m.*) German (*lang.*), 2
**alérgico(-a)** allergic, 17
**alfabetizar** to alphabetize
**alfabeto** (*m.*) alphabet
**alfombra** (*f.*) carpet, rug, 9
**algo** something, anything, 6
**algodón** (*m.*) cotton, 15
**alguien** someone, somebody, anyone, 6
**alguno(-a), algún** any, some, 6
**alguna vez** ever, 15
**algunos(-as)** some, 5
**allí** there, 4
_____ **mismo** right there, 12
**almacén** (*m.*) department store, 15
**almohada** (*f.*) pillow, 13
**almorzar (o:ue)** to have lunch, 5
**almuerzo** (*m.*) lunch, 6
**alojamiento** (*m.*) lodging, 6
**alquilar** to rent, 10
**se alquila** for rent, 13
**alquiler** (*m.*) rent, 13
**alrededor de** around
**alto** stop (*sign*)
**alto(-a)** tall, 3
**alumno(-a)** (*m., f.*) student, 2
**amarillo(-a)** yellow, 1
**ambos(-as)** both
**ambulancia** (*f.*) ambulance, 17
**amigdalitis** (*f.*) tonsilitis
**amigo(-a)** (*m., f.*) friend, 2
**amistad** (*f.*) friendship
**amor** (*m.*) love, 8
**mi** _____ my love, my darling, 8
**amplio(-a)** ample, 6
**amueblado(-a)** furnished, 13
**amurallado(-a)** walled in
**analista de sistemas** (*m., f.*) systems analyst, 1
**anaranjado(-a)** orange, 1
**ancho(-a)** wide, 15
**anhelar** to yearn for
**aniversario** (*m.*) anniversary, 8
_____ **de bodas** wedding anniversary, 8
**anoche** last night, 8
**anotar** to write down, 8
**ansiosamente** anxiously
**anteayer** the day before yesterday, 8
**antes (de)** before, 4
_____ **de que** before, 14
**antibiótico** (*m.*) antibiotic, 17
**antiguo(-a)** old, 12
**antipático(-a)** unpleasant, 3
**anunciar** to announce, 13
**anuncio** (*m.*) ad, 6
**añadir** to add
**año** (*m.*) year, 3
**aparato electrodoméstico** (*m.*) home appliance, 13
**aparcar** to park, 11
**aparecer** to appear
**apartamento** (*m.*) apartment, 9
**apellido** (*m.*) surname, 3; last name
**apenas** hardly
**apendicitis** (*f.*) appendicitis
**apio** (*m.*) celery, 14
**apostar (o:ue)** to bet
**apreciar** to appreciate, 10
**aprender (a)** to learn, 3
**apretar (e:ie)** to be tight, 15
**me aprietan** they feel tight (on me), 15
**aprobar (o:ue)** to pass (*an exam or course*), 16
**aprovechar** to take advantage of, 15
**apuesta** (*f.*) bet
**apurarse** to hurry (up), 14
**apuro** (*m.*): **No hay apuro.** There's no hurry., 7
**aquel(los), aquella(s)** (*adj.*) that, those (*distant*), 7
**aquél(los), aquélla(s)** (*pron.*) that one, those (*distant*), 7
**aquello** (*neuter pron.*) that, 7
**aquí** here, 5
_____ **la tiene.** Here it is. (Here you have it.), 6
**árbol** (*m.*) tree
_____ **de Navidad** Christmas tree, 4
_____ **genealógico** (*m.*) family tree
**arena** (*f.*) sand
**Argentina** Argentina, 10
**argentino(-a)** Argentinian, 16
**armar** to pitch (a tent), 10
**armario** (*m.*) closet, wardrobe, 15
**arrancar** to start (*car*), 18
**arreglar** to fix, to repair, 18
**arreglo** (*m.*) repair, 18
**arriba** upstairs, 12
**arroz** (*m.*) rice, 8
_____ **con leche** (*m.*) rice pudding, 8
_____ **con pollo** (*m.*) chicken with rice, 8
**arte** (*f.*) art
**artículo** (*m.*) article, 3
**asado(-a)** roasted, 8
**ascensor** (*m.*) elevator, 6
**asiento** (*m.*) seat
_____ **de pasillo** (*m.*) aisle seat, 7
_____ **de ventanilla** (*m.*) window seat, 7
**Tome** _____. Have a seat., 2
**asignatura** (*f.*) (*school*) subject, 16
**asistir (a)** to attend, 5
**asma** (*f.*) asthma
**aspiradora** (*f.*) vacuum cleaner, 9
**aspirina** (*f.*) aspirin, 17
**aterrizar** to land (*plane*)
**atraso** (*m.*) delay, 7
**tener... de** _____ to be . . . behind schedule, 7
**atropellar** to run over, 17
**aumentar** to gain
**aún** still
**aunque** although, 9
**auto** (*m.*) car, 5
**autobús** (*m.*) bus, 5
**automático(-a)** automatic, 18
**automóvil** (*m.*) car, 5
**autopista** (*f.*) freeway, highway, 18

**auxiliar de vuelo** (*m., f.*) flight attendant, 1
**avenida** (*f.*) avenue, 2
**avergonzado(-a)** ashamed
**averiguar** to find out, 6
**avión** (*m.*) plane, 7
**ayer** yesterday, 7
**ayudar (a)** to help, to assist, 15
**azafata** (*f.*) female flight attendant, 7
**azúcar** (*m.*) sugar, 14
**azul** blue, 1

## B

**¡Bah!** Bah!, 5
**bailar** to dance, 4
**¿Bailamos?** Shall we dance?, 4
**baile** (*m.*) dance, 4
**bajar** to descend, to go down, 12
**bajo(-a)** (*adj.*) short, 3
**balazo** (*m.*) shot
**baloncesto** (*m.*) basketball
**banano** (*m.*) banana tree
**banco** (*m.*) bank, 11
**bañadera** (*f.*) bathtub, 6
**bañar(se)** to bathe (oneself), 9
**baño** (*m.*) bathroom, 6
 _____ **María** (*m.*) double boiler
**barato(-a)** cheap, inexpensive, 6
**barbería** (*f.*) barber shop, 9
**barbero(-a)** (*m., f.*) barber, 9
**barco** (*m.*) boat, ship, 7
**barrer** to sweep, 9
**barrio** (*m.*) neighborhood, 13
**barro** (*m.*) clay, mud
**básquetbol** (*m.*) basketball
**bastante** enough
**batería** (*f.*) battery, 18
 _____ **de cocina** (*f.*) cookware, 13
**beber** to drink, 3
**bebida** (*f.*) drink, beverage, 4
**beca** (*f.*) scholarship, 16
**béisbol** (*m.*) baseball
**belleza** (*f.*) beauty
**beso** (*m.*) kiss, 8
**biblioteca** (*f.*) library, 3
**bibliotecario(-a)** (*m., f.*) librarian, 16
**bicicleta** (*f.*) bicycle, 10
 **montar en** _____ to ride a bicycle, 10
**bien** well, fine, 1; okay, 7
**bikini** (*m.*) bikini, 15
**billete** (*m.*) ticket, 7
 _____ **de ida** (*m.*) one-way ticket, 7
 _____ **de ida y vuelta** (*m.*) round-trip ticket, 7
 _____ **de primera clase** (*m.*) first-class ticket, 7
**billetera** (*f.*) wallet, 15
**biología** (*f.*) biology
**bisabuela** (*f.*) great-grandmother, 4
**bisabuelo** (*m.*) great-grandfather, 4
**bistec** (*m.*) steak, 8
**blanco(-a)** white, 1
**bluejeans** (*m. pl.*) jeans, 15
**blusa** (*f.*) blouse, 15
**boca** (*f.*) mouth, 17
**bocina** (*f.*) horn, 18
**boda** (*f.*) wedding
**boleto** (*m.*) ticket (*for a show*), 8
**bolígrafo** (*m.*) pen, 2
**bolsa** (*f.*) (*Mex.*) purse, handbag, 9
 _____ **de aire** (*f.*) air bag, 18
 _____ **de dormir** (*f.*) sleeping bag, 10
**bolsillo** (*m.*) pocket
**bolso** (*m.*) purse, handbag, 9
 _____ **de mano** (*m.*) carry-on bag, 7
**bomba de agua** (*f.*) water pump, 18
**bonito(-a)** pretty, 3
**borrador** (*m.*) eraser, 2
**bosque** (*m.*) forest
**bota** (*f.*) boot, 15
**bote** (*m.*) (*Mex.*) can, 14
**botella** (*f.*) bottle, 8
**botiquín** (*m.*) medicine cabinet, 9
**botones** (*m.*) bellhop, 6
**brazo** (*m.*) arm, 17
**brindar** to toast, 4
**brindis** (*m.*) toast (*wine*), 4
**broma** (*f.*) practical joke
**bromear** to joke, to kid, 13
**bronquitis** (*f.*) bronchitis
**bueno(-a), buen** good, 3; hello (*phone*), 3; fine, okay, 7; well, 8
 **¡Buen viaje!** Have a nice trip!, 7
 **buenas noches** good evening, good night, 1
 **buenas tardes** good afternoon, 1
 **buenos días** good morning, 1
**bufanda** (*f.*) scarf
**bujía** (*f.*) sparkplug, 18
**burlarse de** to make fun of
**buscar** to pick up, to get, 17; to look for
**butaca** (*f.*) armchair, 13
**buzón** (*m.*) mailbox, 12

## C

**caballeros** (*m. sing.*) gentlemen, 6
**caballo** (*m.*) horse, 10
 **montar a** _____ to ride a horse, 10
**cabaña** (*f.*) cabin, 10
**cabello** (*m.*) hair, 17
**caber** to fit, 6
**cabeza** (*f.*) head, 17
 **dolor de** _____ (*m.*) headache, 17
**cacerola** (*f.*) saucepan, 13
**cada** (*invariable adj.*) each, 12
**caer(se)** to fall
**café** (*m.*) brown, 1; coffee, 5
 _____ **al aire libre** (*m.*) sidewalk cafe, 5
**cafetera** (*f.*) coffee maker, 13
**cafetería** (*f.*) cafeteria, 3
**cajero automático** (*m.*) automatic teller, 11
**cajuela** (*f.*) trunk (*car*), 18
**calcetín** (*m.*) sock, 15
**calefacción** (*f.*) heater
 _____ **central** (*f.*) central heating, 13
**calentar (e:ie)** to heat up, to warm up
**cálido(-a)** hot, warm
**caliente** hot, 7
**calificativo(-a)** descriptive
**callar** be silent
**calle** (*f.*) street, 2
**calor** (*m.*) heat, 4
**calzar** to take (*a certain size in shoes*), 15
**calzoncillos** (*m. pl.*) men's undershorts, 15
**cama** (*f.*) bed, 11
**cámara (fotográfica)** (*f.*) camera, 6
 _____ **de video** (*f.*) video camera, 6
**camarero(-a)** (*m., f.*) waiter, waitress, 8
**camarones** (*m. pl.*) shrimp, 8
**cambiar** to change, to exchange, 15

**cambio** (*m.*) exchange
_____ **de moneda** exchange rate, 6
**cambios mecánicos** (*m. pl.*) standard shift, 18
**caminar** to walk, 11
**camino** (*m.*) road, 18
_____ **a** on the way to, 18
**camioneta** (*f.*) station wagon, van, 18
**camisa** (*f.*) shirt, 15
**camiseta** (*f.*) T-shirt, 15
**camisón** (*m.*) nightgown, 15
**campo** (*m.*) country, 10
_____ **de batalla** (*m.*) battlefield
**canasto** (*m.*) basket
**cancelación** (*f.*) cancellation, 6
**cancelar** to cancel, 6
**canción** (*f.*) song
**cansado(-a)** tired, 4
**cantar** to sing, 4
**cántaros:**
**llover a** _____ to rain cats and dogs, 8
**caña de pescar** (*f.*) fishing rod, 10
**capital** (*f.*) capital (*city*), 6
**capó** (*m.*) hood, 18
**cara** (*f.*) face, 17
**¡caramba!** gee!, 14
**carbón** (*m.*) coal
**carburador** (*m.*) carburetor, 18
**cárcel** (*f.*) jail
**carne** (*f.*) meat, 8
**carnicería** (*f.*) meat market
**caro(-a)** expensive, 6
**carpintero(-a)** (*m., f.*) carpenter, 16
**carrera** (*f.*) university studies, career, 16; race
**carretera** (*f.*) highway, 18
**carro** (*m.*) car, 5; carriage
**carroza** (*f.*) float
**carta** (*f.*) letter, 5; menu, 8
**cartera** (*f.*) handbag, 9; wallet, 15
**cartero** (*m.*) mailman, 12
**casa** (*f.*) house, home, 3
**casado(-a)** married, 3
**casarse (con)** to get married (to), 13; to marry, 17
**casete** (*m.*) cassette, tape, 4
**casi** almost, 18
**casillero** (*m.*) mailbox, 12
**castaño** brown (*hair, eyes*), 3
**catarata** (*f.*) waterfall
**catarro** (*m.*) cold, 17
**catorce** fourteen, 1
**caudaloso(-a)** abundant
**cebolla** (*f.*) onion, 14
**ceda el paso** yield (*sign*)
**celebrar** to celebrate, 4
**cena** (*f.*) dinner, supper, 6
**cenar** to have dinner, supper, 6
**centro** (*m.*) downtown (*area*), 6; center, 15
_____ **comercial** shopping mall, 15
**cepillo** (*m.*) brush, 9
**cerca (de)** close to, near, 5; around
**cereal** (*m.*) cereal
**cero** zero, 1
**cerrar (e:ie)** to close, 4
**certidumbre** (*f.*) certainty
**certificado(-a)** certified, registered 12
**cerveza** (*f.*) beer, 4
**cesto de papeles** (*m.*) wastebasket, 2
**chaleco** (*m.*) vest, 15
**champán** (*m.*) champagne, 4
**champú** (*m.*) shampoo, 9
**chapa** (*f.*) license plate, 18
**chaqueta** (*f.*) jacket, 15
**charlar** to talk, chat, 4
**chau** bye, 1
**cheque** (*m.*) check, 11
_____ **de viajero** (*m.*) traveler's check, 6
**chequear** to check, 18
**chequeo** (*m.*) checkup, examination, 17
**chequera** (*f.*) checkbook, 11
**chica** (*f.*) girl, young woman, 3
**chico** (*m.*) boy, young man, 3
**Chile** Chile, 10
**chileno(-a)** Chilean, 10
**chino(-a)** Chinese
**chocolate** (*m.*) chocolate, 8
_____ **caliente** (*m.*) hot chocolate, 8
**chorizo** (*m.*) sausage
**cien, ciento** one hundred, 2
**ciencia** (*f.*) science, 16
_____ **ficción** science fiction
**cierto** true
**No es** _____. It's not true., 12
**cinco** five, 1
**cincuenta** fifty, 2
**cine** (*m.*) movie theater, movies, 7
**cinta** (*f.*) cassette, tape, 4
**cinturón** (*m.*) belt, 15
**circo** (*m.*) circus, 14
**cita** (*f.*) appointment, 9; date, 14
**ciudad** (*f.*) city, 3
**claro(-a)** light; clear
**claro** of course, 7
**clase** (*f.*) class, 2; kind
_____ **de alemán** (*f.*) German class, 2
_____ **optativa** (*f.*) elective
_____ **turista** (*f.*) tourist class, 7
**primera** _____ first class, 7
**clasificado(-a)** classified, 13
**clima** (*m.*) climate
**club** (*m.*) club, 4
**cobija** (*f.*) blanket, 13
**cobrar** to charge, 11
**coche** (*m.*) car, automobile, 5
**cochino** (*m.*) pig
**cocina** (*f.*) kitchen, 9; stove, 13; cuisine
**cocinar** to cook, 9
**cocinero(-a)** (*m., f.*) cook, chef, 16
**coctel** (*m.*) cocktail, 4
**cognado** (*m.*) cognate
**cojera** (*f.*) limp
**colchón** (*m.*) mattress, 13
**colombiano(-a)** Colombian, 13
**Colón: Cristóbal Colón** Christopher Columbus
**color** (*m.*) color, 1
**combinar** to match, to go together, 15
**comedia** (*f.*) comedy, 8
**comedor** (*m.*) dining room, 13
**comenzar (e:ie) (a)** to begin, to start, 4
**comer** to eat, 3
_____ **algo** to have something to eat, 14
**cómico(-a)** funny
**comida** (*f.*) food, 6; meal, 8
**cuarto y** _____ room and board
**como** since, 7; as, 16
_____ **si** as if, 18
**cómo** how?, 1; what?
¿_____ **es...?** What is . . . like?, 3
¿_____ **está usted?** How are you? (*form.*), 1
¿_____ **estás?** How are you? (*fam.*), 1
_____ **están ustedes** How are you?, 1
¿_____ **se dice...?** How do you say . . . ?, 2

¿_____ **se llama usted?** What's your name? (*form.*), 1
¿_____ **te llamas tú?** What's your name? (*fam.*), 1
¿_____ **te va?** How is it going (for you) (*fam.*)?, 1
¿_____ **te fue?** How did it go for you?, 10
**cómoda** (*f.*) bureau, chest of drawers, 13
**cómodo(-a)** comfortable, 5
**compañero(-a) de clase** (*m., f.*) classmate, 4
**compañero(-a) de cuarto** (*m., f.*) roommate, 17
**compañía** (*f.*) company, 3
**comparativo(-a)** comparative
**compra** (*f.*) purchase, 15
**comprar** to buy, 6
**comprobante** (*m.*) claim check, 11
**comprometerse con** to get engaged to, 17
**computador(-a)** (*m., f.*) computer, 12
**con** with, 2
_____ **ella habla** this is she (*speaking*), 3
_____ **permiso.** Excuse me., 2
_____ **tal (de) que** provided that, 14
_____ **vista a** overlooking, 6
**concierto** (*m.*) concert, 9
**conclusión** (*f.*) conclusion, 15
**concordancia** (*f.*) agreement
**condicional** conditional
**conducir** to drive (*Sp.*), 5; to conduct, 6
**conferencia** (*f.*) lecture
**confirmar** to confirm, 6
**conmigo** with me, 5
**conocer** to know, to be acquainted, 6; to meet, 7
**conocido(-a)** known
**conseguir (e:i)** to get, to obtain, 6
**consejero(-a)** (*m., f.*) advisor, 16
**consejo** (*m.*) advice, 16
**consulado** (*m.*) consulate, 6
**consultorio** (*m.*) doctor's office, 17
**contabilidad** (*f.*) accounting, 16
**contador(-a)** (*m., f.*) accountant, 16
**contaminación del aire** (*f.*) smog
**contar (o:ue)** to count, 5; to tell, 7
**contento(-a)** happy, 4
**contestar** to answer
**contigo** (*inf. sing.*) with you, 5
**convencer** to convince, 10
**conversación** (*f.*) conversation
**conversar** to talk, to chat, 4
**conversemos** let's talk
**convertirse (e:ie) en** to turn into
**copa** (*f.*) glass, goblet, 4
**corbata** (*f.*) tie, 15
**cordero** (*m.*) lamb, 8
**correo** (*m.*) mail, 12; post office, 12
_____ **electrónico** (*m.*) E-mail, 12
**cortar(se)** to cut (oneself), 9
**cortarse el pelo** to get a haircut, 9
**corte** (*m.*) haircut, cut, 9
**cortesía** (*f.*) courtesy
**cortina** (*f.*) curtain, 13
**corto(-a)** short, 9
**cosa** (*f.*) thing, 14
**costar (o:ue)** to cost, 5
_____ **un ojo de la cara** to cost an arm and a leg, 10
**crecimiento** (*m.*) growth
**creer** to believe, think, 3
**creído** (*p.p. of* **creer**) believed, 15
**crema** (*f.*) cream, 8
_____ **de afeitar** (*f.*) shaving cream, 9
**criollo(-a)** creole
**cruzar** to cross, 12
**cuaderno** (*m.*) notebook, 2
**cuadra** (*f.*) (*Sp. Am.*) city block, 12
**cuadro** (*m.*) picture, painting, 5
**de cuadros** plaid, 15
**cuál** what?, which?, 2
¿_____ **es tu (su) dirección?** What's your address?, 2
¿_____ **es tu (su) número de teléfono?** What is your telephone number?
**cualquier(a)** any; anybody
**cuando** when, 5
**cuándo** when?, 2
**cuánto(-a)** how much?, 4
¿_____ **tiempo hace que...?** How long . . . ?, 7
**cuántos(-as)** how many?, 2
**cuarenta** forty, 2
**cuarto** (*m.*) quarter, 2; room, 6
_____ **de baño** (*m.*) bathroom, 6
_____ **y comida** room and board
**menos** _____ quarter of/to (*time*), 2
**y** _____ quarter after/past (*time*), 2
**cuarto(-a)** fourth, 8
**cuatro** four, 1
**cuatrocientos** four hundred, 3
**cubano(-a)** Cuban, 8
**cubierto(-a)** (*p.p.* of **cubrir** *and adj.*) covered, 15
**cubiertos** (*m. pl.*) place settings, 8
**cubrir** to cover
**cucaracha** (*f.*) cockroach
**cuchara** (*f.*) spoon, 8
**cucharada** (*f.*) spoonful
**cucharadita** (*f.*) teaspoonful
**cucharita** (*f.*) teaspoon, 8
**cuchillo** (*m.*) knife, 8
**cuello** (*m.*) neck, 17
**cuenca** (*f.*) (river) basin
**cuenta** (*f.*) bill, 8; account, 11
_____ **corriente** (*f.*) checking account, 11
_____ **de ahorros** (*f.*) savings account, 11
**cuero** (*m.*) leather, 15
**cuerpo** (*m.*) body, 17
**cuidarse** to take care of oneself, 17
**culpa** (*f.*) blame, fault, 18
**culpable** guilty
**culpar** to blame, 18
**cultura** (*f.*) culture, 9
**cumpleaños** (*m.*) birthday, 4
**cumplir... años** to turn _____ (*age*), 4
**cuñada** (*f.*) sister-in-law, 5
**cuñado** (*m.*) brother-in-law, 5
**curandero** (*m.*) healer
**curita** (*f.*) adhesive bandage, 17
**curso** (*m.*) course, class, 16

## D

**damas** ladies, 6
**dar** to give, 4
_____ **una multa** to give a ticket (*fine*), 18
**darse por vencido(-a)** to give up
**darse prisa** to hurry (*up*), 14
**datos** (*m. pl.*) data, 3
**de** from, 1; of, 3; about, 7
_____ **acuerdo** okay, I agree, 14

_____ **compras** shopping, 10
_____ **cuadros** plaid, 15
_____ **estatura mediana** of medium height, 5
_____ **haber sabido** had I known, 17
_____ **haber seguido** had he followed, 16
_____ **la mañana** A.M., 2
_____ **la tarde** P.M., 2
_____ **manera que** so, 11
_____ **modo que** so, 11
_____ **nada** you're welcome, 2
¿_____ **parte de quién?** Who is speaking?, 3
_____ **postre** for dessert, 8
_____ **quién(es)** whose?, 4
_____ **todo** everything, 10
_____ **vez en cuando** from time to time, 14
_____ **viaje** traveling
_____ **vuelta** back
**deber** (+ *infinitive*) must, to have to, should, 3
**deberse a** to be due to
**decidir** to decide, 3
**décimo(-a)** tenth, 8
**decir (e:i)** to say, to tell, 6
_____ **tonterías** to talk nonsense, 13
**decisión** (*f.*) decision, 13
**dedo** (*m.*) finger, 17
_____ **del pie** (*m.*) toe, 17
**dejar** to leave (*behind*), 8
**del** (*m. sing.*) (*contraction*) of the, from the, 4
**delante de** in front of
**delgado(-a)** thin, slender, 3
**delicioso (-a)** delicious, 4
**demasiado(-a)(s)** too; too much, too many
**demostrativo(-a)** demonstrative
**dentista** (*m., f.*) dentist, 1
**departamento** (*m.*) department, section, 11; apartment
_____ **de (ropa para) caballeros** (*m.*) men's department, 15
_____ **de (ropa para) señoras (damas)** (*m.*) women's department, 12
**dependiente(-a)** (*m., f.*) store clerk, 15
**deporte** (*m.*) sport
**depositar** to deposit, 11
**derecho** (*m., adv.*) straight ahead, 12
**derecho(-a)** (*adj.*) right
**a la derecha** to the right, 6
**derramar** to spill
**derretir (e:i)** to melt
**desafiar** to challenge
**desafortunadamente** unfortunately
**desafortunado(-a)** unfortunate
**desayuno** (*m.*) breakfast, 6
**descomponerse** to break down
**descompuesto(-a)** (*p.p. of* **descomponer** *and adj.*) out of order, not working, 18
**desde** from, 12
**desear** to want, 11
**desierto** (*m.*) desert, 10
**desilusión** (*f.*) disappointment
**desinfectar** to disinfect, 17
**despedida** (*f.*) farewell
**despertador** (*m.*) alarm clock, 11
**despertarse (e:ie)** to wake up, 9
**despreciar** to scorn
**después** afterwards, 4; then, 7
_____ **de** after, 8
**desvestirse (e:i)** to get undressed, 9
**detenerse** to stop
**determinado(-a)** definite
**devolver (o:ue)** to return (*something*), 7
**devuelto(-a)** (*p.p. of* **devolver** *and adj.*) returned, 15
**día** (*m.*) day, 2
_____ **de fiesta** (*m.*) holiday, 14
_____ **de la semana** day of the week
**¿Qué _____ es hoy?** What day is today?, 1
**diamante** (*m.*) diamond
**diario** (*m.*) newspaper, 13
**diciembre** December, 1
**dicho(-a)** (*p.p. of* **decir** *and adj.*) said, told, 15
**diecinueve** nineteen, 1
**dieciocho** eighteen, 1
**dieciséis** sixteen, 1
**diecisiete** seventeen, 1
**diente** (*m.*) tooth, 17
**dieta** (*f.*) diet, 14
**diez** ten, 1
**difícil** difficult, 4
**¡dígame!** hello! (*phone*), 3
**díganos** tell us
**diligencia** (*f.*) errand, 11
**hacer _____s** to run errands, 11
**dinero** (*m.*) money, 3
**Dios** (*m.*) God
**dirección** (*f.*) address, 2
**disco** (*m.*) record
_____ **compacto** (*m.*) compact disc (CD), 4
**discoteca** (*f.*) disco
**diseño** (*m.*) design, 15
**disfrutar** to enjoy
**divertido(-a)** entertaining
**divertirse (e:ie)** to have a good time, to enjoy oneself, 10
**divorciado(-a)** divorced, 3
**doblar** to turn, to bend, 12; to dub
**doce** twelve, 1
**docena** (*f.*) dozen, 14
**doctor(-a)** (*m., f.*) doctor, 1
**documento** (*m.*) document, 12
_____ **de identidad (identificación)** (*m.*) I.D., 12
**doler (o:ue)** to ache, to hurt, 17
**dolor** (*m.*) pain, 17
_____ **de cabeza** (*m.*) headache, 17
**domicilio** (*m.*) address, 2
**domingo** (*m.*) Sunday, 1
**dónde** where?, 1
**dormir (o:ue)** to sleep, 5
**dormirse** to fall asleep, 9
**dormitorio** (*m.*) bedroom, 13
**dos** two, 1
**doscientos** two hundred, 3
**dramático(-a)** dramatic
**ducha** (*f.*) shower, 6
**ducharse** to take a shower, 9
**dudar** to doubt, 12
**dulces** (*m. pl.*) sweets
**durante** during, 7
**durar** to last
**durazno** (*m.*) peach, 14

# E

**echar** to throw
_____ **de menos** to miss, 5
_____ **el bofe** to be out of breath
_____ **una carta al correo** to mail a letter, 12
**edad** (*f.*) age, 3
**edificio** (*m.*) building, 12
**educación** (*f.*) education, 3
**efectivo** (*m.*) cash, 11
**en _____** in cash, 11

**ejército** (*m.*) army
**el** the (*m. sing.*), 1
**él** he, 1; him, 5
**electricista** (*m., f.*) electrician, 16
**elegante** elegant, 8
**elevador** (*m.*) elevator, 6
**ella** she, 1; her, 5
**ellas** (*f. pl.*) they, 1; them, 5
**ellos** (*m. pl.*) they, 1; them, 5
**embajada** (*f.*) embassy, 6
**embarazada** pregnant, 17
**emergencia** (*f.*) emergency, 17
**empezar (e:ie) (a)** to begin, to start, 4
**empleado(-a)** (*m., f.*) clerk, 6; employee
**empleo** (*m.*) job, 3
**en** in, at, 2; on, 3
 _____ **caso de que** in case, 14
 _____ **cuanto** as soon as, 11
 _____ **efectivo** in cash, 11
 _____ **inglés** in English, 2
 _____ **punto** on the dot
 _____ **seguida** right away, 6
 _____ **seguida vuelvo** I'll be right back, 15
 _____ **serio** seriously, 10
 _____ **vez de** instead of, 13
**enamorado(-a)** in love
**enamorarse de** to fall in love with, 17
**encaje** (*m.*) lace
**encantado(-a)** charmed, it's a pleasure
**encantador(-a)** charming
**encantar** to love, to like very much, 8
**encargado(-a) de** in charge of
**encima de** above, on top of
**encontrar (o:ue)** to find, 5
**encontrarse (con)** to meet, 12
**encuentro** (*m.*) encounter
**enero** January, 1
**enfadado(-a)** angry, 4
**enfermedad** (*f.*) disease, sickness
 _____ **de la niñez** childhood disease
**enfermero(-a)** (*m., f.*) nurse, 1
**enfermo(-a)** sick, 4
**enfriar** to cool down
**enojado(-a)** angry, 4
**ensalada** (*f.*) salad, 4
 _____ **de papas** (*f.*) potato salad, 4
**enseñanza** (*f.*) teaching
**enseñar (a)** to show, 6; to teach, 10
**ensuciar(se)** to get (oneself) dirty, 9
**entender (e:ie)** to understand, 4
**enterrado(-a)** buried
**entonces** then, in that case, 3
**entrada** (*f.*) entrance, 7; ticket (*for a show*), 8
**entre** between, among
 _____ **la espada y la pared** between a rock and a hard place
**entregar** to deliver, to turn in, 16
**entremeses** (*m. pl.*) hors d'oeuvres, 4
**entrevista** (*f.*) interview
**entrevistar** to interview
**enviar** to send, 3
**envolver (o:ue)** to wrap, 15
**envuelto(-a)** (*p.p. of* **envolver** *and adj.*) wrapped, 15
**enyesar** to put in a cast, 17
**equipaje** (*m.*) luggage, 7
**equipo** (*m.*) team, 16
 _____ **estereofónico** (*m.*) stereo system, 4
**equivocado(-a)** wrong, 4
**es que...** the fact is . . . , 12
**escalar** to climb, 10
**escalera** (*f.*) stairs, 6
 _____ **mecánica** (*f.*) escalator, 15
**esclavo(-a)** (*m., f.*) slave
**escoba** (*f.*) broom, 9
**escribir** to write, 3
**escrito(-a)** (*p.p. of* **escribir** *and adj.*) written, 15
**escritorio** (*m.*) desk, 2
**escuchar** to listen to
**escuela** (*f.*) school, 5
 _____ **secundaria** (*f.*) high school
**ese(-os), esa(s)** (*adj.*) that, those, (*nearby*), 7
**ése(-os), ésa(s)** (*pron.*) that one, those (*nearby*), 7
**eso** (*neuter pron.*) that, 7
 **a** _____ **de** at about, 14
**Esopo** Aesop
**espalda** (*f.*) back, 17
**España** Spain, 4
**español** (*m.*) Spanish (*lang.*), 1
**español(-a)** (*m., f.*) Spaniard, 12
**especial** special, 16
**especialidad** (*f.*) specialty, 8
**especialización** (*f.*) major (*field of study*), 16
**especialmente** especially, 5
**especie** (*f.*) sort
**espejo** (*m.*) mirror, 9
**esperar** to wait (for), 9; to hope, 11
 **—Espero que sí.** I hope so., 10
**esposa** (*f.*) wife, 3
**esposo** (*m.*) husband, 3
**esquiar** to ski, 10
**esquina** (*f.*) corner, 12
**estación** (*f.*) season, 1; station, 12
 _____ **de policía** (*f.*) police station, 11
 _____ **de servicio** (*f.*) gas (*service*) station, 18
**estacionar** to park, 11
**estadio** (*m.*) stadium, 16
**estado** (*m.*) state
 _____ **civil** (*m.*) marital status, 3
**Estados Unidos** (*m. pl.*) United States, 5
**estampado(-a)** print (fabric), 15
**estampilla** (*f.*) stamp, 12
**estar** to be, 4
 _____ **a... de aquí** to be . . . from here, 12
 _____ **de acuerdo** to agree, 18
 _____ **de moda** to be in style, 9
 _____ **de vuelta** to be back
 _____ **equivocado(-a)** to be wrong, 4
 _____ **invitado(-a)** to be invited, 9
 _____ **listo(-a)** to be ready, 5
 _____ **muerto(-a) de hambre** to be starving, 15
 **¿Está... (*name*)?** Is... (*name*) there?, 3
**estatura** (*f.*) height, 5
**este** east, 10
**este(-os), esta(s)** (*adj.*) this, 5; these, 7
**este semestre** (*m.*) this semester, 2
**éste(-os) ésta(s)** (*pron.*) this one; these, 7
**estilo** (*m.*) style
**estimado(-a)** dear, 16
**esto** (*neuter pron.*) this, 7
**estómago** (*m.*) stomach, 17
**estrecho(-a)** narrow, 15
**estrella** (*f.*) star
**estudiante** (*m., f.*) student, 1

**estudiar** to study, 2
**evitar** to avoid, 17
**exactitud** (*f.*) accuracy
**examen** (*m.*) exam, 3; checkup, 17
_____ **final** (*m.*) final exam, 16
_____ **parcial (de mitad de curso)** (*m.*) midterm exam, 16
**excelente** excellent, 8
**exceso** (*m.*) excess, 7
_____ **de equipaje** (*m.*) excess baggage, 7
_____ **de velocidad** (*m.*) speeding, 18
**excursión** (*f.*) tour, 6; excursion, 10
**experiencia** (*f.*) experience, 3
**expresión** (*f.*) expression, 1
**extranjero(-a)** foreigner, 12; (*adj.*) foreign
**al extranjero** abroad
**extrañar** to miss, 5
**extraño(-a)** strange, 18

## F

**fácil** easy, 4
**fácilmente** easily, 10
**facsímil** (*m.*) fax (*letter*), 12
**facultad** (*f.*) college, school
**de derecho** (*f.*) law school, 16
**falda** (*f.*) skirt, 15
**familia** (*f.*) family, 5
**famoso(-a)** famous, 5
**farmacia** (*f.*) pharmacy, drugstore, 9
**favor** (*m.*) favor, 13
**favorito(-a)** favorite, 6
**fax** (*m.*) fax (*letter*), 12
**febrero** February, 1
**fecha** (*f.*) date, 3
_____ **de nacimiento** (*f.*) date of birth, 3
**fechar** to date (*check or letter*), 11
**feliz** happy, 4
**femenino(-a)** feminine, 3
**feo(-a)** ugly, 3
**feria** (*f.*) fair
**feriado** (*m.*) holiday, 14
**fiebre** (*f.*) fever, 17
**fiesta** (*f.*) party, 4
_____ **de fin de año** (*f.*) New Year's Eve party, 14
**fijarse en** to notice, 17
**filete** (*m.*) tenderloin steak, 8
**filtro** (*m.*) filter, 18
**fin** (*m.*) end
_____ **de año** (*m.*) New Year's Eve, 4
_____ **de semana** (*m.*) weekend, 5
**firma** (*f.*) signature, 11
**firmar** to sign, 6
**Firme aquí.** Sign here., 6
**física** (*f.*) physics, 16
**flan** (*m.*) caramel custard, 8
**formal** (*f.*) formal
**fortaleza** (*f.*) fortress
**fortuna** (*f.*) fortune, 10
**foto** (*f.*) photograph, 5
**fotografía** (*f.*) photograph, 5
**francés** (*m.*) French (*lang.*), 2
**frazada** (*f.*) blanket, 13
**frecuente** frequent
**frecuentemente** frequently
**fregadero** (*m.*) kitchen sink, 13
**freír (e:i)** to fry
**freno** (*m.*) brake, 18
**frente a** in front of, 11; across from, 12
**fresa** (*f.*) strawberry, 14
**frijoles** (*m. pl.*) beans, 8
**frito(-a)** fried, 8
**fruta** (*f.*) fruit, 8
**fuente** (*f.*) fountain; source
**fumar** to smoke
**función** (*f.*) show, 14
**funcionar** to work, to function, 18
**funda** (*f.*) pillowcase, 13
**fútbol** (*m.*) soccer, 16
_____ **americano** (*m.*) football
**futuro** (*m.*) future

## G

**gamba** (*f.*) shrimp (*Sp.*), 8
**ganadería** (*f.*) cattle raising; livestock
**ganador(-a)** (*m., f.*) winner
**ganar** to earn, 13; to win, 13
**ganas: tener** _____ **de** to feel like, 14
**ganga** (*f.*) bargain, 15
**garaje** (*m.*) garage, 13
**garganta** (*f.*) throat, 17
**gasolina** (*f.*) gasoline, 18
**gasolinera** (*f.*) gas (*service*) station, 18
**gastar** to spend (*money*), 16
**gato** (*m.*) car jack, 18
**general** general
**generalmente** generally, 9
**género** (*m.*) gender
**gente** (*f.*) people
**geográfico(-a)** geographical
**giro postal** (*m.*) money order, 12
**gobierno** (*m.*) government
**goma** (*f.*) tire, 18
_____ **de borrar** eraser, 2
**gordo(-a)** fat
**gorro** (*m.*) cap, 15
**gozar (de)** to enjoy
**gracias** thank you, thanks
**—Muchas** _____ Thank you very much, 2
**grado** (*m.*) degree, 17
**graduarse** to graduate, 16
**grande** big, 4
**gratis** free (*of charge*), 11
**gripe** (*f.*) flu, 17
**gris** gray, 1
**gritar** to scream, 11
**grúa** (*f.*) tow truck, 18
**guante** (*m.*) glove, 15
**guantera** (*f.*) glove compartment, 18
**guapo(-a)** handsome, 3
**guardafangos (guardabarros)** (*m.*) fender, 18
**guerra** (*f.*) war
**guía de espectáculos** (*f.*) movie guide, 14
**guía telefónica** (*f.*) telephone book
**gustar** to like, to be pleasing to, 7
**gusto** (*m.*) pleasure
**El** _____ **es mío.** The pleasure is mine., 2
**Mucho** _____**.** How do you do? Nice (*pleased*) to meet you., 2

## H

**haber** (*aux.*) to have, 15
**habitación** (*f.*) room, 6
_____ **doble** (*f.*) double room, 6
**habla: de** _____ **hispana** Spanish-speaking
**hablado(-a)** spoken
**hablar** to speak, to talk, 2
**hacer** to do, to make, 6
_____ **buen tiempo** to be good weather, 6
_____ **calor** to be hot, 6

_____ **caso** to pay attention, 13
_____ **diligencias** to run errands, 11
_____ **frío** to be cold, 6
_____ **juego** to match, to go together, 15
_____ **las maletas** to pack
_____ **mal tiempo** to be bad weather, 6
_____ **sol** to be sunny, 6
_____ **un depósito** make a deposit, 11
_____ **una radiografía** to take an x-ray, 17
_____ **viento** to be windy, 6
**hace** + *time* ago, 11
**hace** + *time* + **que** + *verb* (*present*) to have been doing something for a length of time, 7
**hace** + *time* + **que** + *verb* (*preterit/imperfect*) to have done something in the past (ago), 10
**hacerse** to become
**hacia** toward, 11
**hambre** (*f.*) hunger, 4
**tener** _____ to be hungry, 4
**harto(-a) de** fed up
**hamburguesa** (*f.*) hamburger, 8
**hasta** until, 6; up to
_____ **la vista** until I see you again, 1
_____ **llegar** until you get, 12
_____ **luego** see you later, 1
_____ **mañana** see you tomorrow, 1
_____ **pronto.** See you later., 1
_____ **que** until, 14
**hay** there is, there are, 2
_____ **niebla** it's foggy, 6
**hecho(-a)** (*p.p. of* **hacer** *and adj.*) done, made, 15
**helado** (*m.*) ice cream, 8
**helado(-a)** iced, ice cold, 8
**torta helada** (*f.*) ice cream cake, 8
**herida** (*f.*) wound, 17
**herir (e:ie)** to hurt
**hermana** (*f.*) sister, 5
**hermanastra** (*f.*) stepsister, 5
**hermanastro** (*m.*) stepbrother, 5
**hermano** (*m.*) brother, 5
**hermoso(-a)** beautiful, 6
**hierba** (*f.*) herb; grass
**hija** (*f.*) daughter, 5
**hijastra** (*f.*) stepdaughter, 5
**hijastro** (*m.*) stepson, 5
**hijo** (*m.*) son, 5
**hijo(-a) único(-a)** (*m., f.*) only child, 11
**hijos** (*m. pl.*) children, 3
**hilo** (*m.*) linen, 15
**hipoteca** (*f.*) mortgage
**hoja** (*f.*) leaf
_____ **de papel** (*f.*) sheet of paper, 2
**hola** hello, 1
**hombre** (*m.*) man
_____ **de negocios** (*m.*) businessman, 16
**hora** (*f.*) time, 2; hour, 7
**¿A qué** _____**...?** (At) what time . . . ?, 2
**¿Qué** _____ **es?** What time is it?, 2
**horario** (*m.*) schedule, 16
**horno de microondas** (*m.*) microwave oven, 13
**horror** (*m.*) horror
**hospedarse en** to stay (*at a hotel*), 10
**hospital** (*m.*) hospital, 2
**hotel** (*m.*) hotel, 6
**hoy** today, 2
_____ **mismo** this very day, 15
**hubo** There was, were, 9
**huevo** (*m.*) egg, 8

## I

**ida** (*f.*): **de** _____ one-way (*ticket*), 7
**de** _____ **y vuelta** round-trip, 7
**ido** (*p.p. of* **ir**) gone, 15
**idea** (*f.*) idea, 4
**identidad** (*f.*) identity, 3
**idioma** (*m.*) language
**iglesia** (*f.*) church
**imperativo** (*m.*) command
**imperfecto** (*m.*) imperfect
**imperio** (*m.*) empire
**impermeable** (*m.*) raincoat
**importado(-a)** imported, 15
**importante** important, 16
**importar** to matter, 16
**incómodo(-a)** uncomfortable
**incredulidad** (*f.*) disbelief
**indeterminado(-a)** indefinite
**indicativo(-a)** indicative
**infección** (*f.*) infection, 17
**información** (*f.*) information, 6
**informática** (*f.*) computer science
**informe** (*m.*) report, 3; paper, 16
**ingeniería** (*f.*) engineering, 16
**ingeniero(-a)** (*m., f.*) engineer, 16
**inglés** (*m.*) English (*lang.*), 2
**en** _____ in English, 2
**ingreso(s)** (*m. pl.*) income
**inodoro** (*m.*) toilet, 6
**insistir en** to insist on, 17
**instalar** to install, 18
**institución** (*f.*) institution, 3
**inteligente** intelligent, 3
**interés** (*m.*) interest, 6
**interesante** interesting, 5
**interior** interior, 6
**internacional** international, 6
**interrogativo(-a)** interrogative
**investigación** (*f.*) research, 16
**invierno** (*m.*) winter, 1
**invitación** (*f.*) invitation, 4
**invitado(-a)** invited, 4
**invitar (a)** to invite, 4
**¡Yo invito!** My treat!, 14
**inyección** (*f.*) injection, shot, 17
_____ **antitetánica** (*f.*) tetanus shot, 17
**poner una** _____ to give a shot, an injection, 17
**ir (a)** to go, 4
**ir a** + *infinitive* to be going (to) + *infinitive*, 4
_____ **de compras** to go shopping, 10
_____ **de pesca** to go fishing, 10
_____ **de vacaciones** to go on vacation, 10
_____ **mal** to go wrong
**irse** to go away, to leave, 9
**italiano** (*m.*) Italian (*lang.*), 2
**izquierdo(-a)** left
**a la izquierda** to (on, at) the left, 6

## J

**jabón** (*m.*) soap, 6
**jactarse (de)** to brag (about)
**jamás** never, 6
**jamón** (*m.*) ham, 8
**japonés(-esa)** Japanese

**jarabe** (*m.*) cough syrup, 17
**jardín** (*m.*) garden, 13
**joven** (*m., f.*) young
**joyas** (*f. pl.*) jewels, jewelry
**joyería** (*f.*) jewelry store
**jueves** (*m.*) Thursday, 1
**juez** (*m.*) judge
**jugador(-a)** (*m., f.*) player
**jugar (u:ue)** to play (*game, sport*)
  ______ **al golf** to play golf, 10
  ______ **al tenis** to play tennis, 10
**jugo** (*m.*) juice, 8
**julio** July, 1
**junio** June, 1
**junto a** next to, 10
**juntos(-as)** together, 7

## K

**kilómetro** (*m.*) kilometer, 18

## L

**la** (*f. sing.*) the, 1; (*pron.*) her, it, you (*form.*), 6
**laboratorio** (*m.*) laboratory, 16
  ______ **de lenguas** (*m.*) language lab
**labrador(-a)** (*m., f.*) farmer
**lacio(-a)** straight (*hair*), 9
**ladrón(-ona)** (*m., f.*) robber
**lago** (*m.*) lake, 10
**lámpara** (*f.*) lamp, 13
**lana** (*f.*) wool, 15
**langosta** (*f.*) lobster, 8
**lápiz** (*m.*) pencil, 2
**largo(-a)** long, 7
**las** (*f. pl.*) the, 1; (*pron.*) them, you (*form.*), 6
**lástima** (*f.*) pity, shame
  **es una** ______ it's a pity, 11
  **¡Qué** ______**!** What a pity!, 5
**lata** (*f.*) can, 14
**latinoamericano(-a)** Latin American
**lavabo** (*m.*) sink, 6
**lavado** (*m.*) shampoo, wash, 9
**lavadora** (*f.*) washing machine, 13
**lavaplatos** (*m.*) dishwasher, 13
**lavar(se)** to wash (oneself), 9
  ______ **la cabeza** to wash one's hair, 9
**le** (to, for) her, (to, for) him, (to, for) you (*form.*), 7
**leche** (*f.*) milk, 8
**lechera** (*f.*) milkmaid
**lechón** (*m.*) pork, 8
**lechuga** (*f.*) lettuce, 14
**lector(-a)** (*m., f.*) reader
**leer** to read, 3
**leído** (*p.p. of* **leer**) read, 15
**lejos** (*adv.*) far, 8
**lengua** (*f.*) tongue, 17; language
**lentamente** slowly
**lento(-a)** slow
**les** (to, for) them, (to, for) you, (*form. pl.*), 7
**letrero** (*m.*) sign, 18
**levantar** to lift, to raise, 9
  **levantarse** to get up, 9
**libertad** (*f.*) liberty
**libra** (*f.*) pound
**libre** vacant, 6; off, free, 11
**libreta de ahorros** (*f.*) savings passbook, 11
**libro** (*m.*) book, 2
**licencia de conducir** (*f.*) driver's license, 3
**licuadora** (*f.*) blender, 13
**liebre** (*f.*) hare
**limpiaparabrisas** (*m.*) windshield wiper, 18
**limpiar(se)** to clean (oneself), 9
**limpio(-a)** clean
**lindo(-a)** pretty, 3
**lino** (*m.*) linen, 15
**liquidación** (*f.*) sale, 15
**lista** (*f.*) list, 6; menu, 8
  ______ **de espera** (*f.*) waiting list, 6
**listo(-a)** ready, 11
**literatura** (*f.*) literature, 16
**llamar** to call, 2
  **llamarse** to be called, 9
    **¿Cómo se llama usted?** What is your name? (*form.*), 1
    **¿Cómo te llamas?** What's your name? (*fam.*), 1
    **Me llamo...** My name is . . . , 1
**llano** (*m.*) plain
**llanta** (*f.*) tire, 18
**llanura** (*f.*) plain
**llave** (*f.*) key, 6
**llegada** (*f.*) arrival, 4
**llegar** to arrive, 6
  ______ **tarde** to be late, 7
  ______ **temprano** to be early
**llenar** to fill, to fill out, 11
**lleno(-a)** full, 18
**llevar** to take (*someone or something someplace*), 4; to wear, to use, 15
  **llevarse** to take (away), 11; to buy, to take, 15
**llover (o:ue)** to rain, 5
  ______ **a cántaros** to rain cats and dogs, to pour, 8
**lloviznar** to drizzle, 6
**lluvia** (*f.*) rain, 6
**lo** him, it, you (*form.*), 6
  ______ **cual** which
  ______ **siento** I'm sorry, 3
  ______ **único** the only thing, 16
**loco(-a)** crazy, 7
**Londres** London
**los** (*m. pl.*) the, 1; (*pron.*) them, you (*form.*), 6
**lotería** (*f.*) lottery, 13
**luchar** to fight
**luego** afterwards, then, 6
**lugar** (*m.*) place, 6
  ______ **de nacimiento** (*m.*) place of birth, 3
  ______ **donde trabaja** (*m.*) place of employment, 3
**lumbre** (*f.*) fire
**lunar** (*m.*) mole
  **de lunares** polka dot, 15
**lunes** (*m.*) Monday, 1
**luz** (*f.*) light, 2; headlight, 18

## M

**madera** (*f.*) wood
**madrastra** (*f.*) stepmother, 5
**madre** (*f.*) mother, 4
**maestro(-a)** (*m., f.*) teacher (*elementary school*), 1
**magnífico(-a)** great, 4
**maleta** (*f.*) suitcase, 6
**maletero** (*m.*) (*car*) trunk, 18
**maletín** (*m.*) briefcase
**malo(-a)** bad, 4
**mamá** mom, 4
**manada** (*f.*) herd
**manchar** to stain
**mandar** to send, 7; to order, 11
**manejar** to drive, 5
**manía** (*f.*) bad habit
**mano** (*f.*) hand, 17
**manta** (*f.*) blanket, 13

**mantecado** (*m.*) ice cream (*Mex., Puerto Rico*), 8
**mantel** (*m.*) tablecloth, 8
**mantener** (*conj. like* **tener**) to maintain, 16
**mantequilla** (*f.*) butter, 14
**manzana** (*f.*) apple, 14; (*Sp.*) city block, 12; block (*of buildings*), (*Sp. Am.*), 12
**mañana** (*f.*) morning, 2; (*adv.*) tomorrow, 3
  **de la _____** A.M., 2
**mapa** (*m.*) map, 2
**máquina de afeitar** (*f.*) razor, 9
**mar** (*m.*) sea, 10
  **_____ Mediterráneo** Mediterranean Sea, 10
**marcador** (*m.*) felt-tip marker, 2
**marchito(-a)** faded, withered
**mareo** (*m.*) dizziness, dizzy spell
**margarina** (*f.*) margarine, 14
**mariscos** (*m. pl.*) shellfish, 8
**marrón** brown, 1
**martes** (*m.*) Tuesday, 1
**marzo** March, 1
**más** more, 5
  **el (la) _____... de** the most ... in, 5
  **_____ de** more than, 5
  **_____ o menos** so-so, more or less, 3
  **_____... que** more ... than, 5
  **_____ tarde** later, 3
**masculino** male, 3
**matemáticas** (*f. pl.*) mathematics, 16
**materia** (*f.*) (*school*) subject, 16
**matrícula** (*f.*) registration, tuition, 16
**matricularse** to register, 16
**mayo** May, 1
**mayor** older, 5; bigger, 5
  **el (la) _____** the oldest, 5
**me** me, 6; (to, for) me, 7; (to) myself, 9
  **_____ llamo...** My name is ..., 1
**mecánico** (*m.*) mechanic, 18
**mediano(-a)** medium, 15
**medianoche** (*f.*) midnight, 4
**medicina** (*f.*) medicine, 5
**médico(-a)** (*m., f.*) doctor, 1; (*adj.*) medical, 17
**medida** (*f.*) size, 15
**medio** (*m.*) means
**medio(-a)** half, 8
  **media hermana** (*f.*) half sister, 5
  **media hora** half an hour, 7
  **medio ambiente** (*m.*) environment
  **medio día** half a day; part-time, 13
  **medio hermano** (*m.*) half brother, 5
  **y media** half-past (*telling time*), 2
**mediodía** (*m.*) noon, 4
  **al _____** at noon, 4
**mejor** best; better, 5
  **el (la) _____** the best, 5
**mejorar** to improve
**melocotón** (*m.*) peach, 14
**melón** (*m.*) melon, 14
**menor** younger, 5
  **el (la) _____** youngest, 5
**menos** less, 5
  **a _____ que** unless, 14
  **el (la) _____... de** the least ... in, 5
  **_____ de** + *number* less than + *number*, 5
  **_____... que** less ... than, 5
**mentir (e:ie)** to lie, 8
**menú** (*m.*) menu, 8
**menudo: a _____** often
**mermelada** (*f.*) jam
**mercado** (*m.*) market, 14
**mes** (*m.*) month, 1
**mesa** (*f.*) table, 4
**mesita de noche** (*f.*) nightstand, 13
**metro** (*m.*) subway, 12
**mexicano(-a)** Mexican, 1
**mezcla** (*f.*) mix, mixture, blend
**mi** (*sing.*) my, 3
  **_____ amor** my love, my darling, 8
  **_____ dirección es...** my address is ..., 2
**mí** (*obj. of prep.*) me, 5
**microondas** microwave, 13
**miedo** (*m.*) fear, 4
**mientras** while, 11
  **_____ tanto** meanwhile
**miércoles** (*m.*) Wednesday, 1
**mil** one thousand, 3
**milla** (*f.*) mile, 18
**mío(s), mía(s)** (*pron.*) mine, 9
**mirar** to look at, 5; to watch (*T.V.*), 3
  **_____ vidrieras** to window shop, 15
**mis** (*pl.*) my, 3
**mismo(-a)** same, 13
  **al mismo tiempo** at the same time, 13
**misterio** (*m.*) mystery
**mochila** (*f.*) backpack, 10
**moda** (*f.*) fashion
**modista** (*f.*) dressmaker
**modo** (*m.*) way
  **de _____ que** so, 11
  **de todos modos** anyway
**mojar** to dip
**molino de viento** (*m.*) windmill
**momento** (*m.*) moment, 3
**moneda** (*f.*) currency
**montaña** (*f.*) mountain, 10
  **_____ rusa** (*f.*) roller coaster, 14
**montar** to mount, to ride, 10
  **_____ a caballo** to ride a horse, 10
  **_____ en bicicleta** to ride a bicycle, 10
**monte** (*m.*) mountains
**montón** (*m.*)**: un montón de** a pile of, 12
**morado(-a)** purple, 1
**moreno(-a)** dark, brunette, 3
**morir (o:ue)** to die, 5
**moro(-a)** Moorish, Moor
**mostrador** (*m.*) counter, 9
**mostrar (o:ue)** to show, 6
**moto** (*f.*) motorcycle, 11
**motocicleta** (*f.*) motorcycle, 11
**motor** (*m.*) motor, 18
**mozo** (*m.*) waiter, 8
**muchacha** (*f.*) girl, young woman, 3
**muchacho** (*m.*) boy, young man, 3
**mucho(-a)** much, a lot (of), 4
  **Muchas gracias.** Thank you very much., 2
  **Mucho gusto.** How do you do? Nice to meet you., 1; Pleased to meet you, 2
  **no mucho** not much
**muchos(-as)** many, 4
**mudarse** to move (*from one house to another*), 13
**muebles** (*m. pl.*) furniture, 13
**muerto(-a)** (*p.p. of* **morir** *and adj.*) dead, 15

**mujer** (*f.*) woman
_____ **de negocios** (*f.*) businesswoman, 16
**muleta** (*f.*) crutch, 17
**multa** (*f.*) fine, ticket, 18
**mundo** (*m.*) world, 5
**muralla** (*f.*) wall
**museo** (*m.*) museum, 5
**muy** very, 1
_____ **bien** very well, 1

## N

**nacer** to be born
**nacimiento** (*m.*) birth, 3
**nacionalidad** (*f.*) nationality, 3
**nada** nothing, 3; not anything, 6
**nadar** to swim, 10
**nadie** nobody, no one, not anyone, 6
**naranja** (*f.*) orange, 14
**nariz** (*f.*) nose, 17
**naturaleza** (*f.*) nature, 10
**Navidad** (*f.*) Christmas, 4
**necesario(-a)** necessary, 18
**necesitar** to need, 2
**negación** (*f.*) denial
**negar (e:ie)** to deny, 12
**negarse** to refuse
**negativo(-a)** negative
**negro(-a)** black, 1
**nervioso(-a)** nervous, 4
**neumático** (*m.*) tire, 18
**nevado(-a)** snow-covered
**nevar (e:ie)** to snow, 6
**ni** nor, 6
_____**... ni...** neither . . . nor . . . , 6
**niebla** (*f.*) fog, 6
**nieta** (*f.*) granddaughter, 5
**nieto** (*m.*) grandson, 5
**nieve** (*f.*) snow, 10
**ninguno(-a), ningún** no, none, not any, 6
**niñez** (*f.*) childhood
**niño(-a)** (*m., f.*) child, 10
**no** no, not, 1
_____ **está** he or she is not here, 3
_____ **mucho** not much
_____ **muy bien** not very well, 1
**noche** (*f.*) evening, night, 3
**esta** _____ tonight, 3
**nombrar** to name
**nombre** (*m.*) (*first*) name, 3; noun
**nominado(-a)** nominated, 14
**noroeste** northwest
**norte** north, 10
**norteamericano(-a)** North American, 1
**nos** us, 6; (to, for) us, 7; (to, for) ourselves, 9
_____ **vemos.** See you., 1
**nosotros(-as)** we, 1; us, 5
**nota** (*f.*) grade, 16
**notar** to note
**noticias** (*f. pl.*) news
**novecientos** nine hundred, 3
**noveno(-a)** ninth, 8
**noventa** ninety, 2
**novia** (*f.*) girlfriend, fiancée, bride, 3
**noviembre** November, 1
**novio** (*m.*) boyfriend, fiancé, groom, 3
**nuera** (*f.*) daughter-in-law, 5
**nuestro(-a)** our, 3; (*pron.*) ours, 9
**nuestro(-as)** our (*pl.*), 3
**nueve** nine, 1
**nuevo(-a)** new, 4
**número** (*m.*) number, 2; size (*of shoes*), 15
**nunca** never, 5

## O

**o** or, 3
_____**... o...** either . . . or . . . , 6
**objeto** (*m.*) object, 6
**occidental** western
**océano** (*m.*) ocean, 10
_____ **Atlántico** Atlantic Ocean, 10
_____ **Pacífico** Pacific Ocean, 10
**octavo(-a)** eighth, 8
**octubre** October, 1
**ocupación** (*f.*) occupation, 3
**ocupado(-a)** busy, 4
**ochenta** eighty, 2
**ocho** eight, 1
**ochocientos** eight hundred, 3
**ocultar** to hide
**oeste** west, 10
**oficina** (*f.*) office, 6
_____ **de correos** (*f.*) post office, 12
**oficio** (*m.*) trade, 16
**ofrecer** to offer, 6
**oído** (*m.*) (*p.p. of* **oír**) heard, 15; ear (*inner*), 17
**oír** to hear, 15
**ojalá** I hope, God grant, 11
**ojo** (*m.*) eye, 17
**olvidar(se) (de)** to forget, 9
**once** eleven, 1
**operación** (*f.*) surgery
**oportunidad** (*f.*) opportunity, 5
**optativo(-a)** elective
**optimista** (*invariable adj.*) optimistic, 3
**oración** (*f.*) sentence
**orden** (*f.*) order
**oreja** (*f.*) ear, 17
**orgullo** (*m.*) pride
**orgulloso(-a)** proud
**oriental** eastern
**oro** (*m.*) gold, 6
**orquesta** (*f.*) orchestra, band, 4
**os** you (*fam. pl.*), 6; (to, for) you, 7; (to) yourselves, 9
**oscuro(-a)** dark
**otoño** (*m.*) autumn, fall, 1
**otro(-a)** another, other, 3
**otra vez** again
**oveja** (*f.*) sheep
**oye** listen, 2

## P

**pacer** to graze
**padrastro** (*m.*) stepfather, 5
**padre** (*m.*) father, 5
**padres** (*m., pl.*) parents, 5
**pagar** to pay, 7
_____ **por adelantado** to pay in advance, 6
**país** (*m.*) country, 10
**País Vasco** (*m.*) Basque Country
**palabra** (*f.*) word
**palacio** (*m.*) palace, 12
**palita** (*f.*) dustpan, 9
**pan** (*m.*) bread, 14
**panqueque** (*m.*) pancake
**pantalla** (*f.*) screen, 12
**pantalón** (*m.*) pants, trousers, 11
**pantalones** (*m. pl.*) pants, trousers, 11
**pantalones cortos** shorts
**pantimedias** (*f. pl.*) pantyhose, 15
**pantorrilla** (*f.*) calf (*of leg*)
**pañuelo** (*m.*) handkerchief, 15

**papa** (*f.*) potato, 8
 **____s fritas** (*f. pl.*) French fries, 8
**papá** dad, 5
**papel** (*m.*) paper, 2; role
 **____ higiénico** (*m.*) toilet tissue, 14
**paperas** (*f. pl.*) mumps
**paquete** (*m.*) package, parcel, 12
**par** (*m.*) pair, 15
**para** for, 3; to, in order to, 4; by, 8
 **____ entonces** by then, 16
 **____ que** in order that, 14
**parabrisas** (*m.*) windshield, 18
**parachoques** (*m.*) bumper, 18
**parado(-a)** standing, 12
**paraguas** (*m.*) umbrella
**paraguayo(-a)** Paraguayan, 9
**parar** to stop, 18
**parecerse (a)** to look like, 11
**pared** (*f.*) wall, 2
**pareja** (*f.*) couple, 18
**parque** (*m.*) park, 12
 **____ de diversiones** (*m.*) amusement park, 14
**parquear** to park, 11
**parte** (*f.*): **a (de) todas ____s** everywhere
**partera** (*f.*) midwife
**partido** (*m.*) game, 16
**pasado(-a)** last, 7
 **____ de moda** out of style, 15
**pasaje** (*m.*) ticket, 7
 **____ de ida** (*m.*) one-way ticket, 7
 **____ de ida y vuelta** (*m.*) round-trip ticket, 7
 **____ de primera clase** (*m.*) first-class ticket, 7
**pasaporte** (*m.*) passport, 6
**pasar** to pass; to spend (*time*), 6; to happen, 7
 **____ la aspiradora** to vacuum, 9
 **____ por** to go by, through, 6
**pasarlo bien** to have a good time, 4
**Pase.** Come in., 2
**pasillo** (*m.*) aisle, 7
**paso** (*m.*) step
 **____ de peatones** pedestrian crosswalk
**pastilla** (*f.*) pill, 17
**pavo** (*m.*) turkey, 8
**paz** (*f.*) peace
**pecho** (*m.*) chest, 17
**pedido** (*m.*) order, 8
**pedir (e:i)** to ask for, to request, 6; to order, 8
 **____ prestado** to borrow, 11
 **____ turno (cita)** to make an appointment, 9
 **____ un préstamo** to apply for a loan, 11
**peinado** (*m.*) hairstyle, hairdo, 9
**peinarse** to comb or style one's hair, 9
**peine** (*m.*) comb, 9
**película** (*f.*) film (*for camera*), 11; movie, 14
**pelirrojo(-a)** red-headed, 3
**pelo** (*m.*) hair, 9
**peluquería** (*f.*) beauty parlor, 9
**peluquero(-a)** hairdresser, beautician, 9
**pena** (*f.*) sorrow
**penicilina** (*f.*) penicillin, 17
**pensamiento** (*m.*) thought
**pensar (e:ie)** to think, 4; (+*inf.*) to plan, 4
 **____ en** to think about, 17
**pensión** (*f.*) boarding house, 5
**peor** worse, 5
 **el (la) ____** the worst, 5
**pequeño(-a)** small, little, 4
**pera** (*f.*) pear, 14
**perder (e:ie)** to lose, 4
**Perdón.** (*m.*) Pardon me., 2
**perdonar** to forgive
**perfectamente** perfectly, 5
**perfecto(-a)** perfect
**perfume** (*m.*) perfume
**perfumería** (*f.*) perfume shop
**periódico** (*m.*) newspaper, 13
**periodismo** (*m.*) journalism, 16
**periodista** (*m., f.*) journalist, 16
**permanente** (*m., f.*) permanent (wave), 9
**permiso** (*m.*) Excuse me., 2
**pero** but, 4
**perro(-a)** (*m., f.*) dog, 9
 **____ caliente** (*m.*) hot dog, 14
**personaje** (*m.*) character
**personal** personal, 3
**pesar** to weigh
**pesca** (*f.*) fishing, 10
 **ir de ____** to go fishing, 10
**pescado** (*m.*) fish, 8
**pescar** to fish, to catch (*a fish*), 10
**peseta** monetary unit (*Sp.*)
**pesimista** (*m., f.*) pessimistic, 3
**peso** (*m.*) weight; monetary unit (*Mex.*)
**pesquero(-a)** fishing
**picnic** (*m.*) picnic
**pie** (*m.*) foot, 17
**piedra** (*f.*) stone
**piel** (*f.*) leather
**pierna** (*f.*) leg, 17
**pieza de repuesto** (*f.*) spare part, 18
**pijama** (*m.*) pajamas, 15
**piloto** (*m., f.*) pilot, 1
**pimienta** (*f.*) pepper, 8
**pinchazo** (*m.*) flat tire, 18
**pintura** (*f.*) painting, picture, 5
**piña** (*f.*) pineapple, 14
**piscina** (*f.*) swimming pool, 6
**piso** (*m.*) floor, 6; (*Sp.*) apartment
**pizarra** (*f.*) chalkboard, 2
**placa** (*f.*) license plate, 18
**plan** (*m.*) plan, 5
**plancha** (*f.*) iron, 13
**planchar** to iron, 9
**planear** to plan, 10
**planta baja** (*f.*) ground floor, 15
**plata** (*f.*) silver, 6
**platillo** (*m.*) saucer, 8
**plato** (*m.*) dish, 8; plate, 8
**playa** (*f.*) beach, 10
**plaza** (*f.*) town square, 5
**plazo: a ____s** in installments, 11
**plomero(-a)** (*m., f.*) plumber, 16
**pluma** (*f.*) pen, 2; feather
 **____ estilográfica** (*f.*) fountain pen, 2
**pluscuamperfecto** (*m.*) pluperfect
**población** (*f.*) population
**pobre** poor (*unfortunate*), 11; poor, 13
**poco(-a)** little (*quantity*), 2
 **un poco +** *adjective* a little + *adjective*, 4
**pocos(-as)** few, 6
**poder (o:ue)** to be able to, can, 5; (*m.*) power
**poema** (*m.*) poem
**policía** (*m.*) police officer, 18; (*f.*) police
**policíaco(-a)** (*adj.*) detective
**pollo** (*m.*) chicken, 4
 **____ frito** (*m.*) fried chicken
**pomelo** (*m.*) grapefruit, 14

**ponche** (*m.*) punch, 4
**poner** to put, to place, 6; to turn on (*heat, air conditioning*), 13
_____ **la fecha** to date (check, letter), 11
_____ **la mesa** to set the table, 8
_____ **una inyección** to give an injection, shot, 17
_____ **un multa** to give a ticket (*fine*), 18
_____ **una película** to show a movie, 14
**ponerse** to put on, 9
_____ **a dieta** to go on a diet, 14
**no tener nada que** _____ not to have anything to put on, 15
**por** along, 8; around, 8; because of, 8; by, 8; during, 8; for, 6; in, 8; in exchange for, 8; in search of, 8; on account of, 8; on behalf of, 8; per, 6; through, 8
_____ **aquí** this way, 8
_____ **ejemplo** for example
_____ **eso** that is why, 5
_____ **favor** please, 2
_____ **la mañana (tarde)** in the morning (*afternoon*), 2
¿_____ **qué?** why?, 3
_____ **supuesto** of course, 7
_____ **teléfono** by phone; on the phone, 3
_____ **vía aérea** by airmail, 12
**porque** because, 2
**portaguantes** (*m. sing.*) glove compartment, 18
**Portugal** Portugal
**portugués** (*m.*) Portuguese (*lang.*), 2
**posibilidad** (*f.*) possibility
**posición** (*f.*) position
**postre** (*m.*) dessert, 8
**de** _____ for dessert, 8
**practicar** to practice, 5
**precio** (*m.*) price, 8
**preferir (e:ie)** to prefer, 4
**pregunta** (*f.*) question
**preguntar** to ask (*a question*), 14
**preocupado(-a)** worried, 4
**preocuparse (por)** to worry (about), 9
**preparar** to prepare, 4
**presentación** (*f.*) introduction
**presentar** to introduce, 7
**presente** present
**presión** (*f.*): _____ **arterial** blood pressure
**préstamo** (*m.*) loan
**pedir un** _____ to apply for a loan, 11
**prestar** to lend, 7
**primavera** (*f.*) spring, 1
**primero(-a), primer** first, 8
**primer día de clases** first day of classes, 2
**primo(-a)** (*m., f.*) cousin, 4
**prisa** (*f.*) hurry
**darse** _____ to hurry (up), 14
**No hay** _____. There's no hurry., 7
**tener** _____ to be in a hurry, 4
**privado(-a)** private, 6
**probablemente,** probably, 16
**probador** (*m.*) fitting room, 15
**probar (o:ue)** to try, 9; to taste, 9
**probarse** to try on, 9
**problema** (*m.*) problem
_____ **financiero** (*m.*) money problem, 3
_____ **sentimental** (*m.*) love problem, 3
**profesión** (*f.*) profession, 3
**profesor(-a)** (*m., f.*) professor, teacher, instructor, 1
_____ **de español** Spanish teacher, 1
**profundamente** soundly, 10
**programa** (*m.*) program
**programador(-a)** (*m., f.*) programmer, 1
**prohibido(-a)** prohibited, 14
**promedio** (*m.*) grade point average, 16
**pronto** soon, 16
**propina** (*f.*) tip, 8
**propio(-a)(s)** own
**propia página** (*f.*) home page
**próximo(-a)** next, 7
**psicología** (*f.*) psychology, 16
**psicólogo(-a)** (*m., f.*) psychologist, 16
**pueblo** (*m.*) town, people, nation
**puerta** (*f.*) door, 2; gate
_____ **de salida** (*f.*) airline departure gate, 7
_____ **principal** (*f.*) main exit (*door*), 12
**pues** then, 7
**puesto(-a)** (*p.p. of* **poner** *and adj.*) set, placed, put, 15
**pulmonía** (*f.*) pneumonia
**pulsera** (*f.*) bracelet, 8
**puntual** punctual, 12
**pupitre** (*m.*) desk, 2

## Q

**que** (*rel. pron.*) that, 3; who, 3; which, 6; (*conj.*) than, 5
**qué** what?, 2
**¿A** _____ **hora?** (At) what time?, 2
_____ **diablo** what the heck
¿_____ **hay (de nuevo)?** What's up (new)?, 1
¿_____ **hora es?** What time is it?, 2
¡ _____ **horrible!** How horrible!, 10
¡ _____ **lástima!** What a pity!, 5
¡_____ **pena!** What a pity!, 5
¿_____ **quiere decir… ?** What does . . . mean?, 2
¡ _____ **sorpresa!** What a surprise!, 8
¿_____ **tal?** How's it going? (*fam.*), 1; How was (is) . . . ?, 7
¿_____ **tiempo hace?** What's the weather like?, 6
**quebrar(se) (e:ie)** to break, 17
**quedar** to be located, 8; to fit, 9
_____**le grande (chico) a uno** to be too big (small) on someone, 15
_____ **suspendido(-a)** to fail (*exam or course*), 16
**quedarse** to remain, to stay, 10
_____ **en la cama hasta tarde** to sleep late, 11
_____ **sentado** to remain seated
**queja** (*f.*) complaint
**querer (e:ie)** to want, to wish, 4; to love, 4
**no quise** I refused, 10
**querido(-a)** dear, darling, 8
**queso** (*m.*) cheese, 8
**quien(es)** who, whom, that, 12

**quién** who?, 3
  **¿de ____?** whose?, 4
  **¿____ es?** Who is it?, 3
  **¿____ habla?** Who is speaking?, 3
  **¿De parte de ____?** Who is speaking?, 3
**quiere decir...** it means . . . , 2
**química** (*f.*) chemistry, 16
**quince** fifteen, 1
**quinientos** five hundred, 3
**quinto(-a)** fifth, 8
**quitar** to take away, 9
  **quitarse** to take off, 9

## R

**radiografía** (*f.*) X-ray, 17
**rallado(-a)** grated
**rápidamente** rapidly
**rápido** (*adv.*) fast, rapidly, 18
**raqueta** (*f.*) racket, 10
**raro(-a)** rare
**ratón** (*m.*) mouse, 12
**raya** (*f.*) stripe, 15
**rayón** (*m.*) rayon
**razón** (*f.*) reason
  **tener ____** to be right, 4
**real** royal, 12; real
**realista** realistic, 3
**rebaja** (*f.*) sale, 15
**rebajar** to mark down, 15
**recámara** (*f.*) (*Mex.*) bedroom, 13
**recepción** (*f.*) registration, 6
**recepcionista** (*m., f.*) receptionist, 1
**receta** (*f.*) prescription, 17; recipe
**recetar** to prescribe, 17
**recibir** to receive, 3
**recién casados** (*m. pl.*) newlyweds, 18
**reciente** recent
**recientemente** recently
**recogedor** (*m.*) dustpan, 9
**recoger** to pick up, 11
**recomendar (e:ie)** to recommend, 8
**recordar (o:ue)** to remember, 5
**recurrir a** to turn to
**refresco** (*m.*) soft drink, soda pop, 4
**refrigerador** (*m.*) refrigerator, 13
**regalar** to give (*as a gift*), 9
**regalo** (*m.*) gift, 8
**registro** (*m.*) register, 6
**regla** (*f.*) ruler, 2
**regresar** to return, 2
**relato breve** (*m.*) short story
**reloj** (*m.*) clock, 2
**relojería** (*f.*) watch store
**relleno(-a)** stuffed, 8
**remolcador** (*m.*) tow truck, 18
**remolcar** to tow, 18
**repetir (e:i)** to repeat, 8
**repollo** (*m.*) cabbage, 14
**represa** (*f.*) dam
**reproductor de discos** (*m.*) CD player, 4
**requisito** (*m.*) requirement, 16
**reserva** (*f.*) reservation, 6
**reservación** (*f.*) reservation, 6
**resfriado** (*m.*) cold, 17
**resfrío** (*m.*) cold, 17
**residencia universitaria** (*f.*) dorm
**respuesta** (*f.*) answer
**resta** (*f.*) subtraction
**restaurante** (*m.*) restaurant, 5
**resto** (*m.*) the rest, 14
**retraso** (*m.*) delay, 7
  **tener... de ____** to be . . . behind schedule, 7
**revelar** to develop (*film*), 11
**reventa** (*f.*) resale
**revisar** to check, 18
**revista** (*f.*) magazine, 9
**revolver (o:ue)** to mix
**rey** (*m.*) king
**rezar** to pray
**rico(-a)** tasty, delicious, 8; rich
**rifle** (*m.*) rifle, 10
**río** (*m.*) river, 10
**rizador** (*m.*) curling iron, 9
**rizo** (*m.*) curl, 9
**robar** to steal, 11
**rodilla** (*f.*) knee, 17
**rogar (o:ue)** to beg, to plead, 11
**rojo(-a)** red, 1
**rollo de película** (*m.*) roll of film, 11
**románico(-a)** Romanesque
**romper(se)** to break, 17
**ropa** (*f.*) clothes, clothing, 11
  **____ hecha** (*f.*) ready-to-wear clothes
  **____ interior** (*f.*) underwear, 15
**ropero** (*m.*) closet, wardrobe, 15
**rosado(-a)** pink, 1
**roto(-a)** (*p.p. of* **romper** *and adj.*) broken, 15
**rubio(-a)** blond, 3
**ruido** (*m.*) noise, 18
**ruinas** (*f. pl.*) ruins, 6

## S

**sábado** (*m.*) Saturday, 1
**sábana** (*f.*) sheet, 13
**saber** to know, 6; to find out, 10
**saborear** to taste
**sabroso(-a)** tasty, delicious, 8
**sacapuntas** (*m.*) pencil sharpener, 2
**sacar** to take out, to withdraw, 11; to get, to receive (*a grade*), 16
**saco de dormir** (*m.*) sleeping bag, 10
**sal** (*f.*) salt, 8
**sala** (*f.*) living room, 13
  **____ de emergencia** (*f.*) emergency room, 17
  **____ de rayos X (equis)** (*f.*) X-ray room, 17
**salario** (*m.*) salary, 13
**saldo** (*m.*) balance, 11
**salida** (*f.*) exit, 7; departure, 7
**salir** to leave, to go out, 6
  **____ de viaje** to leave on a trip, 18
**salmón** (*m.*) salmon, 8
**salón** (*m.*) room
  **____ de belleza** (*m.*) beauty parlor, 9
  **____ de estar** (*m.*) family room, 13
**salsa** (*f.*) sauce, 14
**Salto Ángel** Angel Falls
**salud** (*f.*) health
  **¡Salud!** cheers!
**saludo** (*m.*) greeting
  **____s a...** Say hello to . . . , 16
**salvavidas** (*m., f.*) lifeguard, 10
**sandalia** (*f.*) sandal, 15
**sandía** (*f.*) watermelon, 14
**sándwich** (*m.*) sandwich, 4
**sangría** (*f.*) sangría, 4
**sarampión** (*m.*) measles
**sartén** (*f.*) skillet, 13
**sastre** (*m.*) tailor
**sauce** (*m.*) (*weeping*) willow, 10
**se** (to) himself, (to) herself, (to) yourself (*form.*), (to) yourselves, (to) themselves, 9
  **____ dice...** You say . . . , One says . . . , 2
  **____ prohíbe fumar.** No smoking.
  **____ sale por la derecha** exit to the right
  **____ vende** for sale

**secador** (*m.*) blow dryer, 9
**secadora** (*f.*) dryer, 13
**sección** (*f.*) section
 ____ **de (no) fumar** (*f.*) (no) smoking section, 7
**secretario(-a)** (*m., f.*) secretary, 1
**sed** (*f.*) thirst, 4
 **tener** ____ to be thirsty, 4
**seda** (*f.*) silk, 15
**sede** (*f.*) headquarters; campus; seat
**seguir (e:i)** to follow, 6; to continue, 6
 ____ **la moda** to follow fashion, 15
**según** according to, 18
**segundo(-a)** second, 6
 **segundo nombre** (*m.*) middle name
**seguro** (*m.*) insurance
 ____ **de automóvil** (*m.*) auto insurance
 ____ **social** (*m.*) social security, 3
**seis** six, 1
**seiscientos** six hundred, 3
**sello** (*m.*) stamp, 12
**semáforo** (*m.*) traffic light, 12
**semana** (*f.*) week, 9
 **Semana Santa** Holy Week
**sencillo(-a)** single, 6; simple, 6
**sentarse (e:ie)** to sit (down), 9
**sentir(se) (e:ie)** to feel, 9; to be sorry, to regret, 11
 **lo siento** I'm sorry
**señal** (*f.*) sign
**señor** (*abbr.* **Sr.**) Mr., sir, gentleman, 1
**señora** (*abbr.* **Sra.**) Mrs. madam, lady, 1
**señorita** (*abbr.* **Srta.**) Miss, young lady, 1
**septiembre** September, 1
**séptimo(-a)** seventh, 8
**ser** to be, 1
**servicio de habitación (cuarto)** (*m.*) room service, 6
**servicios** (*m. pl.*) restrooms, 6
**servilleta** (*f.*) napkin, 8
**servir (e:i)** to serve, 6
 **no sirve** it's no good, 18
**sesenta** sixty, 2
**setecientos** seven hundred, 3
**setenta** seventy, 2
**sexo** (*m.*) sex, 3
**sexto(-a)** sixth, 8
**si** if, 5
**sí** yes, 2
**sidra** (*f.*) cider, 4
**siempre** always, 4
**siesta** (*f.*) nap
**siete** seven, 1
**silla** (*f.*) chair, 2
 ____ **de ruedas** (*f.*) wheelchair, 17
**sillón** (*m.*) armchair, 13
**simpático(-a)** nice, charming, 3
**sin** without, 12
 ____ **embargo** however, nevertheless, 10
 ____ **falta** without fail
 ____ **que** without, 14
**sino** but
 ____ **que** but rather
**sistema** (*m.*) system
 ____ **de calificaciones** (*m.*) grading system
**situado(-a)** located, 6
**sobre** about, 6; over
**sobrecama** (*f.*) bedspread, 13
**sobrenombre** (*m.*) nickname
**sobrina** (*f.*) niece, 5
**sobrino** (*m.*) nephew, 5
**sociología** (*f.*) sociology, 16
**sofá** (*m.*) couch, sofa, 13
**sol** (*m.*) sun
**solamente** only, 2
**solicitar** to apply for, 3
**solicitud** (*f.*) application, 3
 ____ **de trabajo** (*f.*) job application, 3
**solo(-a)** alone
**sólo** only, 7
**soltar (o:ue)** to turn loose
**soltero(-a)** single, 3
**sollozar** to weep
**sombrero** (*m.*) hat
**son las...** it's . . . (*time*), 2
**sonar (o:ue)** to ring, 11; to go off, 11
**soñar (o:ue) con** to dream about (of), 17
**sopa** (*f.*) soup, 8
 ____ **del día** (*f.*) soup of the day, 8
**sorprender** to surprise, 11
**sorpresa** (*f.*) surprise, 8
**sostén** (*m.*) bra, 15
**su** his, her, its, your (*form.*), their, 3
**subir** to climb, to go up, 12
**subterráneo** (*m.*) subway, 12
**subvencionado(-a)** subsidized
**sucio(-a)** dirty
**sucursal** (*f.*) branch (*office*)
**suegra** (*f.*) mother-in-law, 5
**suegro** (*m.*) father-in-law, 5
**sueldo** (*m.*) salary, 13
**sueño** (*m.*) dream
 **tener** ____ to be sleepy, 4
**suerte** (*f.*) luck
**suéter** (*m.*) sweater, 15
**suficiente** enough, sufficient, 11
**sugerir (e:ie)** to suggest, 11
**Suiza** Switzerland
**sujetador** (*m.*) bra
**suma** (*f.*) addition
**supermercado** (*m.*) supermarket, 14
**suponer** (*conj. like* **poner**) to suppose, 16
**sur** south, 10; southern
**suspendido(-a): quedar** ____ to fail (*exam or course*), 16
**sus** his, her, its, your (*form.*), 3
**suyo(s), suya(s)** (*pron.*) his, hers, theirs, yours, 9

## T

**tablero de anuncios** (*m.*) bulletin board, 2
**tal vez** maybe, perhaps, 13
**talla** (*f.*) size, 15
**tallado(-a)** carved
**taller (de mecánica)** (*m.*) repair shop, mechanic's shop, 18
**talonario de cheques** (*m.*) checkbook, 11
**talones** (*m. pl.*) checks (*Sp.*)
**tamaño** (*m.*) size
**también** also, too, 2
**tampoco** neither, not either, 6
**tan** as, so, 5
 ____**... como...** as . . . as . . . , 5
 ____ **pronto como** as soon as, 11
**tanque** (*m.*) tank, 18
**tanto(-a)** as much, 5; so much, 14
 ____ **como** as much as, 5
**tantos(-as)** as many, 5
 ____ **como** as many as, 5
**tarde** (*f.*) afternoon, 2; (*adv.*) late, 7
 **de la** ____ P.M., 2
 **llegar** ____ to be late, 7
 **más** ____ later, 2
 **por la** ____ in the afternoon, 2

**tarjeta** (*f.*) card, 7
    _____ **de crédito** (*f.*) credit card, 6
    _____ **de embarque** (*f.*) boarding pass, 7
    _____ **de turista** (*f.*) tourist card, 6
    _____ **postal** (*f.*) postcard, 7
**taxi** (*m.*) taxi, 6
**taza** (*f.*) cup, 8
**te** (*pron.*) you (*fam.*), 6; (to, for) you, 7; (to) yourself, 9
**té** (*m.*) tea
**teatro** (*m.*) theater, 8
**teclado** (*m.*) keyboard, 12
**tejanos** (*m. pl.*) jeans, 15
**teléfono** (*m.*) telephone, 3
    _____ **celular** (*m.*) cellular phone, 18
**telegrama** (*m.*) telegram
**televisor** (*m.*) television set, 6
**tema** (*m.*) subject, theme, 2; topic
**temer** to fear, 11
**temperatura** (*f.*) temperature, 17
**temprano** early, 9
**tenedor** (*m.*) fork, 8
**tener** to have, 3
    **no** _____ **nada que ponerse** not to have anything to put on, 15
    **no** _____ **razón** to be wrong, 4
    _____**... años (de edad)** to be . . . years old, 4
    _____ **calor** to be hot, 4
    _____ **correspondencia** to correspond
    _____ **cuidado** to be careful, 4
    _____ **éxito** to be successful, 4
    _____ **frío** to be cold, 4
    _____ **ganas (de)** to feel like (*doing something*), 14
    _____ **hambre** to be hungry, 4
    _____ **la culpa** to be one's fault, 18
    _____ **lugar** to take place
    _____ **miedo** to be afraid, 4
    _____ **prisa** to be in a hurry, 4
    _____ **que** to have to, 3
    _____ **razón** to be right, 4
    _____ **sed** to be thirsty, 4
    _____ **sueño** to be sleepy, 4
    _____ **suerte** to be lucky, 4
    _____**... de retraso (atraso)** to be . . . behind schedule, 7
    _____ **un pinchazo** to have a flat tire, 18
**tercero(-a), tercer** third, 8
**terminar** to finish, 9
**ternero** (*m.*) calf
**terraza** (*f.*) terrace, 4
**terremoto** (*m.*) earthquake
**ti** you (*fam. sing.*), 5
**tía** (*f.*) aunt, 5
**tiempo** (*m.*) weather, 6; time, 16
    _____ **completo** full-time, 13
**tienda** (*f.*) store, 8
    _____ **de campaña** (*f.*) tent, 10
    _____ **por departamentos** (*f.*) department store, 15
**tierra** (*f.*) earth, land
**timbre** (*m.*) (*Mex.*) stamp, 12
**tinto** red (*wine*), 8
**tintorería** (*f.*) dry cleaner's, 11
**tío** (*m.*) uncle, 5
**tirar basura** to litter
**título** (*m.*) title
**tiza** (*f.*) chalk, 2
**toalla** (*f.*) towel, 6
**tobillo** (*m.*) ankle, 17
**tocar** to play (*music, an instrument*)
**tocino** (*m.*) bacon
**todavía** yet, 17
**todo(-a)** all, 7
    **toda la noche** all night long, 10
    **todo el día** all day long
    **todo el viaje** the whole trip, 7
**todo** everything, 4
    _____ **lo que pasó** everything that happened, 7
**todos(-as)** everybody, 4
**tomar** to take, 2; to drink, 8
    _____ **algo** to have something to drink, 14
    _____ **el sol** to sunbathe, 10
    **la temperatura a alguien** take someone's temperature, 17
    _____ **una decisión** to make a decision, 13
    **Tome asiento.** Have a seat., 2
**tomate** (*m.*) tomato, 14
**tonterías** (*f.*): **decir** _____ to talk nonsense, 13
**torneo** (*m.*) tournament
**toro** (*m.*) bull
**toronja** (*f.*) grapefruit, 14
**torta** (*f.*) cake, 8
    _____ **helada** (*f.*) ice cream cake, 8
**tortilla a la española** (*f.*) omelette, 8
**tortilla mexicana** (*f.*) Mexican tortilla, 8
**tortuga** (*f.*) tortoise
**tos** (*f.*) cough, 17
**tostadora** (*f.*) toaster, 13
**trabajador(-a)** hard-working
**trabajar** to work, 2
**trabajo** (*m.*) job, work, 3
**traducir** to translate, 6
**traer** to bring, 4
**tráfico** (*m.*) traffic
**trágico(-a)** tragic
**traído** brought (*p.p. of* **traer**)
**traje** (*m.*) suit, 15
    _____ **de baño** (*m.*) bathing suit, 10
    _____ **de ejercicio** (*m.*) jogging suit, 15
**traslado** (*m.*) transportation
**tratar** to treat
    _____ **(de)** to try (to), 16
**travesía** (*f.*) voyage
**trece** thirteen, 1
**treinta** thirty, 1
**tren** (*m.*) train, 7
**tres** three, 1
**trescientos** three hundred, 3
**trimestre** (*m.*) quarter, 16
**triste** sad, 4
**tropezar (e:ie)** to trip
**trozo** (*m.*) piece
**trucha** (*f.*) trout, 8
**tu** your (*fam. sing.*), 3
**tú** you (*fam. sing.*), 1
**turismo** (*m.*) tourism, 6
**turista** (*m., f.*) tourist, 6
**turno** (*m.*) turn, 9
    **pedir** _____ to make an appointment, 9
**tus** your (*fam. pl.*), 3
**tutear** to use the **tú** form
**tuyo(s), tuya(s)** (*pron.*) yours (*fam. sing.*), 9

## U

**últimamente** lately, 9
**último(-a)** last, 14
    **última vez** the last time, 17

**un(a)** a, an, one, 2
**un momento** one moment, 3
**un poco** + *adj.* a little + *adj.* 4
**un poco de** a little, 2
**una vía** one way
**único(-a)** only, 11
**lo único** the only thing, 16
**universidad** (*f.*) university, 1
**universitario(-a)** (*adj.*) university, 3
**uno** (*m.*) one, 1
**unos(-as)** a few, some, 2; about
**usar** to wear, to use, 9
**se usa** it is used
**usted (Ud.)** you (*form., sing.*), 1; (*obj. of prep.*), 5
**ustedes (Uds.)** you (*form. pl.*), 1; (*obj. of prep.*), 5
**utensilio** (*m.*) utensil, 13
**útil** useful
**uva** (*f.*) grape, 4

## V

**vaca** (*f.*) cow
**vacaciones** (*f. pl.*) vacation, 6
**vacío(-a)** empty, 18
**vale** okay (*Sp.*), 5
**valer** to be worth
**(no) vale la pena** it's (not) worth the trouble, 18
**valija** (*f.*) suitcase, 6
**¡vámonos!** let's go, 13
**¡vamos!** let's go!, 5
**vaqueros** (*m. pl.*) bluejeans
**varicela** (*f.*) chickenpox
**varios(-as)** several, 3
**vasija** (*f.*) pot
**vaso** (*m.*) glass, 4
**vaya a** go to, 6
**veces: a** _____ at times, sometimes, 12
**vecino(-a)** (*m., f.*) neighbor
**vegetal** (*m.*) vegetable, 14
**veinte** twenty, 1
**veinticinco** twenty-five, 1
**veinticuatro** twenty-four, 1
**veintidós** twenty-two, 1
**veintinueve** twenty-nine, 1
**veintiocho** twenty-eight, 1
**veintiséis** twenty-six, 1
**veintisiete** twenty-seven, 1
**veintitrés** twenty-three, 1
**veintiuno** twenty-one, 1
**vela** (*f.*) candle
**velero** (*m.*) sailboat
**velocidad** (*f.*) speed, 18
_____ **máxima** (*f.*) speed limit, 18
**vencer** to beat, defeat
**venda** (*f.*) bandage, 17
**vendar** to bandage, 17
**vendedor(-a)** (*m., f.*) salesperson, 16
**vender** to sell, 3
**venezolano(-a)** Venezuelan, 14
**venir (a)** to come, 3
**venta** (*f.*) sale
**ventana** (*f.*) window, 2
**ventanilla** (*f.*) window (*of a vehicle or booth*), 12
**ventilador** (*m.*) fan, 18
**ver** to see, 6
**a** _____ let's see, 11
**verano** (*m.*) summer, 1
**verbo** (*m.*) verb
**verdad** (*f.*) truth
**¿verdad?** right?, true?, 11
**No es** _____**.** It's not true., 12
**verdadero(-a)** real, 15
**verde** green, 1
**verdura** (*f.*) vegetable, 14
**vermut** (*m.*) vermouth, 8
**vestido** (*m.*) dress, 9
_____ **de noche** (*m.*) evening gown, 15
**vestirse (e:i)** to get dressed, 9
**vez** (*f.*) time (occasion), 7
**a veces** at times, 12
**alguna** _____ ever, 15
**de** _____ **en cuando** from time to time, 14
**en** _____ **de** instead of, 13
**otra** _____ again
**próxima** _____ next time, 7
**tal** _____ maybe, 13
**vía** (*f.*) street, way
**por** _____ **aérea** airmail, 12
**viajar** to travel, 5
**viaje** (*m.*) trip, 6
**de** _____ traveling
**salir de** _____ to leave on a trip, 18
**viajero(-a)** (*m., f.*) traveler, 7
**vida** (*f.*) life, 16
**viejo(-a)** old, 12
**viento** (*m.*) wind, 6
**hacer** _____ to be windy, 6
**viernes** (*m.*) Friday, 1
**vinagre** (*m.*) vinegar, 14
**vino** (*m.*) wine, 4
_____ **tinto** (*m.*) red wine, 8
**visitar** to visit, 6
**vista** (*f.*) view
**con** _____ **a** overlooking, 6
**hasta la** _____ until I see you again, I'll see you later, 1
**visto(-a)** (*p.p. of* ver *and adj.*) seen, 15
**viudo(-a)** widowed, 3
**vivir** to live, 3
**vocabulario** (*m.*) vocabulary
**volante** (*m.*) steering wheel, 18
**volar (o:ue)** to fly, 5
**volver (o:ue)** to return, 5
**vosotros(-as)** (*subject pron.*) you (*fam. pl.*), 1; (*object of preposition*), you (*fam. pl.*), 5
**vuelo** (*m.*) flight, 7
**vuelto(-a)** (*p.p. of* **volver** *and adj.*) returned, 15
**vuestro(-a)** your (*fam. sing.*), 3; (*pron.*) yours (*fam. pl.*), 9
**vuestros(-a)** your (*fam. pl.*), 3

## Y

**y** and, 1; past, after (*time*), 2
**ya** already, 2; now, 7
_____ **no** no longer
**yerno** (*m.*) son-in-law, 5
**yo** I, 1
**yogur** (*m.*) yogurt

## Z

**zanahoria** (*f.*) carrot, 14
**zapatería** (*f.*) shoe department, shoe store, 15
**zapatillas** (*f. pl.*) slippers, 15
**zapato** (*m.*) shoe, 15
**zona postal** (*f.*) zip code, 3
**zoológico** (*m.*) zoo, 14
**zorro(-a)** (*m., f.*) fox

# English–Spanish

## A

**a, an** un(a), 2
**a little** un poco de, 2
**about** sobre, 6; de, 7; acerca de; unos(-as)

**abundant** caudaloso(-a)
**accept** aceptar, 6
**accident** accidente (*m.*), 17
**accommodation** alojamiento (*m.*), 6
**according to** según, 18
**account** cuenta (*f.*), 11
  **checking ____** cuenta corriente (*f.*), 11
  **on ____ of** por, 8
  **savings ____** cuenta de ahorros (*f.*), 11
**accountant** contador(-a) (*m., f.*), 16
**accounting** contabilidad (*f.*), 16
**accuracy** exactitud (*f.*)
**ache** doler (o:ue), 17
**across from** frente a, 12
**action** acción (*f.*)
**activity** actividad (*f.*), 10
**actor** actor (*m.*)
**actress** actriz (*f.*)
**ad** anuncio (*m.*), 6
**add** añadir
**addition** suma (*f.*)
**additional** adicional
**address** dirección (*f.*), 2; domicilio (*m.*), 2
**adjective** adjetivo (*m.*)
**advanced** adelantado(-a)
**advice** consejo (*m.*), 16
**advise** aconsejar, 11
**advisor** consejero(-a) (*m., f.*), 16
**Aesop** Esopo
**affectionately** afectuosamente, 16
**afraid: to be ____** tener miedo, 4
**after** (*time*) y, 2; después (de), 8
**afternoon** tarde (*f.*), 2
  **good ____** buenas tardes, 1
  **in the ____** de (por) la tarde, 2
**afterwards** después, 4; luego, 6
**again** otra vez
**age** edad (*f.*), 3
**ago: . . . ago** hace + *time*, 10
**agree** estar de acuerdo, 18
**agreement** concordancia (*f.*)
**air** aire (*m.*)
  **____ bag** bolsa de aire (*f.*), 18
  **____ conditioning** aire acondicionado (*m.*), 6
**airmail** por vía aérea, 12
**airport** aeropuerto (*m.*), 6
**aisle seat** asiento de pasillo (*m.*), 7
**alarm clock** despertador (*m.*), 11
**all** todo(-a), 7; (*pron.*) todo, 7
  **____ day long** todo el día
  **____ night long** toda la noche, 10
**allergic** alérgico(-a), 17
**almost** casi, 18
**alone** solo(-a)
**along** por, 8
**alphabet** alfabeto (*m.*)
**alphabetize** alfabetizar
**already** ya, 2
**also** también, 2
**although** aunque, 9
**always** siempre, 4
**A.M.** de la mañana, 2
**ambulance** ambulancia (*f.*), 17
**among** entre
**ample** amplio(-a), 6
**amusement park** parque de diversiones (*m.*), 14
**and** y, 1
**angry** enfadado(-a), enojado(-a), 4
**ankle** tobillo (*m.*), 17
**anniversary** aniversario (*m.*), 8
**announce** anunciar, 13
**another** otro(-a), 3
**answer** respuesta (*f.*); contestar
**antibiotic** antibiótico (*m.*), 17
**anxiously** ansiosamente
**any** alguno(-a), algún, 6; cualquier
  **not ____** ninguno(-a), ningún, 6
**anyone** alguien, 6
**anything** algo, 6
  **not ____** nada, 6
**anyway** de todos modos
**apartment** apartamento (*m.*), 9; departamento (*m.*); piso (*m.*) (*Sp.*)
**appear** aparecer
**appendicitis** apendicitis (*f.*)
**applaud** aclamar
**apple** manzana (*f.*), 14
**application** solicitud (*f.*), 3
**apply (for)** solicitar, 3
  **____ for a loan** pedir (e:i) un préstamo, 11
**appointment** cita (*f.*); turno (*m.*), 9
  **to make an ____** pedir (e:i) turno, cita, 9
**appreciate** apreciar, 10
**April** abril, 1
**Argentina** Argentina, 10
**Argentinian** argentino(-a), 16
**arm** brazo (*m.*), 17
**armchair** butaca (*f.*); sillón (*m.*), 13
**army** ejército (*m.*)
**around** por, 8; alrededor de, cerca de
**arrival** llegada (*f.*), 4
**arrive** llegar, 6
**art** arte (*f.*)
**article** artículo (*m.*), 3
**as** como, 16
  **____ . . . ____** tan... como, 5
  **____ if** como si, 18
  **____ many** tantos(-as), 5
  **____ many . . . ____** tantos(-as)... como, 5
  **____ much** tanto, 5
  **____ much ____** tanto como, 5
  **____ soon ____** en cuanto, 11; tan pronto como, 11
**ashamed** avergonzado(-a)
**ask** preguntar, 6
  **____ (for)** pedir (e:i), 6
**asleep: to fall ____** dormirse (o:ue), 9
**aspirin** aspirina (*f.*), 17
**assist** ayudar (a), 15
**asthma** asma (*m.*)
**at** a, 3; en, 2
  **____ noon** al mediodía, 4
  **____ what time . . . ?** ¿a qué hora... ?, 2
  **at** + *time* a la (las) + *time*, 2
**Atlantic Ocean** oceáno Atlántico, 10
**attend** asistir (a), 5
**attention: to pay ____** hacer caso, 13
**August** agosto, 1
**aunt** tía (*f.*), 5
**auto insurance policy** seguro de automóvil (*m.*)
**automatic** automático(-a), 18
  **____ teller** cajero automático (*m.*), 11
**automobile** automóvil (*m.*), auto (*m.*), carro (*m.*); coche (*m.*), 5
**autumn** otoño (*m.*), 1
**avenue** avenida (*f.*), 2
**average** promedio (*m.*), 16
**avoid** evitar, 17

## B

**back** espalda (*f.*), 17; de vuelta
**backpack** mochila (*f.*), 10
**bacon** tocino (*m.*)

**bad** malo(-a), 4
**Bah!** ¡Bah!, 5
**balance** (*bank*) saldo (*m.*), 11
**banana tree** banano (*m.*)
**band** orquesta (*f.*), 4
**bandage** vendar, 17; venda (*f.*), 17; (adhesive) curita (*f.*), 17
**bank** banco (*m.*), 11
**barber** barbero(-a), (*m., f.*), 9
____ **shop** barbería (*f.*), 9
**bargain** ganga (*f.*), 15
**baseball** béisbol (*m.*)
**basin** cuenca (*f.*)
**basket** canasto (*m.*)
**basketball** basquetbol (*m.*), baloncesto (*m.*)
**Basque Country** País Vasco (*m.*)
**bathe (oneself)** bañar(se), 9
**bathing suit** traje de baño (*m.*), 10
**bathroom** baño (*m.*), 6; cuarto de baño (*m.*), 6
**bathtub** bañadera (*f.*), 6
**battery** acumulador (*m.*), batería (*f.*), 18
**battlefield** campo de batalla (*m.*)
**be** ser, 1; estar, 4
____ **able to** poder (o:ue), 5
____ **acquainted with** conocer, 6
____ **afraid** tener miedo (de), 4
____ **bad weather** hacer mal tiempo, 6
____ **. . . behind schedule** tener… de atraso (retraso), 7
____ **bored** aburrirse, 10
____ **born** nacer
____ **called** llamarse, 9
____ **careful** tener cuidado, 4
____ **cold** (*weather*) tener frío, 4; hacer frío, 6
____ **due to** debido a
____ **early** llegar temprano
____ **. . . from here** estar a… de aquí, 12
____ **glad** alegrarse (de), 11
____ **going to +** ***inf.*** ir a + *inf.*, 4
____ **good weather** hacer buen tiempo, 6
____ **hot** (*weather*) hacer calor, 6; tener calor, 4
____ **hungry** tener hambre, 4
____ **in a hurry** tener prisa, 4
____ **invited** estar invitado(-a), 9
____ **late** llegar tarde, 7
____ **located** quedar, 8
____ **lucky** tener suerte, 4
____ **named** llamarse, 9
____ **pleasing to** gustar, 7
____ **ready** estar listo(-a), 5
____ **right** tener razón, 4
____ **right back** volver en seguida, 15
____ **scared** tener miedo, 4
____ **silent** callar
____ **sleepy** tener sueño, 4
____ **sorry** sentir (e:ie), 11
____ **starving** estar muerto(-a) de hambre, 15
____ **successful** tener éxito, 4
____ **sunny** hacer sol, 6
____ **thirsty** tener sed, 4
____ **tight** apretar (e:ie), 15
____ **too big (small) on someone** quedarle grande (chico) a uno, 15
____ **windy** hacer viento, 6
____ **worth the trouble** valer la pena, 18
____ **wrong** estar equivocado(-a), no tener razón, 4
____ **. . . years old** tener… años, 4
**beach** playa (*f.*), 10
**beans** frijoles (*m. pl.*), 8
**beautician** peluquero(-a) (*m., f.*), 9
**beautiful** hermoso(-a), 6
**beauty** belleza (*f.*)
____ **parlor** peluquería (*f.*), 9; salón de belleza (*m.*), 9
**because** porque, 2
____ **of** por, 8
**become** hacerse
**bed** cama (*f.*), 11
**to go to** ____ acostarse (o:ue), 9
**to put to** ____ acostar (o:ue), 9
**bedroom** dormitorio (*m.*); recámara (*f.*) (*Mex.*), 13
**bedspread** sobrecama (*f.*), 13
**beer** cerveza (*f.*), 4
**before** antes (de), 4; antes de que, 14
**beg** rogar (o:ue), 11
**begin** comenzar (e:ie) (a); 4; empezar (e:ie) (a), 4
**behalf: on** ____ **of** por, 8
**believe** creer, 3
**believed** creído (*p.p. of* **creer**), 15
**bellhop** botones (*m.*), 6
**belt** cinturón (*m.*), 15
**bend** doblar, 12
**besides** además, 13
**best** el (la) mejor, 5
**bet** apuesta (*f.*); apostar (o:ue)
**better** mejor, 5
**beverage** bebida (*f.*), 4
**bicycle** bicicleta (*f.*), 10
**big** grande, 4
**to be too** ____ quedar grande, 15
**bigger** mayor, 5
**bill** cuenta (*f.*), 8
**biology** biología (*f.*)
**birth** nacimiento (*m.*), 3
**birthday** cumpleaños (*m.*), 4
**black** negro(-a), 1
**blame** culpa (*f.*), 18; culpar, 18
**blanket** cobija (*f.*), frazada (*f.*), manta (*f.*), 13
**blend** mezcla (*f.*)
**blender** licuadora (*f.*), 13
**block** (*city*) cuadra (*f.*) (*Sp. Am.*), manzana (*f.*) (*Sp.*), 12
____ (*of buildings*) manzana (*f.*) (*Sp. Am.*), 12
**blond** rubio(-a), 3
**blood pressure** presión arterial (*f.*)
**blouse** blusa (*f.*), 15
**blow dryer** secador (*m.*), 9
**blue** azul, 1
**boarding house** pensión (*f.*), 5
**boarding pass** tarjeta de embarque (*f.*), 7
**boat** barco (*m.*), 7
**body** cuerpo (*m.*), 17
**book** libro (*m.*), 2
**boot** bota (*f.*), 15
**bored** aburrido(-a), 4
**to be** ____ aburrirse, 10
**boring** aburrido(-a), 7
**borrow** pedir (e:i) prestado, 11
**both** ambos(-as)
**bottle** botella (*f.*), 8
**boy** chico (*m.*), muchacho (*m.*), 3
**boyfriend** novio (*m.*), 3
**bra** sostén (*m.*), sujetador (*m.*), 15
**bracelet** pulsera (*f.*), 8

**brake** freno (*m.*), 18
**branch** (*office*) sucursal (*f.*)
**bread** pan (*m.*), 14
**break** romper(se), quebrar(se) (e:ie), 17
**breakfast** desayuno (*m.*), 6
**bride** novia (*f.*), 3
**briefcase** maletín (*m.*), 2
**bring** traer, 4
**broken** roto(-a), 15
**bronchitis** bronquitis (*f.*)
**broom** escoba (*f.*), 9
**brother** hermano (*m.*), 5
**brother-in-law** cuñado (*m.*), 5
**brown** marrón, café, 1; (*hair, eyes*) castaño, 3
**brought** traído (*p.p. of* **traer**)
**brunette** morena, 3
**brush** cepillo (*m.*), 9
**building** edificio (*m.*), 12
**bull** toro (*m.*)
**bulletin board** tablero de anuncios (*m.*), 2
**bumper** parachoques (*m.*), 18
**bureau** cómoda (*f.*), 13
**buried** enterrado(-a)
**bus** autobús (*m.*), ómnibus (*m.*), 5
**business administration** administración de empresas (*f.*), 16
**businessman (woman)** hombre (mujer) de negocios (*m., f.*), 16
**busy** ocupado(-a), 4
**but** pero, 4; sino, 14
**butter** mantequilla (*f.*), 14
**buy** comprar, 6; llevarse, 15
**by** para, 8; por, 8
  **____ then** para entonces, 16
  **to go ____** pasar (por), 6
**bye** chau, 1

## C

**cabbage** repollo (*m.*), 14
**cabin** cabaña (*f.*), 10
**cafe** café (*m.*), 5
**cafeteria** cafetería (*f.*), 3
**cake** torta (*f.*), 8
**calf** ternero (*m.*), (*of leg*) pantorilla (f.)
**call** llamar, 2
**called: to be ____** llamarse, 9
**camera** cámara fotográfica (*f.*), 6
  **video ____** cámara de video (*f.*), 6
**camp** acampar, 10
**campus** sede (*f.*)
**can** poder (o:ue), 5; bote (*m.*) (*Mex.*), lata (*f.*), 14
**cancel** cancelar, 6
**cancellation** cancelación (*f.*), 6
**candle** vela (*f.*)
**cap** gorro (*m.*), 15
**capital** capital (*city*) (*f.*), 6
**car** auto (*m.*), automóvil (*m.*), carro (*m.*), coche (*m.*), 5
**caramel custard** flan (*m.*), 8
**carburetor** carburador (*m.*), 18
**card** tarjeta (*f.*), 7
**career** carrera (*f.*), 16
**carpet** alfombra (*f.*), 9
**carpenter** carpintero(-a), (*m., f.*), 16
**carriage** carro (*m.*)
**carrot** zanahoria (*f.*), 14
**carry-on bag** bolso de mano (*m.*), 7
**carved** tallado(-a)
**case** caso (*m.*), 14
  **in ____** en caso de que, 14
**cash** efectivo (*m.*), 11
  **in ____** al contado, en efectivo, 11
**cassette** casete (*m.*), cinta (*f.*), 4
**catch a fish** pescar, 10
**celebrate** celebrar, 4
**celery** apio (*m.*), 14
**cellular phone** teléfono celular (*m.*), 18
**center** centro (*m.*), 15
**central heating** calefacción central (*f.*), 13
**cereal** cereal (*m.*)
**certainty** certidumbre (*f.*)
**certified** certificado(-a), 12
**chair** silla (*f.*), 2
**chalk** tiza (*f.*), 2
**chalkboard** pizarra (*f.*), 2
**challenge** desafiar
**champagne** champán (*m.*), 4
**change** cambiar, 15
**character** personaje (*m.*)
**charge** cobrar, 11
  **in ____ of** encargado(-a) de
**charmed** encantado(-a)
**charming** simpático(-a), 3; encantador(-a)
**chat** conversar, charlar, 4
**cheap** barato(-a), 6
**check** cheque (*m.*), talón, (*m.*) 11; chequear, revisar, 18
**checkbook** talonario de cheques (*m.*), chequera (*f.*), 11
**checking account** cuenta corriente (*f.*), 11
**checkup** examen (*m.*), chequeo (*m.*), 17
**Cheers!** ¡Salud!
**cheese** queso (*m.*), 8
**chef** cocinero(-a), (*m., f.*), 16
**chemistry** química (*f.*), 16
**chest** pecho (*m.*), 17
  **____ of drawers** cómoda (*f.*), 13
**chicken** pollo (*m.*), 4
  **____ and rice** arroz con pollo (*m.*), 8
  **____ pox** varicela (*f.*)
**child** niño(-a), 10
  **only ____** hijo(-a) único(-a), 11
**childhood** niñez (*f.*)
**children** hijos (*m. pl.*), 3
**Chile** Chile, 10
**Chilean** chileno(-a), 10
**Chinese** chino(-a)
**chocolate** chocolate (*m.*), 8
  **hot ____** chocolate caliente (*m.*), 8
**Christmas** Navidad (*f.*), 4
  **____ tree** árbol de Navidad (*m.*), 4
**church** iglesia (*f.*)
**cider** sidra (*f.*), 4
**circus** circo (*m.*), 14
**city** ciudad (*f.*), 3
**claim check** comprobante (*m.*), 11
**class** clase (*f.*), 2; curso (*m.*), 16
**classified** clasificado(-a), 13
**classmate** compañero(-a) de clase (*m., f.*), 4
**clay** barro (*m.*)
**clean (oneself)** limpiar(se), 9; (*adj.*) limpio(-a)
**clerk** empleado(-a) (*m., f.*), 6
**climate** clima (*m.*)
**climb** escalar, 10, subir, 12
**clock** reloj (*m.*), 2
**close** cerrar (e:ie), 4
  **____ to** (*prep.*) cerca de, 5
**closet** amario (*m.*), ropero (*m.*), 15
**clothes** ropa (*f.*), 11
**clothing** ropa (*f.*), 11
**club** club (*m.*), 4
**coal** carbón (*m.*)
**coat** abrigo (*m.*)

**cockroach** cucaracha (*f.*)
**cocktail** coctel (*m.*), 4
**coffee** café (*m.*), 5
   _____ **maker** cafetera (*f.*), 13
**cognate** cognado (*m.*)
**cold** catarro (*m.*), resfriado (*m.*), resfrío (*m.*), 17
   **to be** _____ (*weather*) hacer frío, 6; tener frío, 4
**color** color (*m.*), 1
**Colombian** colombiano(-a), 13
**Columbus** Colón (*m.*)
**comb** peine (*m.*), 9
   _____ **(one's hair)** peinar(se), 9
**come** venir (a), 3
   _____ **in!** ¡pase!, 2
**comedy** comedia (*f.*), 8
**comfortable** cómodo(-a), 5
**command** imperativo (*m.*)
**compact disc** disco compacto (*m.*), 4
   _____ **player** reproductor de discos (*m.*), 4
**company** compania (*f.*), 3
**comparative** comparativo(-a)
**complaint** queja (*f.*)
**computer** computador(-a), (*m., f.*), 12
   _____ **science** informática (*f.*)
**concert** concierto (*m.*), 9
**conclusion** conclusión (*f.*)
**conditional** condicional (*m.*)
**conduct** conducir, 6
**confirm** confirmar, 6
**consulate** consulado (*m.*), 6
**continue** seguir (e:i), 6
**conversation** conversación (*f.*), 2
**convince** convencer, 10
**cook** cocinar, 9; cocinero(-a) (*m., f.*), 16
**cookware** batería de cocina (*f.*), 13
**cool (down)** enfriar
**corner** (*street*) esquina (*f.*), 12
**correspond** tener correspondencia
**cost** costar (o:ue), 5
   _____ **an arm and a leg** costar un ojo de la cara, 10
**cotton** algodón (*m.*), 15
**couch** sofá (*m.*), 13
**cough** tos (*f.*), 17
   _____ **syrup** jarabe (*m.*), 17
**count** contar (o:ue), 5
**counter** mostrador (*m.*), 9
**country** campo (*m.*), 10; país (*m.*), 10
**couple** pareja (*f.*), 18
**course** curso (*m.*), 16
   **of** _____**!** ¡claro!, por supuesto, 7
**courtesy** cortesía (*f.*)
**cousin** primo(-a) (*m., f.*), 4
**covered** cubierto(-a), 15
**cover** cubrir
**cow** vaca (*f.*)
**crazy** loco(-a), 7
**cream** crema (*f.*), 8
**credit card** tarjeta de crédito (*f.*), 6
**creole** criollo(-a)
**cross** cruzar, 12
**crutch** muleta (*f.*), 17
**Cuban** cubano(-a), 8
**culture** cultura (*f.*), 9
**cup** taza (*f.*), 8
**curl** rizo (*m.*), 9
**curling iron** rizador (*m.*), 9
**currency** moneda (*f.*)
**curtain** cortina (*f.*), 13
**customs** aduana (*f.*), 6
**cut** corte (*m.*), 9
   _____ **(oneself)** cortar(se) (9)

## D

**dad** papá (*m.*), 5
**dam** represa (f.)
**dance** baile (*m.*), 4; bailar, 4
**dark** moreno(-a), 3; oscuro(-a)
**darling** (mi) amor (*m.*), 8; (*adj.*) querido(-a), 8
**data** datos (*m.*), 3
**date** fecha (*f.*), 3; (*check or letter*) fechar, poner la fecha, 11; cita (*f.*), 14
   **What's the** _____ **today?** ¿Qué fecha es hoy?, 1
**daughter** hija (*f.*), 5
   _____**-in-law** nuera (*f.*), 5
**day** día (*m.*), 2
   **a** _____ al día, 17
   _____ **before yesterday** anteayer, 8
   **What** _____ **is today?** ¿Qué día es hoy?, 1
   **days of the week** días de la semana (*m. pl.*)
**dear** querido(-a), 8; estimado(-a), 16
**December** diciembre
**decide** decidir, 3
**decision** decisión (*f.*), 13
   **to make a** _____ tomar una decisión, 13
**defeat** vencer
**definite** determinado(-a)
**degree** grado (*m.*), 17
**delay** atraso (*m.*), retraso (*m.*), 7
**delicious** delicioso(-a), 4; rico(-a), sabroso(-a), 8
**deliver** entregar, 16
**demonstrative** demonstrativo(-a)
**denial** negación (*f.*)
**dentist** dentista (*m., f.*), 1
**deny** negar (e:ie), 12
**department** departamento (*m.*), 11
   _____ **store** almacén (*m.*), tienda por departamentos (*f.*), 15
**departure gate** puerta de salida (*f.*), 7
**deposit** depositar, 11
**descend** bajar, 12
**describe** describir
**descriptive** calificativo(-a)
**desert** desierto (*m.*), 10
**design** diseño (*m.*), 15
**desk** escritorio (*m.*), 2; pupitre (*m.*), 2
**despite** a pesar de (que), 10
**dessert** postre (*m.*), 8
   **for** _____ de postre, 8
**detective** (*adj.*) policíaco(-a)
**develop** (*film*) revelar, 11
**diamond** diamante (*m.*)
**die** morir (o:ue), 5
**died** muerto(-a), 15
**diet** dieta (*f.*), 14
   **to go on a** _____ ponerse a dieta, 14
**difficult** difícil, 4
**dining room** comedor (*m.*), 13
**dinner** cena (*f.*), 6
   **to have** _____ cenar, 6
**dip** mojar
**dirty** sucio(-a)
   **to get (oneself)** _____ ensuciar(se), 9
**disappointment** desilusión (*f.*)
**disbelief** incredulidad (*f.*)
**disco** discoteca (*f.*)
**disease** enfermedad (*f.*)
**dish** plato (*m.*), 8
**dishwasher** lavaplatos (*m.*), 13

**disinfect** desinfectar, 17
**divorced** divorciado(-a), 3
**dizziness (dizzy spell)** mareo (*m.*)
**do** hacer, 6
**doctor** doctor(-a) (*m., f.*), 1; médico(-a), (*m., f.*), 1
    **____'s office** consultorio (*m.*), 17
**document** documento (*m.*), 12
**dog** perro(-a), 9
**dollar** dólar (*m.*)
**done** hecho(-a), 15
**door** puerta (*f.*), 2
**dorm** residencia universitaria (*f.*)
**dot: on the ____** en punto
**double: ____ room** habitación doble (*f.*), 6
**doubt** dudar, 12
**downstairs** abajo, 12
**downtown** (*area*) centro (*m.*), 6
**dozen** docena (*f.*), 14
**dramatic** dramático(-a)
**dream about (of)** soñar (o:ue) con, 17
**dress** vestido (*m.*), 9
**dressed: to get ____** vestirse (e:i), 9
**dressmaker** modista (*f.*)
**drink** beber, 3; tomar, 8; bebida (*f.*), 4
**drive** conducir, manejar, 5
**driver's license** licencia de conducir (*f.*), 3
**drizzle** lloviznar, 6
**dry cleaner's** tintorería (*f.*), 11
**dryer** secadora (*f.*), 13
**drugstore** farmacia (*f.*), 9
**dubbed** doblado(-a)
**during** durante, 7; por, 8
**dustpan** palita (*f.*), recogedor (*m.*), 9

## E

**each** cada, 12
**ear** (*inner*), oído (*m.*), 17; (*external*) oreja (*f.*), 17
**early** temprano, 9
    **to be ____** llegar temprano, 7
**earn** ganar, 13
**earthquake** terremoto (*m.*)
**easily** fácilmente, 10
**east** este, 10
**eastern** oriental
**easy** fácil, 4
**eat** comer, 3
**education** educación (*f.*), 3
**egg** huevo (*m.*), 8
**eight** ocho, 1
    **____ hundred** ochocientos, 3
**eighteen** dieciocho, 1
**eighth** octavo(-a), 8
**eighty** ochenta, 2
**either . . . or** o... o, 6
    **not ____** tampoco, 6
**elective** clase optativa (*f.*)
**electrician** electricista (*m., f.*), 16
**elegant** elegante, 8
**elevator** ascensor (*m.*), elevador (*m.*), 6
**eleven** once, 1
**E-mail** correo electrónico (*m.*), 12
**embassy** embajada (*f.*), 6
**emergency** emergencia (*f.*), 17
    **____ room** sala de emergencia (*f.*), 17
**empty** vacío(-a), 18
**encounter** encuentro (*m.*)
**engaged: to get ____ to** comprometerse con, 17
**engine** motor (*m.*), 18
**engineer** ingeniero(-a) (*m., f.*), 16
**engineering** ingeniería (*f.*), 16
**English** (*lang.*) inglés (*m.*), 2; (*nationality*) inglés(-a), 3
**enjoy** disfrutar, gozar de
    **____ oneself** divertirse (e:ie), 10
**enough** suficiente, 11; bastante
**entertaining** divertido(-a)
**entrance** entrada (*f.*), 7
**eraser** borrador (*m.*), 2; goma de borrar, 2
**errand** diligencia (*f.*), 11
    **to run ____s** hacer diligencias, 11
**escalator** escalera mecánica (*f.*), 15
**especially** especialmente, 5
**evening** noche (*f.*), 3
    **____ gown** vestido de noche (*m.*), 15
**ever** alguna vez, 15
**everybody** todos(-as), 4
**everything** todo, 4; de todo, 10
    **____ that happened** todo lo que pasó, 7
**everywhere** a (de) todas partes
**exam** examen (*m.*), 3; (*checkup*) examen (*m.*), 17
**excellent** excelente, 8
**excess baggage** exceso de equipaje (*m.*), 7
**exchange** cambiar, 15
    **in ____ for** por, 8
    **____ rate** cambio de moneda, 6
**excuse me** (con) permiso, 2
**exit** salida (*f.*), 7
    **main ____** puerta principal (*f.*), 12
**expensive** caro(-a), 6
**experience** experiencia (*f.*), 3
**expression** expresión (*f.*)
**eye** ojo (*m.*), 17

## F

**face** cara (*f.*), 17
**fact: the ____ is . . .** es que... , 12
**fail** (*course or exam*) quedar suspendido(-a), 16
**fair** feria (*f.*)
**fall** otoño (*m.*), 1; caer
    **____ asleep** dormirse (o:ue), 9
    **____ in love with** enamorarse de, 17
**family** familia (*f.*), 5
    **____ room** salón de estar (*m.*), 13
    **____ tree** árbol genealógico (*m.*)
**famous** famoso(-a), 5
**fan** ventilador (*m.*), 18
**farewell** despedida (*f.*)
**farmer** labrador(-a) (*m., f.*)
**fashion** moda (*f.*), 15
**fast** (*adv.*) rápido, 18
**fat** gordo(-a), 3
**father** padre (*m.*), 5
**father-in-law** suegro (*m.*), 5
**fault** culpa (*f.*), 18
    **to be one's ____** tener la culpa, 18
**favor** favor (*m.*), 13
**favorite** favorito(-a), 6
**fax** facsímil (*m.*), fax (*m.*), 12
**fear** miedo (*m.*), 4; temer, 11
**feather** pluma (*f.*)
**February** febrero, 1
**fed up** harto(-a)
**feel** sentir(se) (e:ie), 9
    **____ like** (*doing something*) tener ganas de, 14
**feminine** femenino(-a), 3

**fender** guardafangos (*m.*), guardabarros (*m.*), 18
**fever** fiebre (*f.*), 17
**few** pocos(-as), 6; unos(-as), 1
**fiancé** novio (*m.*), 3
**fiancée** novia (*f.*), 3
**fifteen** quince, 1
**fifth** quinto(-a), 8
**fifty** cincuenta, 2
**fight** luchar
**fill** llenar, 3
 ____ **out** llenar, 11
**film** (*for camera*) película (*f.*), 11
**filter** filtro (*m.*), 18
**final exam** examen final (*m.*), 16
**finally** por fin, 10
**financial problems** problemas económicos (*m. pl.*), 3
**find** encontrar (o:ue), 5
 ____ **out** averiguar, 6; saber, 10
**fine** (*adv.*), bien, 1; bueno, 7; multa (*f.*), 18
**finger** dedo (*m.*), 17
**finish** terminar, 9
**finished** acabado(-a)
**fire** lumbre (*f.*)
**first** primero(-a), primer, 8
 ____ **class** primera clase, 7
 ____ **day of classes** primer día de clases, 2
**fish** pescado (*m.*), 8; pescar, 10
**fishing** pesca (*f.*), 10; pesquero(-a)
 **to go** ____ ir de pesca, 10
**fishing rod** caña de pescar (*f.*), 10
**fit** caber, 6; quedar, 9
**fitting room** probador (*m.*), 15
**five** cinco, 1
 ____ **hundred** quinientos, 3
**fix** arreglar, 18
**flat tire: have a** ____ tener un pinchazo (*m.*), 18
**flight** vuelo (*m.*), 7
 ____ **attendant** auxiliar de vuelo (*m.*), 1; azafata (*f.*), 7
**float** carroza (*f.*)
**floor** piso (*m.*), 6
**flu** gripe (*f.*), 17
**fly** volar (o:ue), 5
**fog** niebla (*f.*), 6
**foggy: it's** ____ hay niebla, 6
**follow** seguir (e:i), 6
**food** comida (*f.*), 6
**foot** pie (*m.*), 17
**football** fútbol americano (*m.*)
**for** para, 3; por, 6
**foreign** extranjero(-a)
**foreigner** extranjero(-a), 12
**forest** bosque (*m.*)
**forget** olvidar(se) (de), 9
**forgive** perdonar
**fork** tenedor (*m.*), 8
**form** forma (*f.*)
**fortress** fortaleza (*f.*)
**fortune** fortuna (*f.*), 10
**forty** cuarenta, 2
**fountain** fuente (*f.*)
 ____ **pen** pluma estilográfica (*f.*), 2
**four** cuatro, 1
 ____ **hundred** cuatrocientos, 3
**fourteen** catorce, 1
**fourth** cuarto(-a), 8
**fox** zorro(-a) (*m., f.*)
**free** (*of charge*) gratis; libre, 11
**freedom** libertad (*f.*)
**freeway** autopista (*f.*), 18
**French** (*lang.*) francés (*m.*), 2
 ____ **fries** papas fritas (*f. pl.*), 8
**frequent** frecuente
**Friday** viernes (*m.*), 1
**fried** frito(-a), 8
**friend** amigo(-a), (*m., f.*)
**friendship** amistad (*f.*)
**from** de, 1; desde, 12
 ____ **the** (*contraction*) del, 4
**front: in** ____ **of** frente a, 11; delante de
**fruit** fruta (*f.*), 8
**fry** freír (e:i)
**full** lleno(-a), 18
 ____**-time** tiempo completo, 13
**function** funcionar, 18
**funny** cómico(-a)
**furnished** amueblado(-a), 13
**furniture** muebles (*m. pl.*), 13
**future** futuro (*m.*)

## G

**gain** aumentar
**game** partido (*m.*), 16
**garage** garaje (*m.*), 13
**garden** jardín (*m.*), 13
**gas station** gasolinera (*f.*), estación de servicio (*f.*), 18
**gasoline** gasolina (*f.*), 18
**gate** puerta (*f.*), 7
**gee!** ¡caramba!, 14
**gender** género (*m.*)
**generally** generalmente, 9
**gentleman** señor (*m.*), 1
**geographical** geográfico(-a)
**German** (*lang.*) alemán (*m.*), 2
 ____ **class** clase de alemán (*f.*), 2
**get** conseguir (e:i), 6; (*grade*) sacar, 16; buscar, 17
 ____ **a haircut** cortarse el pelo, 9
 ____ **dirty** ensuciar(se), 9
 ____ **dressed** vestirse (e:i), 9
 ____ **engaged to** comprometerse con, 17
 ____ **married** casarse con, 13
 ____ **undressed** desvestirse (e:i), 9
 ____ **up** levantarse, 9
**gift** regalo (*m.*), 8
**girl** chica (*f.*), muchacha (*f.*), 3
**girlfriend** novia (*f.*), 3
**give** dar, 4; (*as a gift*) regalar, 9
 ____ **a ticket (fine)** poner (dar) una multa, 18
 ____ **an injection** poner una inyección, 17
**glass** vaso (*m.*), 4; copa (*f.*), 4
**glove** guante (*m.*), 15
 ____ **compartment** guantera (*f.*), portaguantes (*m.*), 18
**go** ir (a), 4
 ____ **away** irse, 9
 ____ **by** pasar por, 6
 ____ **camping** acampar, 10
 ____ **down** bajar, 12
 ____ **fishing** ir de pesca, 10
 ____ **off** (*alarm*) sonar (o:ue), 11
 ____ **on a diet** ponerse a dieta, 14
 ____ **on vacation** ir de vacaciones, 10
 ____ **out** salir, 6
 ____ **shopping** ir de compras, 10
 ____ **through** pasar por, 6
 ____ **to** vaya a, 6
 ____ **to bed** acostarse (o:ue), 9
 ____ **together** hacer juego, combinar, 15

**_____ up** subir, 12
**_____ wrong** ir mal
**I'm leaving** me voy, 3
**to be going (to) +** *infinitive* ir a + *infinitive,* 4
**goblet** copa (*f.*), 4
**God grant** ojalá, 11
**gold** oro (*m.*), 6
**gone** ido, 15
**good** bueno(-a), buen, 3
**_____ afternoon** buenas tardes, 1
**_____ evening** buenas noches, 1
**_____ morning** buenos días, 1
**_____ night** buenas noches, 1
**it's no _____** no sirve, 18
**good-bye** adiós, 1
**grade** nota (*f.*), 16
**_____ point average** promedio (*m.*), 16
**grading system** sistema de calificaciones (*m.*)
**graduate** graduar(se), 16
**granddaughter** nieta (*f.*), 5
**grandfather** abuelo (*m.*), 5
**grandmother** abuela (*f.*), 5
**grandson** nieto (*m.*), 5
**grape** uva (*f.*), 4
**grapefruit** toronja (*f.*), pomelo (*m.*), 14
**grass** hierba (*f.*)
**grated** rallado(-a)
**gray** gris, 1
**graze** pacer
**great** magnífico(-a), 4
**great-grandfather (mother)** bisabuelo(-a) (*m., f.*), 4
**green** verde, 1
**greeting** saludo (*m.*)
**groom** novio (*m.*), 3
**ground floor** planta baja (*f.*), 15
**growth** crecimiento (*m.*)
**guilty** culpable

## H

**habit: bad _____** manía (*f.*)
**hair** pelo (*m.*), 9; cabello (*m.*), 17
**to comb one's _____** peinarse, 9
**to wash one's _____** lavarse la cabeza, 9
**haircut** corte (*m.*), 9
**to get a _____** cortarse el pelo, 9
**hairdo** peinado (*m.*), 9
**hairdresser** peluquero(-a) (*m., f.*), 9
**hairstyle** peinado (*m.*), 9
**half** medio(-a), 8
**_____ an hour** media hora, 7
**_____ brother** medio hermano, 5
**_____ past** y media (*time*), 2
**_____ sister** media hermana, 5
**ham** jamón (*m.*), 8
**hamburger** hamburguesa (*f.*), 8
**hand** mano (*f.*), 17
**handbag** bolsa (*f.*), bolso (*m.*), cartera (*f.*), 9
**handkerchief** pañuelo (*m.*), 15
**handsome** guapo(-a), 3
**happen** pasar, 7
**happy** contento(-a), 4; feliz, 4
**hardly** apenas
**hare** liebre (*f.*)
**hat** sombrero (*m.*)
**hate** odiar, 10
**have** tener, 3; haber (*aux.*), 15
**_____ a good time** pasarlo bien, 4; divertirse (e:ie), 10
**_____ a nice trip** buen viaje, 7
**_____ a seat.** Tome asiento., 2
**to _____ been doing something for a length of time** hace + *time* + que + *verb* (*present*), 7
**_____ dinner** cenar, 6
**to _____ done something in the past** hace + *time* + que + *verb* (*preterit/imperfect*), 10
**_____ just . . .** acabar de..., 6
**_____ lunch** almorzar (o:ue), 5
**_____ something to eat** comer algo, 14
**_____ something to drink** tomar algo, 14
**_____ supper** cenar, 6
**_____ to** deber, 3; tener que, 3
**he** él, 1
**head** cabeza (*f.*), 17
**headache** dolor de cabeza (*m.*), 17
**headlight** luz (*f.*), 18
**healer** curandero(-a) (*m., f.*)
**health** salud (*f.*)
**hear** oír, 15
**heard** oído (*p.p. of* oír), 15
**heat** calor (*m.*), 4; calentar (e:ie)
**heater** calefacción (*f.*)
**height** estatura (*f.*), 5
**hello** hola, 1; (*on the phone*) bueno, 3; (*on the phone*) dígame, 3
**say _____ to . . .** saludos a..., 16
**help** ayudar (a), 15
**her** su, 3; ella, 5; la, 6; le, 7
**herd** manada (*f.*)
**here** aquí, 5
**_____ it is.** Aquí la (lo) tiene., 6
**hers** suyo(-a)(s), 9
**herself** se, 9
**hide** ocultar
**high school** escuela secundaria (*f.*)
**highway** autopista (*f.*), carretera (*f.*), 18
**him** él, 5; lo, 6; le, 7
**himself** se, 9
**his** su, 3; suyo(-a)(s), 9
**hit** (*with a car*) atropellar, 17
**holiday** feriado (*m.*), día de fiesta (*m.*), 14
**Holy Week** Semana Santa (*f.*)
**home** casa (*f.*), 3; a casa
**_____ appliance** aparato electrodoméstico (*m.*), 13
**_____ page** propia página (*f.*)
**hood** capó (*m.*), 18
**hope** esperar, 11
**I _____ . . .** ojalá..., 11
**I _____ so.** Espero que sí., 10
**horn** bocina (*f.*), 18
**horror** horror (*m.*)
**hors d'oeuvres** entremeses (*m. pl.*), 4
**horse** caballo (*m.*), 10
**hospital** hospital (*m.*), 2
**hot** caliente
**to be _____** (*weather*) tener calor, 4; hacer calor, 6
**_____ chocolate** chocolate caliente (*m.*), 8
**_____ dog** perro caliente (*m.*), 14
**hotel** hotel (*m.*), 6
**hour** hora (*f.*), 7
**house** casa (*f.*), 3

**how** cómo, 1
_____ **are you?** ¿Cómo está Ud.? (*form. sing.*), ¿Cómo están ustedes? (*form. pl.*), ¿Cómo estás? (*fam.*), 1
_____ **did it go for you?** ¿Cómo te fue?, 10
_____ **do you do?** Mucho gusto, 1
_____ **do you say . . . ?** ¿Cómo se dice...?, 2
_____ **is it going (for you)?** ¿Cómo te va?
_____ **long . . . ?** ¿cuánto tiempo hace que...?
_____ **many** cuántos(-as), 2
_____ **much** cuánto(-a), 4
_____**'s it going?** ¿Qué tal?, 1
_____ **was (is) . . . ?** ¿Qué tal...?, 7
**however** sin embargo, 10
**hug** abrazar, 8; abrazo (*m.*), 10
**hundred** cien, ciento, 2
**hungry: to be** _____ tener hambre, 4
**hurry (up)** apurarse, darse prisa, 14
**to be in a** _____ tener prisa, 4
**There's no** _____**.** No hay apuro (prisa)., 7
**hurt** doler (o:ue), 17; herir (e:ie)
**husband** esposo (*m.*), 3

## I

**I** yo, 1
_____ **have to go.** Tengo que ir., 3
**ice cream** helado (*m.*), mantecado (*m.*) (*Mex., Puerto Rico*), 8
_____ **cake** torta helada (*f.*), 8
**iced (ice cold)** helado(-a), 8
**idea** idea (*f.*), 4
**identification** identificación, 3
_____ **card** documento de identidad (*de identificación*) (*m.*), 12
**if** si, 5
**I'm sorry** lo siento, 3
**imperfect** imperfecto(-a)
**important** importante, 16
**imported** importado(-a), 15
**improve** mejorar
**in** en, 2
_____ **case** en caso de que, 14
_____ **English** en inglés, 2
_____ **exchange for** por, 8
_____ **front of** frente a, 11
_____ **order that** para que, 14
_____ **order to** a, 3; para, 4
_____ **search of** en busca de, 8
_____ **spite of** a pesar de (que), 10
_____ **that case** entonces, 3
_____ **the afternoon** de la tarde, 2; por la tarde, 2
_____ **the morning** de la mañana, 2; por la mañana, 2
**income** ingresos (*m. pl.*)
**indefinite** indeterminado(-a)
**indicative** indicativo(-a)
**inexpensive** barato(-a), 6
**infection** infección (*f.*), 17
**information** información (*f.*), 6
**injection** inyección (*f.*), 17
**to give an** _____ poner una inyección, 17
**insist on** insistir en, 17
**install** instalar, 18
**installments** plazos (*m. pl.*), 11
**in (on)** _____ a plazos, 11
**instead of** en vez de, 13
**institution** institución (*f.*), 3
**instructor** profesor(-a) (*m., f.*), 1
**insurance** seguro (*m.*)
**intelligent** inteligente, 3
**interest** interés (*m.*), 6
**interesting** interesante, 5
**interior** interior, 6
**international** internacional, 6
**interrogative** interrogativo(-a)
**interview** entrevista (*f.*); entrevistar
**introduce** presentar, 7
**introduction** presentación (*f.*)
**invitation** invitación (*f.*), 4
**invite** invitar (a), 4
**invited** invitado(-a), 4
**iron** planchar, 9; plancha (*f.*), 13
**Is... (*name*) there?** ¿Está... (*name*)?, 3
**it** la, 6; lo, 6
_____ **means** quiere decir, 2
**Italian** (*lang.*) italiano (*m.*), 2
**it's... (*time*)** son las..., 2
**its** su, 3

## J

**jack** gato (*m.*), 18
**jacket** chaqueta (*f.*), 15
**jail** cárcel (*f.*)
**jam** mermelada (*f.*)
**January** enero, 1
**Japanese** japonés(-a)
**jeans** vaqueros (*m. pl.*); tejanos (*m. pl.*), bluejeans (*m. pl.*), 15
**jewel** joya (*f.*)
**jewelry** joyas (*f. pl.*)
_____ **store** joyería (*f.*)
**job** empleo (*m.*), trabajo (*m.*), 3
_____ **application** solicitud de trabajo (*f.*), 3
**jogging suit** traje de ejercicio (*m.*), 15
**joke** bromear, 13
**practical** _____ broma (*f.*)
**journalism** periodismo (*m.*), 16
**journalist** periodista (*m., f.*), 16
**journey** viaje (*m.*), 6
**judge** juez (*m., f.*)
**jug** cántaro (*m.*)
**juice** jugo (*m.*), 8
**July** julio, 1
**June** junio, 1

## K

**key** llave (*f.*), 6
**keyboard** teclado (*m.*), 12
**kid: to** _____ (***joke***) bromear, 13
**kilometer** kilómetro (*m.*), 18
**kind** clase (*f.*)
**king** rey (*m.*)
**kiss** beso (*m.*), 8
**kitchen** cocina (*f.*), 9
_____ **sink** fregadero (*m.*), 13
**knee** rodilla (*f.*), 17
**knife** cuchillo (*m.*), 8
**know** conocer, 6; saber, 6
**knowledge** conocimiento (*m.*), 3
**known** conocido(-a)

## L

**laboratory** laboratorio (*m.*), 16
**lace** encaje (*m.*)
**ladies** damas, 6
**lady** señora (*f.*), 1
**lake** lago (*m.*), 10
**lamb** cordero (*m.*), 8
**lamp** lámpara (*f.*), 13

**land** (*plane*) aterrizar
**language** idioma (*m.*); lengua (*f.*)
**large** grande, 5
**last** pasado(-a), 7; último(-a), 14; durar
　**_____ month** el mes pasado (*m.*), 7
　**_____ name** apellido (*m.*)
　**_____ night** anoche, 8
　**_____ time** última vez (*f.*), 17
**late** tarde, 7
　**to be _____** llegar tarde, 7
**lately** últimamente, 9
**later** más tarde, 3
　**(I'll) see you _____** hasta luego, 1; hasta la vista, 1
**Latin American** latinoamericano(-a)
**law school** facultad de derecho (*f.*), 16
**lawyer** abogado(-a) (*m., f.*), 3
**leaf** hoja (*f.*)
**learn** aprender (a), 3
**least** el (la) menos, 5
**leather** cuero (*m.*)
**leave** salir, 5; (behind) dejar, 8; irse, 9
　**_____ on a trip** salir de viaje, 18
**lecture** conferencia (*f.*)
**left** izquierdo(-a)
　**to the _____** a la izquierda, 6
**leg** pierna (*f.*), 17
**lend** prestar, 7
**letter** carta (*f.*), 5
**less** menos, 5
　**_____ . . . than** menos... que, 5
　**_____ than +** *number* menos de + *number*, 5
　**more or _____** más o menos, 3
**let's go** vamos, 5; vámonos, 13
**let's see** a ver, 11
**let's talk** conversemos
**letter** carta (*f.*), 5
**lettuce** lechuga (*f.*), 14
**liberty** libertad (*f.*)
**librarian** bibliotecario(-a) (*m., f.*), 16
**library** biblioteca (*f.*), 3
**license** licencia de conducir (*f.*), 3
　**_____ plate** chapa (*f.*), placa (*f.*) (*Mex.*), 18
**lie** mentir (e:ie), 8
**life** vida (*f.*), 16
**lifeguard** salvavidas (*m., f.*), 10
**lift** levantar, 9
**light** luz (*f.*), 2; (*adj.*) claro(-a)
**like** gustar, 7
**limp** cojera (*f.*)
**linen** hilo (*m.*), lino (*m.*), 15
**list** lista (*f.*), 6
**listen** oye, 2; escuchar
**literature** literatura (*f.*), 16
**litter** tirar hasura
**little** pequeño(-a), 5
　**a _____** un poco de, 2
　**a _____** + *adjective* un poco + *adjective*, 4
**live** vivir, 3
**livestock** ganadería (*f.*)
**living room** sala (*f.*), 13
**loan** préstamo (*m.*), 11
**lobster** langosta (*f.*), 8
**located** situado(-a), 6
　**to be _____** quedar, 8
**London** Londres
**long** largo(-a), 7
**look (at)** mirar, 5
　**_____ for** buscar
　**_____ like** parecerse (a), 11
**lose** perder (e:ie), 4
**lot (of)** mucho(-a), 4
**lottery** lotería (*f.*), 13
**love** querer (e:ie), 4; encantar, 8; love (*m.*), 8
　**_____ problems** problemas sentimentales (*m. pl.*), 3
　**in _____** enamorado(-a)
**luck** suerte (*f.*)
**luggage** equipaje (*m.*), 7
**lunch** almuerzo (*m.*), 6
　**to have _____** almorzar (o:ue), 5

## M

**madam** señora (*f.*), 1
**made** hecho(-a), 15
**magazine** revista (*f.*), 9
**mail** correo (*m.*), 12
　**_____ a letter** echar una carta al correo, 12
**mailbox** buzón (*m.*), 12; casillero (*m.*), 12
**mailman** cartero (*m.*), 12
**main** principal, 12
**maintain** mantener, 16
**major** especialización (*f.*), 16
**make** hacer, 6
　**_____ a decision** tomar una decisión, 13
　**_____ a deposit** hacer un depósito, 11
　**_____ an appointment** pedir (e:i) turno, cita, 9
　**_____ fun of** burlarse de
**male** masculino(-a)
**mall** centro comercial (*m.*)
**man** hombre (*m.*)
**many** muchos(-as), 4
　**as _____** tantos(-as), 5
**map** mapa (*m.*), 2
**March** marzo, 1
**margarine** margarina (*f.*), 14
**marital status** estado civil (*m.*), 3
**mark down** rebajar, 15
**marker** marcador (*m.*), 2
**market** mercado (*m.*), 14
**married** casado(-a), 3
**marry** casarse (con), 17
**match** combinar, hacer juego, 15
**mathematics** matemáticas (*f. pl.*), 16
**matter** importar, 16
**mattress** colchón (*m.*), 13
**May** mayo, 1
**maybe** tal vez, 13
**me** mí, 5; me (*d.o.*), 6; me (*i.o.*), 7
**meal** comida (*f.*), 8
**mean: What does . . . _____?** ¿Qué quiere decir...?, 2
　**It _____s . . .** Quiere decir..., 2
**means** medio (*m.*)
**meanwhile** mientras tanto
**measles** sarampión (*m.*)
**meat** carne (*f.*), 8
**meatball** albóndiga (*f.*), 8
**mechanic** mecánico (*m.*), 18
　**_____'s shop** taller de mecánica (*m.*)
**medical** médico(-a), 17
**medicine** medicina (*f.*), 5
　**_____ cabinet** botiquín (*m.*), 9
**Mediterranean Sea** mar Mediterráneo, 10
**medium** mediano(-a), 15
**meet** conocer, 7; encontrarse (o:ue) (con), 12
**melon** melón (*m.*), 14
**melt** derretir (e:i)

**men** hombres (*m. pl.*)
_____ **'s department** departamento de (ropa para) caballeros (*m.*), 15
_____ **'s room** caballeros, 6
_____ **'s undershorts** bikini (*m.*), calzoncillos (*m. pl.*), 15
**menu** menú (*m.*), lista (*f.*), carta (*f.*), 8
**merry** alegre
**Mexican** mexicano(-a), 1
**microwave (oven)** (horno de) microondas (*m.*), 13
**middle name** segundo nombre (*m.*)
**midnight** medianoche (*f.*), 4
**at** _____ a la medianoche, 4
**midterm exam** examen de mitad de curso (*m.*), examen parcial (*m.*), 16
**midwife** partera (*f.*)
**mile** milla (*f.*), 18
**milk** leche (*f.*), 8
**milkmaid** lechera (*f.*)
**mine** mío(-a), míos(-as), 9
**mineral water** agua mineral (*f.*), 4
**mirror** espejo (*m.*), 9
**miss** echar de menos, 5; extrañar, 5
**Miss** señorita, Srta. (*f.*), 1
**mix** revolver (o:ue)
**modern** moderno(-a), 6
**mole** lunar (*m.*)
**mom** mamá (*f.*), 4
**Monday** lunes (*m.*), 1
**money** dinero (*m.*), 3
_____ **order** giro postal (*m.*), 12
**month** mes (*m.*), 1
**last** _____ mes pasado, 7
**Moor** moro(-a) (*m., f.*)
**more** más, 5
_____ **or less** más o menos, 3
_____ **... than** más... que, 5
_____ **than +** ***number*** más de + *number*, 5
**morning** mañana (*f.*), 2
**mortgage** hipoteca (*f.*)
**most** el (la) más, 5
**mother** madre (*f.*), 4
**mother-in-law** suegra (*f.*), 5
**motor** motor (*m.*), 18
**motorcycle** motocicleta (*f.*), moto (*f.*), 11
**mountain** montaña (*f.*), 10; monte (*m.*)
**mouse** ratón (*m.*), 12
**mouth** boca (*f.*), 17
**move** (*from one house to another*) mudarse, 13
**movie** película (*f.*), 14
_____ **guide** guía de espectáculos (*f.*), 14
_____ **theater** cine (*m.*), 7
**movies** cine (*m.*), 7
**Mr.** señor (*m.*), Sr., 1
**Mrs.** señora (*f.*), Sra., 1
**much** mucho(-a), 4
**mumps** paperas (*f. pl.*)
**mud** barro (*m.*)
**museum** museo (*m.*), 5
**must** deber, 3
**my** mi(s), 3
_____ **address is . . .** Mi dirección es..., 2
_____ **name is . . .** Me llamo..., 1
**myself** me, 9
**mystery** misterio (*m.*)

## N

**name** nombre (*m.*), 3; nombrar
**My** _____ **is . . .** Me llamo..., 1
**first** _____ nombre (*m.*), 3
**What's your** _____**?** ¿Cómo se llama Ud.? (*form.*), 1; ¿Cómo te llamas? (*fam.*), 1
**nap** siesta (*f.*)
**napkin** servilleta (*f.*), 8
**narrow** estrecho(-a), 15
**nation** nación (*f.*); pueblo (*m.*)
**nationality** nacionalidad (*f.*), 3
**nature** naturaleza (*f.*), 10
**near** cerca de, 5; junto a, 10
**necessary** necesario(-a), 18
**neck** cuello (*m.*), 7
**need** necesitar, 2
**negative** negativo(-a)
**neighbor** vecino(-a) (*m., f.*)
**neighborhood** barrio (*m.*), 13
**neither** tampoco, 6
_____ **. . . nor** ni... ni, 6
**nephew** sobrino (*m.*), 5
**nervous** nervioso(-a), 4
**never** nunca, 5; jamás, 6
**nevertheless** sin embargo, 10
**new** nuevo(-a), 4
**New Year's Eve party** fiesta de fin de año (*f.*), 4
**newlyweds** recién casados (*m. pl.*), 18
**news** noticias (*f. pl*)
**newspaper** diario (*m.*), periódico (*m.*), 13
**next** próximo(-a), 7
_____ **day** al día siguiente, 10
_____ **time** la próxima vez, 7
_____ **to** al lado de, 12; junto a, 10
**nice** simpático(-a), 3
_____ **to meet you** Mucho gusto, 1
**nickname** sobrenombre (*m.*)
**niece** sobrina (*f.*), 5
**night** noche (*f.*), 3
**nightgown** camisón (*m.*), 15
**nightstand** mesita de noche (*f.*), 13
**nine** nueve, 1
_____ **hundred** novecientos, 3
**nineteen** diecinueve, 1
**ninety** noventa, 2
**ninth** noveno(-a), 8
**no** no, 1; ningún, ninguna, 6
_____ **one** nadie, 6
_____ **longer** ya no
**nobody** nadie, 6
**noise** ruido (*m.*), 18
**nominated** nominado(-a), 14
**none** ninguno(-a), ningún, 6
**nonsense: to talk** _____ decir tonterías, 13
**noon** mediodía (*m.*), 4
**at** _____ al mediodía, 4
**nor** ni, 6
**neither . . .** _____ **. . .** ni... ni..., 6
**north** norte (*m.*), 10
**North American** norteamericano(-a), 1
**northwest** noroeste (*m.*)
**nose** nariz (*f.*), 17
**not** no, 1
_____ **any** ninguno(-a), 6
_____ **much** no mucho
**note** notar
**notebook** cuaderno (*m.*), 2
**nothing** nada, 3
**notice** fijarse en, 17
**noun** nombre (*m.*)
**November** noviembre, 1
**now** ahora, 4
_____ **that I think about it** ahora que lo pienso, 14

**nowadays** actualmente
**number** número (*m.*), 2
**nurse** enfermero(-a) (*m., f.*), 1

## O

**object** objeto (*m.*), 6
**obtain** conseguir (e:i), 6
**occupation** ocupación (*f.*), 3
**ocean** océano (*m.*), 10
**October** octubre, 1
**of** de, 3;
 ____ **course!** ¡claro!, ¡por supuesto!, 7
**off** libre, 11
**offer** ofrecer, 6
**office** oficina (*f.*), 6
**often** a menudo
**oh** ah, 2
**oil** aceite (*m.*), 14
**okay** vale (*Sp.*), 5; bien, 7; bueno, 7; de acuerdo, 14
**old** antiguo(-a), 12; viejo(-a), 12
 **to be . . . years** ____ tener... años, 4
**older** mayor, 5
**oldest** el (la) mayor, 5
**omelette** tortilla (*f.*), 8
**on** en, 3
 ____ **account of** por, 8
 ____ **behalf of** por, 8
 ____ **the phone** por teléfono, 3
 ____ **the way to** camino a, 18
 **top (of)** encima de
**one** uno, 1
 ____ **hundred** cien, 2; ciento, 2
 ____ **moment** un momento, 3
 ____ **says** se dice, 2
 ____ **thousand** mil, 3
 ____ **way** una vía
 ____**-way (ticket)** de ida, 7
**onion** cebolla (*f.*), 14
**only** solamente, 2; sólo, 7; único(-a), 11
 ____ **child** hijo(-a) único(-a), 11
 ____ **thing** lo único, 16
**open** abrir, 3
**open(ed)** abierto(-a), 12, 15
**opportunity** oportunidad (*f.*), 5
**optimist(ic)** optimista (*m., f.*), 3
**or** o, 3
**orange** anaranjado(-a), 1; naranja (*f.*), 14
**orchestra** orquesta (*f.*), 4
**order** pedir (e:i), 8; mandar, 11; pedido (*m.*), 8; orden
**other** otro(-a), 3
**our** nuestro(-a)(-os)(-as), 3
**ours** nuestro(-a)(s), 9
**ourselves** nos, 9
**out of breath** echando el bofe
**out of order** descompuesto(-a), 18
**outdoor** al aire libre, 10
**outskirts** afueras (*f. pl.*)
**overlooking** con vista a, 6
**own** propio(-a)

## P

**Pacific Ocean** océano Pacífico (*m.*), 10
**pack** hacer las maletas
**package** paquete (*m.*), 12
**page** página (*f.*)
**pain** dolor (*m.*), 17
**painting** cuadro (*m.*), pintura (*f.*), 5
**pair** par (*m.*), 15
**palace** palacio (*m.*), 12
**pancake** panqueque (*m.*)
**pants** pantalón (*m.*), pantalones (*m. pl.*), 11
**pantyhose** pantimedias (*f. pl.*), 15
**paper** papel (*m.*), 2; (*report*) informe (*m.*), 16
**Paraguayan** paraguayo(-a), 9
**parcel** paquete (*m.*), 12
**Pardon me.** Perdón (*m.*), 2
**parents** padres (*m. pl.*), 5
**park** aparcar, estacionar, parquear, 11; parque (*m.*), 12
**part-time** medio día, 13
**party** fiesta (*f.*), 4
**pass** (*an exam or course*) aprobar (o:ue), 16
 ____ **through** pasar por, 6
**passbook** libreta de ahorros (*f.*), 11
**passport** pasaporte (*m.*), 6
**past** (*time*) y, 2
**pay** pagar, 7
 ____ **attention** hacer caso, 13
 ____ **in advance** pagar por adelantado, 6
**peach** durazno (*m.*), melocotón (*m.*), 14
**pear** pera (*f.*), 14
**pedestrian crosswalk** paso de peatones (*m.*)
**pen** pluma (*f.*), 2; bolígrafo (m.), 2
**pencil** lápiz (*m.*), 2
 ____ **sharpener** sacapuntas (*m.*), 2
**penicillin** penicilina (*f.*), 17
**people** gente (*f.*), 9; pueblo (*m.*)
**pepper** pimienta (*f.*), 8
**per** por, 6
**perfectly** perfectamente, 5
**perform** actuar
**perfume** perfume (*m.*)
 ____ **store** perfumería (*f.*)
**perhaps** tal vez, 13
**permanent wave** permanente (*m., f.*), 9
**personal** personal, 3
**pessimist(ic)** pesimista (*m., f.*), 3
**pharmacy** farmacia (*f.*), 9
**phone** teléfono (*m.*), 3
 ____ **book** guía telefónica (*f.*)
**photo(graph)** fotografía (*f.*), foto (*f.*), 5
**physics** física (*f.*), 16
**pick up** recoger, 11; buscar, 17
**picnic** picnic (*m.*)
**picture** cuadro (*m.*), pintura (*f.*), 5
**piece** trozo (*m.*)
**pig** cochino (*m.*)
**pile: a** ____ **of** un montón de (*m.*), 12
**pill** pastilla (*f.*), 17
**pillow** almohada (*f.*), 13
**pillowcase** funda (*f.*), 13
**pilot** piloto (*m., f.*), 1
**pineapple** piña (*f.*), 14
**pink** rosado(-a), 1
**pitch** (a tent) armar, 10
**pity: it's a** ____ es una lástima, 11
 **What a** ____**!** ¡Qué lástima!, 5
**place** lugar (*m.*), 6; poner, 6
 ____ **of birth** lugar de nacimiento (*m.*), 3
 ____ **of employment** lugar donde trabaja (*m.*), 3
 ____ **setting** cubiertos (*m. pl.*), 8
**placed** puesto(-a), 15
**plaid** de cuadros, 15

**plain** llanura (*f.*), llano (*m.*)
**plan** plan (*m.*), 5; pensar (e:ie) (+ *inf.*), 4; planear, 10
**plane** avión (*m.*), 7
**plate** plato (*m.*), 8
**play** tocar; jugar (u:ue)
  **____ golf** jugar (u:ue) al golf (*m.*), 10;
  **____ tennis** jugar (u:ue) al tenis (*m.*), 10
**player** jugador(-a) (*m., f.*)
**plead** rogar (o:ue), 11
**please** por favor, 2
**pleased: ____ to meet you.** Mucho gusto., 2
**pleasure: The ____ is mine.** El gusto es mío., 2
**plumber** plomero(-a) (*m., f.*), 16
**pluperfect** pluscuamperfecto
**P.M.** de la tarde, 2
**pneumonia** pulmonía (*f.*)
**pocket** bolsillo (*m.*)
**poem** poema (*m.*), 2
**police** policía (*f.*)
  **____ officer** policía (*m.*), 18
  **____ station** estación de policía (*f.*), 11
**polka dot** de lunares, 15
**pool** piscina (*f.*), 6
**poor** pobre (*unfortunate*), 11; pobre, 13
**pork** lechón (*m.*), 8
**Portugal** Portugal
**Portuguese** (*lang.*) portugués (*m.*), 2
**position** posición (*f.*)
**post office** correo (*m.*), oficina de correos (*f.*), 12
**postcard** tarjeta postal (*f.*), 7
**pot** vasija (*f.*)
**potato** papa (*f.*), 8; patata (*f.*) (*Sp.*), 8
  **____ salad** ensalada de papas (*f.*), 4
**pound** libra (*f.*)
**pour down raining** llover (o:ue) a cántaros, 8
**power** poder (*m.*)
**practice** practicar, 5
**pray** rezar
**prefer** preferir (e:ie), 4
**pregnant** embarazada, 17
**prepare** preparar, 4
**prescribe** recetar, 17
**prescription** receta (*f.*), 17
**present** regalo (*m.*), 8; presente
**pretty** bonito(-a), lindo(-a), 3
**price** precio (*m.*), 8
**pride** orgullo (*m.*)
**print** (*fabric*) estampado(-a), 15
**private** privado(-a), 6
**probably** probablemente, 16
**problem** problema (*m.*)
**profession** profesión (*f.*), 3
**professor** profesor(-a) (*m., f.*), 1
**program** programa (*m.*)
**programmer** programador(-a), (*m., f.*), 1
**prohibited** prohibido(-a), 14
**proud** orgulloso(-a)
**provided that** con tal (de) que, 14
**psychologist** psicólogo(-a) (*m., f.*), 16
**psychology** psicología (*f.*), 16
**punch** ponche (*m.*), 4
**punctual** puntual, 12
**purchase** compra (*f.*), 15
**purple** morado(-a), 1
**purse** bolsa (*f.*) (*Mex.*), bolso (*m.*), cartera (*f.*), 9
**put** poner, 6; puesto(-a), 15
  **____ in a cast** enyesar, 17
  **____ on** ponerse, 9
  **____ to bed** acostar (o:ue), 9

## Q

**quarter** trimestre (*m.*), 16
  **____ after/past** ... y cuarto (*time*), 2
  **____ of/to** ... menos cuarto (*time*), 2
**question** pregunta (*f.*)

## R

**race** carrera (*f.*)
**racket** raqueta (*f.*), 10
**rain** lluvia (*f.*), 8; llover (o:ue), 5
  **____ cats and dogs** llover a cántaros, 8
**raincoat** impermeable (*m.*)
**raise** levantar, 9
**rapidly** rápido, 18
**rare** raro(-a)
**rayon** rayón (*m.*)
**razor** máquina de afeitar (*f.*), 9
**reach** alcanzar
**read** leer, 3; leído (*p.p. of* **leer**)
**reader** lector(-a) (*m., f.*)
**ready** listo(-a), 11
  **ready-to-wear clothes** ropa hecha (*f.*)
**real** verdadero(-a), 15; real
**realist(ic)** realista (*m., f.*), 3
**reason** razón (*f.*)
**receive** recibir, 3; (*grade*) sacar, 16
**recent** reciente
**recently** recientemente
**receptionist** recepcionista (*m., f.*), 1
**recommend** recomendar (e:ie), 8
**red** rojo(-a), 1; (*wine*) tinto, 8
**red-headed** pelirrojo(-a), 3
**refrigerator** refrigerador (*m.*), 13
**refuse** no querer (e:ie) (*preterit*), 10; negarse(a)
**register** registro (*m.*), 6; matricularse, 16
**registered** certificado(-a), 12
**registration** recepción (*f.*), 6; matrícula (*f.*), 16
**regret** sentir (e:ie), 11
**remain** quedarse, 10
  **____ seated** quedar(-se) sentado(-a)
**remember** recordar (o:ue), 5; acordarse (o:ue) (de), 9
**rent** alquiler (*m.*), 13; alquilar, 10
  **for ____** se alquila, 13
**repair** arreglo (*m.*), 18; arreglar, 18
  **____ shop** taller (de mecánica) (*m.*), 18
**repeat** repetir (e:i), 8
**report** informe (*m.*), 3
**request** pedir (e:i), 6
**requirement** requisito (*m.*), 16
**resale** reventa (*f.*)
**research** investigación (*f.*), 16
**reservation** reserva (*f.*), reservación (*f.*), 6
**rest** resto (*m.*), 14
**restaurant** restaurante (*m.*), 5
**restroom** servicio (*m.*), W.C. (*m.*), 6
**return** regresar, 2; volver (o:ue), 5; (*something*) devolver (o:ue), 7
**returned** devuelto(-a), 15; vuelto(-a), 15
**rice** arroz (*m.*), 8
  **____ pudding** arroz con leche (*m.*), 8
**ride** (*a bicycle*) montar en bicicleta, 10; (*a horse*) montar a caballo, 10

**rifle** rifle (*m.*), 10
**right: to the ___** a la derecha, 6
**___?** ¿verdad?, 11
**___ away** en seguida, 6
**___ now** ahora mismo, 18
**___ there** allí mismo, 12
**to be ___** tener razón, 4
**ring** (*phone*) sonar (o:ue), 11
**river** río (*m.*), 10
**road** camino (*m.*), 18
**roasted** asado(-a), 8
**role** papel (*m.*)
**roll of film** rollo de película (*m.*), 11
**roller coaster** montaña rusa (*f.*), 14
**Romanesque** románico(-a)
**room** cuarto (*m.*), 6; habitación (*f.*), 6
**___ and board** cuarto y comida
**___ service** servicio de habitación (cuarto) (*m.*), 6
**roommate** compañero(-a) de cuarto (*m., f.*), 17
**round-trip** de ida y vuelta, 7
**royal** real, 12
**rug** alfombra (*f.*), 9
**ruins** ruinas (*f. pl.*), 6
**ruler** regla (*f.*), 2
**run errands** hacer diligencias, 11
**run over** atropellar, 17

## S

**sad** triste, 4
**said** dicho(-a), 15
**sailboat** velero (*m.*)
**salad** ensalada (*f.*), 4
**salary** salario (*m.*), sueldo (*m.*), 13
**sale** liquidación (*f.*), rebaja (*f.*), 15; venta (*f.*)
**for ___** se vende
**salesperson** vendedor(-a) (*m., f.*), 16
**salmon** salmón (*m.*), 8
**salon** salón (*m.*), 9
**___ de belleza** (*m.*) beauty parlor, salon, 9
**salt** sal (*f.*), 8
**same** mismo(-a), 13
**sand** arena (*f.*)
**sandal** sandalia (*f.*), 15
**sandwich** sándwich (*m.*), 4
**sangría** sangría (*f.*), 4
**Saturday** sábado (*m.*), 1
**sauce** salsa (*f.*), 14
**saucepan** cacerola (*f.*), 13
**saucer** platillo (*m.*), 8
**sausage** chorizo (*m.*)
**save** ahorrar, 11
**savings** ahorros (*m. pl.*), 11
**___ account** cuenta de ahorros (*f.*), 11
**___ passbook** libreta de ahorros (*f.*), 11
**say** decir (e:i), 6
**scarf** bufanda (*f.*)
**schedule** horario (*m.*), 16
**scholarship** beca (*f.*), 16
**school** escuela (*f.*), 5
**science** ciencia (*f.*), 16
**___ fiction** ciencia ficción (*f.*)
**scorn** despreciar
**scream** gritar, 11
**screen** pantalla (*f.*), 12
**sea** mar (*m.*), 10
**season** estación (*f.*), 1
**seat** asiento (*m.*), 7; sede (*f.*)
**second** segundo(-a), 6
**secretary** secretario(-a) (*m., f.*), 1
**section** departamento (*m.*), 11
**(no) smoking ___** sección de (no) fumar (*f.*), 7
**see** ver, 6
**let's ___ . . .** a ver..., 11
**(I'll) ___ you later** hasta luego, 1; hasta la vista, 1
**___ you soon.** Hasta pronto.
**___ you tomorrow** hasta mañana, 1
**___ you.** Nos vemos., 1
**seen** visto(-a), 15
**sell** vender, 3
**send** enviar, mandar, 7
**sentence** oración (*f.*)
**September** septiembre, 1
**seriously** en serio, 10
**serve** servir (e:i), 6
**service station** gasolinera (*f.*), estación de servicio (*f.*), 18
**set the table** poner la mesa, 8
**seven** siete, 1
**___ hundred** setecientos, 3
**seventeen** diecisiete, 1
**seventh** séptimo(-a), 8
**seventy** setenta, 2
**several** varios(-as), 3
**sex** sexo (*m.*), 3
**Shall we dance?** ¿Bailamos?, 4
**shame: it's a ___** es una lástima, 11
**What a ___!** ¡Qué lástima!, 5
**shampoo** champú (*m.*), 9; lavado (*m.*), 9
**shave** afeitar(se), 9
**shaving cream** crema de afeitar (*f.*), 9
**she** ella, 1
**sheep** ovejas (*f. pl.*)
**sheet** sábana (*f.*), 13
**___ of paper** hoja de papel (*f.*), 2
**shellfish** mariscos (*m. pl.*), 8
**ship** barco (*m.*), 7
**shirt** camisa (*f.*), 15
**shoe** zapato (*m.*), 15
**___ department (store)** zapatería (*f.*), 15
**shopping** de compras, 10
**___ mall** centro comercial, 15
**to go ___** ir de compras, 10
**short** bajo(-a), 3; corto(-a), 9
**___ story** relato breve (*m.*)
**shorts** pantalones cortos (*m. pl.*)
**shot** inyección (*f.*), 17; balazo (*m.*)
**to give a ___** poner una inyección, 17
**should** deber, 3
**show** enseñar (a), 6; mostrar (o:ue), 6; función (*f.*), 14
**___ a movie** poner una película, 14
**shower** ducha (*f.*), 6
**to take a ___** ducharse, 9
**shrimp** camarones (*m. pl.*), gambas (*f. pl.*) (*Sp.*), 8
**sick** enfermo(-a), 4
**sidewalk cafe** café al aire libre (*m.*), 5
**sign** firmar, 6; letrero (*m.*), 18; señal (*f.*)
**___ here.** Firme aquí., 6
**signature** firma (*f.*), 11
**silk** seda (*f.*), 15
**silver** plata (*f.*), 6
**simple** sencillo(-a), 6
**since** como, 7
**sing** cantar, 4
**single** soltero(-a), 3; sencillo(-a), 6

**sink** lavabo (*m.*), 6; (*kitchen*) fregadero (*m.*), 13
**sir** señor, 1
**sister** hermana (*f.*), 5
**sister-in-law** cuñada (*f.*), 5
**sit down** sentarse (e:ie), 9
**six** seis, 1
  ____ **hundred** seiscientos, 3
**sixteen** dieciséis, 1
**sixth** sexto(-a), 8
**sixty** sesenta, 2
**size** medida (*f.*), talla (*f.*), 15; (*of shoes*) número (*m.*), 15; tamaño (*m.*)
**ski** esquiar, 10
**skillet** sartén (*f.*), 13
**skirt** falda (*f.*), 15
**slave** esclavo(-a) (*m., f.*)
**sleep** dormir (o:ue), 5
  ____ **late** quedarse en la cama hasta tarde, 11
**sleeping bag** saco de dormir (*m.*), bolsa de dormir (*f.*), 10
**sleepy: to be** ____ tener sueño, 4
**slender** delgado(-a), 3
**slippers** zapatillas (*f., pl.*), 15
**small** pequeño(-a), 4
  **to be too** ____ **(on someone)** quedar(le) chico(-a) (a uno), 15
**smog** contaminación del aire (*f.*)
**smoking: (no) smoking section** sección de (no) fumar (*f.*), 7
**snow** nevar (e:ie), 6; nieve (*f.*), 10
  ____ **covered** nevado(-a)
**so** tan, 5; de manera que, 11; de modo que, 11
  ____ **much** tanto, 14
**so-so** más o menos, 3
**soap** jabón (*m.*), 6
**soccer** fútbol (*m.*), 16
**social security** seguro social (*m.*), 3
**sociology** sociología (*f.*), 16
**sock** calcetín (*m.*), 15
**soda pop** refresco (*m.*), 4
**sofa** sofá (*m.*), 13
**soft drink** refresco (*m.*), 4
**some** unos(-as), 2; algunos(-as), 5; alguno(-a), algún, 6
**somebody** alguien, 6
**someone** alguien, 6
**something** algo, 6
**sometimes** a veces, 12
**son** hijo (*m.*), 5
**son-in-law** yerno (*m.*), 5
**song** canción (*f.*)
**soon** pronto, 16
  **as** ____ **as** en cuanto, 11; tan pronto como, 11
**sorrow** pena (*f.*)
**sorry: to be** ____ sentir (e:ie), 11
**sort** especie (*f.*)
**soundly** profundamente, 10
**soup** sopa (*f.*), 8
  ____ **of the day** sopa del día (*f.*), 8
**source** fuente (*f.*)
**south (southern)** sur (*m.*), 10
**Spain** España, 4
**Spaniard** español(-a) (*m., f.*), 12
**Spanish** (*lang.*) español (*m.*), 1
  ____**-speaking** de habla hispana
  ____ **teacher** profesor(-a) de español (*m., f.*), 1
**spare part** pieza de repuesto (*f.*), 18
**sparkplug** bujía (*f.*), 18
**speak** hablar, 2
**special** especial, 16
**specialty** especialidad (*f.*), 8
**speed** velocidad (*f.*), 18
  ____ **limit** velocidad máxima (*f.*), 18
**speeding** exceso de velocidad (*m.*), 18
**spend** (*time*) pasar, 6; (*money*) gastar, 16
**spill** derramar
**spoilsport** aguafiestas (*m., f.*), 13
**spoken** hablado(-a)
**spoon** cuchara (*f.*), 8
**spoonful** cucharada (*f.*)
**sport** deporte (*m.*), 16
**spring** primavera (*f.*), 1
**stadium** estadio (*m.*), 16
**stain** manchar
**stairs** escalera (*f.*), 6
**stamp** estampilla (*f.*), sello (*m.*), timbre (*m.*) (*Mex.*), 12
**standard shift** de cambios mecánicos, 18
**standing** parado(-a), 12
**star** estrella (*f.*)
**start** comenzar (e:ie), empezar (e:ie), 4; arrancar (*car*), 18
**starving: to be** ____ estar muerto(-a) de hambre, 15
**station** estación (*f.*), 12
  ____ **wagon** camioneta, 18
**stay** quedarse, 10; hospedarse (en) (*at a hotel*), 10
**steak** bistec (*m.*), 8
**steal** robar, 11
**steering wheel** volante (*m.*), 18
**stepbrother** hermanastro (*m.*), 5
**stepdaughter** hijastra (*f.*), 5
**stepfather** padrastro (*m.*), 5
**stepmother** madrastra (*f.*), 5
**stepsister** hermanastra (*f.*), 5
**stepson** hijastro (*m.*), 5
**stereo system** equipo estereofónico (*m.*), 4
**still** todavía, 17; aún
**stomach** estómago (*m.*), 17
**stone** piedra (*f.*)
**stop** parar, 18; (*moving*) detenerse; (*sign*) alto
**store** tienda (*f.*), 8
**store clerk** dependiente(-a) (*m., f.*), 15
**stove** cocina (*f.*), 13
**straight (hair)** lacio(-a), 9
  ____ **(ahead)** derecho, 12
**strange** extraño(-a), 18
**strawberry** fresa (*f.*), 14
**street** calle (*f.*), 2
  ____ **corner** esquina (*f.*), 12
**striped** a rayas, 15
**student** estudiante (*m., f.*), 1; alumno(-a) (*m., f.*), 2
**study** estudiar, 2
**stuffed** relleno(-a), 8
**style** moda, 15
  **be in** ____ estar de moda, 9
  **out of** ____ pasado(-a) de moda, 15
**subject** asignatura (*f.*), materia (*f.*), 16; tema (*m.*)
**subsidized** subvencionado(-a)
**subtraction** resta (*f.*)
**subway** metro (*m.*), subterráneo (*m.*), 12
**sufficient** suficiente, 11
**sugar** azúcar (*m.*), 14
**suggest** sugerir (e:ie), 11
**suit** traje (*m.*), 15
**suitcase** maleta (*f.*); valija (*f.*), 6
**summer** verano (*m.*), 1
**sun** sol (*m.*)
**sunbathe** tomar el sol, 10
**Sunday** domingo (*m.*), 1
**sunny: to be** ____ hacer sol, 6
**supermarket** supermercado (*m.*), 14

**supper** cena (*f.*), 6
**to have ______** cenar, 6
**suppose** suponer, 16
**surgery** operación (*f.*)
**surname** apellido (*m.*), 3
**surprise** sorpresa (*f.*), 8; sorprender, 11
**sweater** suéter (*m.*), 15
**sweep** barrer, 9
**sweets** dulces (*m. pl.*)
**swim** nadar, 10
**swimming pool** piscina (*f.*), 6
**Switzerland** Suiza
**system** sistema (*m.*)
**systems analyst** analista de sistemas (*m., f.*), 1

## T

**T-shirt** camiseta (*f.*), 15
**table** mesa (*f.*), 4
**tablecloth** mantel (*m.*), 8
**tailor** sastre (*m.*)
**take** tomar, 2; (*someone or something someplace*) llevar, 4; (*buy*) llevarse, 15
**______ a shower** ducharse, 9
**______ advantage of** aprovechar, 15
**______ an X-ray** hacer una radiografía, 17
**______ away** quitar, 9; llevarse, 11
**______ care of oneself** cuidarse, 17
**______ off** quitarse, 9
**______ out** sacar, 11
**______ place** tener lugar
**______ size . . .** (*in shoes*) calzar, 15
**______ someone's temperature** tomarle la temperatura a alguien, 17
**talk** conversar, charlar, 4; hablar
**tall** alto(-a), 3
**tank** tanque (*m.*), 18
**tape** casete (*m.*), cinta (*f.*), 4
**taste** probar (o:ue), 9; saborear
**tasty** sabroso(-a), rico(-a), 8
**taxi** taxi (*m.*), 6
**tea** té (*m.*), 8
**teach** enseñar (a), 10
**teacher** profesor(a) (*m., f.*), 1; (*elementary school*) maestro(-a) (*m., f.*), 1
**team** equipo (*m.*), 16
**teaspoon** cucharita (*f.*), 8
**teaspoonful** cucharadita (*f.*)
**teeth** dientes (*m. pl.*), 17
**telegram** telegrama (*m.*)
**telephone** teléfono (*m.*), 3
**television** (*set*) televisor (*m.*), 6; televisión (*f.*)
**tell** decir (e:i), 6; contar (o:ue), 7
**______ us** díganos
**temperature** temperatura (*f.*), 17
**ten** diez, 1
**tenderloin steak** filete (*m.*), 8
**tent** tienda de campaña (*f.*), 10
**tenth** décimo(-a), 8
**terrace** terraza (*f.*), 4
**tetanus shot** inyección antitetánica (*f.*), 17
**than** que, 5
**thank you** gracias
**______ very much** muchas gracias, 2
**that** (*adj.*) que, 3; aquel(la), 7; (*adj.*) ese, 7; (*adj.*) esa, 7; (*neuter pron.*) aquello, 7; (*neuter pron.*) eso, 7
**______ one** aquél(la),7; ése, 7; ésa, 7
**the** el, 1; la, 1; las, 1; los, 1
**theater** teatro (*m.*), 8
**their** su(s), 3
**theirs** suyo(-a)(s), 9
**them** ellas, ellos, 5; las, 6; les, 7; los, 6
**theme** tema (*m.*)
**themselves** se, 9
**then** entonces, 3; luego, 6; después, 7; pues, 7
**there** allí, 4
**______ are, is** hay, 2
**______ was, were** hubo, 9
**these** (*adj.*) estos(-as), 7; (*pron.*) éstos(-as), 7
**they** ellos 1; ellas, 1
**thin** delgado(-a), 3
**thing** cosa (*f.*), 14
**think** creer, 3; pensar (e:ie), 4
**______ about** pensar en, 17
**third** tercero(-a), tercer, 8
**thirsty: to be ______** tener sed, 4
**thirteen** trece, 1
**thirty** treinta, 1
**this** (*adj.*) este, 5; (*adj.*) esta, 7; (*neuter pron.*), esto, 7
**______ is she (speaking)** con ella habla, 3
**______ one** (*pron.*) éste(-a), 7
**______ semester** este semestre (*m.*), 2
**those** (*adj.*) aquellos(-as), 7; (*pron.*) aquéllos(-as), 7; (*adj.*) esos(-as), 7; (*pron.*) ésos(-as), 7
**thought** pensamiento (*m.*)
**thousand** mil, 3
**three** tres, 1
**______ hundred** trescientos, 3
**throat** garganta (*f.*), 17
**through** por, 8
**Thursday** jueves (*m.*), 1
**ticket** (*for plane, train, bus*) billete (*m.*) (*Sp.*), pasaje (*m.*), 7; (*for a show*) boleto (*m.*), entrada (*f.*), 8; (*fine*) multa (*f.*), 18
**first-class ______** billete (pasaje) de primera clase (*m.*), 7
**to give a ______** poner (dar) una multa, 18
**one-way ______** billete (pasaje) de ida (*m.*), 7
**round-trip ______** billete (pasaje) de ida y vuelta (*m.*), 7
**tie** corbata (*f.*), 15
**tight: to be ______** apretar (e:ie), 15
**they feel ______ (on me)** me aprietan, 15
**tiled sidewalk** acera adoquinada (*f.*)
**till** menos (*telling time*), 2
**time** hora (*f.*), 2; vez (*occasion*) (*f.*), 7; tiempo (*m.*), 16
**at the same ______** al mismo tiempo, 13
**from ______ to ______** de vez en cuando, 14
**have a good ______** divertirse, (e:ie), 10
**What ______ is it?** ¿Qué hora es?, 2
**tip** propina (*f.*), 8
**tire** goma (*f.*), llanta (*f.*), neumático (*m.*), 18
**tired** cansado(-a), 4
**to** a, 3; para, 3
**______ the** al (*m. sing.*) (*contraction*), 3
**toast** (*wine*) brindar, 4; brindis (*m.*), 4
**toaster** tostadora (*f.*), 13
**today** hoy, 2
**toe** dedo del pie (*m.*), 17

**together** juntos(-as), 7
**toilet** inodoro (*m.*), 6
**toilet tissue** papel higiénico (*m.*), 14
**told** dicho(-a), 15
**tomato** tomate (*m.*), 14
**tomorrow** mañana, 3
**tongue** lengua (*f.*), 17
**tonight** esta noche, 3
**tonsilitis** amigdalitis (*f.*)
**too** también, 2; demasiado
**tooth** diente (*m.*), 17
**topic** tema (*m.*)
**tortoise** tortuga (*f.*)
**tour** excursión (*f.*), 6
**tourism** turismo (*m.*), 6
**tourist** turista (*m., f.*), 6
  ______ **card** tarjeta de turista (*f.*), 6
  ______ **class** clase turista (*f.*), 7
**tournament** torneo (*m.*)
**tow** remolcar, 18
  ______ **truck** grúa (*f.*), remolcador (*m.*), 18
**toward** hacia, 11
**towel** toalla (*f.*), 6
**town** aldea (*f.*), pueblo (*m.*)
**town square** plaza (*f.*), 5
**trade** oficio (*m.*), 16
**traffic** tráfico (m.)
  ______ **light** semáforo (*m.*), 12
**tragic** trágico(-a)
**train** tren (*m.*), 7
**translate** traducir, 6
**transportation** traslado (*m.*)
**travel** viajar, 5
  ______ **agency** agencia de viajes (*f.*), 7
  ______ **agent** agente de viajes (*m., f.*), 7
**traveler** viajero(-a) (*m., f.*), 7
**traveler's check** cheque de viajeros (*m.*), 6
**traveling** de viaje
**treat** tratar
  **My** ______**!** ¡Yo invito!, 14
**trimester** trimestre (*m.*), 16
**trip** viaje (*m.*), 6; tropezar (e:ie)
**trousers** pantalón (*m.*), pantalones, (*m. pl.*), 11
**trout** trucha (*f.*), 8
**true** cierto, verdad, 12
  **It's not** ______. No es cierto (verdad)., 12
  **true?** ¿verdad?, 11
**trunk** (*car*) cajuela (*f.*), maletero (*m.*), 18
**truth** verdad (*f.*)
**try** probar (o:ue), 9; tratar (de), 16
  ______ **on** probarse (o:ue), 9
**Tuesday** martes (*m.*), 1
**tuition** matrícula (*f.*), 16
**turkey** pavo (*m.*), 8
**turn** turno (*m.*), 9; doblar, 12
  **. . . years old** cumplir ...años, 4
  ______ **in** entregar, 16
  ______ **into** convertirse (e:ie) en
  ______ **loose** soltar (o:ue)
  ______ **on** (*air conditioning heat*) poner
  ______ **to** recurrir a
**T.V. set** televisor (*m.*), 6
**twelve** doce, 1
**twenty** veinte, 1
  ______**-one** veintiuno, 1
  ______**-two** veintidós, 1
  ______**-three** veintitrés, 1
  ______**-four** veinticuatro, 1
  ______**-five** veinticinco, 1
  ______**-six** veintiséis, 1
  ______**-seven** veintisiete, 1
  ______**-eight** veintiocho, 1
  ______**-nine** veintinueve, 1
**two** dos, 1
  ______ **hundred** doscientos, 3

## U

**ugly** feo(-a), 3
**umbrella** paraguas (*m. sing.*)
**uncle** tío (*m.*), 5
**uncomfortable** incómodo(-a)
**understand** entender (e:ie), 4
**underwear** ropa interior (*f.*), 15
**undress, get undressed** desvestir(se) (e:i), 9
**unfortunate** desafortunado(-a)
**unfortunately** desafortunadamente, 10
**United States** Estados Unidos (*m. pl.*), 5
**university** universidad (*f.*), 1; (*adj.*) universitario(-a), 3
  ______ **studies** carrera (*f.*), 16
**unless** a menos que, 14
**unpleasant** antipático(-a), 3
**until** hasta, 6; hasta que, 14
  ______ **I see you again** hasta la vista, 1
  ______ **you get** hasta llegar, 12
**up to** hasta
**upstairs** arriba, 12
**us** nosotros(-as), 6; nos, 6, 7
**useful** útil
**utensil** utensilio (*m.*), 13

## V

**vacant** libre, 6
**vacation** vacaciones (*f. pl.*), 6
  **to go on** ______ ir de vacaciones, 10
**vacuum** pasar la aspiradora, 9
  ______ **cleaner** aspiradora (*f.*), 9
**van** camioneta (*f.*), 18
**vegetable** verdura (*f.*), vegetal (*m.*), 14
**Venezuelan** venezolano(-a), 14
**verb** verbo (*m.*)
**vermouth** vermut (*m.*), 8
**very** muy, 1
  **(not)** ______ **well** (no) muy bien, 1
  **This** ______ **day** hoy mismo, 15
**vest** chaleco (*m.*), 15
**video camera** cámara de video (*f.*), 6
**vinegar** vinagre (*m.*), 14
**visit** visitar, 6
**vocabulary** vocabulario (*m.*)
**voyage** travesía (*f.*)

## W

**wait (for)** esperar, 9
**waiter** camarero (*m.*), mozo (*m.*), 8
**waiting list** lista de espera (*f.*), 6
**waitress** camarera (*f.*), 8
**wake up** despertarse (e:ie), 9
**walk** caminar, 11
**wall** pared (*f.*), 2; muralla (*f.*)
**walled** amurallado(-a)
**wallet** billetera (*f.*), cartera (*f.*), 15
**want** querer (e:ie), 4; desear, 11
**war** guerra (*f.*)
**wardrobe** armario (*m.*), ropero (*m.*), 15

**warm** cálido(-a)
**warn** advertir (e:ie)
**wash** lavar(se), 9; lavado (*m.*)
**_____ one's hair** lavarse la cabeza, 9
**washing machine** lavadora (*f.*), 13
**wastebasket** cesto de papeles (*m.*), 2
**watch** mirar, 3
**_____ store** relojería (*f.*)
**water** agua (*f.*), 4
**_____ pump** bomba de agua (*f.*), 18
**waterfall** catarata (*f.*)
**watermelon** sandía (*f.*), 14
**we** nosotros(-as), 1
**wear** usar, 9; llevar, 15
**not to have anything to _____** no tener nada que ponerse, 15
**weather** tiempo (*m.*), 6
**to be good (bad) _____** hacer buen (mal) tiempo, 6
**What's the weather like?** ¿Qué tiempo hace?, 6
**wedding** boda (*f.*)
**_____ anniversary** aniversario de bodas (*m.*), 8
**Wednesday** miércoles (*m.*), 1
**week** semana (*f.*), 9
**weekend** fin de semana (*m.*), 5
**weigh** pesar
**welcome: you're _____** de nada, 2
**well** bien, 1; bueno, 9; pues, 10
**not very _____** no muy bien, 1
**very _____** muy bien, 1
**west** oeste (*m.*), 10
**western** occidental
**what** cuál, 2; qué, 2
**_____ a pity!** ¡Qué pena!, ¡Qué lastima!, 5
**_____ does . . . mean?** ¿Qué quiere decir...?, 2
**_____ is . . . like?** ¿Cómo es...?
**_____ is the exchange rate?** ¿A cómo está el cambio de moneda?, 6
**_____ is your address?** ¿Cuál es tu dirección?, 2
**_____ is your name?** ¿Cómo se llama Ud.? (*form.*), 1; ¿Cómo te llamas tú? (*fam.*), 1
**_____ is your phone number?** ¿Cuál es tu número de teléfono?
**_____ the heck** qué diablo
**_____ time is it?** ¿Qué hora es?, 2
**_____'s up (new)?** ¿Qué hay (de nuevo)?, 1
**wheelchair** silla de ruedas (*f.*), 17
**when** cuándo, 2; cuando, 5
**where** dónde, 1; adónde, 4
**_____ are you from?** ¿De dónde eres?, 1
**which** cuál, 2; (*rel. pron.*) que, 6; lo cual
**while** (*conj.*) mientras, 11
**a _____ later** al rato, 11
**white** blanco(-a), 1
**who** (*rel. pron.*) que, 3; quién, 3; quien(es), 12
**_____ is it?** ¿Quién es?, 3
**_____ is speaking?** ¿De parte de quién?, ¿Quién habla?, 3
**whole: the whole trip** todo el viaje, 7
**whom** quien, quienes, 12
**whose** de quién, 4
**why** por qué, 3
**wide** ancho(-a), 15
**widowed** viudo(-a), 3
**wife** esposa (*f.*), 3
**willow** sauce (*m.*), 10
**win** ganar, 13
**windmill** molino de viento (*m.*)
**window** ventana (*f.*), 2; (*of a vehicle or booth*) ventanilla (*f.*), 12
**_____ seat** asiento de ventanilla (*m.*), 7
**to _____ shop** mirar vidrieras, 15
**windshield** parabrisas (*m.*), 18
**_____ wiper** limpiaparabrisas (*m.*), 18
**windy: to be _____** hacer viento, 6
**wine** vino (*m.*), 4
**red _____** vino tinto (*m.*), 8
**white _____** vino blanco (*m.*), 8
**winner** ganador(-a) (*m., f.*)
**winter** invierno (*m.*), 1
**wish** querer (e:ie), 4
**with** con, 2
**_____ me** conmigo, 5
**_____ you** (*fam. sing.*) contigo, 5
**withdraw** sacar, 11
**withered** marchito(-a)
**without** sin, 12; sin que, 14
**_____ fail** sin falta
**woman** mujer (*f.*)
**women's department** departamento de (ropa para) señoras (damas), 12
**wood** madera (*f.*)
**wool** lana (*f.*)
**word** palabra (*f.*)
**work** trabajar, 2; trabajo (*m.*), 3; funcionar, 18
**world** mundo (*m.*), 5
**worried** preocupado(-a), 4
**worry (about)** preocuparse (por), 9
**worse** peor, 5
**worst** el (la) peor, 5
**worth: it's (not) _____ the trouble** (no) vale la pena, 18
**wound** herida (*f.*), 17
**wrap** envolver (o:ue), 15
**wrapped** envuelto(-a), 15
**write** escribir, 3
**_____ down** anotar, 8
**written** escrito(-a), 15
**wrong: to be _____** estar equivocado(-a), no tener razón, 4
**to go _____** ir mal

## X

**X-ray** radiografía (*f.*), 17
**_____ room** sala de rayos X (*f.*), 17

## Y

**year** año (*m.*), 3
**to be . . . _____s old** tener... años, 4
**yearn for** anhelar
**yellow** amarillo(-a), 1
**yes** sí, 2
**yesterday** ayer, 7
**yet** todavía, 17
**yield** ceda el paso
**yogurt** yogur (*m.*)
**you** (*subj.*) tú (*fam.*), usted (Ud.) (*form.*); ustedes, vosotros(-as), 1; (*d.o. pron.*) la(s), lo(s), os, te, 6;

(*i.o. pron.*) le(s), os, te, 7; (*obj. of prep.*) ti, usted(es), vosotros(-as), 5
 _____**'re welcome** de nada, 2
 _____ **say** se dice, 2
 **with _____** contigo (*fam.*)
**young** joven (*m., f.*)
 _____ **man** chico (*m.*), muchacho (*m.*), 3
 _____ **lady** señorita (*f.*), 1
 _____ **woman** chica (*f.*), muchacha (*f.*), 3
**younger** menor, 5
**youngest** el (la) menor, 5
**your** su(s), tu(s), vucstro(-a)(-os)(-as), 3
**yours** suyo(-a)(s), tuyo(-a)(s), vuestro(-a)(s), 9
**yourself** se, te, 9
**yourselves** os, se, 9

## Z

**zero** cero, 1
**zip code** zona postal (*f.*), 3
**zoo** zoológico (*m.*), 14

# Index

# Photo Credits

**Chapter 1:** page 1: © Jeff Greenberg/PhotoEdit; page 2TL: © Beryl Goldberg; page 2CR: © Robert Frerck/Odyssey/Chicago; page 2BL: © Bob Daemmrich/The Image Works; page 3TR: © Richard Hutchings/PhotoEdit; page 3CL: © Robert Fried; page 3CR: © Bob Daemmrich/The Image Works; page 3BL: © David Young-Wolff/PhotoEdit; page 7: © Myrleen Cate/ PhotoEdit; page 10: © Beryl Goldberg; page 19: © Michael Newman/ PhotoEdit; **Chapter 2:** page 23: © Ulrike Welsch; page 45: © Robert Frerck/Odyssey/ Chicago; page 46TR: © Bonnie Kamin/PhotoEdit; page 46CL: © Ulrike Welsch; page 46BR: © Tony Freeman/PhotoEdit; page 47T: © Beryl Goldberg; page 47B: © Beryl Goldberg; page 48L: © Ulrike Welsch; page 48R: © Bob Krist/Leo de Wys; **Chapter 3:** page 51: © Myrleen Cate/PhotoEdit; page 56: © Robert Frerck/Odyssey/Chicago; **Chapter 4:** page 79: © B. Bachmann/The Image Works; page 84: © Robert Frerck/Odyssey/ Chicago; page 97: © David Young-Wolff/PhotoEdit; page 100: © Jon Hicks/Leo de Wys; page 101T: © Mark Antman/The Image Works; page 101BL: © Mark Antman/The Image Works; page 101BR: © Mark Antman/The Image Works; page 102T: © Mark Antman/The Image Works; page 102B: © Jose Fusta Raga/Leo de Wys; page 103TL: © Mark Antman/ The Image Works; page 103TR: © Robert Frerck/Odyssey/Chicago; page 103B: © Robert Frerck/Odyssey/Chicago; **Chapter 5:** page 106: © Rogers/ Monkmeyer Press; page 110: © Beryl Goldberg; page 127: © Wesley Bocxe/The Image Works; **Chapter 6:** page 130: © Bachmann/PhotoEdit; page 135: © Beryl Goldberg; page 158: © Robert Frerck/Odyssey/ Chicago; page 159T: Liaison Agency; page 159B: © Noboru Komine/Photo Researchers; page 160TL: © Robert Frerck/Odyssey/Chicago; page 160TR: © Viccari/Liaison Agency; page 160B: © Peter Menzel; page 161T: © Mark Antman/The Image Works; page 161B: © Mark Antman/The Image Works; **Chapter 7:** page 164: © George Holton/Photo Researchers; page 168: © Robert Frerck/Odyssey/ Chicago; page 181: © Beryl Goldberg; **Chapter 8:** page 187: © Ulrike Welsch; page 192: © David Frazier; page 206: © Beryl Goldberg; page 207T: © Jeff Greenberg/PhotoEdit; page 207B: © Robert Frerck/Odyssey/ Chicago; page 208T: © Robert Frerck/Odyssey/Chicago; page 208B: © Porterfield-Chickering/Photo Researchers; page 209T: © Peter Menzel; page 209B: © Robert Frerck/ Odyssey/Chicago; page 210T: © Spencer Grant/Stock Boston; page 210B: © MacDuff Everton/The Image Works; **Chapter 9:** page 213: © David Young-Wolff/ PhotoEdit; page 217: © Paul Griffin/Stock Boston; **Chapter 10:** page 243: © Ulrike Welsch; page 248: © George Gerster/Comstock; page 258: © B. Bachmann/The Image Works; page 261: © Byron Augustin/DDB Stock Photo; page 262T: © Robert Frerck/Odyssey /Chicago; page 262B: © Chip & Rosa Maria Peterson; page 263T: © Bob Daemmrich; page 263B: © Robert Frerck/Odyssey/Chicago; page 264T: © Francis Lepine/Earth Scenes; page 264B: © Robert Frerck/Odyssey/Chicago; **Chapter 11:** page 267: © Chip & Rosa Maria Peterson; page 271: © Robert Frerck/Odyssey/Chicago; **Chapter 12:** page 289: © Cameramann/The Image Works; page 294: © Beryl Goldberg; page 311: © Chip & Rosa Maria Peterson; page 312T: © Ulrike Welsch; page 312B: © Robert Frerck/Odyssey/Chicago; page 313T: © Peter Menzel; page 313B: © Stuart Cohen/Comstock; page 314T: © Paul Conklin/ PhotoEdit; page 314B: © Robert Frerck/Odyssey/Chicago; **Chapter 13:** page 317: © Beryl Goldberg; page 322: © Robert Frerck/Odyssey/Chicago; **Chapter 14:** page 339: © Robert Frerck/Odyssey/Chicago; page 344: © Robert Frerck/Odyssey/Chicago; page 354: © Robert Frerck/Odyssey/Chicago; page 355T: © Robert Fried; page 355B: © Victor Englebert; page 356T: © Karl Weidman/Photo Researchers; page 356B: © Mark Antman/ The Image Works; page 357T: © Greenberg/Monkmeyer Press; page 357B: © Robert Frerck/Odyssey/Chicago; page 358T: © Anna E. Zuckerman/PhotoEdit; page 358B: © Ulrike Welsch; **Chapter 15:** page 361: © Robert Frerck/Odyssey/Chicago; page 367: © Peter Menzel; **Chapter 16:** page 389: © Robert Frerck/Odyssey/ Chicago; page 395: © Ulrike Welsch; page 406: © Paul Conklin/PhotoEdit; page 408: © Robert Frerck/ Odyssey/Chicago; page 409T: © Ken Haas/Leo de Wys; page 409B: © Robert Frerck/

Odyssey/Chicago; page 410T: © Peter Menzel; page 410B: © Owen Franken/Stock Boston; page 411T: © W. Hille/Leo de Wys; page 411B: © Daniel Rivademar/Odyssey/Chicago; **Chapter 17:** page 414: © Ulrike Welsch; page 418: © Katherine McGlynn/The Image Works; **Chapter 18:** page 433: © Ulrike Welsch; page 437: © Ulrike Welsch; page 453: © Bob Daemmrich; page 454T: © Stuart Cohen/Comstock; page 454B: © Beryl Goldberg; page 455T: © Carolyn Gangi/Liaison Agency; page 455M: © Photofest; page 455B: © Frederic de LaFosse/Sygma; page 456T: © Bob Daemmrich; page 456B: © Susan Greenwood/Liaison Agency

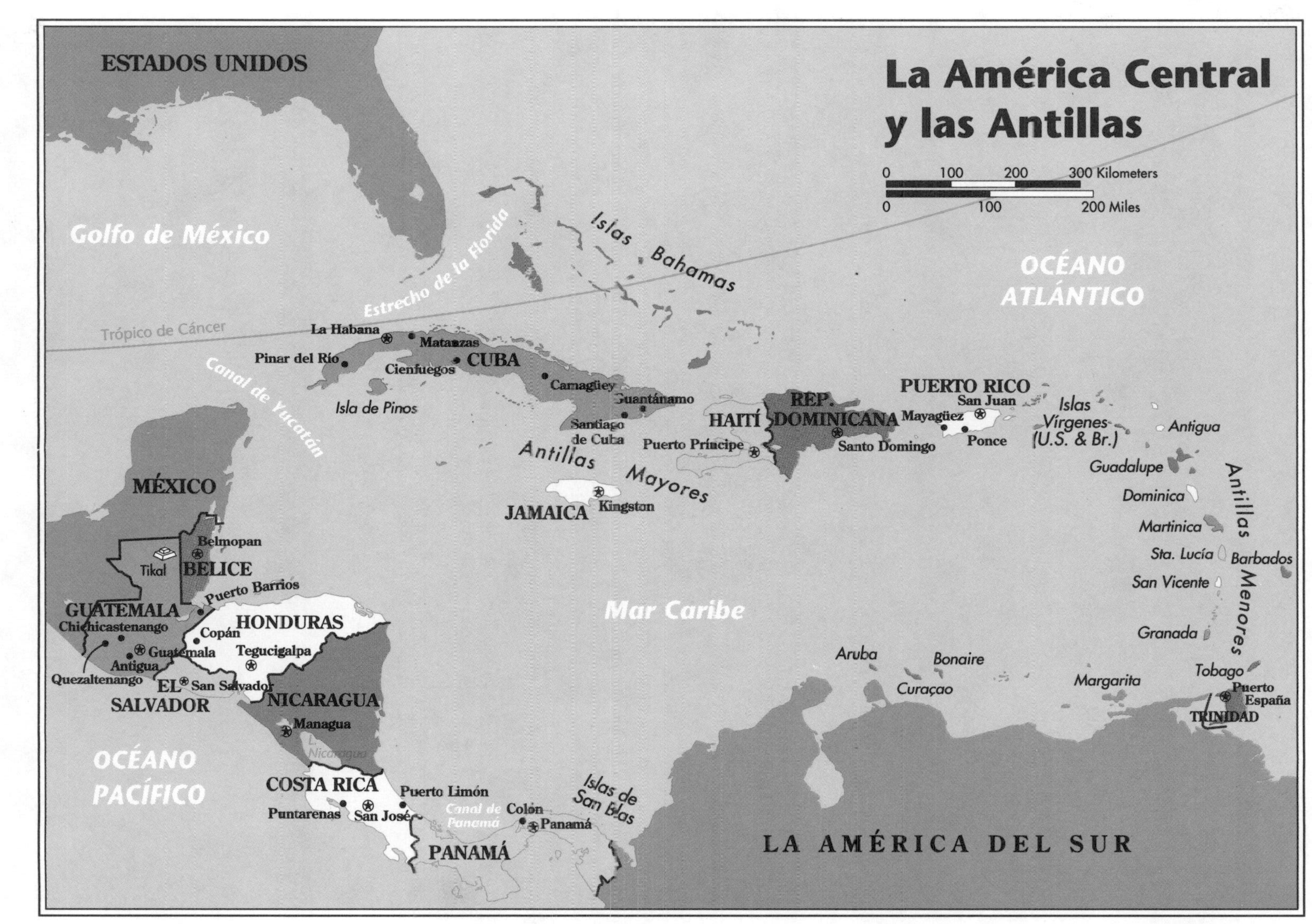
La América Central y las Antillas
0 100 200 300 Kilometers
0 100 200 Miles
ESTADOS UNIDOS
Golfo de México
Estrecho de la Florida
Islas Bahamas
OCÉANO ATLÁNTICO
Trópico de Cáncer
La Habana
Matanzas
Pinar del Río
Cienfuegos
CUBA
Isla de Pinos
Canal de Yucatán
Camagüey
Guantánamo
Santiago de Cuba
HAITÍ
REP. DOMINICANA
Puerto Príncipe
Santo Domingo
PUERTO RICO
San Juan
Mayagüez
Ponce
Islas Vírgenes (U.S. & Br.)
Antigua
Antillas Mayores
JAMAICA
Kingston
MÉXICO
Belmopan
Tikal
BELICE
Puerto Barrios
GUATEMALA
Chichicastenango
Guatemala
Antigua
Quezaltenango
HONDURAS
Copán
Tegucigalpa
EL SALVADOR
San Salvador
NICARAGUA
Managua
L. Nicaragua
OCÉANO PACÍFICO
COSTA RICA
Puntarenas
San José
Puerto Limón
Canal de Panamá
Colón
Panamá
PANAMÁ
Islas de San Blas
Mar Caribe
Guadalupe
Dominica
Martinica
Sta. Lucía
Barbados
San Vicente
Granada
Antillas Menores
Aruba
Bonaire
Curaçao
Margarita
Tobago
Puerto España
TRINIDAD
LA AMÉRICA DEL SUR